THE CRAFTS SUPPLY SOURCE BOOK

A comprehensive shop-by-mail guide
for thousands of craft materials.

MARGARET A. BOYD

REVISED THIRD EDITION

BETTERWAY BOOKS
CINCINNATI, OHIO

ACKNOWLEDGMENTS

My appreciation to all the companies that responded with materials for this new edition. Their information helped me to provide more comprehensive listings.

A special thank-you to Patti DeLette Boyd, my dear daughter-in-law, whose assistance throughout this year has been the basis for joyful steps to completion of this work.

To my family and friends—bless you for your love and understanding.

Library of Congress Cataloging-in-Publication Data

Boyd, Margaret Ann
      The crafts supply sourcebook / Margaret A. Boyd.—3rd ed.
            p.   cm.
      Includes index.
      ISBN 1-55870-355-1 (pb)
      1. Handicraft—United States—Equipment and supplies—Directories. 2. Handicraft—Canada—Equipment and supplies—Directories. I. Title.
TT12.B683   1994
680′.28—dc20   94-20392
                                                                        CIP

Edited by David G. Tompkins
Interior and cover design by Clare Finney

This and other Betterway Books are available at a discount when purchased in bulk. Schools, organizations, corporations and others interested in purchasing bulk quantities of this book should contact the Special Sales Department of F&W Publications at 1-800-289-0963 (8 A.M.—5 P.M. Eastern Time) or write to this department at 1507 Dana Avenue, Cincinnati, OH 45207.

The Crafts Supply Sourcebook is printed on recycled paper.

In memory of my creative grandmothers,
Johanna Pribyl and Elizabeth Jane Munnerlyn.

GUIDE TO LISTINGS IN THIS BOOK

This book is organized into categories (see Table of Contents). Check the index for more detailed source searching.

In listings, references to SASE mean self-addressed, stamped envelope; business-size SASE refers to a #10 envelope. Include an SASE with *every inquiry* to assure receiving a reply.

Listings include information on materials, services, and whether a company gives price breaks.

Some manufacturers are also listed because consumers may want the address; some manufacturers will forward information or aid those wanting business order information.

Even listings with scant information are given because they might be important sources for some people.

Many mail order companies now have toll-free numbers for *orders*. Only those with toll-free numbers for *inquiries* are given in this book.

Comments and contributions of information are welcome for future editions.

May your days be full of the light of creative expression.

Margaret A. Boyd
P.O. Box 6232-FW
Augusta, GA 30906

Contents

INTRODUCTION

The third edition of this sourcebook has many hundreds of new and exciting sources of supplies. These wonderful companies provide materials that inspire us to even more creatively innovative craft design and work.

Behind every catalog are dedicated business professionals who share their wares and often their experience as well. The literature offered on inquiry may include technical hints that help us avoid pitfalls and produce easier, with more satisfying results. Often the value of what we can learn far outweighs any cost for literature.

With that in mind, we urge you to explore your areas of interest and other areas, too—they can lead to other pathways of creation.

Whatever you create, enjoy!

Margaret A. Boyd

General Arts, Crafts and Hobbies

Art Instruction

Also see Artist's Supplies, Graphics and Printing, Books and Booksellers, Publications and Associations.

AMERICAN ARTIST BOOK CLUB
P.O. Box 2012
Lakewood, NJ 08701

Offers: Members are entitled to purchase an introductory selection at substantial savings, and agree to purchase additional books at discounts of 20% to 50%. They receive a club bulletin describing art technique books for painting, pastels, pencil, drawing, perspective and other topics.
For Further Information: Send SASE for full details.

ART VIDEO LIBRARY
P.O. Box 68
Ukiah, OR 97880

Offers: Art instructional videos (sale or rent). Members may rent videos at low cost (and elect to apply rent to purchase). Videos cover acrylics, oils, watercolors, pastels, drawing, color, anatomy, perspective, still life, landscapes and portraits. Instructors include Carter, Demeres, Sargent, Burton, Kelly, Jenkins, Palluth, Blackman, Graham, Flannery, Pike, Marchenko, Boyle, Vilppu, Lee, Pitard and Harris.
For Further Information: Free catalog.
See Also: General Craft Supplies

ARTS AMERICA
12 Havemeyer Place
Greenwich, CT 06830
(203) 869-4693

Offers: Over 300 arts/crafts videos on techniques, artists, exhibitions, museum collections, architecture and other topics.
For Further Information: Free catalog.

ASSOCIATION OF TELEVISION ARTISTS
P.O. Box 2746
Reston, VA 22090
(703) 450-7666

Offers: A membership in this painting association allows discounts on videos, books and supplies, plus a newsletter subscription and notification of artists' seminars, demonstrations, classes and workshops. Among mentioned artists: Gary Jenkins, Bob Ross, Priscilla Hauser and Dorothy Dent.

For Further Information: Send SASE for complete information.

WM. BLACKMAN PRODUCTIONS
2369 Magda Circle
Thousand Oaks, CA 91360

Offers: Over 25 oil instructional painting videos. Subjects include animals, clowns, florals, seascapes, landscapes, exotic birds, barns and others.
For Further Information: Free brochure.

C & L PRODUCTIONS
Brown & Williamson Tower, Suite 2001
Louisville, KY 40202

Offers: Paint-along instructional videos with John Michael Carter (2 hour, as one-to-one workshops), including demonstrations and instruction on mixing oil colors, painting still lifes, landscapes, waterfronts and portraiture.
For Further Information: Free brochure.

CAMELOT PRODUCTIONS
2750 Glendower Ave., Suite 20
Los Angeles, CA 90027

Offers: Oil painting instructional videos by Margaret Holland Sargent (1 to 2 hours), including *Basics*, *Intermediate*, *Succeed in Portraiture* and *Portraits*, plus a sample promotion portfolio.
For Further Information: Send SASE for list.

CANDLELIGHT STUDIOS
P.O. Box 627
Littleriver, CA 95456

Offers: Art instructional videos by E. John Robinson (40 to 82 minutes), covering oil and watercolor seascapes and landscapes.
For Further Information: Send SASE for list.

CARTOONERAMA
P.O. Box 854
Portland, ME 04104
(207) 773-5040

Offers: Cartoon correspondence course with professional instruction.
For Further Information: Free brochures.

DECORATIVE ARTS PAINTING
701 Lee St., Dept. CSS2
Des Plaines, IL 60016

Offers: Oil painting instructional videos by Sherry C. Nelson, including *Learn to Paint a Hummingbird* and *Learn to Paint a Pintail Duck*; videos come with packets. Videos by Buck Paulson include *Dancing Lights*, *Seascape Canvas*, *Paint Skies*, and *Basic Principles of Seascapes*. Also carries resin pieces.
For Further Information: Send SASE for details.
Discounts: Quantity discounts; allows discounts to teachers and institutions; sells wholesale to legitimate businesses.

DEMBER ARTS
P.O. Box 8093
Van Nuys, CA 91409

Offers: Instructional art courses videos covering basic and advanced airbrushing, photo retouching, watercolor, rendering various media and hi-tech rendering (finished, conceptual and cutaway). Also offers demonstrations of mural techniques (materials, paints, airbrush, masking, scaffolding and transferring); plus instructional books.
For Further Information: Send SASE for list.
Accepts: MasterCard, Visa

FAMOUS ARTISTS SCHOOL
19 Newtown Turnpike
Westport, CT 06880

Offers: Art instruction books covering the methods of Norman Rockwell, Ben Stahl, Robert Fawcett and others, with self-correcting overlay sheets. Learn to draw or paint landscapes and portraits, the human figure, animals and other subjects.
For Further Information: Send SASE for details.
Accepts: MasterCard, Visa

FLORA & COMPANY MULTIMEDIA
4801 Marble Ave. NE
Albuquerque, NM 87110
(505) 255-9988

Offers: Silk screen process instructional video, adapted to the home workshop, demonstrating techniques for reproducing patterns on fabric, wood, paper, plastics and other flat surfaces; a workbook is included.
For Further Information: Send SASE for details.
Accepts: American Express

BEEBE HOPPER
731 Beech Ave.
Chula Vista, CA 91910
(619) 420-8766

Offers: Instruction books in decorative arts (featherstroke technique), painting wildfowl and landscapes.
For Further Information: Send SASE for list.

HW PRODUCTIONS
P.O. Box 4273
Burlingame, CA 94011

Offers: The video *Classical Life Drawing With Fred Holle* (a demonstration home-study for watercolor and oil painting with a live model, from the Artist In Residence series).
For Further Information: Free brochure.

DAVID A. LEFFEL
P.O. Box 278
Sanbornton, NH 03269
(603) 934-3222

Offers: Art videotapes covering still life and portraits with palette and brush techniques.
For Further Information: Send SASE for details.
Accepts: MasterCard, Visa

M-M VIDEOS
P.O. Box 158
Freehold, NY 12431

Offers: Drawing instruction video by Stanley Maltzman demonstrating the techniques of landscape drawing, location through finished picture, a demonstration of techniques, rendering, composition and materials for the beginner and intermediate (56 minutes).
For Further Information: Send SASE for details.
Accepts: MasterCard, Visa

MAJIC OF MAINE
P.O. Box 8000
Lewiston, ME 04243
(207) 782-5650

Offers: Instructional videos of painting wildlife into landscapes (bear, fish, birds, moose and deer). Offers sales and rentals. Video production service.
For Further Information: Free brochure.
Store Location: Yes
Discounts: Sells wholesale.

NORTH LIGHT ART SCHOOL
1507 Dana Ave.
Cincinnati, OH 45207

Offers: Home-study art course from professionals including a series of basic studies, perspective, techniques for pencil, color, painting and others.
For Further Information: Write for full information.

NORTH LIGHT BOOKS
1507 Dana Ave.
Cincinnati, OH 45207
(513) 531-2222

Offers: Art instruction books, covering painting portraits, florals. Offers instruction in landscapes, nature, textures, flowers, weather, animals, people, urban settings and wildlife. Covers techniques for basics, such as color, light and values, acrylics, watercolors, oils, airbrush, screen printing and silk fabrics. Drawing and pastel titles are also available. Guides include *The Graphic Artist's Guide to Marketing and Self-Promotion, Market Guide for Young Artists and Photographers*, and the yearly *Artist's Market*.
For Further Information: Send for information.

PAINTER'S CORNER, INC.
108 W. Highway 174
Republic, MO 65738
(417) 732-2076

Offers: Instructional painting videos by Dorothy Dent, covering landscapes and other subjects (1 hour). Also offers painting packets and books.
For Further Information: Send SASE for brochure.

SIGNILAR ART VIDEOS
P.O. Box 278
Sanbornton, NH 03269
(603) 934-3222

Offers: Instructional painting videos by Ken Davies on sharp focus still life and trompe l'oeil, including subject selection, lighting, drawing, painting and perspective. Videos by David

A. Leffel cover methods and techniques for backgrounds, design and other techniques after the style of Rembrandt. Videos by Bruno Lucchesi demonstrate sculpture, including portraits, reclining figures, firing and patina.
For Further Information: Send SASE for details.
Accepts: MasterCard, Visa

STACKPOLE BOOKS
P.O. Box 1831
Harrisburg, PA 17105

Offers: Painting books, such as *Shorebirds, Songbirds*, by David Mohrhardt, which offer instruction in gouache and acrylic techniques, and an overview of painting media and surfaces, practices and anatomical references.
For Further Information: Catalog, $3 (refundable).
Discounts: "Dealer inquiries invited."

TIPS FROM THE STUDIO
P.O. Box 6297
East Brunswick, NJ 08816

Offers: Watercolor painting instructional video, with step-by-step demonstration by Richard Jaedicke, covers all aspects of painting.
For Further Information: Send SASE for details.

WORKSHOP — THE ARTIST'S STUDIO
1507 Dana Ave.
Cincinnati, OH 45207

Offers: Ten different artist's painting workshops. Professional instruction and contacts aid in a guided home-study approach for oils, watercolors or acrylics.
For Further Information: Free details.

Artist's Supplies, Graphics and Printing

Also see Paints, Finishes and Adhesives, Tole and Decorative Crafts, Books and Booksellers, Publications, Associations and other specific categories.

AIKO'S ART MATERIALS IMPORT
3347 N. Clark St.
Chicago, IL 60657

Offers: Oriental art supplies including brushes, inks and papers. Also carries Japanese handmade paper (for printing, painting, collage, restoration, crafts, bookbinding), homespun (Kizuki), solid colors, textured with fiber, plus Masa, Hsho and Torinoko paper, designed (paper on paper), stencil designed, metallics and gossamer types. Fabric dyes and equipment are also available.
For Further Information: Catalog, $1.50.

ALEXANDER ART CORP.
P.O. Box 20250
Salem, OR 97308

Offers: Specially formulated oil paints (extra thick), personally designed brushes (by Bill Alexander, as seen on TV), instructional videos (techniques, hints and tips) and books. Publishes a bimonthly newsletter.
For Further Information: Free supply catalog.
Accepts: MasterCard, Visa

ART EXPRESS
1561 Broad River Rd.
Columbia, SC 29210

Offers: Art supplies in known brands such as Holbein, Grumbacher, Canton, Artograph, Badger and LeCornell. Carries paints, papers, canvas, inks, pastels, equipment and accessories.
For Further Information: Free catalog.
Discounts: Wholesale and quantity discounts.

ART SUPPLY WAREHOUSE
360 Main Ave.
Norwalk, CT 06851

Offers: Artist's supplies including a full line of paints (watercolors, oils, acrylics), markers, brushes, papers, canvas, equipment and tools.
For Further Information: Catalog.
Discounts: "At savings up to 60% off."
Accepts: MasterCard, Visa

THE ARTIST'S CLUB
5750 NE Hassalo St.
Portland, OR 97213

Offers: Pecan shell resin figures, ready to paint—rabbits, figures, children. Also carries Master Stripper and other items.
For Further Information: Free catalog.
Accepts: MasterCard, Visa

ARTISTS' CONNECTION
20 Constance Ct.
P.O. Box 13007
Hauppauge, NY 11788
(800) 951-9333

Offers: Artist's supplies by Badger, Winsor & Newton, Paasche, Koh-I-Noor, Rotring, Stanrite, Eurofold, Rembrant and others. Carries art equipment and furniture.
For Further Information: Free catalog.
Store Location: Yes
Discounts: May run sales.

BADGER AIR-BRUSH CO.
9128 W. Belmont Ave.
Franklin Park, IL 60131

Offers: Airbrushes (large cup gravity feed) for painting and finishing, in sets/outfits. Carries Air-Opaque paints in 35 non-toxic colors and 8 pearlescents that are intermixable—light-fast, waterproof, non-bleed paints for airbrushes, paint brushes and technical pens.
For Further Information: Project information sheet and catalog, $1.50.

DICK BLICK
P.O. Box 1267
Galesburg, IL 61402
(309) 343-6181

Offers: Extensive art supplies (including known brands), papers, paint mediums, canvas, painters' supplies and graphic arts materials. Carries supplies/equipment for intaglio, screen process, etching, block printing, lithography, laminating, dry mounting, signmaking, air brushing, picture framing, woodworking, sculpture and ceramics. Also carries adhesives, tapes, tools, easels, furniture, books, videos and computer software.
For Further Information: Catalog, $4.
Store Location: Yes

Accepts: American Express, Discover, MasterCard, Visa
See Also: General Craft Supplies, Sculpture and Sign Making

CHARLES BRAND MACHINERY, INC.
45 York St.
Brooklyn, NY 11201
(718) 797-1887

Offers: A line of etching and lithography presses, inking rollers and electric hot plates. Manufacturer.
For Further Information: Free catalog and price list.

ARTHUR BROWN & BRO., INC.
P.O. Box 7820
Maspeth, NY 11378
(718) 628-0600

Offers: An extensive inventory of art supplies in known and less-known brands—colors, mediums, finishes and papers. Carries supplies/equipment/tools for lithography, calligraphy, graphics, dry mounting, framing, airbrush, silkscreen, wood carving, textile painting, engraving, block printing, etching and others. Also carries glues and equipment such as lettering guides, lighting, magnifiers, paper cutters, furniture and tracing units. Stocks tools by X-Acto, Paasche, Badger, Dremel, Koh-I-Noor and others, plus drafting items and books.
For Further Information: Catalog, $3.75.

STAN BROWN'S ARTS & CRAFTS, INC
13435 NE Whitaker Way
Portland, OR 97230
(503) 257-0559

Offers: Artists' supplies—a full line of paints, brushes, papers, canvas and other material, including known brands and books.
For Further Information: Catalog, $2.50.

CHATHAM ART DISTRIBUTORS, INC.
11 Brookside Ave.
Chatham, NY 12037
(800) 822-4747

Offers: Decorative art supplies, including painting surfaces, tools, paints and brushes. Also carries books.
For Further Information: Write for catalog.
Store Location: Yes

CHEAP JOE'S ART STUFF
300A Industrial Park Rd.
Boone, NC 28607

Offers: Artist's supplies, such as papers (known brands) and a line of art supplies at reduced cost including professional colors (oils, watercolors, acrylics and others).

For Further Information: Free catalog.

CHROMA ACRYLICS, INC.
205 Bucky Dr.
Lititz, PA 17543
(717) 626-8866

Offers: Atelier acrylic paints (for impasto or wash). Has an 800 number for orders.
For Further Information: Write for information.

CO-OP ARTISTS' MATERIALS
P.O. Box 53097
Atlanta, GA 30355

Offers: Known brand supplies/equipment in all mediums/colors. Carries modeling paste, drawing inks, calligraphy pens/sets, markers, pastels, pencils/sets, brush-pans, and paper/mat cutters. Also carries sumi kits, ink sticks, pigments, grindstones, palettes, easels, stretchers, canvas, tools, brushes, 73 plus art papers, boards, acetate, films, tapes, pens, erasers, sharpeners, wax, adhesives and burnishers. Also offers supplies for drafting, framing, airbrushing (30 plus units), compressors and parts. Bronze powders, sign painting items, modeling materials/tools, drafting units, magnifiers, tracing boxes, projectors and books are also available.
For Further Information: Free catalog.
Discounts: All at discount; runs sales.

CONRAD MACHINE CO.
1525 S. Warner
Whitehall, MI 49461
(616) 893-7455

Offers: Etching and lithography presses (2 sizes), Convertible Press (hand-driven model) and optional accessories. Carries table and floor model presses, plus re-manufactured presses in 12- to 36-inch sizes.
For Further Information: Free catalog. Request trade-ins list.
Discounts: Sells wholesale; quantity discounts.

FLETCHER-LEE & CO.
P.O. Box 007
Elk Grove Village, IL 60009

Offers: Liquitex watercolors (professional grade), watercolor sets and others at savings.
For Further Information: Send SASE for list.
Accepts: MasterCard, Visa

GRAPHIC CHEMICAL & INK CO.
728 N. Yale Ave.
P.O. Box 27
Villa Park, IL 60181

Offers: Printmaking supplies. Block printing line includes linoleum and wood blocks, brayers and cutting tools. Lithographic line includes gums, asphaltum, tusche and rollers (rubber, NuClear). Carries litho stones in many sizes, KU Leather and composition, inks, a variety of papers and other supplies.
For Further Information: Write for catalog.

GRAPHIC MEDIA CO.
13916 Cordary Ave.
Hawthorne, CA 90250

Offers: Art supplies in a wide range of name brands, including Grumbacher, Winsor & Newton, Liquitex, Parker, Pelikan, 3M, Letraset, Lamy, K&E and others.
For Further Information: Catalog, $5 (refundable).
Discounts: "20% to 60% off."

GRUMBACHER
30 Englehard Dr.
Cranbury, NJ 08512

Offers: Full lines of artist's supplies, including brushes for artists and signpainters, Golden Edge synthetic brushes, and other tools and equipment.
For Further Information: Contact dealer or send SASE for information.

HK HOLBEIN, INC.
P.O. Box 555
Williston, VT 05495

Offers: A variety of artists' colors—oils, oil sets, pastel/blend brushes, watercolors, acrylics, Aeroflash inks and acrylic gouache.
For Further Information: Catalog and color charts, $3.50.

THE ITALIAN ART STORE
84 Maple Ave.
Morristown, NJ 07960
(800) 643-6440

Offers: European artist's supplies—colors, oils, acrylics, watercolors and others.
For Further Information: Free catalog.

JERRY'S ARTORAMA
117 S. 2nd St.
P.O. Box 1105
New Hyde Park, NY 11040
(516) 328-6633

Offers: Full line of artist's supplies, reducing lenses and opaque projectors in a variety of models.
For Further Information: Catalog, $2 (refundable).
Store Location: Yes

Discounts: Quantity prices; allows discounts to teachers and institutions.

KOH-I-NOOR RAPIDOGRAPH, INC.
100 North St.
P.O. Box 68
Bloomsbury, NJ 08804
(201) 479-4124

Offers: Colors, art instruments and accessories including papers, Pelikan opaque and transparent colors, metallics and drawing inks. Pens available include technical, calligraphy, lettering, sketch and others. Also carries water box, Goldstar brushes, sharpeners, pen holders and accessories, portable drawing board/case, templates, triangles and other drawing instruments.
For Further Information: Send SASE for details and nearest dealer.

JOE KUBERT ART & GRAPHIC SUPPLY
37A Myrtle Ave.
Dover, NJ 07801
(201) 328-3266

Offers: Artist's, cartoonist's, and graphic materials, including boards, papers (art, parchments, drafting, etching, rag, others), paints, finger paints, brushes, palettes, pens, crayons, chalk, pencils, pastels, airbrushes, airbrush sets, calligraphy pens/inks, drafting materials/equipment and Pantographs. Also carries mat/paper cutters, projectors, easels, canvas, stretcher strips, graphic and printing supplies, frisket, grids, films, Letraset letters, tapes, film, waxers, light boxes, projectors, furniture, plus etching, block printing and silkscreen supplies and equipment, tools, knives and books.
For Further Information: Catalog, $4.
Discounts: Allows discounts to professionals, teachers and institutions.

SUE LARUE'S
49-6A The Donway West, Suite 1906
Don Mills, Ontario M3C 2E8 Canada

Offers: Folk art supplies including a full line of paints, brushes, decorative books and others.
For Further Information: Catalog, $4.

Paint of any type, even water-based paint, should never be allowed to dry in the paintbrush.

—Dick Blick

NAPA VALLEY ART STORE
1041 Lincoln Ave.
Napa, CA 94558
(707) 247-1111

Offers: Artist's supplies including Winsor & Newton water-color papers and blocks, watercolor series and others.
For Further Information: Free catalog.
Accepts: MasterCard, Visa

NEW YORK CENTRAL ART SUPPLY
62 3rd Ave.
New York, NY 10003
(800) 950-6111

Offers: Fine arts supplies including colors (oils, watercolors, acrylics, sets), markers, pens, pastels, brushes and pencils. Also carries over 150 types of canvas (widths up to 197 inches), supplies, tools and accessories for silkscreen, woodcut, etching and lithography. Stocks handmade papers by Fabriano, Arches and others, plus marbling supplies and other supplies and equipment.
For Further Information: Call or write for catalog.
Discounts: Sells wholesale; quantity discounts.

OTT'S DISCOUNT ART SUPPLY
714 Greenville Blvd. SE
Greenville, NC 27858
(919) 756-9565

Offers: A full range of pencils, charcoal, artist's papers and other materials.
For Further Information: Free catalog.

PAASCHE AIRBRUSH CO.
7440 W. Lawrence Ave.
Harwood Heights, IL 60656
(708) 867-9191

Offers: Airbrushes, both gravity feed double action and other models, airbrush sets for paints, varnish, lacquers and others. Accessories, air compressors, sprayers, equipment and supplies for air etching/spraying are also available. Also offers an air etching video. Manufacturer.
For Further Information: Free literature.
Discounts: "Call for current discount quantities."

PEARL PAINT CO.
308 Canal St.
New York, NY 10013
(212) 431-7932

Offers: Extensive artist's supplies (including known brands). Carries paints—oils, acrylics, watercolors, gouache, egg temperas, encaustics, vinyl matte, lettering enamel, gold leaf, specialty paints and various mediums. Also carries paint accessories, knives, brushes, cleaners, pencils, charcoal, pastels, markers, papers and specialty types. Airbrushes and supplies, studio accessories, easels, mannequins, canvas and boards are available. Provides international mail order. "We special order anything."
For Further Information: Send SASE for list.

Store Location: Yes
Discounts: Quantity discounts; allows discounts to teachers, institutions and professionals; large order discounts negotiable.
Accepts: American Express, MasterCard, Visa

PENTEL OF AMERICA, LTD.
2805 Columbia St.
Torrance, CA 90503

Offers: An extensive line of pens, including porous, color brush, fluorescents, markers, projection, white, porcelain, ceramic tip, correction and seven permanent pens. Also offers 15 drafting pencils, erasers and Roll'N Glue adhesive.
For Further Information: Contact your dealer or send SASE for details.

PERMA COLOR
226 E. Tremont
Charlotte, NC 28203
(704) 333-9201

Offers: 200 dry pigments including pearlescents, bronze powders, iridescents and standard pigments. Also carries rabbit-skinned glue gesso primed panels, Kolinsky sable brushes (factory direct, "at least half" price), binders and specialty items, such as gum, beeswax, talc, kaolin, gessos, graphite and others.
For Further Information: Send SASE for information.
Discounts: Quantity discounts; allows discounts to teachers and institutions; sells wholesale to legitimate businesses and professionals.

PRINTMAKERS MACHINE CO.
P.O. Box 71
Villa Park, IL 60181
(708) 832-4888

Offers: Presses, including Sturges and etching presses, printmaker combination and lithopresses and Bunch etching presses.
For Further Information: Free brochure.

REX GRAPHIC SUPPLY
P.O. Box 6226
Edison, NJ 08818
(201) 613-8777

Offers: "The Creator" table for graphic artists and draftsman. The table has a melamine top, steel base (enamel finish), dual position foot rest, rear stabilizing bar and built-in floor levelers; it's adjustable for height and angle and comes in 2 size models.
For Further Information: Send SASE or call.

SAX ARTS & CRAFTS
P.O. Box 51710
New Berlin, WI 53151

Offers: Artist's supplies (known brands), including a line of paints, brushes, palette knives, boxes, organizers, trays, markers, pens. Also carries sumi supplies, airbrush kits/accessories and compressors, paints, inks, canvas, stretchers, tools, easels, boards, plus a full line of papers, boards, mats and cutters. Also offers frames, framing tools and supplies, knives, scissors, adhesives, paper cutters, waxers, glue guns, tapes, punches and pencils. Carries artists' aids, such as mannequins and models. Drafting items, calligraphy and lettering tools, light boxes, mounting presses, film, projectors, photography supplies, magnifier lamps and furniture are also available. Stocks block printing supplies, offset printing kits and presses, etching, lithography and screen printing items/kits, T-shirt printing machines, photo and speed screen supplies, videos (art, craft), film strips and books.
For Further Information: Catalog, $4 (refundable).
Discounts: Quantity discounts.
Accepts: American Express, MasterCard, Visa
See Also: General Craft Supplies

ROBERT SIMMONS, INC.
45 W. 18th St.
New York, NY 10011

Offers: Brushes for watercolors, oils and acrylics, plus brushes for crafts, artwork, ceramics, hobbies and lettering. Styles avalable include Priscilla Hauser tole decorative brushes and ceramic brushes, such as Mary Gilbertson, Marc Bellaire and Helen Altieri types. Also offers Fabric Master brushes—design book, base coaters (flat, round) and scrubbers (nylon). Bamboo brushes, brushes for plaster crafts and china painting, brush roll pack sets in most sizes and styles, and books are also available. Manufacturer.
For Further Information: Contact dealer or write for information.

DANIEL SMITH, INC.
4150 1st Ave. S.
P.O. Box 84268
Seattle, WA 98124
(800) 426-6740

Offers: Artist's supplies in extensive colors including oils, acrylics, watercolors, egg tempera, inks, airbrush, metallics, dry pigments, mediums, pastels and pencils. Has a full line of papers—marbled, textured and specialty. Carries brushes and specialty types, art boards, canvas and linen. Print-making supplies for etching, relief and lithography (including known brands) are available, plus supplies for arts, graphics and framing. Also carries easels, furniture, projectors, magnifiers, books and others.
For Further Information: Write for information.
Store Location: Yes
Discounts: Sells wholesale; quantity discounts.
Accepts: American Express, Discover, MasterCard, Visa

UTRECHT MANUFACTURING CORP.
33 35th St.
Brooklyn, NY 11232
(718) 768-2525

Offers: Professional artists' colors, stretchers, paper converters and other major brand art supplies, such as papers, colors, brushes, canvases and others.
For Further Information: Free catalog.
Store Location: Yes
Discounts: "Impressive savings."

WINSOR & NEWTON
P.O. Box 1396
Piscataway, NJ 08855

Offers: Artist's brushes, including the Sceptre 6-brush series that blends synthetic fibers with genuine sable. Offers other brushes for a variety of mediums.
For Further Information: Contact dealer or send SASE for information.

ZIEGLER
P.O. Box 50037
Tulsa, OK 74150

Offers: Artist's supplies including paints, brushes, a variety of papers, miniature easels (brass or wood), picture frames (miniature, shadowbox and others in a variety of sizes).
For Further Information: Catalog, $2 (refundable).

Basketry and Seat Weaving

Also see Batik and Dyeing, Indian and Frontier Crafts, Nature Crafts and Knitting and Crochet

ACP INC.
P.O. Box 1426
Salisbury, NC 28145
(704) 636-3034

Offers: Basketry supplies including reed, raffia, cane, cane binder, spline, seagrass, fiber rush and prewoven cane. Also carries basket hoops, kits (egg, berry and square handle) for wall, mini-, homestead, wine, other types of baskets. Tools available include awls, cutters. Also stocks dyes, acrylics, various aids, brushes, and 50 plus basketry books.
For Further Information: Catalog, $1.
Store Location: Yes
Discounts: Allows discounts to teachers, institutions and professionals; sells wholesale to legitimate businesses.
Accepts: MasterCard, Visa

ADIRONDACK SEATWEAVERS
337 Old Trail Rd.
Fonda, NY 12068
(518) 829-7241, (800) 724-9862

Offers: Basketry and seat-weaving supplies, including chair and binder cane and webbing. Reed types available include flat, oval, round and smoked. Also carries slab rattan, seagrass, fiber rush and paper twist. Carries kits and a full line of tools, Napier and reed dyes, hoops, 25 handles, frames, Shaker tape, feet and books.
For Further Information: Free catalog.
Store Location: Yes
Discounts: Quantity discounts; allows discounts to teachers and institutions.
Accepts: MasterCard, Visa

ALLEN'S BASKETWORKS
8624 SE 13th Place
Portland, OR 97202
(503) 238-6384

Offers: Basketry supplies (domestic and imported) and 3 basic basket kits. Also carries reeds (round, flat, half round and oval), rattan, poles, cane, raffia, pine needles, seagrass, fiber rush (paper), corn husks, "Richard's bean twine," generic papers, fiber core, basket feet, hoops, many handles, wood strips, bases, wire, hearts and dyes. Tools available include awls, pliers and scissors.

For Further Information: Catalog, 45¢.
Store Location: Yes
Discounts: Sells wholesale.

BASKET BEGINNINGS
25 West Tioga St.
Tunkhannock, PA 18657
(717) 836-6080

Offers: California and Pacific Northwest basketry materials, hand-dyed fibers, kits, tools, beads, books and 38 colors of waxed linen.
For Further Information: Free catalog. Material samples, $4; waxed linen samples, $2.
Store Location: Yes

THE BASKET WORKS
77 Mellor Ave.
Baltimore, MD 21228

Offers: Basketmaking items including reed, ash, oak, pine needles, raffia, oak hoops, handles, kits, dyes and books. Also carries Sculpey and Fimo.
For Further Information: Catalog, $1.
Store Location: Yes
Discounts: Quantity discounts; sells wholesale to businesses; allows discounts to teachers and institutions.

When replacing a prewoven cane seat, remember to sand any sharp edges in the groove and along the inside of the seat. This will help prevent the cane from breaking when putting in the new piece.

—Adirondack Seat Weavers

THE BASKETRY SCHOOL
3516 Fremont Place N.
Seattle, WA 98103
(206) 632-6072, (800) 87-WEAVE

Offers: Supplies including dyed (over 40 colors) and natural reed, cedar and birch bark, pine needles and basket kits.
For Further Information: Free catalog.

THE CANING SHOP
926 Gilman St.
Berkley, CA 94710
(510) 527-5010

Offers: Basketry and chair caning supplies including cane and webbing, spline, Danish seat cord, rawhide and rubber webbing, Shaker tapes, reed splint, fiber rush, Hong Kong grass, ash splint, braided raffia, willowsticks and reed. Also carries rattan poles, Kooboo and whole rattans, pine needles, hickory and palm bark, paper rush, jute roving, date palm stalks, pressed fiber seats, basket kits and hoops. Tools available include awls, chisels, clamps, knives, clippers, shears, sliver grippers and cutters. Gourds, videos, books, and Ukranian egg decorating supplies are also available.
For Further Information: Catalog, $2 (refundable).
Store Location: Yes
Discounts: Quantity discounts; allows discounts to teachers and institutions.
Accepts: MasterCard, Visa

CONNECTICUT CANE & REED CO.
134 Pine St.
P.O. Box 762
Manchester, CT 06045
(203) 646-6586

Offers: Basketry supplies, including a full line of Nantucket basket molds (purse ovals, fruit basket, Shaker style, bushel, pushbottom and hardwood) and Nantucket accessories (rims, rivets, bolts, pins, ears, handle, bases, ribs and weavers). Also carries a variety of basket kits. Materials available include seagrass, reeds, handles, ash and oak splints and dyes. Books are also available.
For Further Information: Free catalog.

COUNTRY SEAT
P.O. Box 24
Kempton, PA 19529
(215) 756-6124

Offers: Basketry and chair seating supplies including oval and other reeds, hoops, handles, basket kits, and over 100 instructional books.
For Further Information: Send business-size SASE ($.65 postage) for list.
Discounts: "Lowest prices."
Accepts: MasterCard, Visa

FRANK'S CANE & RUSH SUPPLY
7252 Heil Ave.
Huntington Beach, CA 92647
(714) 847-0707

Offers: Basket and seat-weaving supplies, including 5 rattans and shredded rattan, poles, cane and binder cane, cane webbing, reed spline, fiber and wire rush, Danish cord, flat fiber, fiber wicker and braids, round reeds, oriental seagrass and coir, rice straw, raffia, sisal, hoops, handles, bases, dowels, braces, plugs and pins. Also carries candle cups, mugs, pegs, hearts, wheels, basket kits and furniture kits. Upholstery supplies available include cords, strips, tools, edgings, polyfilament and brass hardware. Tools available include awls, chisels, cutters, staple guns, templates and calipers.
For Further Information: Free catalog.
Store Location: Yes
Discounts: Quantity discounts; sells wholesale to legitimate businesses.
Accepts: MasterCard, Visa

GH PRODUCTIONS
521 E. Walnut St.
Scottsville, KY 42164

Offers: Basket kits. Supplies available include handcrafted white oak basket handles and splints, reed, cane, waxed linen thread, tools and books.
For Further Information: Catalog, $1 (refundable).

GRATIOT LAKE BASKETRY
Star Rt., P.O. Box 16
Mohawk, MI 49950
(906) 337-5116

Offers: Basketry supplies, including white pulute, maple, black walnut, cherry, 6 types of reeds, ash splint, red oak, poplar, seagrass, cane bindings, slab and chair rattan and cane webbing. Hoops are available in 9 sizes, including oak rims/hoops and poplar hoops. Also carries spline, 5 swing handles, bushel handles, D-shape handles, ash handles, oak handles, and round double-notched handles. Florida materials available include grapevines and philodendron sheaths. Patterns and books are also available.
For Further Information: Free catalog and newsletter.
Discounts: Quantity discounts; allows discounts to teachers and institutions; sells wholesale to legitimate businesses.

A branch from a tree can be carved for a handle on the shavehorse, then carefully bent fresh or boiled. A relatively twig-free branch cut in half and boiled may serve for rims.
—John McGuire Basket Supplies

GREAT AUNT VICTORIA'S WICKER
P.O. Box 99
Waubaushene, Ontario L0K 2C0 Canada

Offers: Basket kits, round and flat reed, seagrass, dyes and books.
For Further Information: Send SASE with inquiry.

THE HANDLE WORKS
8400 Old Hartsville Rd.
Adolphus, KY 42120

Offers: Basket handles handcrafted of white oak (swing handles with ears), plus basket rims, tools and books.

For Further Information: Catalog, $1 (refundable).

JAM CREATIONS
P.O. Box 31024
Highland, MI 48031

Offers: Books, including *Friendship Baskets* (patterns for beginner to advanced), *Tribute* (23 patterns for all levels, as a tribute to basketmakers who added sparkle to weaving) and *Tole Sampler* (weaving patterns and painting instructions).
For Further Information: Send SASE for price list.

MADE IN THE SHADE
4842 W. Flamingo Rd.
Tampa, FL 33611
(813) 837-5243

Offers: Basket weaving materials, including multi-reed, handspun yarns, philodendron sheaths and palm sprays.
For Further Information: Send $1 for samples and prices.

JOHN MCGUIRE
398 S. Main
Geneva, NY 14456
(315) 781-1251

Offers: Basketry supplies including Nantucket-style kits, molds, resin molds, Nantucket cane, reed and white oak rims and bases. Materials available include black ash, white ash and oak, red cedar bark, bear grass, reeds, cane. Also carries splint-cutting machines, table-top shavehorses and tools such as cutters, nippers and knives. Bindings, handles and dyes (Basket Tree, Comcraft, W. Cushing) are available.
For Further Information: Send business-size SASE with 52¢ postage for information.
Store Location: Yes
Discounts: Quantity discounts.

THE NORESTA
320 Western Ave.
Allegan, MI 49010
(616) 673-3249

Offers: Basketry supplies including press cane, hank cane, rush, splint, wicker, flat and round reeds, hoops, handles, dyes, basketry tools and books.
For Further Information: Send SASE for price catalog.
Discounts: Sells wholesale.

NORTH CAROLINA BASKET WORKS
1808 Phillips Dr.
Sanford, NC 27330

Offers: A distinctive selection of basketry kits, plus a complete line of supplies, including reeds, other naturals, and a large selection of handmade white oak handles. Also carries Nantucket and Shaker hardwood molds—accurate repro-

ductions; rental is available on selected molds.
For Further Information: Send a 45¢ stamp for price list.
Discounts: Sells wholesale.

OZARK BASKETRY SUPPLY
599 FA
Fayetteville, AR 72702

Offers: Supplies including basketry kits, tools, chair canes, handles, hoops, materials, chair seating supplies, dyes— "low priced." Carries 100 plus books.
For Further Information: Catalog, $4.
Discounts: Sells wholesale.
Accepts: MasterCard, Visa

J. PAGE BASKETRY
820 Albee Road W., Casey Key Plaza
Nokomis, FL 34275
(813) 485-6730

Offers: Full line of basketmaking supplies, equipment and books.
For Further Information: Catalog, $2 (refundable).
Store Location: Yes

When cutting spokes for your baskets, cut long spokes diagonally at ends and short spokes blunt. You won't have to remeasure when you are ready to weave.

—Gratiot Lake Baketry

H.H. PERKINS CO.
10 S. Bradley Rd.
Woodbridge, CT 06525
(203) 389-9501

Offers: Caning supplies, strands (over 5 widths) by bunch; plastic cane (3 widths) by coils. Also carries fiber splinty and rush, Hong Kong grass, reed—flat, ash, flat oval. Carries kits for bench, barstool, ladder back chairs, rockers and others. Reed kits available include doll cradlestools and others. Reeds, raffia (color), basket bases, hoops and books are also available.
For Further Information: Seat/basket weaving booklet and catalog, $1.
Accepts: MasterCard, Visa

PLYMOUTH REED & CANE SUPPLY
1200 W. Ann Arbor Rd.
Plymouth, MI 48170
(313) 455-2150

Offers: Basketmaking supplies including natural weaving products, handles, hoops, tools, Old Village Collection basketry kits, chair seating materials, dyes and books.
For Further Information: Send for catalog.

Store Location: Yes
Discounts: Quantity discounts; sells wholesale to teachers, institutions and legitimate businesses.
Accepts: Discover, MasterCard, Visa

QUIST CO.
16484 Highway 202
Rocky Ford, CO 81067

Offers: Rope-making machine (for swings, jump ropes, etc.).
For Further Information: Send SASE for details.

ROYALWOOD LTD.
517 Woodville Rd.
Mansfield, OH 44907
(419) 526-1630

Offers: Basketry supplies including Irish waxed linen, a line of reed and other naturals, hoops, handles, dyes, accessories, basketry kits, brown ash, tools and molds.
For Further Information: Catalog, $1.50.
Store Location: Yes
Discounts: Quantity discounts.

V.I. REED & CANE
Rt. 5, P.O. Box 632
Rogers, AR 72756
(501) 789-2639

Offers: Over 18 basketry kits, instructions and sets for mail, flower, Cape Cod, tray, "tulip," bushel, Easter, heart and other baskets. Also carries reeds, smoked reed, cane and cane webbing, raffia, handles, wood hoops and others.
For Further Information: Catalog, $1.
Discounts: Quantity discounts; allows discounts to legitimate businesses.
Accepts: MasterCard, Visa

VICTORIAN VIDEO PRODUCTIONS
P.O. Box 1540
Colfax, CA 95713
(916) 346-6184

Offers: Instructional videos, including basketry demonstrating techniques for splint, Appalachian egg and melon-type baskets with handle decoration choices. Offers 19 other craft videos.
For Further Information: Free catalog.
Discounts: Allows discounts to schools and libraries; sells wholesale to legitimate businesses.
Accepts: MasterCard, Visa
See Also: General Needlecraft Supplies, Lace Making and Spinning and Weaving

WALTERS, LTD.
Mountain Rd.
Washington Island, WI 54246
(414) 847-2276

Offers: Basketry materials include English basket willow (imported from Bristol, England) and propagated root, which comes with rooting powder and instructions for growing your own materials.
For Further Information: Send SASE for full information.

THE WOOL ROOM
Laurelton Rd.
Mount Kisco, NY 10549
(914) 241-1910

Offers: Line of basketry supplies. (Also weaving and knitting equipment and yarns.)
For Further Information: Send $1 and SASE for catalog.
Discounts: Quantity discounts; allows discounts to teachers and institutions.

When lashing on a border with cane, pull up your cane to its mid-point. Then lash in one direction with one half and in the other direction with the second half. This will mean less friction on the piece of cane, and less breakage.

—V.I. Reed & Cane

Bead Crafts

Also see General Craft Supplies, Indian and Frontier Crafts, Jewelry Making and Lapidary, Miniature Making and related categories.

ALOHALEI HAWAII
P.O. Box 3070
Pueblo, CO 81005

Offers: A line of beads (pearl and others) and craft supplies, "How to Bead" books and others.
For Further Information: Catalog and pattern, $1 (refundable).
Discounts: "Lowest prices."

ART TO WEAR
4202 Water Oaks Lane
Tampa, FL 33624
(813) 265-1681

Offers: Bead stringing (jeweler's) tools such as pliers, tweezers, scissors, pin vises and awls. Also carries bead boards, needles, tips, crimps, tigertails, cable chains, foxtails, boullion wire, needle cards, silk cones, spool cord kits and jewelry findings. Beads include sterling, 13 kt, gold-filled types, semi-precious gemstone beads and cultured and freshwater pearls. Carries designer bead kits and books.
For Further Information: Catalog, $1.
Discounts: Sells wholesale to dealers.

ARTWAY CRAFTS
P.O. Box 1369
Van Alstyne, TX 75495

Offers: Beads, including acrylics, plastics, woods, crystal, alphabet, pearls, rocailles, glass fruit, seed aurora borealis and teardrops. Also carries bead ornament kits and baskets, rhinestones and setters, spangles, 14 Ming tree kits (with wire forms), brass and beading wires and tigertails.
For Further Information: Catalog, $1 (refundable).
Discounts: Quantity discounts.
Accepts: Discover, MasterCard, Visa

BALLY BEAD CO.
P.O. Box 934
Rockwall, TX 75087

Offers: Jewelry making supplies, including gemstones, fetishes, Heishi, old coins and other ethnic items. Beads include wood, Czech crystal, seed, antique silver, 14 kt, gold-filled, sterling and plated types. Carries designer jewelry parts (specalizes in ethnic and Santa Fe looks) and beading supplies. Offers knotting and beading lessons. (Also has finished jewelry.)
For Further Information: Catalog, $4.95 (refundable).
Accepts: Discover, MasterCard, Visa

THE BEAD DIRECTORY
P.O. Box 10103
Oakland, CA 94610

Offers: Directory listing over 250 bead sellers, bazaars, sources, how-tos and classes, and includes coupons.
For Further Information: Write for further details.
Discounts: Sells wholesale.

BEAD LADY DESIGNS
P.O. Box 1060
Freeland, WA 98249
(206) 221-8412

Offers: Maple wood bead loom, adjustable/interchangeable, to serve as 3 size looms in one—6 inches × 12 inches, 24 inches, 36 inches—with double weft or heddle beadweaving.
For Further Information: Write for information.
Accepts: MasterCard, Visa

THE BEAD SHOP
177 Hamilton Ave.
Palo Alto, CA 94301

Offers: Line of beads and bead kits, and sampler boxes including exotics, ancient, "jeweled," gemstone, metal and glass beads. Also carries charms, findings, threads and other supplies.
For Further Information: Catalog, $3.
Discounts: Sells wholesale.

BEADASIAN
P.O. Box 795
Carteret, NJ 07008

Offers: Philippine beads—wood, bone, horn, shell and other types in a variety of sizes and shapes.
For Further Information: Send business-size SASE for catalog.

BEADS-BY-THE-BAY
P.O. Box 5488
Novato, CA 94948
(415) 883-1098

Offers: Beads (specializes in Czechoslovakian beads)—seed, bugle, fire polish and others. Also carries jewelry findings and supplies.
For Further Information: Catalog, $4.25.
Discounts: Sells wholesale.

BEADWORKS
139 Washington St.
South Norwalk, CT 06854
(203) 852-9194

Offers: Contemporary beads from areas worldwide—over 2,000 styles, sizes and colors.
For Further Information: See your dealer, or send SASE for details.

BOONE TRADING COMPANY
562 Coyote Rd.
Brinnon, WA 98320
(206) 796-4330

Offers: Antique glass trade beads (strung), including circa 1800s "white hearts," translucent red/white center, blue smalls, jade green or medium blue glass. Carries padre beads (⅜-inch turquoise round, circa 1500s) and Russian blues (⅜-inch faceted opaque blue, circa 1800s).
For Further Information: Catalog, $1.
Discounts: Quantity discounts; sells wholesale to businesses.
See Also: Scrimshaw

BOVIS BEAD CO.
23 Main St.
P.O. Box 111
Bisbee, AZ 85603
(602) 432-7373

Offers: Rare antique beads from areas worldwide, including religious, traders and merchants of antiquities. Other items include ceramic beads from Mexico, Peru and Guatemala and Navajo sterling beads. Also carries malachite, garnet, azurite and other gemstone beads in a wide array of sizes, colors and types. Beading supplies available include needles, cords and jewelry findings. Books are also available.
For Further Information: Illustrated catalog, $10 (refundable).

BRAHM LIMITED
P.O. Box 1
Lake Charles, LA 70602

Offers: A wide array of precious and semi-precious stones (abalone, agate, amethyst, aquamarine, carnelian, coral, facet jasper, onyx, obsidian, malachite, peridot, rose quartz, turquoise, topaz and others). Also carries acrylic beads (simulated tones in a variety of shapes and colors), costume jewelry beads (in glass, acrylic and wood), bead wire, threads, jewelry findings in 14 kt and gold-filled, sterling, rhodium and surgical steel, plus rattail ribbons. Wires are available in sterling, gold-filled, tigertail, square brass, copper and sterling silver.
For Further Information: Catalog, $2.50.
Discounts: Quantity discount; allows discounts to teachers and institutions.

CANYON RECORDS & INDIAN ARTS
4143 N. 16th St.
Phoenix, AZ 85016
(206) 266-4823

Offers: Beads in a variety of types and sizes—seeds, recailles, bugles, crow, hexagon, metal and bone. Also carries threads, quills, furs, shells, feathers, findings and shawl fringes.
For Further Information: Request craft list.

CENTER FOR THE STUDY OF BEADWORK
P.O. Box 13719
Portland, OR 97213
(503) 249-1848

Offers: Native American beadwork books, resources and a newsletter. Books include authentic techniques and data, specific tribal and regional beading, patterns and data.
For Further Information: Catalog and sample newsletter, $2.50.

BETTY FENSTERMAKER COCHRAN
845 Willow Rd.
Lancaster, PA 17601
(717) 392-1865

Offers: G.B. Fenstermaker's glass trade bead book series including *Chinese Beads*, *Medicine Man*, *Late Beads in African Trade*, *Early Trading Post Beads*, *The Russian Bead*, *Colonial Turkish Colored Bead Chart* and others.
For Further Information: Send SASE for list.

SIDNEY COE, INC.
65 W. 37th St.
New York, NY 10018
(212) 391-6960

Offers: Full line of beads in many styles, colors, sizes and types, including glass, plastic and others.
For Further Information: Catalog, $2.

COLUMBINE BEADS
2723 Loch Haven Dr.
Ijamsville, MD 21754
(800) 638-6947

Offers: Beads, including glass seed and bugles, plus bead looms, threads and needles.
For Further Information: Catalog, $3.
Discounts: "Bimonthly specials."

DIANE'S BEADS
1803 W. Main St.
Medford, OR 97501
(503) 779-5139

Offers: Beads, including seed, bugle, crow and pony, bead supplies, looms and books. Buys glass beads.
For Further Information: Catalog, $4.

DISCOUNT BEAD HOUSE
P.O. Box 186
The Plains, OH 45780
(800) 793-7592

Offers: Line of designer beads in large quantity lots.
For Further Information: Catalog, $3.
Discounts: Sells wholesale.

FIREFLY EMBROIDERIES
P.O. Box 304
Davisburg, MI 48350
(313) 634-3649

Offers: Beaded appliqué kits (with glass beads, sequins, pattern, needles and fabric) and a variety of designs for clothes, jewelry and accessories.
For Further Information: Send SASE for details.

THE FREED CO.
415 Central NW
P.O. Box 394
Albuquerque, NM 87102
(505) 247-9311

Offers: Beads, including collector types, gemstones (coral, amber, ivory and others), clay, wood, glass, cinnabar, metal, cloisonne and oddities. Also carries fetishes, netsuke, sequins, appliqués and milagros.
For Further Information: Send SASE for list.

THE GARDEN OF BEADIN'
P.O. Box 1535
Redway, CA 95560
(707) 923-9120

Offers: Beads, including clay shapes, bugles, glass seed (in a full range of colors), crow, pony, nex, crystal and other gemstone colors, plus Czech drops, crystal faceted, glass, crystal and other gemstone colors. Carries odd-shaped wood beads, including large holed. Ethnic beads include Peruvian, Venetian, satin glass and pseudo trade. Also carries metal and semi-precious beads, hearts, chips and rounds, plus needles and findings.
For Further Information: Catalog, $2.
Discounts: Quantity discounts; sells wholesale.
Accepts: MasterCard, Visa

ROXY GRINNELL
P.O. Box 1155
Paonia, CO 81428
(303) 527-0365

Offers: Beads, including crow, pony, 9/0-3 cuts, 11/0 and 14/0 seeds, bugles, rounds, tubes, chevrons, mosaics, metal, bone, quills and mother-of-pearl, plus supplies.
For Further Information: Free catalog.

HANSA
4315 Upton Ave. S.
Minneapolis, MN 55410
(612) 925-6014

Offers: Venetian glass beads and hand-formed beads, including millefiori, chevron, fiorato, floral, foil and lamp.
For Further Information: Catalog, $2.

KAYDEE BEAD SUPPLY
P.O. Box 07340
Fort Myers, FL 33919

Offers: Full line of beads, pearls and buttons.
For Further Information: Catalog, $2 (refundable).
Discounts: Quantity discounts.

KUMACO
P.O. Box 25049
Glenville, NY 12325

Offers: Gemstone beads including jade, coral, turquoise, ivory, Chinese porcelain, crystal, bone, horn, shell, liquid silver and others. Also carries jewelry findings, supplies, tools, stringing kits and books.
For Further Information: Catalog, $1.

MANGUM'S WESTERN WEAR
P.O. Box 362
Blackfoot, ID 83221
(208) 785-9967

Offers: Seed beads (down to size 24); will match color swatches.
For Further Information: Catalog, $1.

99 BEADS
2263 Old Middlefield Way
Mountain View, CA 94043

Offers: A line of beads in a variety of shapes, styles and sizes.
For Further Information: Catalog, $5.

ORNAMENTAL RESOURCES, INC.
P.O. Box 3010
Idaho Springs, CO 80452
(303) 567-4988

Offers: Full and complete lines of beads, including glass (faceted, cut, pearlized, foiled, decorated, fancy and Pekina types, in variety of sizes, shapes and colors), pendants and drops of glass. Other bead types include metal, wood, ceramic, plastic, bone, stone and shell. Carries bugle beads up to 1½ inches long and pony and seed beads in all sizes. Offers rare and unusual beads for collectors, plus plastic and glass bead chains, metal stampings, appliqué materials and motifs, rhinestones and studs, beading tools/supplies, sequins, glass jewels, old bullion trims, tassels, buckles, buttons, jewels. Offers a custom design service. ($50 minimum order.)
For Further Information: Catalog, $25 (with one year's supplements), or send SASE for details.

PROMENADE'S
P.O. Box 2092
Boulder, CO 80306
(303) 440-4807

Offers: Full line of beadwork supplies (for beaded jewelry, trim on clothing and other). Also carries beading kits, threads, needles and bead instruction booklets for earrings, clothing and other articles.
For Further Information: Catalog, $2.50 (refundable).

SHIPWRECK BEADS
5021 Mud Bay Rd.
Olympia, WA 98502
(800) 950-4232

Offers: Full line of beads: glass, metal, wood, plastic, antique types and others.
For Further Information: Catalog, $3.
Discounts: Sells wholesale.

TOUCH THE EARTH
30 S. Main St.
Harrisonburg, VA 22801

Offers: Beads, including trade beads (chevrons, ovals, white hearts and Hudson Bay), faceted (lead crystal and colors), crow, abalone discs, pink conch beads, metal (hawk bells, mellon, solid brass, fluted) and bone hairpipe. Also carries glass strung beads, fancies (lined, pearls 3-cut, bugles), jewelry findings such as surgical steel, plated and sterling ear wires, clips and parts, needles, nymo thread and supplies. Stocks finished items as well.
For Further Information: Catalog, $2.

UNIVERSAL SYNERGETICS
16510 SW Edminston Rd.
Wilsonville, OR 97070
(503) 625-7168

Offers: Seed beads (11/0-22/0), bugles, findings, threads, needles and books.
For Further Information: Catalog, $2 plus 52¢ postage.
Discounts: Sells wholesale.

WESTCROFT BEADWORKS
139 Washington St.
South Norwalk, CT 06854
(203) 852-9194

Offers: Over 1,500 different beads including plastics, acrylics, glass types, wood, metal and others in a variety of sizes and shapes.
For Further Information: Catalog, $10 (refundable).
Discounts: Sells wholesale.

Ceramics

Also see Artist's Supplies, General Craft Supplies, Sculpture and Modeling, and Doll and Toy Making—Rigid. And note the many custom services available in this chapter.

AEGEAN SPONGE CO., INC.
4722 Memphis Ave.
Cleveland, OH 44144
(216) 749-1927

Offers: Imported water-mount decals including farm animal motifs (ducks, cows and others), plus ceramic and design tools. Ceramic supplies available include Christmas tree lights and sets, strobe and other bulbs, clocks, music boxes, turntables, touch banks, "twinkle-tone" and liquid gold.
For Further Information: Write for price list and supply catalog.

AFTOSA SPONGE CO., INC.
1034 Ohio Ave.
Richmond, CA 94804
(510) 233-0334

Offers: Supportive items including votive chimneys (clear, frosted), lamp kits, candles, mini-lamp kits/shades, lamp oil cartridges and oil, stoppers, dispenser pumps and wire whips. Also carries jewelry findings for pins and earrings, plus wax resist.
For Further Information: Free catalog.
Accepts: MasterCard, Visa

AIM KILNS
369 Main St.
Ramona, CA 92065

Offers: Doll kiln (designed by doll makers for doll makers), 15 amps, cone 10, 8-inch square, with shut off infinite switch.
For Further Information: Write or call for free literature.
Discounts: "Dealer and distributor inquiry invited."

ALBERTA'S MOLDS, INC.
P.O. Box 2018
Atascadero, CA 93423
(805) 466-9255

Offers: Full line of ceramic molds including classic, early American, novelty/holiday figures, animals, music box carousels and dinnerware.
For Further Information: Catalog, $6.

AMERICAN ART CLAY CO., INC.
4717 W. 16th St.
Indianapolis, IN 46222

Offers: AMACO ceramic supplies and glazes. Clays include firing, nonfiring, modeling and other types. Electric kilns include cone 10 gas models and others. Potter's wheels include a rehabilitation model and electric types. Also offers custom decal supplies to make your own ceramic decals, including a handbook, screen bed, light post, clamp light with photo flood, hinges, screen, foam, plate glass, acetate, squeegees and film packet, plus an instructional video. Manufacturer.
For Further Information: Contact dealer, or send SASE for details.
See Also: Sculpture

ANN'S CERAMICS
282 St. Martins Rd.
Vine Grove, KY 40175

Offers: Line of Alberta bisque Christmas ornaments, plus others.
For Further Information: Send 35¢ and a business-size SASE for list.

ARNEL'S, INC.
2330 SE Harney St.
Portland, OR 97202
(503) 236-8540

Offers: Arnel's molds for ceramics including 65 plus mugs with decorative fronts, boxes (ring, powder, tissue, cigarette, flowered egg and others), cornucopias, plates, bowls, cups, serving dishes, wall plaques, 2 chess sets, animals, pedestals, kitchen ware, Christmas items, and religious and other figures.
For Further Information: Color catalog, $5.

ART DECAL CO.
1145 Loma Ave.
Long Beach, CA 90804
(213) 434-2711

Offers: Custom ceramic decals with complete art service. Minimum order of 125; food-safe colors available.
For Further Information: Send SASE with inquiry.

ARTFARE PRODUCTS
1 Village Green
Longwood, FL 32779
(407) 322-7187

Offers: Decals, including graphics, verses, country motifs and others. Also offers a custom decal service, including artwork and typesetting, with low minimum orders.
For Further Information: Send business-size SASE with 45¢ postage for flyer.
Discounts: Call for price quotes.

ATLANTIC MOLD CORP.
55 Main St.
Trenton, NJ 08620

Offers: Molds for figurines (children, historical, doll parts, birds, animals and others), Christmas items (nativity, angels, candles, dishes, Santas), and Easter and other holiday designs. Also offers spaceman/craft molds, decoratives, plaques, vases, clocks, containers, beer steins, emblems, chess sets, planters, platters, casseroles, cookie jars, bathroom items and bases. Accessories available include lamp parts, sets, Lanshire clock movements, Lucite lights. Manufacturer.
For Further Information: Contact your dealer; color catalog, $6.50.
Accepts: MasterCard, Visa

AV PRODUCTIONS
P.O. Box 1796
Troy, MI 48099
(313) 879-1884

Offers: Videos (with Daphne Smith) for beginners, plus instruction on casting/molds, firing various glazes and other techniques, plus *What the Judges See*. Also carries dollmaking books.
For Further Information: Write for information.
Accepts: MasterCard, Visa

BRICKYARD HOUSE OF CERAMICS
4721 W. 16th
Speedway, IN 46224
(317) 244-5230

Offers: Parts for kilns and wheels from Amaco, Brent, Reward, Skutt, Duncan, Paragon and Crusader, plus molds, glazes and tools.
For Further Information: Write or call for information.

BRYNE CERAMICS
95 Bartley Rd.
Flanders, NJ 07836
(201) 584-7492

Offers: Stoneware slip in 5 colors for kilns with cones 6 to 10, plus other slips, clays (earthware, raku, reduction, black and grogged), porcelains, glazes and marbleizers. Equipment available includes wheels, kilns and tools.
For Further Information: Free brochures.

CER CAL, INC.
626 N. San Gabriel Ave.
Azusa, CA 91702
(818) 969-1456

Offers: Custom decals, complete art service, color matching, sheet runs, gold and combination colors.
For Further Information: Send SASE for full details.

CERAMIC BUG SUPPLIES
17220 Garden Valley Rd.
Woodstock, IL 60098
(815) 568-7663

Offers: Ceramic bug slip marbleizer and 20,000 ceramic molds.
For Further Information: Send SASE for list.

CERAMIC RESTORATION
2622 N. Dobson Rd.
Chandler, AZ 85224

Offers: Instruction for restoration of damaged porcelains, ceramics and collectibles.
For Further Information: Send business-size SASE for information.

CERAMIC TILE ART
P.O. Box 28217
Oakdale, MN 55128
(612) 735-3715

Offers: Ceramic decals and art facilities.
For Further Information: Free brochure and samples.

CERAMICORNER, INC.
P.O. Box 1206
Grants Pass, OR 97526

Offers: Decals in over 800 designs, including floral, kitchen verses, labels, and others in traditional motifs.
For Further Information: CeramiCorner color decal catalog, $6; Matthey Florals color catalog, $6.

Use a quality venting system for a cleaner and healthier working environment.

—Skutt Ceramic Products

CHRISTIAN ART CO.
P.O. Box 200262
Austin, TX 78720

Offers: Jewelry molds, bisque and greenware selections.
For Further Information: Catalog, $4.50 (refundable).

CLAY MAGIC, INC.
21201 Russell Dr.
P.O. Box 148
Rockwood, MI 48173
(313) 379-3400

Offers: Ceramic molds (whimsical/fantasy) for holidays (Halloween, Christmas and others), plus wreaths, containers, lanterns and other items.
For Further Information: Catalog, $6.50.

CREATIVE CERAMICS
9815 Reeck
Allen Park, MI 48101
(313) 382-1270

Offers: Line of ceramic supplies in known brands.
For Further Information: Write or call for information.
Accepts: MasterCard, Visa

CREATIVE CORNER
P.O. Box 121
Canistota, SD 57012
(605) 296-3261

Offers: Over 1,200 items in bisque ware, including vases, covered dishes, mugs/cups and other dinnerware, fruits, bookends, racks and canisters. Animal figures include rabbits, squirrels, dinosaurs, and domestic animals. Offers holiday items for Christmas, Halloween and others, plus trees and lights, wide-base vases with Indian motifs, open mailboxes, figures (Pilgrims, Indians, angels, others), carousels (with ducks, bears, etc.) and carousel horses. Carries Duncan paints, brushes and accessories.
For Further Information: Catalog, $4.50.
Discounts: Sells wholesale to businesses.

CRIDGE, INC.
P.O. Box 210
Morrisville, PA 19067
(215) 295-3667

Offers: Full line of porcelain jewelry blanks, plus ornaments, findings and inserts.
For Further Information: Free catalog.
Discounts: Quantity discounts.

CUSTOM CERAMIC MOLDS
P.O. Box 1553
Brownwood, TX 76804
(915) 646-0125

Offers: Molds for ceramics, including jewelry, Indian thunderbird, desert cactus, buffalo, Indian fetish bear, chili pep-

per and Indian pot jewelry. Carries large chili peppers for Ristras pepper strings, Indian pots and peace pipe bowls.
For Further Information: Brochure, $5.

DAIZY BOOKS
3824 Smith Ave.
Everett, WA 98201
(206) 252-1684

Offers: Ceramic books including *Pour Molds*, *Christmas Projects*, *Ceramic Stains*, *Cleaning Greenware*, *Leaves Motifs* and others.
For Further Information: Free catalog.
Discounts: Sells wholesale.

DAKOTA SPECIALTIES
P.O. Box 655
Mandan, ND 58554
(701) 663-3682

Offers: Mold-making kit—"How to Make Your Own Molds"—and materials and instructions for making 2-piece molds. Book: *Advanced Mold Making*.
For Further Information: Send SASE for price information.

LOU DAVIS WHOLESALE
N3211 Highway H N.
Lake Geneva, WI 53147
(800) 748-7991

Offers: Ceramic supplies/equipment, including Kemper and Alcraft tools, Paasche airbrushes, adhesives, flan, clock parts, kiln accessories, desk pens and LCD clocks. Accessories include stoppers, lamp parts and bulbs, carousel bases, rods and parts. Carries gold, lusters, paints, brushes and finishes, plus musical movements and keys, jewelry findings and magnets.
For Further Information: Free catalog.
Discounts: Has discounts.
See Also: General Craft Supplies

DEBCOR
513 W. Taft Dr.
South Holland, IL 60473

Offers: Art/ceramic furniture, including drying and damp cabinets, kiln carts, kiln stands, wedging boards and clay carts. Also offers graphic arts furniture—write for details.
For Further Information: Free catalog.

DECAL LIQUIDATORS
229 Shelby St.
Indianapolis, IN 46202

Offers: Ceramic decals, including quality production designs, fires at cone 017/018 (016 on china); offers new patterns monthly ("not seconds or misprints"). Carries open

stick decals. Designs include traditional, holiday, floral, children, animals and others.
For Further Information: Sample decals, $1; stock catalog, $1.50.

DONGO MOLDS
15 School St.
Morriston, FL 32668
(904) 528-5385

Offers: Over 150 molds for aquariums, terrariums and other items for medium to large tanks. Offers custom mold making from specifications.
For Further Information: Catalog, $3.

DONNA'S MOLDS
P.O. Box 145
West Milton, OH 45383
(513) 947-1333

Offers: Molds including traditional, whimsical, holiday and novelty figures and sets.
For Further Information: Catalog, $7; SASE for flyer.

DURALITE, INC.
15 School St.
P.O. Box 188
Riverton, CT 06065
(203) 379-3113

Offers: Supplies for all brands/types kilns and furnaces, including rapid replacement coils (electric elements), plus straight wire and continous coil, and design services.
For Further Information: Write for brochure and price list.
Discounts: Quantity discounts.

ENGELHARD CORP.
70 Wood Ave. S.
Iselin, NJ 08830

Offers: Hanovia overglaze products, including lusters, metallics, ipal and mother of pearl (for ceramics, china and glass). Also offers Cerama-Pen gold or platinum applicator. Manufacturer.
For Further Information: Contact a dealer. Free technique sheets.

EVENHEAT KILN, INC.
6949 Legion Rd.
Caseville, MI 48725
(517) 856-2281

Offers: Line of kilns (variety of sizes and types), kiln accessories, supplies and parts.
For Further Information: Free brochure.

FAVOR-RITE MOLD CO.
516 Sea St.
Quincy, MA 02169
(617) 479-4107

Offers: Molds for ceramics—Aficana and Fash-en Hues lines.
For Further Information: Catalog, $3.50.

GARE, INC.
165 Rosemont St.
P.O. Box 1686
Haverhill, MA 01832
(508) 373-9131

Offers: Molds, including traditional figures, "The Sophisticates" (1920s stylized figures), holiday designs (including Christmas Windows series) and others. Also offers texture glazes, stains, fired colors, tools, brushes and kilns.
For Further Information: Flyer, $1.

GOLDLINE CERAMICS
3024 Gayle St.
Orange, CA 92665
(714) 637-2205

Offers: Ceramic decals, including 1,500 personal names. 20 minimum order, name.
For Further Information: Send SASE for list.

HILL DECAL CO.
5746 Schutz St.
Houston, TX 77032
(713) 449-1942

Offers: Custom decal service from your artwork, photo or sketch, or complete art services for glass, china and ceramics.
For Further Information: Write or call for information and supplies.

For more even firing, load ware directly onto the kiln brick bottom.

—Paragon Industries, Inc.

HOLLAND MOLD, INC.
P.O. Box 5021
Trenton, NJ 08638

Offers: Molds including the Country Pets series, featuring straw ducks, kittens and others. Also offers holiday items and sets, historical figures, wild animals, birds, eggs, steins, mugs, bowls, serving pieces, canisters, candlesticks, picture frames, plaques (marriage, birth, graduation, others), clocks, lamp bases, pedestals, jewelry, bells, boxes, accessories (clock movements, tree lights), and glaze and porcelain

slip. Custom mold service available. (Write for information. Ideas for new designs welcomed.) Manufacturer.
For Further Information: Mold catalog, $7.
Accepts: MasterCard, Visa

HOWE TO PUBLICATIONS
576 Carroll Ave.
Sacramento, CA 95838

Offers: The book *How to Repair Your Kiln at Home in Easy Step by Step Directions* (repair manual), by C.A. Wier, Kiln Design Engineer. Also carries replacement parts for all kilns, plus brick, elements, switches, lids and other supplies.
For Further Information: Free catalog.
Discounts: Discounts to distributors, dealers and service people.

JAY-KAY MOLDS
P.O. Box 2307
Quinlan, TX 75474
(903) 356-3416

Offers: Molds, including the Leather Wrap collection of vases with oval inserts (changeable faces) and other molds.
For Further Information: Color catalog, $4.
Discounts: Distributorships available.

KAIS, INC.
11943 Discovery Ct.
Moorpark, CA 93021
(805) 523-8986

Offers: Kais Tru Best china paint (use with waterbase or oil-base media), by vial or jar, plus acrylic and dry paint series.
For Further Information: Send SASE for information.
Discounts: Distributor and dealer discounts available.

KELLY'S CERAMICS, INC.
3016 Union Ave.
Pennsauken, NJ 08110
(609) 665-4181

Offers: Molds, including Gare, Atlantic, Dona, Holland, Iandola, Duncan, Kimple, Kansas, Nowell, Provincial, Trenton, Scioto, Macky, New Ocean State, Ceramichrome, Mayco, plus White Horse and Clay Magic. Gare distributor.
For Further Information: Send SASE for a flyer or reply.
Accepts: MasterCard, Visa

KIDCO, INC.
#16 Capri Ct.
Dix Hills, NY 11746

Offers: Line of ceramic decals featuring dogs and cats, and illustrating 90 breeds.
For Further Information: Sample and list, $2 (specify breed).

LAGUNA CLAY CO.
14400 Lomitas Ave.
City of Industry, CA 91715
(818) 330-0631

Offers: Line of ceramic supplies, including clays, glazes, equipment, tools and others. Lab assistance service is available.
For Further Information: Catalog, $5.
Store Location: Yes
Discounts: Quantity discounts; sells wholesale to dealers and distributors.

LAMP SPECIALTIES, INC.
P.O. Box 204
Westville, NJ 08093
(800) CALL-LAMP

Offers: Electronic music boxes with Touch-Me (including blinking lights or harmony types) and multi-tunes. Also carries carousels, lamp making parts (including kits and shades), sheet decals, foil leafing, gold leaf, clock parts (including fit-ups, quartz and electric), brushes (known brands), and Paasche and Badger airbrushes. Carries electrical items, such as tree kits, cord sets, bulbs and strobes. Overglazes, tools, pouring and cleaning items and accessories such as chenille, felt, stoppers, magnets, trims and findings are also available.
For Further Information: Catalog, $3.
Store Location: Yes
Discounts: Quantity discounts; sells wholesale to legitimate businesses.
Accepts: Discover, MasterCard, Visa

LAUKHUFF MOLD CO.
P.O. Box 306
New Holland, PA 17557

Offers: Custom service. Molds rebuilt from old molds; custom molds from sculpture or model.
For Further Information: Send SASE with inquiry.

LEE'S CERAMIC SUPPLY
103 Honeysuckle Dr.
West Monroe, LA 71291

Offers: Over 600 ceramic products; brand name and other lines.
For Further Information: Catalog and sales flyer, $2 (refundable).
Accepts: MasterCard, Visa

LEHMAN
P.O. Box 46
Kentland, IN 47951

Offers: Slip handling equipment, such as Paint Safe drying

table, Trim'N Clean tools, STK-1 slip testing kit, slip-doppe, and original and jumbo stencil pencils. Manufacturer.
For Further Information: Free information.

LILY POND PRODUCTS
2051 E. Tyler
Fresno, CA 93701
(209) 485-5115

Offers: Lil' Pumper ⅓ HP pump—heavy-duty and operates on 1 to 5 gallons of slip. Also offers Lil' Puddle table and Big Puddle mix/pour and reclaim machine with mixer, plus others.
For Further Information: Send SASE for further information.

MAGIC MUSICLAND
18312 Hollister Rd.
Orlando, FL 32820
(407) 548-1550

Offers: Touch music boxes (50 tunes) and bank coin-slot boxes (20 tunes).
For Further Information: Catalog, $1.50.

MARJON CERAMICS
3434 W. Earl Dr.
Phoenix, AZ 85017
(602) 272-6585

Offers: The instructional video, *Mold Making*, with Bill Anderson (creating molds step-by-step) and a complete mold-making kit (mold box, textbook, tools and supplies). Order the video and kit together for savings.
For Further Information: Send SASE for full details.
Accepts: MasterCard, Visa

MARYLAND CHINA CO.
54 Main St.
Reisterstown, MD 21136

Offers: Over 850 white porcelain blanks: tableware, giftware, novelty, souvenir items, white and gold banded dinnerware, coffee and beer mugs, promotional items, ashtrays and trivets, bells, plaques, desk accessories and others.
For Further Information: Contact dealer or send SASE for information.

MAYCO COLORS
4077 Weaver Ct. S.
Hilliard, OH 43026

Offers: Ceramic colors, finishes, glazes (Satina matte colors, exotics and others), stoneware glazes, lead-free glazes and crystal patterned. Also offers bisque colors and underglazes, non-firing opaque stains, translucents, metallics, non-fired pearl, stain kits, sealers, accent glazes and wax resist. Manufacturer.
For Further Information: Contact your dealer, or write for information.

MINNESOTA/MIDWEST CLAY
8001 Grand Ave. S.
Bloomington, MN 55420
(612) 884-9101, (800) 252-9872

Offers: Clays including Rainbow Air-Dry Clay (no firing needed), clay bodies, stonewares and porcelains, glazes (liquid and dry), chemicals, stains, lusters, overglazes, plaster and pouring tables. Also offers kilns and kiln parts, the products of Creative Industry, Skutt, Cress, Amaco, Brent, Lehman, Ohaus and others.
For Further Information: Free catalog.
Store Location: Yes
Discounts: Quantity discounts; allows discounts to teachers and institutions; sells wholesale to legitimate businesses.

MITIZI'S EXCLUSIVE MOLDS
141 Highway 22
Waupaca, WI 54981
(414) 622-3515

Offers: Service, producing custom-made specialty molds per specifications.
For Further Information: Send SASE with inquiry; send a model for evaluation.

NATIONAL ARTCRAFT CO.
23456 Mercantile Rd.
Beachwood, OH 44122
(216) 292-4944, (800) 793-0152

Offers: Ceramic and china paints and kits, brushes, tools and Evenheat kilns. Also offers china blanks, dinnerware, bells and accessories, plus porcelain bisque tiles and figurines. Carries dollmaking items, containers and extensive electrical parts in sets and kits, as well as clock making and kaleidoscope items.
For Further Information: Handcrafts catalog, $4.
Discounts: Quantity discounts.
See Also: General Craft Supplies

NATIONAL CERAMIC EQUIPMENT SALES & LEASING
32784 U.S. Highway 441
Leesburg, FL 34788
(904) 787-2267

Offers: Lease-to-own kiln program that features a "no interest lease" of a Reward Shurefire kiln for one year, then ownership; four kiln sizes available.
For Further Information: Write for information.
Accepts: MasterCard, Visa

NOWELL'S MOLDS
1532 Pointer Ridge Place
Bowie, MD 20716
(301) 249-0846

Offers: Molds for ceramics, including whimsical shadowbox plaques — 3 molds make over 20 combinations, including window seat, rocking chair and oval shadowbox. Also carries molds for bears, rabbits, dogs, oil lamps, table lamps, bells, boots, bonnets, parasols, ballet dancers, vases, pitchers, bowls, cat picture frames, grapevine wreaths, bicycles and others. Sizes vary from ½-inch to 3 inches. Carries Super Brute ¾-inch disc magnets (3 times as strong as ordinary).
For Further Information: Card catalog, $3.
Discounts: Quantity discounts.
Accepts: MasterCard, Visa

Seating a warm element with plastic can ruin the element.
— Paragon Industries, Inc.

O.P.R.
P.O. Box 3543
Lennox, CA 90304
(213) 973-5281

Offers: Quick paint remover for ceramics that removes fired-on paint, decals, gold and lusters from china, bisque or glass; 12 bottle minimum.
For Further Information: Send SASE for price lists.
Discounts: Sells wholesale.

EDWARD ORTON JR. CERAMIC FOUNDATION
6991 Old 3C Highway
P.O. Box 460
Westerville, OH 43081
(614) 895-2663

Offers: Pyrometric products, including self-supporting cones, pyrometric bars, others to measure heat treatment, indicate or control kiln shut-off and monitor firings, plus kiln ventilation systems and supplies, and firing items.
For Further Information: See your dealer or send for catalog.
Discounts: Sells wholesale to legitimate businesses.

PARAGON INDUSTRIES, INC.
2011 S. Town E. Blvd.
Mesquite, TX 75149
(214) 288-7557

Offers: Full line of ceramic kilns, china painting kilns, heat-treating and knife-making furnaces, glass fused jewelry kilns and kiln accessories. Manufacturer.
For Further Information: Free catalog.
Discounts: Sells to consumers only if there is no area dealer.

PEACHTREE ENTERPRISES
1804 Pershing Ct.
Davenport, IA 52803
(319) 324-3383

Offers: Peachtree brand porcelain slip, including Alaskan snow white, translucent self glazing, doll flesh colors and CDW slip.
For Further Information: Write for information.
Discounts: Sells wholesale.
Accepts: MasterCard, Visa

PIERCE TOOLS
1610 Parkdale Dr.
Grants Pass, OR 97527
(503) 476-1778

Offers: "Gold line" ceramic modeling tools and sets.
For Further Information: Free catalog.
Accepts: MasterCard, Visa

PINE TREE MOLDS
14596 S. Main St.
P.O. Box 33
Mill Village, PA 16427

Offers: Ceramic molds, including Victorian houses, gazebos, plaques (doves/bells, duck/daisies, church, lighthouse and others) and planters.
For Further Information: Send SASE for information.

CAROL REINERT CERAMICS
1100 Grosser Rd.
Gilbertsville, PA 19525
(215) 367-4373

Offers: Ceramic molds by Dona's Molds, Scioto, Nowell, Georgie's Bulldog, Starlight, Catskill, Gator, Kimple. Also carries Dona's Hues, Kimple stains, Royal brushes, music boxes, decals, electrical supplies, plastic lights and others.
For Further Information: Send SASE or call for list.

REWARD CERAMIC COLOR MANUFACTURING CO.
4717 W. 16th St.
Indianapolis, IN 46222
(317) 244-6871

Offers: Glazes, stains, tools and brushes, plus a wide variety of ceramic molds in traditional and other styles, including figures, figure groupings, scenes, animals and others. Manufacturer.
For Further Information: Contact your dealer, or send SASE for details.

RIVER VIEW MOLDS
2141 P. Ave.
Williamsburg, IA 52361

Offers: Line of molds including holiday designs, figures and others.
For Further Information: Color catalog, $6.

ROCKING B MANUFACTURING
3924 Camphor Ave.
Newbury Park, CA 91320
(805) 499-9336

Offers: Music boxes including Sankyo 18-jewel movement, mini, mobile, electronic Touch-Me, bank slot and Touch-Me with blinking lights, Waggie Arm and accordion sleeve movements. Accessories available include turntables, keys and extenders.
For Further Information: Send SASE for catalog.
Discounts: Quantity discounts; allows discounts to teachers and institutions; sells wholesale to legitimate businesses.

RYNNE CHINA CO
222 W. Eight Mile Rd.
Hazel Park, MI 48030

Offers: Full and complete line of china blanks—plates, bowls, cups, saucers, creamers, sugar bowls, serving dishes and others. Also offers gold-rimmed items. Manufacturer.
For Further Information: Free catalog.

SCHOOLHOUSE CERAMICS
3860 Columbia Rd.
North Olmsted, OH 44070
(216) 777-5155

Offers: Line of bisque with many popular breeds of dogs and cats.
For Further Information: Send SASE for pictures of specific breeds.

SCIOTO CERAMIC PRODUCTS, INC.
2455 Harrisburg Pike
Grove City, OH 43123
(614) 871-0090

Offers: Molds, including classical, whimsical, contemporary, traditional, fantasy, holiday, Western and other motifs, plus cherubs and other angels, animals, fowl, figures, villages, creches and Christmas ornaments. Also offers vases, planters, pots, pedestals, scenes, bird feeders, 2 chess sets and others.
For Further Information: Mold catalog, $5 plus $2 postage.
Store Location: Yes
Discounts: Sells wholesale to legitimate businesses.

SCOTT PUBLICATIONS
30595 Eight Mile Rd.
Livonia, MI 48152
(313) 477-6650

Offers: Instructional books and videos: Subjects include airbrush, brush stroke, mold making, pottery, clay, sculpting, general techniques, patterns, china painting and porcelain.
For Further Information: Send SASE for list.
Discounts: Sells wholesale to legitimate businesses.
See Also: Doll and Toy Making—Rigid

SKUTT CERAMIC PRODUCTS
2618 SE Tibbetts St.
Portland, OR 97202
(503) 231-7726

Offers: Electric kilns, featuring multi-sided models in modular-section construction, stainless steel jackets, reversible fire-brick bottom slabs; cone 1 to cone 10 models. Also offers cone 6 portable, supersized models, Enviro-Vent for kilns (vents fumes outdoors), kiln furniture, accessories and parts, plus Potter's tools and aids. Manufacturer.
For Further Information: Write for information and nearest dealer.

SPECTRUM CERAMICS, INC.
2576 Overlook Dr.
Germantown, TN 38138

Offers: Casting equipment including 18-gallon caster, submersible pump, removable mold rack, plus slip, modeling clay and molds.
Manufacturer.
For Further Information: Contact your dealer, or write for catalog.

STAR STILTS CO.
P.O. Box 367
Feasterville, PA 19053
(215) 357-1893

Offers: Stilts product's including napkin ring, star tree, rods (setter for beads, buttons, trinkets and others), bell type, junior shelves, high stilts (5 sizes), element retaining stables and others.
For Further Information: Contact dealer, or write for catalog.

SUGAR CREEK INDUSTRIES, INC.
P.O. Box 354
Linden, IN 47955
(317) 339-4641

Offers: Pouring room equipment, including over 60 items such as pouring machines (from a 4 gallon Flow Baby to a basic 125 gallon unit), pumps (immersion red heads, reversible/external), mixers and reclaimers (from 1 gallon porcelain to 200 gallons), tables (4 foot through 16 foot in 6 sizes) and the Spraymaster booth for greenware, airbrush and other uses.
For Further Information: Free catalog.

Achieve brighter and more vibrant colors when firing ceramics by using a down-draft kiln vent to bring the proper amount of air into the kiln.

— Orton Ceramic Foundation

TAMPA BAY MOLD CO.
2724 22nd St. N.
St. Petersburg, FL 33713

Offers: Original molds in a full line of traditional designs.
For Further Information: Catalog, $2.

TRENTON MOLD
329 Whitehead Rd.
Trenton, NJ 08619
(609) 890-0606

Offers: Molds, including dog figurines (32 popular breeds), other animals, holiday items, figures, plaques, vases, pitchers and others.
For Further Information: Color catalog, $4.

VITO'S CERAMIC SUPPLY
P.O. Box 422
Tewksbury, MA 01876
(508) 851-4232

Offers: Ceramic bisque from the molds of a variety of manufacturers.
For Further Information: Catalog, $3.
Discounts: Quantity discounts.
Accepts: MasterCard, Visa

WESTWOOD CERAMIC SUPPLY
14400 Lomitas Ave.
City of Industry, CA 91715

Offers: Casting clay bodies in earthenware, stoneware and porcelain (50 pounds and up). Also offers special clay formulas, low-fire clays, raku, high/low-fire casting bodies, chemicals, colors and finishes (including metallics, texture and other glazes, and lusters), Egyptian paste, Engobe stains, and equipment (of known brands such as Kemper, Kingspin, Ohaus, Cress, Olympic and others). Books are also available. Manufacturer, distributor.
For Further Information: Catalog, $5.

WISE SCREENPRINT, INC.
1015 Valley St.
Dayton, OH 45404
(513) 223-1573

Offers: Custom ceramic and glass decals from customer's rough sketch, photo or artwork. Complete art services, design and technical assistance are available.
For Further Information: Free color card, price list and samples.

ZEMBILLAS SPONGE CO., INC.
P.O. Box 24
Campbell, OH 44405
(216) 755-1644

Offers: Mediterranean silk sponges in a variety of sizes, plus imported ceramic decals in a wide assortment of traditional motifs.
For Further Information: Catalog, $3.50 ($4.50 outside U.S.).

ZIP MANUFACTURING
13584 East Manito Rd.
Pekin, IL 61554
(309) 346-7916

Offers: Zip porcelain slip in 40 colors.
For Further Information: Send SASE for price list.

Clock Making

AMERICAN MINERAL GIFT
326 Steel Rd.
Feasterville, PA 19053
(215) 364-1114

Offers: Mini-quartz clock movements (3 shaft sizes) by 15 plus lots.
For Further Information: Free catalog.
Discounts: Quantity discounts.

B&J
620 Claymont Estate Dr.
Ballwin, MO 63011
(314) 394-4567

Offers: Line of clock kits (clock movements with hands and numbers, polished/drilled agate clock faces and clear Lucite stands), desk clock kits and large models (with 5-inch to 6½-inch faces). Carries quartz clock movements—Seiko, battery with 5/16-inch or 11/16-inch shaft (with hour, minute and second hands, hangers, hardware, numbers/dots).
For Further Information: Catalog, $3 (refundable).
Discounts: Quantity discounts.

BEEMAN'S CLOCK MANUFACTURING
109 W. Van Buren
Centerville, IA 52544

Offers: Clock movements, over 400 clock faces (classic, contemporary and others), wood cutouts and foil prints.
For Further Information: Catalog, $2.
Discounts: "All at wholesale."

CREATIVE CLOCK
P.O. Box 565
Hanson, MA 02341
(617) 293-2855

Offers: Clock components, movements and others.
For Further Information: Free catalog.

DECOR TIME
P.O. Box 277698
Sacramento, CA 95827
(916) 362-4777, (800) 487-2524

Offers: Full line of clock parts, dials, quartz motors and accessories. Also carries epoxy, resin, pen sets and others.
For Further Information: Free catalog.

EMPEROR CLOCK CO.
Emperor Industrial Park
Fairhope, AL 36532
(205) 928-2316

Offers: Clock kits, including grandfather, mantel and wall models in black walnut, cherry or oak with solid brass West German movements and dials. Also carries furniture kits and assembled clocks.
For Further Information: Color catalog, $1.

HASKELL'S
40 College
Waterville, ME 04901

Offers: Clock kits, parts and accessories, plus books.
For Further Information: Catalog, $6 (refundable).

HURST ASSOCIATES LTD.
405 Britannia Rd. E., #10
Mississauga, Ontario L4Z 3E6 Canada
(416) 890-0269

Offers: Folk art clock-making supplies, including folk art dials, decoy patterns, cross-stitch clocks and basic clock supplies.
For Further Information: Send SASE for full information.

KLOCKIT
P.O. Box 542
Lake Geneva, WI 53147
(414) 248-7000, (800) 556-2548

Offers: Clock kits (quartz or quartz Westminster chime movements), including wooden gears, shelf, schoolhouse or Alpine steeple models. Also carries wood blanks for clocks in various shapes, stitchery clocks, country wood kits (easy), desk clocks, wall clocks and jumbo watches. Grandfather, grandmother, and cypress clocks, desk sets, contemporary wood/brass, time and weather, mantel, banjo/cloth, gallery, nautical, carriage, time zone, cottage, carriage/moving moon, 400-day crystal and wood and regulator types are also available. Parts available include chimes, hardware, fit-ups, movements, pendulums, wood shapes, brass name plates, plus lamp items.
For Further Information: Free catalog.
Store Location: Yes
Discounts: Quantity discounts; allows discounts to teachers and institutions.
Accepts: Discover, MasterCard, Visa

KUEMPEL CHIME
21195 Minnetonka Blvd.
Excelsior, MN 55331

Offers: Redi-Kut clock kits (grandfather and other types) of walnut, cherry, mahogany or oak, with precision West German movements, handcrafted pendulums and hand-painted moon wheels. Also carries brass pendulums, tubular bells or Westminster rod chimes. Offers traditional styles.
For Further Information: Catalog, $2.

MASON & SULLIVAN
210 Wood Country Industrial Park
Parkersburg, WV 26101
(800) 542-9115

Offers: Antique reproduction clock kits, over 20 precut models, including grandfather, grandmother, wall, desk, mantel and others. Also carries clock parts and accessories, including hardware, imported precision movements, chimes and brass dials. Books are also available.
For Further Information: Free catalog.

MURRAY CLOCK CRAFT LTD.
510 McNicoll Ave.
Willowdale, Ontario M2H 2E1 Canada
(416) 499-4531

Offers: Clock plans and kits for grandfather, grandmother, wall and shelf models. Also carries battery, weight and spring driven movements and dials.
For Further Information: Catalog, $2 (refundable).

PRECISE CLOCK, INC.
8107 Braeburn Lane
Orland Park, IL 60462
(708) 403-0515

Offers: Clock fit-ups and mini-quartz movements, plus many styles of dials and hands.
For Further Information: Write or call for brochure.
Discounts: Sells wholesale.

PRECISION MOVEMENTS
4251 Chestnut St., P.O. Box 689
Emmaus, PA 18049
(215) 967-3156, (800) 533-2024

Offers: Full line of clock-making needs, including clock hands, dials, bezels, quartz movements, and a variety of clock styles and accessories.
For Further Information: Write or call for color catalog.
Discounts: "Quotations upon request."

PSMC, INC.
P.O. Box 5099
Oroville, CA 95966
(916) 589-1840

Offers: Clock-making parts, including quartz motors (SPD, NSN, Rhythm, Takane) — 5 mini and standard sizes, 4 pendulum types, 7 chimes/double chimes, 30 fit-ups, LCDs, alarms and reverse motors. Carries over 50 number sets, over 180 painted dials, over 60 starbursts, over 50 styles of hands, plus dials and bezel dial combinations.
For Further Information: Free catalog.

SCHOOL OF CLOCK REPAIR
6313 Come About Way
Awendaw, SC 29429
(803) 928-3489

Offers: Instructional videos on clock repair, a comprehensive home-study course "approved for veterans." Also carries clock-making tools.
For Further Information: Free catalog.

STEEBAR
P.O. Box 463
Andover, NJ 07821

Offers: Complete clock kits, music movements, components, plans, epoxy, prints and over 800 clock-making supplies (chimes, hands, dials, faces, blanks and others).
For Further Information: Catalog, $3 (refundable).

VILLAGE ORIGINALS
24140 Detroit Rd.
Cleveland, OH 44145
(800) 899-1314

Offers: Quartz movements — regular, miniature, pendulum and electronic chime, plus clock accessories and parts.
For Further Information: Free catalog.

WEISBECK DESIGN
25 E. Huron
Buffalo, NY 14203

Offers: Plans/pattern for contemporary classic mantel clock "by award winning designer." Others.
For Further Information: Write for information.

YANKEE INGENUITY
P.O. Box 113
Altus, OK 73522
(405) 477-2191

Offers: Line of battery clock movements in a variety of styles and sizes, plus accessory items.
For Further Information: Free catalog.
Discounts: Quantity discounts.

Construction — Full-Size Structures

Includes Houses, Barns, Garages, Shops, Docks, Studios, Tipis, Shelters, Gazebos, Saw Mills, Tepees.
Also see Miniature Making, Model Making, Tools and Equipment, Woodworking and related categories.

ASHLAND BARNS
990 Butler Creek
Ashland, OR 97520

Offers: Plans/blueprints for the construction of 82 classic (traditional) barns, mini-barns, garages and craftshops.
For Further Information: Catalog, $5 (refundable).

BARTON'S BARNWOOD
RR 3
Carp, Ontario K0A 1L0 Canada
(613) 839-5530

Offers: Weathered barn siding, old flooring, hand-hewn beams and other barn material by the square foot.
For Further Information: Send SASE for full details.

BETTER BUILT CORP.
845 Woburn St.
Wilmington, MA 01887
(508) 657-5636

Offers: Portable Sawmill, a one-man band sawmill that cuts 20-inch diameter logs into lumber ⅛ inch to 9 inches in thickness. Instructional video available.
For Further Information: Write for brochure.

BROWN ENGINEERING
P.O. Box 40
West Point, CA 95255

Offers: Lumberjack chainsaw sawmills with power-feed, cuts forward and reverse.
For Further Information: Send SASE for full information.

CARLISLE RESTORATION LUMBER
HCR 32, P.O. Box 679
Stoddard, NH 03464
(603) 446-3937

Offers: Wide pine flooring and paneling in Eastern white or Southern yellow pine, or wide oak. Installation service nationwide.
For Further Information: Send SASE for full information.

CONKLIN'S
RD 1, P.O. Box 70
Susquehanna, PA 18847
(717) 465-3832

Offers: Authentic antique barnwood and hand-hewn beams, old flooring, plus Pennsylvania flagstone and wall stone.
For Further Information: Send SASE for information.
Discounts: Sells wholesale.

DESIGN WORKS, INC.
11 Hitching Post Rd.
Amherst, MA 01002
(413) 549-9763

Offers: Model designing kit (cardboard) that aids in visualizing designs before building or adding to a home. Includes miniature items, floor-plan grids, scale ruler roof-slope calculator and appliance cut-outs.
For Further Information: Send SASE for full details.
Discounts: Quantity discounts; sells wholesale to teachers, institutions and professionals.

EBAC LUMBER DRYERS
5789 Park Plaza Ct.
Indianapolis, IN 46220
(317) 577-7870

Offers: Lumber dryer system (construct kiln, and Ebac supplies this drying equipment) for drying green lumber.
For Further Information: Write or call for information.

FANTASIA TRAINS
P.O. Box 1199
Port Washington, NY 11050
(516) 883-1120

Offers: Railroad cabooses in operating condition for remodeling as guest cabins, restaurants, stores or offices.
For Further Information: Send SASE for price list and availability.

FOLEY-BELSAW CO.
6301 Equitable Rd.
Kansas City, MO 64120

Offers: One-man sawmill—portable, use with PTO or low HP diesel or electric unit.
For Further Information: Free book: *How to Saw Lumber*.
Discounts: "Factory-direct selling."

FOLLANSBEE DOCK SYSTEMS
State St.
Follansbee, WV 26037
(304) 527-4500, (800) 223-3444 (except WV)

Offers: Dock products including heavy galvanized wood dock hardware, hinges, pipe and pile holders, ladders, dock boxes, power systems, boarding steps, uprights, fasteners, accessories, floating and stationary docks and float drums (air or foam filled), plus swim float kits.
For Further Information: Write or call for catalog.
Discounts: Sells at discount prices.

GRANBERG INTERNATIONAL
P.O. Box 425
Richmond, CA 94807
(510) 237-2099

Offers: Portable chainsaw lumber mill attachment (clamps to chain saw) that makes lumber from rough logs for furniture, beams, decks, cabins, etc.
For Further Information: Write for details.

GREATWOOD LOG HOMES, INC.
P.O. Box 707
Elkhart Lake, WI 53020

Offers: Traditional full log or insulated log home kits, with R-40 roof system of white cedar or pine.
For Further Information: Free booklet. Plan book (100 models), $8.95.

When planning a home building project, there's no substitute for seeing your plans in three dimensions.
—Design Works, Inc.

HOMESTEAD DESIGNS, INC.
P.O. Box 1058
Bellingham, WA 98227

Offers: Floor plans for small barns, workshops, garages, studios and compact country homes (including the Barnhouse series of starter homes); new designs in traditional styling combined with modern construction methods.
For Further Information: Designs book, $3.

THE IRON SHOP
400 Reed St.
P.O. Box 547
Broomall, PA 19008
(215) 544-7100

Offers: Oak stair kits (to-be-assembled) with hardware, handrail kit, in-between spindle kits and rail kits for enclosed landings.

For Further Information: Send SASE or call for free brochure.
Accepts: American Express, MasterCard, Visa

KEY DOME
P.O. Box 430253
South Miami, FL 33243

Offers: Dome home plans for 14 foot to 50 foot domes in a variety of shape combinations.
For Further Information: Plans/how-to book, $5.

LINDAL CEDAR HOMES
P.O. Box 24426
Seattle, WA 98124

Offers: Full line of plans for contemporary homes including A-frames, modified A-frames, houses for full-time use, vacation homes, and one- and two-story models.
For Further Information: Order catalog with 200 pages of plans for $15.

OREGON DOME, INC.
3215 Meadow Lane
Eugene, OR 97402
(503) 689-3443

Offers: Geodesic dome plans in a variety of design arrangements.
For Further Information: Catalog, price and planning set, $12.

PANTHER LODGES
P.O. Box 32
Normantown, WV 25267

Offers: Tepees, tepee poles and other pre-1840s products.
For Further Information: Catalog, $2 (refundable).
See Also: Indian and Frontier Crafts

SALTER INDUSTRIES
P.O. Box 183
Eagleville, PA 19408
(215) 631-1360

Offers: Metal spiral staircases, in install-it-yourself kit form for 3½ foot to 6 foot diameters, adjustable to any height; oak and brass options available. Manufacturer.
For Further Information: Free brochure.
Accepts: MasterCard, Visa

SANDY POND HARDWOODS
921 A Lancaster Pike
Quarryville, PA 17566
(717) 284-5030

Offers: Tiger and bird's eye lumber and flooring, plus other figured woods.
For Further Information: Send SASE for full information.

SHELTER SYSTEMS
P.O. Box 67
Aptos, CA 95001

Offers: Instant dome shelters, many quick-assemble models.
For Further Information: Catalog, $1.

TIMBERLINE GEODESICS
2015 Blake St.
Berkley, CA 94704
(415) 849-4481

Offers: Prefabricated dome home kits (precut and pre-drilled, with steel connector systems; iron, with heavy-duty steel connector system); as complete kit, street framing kit (all but pre-cut plywood), connector kit (with assembly instructions) in a variety of dome sizes/design combinations.
For Further Information: Information packet/catalog, $12.

TROY-BUILT MANUFACTURING CO.
102nd St. 9th Ave.
Troy, NY 12180

Offers: Greenhouse kit (to-be-assembled with hand tools) with over 50 square feet of usable space beneath a 7½ foot peak; includes glass (with double-strength glazing) and aluminum frame, with sliding door and built-in rain gutter.

For Further Information: Write for full details.

VINTAGE WOOD WORKS
Highway 34, P.O. Box 2265
Quinlan, TX 75474

Offers: Victorian and country gingerbread trims for buildings (solid wood), including brackets (for openings), porch turnings, gable decorations, spandrels and doorway embellishments in a wide range of styles and sizes.
For Further Information: 50-page illustrated catalog, $2.

VIXEN HILL
Elverson, PA 19520

Offers: Gazebo kits. Offers a wide selection of architecturally authentic gazebos, pre-engineered for easy assembly by the non-carpenter. Available in a variety of styles and sizes.
For Further Information: 20-page color catalog, $3.

WOOD MIZER PRODUCTS
8180 W. 10th St.
Indianapolis, IN 46214
(317) 271-1542

Offers: Portable sawmills with remote hydraulic log handling, capacities to 32 inches in diameter by 33 inches long; includes bandsaw cutting head. Solar Dry Kiln and Vacu-Kiln also available.
For Further Information: Catalog, $2; demonstration video, $10.
Accepts: MasterCard, Visa

Construction—Full-Size, Operating Vehicles

Includes Cars, Boats/Hovercraft, Trailers, Go Carts, Tractors.
Also see Model Making, Tools and Equipment and related categories.

A-1 RACING PARTS, INC.
770 Rt. 28, P.O. Box 4
Middlesex, NJ 08846
(201) 968-2323

Offers: For cars—Mustang II/Pinto-type struts, heavy-duty strut rods (production struts made from 1 inch stock, originals were ¾ inch), with same angle as Ford D5FZ3468 units, includes strut bushings and retainers.
For Further Information: Send SASE or call with inquiry.
Accepts: MasterCard, Visa

AERO-PROJECTS
P.O. Box 5118
Clinton, NJ 08809

Offers: Aero-Car hovercraft plans, for you-build (using ordinary tools). Is lawnmower engine powered, carries one person, and flies over any terrain.
For Further Information: Send SASE for full details.

ANTIQUE & CLASSIC AUTOMOTIVE, INC.
100 Sonwil Dr.
Buffalo, NY 14225
(716) 684-1167

Offers: Car kits, including a reproduction of the 1937 Jaguar SS-100, with the chrome features of the SS-100, and many pre-assembled components.
For Further Information: Free brochure and information package.
Accepts: American Express, MasterCard, Visa

ARIZONA Z CAR
2110 W. Devonshire St.
Mesa, AZ 85201
(602) 844-9677

Offers: Performance parts for Datsun 240Z through 280ZX. Comes with exotic GTO body kit, race bodies, spoilers, springs, swaybars, racing brakes, tube chassis, roll cages, carb kits, turbos, G-nose. Headers, flywheels, shocks available.
For Further Information: Catalog, $2.

ATLANTA KIT & CUSTOM CARS
2560 S. Hairston Rd.
Decatur, GA 30035
(404) 981-4143

Offers: Custom kit car assembly service for any model, from crate to turnkey. Also offers kit car accessories, aero packages, lowering kits, and aluminum and ceramic thermal coating.
For Further Information: Send SASE or call with inquiry.

BERNIE BERGMANN, VW MOTOR SPEC.
340 N. Hale Ave.
Escondido, CA 92029

Offers: Car parts including Turbocharged VW motors, both single and dual carbureted, single/dual carbureted engines for sedans, Baja, Rail, kit cars and others. Also carries engine kits/parts, hydraulic lifters, unleaded heads, shuffle pins and others.
For Further Information: Photo products display, $2.

CLARKCRAFT
16 Aqualane
Tonawanda, NY 14150

Offers: Boat kits/plans/patterns, over 250 designs, 8 foot to 70 foot models in plywood, fiberglass or steel, including powerboats, inboards, outboards, jets, cruisers, sports fishers, hydroplanes, houseboats, runabouts, sailboats, motorsailers, multihulls, kayaks and canoes (over 35 models). Kit materials include hardware, fastenings, master rigging, sails, plywood, fiberglass, foams, resins, glues, polyesters, mats, cloth, others, depending on type. Books also available.
For Further Information: Catalog, $3.

CLASSIC INSTRUMENTS, PK
P.O. Box 1216
Crooked River Ranch, OR 97760

Offers: Original instruments for classic vehicles, including speedometers, indicators for oil pressure, petrol, battery voltage and water temperature, programmable electric instruments, electric senders, lighting and matching quartz clocks. "Factory direct . . . at below dealer cost."
For Further Information: Information and catalog, $2.

CLASSIC MOTOR CARRIAGES
16650 NW 27th Ave.
P.O. Box 10

Opa Locka, FL 33054
(305) 625-9700

Offers: Car kits for classic 359 sports car, Classic Speedster model with yesterday styling, and Classic Speedster of near-today. Other replica kits include '34 Ford street rod and the Gazelle classic.
For Further Information: Color information kit, $1 per model.
Accepts: American Express, Discover, MasterCard, Visa

CLASSIC ROADSTERS, LTD.
1617 Main Ave.
Fargo, ND 58103

Offers: Automobile kits including Classic Roadsters—reproductions of The Marlene, '365 Mercedes, 500K, and Sebring Austin-Healey. Reproduction kits for the Jaguar, MG and 4-passenger Mercedes. Cars are equipped with V-8 power.
For Further Information: Information on you-assemble kit, or brochure.
Accepts: MasterCard, Visa

COPY CARS, INC.
1980 Rt. 30, Unit 13
Sugar Grove, IL 60554
(312) 466-7540

Offers: Cobra car kits, and a line of parts and accessories, plus powder coating. Custom services are available for restoration, assembly or partially completed kits.
For Further Information: Send SASE or call for information.

CUSTOM CARS BY ROBBIE
17115 Alburtis Ave.
Artesia, CA 90701
(213) 860-5092

Offers: Custom services—partially built kits finished, new kits assembled; builds to personal preference. Artesia electric auto repair. Custom exhaust systems and engine work.
For Further Information: Write or call for information.

EAGLE COACH WORK, INC.
760 Northland Ave.
Buffalo, NY 14211
(716) 897-4292

Offers: Replica car kits for the Jaguar SS100 and XK120G sports cars. Both cars are built on custom-engineered steel chassis—bolt to Ford Pinto or Mustang II running gear.
For Further Information: Color brochure, $3.

EVA SPORTSCARS
Pleasant Corners
Vankleek Hill, Ontario K0B 1R0 Canada
(613) 678-3377

Offers: The Beva sports car kit, with Toyota drive train/parts, MIG welded space frame chassis with mounting brackets for all components, tilting front body section, fiberglass body and wet weather equipment.
For Further Information: Send $3 for full information.

EVERETT-MORRISON MOTORCARS
5137 W. Clifton St.
Tampa, FL 33634
(813) 887-5885

Offers: Replica 427SC Cobra car kits (Mustang or Pinto components bolted on 4-inch round tube frame kit) including Cobra bodies, body frame kits, optional Jaguar front and rear end, and optional Corvette suspension.
For Further Information: Product literature, $4.
Discounts: "Factory direct."

FIBERFAB INTERNATIONAL, INC.
16650 NW 27th Ave.
Opa Locka, FL 33054

Offers: "Replicars" kits—replicas of 1952 MG-TD (with front or rear engine drive), 1929 Mercedes Benz SSK, 1955 356-A Speedster, and Speedster Californian models; "easier to build" with average mechanical skills, ordinary tools. Kits come with step-by-step assembly guide.
For Further Information: Color brochure and information, $1.
Accepts: American Express, MasterCard, Visa

FLOBOT
P.O. Box 70877
Charleston, SC 29415

Offers: Boat kits—Flobot kayaks, folding boats and rigid models; includes "rotomolded" polyethylene and fiberglass for sailrigs, plus a variety of other accessories.
For Further Information: Send SASE for full details.

GAS SAVER/DORY SKIFFS
P.O. Box 720
Galveston, TX 77553

Offers: Gloucester Gull rowing dory—boat plans for fishing, surfing, sailing power dories, classic runabouts, motor cruisers, prams skiffs and schooners.
For Further Information: Send SASE for full information.
Discounts: "Low-cost boats you can build."

GENNIE SHIFTER CO.
930 S. Broadmoor Ave.
West Covina, CA 91790
(818) 337-2536

Offers: Street and racing hot rod parts, including Gennie shifter and hand brakes for GM, Ford and Mopar. Rear mount shifter, boot kits, brake pedal pads, Lo-Line hand brakes, Gennie hood props, throttle cables, kick-down cables. Headlight bars, brake cables and flushmount mini antenna kit are available. Gas pedals with splined shift knobs, Billet aluminum mirrors, column dress-up kit are also stocked.
For Further Information: Send SASE for list.

GLEN-L MARINE
9152 Rosecrans, P.O. Box 1804
Bellflower, CA 90707

Offers: Boat kits, plans and full-size patterns for fishing boats, duck boats, sailboats, inboards, outboards, cruisers, jets, runabouts, dories, workboats, hydroplanes, pontoons and houseboats. Models are from 8 foot to 49 foot, of wood, steel, aluminum or fiberglass. Boat-builder's supplies available include fiberglass, resins, glues, hardware and other equipment, plus books, plans and patterns.
For Further Information: Free catalog.

GOLDBERGS' MARINE
201 Meadow Rd.
Edison, NJ 08817
(800) BOATING

Offers: Boating products—a full line of parts, accessories, kits and others. Carries "everything for boating, sailing and fishing."
For Further Information: Call or write for catalog.
Discounts: "Great discount prices."

GOLDEN WEST MOTORSPORT, INC.
27732 Industrial Blvd.
Hayward, CA 94545
(415) 783-7555

Offers: Cobra replica car kits, rolling chassis and turn-key cars, plus replicas from ERA, NAF and contemporary "award winning" sports convertibles. Also offers Gran Sport Vette and Daytona Spyder replicas.
For Further Information: Catalog, $5.

KEN HANKINSON ASSOCIATES
P.O. Box 255
La Habra, CA 90633
(213) 947-1241

Offers: Boat plans and kits for hundreds of models from world famous designers—powerboats, inboards, outboards,

rowboats and sailboats in a wide variety of types and sizes.
For Further Information: Catalog, $5 (includes dinghy plans).

HARRIS ENGINEERING
P.O. Box 885192
San Francisco, CA 94188
(415) 469-8966

Offers: Kit cars—Countach SRT 9000 body kits, round tube space frames for Countach or Cobra, plus any suspension or drive train equipment. Also carries equipment for V8-ZF/Porsche, V6 Transverse and Fiero.
For Further Information: Information package, $5.

JAMESTOWN DISTRIBUTORS
28 Narraganette Ave.
P.O. Box 348
Jamestown, RI 02835

Offers: A line of boatbuilding and woodworking supplies.
For Further Information: Free catalog.
Store location: At Highway 27 and 21 Gardens Corner, Rt. 1, P.O. Box 375, Seabrook, SC 29940.

KART WORLD
1488 Mentor Ave.
Painesville, OH 44077
(216) 357-5569

Offers: Go Karts—kits, engines and parts. Also has kits, engines and parts for minicars and minibikes.
For Further Information: 80-page catalog, $3 (refundable).
Discounts: "Discount prices."

LEGENDARY MOTORCARS, INC.
1 Wayside Village, #350
Marmora, NJ 08223
(800) 926-3950

Offers: Car kits of yesterday's wood-paneled four-passenger wagon, delivery van and pickup.
For Further Information: Complete information package, $1.

MARAUDER & CO.
Rt. 2
Potomac, IL 61865

Offers: Marauder kit cars—replicas of the Lola, McLaren, Ferrari and Chevron sport racers in VW versions, with 35 MPG, to full Can-Am street cars with 25 MPG. Kits combine VW components with aluminum/steel monocoque.
For Further Information: Catalog and complete information, $12.

POLI-FORM INDUSTRIES

783 San Andreas Rd.
La Selva Beach, CA 95076
(408) 722-4418

Offers: Kit cars from individual parts to complete kits, including Track roadster kit using molded fiberglass parts, and Ford bodies including the '27 Roadster, '27 four-door Touring car, '29 Roadster, '29 Highboy and '34 3-Window Coupe. Full line of bodies, fenders, aprons, dashes and other parts for '26 to '34 Fords, and '29 to '34 Chevrolets. Also stocks wiring components, frames and custom windshield posts.
For Further Information: Catalog, $3.

REDLINE ROADSTERS

30251 E. Acre Place
Orange, CA 92669
(714) 771-0533

Offers: Donor car parts for Sebring, Speedster, Cobra, Corvette, VW-based or whatever car is being built. Donor parts are rebuilt, with new bushings and bearings—reconditioned arms, rack and pinions, springs, differentials, custom power steering units, motors, trannys—all built to specification. Custom kit building to any step of completion.
For Further Information: Send SASE or call with inquiry.

ROWAN REPLICARS

P.O. Box 2133
Salisbury, NC 28145
(704) 636-7020

Offers: Car component kits for the 427 SC Cobra, including heavy-duty frames, one-piece molded bodies with hinged doors, hoods and trunks, and extra features to aid the assembler.
For Further Information: Color brochure, $2.

SEVTEC

P.O. Box 846
Monroe, WA 98272

Offers: Hovercraft plans, for crafts that fly over land, sea or air, with 3 to 160 HP.
For Further Information: Information package, $4 (refundable).

SPORTSCRAFT

P.O. Box 640
Meeker, OK 74855

Offers: Airboats—hovercraft plans, kits, propellers, engines and other supplies and accessories, plus wind machines.
For Further Information: Catalog, $3.

STRUCK-KIT

P.O. Box 307
Cedarburg, WI 53012

Offers: Kits and plans for mini-dozer tractors including Magratrac, which can landscape homes or roads. It excavates (for basement, pool, etc.), hauls and clears areas. Available in kit form or assembled. Technical manual (with construction details) available.
For Further Information: Catalog of uses, $1.

SUN RAY PRODUCTS CORP.

8017 Ranchers Rd. NE
Fridley, MN 55432
(612) 780-0774

Offers: Bradley GT parts—original equipment replacements, including doors, windows, gaskets, wiring harnesses and other items, some of limited quantity.
For Further Information: Free parts list.

TAG-ALONG

P.O. Box 15107
Salem, OR 97309

Offers: 172 trailer plans for motorcycle trailer, utility trailer, car trailer construction and others.
For Further Information: Catalog, $4 (refundable).

UNIVERSAL HOVERCRAFT

1204 3rd St., P.O. Box 281
Cordova, IL 61242

Offers: Hovercraft plans. (Hovercraft are air cushion vehicles that travel inches from any surface on a bubble of air.) Plans include performance and operating data for over 15 models, from 10 feet to 26 feet. Lift fans and propellers are available. (Hovercraft of America, P.O. Box 216, Clinton, IN 47842 is the only association of amateur/pro Hovercraft enthusiasts.)
For Further Information: Catalog, $1.

Doll and Toy Making—Rigid

Also see Ceramics, Miniature Making, Model Making, Woodworking and related categories.

ADOPT-A-DOLL
1041 Lincoln Ave.
San Jose, CA 95125
(408) 298-DOLL

Offers: Doll supplies, greenware and bisque kits; accessories for Playhouse, Seeley, Global, Jean Nordquist, Kemper, Virginia La Vorgna, Connie Lee Finchum Patterns and Royal.
For Further Information: Catalog, $3.
Store Location: Yes
Discounts: Sells wholesale.

AIM KILNS
369 Main St.
Ramona, CA 92065
(800) 647-1624, (800) 222-5456 (in CA)

Offers: AIM Doll Kiln, 8 inches high, 8 inches wide, 9 inches deep, 120V, to cone 10 with kiln sitter shut off and infinite switch; an optional timer is available.
For Further Information: Free literature.
Discounts: Sells wholesale.
See Also: Ceramics

THE AMERICAN COASTER
7106 Lake Rd.
Montrose, MI 48457

Offers: Early American wagon kits and full-scale blueprints for farm and flat wagons, wheelbarrows and others. Wood and rubber wheel kits and metal parts are also available.
For Further Information: Brochure, $1.

& EVERYTHING NICE
1108 1st Ave.
Toms River, NJ 08757
(908) 349-8859

Offers: "Jade" doll body and costume patterns, headpieces, and other porcelain dolls and supplies.
For Further Information: Send for information.
Store Location: Yes

ANNE
P.O. Box 371
West Linn, OR 97068
(503) 656-9556

Offers: Doll eyes (hand glass—all styles, German glass) and doll teeth.
For Further Information: Send stamp for list.

BANNER DOLL SUPPLY, INC.
P.O. Box 32
Mechanicsburg, PA 17055
(800) 637-8305

Offers: Doll stands (adjustable height, vinyl-coated steel wire) in 10 sizes for dolls from 3½ inches to 48 inches; available in lots of 6 or 12.
For Further Information: Call or write for catalog.
Discounts: Quantity discounts.
Accepts: Discover, MasterCard, Visa

BB DOLL SUPPLIES
4216 Grandview Rd.
Kansas City, MO 64137
(816) 761-4900

Offers: Doll supplies, including doll molds, materials, tools, accessories, wigs, lashes, shoes, socks, tights, pellets, dresses (Vee's Victorian), plus Granny molds and wigs. Also carries vinyl doll kits and porcelain materials.
For Further Information: Catalog, $6 plus $2 postage and handling.
Store Location: Yes
Discounts: Quantity discounts; allows discounts to teachers and institutions; sells wholesale to legitimate businesses.
Accepts: MasterCard, Visa

BELL CERAMICS
P.O. Box 120127
Clermont, FL 34712
(904) 394-2175

Offers: Doll molds for over 200 modern and antique reproduction styles. Carries the Gold Marque Artist Series and others, plus porcelain and composition slip, dry and premixed china paints, wigs, patterns, eyes and other items.
For Further Information: Catalog, $8.

JOANN BENTSON
15612 Erin Lane
Orland Park, IL 60462
(708) 403-0270

Offers: Doll blanks, painted kits, eyes, wigs and patterns for antique reproductions and modern dolls. Carries milette to 30 inch sizes.
For Further Information: Catalog, $3.

BOBEL BROS.
5134 Simpkins Rd.
Whites Creek, TN 37189
(615) 876-6714

Offers: Wagon wheels, aluminum, bushings, plus plans and kits.
For Further Information: Write for information.
Discounts: Quantity discounts.

BROWN HOUSE DOLLS
3200 N. Sand Lake Rd.
Allen, MI 49227
(517) 869-2833

Offers: Over 230 doll clothing pattern designs (in several sizes) including those of antique vintage, babies, toddlers and known dolls. Also carries doll accessories patterns.
For Further Information: Catalog, $2 ($3 foreign).
Accepts: Discover, MasterCard, Visa

BYRON MOLDS, INC.
4710 Beidler Rd.
Willoughby, OH 44094
(215) 946-9232

Offers: Doll molds and supplies, including bodies, wigs, eyes and others.
For Further Information: Doll catalog, $6.50; pattern catalog, $9.95.
Accepts: MasterCard, Visa

CARVERS' EYE COMPANY
P.O. Box 16692
Portland, OR 97216
(503) 666-5680

Offers: Glass or plastic eyes, noses, joints, growlers and eye glasses for teddy bears and dolls.
For Further Information: Send $1 for information.
Discounts: Sells wholesale.

COLLECTIBLE DOLL
1421 N. 34th St.
Seattle, WA 98103

Offers: Instructional video—*Painting Reproduction Antique*

Dolls, with Jean Nordquist. Also carries China paints and over 170 rare, classic molds, plus eyes, wigs, kilns, books.
For Further Information: Send SASE for further details.

COLORADO DOLL FAIRE
3307 S. College Ave.
Fort Collins, CO 80525
(303) 226-3655

Offers: Composition doll repair kit. Craze Control restores minor crazing cleans; Care-Repair flesh-tinted compound fills cracks, rebuilds fingers and toes and resurfaces chips.
For Further Information: Send SASE for further details.

CREATE AN HEIRLOOM
160 West St.
P.O. Box 1068
Berlin, MA 01503
(508) 838-2130

Offers: Over 50 painted porcelain doll kits (includes dress and body patterns)—Goose Girl, Peddler, Bye-Lo babies, Mammy, Pierrot, Gibson girl, Little Women, Scarlett. Also carries wax doll kits, porcelain doll heads and molds, dollhouses, character and toddler dolls, doll skull crowns, pates, acrylic eyes, teeth, lashes, plastic pellets, wigs, furniture and doll dress patterns.
For Further Information: Catalog, $1.
Store Location: Yes
Discounts: Quantity discounts.

CREATIVE IMPRESSIONS
5207 Sunnyslope Rd. SW
Port Orchard, WA 98366
(206) 674-2935

Offers: Used doll molds for heirloom quality dolls and kits, soft-fired bisque, plus mohair and sheepskin wigs.
For Further Information: Catalog, send $3 and SASE.

CREATIVE PAPERCLAY CO.
1800 S. Robertson Blvd., Suite 907
Los Angeles, CA 90035
(310) 839-0466

Offers: Creative Paperclay, an air hardening, lightweight material for doll heads and other parts. Also carries kits, molds and books.
For Further Information: Send SASE for details.
Discounts: Allows discounts to teachers and institutions; sells wholesale to legitimate businesses.

CR'S CRAFTS
P.O. Box 8-CZ
Leland, IA 50453
(515) 567-3652

Offers: Extensive lines of doll-making supplies—designer porcelain kits, sets and heads, pre-sewn and composition bodies, plus patterns, wigs, hair and eyes. Carries vinyl dolls and parts, wood toy parts, doll furniture, wicker furniture, accessories and novelties, bases, patterns and books.
For Further Information: Catalog, $2 U.S., $4 Canada.
Store Location: Yes
Discounts: Quantity discounts "by written quotes."
Accepts: MasterCard, Visa
See Also: Doll, Toy and Clothes Making—Soft

DEAR DOLLY
1602 Edgewater Dr.
Orlando, FL 32804
(407) 839-2041

Offers: Doll-making porcelain bisque and greenware, plus a line of supplies, books and patterns.
For Further Information: Send SASE for details.
Store Location: Yes

THE DOL-LEE SHOP
946 Tyler St., Studio B
Benicia, CA 94510
(707) 745-5015

Offers: Doll greenware of past times, including Kays Klowns, Bell, Jan Garnett and Donna RuBert. Also carries cloth body patterns and pre-made bodies.
For Further Information: Send double SASE for list.

THE DOLL ADVENTURE
2111 S. U.S. Highway 1
Jupiter, FL 33477
(407) 575-4292

Offers: Doll supplies and parts, including composition bodies, eyes, bisque kits and greenware, armatures and pellets of Playhouse, Maimie, Connie Lee Finchum, Byron, Vee's Victorian, Bell, Karl, Judith Howe and others.
For Further Information: Send SASE for information.
Store Location: Yes
Discounts: Sells wholesale.
Accepts: MasterCard, Visa

DOLL ANNEX
2609 E. Business 98
Panama City, FL 32401
(904) 769-1707

Offers: Doll supplies, bisque and kilns for Playhouse, Bell, Kemper, Byron, Brown House, Doll Emporium and others.
For Further Information: Send SASE for list.
Store Location: Yes
Discounts: Sells wholesale.
Accepts: MasterCard, Visa

DOLL BOOKS
P.O. Box 446
Florence, OR 97439
(503) 997-9725

Offers: Out-of-print doll books, auction catalogs and notices.
For Further Information: Catalog, $2.

DOLL CRAFTING DEPOT
4224 Louis Ave.
Holiday, FL 34691
(800) 526-DOLL

Offers: Line of wigs, eyes, armatures, and shoes, socks and outfits.
For Further Information: Free catalog.

THE DOLL DEPOT
3053 Haggerty, Unit 6
Walled Lake, MI 48390
(313) 960-3370

Offers: Dolls—soft-fired and greenware, plus doll wigs, eyes, pellets and sculpting supplies. Also carries Evenheat kilns and supplies and patterns.
For Further Information: Catalog, $5.95.
Discounts: Sells retail and wholesale.

DOLL GALLERY, INC.
1137 Susan Rd.
Columbia, SC 29210
(803) 798-7044

Offers: Doll supplies for Playhouse, Kemper, Global, Seeley and others.
For Further Information: Free catalog.
Discounts: "We discount with no minimums required."

THE DOLL HOUSE
17535 Highland
Tinley Park, IL 60477
(708) 532-4797

Offers: Doll kits—soft-fired or painted bisque for antique and modern reproduction dolls.
For Further Information: Price list, $1.50.

DOLL SCULPTING VIDEOS
22930 SW Schmeltzer
Sherwood, OR 97140
(503) 628-2098

Offers: Doll-making instructional videos by Lewis Goldstein on head and mold making, hands and feet, fashion doll mold making, working Cernit and Sculpey, full bodies and miniatures.

For Further Information: Send SASE for list.
Accepts: MasterCard, Visa

DOLL SUPPLIES, INC.
Don Park Rd., #2
Markham, Ontario L3R 2V2 Canada
(905) 477-3655

Offers: Doll molds for Doll Supplies, Byron, Thelma Resch, T.J., Bell, Scioto, Little Darling and others. Also carries doll porcelain, composition slip (in large quantities), kilns and accessories, Opti-visors, brushes, paints, pellets, silica sand and other supplies.
For Further Information: Send business-size SASE for catalog list.
Store Location: Yes
Discounts: "Dealers welcome."

THE DOLL TRUNK
226 Stratford Way
Signal Mountain, TN 37377

Offers: Doll trunks for 18-inch American dolls and doll accessories.
For Further Information: Catalog, $2.

THE DOLL'S NEST
P.O. Box 13222
Akron, OH 44334

Offers: Doll reproduction leather bodies, body and clothing patterns, antique and modern porcelain doll kits, wigs, bisque and China parts, plus supplies.
For Further Information: Catalog, $3.

THE DOLLMAKERS
109 E. Lemon Ave.
Monrovia, CA 91016
(818) 357-1091

Offers: Line of doll supplies (and finished dolls and bears) from Raikes, Pauline, Carolle and Custom Designers.
For Further Information: Send SASE for details.

DOLLS AND TREASURES
127 Ridgewood Village Center
Garland, TX 75041
(214) 271-8996, (800) 222-7073

Offers: Doll greenware, molds and bisque kits, products of Kemper, Bell, Byron, Jean Nordquist, Syndee, Brown House and others.
For Further Information: Send SASE for details.
Store Location: Yes

DOLLS, BEARS & SURPRISES
3743 E. Indian School Rd.
Phoenix, AZ 85018
(602) 956-8648

Offers: Full line of doll supplies, glass eyes, composition bodies, and a doll repair service. Also carries antiques and reproductions.
For Further Information: Send business-size SASE for list.

DOLLS BY BJ
2806 Ave. E
Kearney, NE 68847
(308) 234-4659

Offers: Soft-fired and bisque doll kits and supplies, a complete line of Seeley porcelain slip and products, and those of Doll Center, Kemper and Playhouse.
For Further Information: Send SASE for list.

DOLLSPART SUPPLY CO.
4650 54th Ave.
Maspeth, NY 11378
(718) 361-1833

Offers: Full and complete line of doll-making supplies, including kits for baby, fashion, ethnic and other dolls, plus doll parts, bodies, heads, hands, feet, eyes, wigs, ceramic supplies and paints, doll shoes, clothing, costumes, hats and stands. Also carries elastic cordrubber loops, doll sewing notions and trims.
For Further Information: Free color catalog.
Accepts: Discover, MasterCard, Visa

DOLLY DELITES
555 S. Cloverdale Blvd.
Cloverdale, CA 95425
(707) 894-2180

Offers: Doll supplies, patterns and tools from Kemper, Heinz-Scharff, Carlisle, Doll Emporium, Jean Nordquist, San A Flex, Marx, Seeley's, Virginia La Vorgna, Dove, Connie Lee Finchum, Judith Howe and Masterpiece. Also carries doll pellets and other supplies.
For Further Information: Send SASE for list.
Store Location: Yes
Discounts: Sells wholesale.
Accepts: MasterCard, Visa

DOVE BRUSH MANUFACTURING, INC.
280 Terrace Rd.
Tarpon Springs, FL 34689
(813) 934-5283

Offers: Line of doll-making tools and brushes.
For Further Information: Send SASE for details.

When using plastic molds there are several methods for release:

1. Leave Paperclay in the mold overnight; it will dry and shrink slightly.
2. Cover the mold with a thin coat of liquid soap.
3. Sprinkle talcum powder in the mold.
4. Spray the mold with a mold release.

—Creative Paperclay Co.

THE ENCHANTED ATTIC

Rt. 5, P.O. Box 165, Oakview Addition
El Dorado Springs, MO 64744

Offers: Doll patterns for 16½-inch brides, Spring Maiden, 7-inch Raggedy helpers, 13-inch Mr. & Mrs. Claus and others.
For Further Information: Brochure, $2 (refundable).

THE FIBER STUDIO

P.O. Box 637
Henniker, NH 03242
(603) 428-7830

Offers: Lambskins for doll making—Tibetan, Lincoln, Kalgon and Pearl.
For Further Information: Send SASE for price list.
Discounts: Sells wholesale.

FUN STUF

P.O. Box 999
Yuma, AZ 85366

Offers: Line of porcelain and vinyl doll kits in a variety of sizes.
For Further Information: Send SASE for list.

ADOLA GALLOWAY

3430 Walhalla Highway
Six Mile, SC 29682
(803) 868-2285

Offers: Doll kits, bisque, painted kits and others.
For Further Information: Price list, $2.

GLASS HOUSE

Woonsocket, SD 57385

Offers: Line of doll eyes including sleeping, movable with lashes and others for a variety of doll types and sizes, and for toys.
For Further Information: Free catalog.

GLOBAL DOLLS CORP.

1903 Aviation Blvd.
Lincoln, CA 95648
(916) 645-3000

Offers: Doll wigs in modacrylic, mohair and human hair, plus doll molds and parts.
For Further Information: Send SASE for details.

GOLDENWEST MANUFACTURING, INC.

P.O. Box 1148
Cedar Ridge, CA 95924
(916) 272-1133

Offers: Resin cast dolls and supplies ("F1 Fast Cast") and rubber molds.
For Further Information: Send SASE for information.

GOOD-KRUGER DOLLS

1842 William Penn Way
Lancaster, PA 17601
(717) 687-7208

Offers: Doll molds for heads and hands, including Hard Lessons and Simple Pleasures, 15-inch soft-body types that share the same hand mold and body pattern. Also carries Loreli doll molds.
For Further Information: Send SASE for further details.

HAMILTON EYE WAREHOUSE

P.O. Box 450
Moorpark, CA 93020
(805) 529-5900

Offers: Doll and toy eyes—hollow blown glass, acrylics—plus solid glass paperweights (antique-look). Eyes are available in over 8 colors, 8mm to 28mm sizes, each pair matched.
For Further Information: Catalog, $1.
Discounts: Quantity discounts of up to 50% for large orders.

HANDCRAFT DESIGNS

63 E. Broad St.
Hatfield, PA 19440

Offers: Cernit modeling compound in 3 flesh tones.
For Further Information: Send SASE for details.

HAUS OF DOLLS

3009 Abingdon Rd.
Abingdon, MD 21009
(410) 515-2555

Offers: Doll supplies from Playhouse, Monique, Kemper, Global, Seeley and Judith Howe.
For Further Information: Send SASE for list.
Store Location: Yes
Discounts: Sells wholesale; quantity discounts.
Accepts: MasterCard, Visa

HEARTCRAFT GIFTS
3855 S. Highway 79, #113
Rapid City, SD 57701

Offers: Line of porcelain doll kits.
For Further Information: Catalog, $4.

HEARTWARMERS
P.O. Box 517
Lennox, SD 57039

Offers: Over 450 doll kits (bisque, soft-fired, painted antique-to-modern types), in a variety of sizes.
For Further Information: Catalog, $4.

HEIRLOOM TOYS
8393 Strato Dr.
Sandy, UT 84093
(801) 562-2546

Offers: Barbie-size doll house kits and wood furniture.
For Further Information: Business-size SASE and $1 for brochure/coupons.

HELLO DOLLY
6550 Mobile Highway
Pensacola, FL 32526
(800) 438-7227

Offers: Doll greenware for over 12,000 modern dolls and reproductions, soft-fire or bisque. Also carries doll finishing supplies.
For Further Information: Free list.
Discounts: Sells wholesale.

JUDITH HOWE
1240 N. Jefferson St.
Anaheim, CA 92807
(714) 630-0677

Offers: Porcelain doll eyes in 16 shades of gray, green, brown, lavender, aqua, blue, amber and bronze, plus designer doll armatures and stands.
For Further Information: Send SASE for catalog sheets.

HOWEE'S, INC.
Rt. 7, P.O. Box 633
Joplin, MO 64801
(417) 623-0656

Offers: Wooden toy plans for vehicles (antique cars, Model A and T Fords, jalopies, roadsters, coupes, trains, farm equipment, heavy haulers and trucks). Also carries hardwood wheels, balls, Shaker pegs, drums, barrels, milk cans, candle cups/inserts, toy parts, axle pegs, plugs, spindles, hardwood dowels, and 5-inch scroll saw blades.
For Further Information: Free catalog.

Discounts: Quantity discounts; sells wholesale to businesses.

HUSTON'S
7960 U.S. Rt. 23
South Chillicothe, OH 45601

Offers: Over 200 handmade porcelain doll kits (and dolls) plus old-fashioned girls, babies and others.
For Further Information: Catalog, $2.

HY VIEW TERRACE
Cold Spring, NY 10516

Offers: Mini-curls for small dolls and dollhouse dolls.
For Further Information: Samples, $1 plus business-size SASE.

IMSCO
1620 S. Sinclair St.
Anaheim, CA 92806

Offers: Great American Doll Company's artist and antique doll molds, including Puyi & Suzi (by Rotraut Schrott), doll wigs (full line of styles and colors), eyes (blown glass, Puppenaugen eyes with glass lens), doll parts, elastic cords, body and clothing patterns. Also carries porcelain or composition slip, stands, shoes and hats.
For Further Information: Color catalog, $5.

INTERNATIONAL PORCELAIN & GLASS REPAIR, INC.
P.O. Box 205
Kulpsville, PA 19443

Offers: Instructional video (52 minutes)—*Doll Repair and Restoration*, detailing repairing a German China head and Jumeau, with step-by-step views of techniques (replacing missing pieces, filling cracks, repainting and others).
For Further Information: Send SASE for further details.

IRENE'S DOLLS
4716 64th St.
Lubbock, TX 79414
(806) 792-9114

Offers: 70 doll kits (greenware to finished, with instructions).
For Further Information: Send business-size SASE for list; photocopied picture, $4.
Discounts: "Volume and supply discounts."

JENNELL'S DOLL HOUSE
7662 Krosp Rd.
Millington, TN 38053
(901) 872-1664

Offers: Bisque doll kits from Doll Artworks and others.
For Further Information: List, $2 (refundable).

JONE'S CERAMIC STUDIO
8620 Wright Rd.
Hillsboro, OH 45133

Offers: Reproduction antique doll kits—China head and porcelain. Also carries doll clothes patterns.
For Further Information: Catalog, $1.

KAIS, INC.
11943 Discovery Ct.
Moorpark, CA 93021
(805) 523-8985

Offers: Doll-making supplies, including eyes, wigs (moda-crylic or mohair for new release dolls), porcelain slip and China paint, plus leather shoes and other accessories.
For Further Information: Send SASE for list.

KAREN KAY PORCELAIN ARTS
P.O. Box 4028
El Paso, TX 79914
(915) 751-0966

Offers: "Heirloom" doll-making kits for 16-inch to 43-inch dolls. Also carries supply packets (eyes, lashes, wigs, body patterns/stringing and other items).
For Further Information: Send business-size SASE for list.
Discounts: Some discounts for quantity orders.
Accepts: MasterCard, Visa

KAREN'S DOLL KLOSET
P.O. Box 71
Clementon, NJ 08021

Offers: Doll stands, clothes hangers, miniature furniture and other items. Also carries containers (crafts organizers).
For Further Information: Catalog, $1 (refundable).

LAND OF OZ DOLLS
1723 Portland Ave.
Savanna, IL 61074
(815) 273-3964

Offers: Doll supplies including wigs, eyes, eyelashes, stands and others. Carries patterns by Brown House, Jean Nord-quist, Yesterday's, Maimie's. Also carries Virginia LaVor-gna China paints. Brands available include Playhouse, Kemper, Monique, Global and La Sioux.
For Further Information: Catalog, $5.
Store Location: Yes
Discounts: Sells wholesale.
Accepts: MasterCard, Visa

LIBRARY CORNER
P.O. Box 3332
Quartz Hill, CA 93551
(805) 943-3028

Offers: Doll-making books, plus books on ceramics, pottery and porcelain techniques and other crafts.
For Further Information: Send business-size SASE for list.

LIFETIME CAREER SCHOOLS
101 Harrison St.
Archbald, PA 18403

Offers: Doll repair/restoration home-study course, plus courses on dressing antiques, other aspects of doll repair and restoration for business or hobby.
For Further Information: Free booklet.
See Also: Sewing

LONETREE ENTERPRISES
1804 Pershing Ave.
Davenport, IA 52803

Offers: Doll wigs, silk products and unusual accessories (such as shoes and dresses).
For Further Information: Send business-size SASE for list.

MA'S BODY SHOP
1628 Eifert Rd.
Holt, MI 48842
(517) 694-9022

Offers: Composition bodies for dolls—finished or straight from the mold, in a variety of sizes and types.
For Further Information: Send SASE for price list.

MAYBELLE'S DOLLWORKS
140 Space Park Dr.
Nashville, TN 37211
(615) 831-0661

Offers: Doll molds and supplies from Playhouse, Bell, Kemper, Monique, Global, Brown House, Doll Artworks, Sugar Creek, Royal and others. Carries Paragon kilns, plus armatures, pellets, tools, equipment and porcelain prop—in bulk or blanket.
For Further Information: Catalogs, $6.50.
Store Location: Yes
Discounts: "Dealer inquiries invited."
Accepts: MasterCard, Visa

JANICE NAIBERT
16590 Emory Lane
Rockville, MD 20853
(301) 774-9252

Offers: French human hair doll wigs (for antique and contemporary dolls). Also carries leather shoes and cotton socks.
For Further Information: Send business-size SASE for list.
Discounts: "Excellent trade discounts."

PAPER DOLLS & CO.
17421 Brimhall Rd.
Bakersfield, CA 93312
(805) 589-2831

Offers: U.S. Kids Collection doll molds and patterns.
For Further Information: Color photos, $3 plus SASE.
Accepts: MasterCard, Visa

PEKIN PORCELAIN SLIP CO.
RR 3, P.O. Box 403
Pekin, IL 61554
(309) 346-7916

Offers: Porcelain slip for doll making and other uses in 39 colors. Carries ceramic and stoneware slip.
For Further Information: Send SASE for price list.

PETITE AMIE
41 Mountain Rd.
Suffield, CT 06078
(203) 668-6380

Offers: Porcelain doll kits, greenware and line of doll supplies.
For Further Information: Send SASE for details.

PIPPIN'S HOLLOW
23456 Mercantile Rd.
Beachwood, OH 44122
(216) 292-4944

Offers: Porcelain doll kits, wigs, pates, wire frames, hookups and stringing items, wires, hooks and connectors. Also carries accessories, acrylic and animal eyes, whiskers, doll teeth, pellets, Friendly Plastic, fiberfill, plus baby sounds, cries and growlers. Stocks fabric and composition bodies, Cernit model compound, Fimo, Evenheat kilns, Kemper and Narco tools, Seeley China colors and kits. Cleaning items, adhesives, stands, music movements and parts, containers and display cases are also available.
For Further Information: Catalog, $2 (refundable).
Discounts: Quantity discounts.

PLEASURE CRAFT
Rt. 2, P.O. Box 1485
Mannford, OK 74044

Offers: Balancing toys, with instructions/plans for wooden "performing" animals and people.
For Further Information: Details free.

PROVINCIAL CERAMIC PRODUCTS, INC.
140 Parker Ct.
Chardon, OH 44024
(216) 286-1277

Offers: Line of doll molds, porcelain, China paint, kilns, doll eyes, wigs and shoes.
For Further Information: Doll mold catalog, $6.50; doll pattern catalog, $6.95.
Discounts: Quantity discounts; allows discounts to teachers and institutions; sells wholesale to businesses.

KAREN RAUM'S FANTASY DOLLS
202 Ridgeview Lane
Boulder, CO 80302
(303) 499-8998

Offers: Doll-making supplies, including mohair wig-making items, silks and other fabrics, purse handles, patterns, books, accessories and other items.
For Further Information: Catalog, $3.75.
Accepts: MasterCard, Visa

REJA DOLLS
517 Hartford Rd.
Manchester, CT 06040
(203) 742-9090

Offers: Doll supplies, including kilns, molds, greenware, fabrics, trims and patterns. Brands include Playhouse, Kemper, IMSCO, Brown House, Global, La Sioux, Karl, Monique, Connies, Dollspart, Wee 3 and others. Also carries notions.
For Further Information: Send SASE for list.
Store Location: Yes
Discounts: Sells wholesale.
Accepts: MasterCard, Visa

BRYNN RIORDAN
P.O. Box 42
Tuppers Plains, OH 45783
(614) 667-6802

Offers: Technical assistance in vinyl doll production (client list includes Klowns by Kay, Johannes Zook, Connie Walser Derek and others).
For Further Information: Free consultation.

RIVENDELL, INC.
8209 Proctor Rd.
Painesville, OH 44077
(216) 254-4088

Offers: Dolls, doll parts and supplies by Seely's, Wee3, Kemper, Playhouse, Virginia La Vorgna, Global, Judith Howe, Kais, Sugar Creek Scharff, Langnickell, Bell Research, European Colours, Kaiser, Orton and others. Also carries doll clothes and patterns.
For Further Information: Catalog, $3.
Discounts: Sells wholesale.
Accepts: MasterCard, Visa

ROMAN'S
9733 Palmetto Ave.
Fontana, CA 92335
(909) 823-1100

Offers: Doll-making molds, cloth bodies and patterns.
For Further Information: Mold catalog, $4.50; pattern catalog, $4.50.
Accepts: MasterCard, Visa

SANDCASTLE CREATIONS
126 SE 1st St.
Newport, OR 97365
(503) 265-2499

Offers: Doll wig-making kit (5 shades), cleaned and combed mohair.
For Further Information: Send for samples and price list. Free doll dress list.
Discounts: Quantity discounts.
Accepts: Discover, MasterCard, Visa

SCOTT PUBLICATIONS
30595 Eight Mile Rd.
Livonia, MI 48152
(313) 477-8237

Offers: Doll-making instructional books and videos. Subjects include doll sculpting, mold making, doll making, China painting, head and eyes, body stringing, hair and wigs, repair and restoration, costuming and patterns. Paper dolls and magazines are also available.
For Further Information: Free catalog.
See Also: Ceramics

SEELEY DOLL CENTER
2200 Charleston Dr.
Aurora, IL 60506
(708) 892-3081

Offers: Complete line of porcelain doll-making supplies.
For Further Information: Send SASE for details.

SHEAR DELIGHT FIBERS
4561 SW 39
Redmond, OR 97756
(503) 923-4723

Offers: Doll-making—Alpaca, wool, mohair, flax.
For Further Information: Catalog and samples, $2.50.
Discounts: Sells wholesale.

JEWEL SOMMARS
P.O. Box 62222
Sunnyvale, CA 94088
(408) 732-7177

Offers: Instructional video (on Beta or VHS) entitled *Delightful Dolls—Collecting and Making*, which demonstrates techniques for portrait, original and reproduction dolls, and offers expert instruction in sculpting, molds, casting finishing, wigs, eyes, costume making and more.
For Further Information: Send SASE for further information.

SOUTH FORTY FARMS
1272 16½ Rd.
Fruita, CO 81521
(303) 858-3687

Offers: Mohair for doll wigs—colors or natural shades, in all stages of preparation.
For Further Information: Send SASE for details.

STANDARD DOLL CO.
2383 31st St.
Long Island City, NY 11105
(718) 721-7787

Offers: Doll-making supplies, including China doll kits (old fashioned, pincushion, character and *Gone With the Wind* characters, and American portraits), porcelain bisque kits (reproductions), and bisque doll heads and parts. Also carries body patterns (12 sizes), plastic head parts, teen dolls, doll stands, covers, accessories, voices, squeakers, music boxes, growlers, stringing items, eyes, wigs, leather body skins, magnifiers, patterns, books, Fimo, Sculpy, laces, notions and other supplies.
For Further Information: Catalog, $3.
Discounts: Quantity discounts.
Accepts: American Express, MasterCard, Visa
See Also: Doll, Toy and Clothes Making—Soft

T.L.C. DOLL HOSPITAL
2479 Sheridan Blvd.
Edgewater, CO 80214
(303) 233-3006

Offers: Line of doll parts, mechanicals and accessories. Professional doll restoration services.
For Further Information: Send SASE for details.

TALLINA'S DOLL SUPPLIES, INC.
15790 SE Highway 224
Clackamas, OR 97015
(503) 658-6148

Offers: Doll-making kits, bodies, eyes, lashes, wigs and other extensives supplies for collectors and craftspersons.
For Further Information: Catalog, $1.

TDI DOLL CO.
P.O. Box 690
Cave Creek, AZ 85331

Offers: Scarlet porcelain doll kit, including head, arms, legs, wig, body and dress patterns.
For Further Information: Write for information.

To make any doll pattern fit your doll, first cut the pattern out of paper towel. Sew the pieces together. Make adjustments to the paper pattern before cutting your fabric. Save the paper pattern with the original pattern for future doll-making.

— Create an Heirloom Doll Kit Co.

THE TEDDY WORKS
4650 54th Ave.
Maspeth, NY 11378
(718) 361-1833

Offers: Teddy bear supplies.
For Further Information: Catalog, $2.
Accepts: Discover, MasterCard, Visa

TM PORCELAIN CO.
108 N. Henry St.
Bay City, MI 48706
(517) 893-3526

Offers: Doll molds, porcelain slip, China paint, body frames, wigs and beard specialty items. Lambskins include — Lincoln, Kalgon, Icelandic and alpaca. Also carries suede leather, rabbit furs and plates. Stocks supplies, equipment and patterns by Connie, Monique, Kemper, La Sioux, Karl, Royal, Brown House and others. Carries Blue Diamond high fire kilns, and offers a custom mold service.
For Further Information: Catalog, $5.
Accepts: MasterCard, Visa

TOTAL NONSENSE CERAMICS
9330 B Mira Mesa Blvd.
San Diego, CA 92126
(619) 695-3071

Offers: Doll greenware and supplies by Bell, Connie Lee Finchum, Seeley's, Playhouse and others.
For Further Information: Send SASE for list.
Store Location: Yes
Discounts: Sells wholesale.
Accepts: MasterCard, Visa

THE ULTIMATE COLLECTION, INC.
12773 W. Forest Hill Blvd., Suite 1207
West Palm Beach, FL 33414
(407) 790-0137

Offers: Doll molds including baby heads — Sweetness (eyes open), Serenity (eyes closed), plus hands, wigs, patterns and body joints, 21-inch baby and others available.

For Further Information: Catalog, $5.
Accepts: MasterCard, Visa

VAN DYKE'S
P.O. Box 278, Dept. 15
Woonsocket, SD 57385

Offers: Doll restoration products, including eyes (for all purposes), plus modeling, casting and filling materials.
For Further Information: Catalog, $1.

VICKIE'S ANGUISH ORIGINAL MOLDS
1704 SE Morrison St.
Topeka, KS 66605
(913) 232-5676

Offers: Doll head and hand molds (and body and clothing patterns) including those for 19-inch baby Cuddle-bug, Elizabeth, Rachel, with darker skin (head only can be used on Phylis dolls), Melody (head only 8 inches in circumference) with darker skin, the 25-inch Phylis doll (head circumference 8½ inches) with light skin and open crown head. Hand and foot molds are available.
For Further Information: Mold list and photo, send $3 and business-size SASE.
Accepts: MasterCard, Visa

VICKI'S ORIGINAL DESIGNS
2100 East 85th St. N.
P.O. Box 363
Valley Center, KS 67147
(316) 755-1504

Offers: Doll parts including one-piece head-to-waist torsoes and, others for Lil Women and Lil Vivien, Rhett and others that wear Barbie-size patterns. Wigs and other items available.
For Further Information: Catalog, $6; pattern catalog, $6.

WEE WORLD OF DOLLS, INC.
112 W. Tarrant Rd.
Gardendale, AL 35071
(205) 631-9270

Offers: Porcelain doll kits and a line of supplies for antique and modern dolls by Playhouse, Seeley, Bell, Brown House, IMSCO and others.
For Further Information: Send SASE for list.
Store Location: Yes
Discounts: Sells wholesale.

WEEFOKE EMPIRE
619 4th St.
Bremerton, WA 98310
(206) 792-9293

Offers: Line of collectible doll supplies and clays (also

finished dolls, furniture).
For Further Information: Send SASE for details.

WOODEN TOY

P.O. Box 40344
Grand Junction, CO 81504

Offers: Wood toy patterns and wood parts.
For Further Information: Catalog, $1.

YESTERDAY'S CHILDREN

413 Harvey St.
Des Plaines, IL 60016
(708) 635-3049

Offers: Over 250 easy-sew design patterns for doll clothes, antique to country styles, for 8-inch to 36-inch dolls. Fabrics and notions are also available.
For Further Information: Catalog, $3.
Discounts: "Dealer inquiries welcome."

Fishing Items

JANN'S
P.O. Box 4315
Toledo, OH 43609

Offers: Materials/accessories for tackle building, including lure making, fly tying and rod building.
For Further Information: Free catalog.

JERRY'S TACKLE
604 12th St.
Highland, IL 62249

Offers: Line of components for lures, jigs, fly tying and rod building.
For Further Information: Free catalog.

LURE-CRAFT INDUSTRIES, INC.
P.O. Box 1
Solsberry, IN 47459

Offers: Fishing lure maker's supplies: Full line of plastic worm-making supplies, Poly-Sil paint and lead castings, skirts, hooks, other lure-making items.
For Further Information: Catalog, $1.

MIDLAND TACKLE
66 Rt. 17
Sloatsburg, NY 10974

Offers: Fishing rod building equipment, lure parts, molds and others.
For Further Information: Free catalog.

THE TACKLE SHOP
P.O. Box 830369
Richardson, TX 75083

Offers: Supplies/accessories for lures, including skirts, blades, worms, bulk plastics and others.
For Further Information: Free catalog.

Frames and Picture Framing

Also see General Craft Supplies, Artist's Supplies, Woodworking, General Needlecraft Supplies, Quilting and other related categories.

AMERICAN FRAME CORP.
400 Tomahawk Dr.
Maumee, OH 43537
(800) 537-0944

Offers: Laminated frame sections, metal frames, section pairs and custom cut frames. Also carries hardwood section frames, Plexiglas, matboards and foam core.
For Further Information: Free catalog.
Store Location: Yes
Accepts: American Express, MasterCard, Visa

Courtesy of Dover Publications.

COS-TOM PICTURE FRAME
1121 Bay Blvd.
Chula Vista, CA 91911
(619) 429-9500

Offers: Frames in a wide array of finishes and styles — contemporary, classical, traditional, baroque and others.
For Further Information: Free catalog.

DOCUMOUNTS
3709 W. 1st Ave.
Eugene, OR 97402

Offers: Full assortment of wood picture frames in a variety of sizes, styles and colors, plus bevel-edged mats.
For Further Information: Call for free information.

THE FLETCHER-TERRY CO.
65 Spring Lane
Farmington, CT 06032

Offers: Picture-framing tools — FrameMaster stapler (fires flat points), FrameMate unit (flat framers, points or brads into moulding).
For Further Information: Send SASE for full details.

FRAME FIT CO.
P.O. Box 8926
Philadelphia, PA 19135
(215) 332-0683

Offers: Picture frames — custom aluminum frames in sections and pairs (colors and metallics), and bulk copy frame sections and pairs.
For Further Information: Send SASE for information.
Discounts: Has discounts.

FRAME STRIPS
P.O. Box 1788
Cathedral City, CA 92235
(619) 328-2358

Offers: Framestrips, clear self-adhesive channel for mounting, framing and attaching; good for changeable artwork, signs and others.
For Further Information: Send for free samples.

FRAME WEALTH
RD 2, P.O. Box 261-7
Otego, NY 13825

Offers: Frames in wood and metal, length mouldings, tools, hardware and how-to books.
For Further Information: Write for catalog.

FRAMES BY MAIL
1155 Addie Rd.
St. Louis, MO 63144

Offers: Picture frames in wood and metal, in a wide range of sizes, styles and colors, plus bevel-edged mats.
For Further Information: Free catalog.

FRANKEN FRAMES
214 W. Holston Ave.
Johnson City, TN 37604

Offers: Picture frames with quality wood mouldings, in a variety of styles, sizes and colors; custom sizes available.
For Further Information: Write for catalog.
Discounts: "Low prices."

GRAPHIC DIMENSIONS LTD.
2130 Brentwood St., #10002
High Point, NC 27263

Offers: Picture frames in a full line of modern metals, lacquered styles and classic woods, plus frames with linen, burlap or suede liners. Other styles include rustic, traditional, contemporary, Oriental, European.
For Further Information: Free color catalog.
Discounts: Has discounts.

IMPERIAL PICTURE FRAMES
P.O. Box 598
Imperial Beach, CA 91933

Offers: Frames in many styles, types and sizes.
For Further Information: Free color catalog.
Discounts: Sells wholesale.

THE METTLE CO.
P.O. Box 525
Fanwood, NJ 07023
(908) 322-2010

Offers: Aluminum picture frame sides in 40 colors and a variety of sizes and widths, plus other metallic and color finished styles.

For Further Information: Send SASE for list.
Accepts: Discover, MasterCard, Visa

STU-ART
2045 Grand Ave.
Baldwin, NY 11510
(516) 546-5151

Offers: Mats/picture frames. Mats include conservation types, ready-mats and hand-cut beveled. Frames include aluminum sections, wood, Tenite and ash frame sections, and pre-assembled aluminum and wood frames in a variety of sizes. Also carries plastic picture saver panels and shrink wrap.
For Further Information: Free catalog and mat samples.

TENNESSEE MOULDING & FRAME CO.
1188 Antioch Pike
Nashville, TN 37211

Offers: Picture frames, a full line, including 450 choices of metals and woods, including oaks, pines, poplar, painted colors/metallics, soft-shades, art deco look, gilded and others. Also carries designer moulding, Crescent mat board (63 colors), foam center and newsboards, black core and simulated fabrics, plus oversizes, barrier papers and museum boards.
For Further Information: Full color catalog, $5.

VALLEY MOULDING & FRAME
10708 Vanowen St.
North Hollywood, CA 91605
(800) 932-7665, (800) 524-1413

Offers: Over 9,000 framing products—metal and mica sectionals, ready-made frames, framing supplies and equipment, mat cutters, matboard, picture lights, display easels, stretcher bars and others.
For Further Information: Write for catalog.

WORLD FRAME DISTRIBUTORS
107 Maple St.
Denton, TX 76201
(817) 382-3442

Offers: Frames—traditional, ready-made types and sizes, plus gallery-style, ornately crafted frames, supplies and canvas.
For Further Information: Free brochure and price list.

Furniture Making and Upholstery

Also see Basketry and Seat Weaving, Miniature Making, Paints, Finishes and Adhesives, Woodworking and other related categories.

ARROW DESIGNS CO.
P.O. Box 680968
Franklin, TN 37068

Offers: Furniture plans for a Shaker entertainment center (pivot pocket doors, stereo compartments, storage drawers, TV shelf) with material list.
For Further Information: Catalog #100 (10 easy pieces), $2.

COUNTRY LANE SHOP
6785 Ellman
Oconto, WI 54153

Offers: Hexagonal picnic table plans (2×6 construction), instructions and illustrations.
For Further Information: Send for information.

CRAFTY CHIP
P.O. Box 1028
Atkinson, NH 03811

Offers: Plans for tavern mirrors, pyramid cupboards, sugar bin end tables, Shaker storage benches, sled shelfs and others.
For Further Information: Send for details.

DESIGNER FURNITURE PLANS
179 Davidson Ave.
Somerset, NJ 08873

Offers: Jewelry armoire plans—classic chests with/without mirrors, secret compartments, necklace storage doors, divided surfaces; comes in a variety of sizes and styles.
For Further Information: Send for catalog (50 designs), $3.

EAGLE WOODWORKING
24 Webster Ave.
Somerville, MA 02143
(617) 628-4343

Offers: Dovetailed drawers of ½-inch maple, assembled and custom-sized width and depth, for cabinets.
For Further Information: Send for information.

EASY PROJECTS
P.O. Box 0286
Ashburn, VA 22011

Offers: Desk and storage drawers "in minutes . . . no expensive tracks."
For Further Information: Send for details.

EMPEROR CLOCK CO.
Emperor Industrial Park
Fairhope, AL 36532

Offers: Furniture kits—traditional-style cabinets, chests, tables, chairs, desks and others in black walnut, cherry or oak. Also carries grandfather and other clock kits, movements and dials.
For Further Information: Color catalog, $1.

FAMILY HANDYMAN/PLAN SERVICE
P.O. Box 695
Stillwater, MN 55082

Offers: Furniture plans for game and coffee tables, low-buck outdoor pieces, lawn glider swings, redwood lounges and tables, PVC pipe outdoor furniture, outdoor dining sets, captains's desks, children's rockers and baby cradles.
For Further Information: Send SASE for list.

FURNITURE DESIGNS, INC.
1827 Elmdale Ave.
Glenview, IL 60025
(708) 657-7526

Offers: Plans for furniture—over 200 professional designs in traditional, Early American, Spanish and modern styles. Carries full-sized plans for tables, desks, chairs, cabinets, dry sinks, buffets, corner cupboards, cupboards, hutches, cradles, chests, rockers, tea carts, trestle tables, benches, chests, cabinets, shelves, bookcases, lamps, mirrors, racks, stools, credenzas, cribs, highchairs, gun cabinets, beds and headboards.
For Further Information: Catalog, $3.
Discounts: Allows discounts to teachers and institutions; sells wholesale to businesses.

GENESIS
P.O. Box 1526
Mendocino, CA 95460

Offers: Instructions for willow-chair making.

For Further Information: Send SASE for details.

HOWARD CAROL CHAIRS, INC.
5116 Jennings Drive
Fort Worth, TX 76180

Offers: Pattern and detailed instructions for folding rocking chair (with fabric sling-seat/back).
For Further Information: Send SASE for further information.

INFORMATIVE INFO
425 State, P.O. Box 5
LaCrosse, WI 54601

Offers: Spin-seat stool plans with construction techniques, materials and data. Stool attaches to person, use for camping, etc.
For Further Information: Write for further information.

INGERSMITH
P.O. Box 87
Hamburg, NY 14075

Offers: Bed patterns including bunk beds and other sizes and styles of beds and furniture.
For Further Information: Send SASE for list.

J & L CASUAL FURNITURE CO.
P.O. Box 208
Tewksbury, MA 01876
(508) 851-4514

Offers: Full line of PVC pipe furniture kits, plans and supplies.
For Further Information: Send SASE for details.

OWEN CO.
Battle Ground, WA 98604
(206) 887-8646

Offers: Starter guide to PVC furniture making (indoor and outdoor), including chairs, tables, love seats, couches, chaise lounges, swing sets, recreation items, children's items, wood stackers and others. Includes plans and diagrams. Also carries cushion patterns, data on PVC furniture and others.
For Further Information: Send SASE for complete details.

SHAKER WORKSHOPS
P.O. Box 1028
Concord, MA 01742
(617) 646-8985

Offers: Shaker kits for rockers, dining chairs, tables, beds, pegboards and pegs. Also carries dolls, needlework kits and custom-finished furniture.
For Further Information: Catalog and tape samples, $1.

TERRY CRAFT
12 Williams Ct.
Shelby, OH 44875
(419) 342-6376

Offers: Adirondack chair kit with instructions, including an optional leg rest.
For Further Information: Send SASE for further details.

THE ROUDEBUSH CO.
P.O. Box 348
Star City, IN 46985
(800) 847-4947

Offers: Buckboard bench kit with "authentically designed" steel springs that "give," metal arms and backrails; comes with complete hardware and instructions. Also carries pre-cut and drilled red oak.
For Further Information: Write for information.
Accepts: MasterCard, Visa

THOM'S, INC.
2012 Wilkins
Laurel, MT 59044

Offers: Picnic patio table plans for an octagonal table that seats 8, includes a lazy susan and umbrella holder, and measures about 7 feet in diameter.
For Further Information: Send SASE for further details.

V. WILMOTH
1202 Vine St.
Norman, OK 73072

Offers: Polystyrene beads (washable, dryable filler) for bean bag chairs and infant "cuddle sac."
For Further Information: Send SASE for price list.

V.U.E.
P.O. Box 128-CSS
El Verano, CA 95433
(800) 635-3493

Offers: Upholstery instructional/training videos, covering the fundamentals, as well as auto/marine recovering (car, truck and boat seats). Carries tools and upholstery supplies.
For Further Information: Free brochure.
Store Location: 17421 Sonoma Highway, El Verano CA.
Discounts: Sells wholesale to legitimate businesses; quantity discounts.
Accepts: MasterCard, Visa

VAN DYKE'S
P.O. Box 278
Woonsocket, SD 57385

Offers: Furniture components, including fiber and leather seats, table and posterbed parts, Queen Anne legs, rolltop desks, and chair and piano stool kits/parts. Also carries cane web, cane, rush and reeds. Carries wood turnings and wood carvings, such as gingerbread, filigrees and others. China cabinet glass, plywood, spring straps, metal tacking straps, fastener strips, Klinch-It tool, zippers and chains, heavy-duty sewing machines, rubber webbing, hemp and jute webbing, cord, super steamer, threads, clips, helicals, torsion, rocker springs, and a variety of fabrics and trims are available. Tools include awls, pinking machines, stuffing irons, stretchers, punches, nippers, mallets, staple guns and shears, plus fasteners and kits. Videos and hardware (brass, wood, cast iron) are also available.

For Further Information: Catalog, $1.
Discounts: Quantity discounts.
See Also: Mold Crafts and Woodworking

WOODINS' WATERBED CONNECTION
45 Industrial Park Rd.
Albany, NY 12206

Offers: Waterbed items for you-build: Heaters, massage systems, mattresses, others.
For Further Information: Catalog and plan set, $2.

General Craft Supplies

Also see specific art/crafts chapters, Books and Booksellers, Publications and Associations.
Browse through this sourcebook for unexpected, unusual and often valuable items for your personal creative expression.

ALPEL PUBLISHING
P.O. Box 203-CSS
Chambly, Quebec J3L 4B3 Canada

Offers: Books: *Kit's Gift Making Ideas.* Pattern books: *Easy Sewing for Infants* (for Children, for Adults, Halloween Costumes). *Catalogue of Canadian Catalogues* (directory). Includes information on crafts, graphics, books, knitting and crochet, sewing, tole, jewelry making, doll making, woodworking and others. Also offers Dupli-cut reusable grid (enlarges miniature patterns).
For Further Information: Free brochures—specify interest.
Discounts: Allows discounts to teachers and institutions; sells wholesale to legitimate businesses and professionals.

AMERICAN ART CLAY CO., INC.
4717 W. 16th St.
Indianapolis, IN 46222
(317) 244-6871

Offers: Craft supplies, including Friendly Plastic, Friendly Clay, Sculptamold and Claycrete for modeling. Also carries jewelry accessories and findings, metallic acrylics, translucent paints and glitters, phosphorescent paints, Batik It cold water fabric dyes, metallic and other wood finishes.
For Further Information: Free catalog and literature.
Discounts: Sells wholesale through distributors only.
See Also: Ceramics, Metalworking and Mold Crafts

THE ART STORE
935 Erie Blvd. E.
Syracuse, NY 13210
(315) 474-1000

Offers: Surface design supplies and equipment for screen printing, papermaking, marbling, gold leaf, airbrush, modeling, batik, silk painting and dyeing. Also carries beads and jewelry findings and others.
For Further Information: Complete list, $3.

ART VIDEO LIBRARY
P.O. Box 68
Ukiah, OR 97880

Offers: Craft instructional videos available to members for sale or rent at low cost on payment of a yearly fee at low cost (rental can apply to purchase). Videos demonstrate paints, color, candy making, stencil, theorem, bronzing, soft-sculpture dolls, cake decorating, tole, stained glass, sculpting, plaster, waste and other molds, bas relief, bronze casting, etching and engraving. Also offers videos on sewing basics, including knits, lingerie, jeans, embroidery, teddy bears and others.
For Further Information: Free catalog.
See Also: Artist's Supplies

ARTWAY CRAFTS
ATTN: Publicity Director
Tom Bean, TX 75489

Offers: Cut-outs. Wide range of supplies in each category. Also offers boutique items (teardrops, sequins, spangles, ultrasuede fringe, rhinestones and setter tools), rock tumblers (2 barrel) and supplies, fabric paints (puffy, slick, glitter, iridescent), T-shirts and sweatshirts, and Ming tree kits and wires.
For Further Information: Catalogs, $1 each: Specify Leather, Bead, Artist or Wood.
Discounts: Quantity discounts.
Accepts: Discover, MasterCard, Visa
See Also: Bead Crafts

DICK BLICK
P.O. Box 1267
Galesburg, IL 61402
(309) 343-6181

Offers: Videos, books, and a complete line of artist's supplies. Crafts: Paints, markers, art and specialty papers, and wearable art supplies. Supplies and equipment for: Airbrushing, sign making, wood carving, printing, modeling, stencils, resin, plaster, mâché, molding and casting, enameling, jewelry making and basketry. Also carries ceramic clays, equipment, kilns, tools and glazes, metal punch and leather supplies, power tools, stitchery and fabric decorating supplies, wood ware and boxes. Group valuepacks are available.
For Further Information: Catalog, $4.
Store Location: Yes
Accepts: American Express, MasterCard, Visa
See Also: Artist's Supplies and Sculpture and Modeling

BOUTIQUE TRIMS, INC.
21200 Pontiac Trail
South Lyon, MI 48178
(313) 437-2017

Offers: Woodenware, stencils, paint and art supplies, silk flowers, floral supplies and dried materials. Also offers resin figures, fabrics, papier-mâché and others.
For Further Information: Send SASE for list.
Discounts: Quantity discounts; allows discounts to teachers, institutions and professionals.

BOYD'S
P.O. Box 6232-C
Augusta, GA 30916

Offers: Formulas (from home materials) for carving "stones," casting and modeling materials, over 16 air-dry modeling "clays," glues, paints and candle-making materials; includes instructions and hints.
For Further Information: Booklet, $6.

BRIAN'S CRAFTS UNLIMITED
1421 S. Dixie Freeway
New Smyrna Beach, FL 32168
(904) 672-2726

Offers: Wearable art supplies including T-shirts, sun visors, ribbon roses, pens (markers, transfer, others) and Tulip, Paintstitch, Art Deco, and other paints and glitters. Carries stamps, inks and tints. Also offers beads and floral supplies including wreaths, moss, grapevine novelties, others. Other items carried include bears, doll items, porcelain-look resin faces, Friendly Plastic, rhinestones, lace, pins, foam, feathers, chenille, felt, adhesives, macrame accessories, wood beads and blocks, rings, ribbon, paper twist, plastic canvas and cross-stitch supplies. Bargain grab bags are available.
For Further Information: Catalog, $1 (refundable). (Canada, $2.)
Discounts: "Discounted prices to everyone."
Accepts: MasterCard, Visa
See Also: Macrame

MARTIN R. CARBONE, INC.
2519 Bath St.
Santa Barbara, CA 93105
(805) 682-0465

Offers: The Carbone Cutter foam cutting machine, for polystyrene and other lightweight plastics; cuts foam up to 12 inches thick; cutting wire works by melting a fine cut through the material.
For Further Information: Send SASE for full information.

CHARLOTTE'S HOBBYS
782 Shield Rd.
Hemmingford, Quebec J0L 1H0 Canada
(514) 247-2590

Offers: Kits and supplies for candle making, costume dolls, jewelry, naturals and boutique items (ribbons, novelties). Also carries basic craft supplies and equipment, accessories and aids.
For Further Information: Write or call for detailed literature.

CRAFT KING
P.O. Box 90637, Dept. CSS
Lakeland, FL 33804
(941) 648-2898

Offers: Over 6,000 art/craft supplies, including paints, papers, canvas board, Ceram tole kits, wood shapes, plastic canvas, macrame, doll-making items, wood, wearable art, trims including rhinestones, sequins, buttons, felt and pompoms. Also carries music box movements, adhesives, foam, glue guns, modeling and floral items, iron-on transfers, jewelry findings, beads, lampshades and supplies for rag baskets. Miniatures available include sports figures, teddies, trees, vehicles, hats, holiday items and flowers. Naturals include wreaths, baskets, raffia, excelsior and moss. Books are also available.
For Further Information: Catalog, $2.
Store Location: Yes
Discounts: Sells wholesale to legitimate businesses.

CRAFT SUPPLIES 4 LESS
13001 Las Vegas Blvd. S.
Las Vegas, NV 89124

Offers: Supplies for a variety of crafts, including laces, appliques, ribbons, cords, beads, wood items, silk painting supplies and others.
For Further Information: Catalog, $2.50.
Discounts: Has discounts.

CREATIVE CRAFT HOUSE
897 San Jose Circle, HC 62
P.O. Box 7810
Bullhead City, AZ 86430
(602) 754-3300

Offers: Full lines of pinecone and seashell projects, plus other natural materials—pods, cones, foliages and Christmas materials. Also carries jewelry findings and parts, dollmaking items, party and wedding favors, and animal and doll parts. Miniatures, beads, novelties, conchos, foil and mirrors are also available.
For Further Information: Catalog, $2.
Discounts: Quantity discounts.

LOU DAVIS WHOLESALE
N3211 Highway H N.
Lake Geneva, WI 53147
(414) 248-2000, (800) 748-7991

Offers: Lamp parts and accessories, bulbs, cork and plastic stoppers, music movements, brushes, paint, pastels, chalks. Also carries airbrush kits and accessories, air compressors, clock parts, doll novelties, fiber bodies, pellets, armatures, bells, caps, jewelry findings, ornament stands, water balls and bases and adhesives.
For Further Information: Free catalog.
Discounts: "We discount everything."
Accepts: Discover, MasterCard, Visa
See Also: Ceramics

Work Friendly Plastic in low temperatures (140 degrees-150 degrees) for jewelry. As a helpful hint — use molds for design.

— American Art Clay Co., Inc.

DOVER PUBLICATIONS, INC.
31 E. 2nd St.
Mineola, NY 11501

Offers: Craft and needlecraft books. Carries a series of copyright-free design books, including clip art (holiday designs, borders, layout grids, old-fashioned animals, transportation, patriotic, sport, wedding, humorous, nautical and alphabets); designs from various eras, including Japanese, Chinese, Art Nouveau, Early Arabic and Mayan designs; stencil books; and folk designs. Also carries books on stained glass, calligraphy costumes, art, silk screen, bookbinding, paper, beads, jewelry, basketry, marionettes, leather, tole, miniatures, dollhouses, and 30 cut/use stencils. Needlecraft books include 38 plus quilting titles, appliqué, knitting/crochet, lace, 14 plus embroidery titles, patterns, needlepoint, and 54 plus charted doll-making books.
For Further Information: Free catalog.

ENTERPRISE ART
12333 Enterprise Blvd.
P.O. Box 2918
Largo, FL 34649
(813) 536-1492

Offers: Beads, bead patterns and kits, jewelry findings and parts. Wearable art supplies include colors and trims. Bulk supplies are available for doll parts, beads and plastic canvas. Also carries wood and clock items.
For Further Information: Free catalog.
Store Location: Yes
Discounts: Quantity discounts.

HANDS ON
203 N. Main
Paris, MO 65275
(816) 327-4435

Offers: Supplies, equipment and tools. Carries a line of

bisque porcelain items to paint, plus paints, finishes and glazes. Also carries dyes, T-shirts with screen printed design outlines, basketry materials, handles and kits. Offers 60 plus baskets, 55 plus wreaths, bird nests, rattan chain, seagrass, bells, brooms, straw and naturals. Floral supplies include fabric, tools, wire, clays and dried naturals. Fruit, woodenware (145 plus cutouts, rings, 42 clipboards/shaped-clips, toys, knobs, wheels, carousels, boxes, weathervanes, buckets, 55 plaques, frames), balsa and basswood are also available. Clock parts, clips, tinware (pots, buckets) and candy/cake-making items, and books are also stocked.
For Further Information: Catalog, $5 (refundable).

HEARTLAND CRAFT DISCOUNTERS
Rt. 6 E., P.O. Box 65
Geneseo, IL 61254
(309) 944-6411

Offers: Arts, crafts and needlecrafts items, including brushes, pens, inks, canvas, paints, dyes, finishes and jewelry findings. Also carries floral supplies, potpourri, musical movements, wires, threads, beads, resin figures, wood novelties, plaques, balsa, dowels, blackboards, letters, woodburning pens, clock parts, stencils and kits, wedding supplies, adhesives, magnets, novelties, miniatures and toy parts. Naturals include moss, wreath forms, wire and excelsior. Carries frames, including wood, shadowbox, shell, metallic and sectional. Model kits for balsa planes and Hobbycraft cars are available.
For Further Information: Catalog, $2 (includes monthly flyers).
Discounts: Quantity prices; allows discounts to institutions; sells wholesale to legitimate businesses.
See Also: General Needlecraft Supplies

KEMPER MANUFACTURING CO.
13595 12th St.
Chino, CA 91710

Offers: Darwi modeling compound (non-toxic, air dries, attaches easily to anything), which can be modeled by hand and/or by using Kemper modeling tools; it can be carved, sanded, painted, used to cover household items — even primed (painted or sealed) styrofoam. Darwi compound can be used to make molds for metal or other casting, as it is heat-proof.
For Further Information: Contact dealer.
See Also: Mold Crafts and Tools and Equipment

KIRCHEN BROS.
P.O. Box 1016
Skokie, IL 60076
(312) 676-2692

Offers: Doll Baby parts and animal parts. Also carries fashion dolls and crochet patterns and accessories, pre-painted wood and tin items, baskets, wreaths, paints, brushes, craft kits (holiday items, ornaments and others). Other items offered include burlap, felt, "fur," foam, various trims, Shrink Art, magnets, miniatures, novelties, small mirrors, butterflies and quilling papers and tools. Naturals include cones, brooms, mats, wreaths, corn husks, wheat, feathers and baskets. Also stocks books.

For Further Information: Catalog, $1.50 (refundable).
Discounts: Sales and quantity prices.
Accepts: Discover, MasterCard, Visa

JOE KUBERT ART & GRAPHIC SUPPLY
37A Myrtle Ave.
Dover, NJ 07801
(201) 328-3266

Offers: Crafts, artist's and graphics materials (major brands), including papers (15 rice types and others), boards, markers, paints, sets, adhesives, and 15 plus airbrushes and compressors. Also carries silk screen supplies, kits and equipment, plus magnifiers, lamps, 6 modeling compounds, casting plaster, clays, mold rubber, plaster gauze, and batik and cold water dyes. Textile, fabric and stained glass colors, stencils, vinyl letters, frames and airbrushes are also offered. Tools available include Moto Tool and lathe, flex shaft, Moto Shop, potter's wheels, turntables and wire/sculpting tools. Books are also stocked.

For Further Information: Catalog and flyers, $4.
Store Location: Yes
Discounts: Allows discounts to teachers and institutions.

NATIONAL ARTCRAFT CO.
23456 Mercantile Rd.
Beachwood, OH 44122
(216) 292-4944

Offers: Extensive electrical items, including lamp parts, hardware, lamp sets and kits, metal rods, pipes and tubing, bases, chains, prisms, bulbs and tree lights. Also carries fountain pumps and parts, oil lamp burners and chimneys, clock parts, including quartz and electric parts, movements, hands, dials and faces. Water globes and bases, kaleidoscope kits and parts, mirrors, stoppers, handles, spigots, plastic tubing, bells, excelsior and raffia are also available. Candle cartridges, glass wicks, jewelry findings (gold fill, s/s, 14 kt), chains, doll items, Friendly Plastic, modeling clays, beveled glass, foam, airbrushes and parts, magnifiers, containers and display items are also stocked.

For Further Information: Crafts/ceramics catalog, $4.
Discounts: Quantity discounts.
See Also: Ceramics

NANCY NEALE TYPECRAFT
Steamboat Wharf Rd.
Bernard, ME 04612
(204) 244-5192, (800) 927-7469

Offers: Antique and old wood printing type (letters, num-

bers, punctuation, in 1 inch to 5 inch sizes, in a variety of styles. Most type is in English, some in German and Hebrew [inquire]; sold by 100 plus lots. Type can be used for printing, as ornaments, for collages, for nameplates, door knockers, inlaid wood patterns, etc.) Also carries old copper and zinc engravings, metal dingbats, printer's galleys, initials and others.

For Further Information: Free catalog.
Discounts: May run sales.

PATCHWORK TURTLE
825 W. 11th St., #158
Austin, TX 78701

Offers: Line of craft supplies.
For Further Information: Catalog, $3 and SASE.
Discounts: "Guaranteed discount." Sells wholesale.

PATTERNCRAFTS, INC.
P.O. Box 25370
Colorado Springs, CO 80936

Offers: Instructional videos on folk art, tole painting, quilting, kid's crafts, naturals, ribbon crafts, floral arranging, calligraphy, cake decorating, etching/mirror removal, fabric painting and others. Also carries over 600 craft patterns — country, unusual, "critters," sweatshirt, decorating, Christmas boutique, paper cutting, dolls, cookie cutters, no-sew, folk art, wood, seasonal motifs and gift ideas, accessories and others.

For Further Information: Catalog, $2.

POLYFORM PRODUCTS CO.
9420 W. Byron St.
Schiller Park, IL 60176
(708) 678-4836

Offers: Super Sculpey, a ceramic-like sculpturing compound for miniatures, plaques, jewelry and sculpture. It's workable until baked in a home oven at 300 degrees; it can be molded by hand, and later sanded, drilled, painted, engraved, carved, antiqued, glazed or bronzed. Thirty colors are available.

For Further Information: Contact dealer or write for details.

S & S ARTS & CRAFTS
P.O. Box 513
Colchester, CT 06415
(800) 243-9232, Dept. 2007

Offers: Low-cost/group projects, including arts, crafts, beads, toys, scraps, mosaics, multi-cultures, naturals, metals/tools, papers, clays, paints, woods, jewelry, decoupage, masks, costumes and educational projects. Also carries sticks, chenille, shapes, puzzles, blocks, rubber stamps, science items, novelties, papers, paints, foam, ribbons, sand, beads and looms. Projects for modeling, plaster, papier mâché, stencil and baking crystals are available. Also offers leathercraft tools, sets, lacings and kits, plus wood items and kits, basketry supplies, tools, games and musical instruments.

For Further Information: Free catalog.
Store Location: Yes
Discounts: Quantity discounts.
Accepts: American Express, Discover, MasterCard, Visa
See Also: General Needlecraft Supplies

SAX ARTS & CRAFTS
2405 S. Calhoun Rd., P.O. Box 51710
New Berlin, WI 53151

Offers: A variety of supplies (known brands), including a full line of enameling products—kits, enamels, tools, aids, class pack, copper forms and others. Also carries tooling metals, weaving looms and aids, yarns, weaving kits, rug/craft yarns, embroidery/crewel threads, rug hook frames and aids, canvas, hoops, burlap, felt and soft sculpture and string art items. Indian beading, beads, feathers, macrame, basketry and batik supplies, fabric paints, airbrush kits and inks, stencil films, trims, foam, mosaics, stained glass kits, etching and beveled glass supplies and supplies for decoupage, jewelry making, leather, casting, plastics, wood and metal working are also available.

For Further Information: Catalog, $4 (refundable).
Discounts: Quantity discounts; sells wholesale to legitimate businesses.

ZIMMERMAN'S
2884 35th St. N.
St. Petersburg, FL 33713
(813) 526-4880

Offers: Craft supplies, including beads, ribbons, doll-making items, yarns and crochet threads, plastic canvas, knitting and crochet needles and aids, miniatures, wood products, macrame cords, sewing aids, flowers and flower parts. Carries basic supplies such as paints, finishes, glues and others.
For Further Information: Catalog, $2 (refundable).
Discounts: Has discounts.
Accepts: MasterCard, Visa

Glass Crafts and Stained Glass

Also see General Craft Supplies, Bead Crafts, Ceramics and other related categories.

ALICE'S STAINED GLASS
7015 N. 58th Ave.
Glendale, AZ 85301
(602) 939-7260

Offers: Stained glass supplies, tools, equipment and books, plus glass beadmaking tools, supplies, videos and books.
For Further Information: Free list.
Store Location: Yes
Discounts: Sells wholesale; quantity discounts.

AMERIGLAS
P.O. Box 27668
Omaha, NE 68127

Offers: Full line of stained glass tools, supplies, kits, others—for novice or artisan.
For Further Information: Catalog, $1.

ANYTHING IN STAINED GLASS
1060 Rt. 47 S.
P.O. Box 444
Rio Grande, NJ 08242
(609) 886-0416

Offers: Stained glass—over 14 types in a full range of colors, plus bargain packs. Also carries beveled glass shapes, nuggets, 20 lead castings, 65 filigrees, copper foil, solder, foil machines and dispensers. Carries tools, including 15 cutters and others, as well as chemicals, 10 soldering irons, saws, grinders, Morton systems items, chains, glass stains, kaleidoscope parts, over 150 Tiffany style shades/forms, lamp parts and bases (table, floor). Etching stencils, patterns and books are also available.
For Further Information: Free catalog.
Store Location: Yes
Discounts: Quantity prices; sells wholesale to legitimate businesses and professionals.

C&R LOO, INC.
1085 Essex Ave.
Richmond, CA 94801
(415) 232-0276

Offers: Flashed color/clear glass in over 20 combinations, plus double flashes on clear and color.

For Further Information: Contact dealer or send SASE for information.

CORAN-SHOLES INDUSTRIES
509 E. 2nd St.
Boston, MA 02127

Offers: Stained glass supplies, including stained glass and came, leads, solders, plus a variety of glass cutters, soldering irons and other tools. Manufacturer.
For Further Information: Free catalog.

COVINGTON ENGINEERING CORP.
715 W. Colton Ave.
P.O. Box 35
Redlands, CA 92374
(909) 793-6636

Offers: Glass machinery, including a glass beveling system, a 2-station unit with polisher, horizontal glass lap, sphere cutting cups and glass smoothing beveler. Also offers a glass lap kit, diamond mini-lap, arbors (for vertical glass units), belt sanders/polishers, web sanders, large sphere maker, cutter cups and supplies. Trim saws/cutters, arbors and accessories, lathes (engraver/cutter), diamond glass routers, Koolerant pumps, water and drain items are also available.
For Further Information: Send SASE for list.
See Also: Jewelry Making and Lapidary

Before applying a patina to your stained glass solder seam:
1. Wash project clean with a good, grease-cutting, dish detergent.
2. Rinse clean with clear water—dry.
3. Buff all seams with 0000 steel wool—wipe any steel wool off the project.
4. Use cotton swabs to apply patina to the solder seam.
5. Then apply a good glass wax over the patina on the seam and buff with a soft rag. This will make your copper patina shine and your black patina will have a deep black luster.

—Anything in Stained Glass

CREEK-TURN, INC.
Rt. 38
Hainesport, NJ 08036
(609) 261-1170

Offers: Glassmold mix for mold making, kiln fired glass, an-

tique reproductions, Tiffany-style lamps, dimensional glass, draping, and slumping. Also offers self-stacking slumping molds (no shelves needed), glass separator, mold release, mold makers' clays, a line of glass fusing kilns and firing kilns, plus kiln lids with elements. Glass crafting tools and complete instructions are also available.
For Further Information: Write or call for information.

DELPHI STAINED GLASS
2116 E. Michigan Ave.
Lansing, MI 48912

Offers: Stained glass kits/projects in a variety of designs, including lampshades, windows (over 90 shapes/sizes). Carries stained glass, both imported and domestic opalescent, iridescent, Chicago Art, streaky, confetti types, antique, ripplebacked, cathedral, handblown types and others in "hundreds" of colors. Also carries glass cutters, circle cutters, drills, pliers, soldering irons and routers. Supplies available include lead came, copper foil, glass paints and others.
For Further Information: Catalog, $4.50 (refundable).
Discounts: Quantity discounts.
Accepts: MasterCard, Visa

DENVER GLASS MACHINERY, INC.
3065 S. Umatilla St.
Englewood, CO 80110
(303) 781-0980

Offers: Glass machinery—hot glass and glory hole—electric glass furnace and propane glory hole (requires no special hookups), runs on 110V circuit. Also carries glass bevelers—industrial model with 2 units, professional compact unit, studio beveler for tabletop use (works glass up to 15 inches), plus engravers, bandsaws and kilns for fusing, slumping or painting.
For Further Information: Write or call for full information.

EASTERN ART GLASS
P.O. Box 341
Wyckoff, NJ 07481
(201) 847-0001

Offers: Glass etching kits (framed table mirrors, etching kits, others) and a glass engraving course. Carries rotary engraving power tools (to carve or engrave on glass, plastic, metal, wood). Supplies available include stencils and slab glass (standing shapes). Glass etching and mirror decorating video course also available.
For Further Information: Catalog, $3 (refundable).
Accepts: MasterCard, Visa

FRANKLIN ART GLASS
222 E. Sycamore St.
Columbus, OH 43206

Offers: Stained glass tools including metal running pliers,

glazing hammers, lead nippers, breaker-groziers, breakers and other pliers. Carries foil, lead, two-in-one patterns and other shears.
For Further Information: Send SASE for list.

GLASS CRAFT, INC.
626 Moss St.
Golden, CO 80401
(303) 278-4670

Offers: Line of glass-blowing equipment, tools, supplies and books.

HOUSTON STAINED GLASS SUPPLY
2420 Center St.
Houston, TX 77007
(713) 868-5296

Offers: Beveled glass, including the ComboClusters series—modular clusters in 28 designs to use alone or to mix with any other clusters for 175 designs in all (also comes in bevel graphic layout design sheets).
For Further Information: Send SASE or call for information.

ED HOY'S STAINED GLASS DISTRIBUTORS
1620 Frontenac Rd.
Naperville, IL 60563
(312) 420-0890

Offers: Glass crafting supplies, including glass bevels (shapes, clusters, color, mirror, panel and engraved), painted/fired shapes, gems, marbles, nuggets, jewels. Carries colored sheets including antiques, glashed, streakies, crackles, mirror, Oceana, textures, art, Bullseye, cathedral, Spectrum and others. Also carries scraps, microsave fuser, fusing kilns, clay molds and supplies, fusing supplies and tools, plus fusible glass, fusing kits and projects, glass paints, brushes and stains. Tools available include circle and other cutters,

Etched glassware. Courtesy of Eastern Art Glass.

pliers, shears, engravers, soldering irons, tools to bend foil, glass drills, burnishers, grinders, routers, belt sanders and saws. Also offers projectors, foil, came, channel, chemicals and Lamp forms and bases.
For Further Information: Contact dealer or send SASE for order details.
Discounts: Sells wholesale to businesses.

HUDSON GLASS CO., INC.
219 N. Division St.
Peekskill, NY 10566
(914) 737-2124

Offers: Stained glass supplies from Glastar, Inland, Motron, Worden, Reusche, Venture, Quicksilver, Ungar, Weller, Pop Lock, McNeil, Diamond, Fletcher, Seerite, Siegel, Sunray, Carolyn Kyle, Armstrong and others. Carries glass fusing and etching supplies, stained and other types glass, crystals, chemicals, foils, patterns, tools and equipment, electrical parts, box accessories and books.
For Further Information: Catalog, $3 (refundable).
Store Location: Yes
Discounts: Allows discounts to teachers and institutions; sells wholesale to legitimate businesses.

IPGR, INC.
P.O. Box 205
Kulpsville, PA 19443
(215) 256-9015

Offers: Materials for restoring china and glass, plus jade, ivory and other materials.
For Further Information: Catalog, $3.

LVR PRODUCTS
P.O. Box 4907
Gardena, CA 90249
(213) 217-8823

Offers: Micro-Kiln EZ-5 for small fusing glass projects. Reaches fusing temperature in 3 to 5 minutes; cools in about 20 minutes. Micro-Kiln EZ-5 can be heated in a microwave oven. Useful for professionals and hobbyists.
For Further Information: Send SASE for further information.

P & E MANUFACTURING
45698 Samuel St.
Sarasota, FL 34233
(813) 924-6401

Offers: Jen-Ken glass kilns in 4 models. One model runs on 120V household current, others on 240V. Carries slumping molds, automatic kiln shutoff and soak control.
For Further Information: Contact dealer or send SASE for information.

PARAGON INDUSTRIES, INC.
2011 S. Town E. Blvd.
Mesquite, TX 75149
(214) 288-7557, (800) 876-4328

Offers: Glass fusing kiln with digital temperature controller.
For Further Information: Free catalog.
Discounts: Sells wholesale to legitimate businesses.
See Also: Ceramics

PREMIUM PRODUCTS OF LOUISIANA, INC.
424 E. Vermilion St.
Lafayette, LA 70501
(318) 237-5691

Offers: Beveled glass (tempered and insulated) in a variety of designs and mirrored bevels. Carries stained glass sheets, painted, fired and etched glass. Custom beveling and mirror resilvering available.
For Further Information: Send SASE for information.

SETH ROSEN STUDIO
19 Curtis Lane
Dennis, MA 02638
(508) 385-5413

Offers: Line of mirrors, clear glass and bevels—any size and shape.
For Further Information: Price list, $1.
Discounts: Quantity discounts.

UNITED ART GLASS, INC.
1032 E. Ogden Ave.
Naperville, IL 60563
(312) 369-8168

Offers: Supplies/equipment including bevels, engraved, star, faceted, mirror, color, clusters, jewels, nuggets and marbles. Glass includes Bulleye, Chicago Art, Cotswold, Emaille, flashed, Flemish, antique Kokomo, Oceana, Waser, Wissmach, mirror, plate and others. Carries chemicals and tools, including 10 cutters, lead cames, shears, engravers, flexible shafts, glass drills, foiling machines, Foilomatic guide rollers and Glastar tools, Motron Surface systems (cutting shops), routers, saws, soldering irons and etching items. Metal lamp bases, fusing projects, Jen-Ken fusing kilns, packs, equipment, Badger spray guns, paints. Kiln firing items and patterns for lamp forms also available.
For Further Information: Catalog, $5.
Discounts: Sells wholesale; quantity discounts.

V.E.A.S., INC.
P.O. Box 278
Troy, MI 48099
(313) 443-9000

Offers: Instructional video on Glass Erasing (a controlled form of sandblasting) — can also be used for wood, plastic or metal — program teaches techniques for professional results, for mirror decorating, monogramming and other projects, plus embellishing on glass.

For Further Information: Send SASE for brochure.
Discounts: "Dealer inquiries welcome."
Accepts: MasterCard, Visa

WHITTEMORE-DURGIN
P.O. Box 2065
Hanover, MA 02339

Offers: Stained glass including French and German antique, cathedral types (in sheets and by the pound), antique, opalescent, clear beveled, jewels and others. Carries stained glass kits with tools, basics and precut lamps. Also carries tool and supplies kits, Suncatcher kits, lampshade maker kits. Tools available include glass cutters, pliers, lead straighteners, soldering irons, glass grinders and accessories. Also offers lead came, copper foil, brass channel and banding, lamp parts, decorative chains, hinges, metal lamp bases, lead castings, patterns and books.

For Further Information: Catalog, $2.
Discounts: Quantity discounts.

Indian and Frontier Crafts

Also see Basketry and Seat Weaving, Bead Crafts, Leather Crafts and General Needlecraft Supplies.

BUFFALO TIPI POLE CO.
3355 Upper Gold Creek
Sandpoint, ID 83864

Offers: Tipis (variety of sizes) and tipi poles.
For Further Information: Send SASE for information.
Discounts: "Best prices."

CHARLES A. CASPAR
Rt. 1, P.O. Box 379
May, TX 76857
(915) 643-2388

Offers: Peace pipe kits, molds, wooden stems and Indian pot molds.
For Further Information: Send #10 envelope and 4 stamps for details.

CRAZY CROW TRADING POST
P.O. Box 314
Denison, TX 75020
(214) 463-1366

Offers: Native American/historic kits, including coats, leggings, dress, pants and shirts. Costume kits include war bonnets, breechclout, roaches, breast plates. Also carries tinware, wood kegs and buckets, tipi poles/covers, jewelry findings, leather items including thongs, sinew, hides, skins of various animals, plus horns, skulls, claws, quills, hair, garment leathers, suedes, latigo and others. Nails, cones, buttons, brass and silver sheets, feathers, fabrics, buckles, conchos and hair-pipes are also available. Tools include awls, cutters, scissors and pliers. Stocks beads, glass seed, trade, metal, plus kits, looms and books.
For Further Information: Catalog, $2.50.
Discounts: Quantity prices.

DIAMOND FORGE SHOP
12955 Archibald Whitehouse Rd.
Whitehouse, OH 43571
(419) 875-6868

Offers: An instructional video, *How to Make a Tipi*, by Charlie Two Feathers, giving step-by-step instructions, from peeling poles to complete set-up. Tipis are available complete and ready to set up, with critter beds, canvas, poles, stakes, ropes and instructions.
For Further Information: Send SASE for complete information.

EAGLE FEATHER TRADING POST
168 W. 12th St.
Ogden, UT 84404
(801) 393-3991

Offers: American Indian costume kits, including single feather, beaded pouch, 17 chokers, 4 headdresses, bustles, necklaces, bandoliers, breastplates, bell sets and medicine pouches. Authentic clothing patterns are available for war shirts, frontiersman's shirts, leather dresses and others. Beads available include bugle, striped pony, wood and large holed beads; faceted glass and plastic, tile loose seed and trade beads. Conchos, tin cones and cowrie shells also available. Stocks scissors and glue, punches, awls, cutters, chisels, buckle blanks, fringes, blankets and books.
For Further Information: Catalog, $3.
Store Location: Yes
Discounts: Quantity discounts; allows discounts to teachers and institutions; sells wholesale to legitimate businesses.

EARTHWORKS
P.O. Box 28
Ridgway, CO 81432

Offers: Tipis—buffalo hide reinforced, mildew/flame retardant, in a variety of sizes.
For Further Information: Brochure, $1.

GRAY OWL INDIAN CRAFT CO., INC.
13205 Merrick Blvd.
P.O. Box 340468
Jamaica, NY 11434
(718) 341-4000

Offers: Over 4,000 Native American and craft items, including costume kits and parts (roaches, headdresses, others), beading and beads (trade, seed, cut beads, crow, pony, brass), bone hairpipes, elk teeth, tin cones, feathers, shawl fringe, leathers (cowhide and others), furs, bones, skins, animal parts, blankets, videos and books.
For Further Information: Catalog, $3.
Store Location: Yes
Discounts: Quantity discount; allows discounts for teachers and institutions; sells wholesale to businesses.
Accepts: American Express, Discover, MasterCard, Visa

THE MUSKRAT TRADER
P.O. Box 20033
Roanoke, VA 24018
(703) 344-1567

Offers: Native American-oriented items, including furs, quills, leather, animal parts (skulls, teeth, bones, claws, others), beads, feathers (turkey, pheasant, peacock, ostrich, others) and buffalo items. Carries do-it-yourself kits and hard to find items.
For Further Information: Catalog, $2.
Discounts: Quantity discounts; allows discounts to teachers and institutions; sells wholesale to legitimate businesses.

NORTHWEST TRADERS
5055 W. Jackson Rd.
Enon, OH 45323

Offers: Frontier apparel kits including capotes precut from blanket of choice, (with directions) and buckskin pants. Frontier patterns available include pants (French fly front), trousers (side button), war shirt, frontier shirt, capote jackets. Carries traditional and Hudson's Bay blankets, mountain hats, sashes, books and ready-made apparel.
For Further Information: Free catalog.

PANTHER PRIMITIVES
P.O. Box 32
Normantown, WV 25267
(304) 462-7718

Offers: Tipi poles, lacing pins, instruction books (also ready-made items for store booths), waterproof canvas and cottons by the yard, frontier clothing kits and patterns, bead kits, plus beads, looms and supplies. Stocks bone choker kits, 15 flags (historical), tinware, oak kegs, wood buckets, metal tinder boxes, candle molds, quills, quillwork kits and finished items.
For Further Information: Catalog, $2 (refundable).
Discounts: Sells wholesale to legitimate businesses.
Accepts: MasterCard, Visa

SWEET MEDICINE
P.O. Box 30128
Phoenix, AZ 85046
(602) 788-3840

Offers: Feathers, leather, beads, crystals, animal bones (claws, teeth, jaws, others) and herbs.
For Further Information: Catalog, $3.
Discounts: Sells wholesale to legitimate businesses.

WAKEDA TRADING POST
P.O. Box 19146
Sacramento, CA 95819
(916) 485-9838

Offers: Native American crafts and garment patterns for authentic, early American fur hats, shirts, pants, leggings, breechclouts, dresses, capotes, coats and accessories. Costume kits include chokers, war bonnets, quillwork, moccasins, fans, hair roaches, breechclouts. Carries shawls and metallic fringes, trade cloths, wool, calico, blankets, beads (seed, pony, iris, luster, crow, tile, others), bead supplies, looms, mirrors, brass nails, tin cones, buckles, metal spots, bells. Naturals available include sweet grass, ropes, sage, gourds and cedar. Also carries hides, furs including sheep, beaver, coyote, red fox, ermine, plus tails. Carries leathers for garment buckskins, thongs, straps, rawhide, latigo. Porcupine quills and teeth are also available.
For Further Information: Catalog, $1.
Discounts: Quantity discounts; sometimes sells wholesale to legitimate businesses.
Accepts: MasterCard, Visa

WESTERN TRADING POST
P.O. Box 9070
Denver, CO 80209
(303) 777-7750

Offers: Beads (metal, brass, wood, bone, hairpipe, seed, tile, others), beading supplies, looms, cones, feathers, conchos, jewelry findings, bells (sheep, dance, sleigh, sets), buckles, shells, buttons, blanks. Carries animal parts, including buffalo horns, bladders and skulls, claws, teeth, porcupine hair, pheasant skins, ermine, horse tails and leather (latigo, rawhide, buckshin, white deer, others). Dance accessories include chainette fringewool trade cloth. Patterns available for Indian and frontier garments. Kits include beading, feather headdresses and feather bonnets. Books also available.
For Further Information: Catalog, $3.
Discounts: Quantity discounts.
Accepts: Discover, MasterCard, Visa

Jewelry Making and Lapidary

Also see General Craft Supplies, Bead Crafts, Indian and Frontier Crafts, Metalworking, Tools and Equipment and other related categories.

A.A. CLOUET
369 W. Fountain St.
Providence, RI 02903
(401) 272-4100

Offers: Earring parts—fasteners, earnuts, clutch backs, clip pads, disks, guards, cushions, jewelers staples, elastic barbs and others.
For Further Information: Send SASE for list.

ACKLEY'S
3230 N. Stone Ave.
Colorado Springs, CO 80907

Offers: Lapidary and silversmithing supplies, rough rock. Jewelry findings include earwires, beads, chains, mountings.
For Further Information: Catalog, $1 (refundable).

AFFORDABLE GEMS
Rt. 1, P.O. Box 81
Novinger, MO 63559
(816) 488-6690

Offers: Faceted gemstones—sunstone, topaz, white sapphire, garnet, smokey quartz. Carries quartz crystal points, clusters and others.
For Further Information: Send for list.

ALETA'S ROCK SHOP
1515 Plainville Ave. NE
Grand Rapids, MI 49505
(616) 363-5394

Offers: Rocks, cutting and tumbling. Lapidary equipment includes machines and tumblers. Carries findings, tools and silversmith supplies.
For Further Information: Catalog, $1.50 (refundable). Free rock list.
Store Location: Yes

ALPHA FACETING SUPPLY, INC.
1225 Hollis St.
P.O. Box 2133
Bremerton, WA 98310
(206) 377-5629

Offers: Over 10,000 items for casting, jewelry making, faceting, wax casting and display. Carries equipment for lapidary, casting, faceting and prospecting.
For Further Information: Supply catalogs, $1.
Discounts: Quantity discounts; allows discounts to institutions and professionals; sells wholesale to businesses.
Accepts: MasterCard, Visa

AMBER CO
5643 Cahuenga Blvd.
North Hollywood, CA 91601
(818) 509-5730

Offers: Beads—unusuals and ethnic, of a variety of materials/sizes/styles, plus ethnic beading accents, bead stringing, knotting, and custom design and repair services.
For Further Information: Free catalog.
Store Location: Yes
Discounts: Quantity discounts; allows discounts to teachers and institutions; sells wholesale to legitimate businesses.

APACHE CANYON MINES
P.O. Box 530
Baker, CA 92309
(619) 733-4271

Offers: Gem grade turquoise, rough or stones.
For Further Information: Free price lists and information sheets.

APL TRADER
P.O. Box 1900
New York, NY 10113
(718) 454-2954

Offers: Faceted gemstones—emeralds, rubies, sapphires, amethysts, citrines, peridots, rhodolites, topaz, tourmalines and others. Also offers cabochons, pearls and beads.
For Further Information: Send for price list.
Discounts: Has discount.

ARA IMPORTS
P.O. Box 41054
Brecksville, OH 44141
(216) 838-1372

Offers: Jewelry findings, including precious and semi-precious beads, plus pearls and corals.
For Further Information: Catalog and price list, $1.

ARE, INC.
P.O. Box 8
Greensboro Bend, VT 05842

Offers: Jewelry-making items including a line of gemstone cabochons, faceted and gemstone beads, jewelry findings (gold filled, s/s), sheet metals (14 kt, gold filled, fine silver), wire (s/s, 14 kt, gold filled), tubing, bezel, silver casting grain, easy and hard solder wires, discs, IT solder and 30 gauge sheet. Carries craft metal wires and sheet in brass, copper, Nugold, nickel silver, pewter, titanium and casting alloys, includes jeweler's bronze, nickel silver, pewter ingots and scrap silver.
For Further Information: Catalog, $3 (refundable).

ARIZONA GEMS & MINERALS, INC.
6370 E. Highway 69
Prescott Valley, AZ 86314
(602) 772-6443

Offers: Beads (Austrian types, metal, plastic, glass, s/s, gold filled, 14 kt, others), beading and bolo supplies, cabochons, charms, chains, crystals and jewelry findings. Equipment includes grinding wheels, silversmithing, buffing wheels and jewelry making tools.
For Further Information: Catalog $4 (refundable).
Store Location: Yes
Discounts: Quantity discounts; sells wholesale to legitimate businesses.
Accepts: American Express, Discover, MasterCard, Visa

ART TECH CASTING CO.
P.O. Box 54
Scottsville, NY 14546
(716) 889-9187

Offers: Casting services—karat gold, sterling and bronze—for one-of-a-kind or production run, from professionals.
For Further Information: Send for details.

AUSTRALIAN OPAL IMPORTS
P.O. Box 44208
Victoria, British Columbia V9A 7H7 Canada
(604) 385-1639

Offers: Australian opals, rough and cut, black and boulders, doublets, triplets, cameos, calibrated, freeform and opal matrix.
For Further Information: Send for price list.

B&J ROCK SHOP
620 Claymont Estate Dr.
Ballwin, MO 63011
(314) 394-4567

Offers: Faceted gemstones, including assorted amethyst and others. Carries quartz crystals, amethyst crystal clusters,

bead stringing supplies, gemstone beads (14 kt, s/s and others) and big earring mountings. Also carries quartz clock movements and kits.
For Further Information: 50-page catalog, $3 (refundable).
Store Location: Yes
Discounts: Quantity discounts.

PAUL J. BADALI
944 S. 200 E.
Layton, UT 84041
(801) 546-4086

Offers: Instructional video (VHS)—*Making Gold Nugget Jewelry*, with Paul J. Badali, covers design, tools, crafting items and mounting for the beginner through advanced silversmith or jeweler. Carries gold ore concentrate with directions, gold samples and jewelry findings (s/s, gold filled).
For Further Information: Send business-size SASE for catalog.
Discounts: Sells wholesale; quantity discounts.

BEADBOX, INC.
10135 E. Via Linda
Scottsdale, AZ 85258
(800) BEADBOX

Offers: Beads from 30 countries, exotics and unusuals, in a line of sizes/shapes, plus beading kits for jewelry, others.
For Further Information: Catalog, $8 (refundable).
Accepts: MasterCard, Visa

BEADNIKS
1197 W. 5th Ave.
Eugene, OR 97402

Offers: Art Deco style beaded earring kits, others.
For Further Information: Details, $1.

BLAKE BROTHERS
451 E. 58th Ave., Suite 2294
Denver, CO 80216
(303) 292-2011, (800) 78-BLAKE

Offers: Stone animal beads in 6 stones and a wide range of animal species.
For Further Information: Send SASE for list.

BOMBAY BAZAAR
P.O. Box 07196
Lakewood, OH 44107
(216) 521-6548

Offers: Lapidary/jewelry-making supplies, including Crystalite equipment and supplies, Diamond saw blades, Raytech and Covington equipment, Rock Rascal gemmaker, saws and arbor, Graves/Raytech machines (faceting and units). Genie and Titan units, Foredom mini and other power tools

and tumblers. Carries hand tools including 18 tweezers, Eastwing line. Rough facet material, synthetics, preforms, cabochons and faceted gemstones are also available.
For Further Information: Catalog, $1.50.

BOURGET BROS.
1636 11th St.
Santa Monica, CA 90404
(310) 450-6556

Offers: Lapidary/jewelry equipment/tools—full lines to cast, weld, drill, enamel, plate, engrave, others. Carries furnaces, saws, flexible shafts, magnifiers, files, torches, tumblers and metals (s/s, kt gold and filled, copper in sheets, wires, channels, bezels and fancies). Also carries jewelry findings, wires, threads—full lines. Beads include turquoise, amber, gemstones, cabochons and synthetics. Stocks pearls, metal and s/s coil types, s/s button covers, chains, mounts and books.
For Further Information: Tool/jewelry catalog, $3; lapidary catalog, $5.
Store Location: Yes
Discounts: Quantity discounts.
Accepts: MasterCard, Visa

C & N ROCKS & GIFTS
350 Keller
Ashdown, AR 71822
(501) 898-3485

Offers: Quartz crystals of various locations; wide range of sizes/types, rough and finished rock materials and supplies.
For Further Information: Free catalog.
Discounts: Wholesale discounts.

CGM, INC.
19562 Ventura Blvd., Suite 231
Tarzana, CA 91356
(818) 609-7088, (800) 426-5CGM

Offers: Jewelry findings (14 kt, sterling, gold filled), mountings, earring and other parts, beads, beading hoops, add-a-bead chains, others. Gemstones include emerald, ruby, sapphire, aqua, amethyst, peridot, garnet, opal and others.
For Further Information: Free catalog.

COVINGTON ENGINEERING CORP.
P.O. Box 35
Redlands, CA 92373
(714) 793-6636

Offers: Lapidary/glass equipment, including lapidary machines (mills, carvers, combos, drum units, gem shops, grinders, slab saws, laps, sanders, sphere makers, tumblers, others), glass machines (bevelers, carving tools, coolerant systems, drills, engravers, laps, polishers, sanders, saws, smoothers, grinders, others), equipment/supplies (adhesives, beading items, dressers, drill bits, drums, Eastwing and

jewelry tools), plus motors, templates and grinding wheels.
For Further Information: Free catalog.
Store Location: Yes
Accepts: MasterCard, Visa

CRAFT SUPPLIES 4 LESS
13001 Las Vegas Blvd. S.
Las Vegas, NV 89124
(702) 361-3600

Offers: Glass beads from areas worldwide including grab bag assortments (crystal, antique, handmade, mosaic, trade, unusuals). Other beads include metal, plastic, acrylic. Carries jewelry findings, rhinestones, pewter and metal charms, beading supplies, Fimo, Sculpey, tools, adhesives, Friendly Plastic, kits and books.
For Further Information: Catalog, $4 (with filigree sample).
Store Location: Yes
Accepts: MasterCard, Visa

For cutting slabs: To get rid of excess oil, drop slabs in kitty litter for one-half hour, then sprinkle Ajax or Comet on the wet slab, scrub with a brush, and rinse.

—Stone Age Industries, Inc.

CROOKED-RIVER
413 Main St.
P.O. Box 129
La Farge, WI 54639
(608) 625-4460

Offers: Line of polymer and glass beads, plus watch parts and faces for jewelry making.
For Further Information: Send SASE for catalog.
Discounts: Quantity discounts; sells wholesale to legitimate businesses.

DAWN FOR NEW DIRECTIONS
P.O. Box 2034
Simi Valley, CA 93062
(805) 584-2567

Offers: Gemstones, including ruby, sapphire, emerald, tanzanite, amethyst, garnet, peridot, star sapphire, moonstone, topaz, sunstone, tourmaline, others.
For Further Information: Free list.
Discounts: "May have sales."
Accepts: MasterCard, Visa

DENDRITICS, INC.
223 Crescent St.
Waltham, MA 02154
(800) 437-9993

Offers: Pocket-sized professional electronic gem scale (5

inches × 3 inches × 1 inch) to weigh 50.50 × .01 cts.
For Further Information: Call for information.

DIAMOND PACIFIC TOOL CORP.
25647 W. Main St.
Barstow, CA 92311
(800) 253-2954

Offers: Jeweler's tools and supplies, diamond lapidary equipment, Vanguard saw blades, Foredom power tools, Eastwing tools, Rockhound products and others.
For Further Information: Free catalog.
Store Location: Yes
Discounts: Sells wholesale to legitimate businesses.

DISCOUNT AGATE HOUSE
3401 N. Dodge Blvd.
Tuscon, AZ 85716
(602) 323-0781

Offers: Cutting rocks from areas worldwide, lapidary machinery, accessories, sterling silver and smithing supplies and jewelry findings.
For Further Information: Send for rough rock list.
Store Location: Yes
Discounts: "Wholesale with a tax number."
Accepts: MasterCard, Visa

EASTGEM, LTD.
P.O. Box 7454
North Brunswick, NJ 08902
(908) 545-9726

Offers: Cut gemstones—cabachons and faceted, plus custom cutting service and appraisals.
For Further Information: Free price list.
Discounts: Quantity discounts; allows discounts to teachers and institutions.

EBERSOLE LAPIDARY SUPPLY, INC.
11417 E. Highway 54
Wichita, KS 67230

Offers: Lapidary equipment and supplies, plus jeweler's supplies, mountings, cabs, and other gemstones and beads.
For Further Information: Catalog, $2.

ELIZABETH WARD & CO.
4 Mount Vernon St.
Arlington, MA 02174
(617) 648-3612

Offers: Lampworked glass beads, semi-precious stone beads, animal fetishes, freshwater pearls, others.
For Further Information: Catalog, $2.
Store Location: Yes

ELOXITE CORP.
806 10th St.
Wheatland, WY 82201
(307) 322-3050

Offers: Jewelry mountings—full line of buckles and inserts, bracelets, pendants, bolos, others, plus jewelry making tools and supplies, 5 tumblers, clock parts and movements, display boxes, racks and earring displays. Beads include gemstone, seed, others. Books available.
For Further Information: Catalog, $1.
Store Location: Yes
Discounts: Quantity discounts; sells wholesale to legitimate businesses.
Accepts: MasterCard, Visa

ENGRAVING ARTS
P.O. Box 787
Laytonville, CA 95454
(707) 984-8203

Offers: Custom services—dies, embossing, coining, striking, blanking, trim dies.
For Further Information: Free brochure.

DAVID H. FELL & COMPANY, INC.
6009 Bandini Blvd.
City of Commerce, CA 90040
(213) 722-9992, (800) 822-1996

Offers: Sheet (all karats, platinum, silver) all gauges, shaped wire—round, half round, triangle, bezel, flat, square all karats, all gauges. 14 kt tubing, 14 kt rod stock, discs. Karat gold, sterling fine silver, platinum, palladium casting grain or pieces, alloys and solders. Variety of karat gold colors. Pattern sheet—photo etched on sterling, fine silver, 10 kt and 14 kt, all gauges. 325 patterns, including gallery sheet and ribbon sheet. Refining services, fast turnaround. Technical services.
For Further Information: Free catalogs; specify Product, Pattern Sheet or Refining Schedule.
Store Location: Yes: 712 Olive St., Suite 305, Los Angeles, CA 90014
Accepts: MasterCard, Visa

FOB VILLAGE ORIGINALS
24140 Detroit Rd.
Westlake, OH 44145
(216) 835-2144

Offers: Brazilian and Uruguayan amethyst, agates, tumbled stones and others.
For Further Information: Free catalog.
Discounts: Quantity discounts.

GABRIEL'S
P.O. Box 222
Unionville, OH 44088
(216) 428-6163

Offers: Cabochons and shapes (including hard-to-find) — teardrops, wedges, triangles, others in a variety of materials.
For Further Information: Free catalog.
Accepts: American Express, MasterCard, Visa

GEM ODYSSEY
P.O. Box 5258
El Dorado Hills, CA 95762
(916) 933-0318

Offers: Jewelry findings, mountings — easy-mounts and chains in sterling, 14 kt gemstones, faceted, calibrated, include amethyst, citrine, peridot, thodolite, blue topaz, others.
For Further Information: Free catalog.

GEMCO INTERNATIONAL
Howard Bank Building
P.O. Box 833
Fayston, VT 05673

Offers: Gem facet rough — ruby, tsavorite, emerald, kunzite, hiddenite, aquamarine, tourmaline, sapphire, golden beryl, imperial topaz, rhodolite garnet, Malaya rhodolite, almandite garnet, amethyst, citrine, gilson emerald opal, facet opal, peridot and melee. Gemstones may also include beryl, spinel, rubellite, Kashan ruby, others.
For Further Information: Free catalog.
Discounts: "Big discounts."

THE GEMMARY
P.O. Box 816
Redondo Beach, CA 90277
(310) 372-5969

Offers: Out of print and rare books on gemology, jewelry (history and making), mineralogy and mining.
For Further Information: Catalog, $2.
Store Location: Yes

GEMSTONE EQUIPMENT MANUFACTURING
750 Easy St.
Simi Valley, CA 93065
(805) 527-6990

Offers: Lapidary equipment, including slant cabbing machine, also available as a kit in 4 models, 5 vibratory tumblers, bench rollaway sand blasters, saws (4-inch, 6-inch and 10-inch trim, 8-inch dynamotrim and drop saw, 16-inch gravity drop type) and saw blades. Also carries diamond products — 6 carving points, blades, discs, 15 drills, points, dressers, files, 9 compounds, plus stone and metal finishing kits,

router bevelers, sculpture router, super buffer and plastic gold pans.
For Further Information: Write or call for information.

GLOBE UNION INTERNATIONAL, INC.
1237 American Pkwy.
Richardson, TX 75081
(214) 669-8181, (800) 765-5339

Offers: Gemstone beads and chips, including rose quartz, aventurine, jaspers, unakite, hematite, black quartz, onyx, dyed fossil, agate, tiger eye, carnelian, malachite, lapis, amethyst, others, plus color-treated quartz.
For Further Information: Free catalog.

A. GOODMAN
949 Beaumont Ave.
P.O. Box 667
Beaumont, CA 92223
(909) 845-8525

Offers: Lapidary instructional videos covering lost wax casting, meet-point faceting carving techniques, crystal and mineral energy, jewelry design, handcrafting, faceting, forming, plating, sphere making, emerald cutting, soldering, faceting, plus videos on opal, bead stringing, gemstone carving and lapidary basics.
For Further Information: Send SASE for list.
Discounts: Sells wholesale to legitimate businesses.
Accepts: MasterCard, Visa

GOODNOW'S
3415 S. Hayden St.
Amarillo, TX 79109

Offers: Rough gemstone material, which may include azuamarine crystal, piranha agate, black fire agate, Afghanistan lapis lazuli, St. Mary's star garnet, Australian tiger iron and tigereye in jasper, rutilated quartz, Botswanna agate, golden tigereye, plus tourmaline crystal assortments, quartz (Angel's hair, raspberry, others).
For Further Information: Send SASE with inquiry.
Discounts: Quantity discounts.

GRAVES
1800 Andrews Ave.
Pompano Beach, FL 33069
(305) 782-8000

Offers: Lapidary equipment, including Cab-Mate (grinds, polishes, sands, rock vise, electric preformer), saws, cabochon preforms, metal polisher, cabaret unit, crowner, spool polisher, 6-wheeler unit, faceting preforms and faceting machine.
For Further Information: Write for free catalog and nearest dealer.

GRIEGER'S

P.O. Box 73070
Pasadena, CA 91109
(800) 423-4181

Offers: Jewelry-making/lapidary supplies, equipment, tools and accessories. Jewelry-making supplies include kits, display items (cases, boxes, trays, stands), and jewelry findings (in 14 kt, s/s, filled, others) — a full line — plus gemstone beads, baroque chip necklaces, chains, cabochons, stones (large variety — diamonds, pearls). Carries beading supplies and accessories. Also carries a full line of hand and power tools for lapidary, jewelry making, silversmithing and lost wax casting. Scales, casting metals, s/s sheet and wires, gold-filled and 14 kt wires, gold sheet, clock parts and books are available.
For Further Information: Free catalog.
Store Location: Yes
Discounts: Quantity discounts; sells wholesale to legitimate businesses.
Accepts: American Express, Discover, MasterCard, Visa

GRYPHON CORP.

101 E. Santa Anita Ave.
Burbank, CA 91502
(818) 845-7807

Offers: Diamond band saw (cuts glass, tile, minerals) and other lapidary equipment, including 10-in-1 lapidary workshop, which has a cabber, trim saw, faceter, slicer/slabber, cab crowner, Starmaster, sapphire cup, sphere maker, tumbler, glass beveler (with a flexible shaft), diamond drills, carving points and burrs, metal burrs, metal buffs and deburring tools. Also carries diamond gem lathes, diamond micro wire saws and others. Manufacturer.
For Further Information: Free catalog.

T.B. HAGSTOZ & SON, INC.

709 Sansom St.
Philadelphia, PA 19106
(215) 922-1627

Offers: Metals: Gold, silver, gold filled, platinum, pewter, copper, bronze, brass, nickel silver. Carries jewelry tools and equipment, waxes, accessories. Brands available include GFC, Vigor, Dremel, Foredom, Kerr, Af USA. Findings: 14 kt, sterling, gold filled, base metals. Solders: Gold, silver, platinum, soft. Wire wrapping and bead stringing supplies are also available.
For Further Information: Catalog, $5 (refundable).
Accepts: MasterCard, Visa

When gluing any object to any type of finding, remember to sand the surfaces for a better glue job.

— Arizona Gems & Minerals, Inc.

HEAVEN & EARTH

P.O. Box 224
Marshfield, VT 05658
(800) 348-5155

Offers: "Mystical" minerals: Azeztulite, merlinite, sphrodite, strombolite, moldavite, phenacite, tanzanite, danburite, charoite, lithium silica, others. Also carries jewelry templates, tools and an array of gemstones and crystals.
For Further Information: Free catalog.

HONG KONG LAPIDARIES, INC.

2801 N. University Dr.
Coral Spring, FL 33065
(305) 755-8777

Offers: Beading threads: Silk, nylon (over 16 colors). Also carries beading needles.
For Further Information: Send SASE for list.
Discounts: Quantity discounts.

HOUSE OF ONYX

120 Main St.
Greenville, KY 42345

Offers: Gemstones and assortments — faceted smoky quartz, Brazil mix, moonstone catseye cabs, blue topaz, white sapphire, amethyst, emerald cabs, blue sapphire, aquamarine, Mozambique garnets, others.
For Further Information: Free 120-page catalog.
Discounts: "Has 15% discount on large orders."
Accepts: MasterCard, Visa

HUBERS

20012 Enadia Way
Canoga Park, CA 91306
(800) 424-8237

Offers: Jewelry findings and beads (14 kt, gold filled), faceted CZ in emerald, ruby, sapphire colors.
For Further Information: Send SASE for list.

INTERNATIONAL BEAD & JEWELRY

P.O. Box 767
Clifton, NJ 07015

Offers: Line of beads — semi-precious stones, sterling silver, bone, Southwest clay, others. Also carries jewelry findings, parts and kits, other jewelry-making and craft supplies, plus polybags.
For Further Information: Catalog, $2.
Discounts: Sells wholesale.

JEWELRY PLUS
P.O. Box 4397
Culver City, CA 90231
(310) 838-1440

Offers: Semi-precious stone charms (heart, star, moon, teardrop, dolphins, whales, tortoises, arrowheads, points, others): amethyst, azurite, malachite, lace agate, hematite, quartz, snowflake obsidian, lapis, tiger eyes, amazonite, others.
For Further Information: Artisans or dealers only: Catalog request on letterhead or with copy of resale number.

JIM'S GEMOLOGY
1322 Harrisburg Rd. NE
Canton, OH 44705

Offers: Faceted gemstones-emerald, ruby, sapphire melee, amethyst, andalusite, aquamarine, chrysoberyl, chrome diopside, citrine, epidot, rhodolite garnets, helidor green beryl, lolites, peridot, spinels (blue, lavender), smoky quartz, tourmaline, tsavorite, zircon. Also carries cabochons: amethyst, apatite cat's eyes, aquamarine cat's eyes, blue lolites, black star sapphires (or blue), emeralds, enstatite, garnets, star garnets, 6-color jade, moon agates, others, including carved cabachons. Beads available include agate, amethyst, bloodstone, aventurine, quartz, others. Strung. Metaphysical cut stones and items.
For Further Information: Send SASE for list.

ESTHER KENNEDY, F.G.A.
P.O. Box 220014
Charlotte, NC 28222
(704) 364-7460

Offers: Gemstones—tourmaline, amethyst, tanzanite, andalusite, emerald, garnet, opal, ruby, sapphire, lapis, zircon.
For Further Information: Send SASE for prices.
Discounts: "Dealers welcome."

KINGSLEY NORTH, INC.
910 Brown St.
P.O. Box 196
Norway, MI 49870
(906) 563-9228

Offers: Lapidary tools, equipment and supplies: Diamond tools, saws, tumblers, soldering torches, gauges, cutters, gravers, pliers, screwdrivers, gripper and clamp, plus third hand, pick-hammer, jewelry waxer kit, machine super kit, Flex shaft equipment, electroplating items and rolling mills. Gemstones include jaspers, quartz, agate, hematite, obsidian, others. Jewelry findings available include necklaces, earrings, ring and pendant mountings, bolos, chains and others.
For Further Information: Free catalog.
Store Location: Yes

Discounts: Quantity discounts; allows discounts to teachers and institutions; sells wholesale to legitimate businesses.
Accepts: MasterCard, Visa

KNIGHT'S
P.O. Box 411
Waitsfield, VT 05673
(802) 496-3707

Offers: Gem roughs—emerald, tourmaline, black star sapphire, jade, star garnets, amethyst, opal, topaz, cat's eye, turquoise, snowflake jade, smoky quartz, India star ruby, moonstone, chrysoprase, lapis lazuli, peridot.
For Further Information: Free price list.
Discounts: Sells wholesale.

KRONA INTERNATIONAL
P.O. Box 9968
Colorado Springs, CO 80932
(719) 597-8779

Offers: Faceted gemstones—emerald (Brazilian, Colombian), amethyst, andalusite, aquamarine, citrine, enstatite, helidor, hiddenite, iolite, kunzite, moonstone, morganite, rubelite, tsavorite, and many rare, unique types.
For Further Information: Free lists.

LANEY CO.
6449 S. 209 E. Ave.
Broken Arrow, OK 74014
(918) 355-1955

Offers: Gold metal letter cutouts (computer/laser) in Old Timer and trophy styles. Wire available round and half, square, dome, rectangle, triangle, fancy and channel. Metal sheets, solders, fluxes, nickel pickle, leaves, bezel cups, ring shanks, beads, bolos, buckle backs and squash blossoms also available.
For Further Information: Free catalog.
Discounts: Quantity discounts; allows discounts to teachers and institutions; sells wholeale to legitimate businesses.

LAPCRAFT CO., INC.
195 W. Olentangy St.
Powell, OH 43065

Offers: Diamond tools—pre-forming/diamond grinding wheels, drilling/diamond drills, core drills, faceting/diamond discs, carving/diamond points, polishing/diamond powders.
For Further Information: Free catalog.

LAPIDABRADE, INC.
8 E. Eagle Rd.
Havertown, PA 19083
(215) 789-4022

Offers: Full range of jewelry findings and tools, lapidary equipment, tools and supplies.
For Further Information: (Catalogs listed are refundable.) Findings Catalog, $4; Jewelry Makers Tool Catalog, $2; Lapidary Equipment & Supply Catalog, $2.
Discounts: Sells wholesale.

LH MINING
4617 W. Ave., K10
Quartz Hill, CA 93551
(805) 943-9654

Offers: Turquoise—natural, stabilized, spider web rough, cabochons and carving material.
For Further Information: Send for price list.

LORTONE, INC.
2856 NW Market St.
Seattle, WA 98107

Offers: Rotary tumblers in 13 models, 1½ to 40 lb. capacity, plus other lapidary equipment.
For Further Information: Send SASE for catalog.

M. NOWOTNY & CO.
8823 Callaghan Rd.
San Antonio, TX 78230
(512) 342-2512

Offers: Gemstone material—amethyst and quartz clusters, crystals, faceted smoky quartz, Brazilian agate slabs, mosaic opal cabs, blue topaz, freshwater pearls, others.
For Further Information: Catalog, $1 (refundable).
Accepts: MasterCard, Visa

MAXANT INDUSTRIES
P.O. Box 454
Ayer, MA 01432
(508) 772-0576

Offers: Lapidary equipment and supplies–saws (4 inch to 16 inch), grinders, sanders, polishers, automatic cabachon maker, others.
For Further Information: Catalog, $1.

METALLIFEROUS
34 W. 46th St.
New York, NY 10036
(212) 944-0909

Offers: Metals—brass, copper, nickel silver, sterling silver, mobium, pewter, aluminum—sheet, wire, circles, rod, tube, stampings, machined parts, hoops, findings, solders, casting alloys. Carries enameling shapes and supplies, plus tools.
For Further Information: Catalog, $5 (refundable).

MINNESOTA LAPIDARY SUPPLY CORP.
2825 Dupont Ave. S.
Minneapolis, MN 55411
(612) 872-7211

Offers: Lapidary equipment—rock cutting and polishing: Diamond saw blades, sanding belts and grinding wheels, diamond wheels and belts. Diamond products, tumbling grit.
For Further Information: Free catalog.
Discounts: Allows discounts to institutions; sells wholesale to legitimate businesses.

MOUNTAIN-MARK TRADING
268 SW 31st St.
Fort Lauderdale, FL 33315
(305) 525-6310, (800) 346-3691

Offers: Blue pectolite (Caribbean) rough, slabs, cabochons, carvings.
For Further Information: Free catalog, price list.

MT TURQUOISE
2530 S. Harrison Rd.
Tucson, AZ 85748
(800) 972-1140

Offers: Turquoise: Block, synthetic block.
For Further Information: Free catalog.
Discounts: Wholesale discounts.

NCE ENTERPRISES
107 W. Van Buren, Suite 207
Chicago, IL 60605
(312) 663-9738

Offers: Gemstone: Facet and cabbing rough from areas worldwide, by piece or kilo.
For Further Information: Send SASE for price list.
Accepts: MasterCard, Visa

NGRAVER CO.
879 Raymond Hill Rd.
Oakdale, CT 06370
(203) 848-8031

Offers: Hand-engraving, flexible shaft machines, gravers and liners, rotary handpieces, engravers blocks, chasing hammers, engravers pencils, electric etchers, graver sharpeners, sharpening stones, plus practice mediums, magnifiers, fixtures, punches, Florentine tools, others.
For Further Information: Catalog, $1 (refundable).

When using Nymo or any nylon thread for beading, be sure to bring it through a block of beeswax to prevent fraying.

— Craft Supplies 4 Less

OPITMAGEM
P.O. Box 4321
Thousand Oaks, CA 91359
(805) 492-8201

Offers: Gemstones: Ruby, sapphire (colors), garnet, amethyst, topaz, tanzanite, tsavorite, beryl (green, blue), peridot, opal, star sapphire. Rough stones.
For Further Information: Send for list.
Discounts: "May have closeouts."
Accepts: American Express, MasterCard, Visa

OPTIONAL EXTRAS
P.O. Box 1421
Burlington, VT 05402
(802) 658-0013

Offers: Jewelry supplies: Beads (glass, crystal, ceramic, metal, bugles, seed, others). Carries findings, cords, adhesives, starter kits and books.
For Further Information: Catalog, $2.

ORNAMENTAL RESOURCES, INC.
P.O. Box 3010
Idaho Springs, CO 80452
(303) 279-2102

Offers: Beads—full line of types, styles, sizes and shapes. Carries brass stampings, charms, plus jewelry findings, parts, tools and supplies, rhinestones and books.
For Further Information: Catalog, $25 (with year's supplements/"discount").

PARSER MINERALS CORP.
P.O. Box 1094
Danbury, CT 06813
(213) 744-6868

Offers: Rare and unusual gemstone cutting materials (rough): From Brazil—watermelon tourmaline, andalusite, jacobina amethyst, rutilated quartz, water clear topaz, rose quartz crystal, blue (indicolite) tourmaline. Others include rhodochosite (Argentina), wine red garnet (India), Labradorite moonstone and apatite (Madagascar), iolite (Tanzania). Diamonds.
For Further Information: Send SASE for list.

THE PERUVIAN BEAD CO.
1601 Callens Rd.
Ventura, CA 93003
(805) 642-0952

Offers: Pre-Colombian collection of beads—contemporary ethnic types in a variety of sizes/styles in sterling silver and brass, designed/manufactured in U.S.
For Further Information: Send for catalog.

PIONEER GEM CORP.
P.O. Box 1513
Auburn, WA 98071
(206) 833-2760

Offers: Cabachons: Opals, black opal, malachite, paua shell, jade, lapis, sapphires, others. Carries bulk bags mixed, plus faceted gemstones: Citrine, amethyst, emerald, lapis, opal, ruby, sapphires, blue topaz, others.
For Further Information: Catalog/price list, $5 (6 times yearly).
Discounts: Quantity discounts; allows discounts to teachers and institutions; sells wholesale to legitimate businesses; large order discounts.

PUEBLO TRADING
P.O. Box 1115
Zuni, NM 87327
(505) 782-5555

Offers: Tibetan turquoise cabochons (calibrated and free form), polished nuggets (drilled, undrilled, by pound), beads (rondels, rounds), lapidary supplies.
For Further Information: Send SASE for list.

REACTIVE METALS STUDIO, INC.
P.O. Box 890
Clarkdale, AZ 86324
(602) 634-3434

Offers: Titanium and niobium (shining wave) metal sheet and wire, plus jewelry findings, beads, miniature nuts and bolts.
For Further Information: Free catalog.
Discounts: Quantity discounts.

RIVER GEMS AND FINDINGS
6901 Washington St. NE
Albuquerque, NM 87109

Offers: Lines of over 2,500 beads, over 5,000 gemstones, over 7,500 jewelry findings and parts in a variety of sizes, styles and types for jewelry making, fashions, other.
For Further Information: Catalog, $10.

RK SERVICE CORP.
P.O. Box 1199
Haines City, FL 33844

Offers: Plans for build-your-own equipment, including tumblers, saws, grinders, lap machines.
For Further Information: Send SASE for information.

ROUSSELS
1225 Dow
Arlington, MA 02174

Offers: Jewelry supplies: Neckchains, variety of ear wires, others, plus polybags.
For Further Information: Wholesale catalog, 25¢.

ROYAL FINDINGS, INC.
301 W. Main St.
P.O. Box 92
Chartley, MA 02712
(617) 222-8173

Offers: Jewelry findings: Complete line of precious metal findings for Sparkle Midget Welder. Friction ear nuts, ball earrings, diamond settings, pendants, beads (rondels, corrugated), Karat Katch, lobster claws, bead clasps, Omega ear clips including Easy Loc and others.
For Further Information: Write or call for complete catalog.

RUNNING T TRADING CO.
1201 Iron Springs Rd., #6
Prescott, AZ 86301
(602) 778-2739

Offers: Jewelry mounts (pre-notched types, earring types, for emerald cut) in 14 kt, sterling, gold-filled, plus colored gemstones and diamonds. Carries jewelry findings in 14 kt, s/s and base metal.
For Further Information: Free catalog.
Store Location: Yes
Discounts: Quantity discounts; sells wholesale to legitimate businesses; large order discounts.
Accepts: MasterCard, Visa

SHIPWRECK BEADS
5021 Mud Bay Rd. W.
Olympia, WA 98512
(206) 866-4061

Offers: Beads: Czechoslovakian glass, gemstone, metallics, crystal, seed, wood, bone, buffalo horn, plastic, antique, trade and others, plus beading supplies and tools, jewelry findings and books.
For Further Information: Catalog, $3.
Store Location: Yes
Discounts: Quantity discounts; sells wholesale to legitimate businesses and professionals.
Accepts: MasterCard, Visa

SILVER ARMADILLO
40 Westgate Pkwy.
Asheville, NC 28806

Offers: Line of jewelry parts, beads, lapidary and rockhound equipment, minerals, others.

For Further Information: Catalog, $4 (refundable).
Store Location: Yes

SMITH EQUIPMENT
Watertown, SD 57201
(800) 48-TORCH

Offers: The Little Torch welding torch (works with any fuel gas), with temperatures to 6,300 degrees (solders, melts, welds, brazes), lightweight hand-held model, with flexible hose.
For Further Information: Call for free brochure.

SOUTHWEST AMERICA
1506 Wyoming Blvd. NE
Albuquerque, NM 87112
(505) 299-1856

Offers: Beads: Ornamental and ethnic (old, new) seed, bugles (including antique) in a variety of colors.
For Further Information: Brochure, $1.50.
Store Location: Yes

SPARKLING CITY GEMS
P.O. Box 905
Kingsville, TX 78364
(512) 296-3958

Offers: Gemstones: Ametrine, emerald, hessonite, garnet, pink sapphire, orthoclase, others.
For Further Information: Gem list, $3.
Accepts: MasterCard, Visa

STARR GEMS, INC.
220 West Drachman St.
Tuscon, AZ 85705
(602) 882-8750, (800) 882-8750

Offers: Jewelry findings and chains in silver and 14 kt gold, plus jewelery supplies, tools. Carries sterling concha stampings, E-Z Mount settings, beads and how-to books.
For Further Information: Catalog, $3.50 (refundable).

STONE AGE INDUSTRIES, INC.
P.O. Box 383
Powell, WY 82435
(307) 754-4681

Offers: Full line of Covington lapidary equipment, motors, commercial equipment, plus Eastwing tools, Foredom flexible shafts and brand tumblers. Carries gemstone rough and slaps from India, Brazil, Mexico, Africa, U.S. and petrified palmwood, picture rock and others.
For Further Information: Catalog, $1.50.
Discounts: Quantity discounts; sells wholesale to legitimate businesses.
Accepts: MasterCard, Visa

SWAYAMBHU

P.O. Box 4137
Berkeley, CA 94704
(510) 644-9449

Offers: Jewelry findings, chains, beads and Chinese coins. Gemstones: Turquoise, crystals, moonstone, tourmaline, others. Ear piercing supplies, displays and others.
For Further Information: Catalog, $2.
Discounts: Wholesale discounts call (510) 644-0110.

TRIPPS, INC.

407 California NW
Socorro, NM 87801

Offers: Jewelry-making supplies: Easy mounts in 14 kt gold and sterling including pendants, ladies' and men's rings in plain and fancy shapes, plus rings and other mountings. Line of chains: Gold filled, 14 kt, s/s and findings. Carries sterling castings, synthetic stones, natural faceted gemstones, including peridot, garnet, ruby, others.
For Further Information: Free catalog.
Discounts: Quantity discounts.
Accepts: American Express, MasterCard, Visa

TSI

101 Nickerson St.
P.O. Box 9266
Seattle, WA 98109
(206) 282-3040, (800) 426-9984

Offers: Full line of lapidary and jewelry-making tools, equipment, supplies, plus beads and beading supplies.
For Further Information: Free catalog.
Discounts: Quantity discounts; allows discounts to teachers, institutions and professionals; sells wholesale to businesses.

UNITED STATES PEARL CO., INC.

4805 Old Hickory Blvd.
Hermitage, TN 37076
(615) 391-0920, (800) 248-3064

Offers: Freshwater pearls: American, Chinese, Japanese, also Japanese cultured pearls, mother-of-pearl.
For Further Information: Send SASE for list.

To make a loop in eye pins, be sure to make the first bend very sharp, 90 degrees, ¼ inch down from tip, then roll it around round-nose pliers for an even-centered over-stem drop.

— Running T Trading

UNIVERSAL WIRECRAFT CO.

P.O. Box 20206
Bradenton, FL 34203
(813) 745-1219

Offers: Solderless wirecraft supplies: 18 kt gold and sterling silver wire, gold-filled wire (in square, round and half round; gauges 24 to 16 on some), by 1 oz. and 3 oz. coil. Carries gold plate and silver filled square and round wires, by 3 oz. coils and up. Wirecraft tools: Round, flat and chain nose pliers, side cutters, pin vise, iron ring mandrel. Carries a variety of cabochons, including onyx, goldstone, hematite, amethyst, agates, tigereye, others. Also carries gemstone beads, books.
For Further Information: Send business-size SASE for price list.
Discounts: Sells wholesale; quantity discounts.

WEIDINGER, INC.

19509 Kedzie Ave.
Flossmoor, IL 60422
(312) 798-6336

Offers: Full lines of lapidary machinery and equipment, tools, cutting materials, plus jewelry mountings/findings in gold filled, s/s. Display items include boxes, cards. Chains sold by yards, 14 kt, s/s, link, others. Desk sets, other accessories available.
For Further Information: 128-page Findings Catalog, $2; 180-page Machinery Catalog, $2 — both catalogs are refundable.
Accepts: MasterCard, Visa

WOOD-MET SERVICES

3314 Shoff Circle, Dept CSS
Peoria, IL 61604
Offers: Plans for the home workshop person to build his own machines, tools and attachments, including investment casting equipment, and items for welding, metalworking, hand tools, grinding wheels, drill presses, and a wide range of others.
For Further Information: Catalog, $1 (refundable).
Discounts: Quantity discounts.
See Also: Metalworking

Kite Making

Also see Fabrics and Trims, Outdoors and Outerwear and other related categories.

BFK
19306 E. Windrose Dr., #101
Rowland Heights, CA 91748
(818) 912-1272

Offers: Over 50 kite models (3 feet to 21 feet), including kits by Action, Flexifoil, Jordan Air, Skyward, Crystal, Highflyers, Rainbow, Advantage, AFC, Renegade, Gayla Wind, Peter Powell, Revolution, Wolfe, Force 10, Shanti, Moran Precision, others.
For Further Information: Free catalog.
Discounts: "Guaranteed lowest prices."

BOISE KITES
1122 E. Hays St.
Boise, ID 83712
(208) 344-2844

Offers: Variety of kite kits.
For Further Information: Call or write for information.

FLYING THINGS
130 SE Highway 101
Lincoln City, OR 97367
(503) 996-6313

Offers: Kite accessories and kits; major brands.
For Further Information: Write for catalog.
Discounts: "Factory direct prices."

GASWORKS PARK KITE SHOPPE
3333 Wallingford Ave. N.
Seattle, WA 98103
(206) 633-4780

Offers: Kite-making supplies—full range.
For Further Information: Write for catalog.
Discounts: "Dealer inquiries welcome."

GREAT WINDS KITE CO.
402 Occidental Ave. S.
Seattle, WA 98104
(206) 624-6886

Offers: Kite kits, including those for beginners and advanced flyers. Materials include Tyvek and others. Carries Frustra-

tionless Flyer to be colored, made of waterproof plastic paper, requires minimal assembly. Custom printing of kites.
For Further Information: Send SASE for details.

GRIZZLY PEAK KITEWORKS
1305 Alvarado Rd.
Berkeley, CA 94705
(510) 644-2981

Offers: Kite-making materials—full line including known brands; carries finished kites.
For Further Information: Free catalog.
Accepts: MasterCard, Visa

HANG-EM HIGH FABRICS
1420 Yale Ave.
Richmond, VA 23224
(804) 233-6155

Offers: Kite kits, fabrics/materials: Ripstop nylon, dacron. Carries adhesives, tubes, poles, webbing, dihedrals, line, fiberglass and aluminum couplings, caps, swivels, tapes, spools, eyelet tools and others.
For Further Information: Send SASE for details.
See Also: Outdoors and Outerwear

HIGH FLY KITE COMPANY
P.O. Box 2146
Haddonfield, NJ 08033
(609) 429-6260

Offers: Kites and kite kits—over 75 fabric styles, 26 stunt kites in a variety of sizes and color combinations. Supplies include over 10 types of reels and handles, 100 plus building items, and over 10 colors/types of ripstop material.
For Further Information: Free catalog.

INTO THE WIND
1408 Pearl St.
Boulder, CO 80302
(800) 541-0314

Offers: Kite kits: Over 56 sport, and other kites. Carries kite-making supplies and tools, packs, wind meters, lighting systems, plus a full range of line, accessories and spare parts for sport (and other) kites.
For Further Information: Free catalog.

JACKITE, INC.
2868 West Landing Rd.
Virginia Beach, VA 23456
(804) 426-5359

Offers: Jackite kite kits, which depict a bird (osprey or eagle) in flight; beating wings are made of Tyvek, poles are fiberglass or bamboo.
For Further Information: Write for details.

KITE STUDIO
5555 Hamilton Blvd.
Wescosville, PA 18106
(215) 395-3560

Offers: Kite parts: Fabrics (ripstop, others), spray paints, tools, spars, adaptors, caps, others.
For Further Information: Write for details.
Store Location: Yes
Discounts: "May run sales."

KITELINES
P.O. Box 466
Randallstown, MD 21133
(410) 922-1212

Offers: Reprints of articles important for kite crafting: (1) "Mastering Nylon," by G. William Tyrrell, Jr. (fabric types, tools, hot/cold cutting, seams, hems, edging, design transferring and coloring; source list, $1 ppd.); (2) "New American Tradition: Kite Festivals!" by Valerie Govig (guidance in festival organizing, beginning to end; includes "Figure Kiting," by Red Braswell, $3 ppd.).

For Further Information: Send SASE for book list.

KITEMANDU
P.O. Box 486
Neepawa, Manitoba R0J 1H0 Canada
(204) 476-3949

Offers: Stunt kite assembly kits, frames (Glasspar, Prospar), others.
For Further Information: Through dealer or write for catalog.
Discounts: "Dealer inquiries always invited."
Accepts: MasterCard

THE UNIQUE PLACE/WORLD OF KITES
525 S. Washington Ave.
Royal Oak, MI 48067
(313) 398-5900

Offers: Kite accessories (for Oriental, sport, custom, fine art, stunters, fighters), plus lines, reels. Over 250 kites.
For Further Information: Write for information.

WIND UNDER YOUR WINGS
P.O. Box 351
Butler, WI 53007
(414) 461-3444

Offers: Stunt kite kits and spare parts including those for Shadow and team kite models; include carbon graphite frames and ripstop.
For Further Information: Write for brochure.
Accepts: MasterCard, Visa
For Further Information: Send SASE for list.

Leather Crafts

Also see General Craft Supplies, Indian and Frontier Crafts, Fabrics and Trims and other related categories.

ATLAS COMPRESSION ENGINEERING
955 Massachusetts Ave., Suite 200
Cambridge, MA 02139

Offers: "Little Atlas" embossing press (steel unit), which embosses and patterns leather and metals (also plastic).
For Further Information: Free details.

BELVINS MANUFACTURING CO., INC.
Wheatland, WY 82201

Offers: Stirrup buckles in 3 widths, all stainless steel and heat-treated aluminum, sleeves leather covered, in improved, regular or four-post types. All metal buckles in 3 widths. Manufacturer.
For Further Information: Send SASE for full information.

BERMAN LEATHERCRAFT
25 Melcher St.
Boston, MA 02210
(671) 426-0870

Offers: Leathers: Pigskin, sheepskin, cowhide suede splits, deerskin, elk, antelope, rabbit, garment cowhide, bat leathers—by skins. Carries English line back, latigo, crepe, elk butt, English sip, wallet leathers, calfskin in assortments. Also carries belt blanks, a full line of buckles, leather kits and garment leathers in smooth, sueded, unusuals, including cowhide, calfskin, others. Tools: Knives, edgers, gauges and shears, cutters, anvils, strippers, plus stamping/sewing tools. Embossing machines, carver kits, finishes, hardware, accessories and books also available.
For Further Information: Catalog, $3 (refundable).
Discounts: Large order discounts.

C.S. OSBORNE & CO.
126 Jersey St.
Harrison, NJ 07029
(201) 483-3232

Offers: Leather crafting tools: Snap setters (snaps), edgers, pliers, hot glue guns, shoe and other hammers, punches, rawhide hammers, scratch compasses, nippers, creasers, gauges, gasket cutters, splitting machines, knives, shears, pincers, grommet dies (and grommets), hole cutters, awl hafts and awls, modeler tools, chisels, eyelet setters, space

markers, embossing wheel carriages, needles. Carries upholstery repair kits, sail and palm thimbles and others. Manufacturer.
For Further Information: Write for free catalog and name of dealer.

CAMPBELL BOSWORTH MACHINERY CO.
720 N. Flagler Dr.
Fort Lauderdale, FL 33304
(305) 463-7910

Offers: Leather machines and hand tools for splitting, plus airbrushes and compressors, overlocks, embossers, new/used and reconditioned machinery, heavy-duty sewing machines, hot stamping and cut-out units, hand/kick presses. Line of hand tools includes punches, shears, measurers, cutters, modeling and edging tools, awls, others, plus jewels, rivets and snap setters.
For Further Information: Free catalog.

AL CHANDRONNAIT
29 Winnhaven Dr.
Hudson, NH 03051

Offers: Ultra thin, soft leather for models, doll making, miniature work, jewelry, etc.; comes in 3-inch × 6-inch sheets, in offwhite (can be dyed), brown, blue.
For Further Information: Send SASE for full details.
Discounts: Quantity discounts.

FEIBING COMPANY, INC.
516 S. 2nd St.
Milwaukee, WI 53204
(414) 271-5011

Offers: Leather dyes: 27 colors (mixable/range of shades). Also carries paints and Rosolene finish. Manufacturer.
For Further Information: Send SASE for information.

FLANNAGAN
370 Mclean Ave.
Yonkers, NY 10705
(914) 968-9200

Offers: Leathers: Harness, bridle, skirting, others. Carries buckles, horse bits, stirrups, spurs, spots, snaps, rivets, chains, rings, others, plus Osborne tools, Fiebing dyes and finishes.
For Further Information: Write or call for catalog.

GOMPH-HACKBARTH TOOLS
Rt. 1, P.O. Box 7
Elfrida, AZ 85610

Offers: Leather crafting tools: Swivel knives (½-inch and ⅝-inch barrels with ball bearing curved finger yoke), letter beveler sets, edgers (for strap leather, with concave-convex cutting edge) and others in a variety of sizes and types.
For Further Information: Send SASE for information.

HORWEEN LEATHER CO.
2015 N. Elston Ave.
Chicago, IL 60614
(312) 772-2026

Offers: Leathers: Latigo, Chromexcel, waxed flesh, horse fronts, side leathers and shell cordovan.
For Further Information: Write for catalog/swatches.

THE LEATHER FACTORY, INC.
P.O. Box 50429
Fort Worth, TX 76105
(817) 496-4874

Offers: Full line of leathers for seating, harness, tooling and lining, plus garment leathers. Specialty leathers include remnant packs, exotics, upholstery, sole and moccasin chap sides and others. Carries belt/strap embossing machines/design rolls, hand-sewing supplies and tools including full line of punches, hammers, stampers and strippers, cutters (also sold in sets). Dyes, stains, finishes, adhesives, buckles, accessories and kits, starter sets, learning moccasins and books are also available.
For Further Information: Catalog, $3.
Discounts: Allows discounts to teachers and institutions; sells wholesale to businesses.

LEATHER UNLIMITED
7155 Highway B.
Belgium, WI 53004
(414) 994-9464

Offers: Leather kits: Bags, accessories, moccasins, others. Leathers include garment/bag sides, splits, oak cowhide, deerskin, sheepskin, cowhide splits, chamois, elk, exotics, pieces (variety) and laces. Causes a line of buckles and conchos, plus hardware, dyes, finishes, Missouri River Frontier clothes patterns, hand tools, stamp units, punches, rivets, snaps and others. Custom fabrication of cutting dies.
For Further Information: 64-page catalog, $2 (refundable).
Discounts: Quantity discounts; sells wholesale to businesses.
Accepts: MasterCard, Visa

M. SIEGEL CO., INC.
120 Pond St.
Ashland, MA 01721
(508) 881-5200

Offers: Leathers: Cowhide vesting, garment, luxury garment (deer, chamois, elk, horse, suedes, antelope, lambskin, others), plus bag, belt, wallet, tooling, sandal (buffalo, calf, kip, pig, sheepskin skiver). Specialty leathers: Chrome moccasin sides, lizard, shearling, plus saddlery and briefcase leathers. Carries close-out lots (inquire), full line of buckles in brass, copper/brass and other metals, plus bag closures/fasteners, and a full line of tools and supplies.
For Further Information: Catalog, $3.
Store Location: Yes
Discounts: Quantity discounts.

MID-CONTINENT LEATHER SALES CO.
1539 S. Yale Place
Tulsa, OK 74136
(918) 747-2061

Offers: Leathers: Saddle (skirting, latigo, others), rawhide, tooling (sides, English sides, strap sides, shoulders, others), plus chap and garment leathers (sides, splits, deerskin), lacing and stirrup leather. Carries conchos, snaps, grommets, inserting dies, buckles, rings, rigging plates, fasteners and zippers. Threads available include nylon, waxed linen, Nytex. Tools include hammers, knives, blades, chisels, anvils, rivet and spike setters, bevelers, groovers, skivers, plus Osborne tools such as glue guns, canvas pliers, hammers, nippers, rivets and others. Conditioners and finishes also available.
For Further Information: Free catalog.
Discounts: Quantity discounts; allows discounts to teachers and institutions; sells wholesale to legitimate businesses.

W. PEARCE & BROTHERS, INC.
38 W. 32nd St.
New York, NY 10001
(212) 244-4595

Offers: Leathers: Tooling kits, variety of garment leathers, and belt and wallet leathers. Carries exotics: Snake, elephant, lizard, python, alligator and ostrich leathers. Stencil springbooks in 15 patterns.
For Further Information: Send SASE for price list and description.
Accepts: MasterCard, Visa

PILGRIM SHOE & SEWING MACHINE CO.
21 Nightingale Ave.
Quincy, MA 02169
(617) 786-8940

Offers: New, used and rebuilt shoe and leather machines, sewing machines, eyelet setters, patchers, clickers, skivers, splitters, cementers, trimmers, 5-in-1 bench cutters, others, plus needles and awls for all machines. Machine parts: Singer, U.S.M., Landis, American, Fortuna, Puritan, Consew, Union Special, Adler, Pfaff, Juki and others, plus obsolete and hard-to-find parts.

For Further Information: Free parts catalog or send SASE with inquiry.

POCAHONTAS LEATHER
P.O. Box 253
Garrettsville, OH 44231
(216) 527-5277

Offers: Deer and elk skins (lots by the foot and up), tannery deep-Scotchgarded for water and soil resistance and pre-stretched "for honest, useable footage."
For Further Information: Send SASE for price list.

S-T LEATHER CO.
P.O. Box 78188
St. Louis, MO 63178
(314) 241-6009

Offers: Leathers: Specialty types, including calf, upholstery and suede. Carries a line of garment leathers and furs, suede and scraps. Kits/patterns include moccasins, accessories, bags. Carries snaps, grommets, rivets, laces, dyes, acrylics, finishes, and a line of hand tools including a variety of punches and chisels: Midas tools, modelers and sets. Buckles and books also available.
For Further Information: Write or call for catalog.
Discounts: Quantity discounts.

SAV-MOR LEATHER & SUPPLY
1626 S. Wall St.
Los Angeles, CA 90015
(213) 749-3468

Offers: Leathers: Sandal, saddlery, scrap, garment types, belt blanks (odd lots), leathers. Also carries buckles, wallet and bag kits, tools and Fiebing dyes.
For Further Information: Catalog, $2.
Discounts: Sells wholesale.

SOLMON BROTHERS
12331 Kelly Rd.
Detroit, MI 48224
(313) 571-9466

Offers: Industrial sewing machines (for leather, other); buys, sells, trades, repairs. Carries machine parts. Attachments made.
For Further Information: Send SASE.

TANDY LEATHER CO.
P.O. Box 2934
Fort Worth, TX 76113

Offers: Leathers: Full line, including pigskin, deerskin, cowhides (smooth, suede), sheepskin, grain leathers, saddle skirting and others for garments, upholstery and utility use. Carries exotic leathers, leather crafting kits for accessories (belts, billfolds, purses, moccasins, credit card wallets, others) and suede items. Also carries leather crafting tools (full line including dyes, laces, patterns), Kodel lining (like sheepskin), saddle trees, stirrups, hardware, patterns, instructional videos and books.
For Further Information: Catalog, $2.50.
Discounts: Quantity discounts.

VETERAN LEATHER CO.
204 25th St.
Brooklyn, NY 11232
(718) 768-0300

Offers: Leathers: Grained cowhide, splits, skivers, chrome and kip sides, English morocco, sueded cowhide splits, others; sells remnants by the pound. Sells belt blanks. Tools available include stamps, rivets, punches, cutters, fasteners, lacing and stitching types, eyelet setters, others. Buckles, leather kits for handbags, dyes, laces and sewing items also available.
For Further Information: Write for catalog.
Discounts: Quantity discounts.

WEAVER LEATHER
P.O. Box 68
Mt. Hope, OH 44660
(216) 674-1782, (800) WEAVER-1

Offers: Leather hides: Chap, suede, strap, skirting, harness, bridle, latigo, others. Hardware includes snaps, loops, rings, dees, buckles, others. Also carries leather crafting tools, thread, nylon webbing, poly rope, oils and dyes.
For Further Information: Free catalog.
Discounts: "Savings."

WORLD TRADING, INC.
121 Spencer Plain Rd.
Old Saybrook, CT 06475
(203) 399-5982

Offers: Imported leathers: Kangaroo, buffalo, calfskins and exotics (ostrich, elephant, shark). Also carries lizardskins and snake skins (rattlers, pythons, others).
For Further Information: Send SASE for list.

Metalworking

Also see Jewelry Making and Lapidary, Miniature Making, Model Making and Sculpture and Modeling.

AMERICAN ART CLAY CO., INC.
4717 W. 16th St.
Indianapolis, IN 46222
(317) 244-6871

Offers: Metal enameling—carries a full line of enamels, kilns (3) and kits, plus glass/metal enameling colors, overglaze colors, liquid metals, lusters. Copper shapes: Circles, squares, bowls, drops, pendants, findings, others. Also carries accessories, cleaners, flux, tools (scrolling, punch, others) and kiln accessories.
For Further Information: Free information packet.
Discounts: Sells wholesale.
See Also: Ceramics and Mold Crafts

ATLAS METAL SALES
1401 Umatilla St.
Denver, CO 80204
(303) 623-0143

Offers: Silicone bronze: Sheets and plate (1/16-inch to 3/8-inch thicknesses), rods, rectangles, circles, plus thin-gauge strips, ingots (1/2 pound to 20 pounds).
For Further Information: Send SASE or call for quotations.

CEI
Rt. 1, P.O. Box 163
Cameron, IL 61423

Offers: Line of metals (sheet, bar): Brass, aluminum. Also carries supplies and plans.
For Further Information: Send SASE for list.

EAST WEST DYE CO.
5238 Peters Creek Rd. NW
Roanoke, VA 24019
(703) 362-1489

Offers: Anodized aluminum as wire, sheets, tubing, beads and other components. Carries aluminum dye starter kits, dyes and sealers, gloves and books. Offers a dyeing and sealing service.
For Further Information: Catalog, $5 (refundable).
Discounts: Quantity discounts; sells wholesale to legitimate businesses.

EDMUND SCIENTIFIC
101 E. Gloucester Pike
Barrington, NJ 08007
(609) 573-6260

Offers: Technical and scientific products, including some for metal crafting or useful aids: Electroplating kits, 6 submersible pumps, compressors and over 20 small motors. Carries a wide array of miniature tools: Dremel Moto Tools, pin vises, drills, hammers, jeweler's drill presses, mini-torches and table saws. Engraver's tools, wire benders. 30 plus magnifiers and loupes, diffraction grating and others also available.
For Further Information: Write for catalog.

Do your forge welding without flux and you'll learn to weld.
—Kayne & Son Custom Hardware

EXTRA SPECIAL PRODUCTS CORP.
P.O. Box 777
Greenville, OH 45331
(513) 548-3793, (800) 648-5945

Offers: House of Copper line of die-cut copper shapes (to punch, bend, burnish, antique, paint, use as trims, window decorations, tree ornaments, candle trims, quilt templates, applique templates, wreath decorations, others), and over 24 project booklets.
For Further Information: Contact your dealer, or write for catalog.
See Also: Fabric Decorating

PYRAMID PRODUCTS
85357 American Canal Rd.
Niland, CA 92257
(619) 354-4265

Offers: Small foundry furnaces for home craftspeople—chamber, lid, motor, components and accessories (in complete, short sets or commercial units) for casting gold, silver, aluminum, brass, bronze, gray iron. Also good for lost wax casting and glass blowing. Carries ingots: Fluxing aluminum and alloy, and brass.
For Further Information: Catalog, $1.
Store Location: Yes
Discounts: Allows discounts to teachers and institutions.

DAVID SHELTON

4207 Lead Ave. SE

Albuquerque, NM 87108

(505) 256-7073

Offers: Custom RT Stamping dies for cutting parts from sheet metal (heat-treated tool steel). Blanking service with dies.

For Further Information: Send SASE for information.

WOOD-MET SERVICES

3314 Shoff, Circle, Dept. CSS

Peoria, IL 61604

(306) 637-9667

Offers: Over 250 plans to build home workshop machines/equipment for wood and metal work: Universal clamping system, metal spinning, metal lathe, 9 wood turning chisels, miter arm for bandsaw and router, electric band sander, photographic equipment, air compressor, drill press items, router and bandsaw items, shop metal benders, welding and hand tools, fixtures, wood lathe items, sander with power feed, circular saw items, power rasps, 6 tools for grinding wheels, milling machine and metal shaper items. Investing cast equipment. Also offers circular saws, wood jointer, belt sander items and woodworker's kits and sets.

For Further Information: Catalog, $1.

Discounts: Quantity discounts; sells wholesale to legitimate businesses.

Save shop space by using your Black & Decker WorkMate to hold your bench-type power tools.

—Wood-Met Services, Inc.

Miniature Making, Miniatures & Dollhouses

Also see Model Making, Paints, Finishes and Adhesives, Tools and Equipment and specific categories of interest.

JOAN ADAMS
2706 Sheridan Dr.
Sarasota, FL 34239

Offers: Miniature needlepunch rug sets of 22 mesh canvas in a variety of designs.
For Further Information: Send SASE for new designs; catalog, $2.75.

AMERICAN VICTORIANS
P.O. Box 65126
Vancouver, WA 98665
(206) 573-2488

Offers: Half-inch scale dollhouses—Victorian, components, interior and exterior trims, shingles, chimneys, brick work, others.
For Further Information: Brochure, $2.

APPLIED DESIGN CORP.
P.O. Box 3384
Torrance, CA 90510

Offers: Tools for miniatures/models crafting: Mini sander, 6-inch blade mini-hacksaw (for plastic, metal, wood), plus papers, T-bar sanding block and others.
For Further Information: Catalog, 50¢.

B.J.'S MAILBOX
4401 Westward Circle
Forest Grove, OR 97116

Offers: Small-scale knitting needles and kits, including ladies' sweaters, infant christening gown, cap and others.
For Further Information: Write for information.
Discounts: "Dealer inquiries welcome."

BEAUVAIS CASTLE
P.O. Box 4060
Manchester, NH 03108
(603) 625-8944

Offers: Over 6,000 miniatures and accessories of known brands—furniture, figures, components, others.
For Further Information: 300-page catalog, $5.

BODKIN CRAFT
P.O. Box 202
Clintonville, PA 16372

Offers: Miniature lazy Susan plans, instructions.
For Further Information: Write for information.

BRAMSCH VIDEO GROUP
P.O. Box 515165
St. Louis, MO 63151
(314) 638-3161

Offers: How-to video on miniature landscaping, with Vicki Metzger.
For Further Information: Call or write for information.
Accepts: MasterCard, Visa

BRODNAX PRINTS
2338 Reagan St.
Dallas, TX 75219
(214) 528-7773

Offers: Quarter-inch scale wallpapers in over 70 patterns, plus matching tile designs and borders (country colors and jewel tones).
For Further Information: Send $1 for color catalog sheets.
Discounts: "Dealer inquiries welcome."

BUILDERS CHOICE
71 Hilliard St.
Manchester, CT 06040

Offers: Miniature landscaping systems including a line of scenic pre-made timbered flower-shrub beds, pre-made bricked flower-shrub beds, and a variety of shrubs and vines, earth and cedar chips, plus paths, sidewalks and accessories.
For Further Information: Send SASE for full information.

AL CHANDRONNAIT
19 Winnhaven Dr.
Hudson, NH 03051

Offers: Leather for miniature work, thin and pliable for scale upholstery, purses, shoes, gloves, trunks, luggage, others; in off-white (can be dyed).
For Further Information: Send SASE for details.
Discounts: Quantity discounts.

CIR-KIT CONCEPTS, INC.
407 14th St. NW
Rochester, MN 55901
(507) 288-0860

Offers: Complete line of wiring kits and lamps including the deluxe wiring kit (for 10 to 12 room dollhouses) and others.
For Further Information: See your dealer, or send $3 for catalog.

CJ ORIGINALS
P.O. Box 538
Bridgeville, PA 15017

Offers: Over 100 scale miniatures kits (40 silk gauze, DMC floss, needle, chart, instructions) for Rose Trellis chair seats and Cluny pillows in a variety of designs.
For Further Information: Catalog, $3.

CONCORD MINIATURES
400 Markley St.
P.O. Box 99
Port Reading, NJ 07064

Offers: Over 200 pieces of Concord miniature furniture and accessories—mahogany furniture, some ½-inch scale items, plus baby's, children's and teen's bedroom pieces and others. Manufacturer.
For Further Information: Contact your miniatures or hobby dealer.

CRISS-CROSS
P.O. Box 324
Wayne, NJ 07474
(201) 835-9339

Offers: Plans (in 1-inch to 1-foot scale, with full-size cutting details, hints, assembly views and photos) for replicas of Peddlers wagons (of late 1800s), like the one at Longstreet Farm Museum, Homdel, NJ, plus plans for the Concord stage coach and Conestoga covered wagon. Miniature wheel-making plans also available.
For Further Information: Catalog, $1.
Accepts: MasterCard, Visa

DEE'S DELIGHTS, INC.
3150 State Line Rd.
North Bend, OH 45052
(513) 353-3390

Offers: Fimo modeling compound in a variety of colors (oven-bakes). Also offers scale miniatures, including hillbilly figures, cowboys, animals, a log cabin (unfinished or stained) and others.
For Further Information: Contact dealer, or send SASE for information.
Discounts: Sells wholesale to legitimate businesses.

THE DEPOT DOLLHOUSE SHOP
215 Worchester Rd., Rt. 9
Framingham, MA 01701
(617) 431-1234

Offers: Full line of scale miniatures, including ⅜-inch cabinet grade dollhouses from known manufacturers, also offers a children's line of dollhouses and furniture, plus handcrafted accessories for all rooms, by established artisans.
For Further Information: Send $3 for periodic newsletter.

DESIGNS BY JUDI
Rt. 2, P.O. Box 204
Scotland Neck, NC 27874

Offers: Miniature scale buttons in a variety of styles.
For Further Information: Send 29¢ stamp/SASE for samples.

DIAMOND "M" BRAND MOLD CO.
15081 91st St.
Hinsdale, IL 60521
(312) 323-5691

Offers: 1-inch scale miniature molds (poured in ceramic) including 3-mold Victorian bath set (claw tub, pedestal sink, water-close toilet). Other molds, for tea sets, variety of pots, vases, and country accessories, plus dolls and various items of furniture and fireplaces and others are available.
For Further Information: Catalog, $2 ($3 foreign).

DIMINUTIVE SPECIALTIES
10337 Ellsworth Dr.
Roscoe, IL 61073
(815) 623-2011

Offers: Nite-Lite Boxes (holds miniatures) for any occasion; miniature photos.
For Further Information: Send business-size SASE for information.
Accepts: MasterCard, Visa

THE DOLLHOUSE FACTORY
157 Main St.
P.O. Box 456
Lebanon, NJ 08833
(908) 236-6404, (800) DOLL-HOUSE

Offers: Over 8,000 miniatures products: 50 plus 1-inch scale dollhouse kits/plans, stores/buildings kits, ½-inch scale dollhouse kits and furniture. Also offers display items and scale furniture kits by X-acto, Realife, Shendoah, Chnrysnbon, others. Carries needlework Shadowits, a full line of building hardware, plus windows and other components, Fimo, stencils, decals, wallpapers, carpet, cords, finishing materials, electric lighting items, hand/power tools, magnifiers, landscape supplies.

For Further Information: Catalog, $5.50.
Store Location: Yes
Discounts: Sells wholesale to legitimate businesses.
Accepts: MasterCard, Visa

DOLLHOUSES BY DAD
1020 E. 146 St., #110
Burnsville, MN 55337
(612) 432-8200

Offers: Service: Custom miniature dollhouse construction from your blueprints or photographs.
For Further Information: Send SASE for details.

THE DOLL'S COBBLER
P.O. Box 906
Berlin, MD 21811

Offers: Full line of miniature doll shoes in leather and other materials, in a variety of styles including boots, slippers, high-button shoes, flats, sandals, heels, shoe ice skates and others.
For Further Information: Catalog, $3.75.

LIGIA DURSTENFELD
2315 Caracas St.
La Crescenta, CA 91214
(818) 248-8058

Offers: Scale enameled miniatures, including Fabrege flower arrangements, other flowers, Oriental screens (enamel on copper) and others. Will custom enamel miniatures to specification.
For Further Information: Catalog, $2 and SASE (refundable).

DWYER'S DOLL HOUSE
1944 Warwick Ave.
Warwick, RI 02889
(401) 738-3248

Offers: Over 4,000 miniatures and dollhouses, including miniatures kits and accessories, others.
For Further Information: Catalog, $2.
Accepts: MasterCard, Visa

ELECT-A-LITE, INC.
P.O. Box 388
Honeoye Falls, NY 14472
(800) EAL-KITS

Offers: Scale dollhouse lighting system kits and accessories (copper tape wiring system, fabricated for shadow boxes, for from 3- to 5-room dollhouses to the largest 9- to 12-room models); complete with patented connectors, parts and instructions.

For Further Information: Contact dealer, or send SASE for information.

Fimo bakes well in a toaster oven set to "defrost." A ceramic tile is an excellent baking sheet for it.

–Pike Creek Miniatures

THE ENCHANTED DOLL HOUSE
Manchester Center, VT 05255
(802) 362-3030

Offers: 6,000 miniatures, dollhouses, miniatures kits and room settings workshop materials, plus kits and books. Many handmade or exclusive by reknowned artisans. Has a collectors club.
For Further Information: Catalog, $3.

FANTASY CRAFT
933 E. Carson Lane
Pomona, CA 91766
(909) 591-8252

Offers: Limited edition miniature room box and house kits — unassembled or assembled, plus finishing kits.
For Further Information: Catalog, $5 (refundable with first $50 order).

FERNWOOD MINIATURES
12730 Finlay NE
Silverton, OR 97381
(503) 873-2397

Offers: Scale miniature furniture kits (basswood): Victorian, Empire and other period pieces (dressers, stands, tables, desks, chairs, cabinets, washstands, cradles, canopy beds and other beds, dry sinks, benches, wardrobes, others).
For Further Information: Send business-size SASE for information.

THE FIELDWOOD CO., INC.
P.O. Box 6
Chester, VT 05143
(802) 875-4127

Offers: "Precious Little Things" scale miniature accessories, including food (artichokes in a pewter bowl, apples in a wicker basket, vegetables in wicker basket, wire egg basket with eggs, banana stalk and others). Also offers other miniature furnishings and accessories in 1-inch and ½-inch scales.
For Further Information: 34-page illustrated catalog, $3.

FRED'S CARPENTER SHOP
Rt. 7
Pittsford, VT 05763
(802) 483-6362

Offers: Complete line of building materials, dollhouse kits, furniture and accessories. Also offers custom service, including replicas of homes, remodeling, wiring and wallpapering of dollhouses.
For Further Information: 136-page catalog, $4.

MARCIA GAIL MINIATURES
P.O. Box 880
Langley AFB, VA 23665

Offers: Kits in cross-stitch (40-count gauze, supplies), in a variety of designs.
For Further Information: Brochure, $2 (refundable).

GINGERBREAD HOUSE OF MINIATURES
2170 Lawndale Dr.
Greensboro, NC 27408
(919) 273-2831

Offers: Marklin miniatures, plus a custom finishing service—inside and outside of dollhouses.
For Further Information: Call or write for information.
Store Location: Yes
Accepts: MasterCard, Visa

GREENBERG DOLLHOUSE PUBLICATIONS
7566 Main St.
Sykesville, MD 21784
(301) 795-7447

Offers: Book: *Finishing Touches*, by Jack Robinson (techniques for creating realistic miniature bricks, actual wood floors, foundations, trims and others, with detailed diagrams).
For Further Information: Send SASE for full information.

J. HERMES
P.O. Box 4023
El Monte, CA 91734

Offers: Miniatures—½-inch scale wallpapers and floor papers in 100 designs and color combinations, plus smaller ¼-inch scale wallpapers and projects (breakaway box kit and others).
For Further Information: Catalog, $3; smaller-scale swatch book, $2.

HIS & HER HOBBYS
15 W. Busse Ave.
Mt. Prospect, IL 60056

Offers: Miniature dollhouse kits (and built), furniture kits, lighting, mouldings, siding, staircases, roofing, landscaping, hard and soft wood selections and hardware. Miniatures include furniture, figures, others. Services: Custom modeling and wiring of dollhouses.
For Further Information: Send SASE for list.

THE HOBBY SUITE
P.O. Box 613
McComb, MS 39648

Offers: Over 16,000 brand-name miniatures including furniture kits (and finished), dollhouses and components, wallpapers, rugs, accessories, electrical systems and other items, plus tools.
For Further Information: Mail-order catalog, $8.50.

HOMESTEAD HOMES
5769 Cottonwood Rd.
Bozeman, MT 59715

Offers: Corrugated aluminum roofing/siding; can cut, bend, age.
For Further Information: Write for product information.

HOUSE OF CARON
10111 Larryln Dr.
Whittier, CA 90603
(310) 947-6753

Offers: Miniature doll molds by Parker-Levi, Keni, Paulette Stinson, Mystic, Theresa Glisson, Ayanna, Little Old Dollmaker. Carries doll clothes patterns, books, doll-making supplies, tools, doll props and accessories.
For Further Information: Illustrated price lists, $2.50.
Discounts: Quantity discounts.

THE HOUSE OF MINIATURES
147 Lake St.
Delaware, OH 43015

Offers: Members of this society receive miniature furniture kits monthly with no obligation to buy. Furniture kits include classic Chippendale styles, Queen Anne and other traditional styles, scaled 1/12 of full-size originals; with hardwoods and solid brass fittings.
For Further Information: Send SASE for full information.

INNOVATIVE PHOTOGRAPHY
1724 NW 36th
Lincoln City, OR 97367
(503) 994-9421

Offers: Framed miniature photos of old masters, impressionist and modern paintings by Da Vinci, Rembrandt, Boticelli, Van Gogh, Degas, Gainsborough, Picasso, Marin, Pollack and others, plus Gutmann babies, Eisley, C.B. Barber, J.W. Carries Victorian photos—framed or in folders, stereoview cards, diplomas, certificates, postcards, color maps (U.S., world, states, antique), postcard and hanging display racks and others. Will do custom reduction of any photos.
For Further Information: Catalog, $2.

IT'S A SMALL WORLD
560 Green Bay Rd.
Winnetka, IL 60093
(312) 446-8399

Offers: Miniatures including flowers by Bagot, Robin's Roose, M. Meyer, fruit by Kim's, dolls by Hantel, Nix, Innes. Picnic baskets by Maryn Johnson, Mirrors by Leeds, silver and gilt items by Fisher, Kupjack, Acquisto and finished miniatures.
For Further Information: Catalog, $6 ($9 outside the U.S.).

JACQUELINE'S
1155 5th St., #405
Oakland, CA 94607

Offers: Dollhouse-making catalog: Plans, building supplies, accessories, dolls, others.
For Further Information: Catalog and newsletter, $3 (refundable).
Discounts: "Bonuses, freebies, discounts."

JANNA JOSEPH
P.O. Box 1026
Tarpon Springs, FL 34688
(813) 934-6977

Offers: Line of scale miniature doll molds.
For Further Information: Brochure, $3.

KARIN'S MINI GARDEN
6128 McLeod Rd. NE, Apt. 15
Albuquerque, NM 87109
(505) 883-4561

Offers: Miniature garden items: Variety of indoor and outdoor plants (in containers), cacti, succulents and arrangements, plus other realistic items.
For Further Information: Catalog, $1.50 (refundable).

KILKENNY MINIATURES
10685 Johansen Dr.
Cupertino, CA 95014

Offers: Ultra-fine glitter kits, including 1-inch Romantic glitter masks and others.
For Further Information: Send SASE for list.

LH STUDIO
1280 Orchard Lane
Elm Grove, WI 53122

Offers: Costuming kits in 1:12 scale including bridal fashions, bridal fabrics and laces.
For Further Information: Bridal brochure, business-size SASE; catalog, $3

LADY LOCKS
4147 Laverock
Spring, TX 77388

Offers: Styled miniature wigs in a variety of styles and colors.
For Further Information: Send SASE for information.

BETTY LAMPEN
2930 Jackson St.
San Francisco, CA 94115

Offers: Miniature knitting pattern books—sweaters for Teddies, people.
For Further Information: Send SASE for list.

LITTLE GOODIES
P.O. Box 1004
Lewisville, TX 75067
(214) 625-9303

Offers: Over 95 precut paper flower kits (1-inch to 1-foot scale): Marigolds, hollyhocks, lilies of the valley, violets, lilies, carnations, irises, tulips, poppies, dandelions, rose bushes, ivy and others.
For Further Information: Catalog, $2 (refundable).
Discounts: Sells wholesale to legitimate businesses.

LITTLE HOUSE OF MINIATURES ON CHELSEA LANE
621½ Sycamore St.
Waterloo, IA 50703
(319) 233-6585

Offers: Over 20,000 miniature items, including dollhouse and furniture kits, dolls, wallpapers and other decorator components, electric wiring and building supplies and others.
For Further Information: Catalog, $15 (refundable).
Store Location: Yes

To make tiny curls, wrap mohair around a metal knitting needle and bake at 250 degrees for 10 minutes, slide off the needle, cut and glue the hair on the head.

—House of Caron

A LITTLE SOMETHING FOR EVERYONE
6203 S. Dover
Littleton, CO 80123

Offers: Southwestern kits: Pottery and other items to scale.
For Further Information: Catalog, $2.

MASTERPIECE MUSEUM MINIATURES
16007 Scenic Oaks Trail
Buda, TX 78610

Offers: Miniature human figures, a line of realistic stock figures with custom detailing to specifications.

For Further Information: Business-size SASE with 65¢ postage and $3 for list.

MASTERPIECES IN MINIATURE

13083 Drummer Way
Grass Valley, CA 95949
(916) 268-1429

Offers: "Instant Age" weathering liquid wood, painted or unpainted—ages shingles, others. Carries PeteCo electric picture lights and scale model artist's items: Blank stretched canvas, palette, brush/paints, sketch pad/pencil, table with palette setting, others.

For Further Information: Send business-size SASE for full details.

Discounts: Sells wholesale to legitimate businesses.

MICROSCALE INDUSTRIES, INC.

P.O. Box 11950
Costa Mesa, CA 92627

Offers: Line of miniature model decals for 1-inch scale, traditional and other periods.

For Further Information: See your dealer, or catalog, $2.

MINI GRAPHICS

2975 Exon Ave.
Cincinnati, OH 45241

Offers: Lines of miniature wallpapers, variety of fabrics, carpeting, others. Miniature needlecraft book (needlepoint, cross stitch for rugs, bedspreads, others).

For Further Information: Catalog, $3.50.

MINI STITCHES

Rt. 3, P.O. Box 143
Clinton, TN 37716

Offers: Miniature needlepoint sampler kits on #40 or #48 silk gauze.

For Further Information: Color photo/price list, $1 and business-size SASE.

MINIATURE ACCESSORIES OF THE MONTH

P.O. Box 90686
Henderson, NV 89009

Offers: Members of this club receive a 1-inch scale miniature accessory designed and created for the club (not found elsewhere).

For Further Information: Send $1 and SASE for introductory offer.

Discounts: "One low price per month."

THE MINIATURE CORNER

12782 Veterans Memorial Dr.
Houston, TX 77014

Offers: Dreamland Babies human figures (1-inch and ½-inch scales) kits, wigs and dresses.

For Further Information: Brochure, SASE and $4 (refundable).

MINIATURE IMAGE

P.O. Box 465
Lawrenceburg, IN 47025

Offers: Scale dollhouses, dollhouse kits and basic building supplies, scale miniatures including furniture kits and finished, accessories including hard-to-find items. Carries reference and how-to books, others.

For Further Information: Full catalog, $12 (refundable).

Accepts: MasterCard, Visa

MINIATURE LUMBER SHOPPE

812 Main St.
Grandview, MO 64030

Offers: ¼-inch scale miniature 1920s style appliances/fixtures: Kitchen stoves, sinks, refrigerators, bathroom tubs, toilets. All have cast-metal components, with instructions and picture. Others.

For Further Information: Catalog, $2.

MINIATURE MAKER'S WORKSHOP

4515 N. Woodward Ave.
Royal Oak, MI 48073
(313) 549-0633

Offers: Magic Mitre miniature mitering kit (for door, window and picture frames, other uses).

For Further Information: Send SASE for details.

THE MINIATURE MERCHANT

10321 Allendale Dr.
Arvada, CO 80004

Offers: Miniature supplies—all major miniature lines are represented with this supplier, with building supplies, finishing material, furniture and accessories; offers kits and components.

For Further Information: 467-page catalog, $12.50 (part refundable).

MINIATURE SAW WORKS

12740 Corydon Ramsey Rd. SW
Palmyra, IN 47164

Offers: Miniature metal items to paint: Saws (hand, crosscut, round types), flat irons, skillets and others.

For Further Information: Send business-size SASE for details and prices.

MINIATURES AND MORE, LTD.
39 Hibert Pkwy.
Eatontown, NJ 07724

Offers: Custom miniature landscaping—portable landscaping system on wood bases, adaptable to any environment; includes landscape components, parts, accessories.
For Further Information: Catalog, $2.

PAUL C. MOORE
6127 Boughton Hill Rd.
Farmington, NY 14425

Offers: Scale miniatures (including traditional styles)—handcrafted furniture, dollhouses, room boxes and cabinet houses.
For Further Information: Catalog, $2.

MOREY'S MINIATURES
RD 2
Unadilla, NY 13849
(607) 369-9578

Offers: Full line of miniature "pedigree inches dogs in 1-inch, ½-inch and ¼-inch scales.
For Further Information: Send $1 and SASE for list.

THE MOUNTAIN VALLEY MINIATURE SHOP
199 Union St.
P.O. Box 94
Occoquan, VA 22125

Offers: Miniature dollhouse kits, finishing and decorating supplies, plus furniture kits and books.
For Further Information: Send SASE for list.
Store Location: Yes
Accepts: MasterCard, Visa

MY SISTER'S SHOPPE, INC.
1671 Penfield Rd.
Rochester, NY 14625

Offers: Collection of scale dollhouses and miniatures (authentic detailed reproductions, and/or whimsical in style) including Laura's Linens English coordinated bedding ensembles in florals and stripes, plus English country gifts (soaps, fragrances, geraniums in pitcher/bowl, lace pillows, luggage, potpourri jar) and others.
For Further Information: Catalog, $2.

NATIVE AMERICAN MINIATURES
13415 Lamel St.
North Edwards, CA 93523
(619) 769-4144

Offers: Scale miniature pottery (each painted and signed by a Navajo Indian), horsehair baskets (woven by Papagos).
For Further Information: Send SASE for information.
Discounts: Quantity discounts.
Accepts: MasterCard, Visa

NOONMARK
P.O. Box 75585
Seattle, WA 98125

Offers: Extra-thin micro glass in bulk size or custom cut to specification.
For Further Information: Send business-size SASE for information.

NORTHEASTERN SCALE MODELS, INC.
99 Cross St.
P.O. Box 727
Methuen, MA 01844
(508) 688-6019

Offers: Model-building components and laser-cut items: Precision scale basswood structural shapes, dollhouse moulding, carving blocks, decking, strips and sheets. Also offers hardware and model railroad kits.
For Further Information: Catalog, $1.
Store Location: Yes
Discounts: Sells wholesale to legitimate businesses.

THE OAKRIDGE CORPORATION
P.O. Box 247
Lemont, IL 60439

Offers: Dollhouse kits (1-inch scale) in a variety of models. Also offers a line of building supplies and accessories by many manufacturers including: Real Good, Greenleaf, American Craft Products, Hofco House, Houseworks, others. Carries ¼-inch and ½-inch scale wooden craft kits, scratchbuilder's supplies, landscaping, miniature accessories and dollhouses.
For Further Information: Catalog, $3 (refundable).

J. PARKER
P.O. Box 34
Midland, Ontario L4R 4K6 Canada

Offers: Swallowhill miniature porcelain doll kits, patterns, trims, mohair, other items.
For Further Information: Catalog, $3 (refundable).

DON PERKINS MINIATURES
1708 59th St.
Des Moines, IA 50322

Offers: Cords for miniature wicker work: White linen, by the half-pound spool (or pound); (natural linen spool) or quarter-pound spools of 3-cord (for ½-scale work).

For Further Information: Send SASE for price list.

PIKE CREEK MINIATURES
8904 24th Ave.
Kenosha, WI 53143
(414) 694-5799

Offers: Houseworks ½-inch scale dollhouse and components kits, and ¼-inch scale dollhouse series kits (6 houses, church, lumber and items). Carries Fimo, Cernit, tools, books.
For Further Information: Send SASE for information.

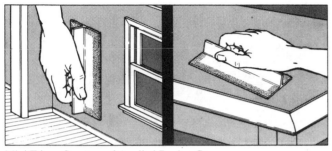

Mini T-bar. Courtesy of Applied Design Corp.

PINOCCHIO'S MINIATURES
465 Main St.
Frankenmuth, MI 48734
(517) 652-2751

Offers: Complete lines of miniature supplies, including Jack Nash assembled houses and kits, others.
For Further Information: Send SASE for information.

CLAUDETTE PRIDDY
840 N. Robinson St.
Los Angeles, CA 90026

Offers: Miniature beads: Full inventory of hard-to-find antique Victorian glass beads, French-cut steel beads, tiny no-hole glass beads, French sequins, tiny Austrian crystals, no-hole pearls, plus jewelry making items.
For Further Information: Catalog, $1 and SASE.

BARBARA J. RAHEB
30132 Elizabeth Ct.
Agoura Hills, CA 91301

Offers: Miniature books: Over 275 selections of abridged and unabridged editions of well-known favorites, classics, reproduced antique books, masterpieces (professionally typeset, illustrated, handsewn, hardbound with titled decorative spines and cover designs stamped in 23 kt gold). Books are limited, numbered, fully readable editions in 1-inch scale.
For Further Information: Catalog, $4.
Discounts: Dealer inquiries invited.

GOLD AND BETTY RIMER
515 Crystal Ave.
Findlay, OH 45840
(419) 423-2016

Offers: Handcrafted scale miniatures including furniture (hutch, cabinet, dry sink, others). Custom-made miniatures by special request (send picture or good description).
For Further Information: Send SASE for price list.

RONDEL WOOD PRODUCTS
2679 Washington Rd.
Waldoboro, ME 04572
(207) 832-6837

Offers: Wood wagon and carriage kits at 1/12 scale: Blueprints, patterns and components.
For Further Information: Brochure, $2.

RUGS GALORE
P.O. Box 339
Cobb Island, MD 20625

Offers: Dollhouse needlepoint rugs (charts and kits) in a variety of designs including Oriental, Colonial, Victorian and contemporary. Also has finished rugs.
For Further Information: Business-size SASE and $4 for photo brochure.

SHARON E. RUSSELL
P.O. Box 2124
Chino, CA 91708

Offers: Wicker furniture kits (1-inch and ½-inch scales) and finished furniture.
For Further Information: Brochure/price list, $1 plus business-size SASE.

SHENANDOAH DESIGNS, INC.
P.O. Box 313
Brookfield, CT 06804

Offers: Miniatures collections at 1/12 scale (kits, unfinished or finished): Chippendale, Colonial, kitchen, porch/patio, builders, dolls, plus ½-inch scale kitchen collection kits.
For Further Information: Send $1 for complete set of literature.
Discounts: "Dealer inquiries welcomed."

THE SIDE DOOR
Rt. 28, P.O. Box 573
Dennisport, MA 02639

Offers: Bisque dollhouse/doll kits, patterns, dressed dolls, trims, accessories.
For Further Information: Brochure, $2.

SMALL HOUSES
8064 Columbia Rd.
Olmstead Falls, OH 44138

Offers: Full line of dollhouse components: Furniture, wallpapers, carpet, building supplies and accessories.
For Further Information: Catalog, $5.

PHYLLIS STAFFORD
939 North St.
Suffield, CT 06078

Offers: Scale miniature carpet kits, including Armenian design reproductions (from 17th Century) on 40 silk gauze mesh with DMC floss (7¾ inches × 3⅞ inches); also offers *Our Lady of Czestochowa* design kit. Has finished carpets.
For Further Information: Send SASE for full information.

RON STETKEWICZ
HCR 1, P.O. Box 61B
Cairo, NY 12413

Offers: Miniature brass hardware: Hinges, drawer pulls, lock plates, screens, others.
For Further Information: Catalog, $6 (refundable).

LINDA TAYLOR
2228 Leif Ave.
Muskegon, MI 49441

Offers: Stuffed bears and bunnies kits (1 inch tall when seated); others.
For Further Information: Send business-size SASE for brochure.

RUSSELL TINGLE
P.O. Box 1501
New Bern, NC 28563

Offers: Miniature figures kits: Celebrities, characters, others—men, women and seniors.
For Further Information: Price list/photos, $4 (refundable).

A TOUCH OF THE PAST
2853 Acushnet Ave.
New Bedford, MA 02745
(508) 998-1277

Offers: Lighthouse scale miniature kits and other dollhouses (lighthouse has 4 levels with central stairway, front opening) and finished. Line of miniature furniture and electrical kits also available.
For Further Information: Send SASE for full information.
Accepts: MasterCard, Visa

TWIN PALMS MINIATURES
1071 Borden Rd.
San Marcos, CA 92069

Offers: Miniature (1-inch scale) cane furniture kits: Cushioned living room group (loveseat, sofa, chair, ottoman, lattice under "glass" table, coffee table, étagère).
For Further Information: Brochure, $1 and SASE (refundable).
Discounts: "Dealer inquiries invited."

PATRICIA VERDUGO
P.O. Box 993
Lawndale, CA 90260

Offers: Miniature accessories (1-inch scale) for holidays, medical, sales, home, others; also offers Fimo and color recipe books.
For Further Information: Catalog, $2.50.

VESTA'S FOREGROUND DESIGNS
P.O. Box 218196
Columbus, OH 43221

Offers: Miniature estate interior accents, seasonal accessories, landscaping details, patio tile, planters, others.
For Further Information: Catalog, $2.
Discounts: "Dealer inquiries welcomed."

VICTORIAN TIMES
2888 S. Highland Dr.
Salt Lake City, UT 84106
(801) 486-0328

Offers: Kits for scale miniature buildings, including a Country Victorian store (large building with a 2-bedroom flat and balcony upstairs).
For Further Information: Contact dealer, or send SASE for information.

VILLAGE MINIATURES
P.O. Box 142
Queenston, Ontario L0S IL0 Canada
(416) 262-4779

Offers: Miniatures: Wallpaper and floor coverings, electrical wiring, doors, windows, stairways. Also offers dollhouses, kits and plans, porcelain doll kits, specialized lumber, landscaping materials, mini holiday decorations, handmade accessories. Carries Dremel and X-acto tools and others.
For Further Information: First-time catalogs, $5 ($4 after).

When cutting window and door openings in plywood with an electric jigsaw, put masking tape on the top surface of the plywood. Mark the cutout lines on the masking tape and cut right through the tape. This will eliminate split-out and give you a smooth cut.

— The Dollhouse Factory

W & D MINI HOMES
415 E. 4th St.
P.O. Box 1654
Bloomington, IN 47402
(812) 332-2499

Offers: American Indian scale miniatures (of clay, fiber, wood, etc.), including a variety of clothing, costumes, pottery, baskets, blankets, rugs, figures, paintings, others.
For Further Information: Send SASE (50¢ postage) and $1 for brochure.

WARLING MINIATURES
22453 Covello St.
West Hills, CA 91307
(818) 340-9855

Offers: Miniatures (1 inch and ½ inch) wicker furniture kits of Victorian to modern styles, including chairs, rockers, tables, peg beds, sofas, chests, others.
For Further Information: Send business-size SASE and $1 for brochure.

WEE THREE
53 Miller Rd.
Bethany, CT 06524

Offers: Scale needlework items: Knitting needles, crochet hooks, flosses and fine threads (for knitting, crochet, sewing, tatting).
For Further Information: Catalog, $2.

THE WILLOW TREE
P.O. Box 16164
Newport Beach, CA 92659

Offers: Raggedy Ann or Andy kits (poseable, 2 inches).
For Further Information: Call.
Discounts: "Dealers inquire."

WOODWORKS-N-MINIATURES
36 Mellen St.
Hopedale, MA 01747

Offers: Dollhouse furniture kits.
For Further Information: Brochure/price list, $1.
Discounts: "Save 15% to 30%."

Model Making—Aircraft

Also see Miniature Making, Model Making—General, Model Making—Railroad and other related categories.

AMERICAN SAILPLANE DESIGNS
2626 Coronado Ave., #89
San Diego, CA 92154

Offers: Model aircraft: Ultima (129-inch wingspan, airfoil), "for the serious competitor." Others.
For Further Information: Catalog, $3.

ASTRO FLIGHT, INC.
13311 Beach Ave.
Marina Del Rey, CA 90292
(213) 821-6242

Offers: Model airplane kits (electric powered), including Astro Sport (37-inch wing span) high wing sport trainer, Partenavia P68 Victor Twin, Challenger sailplane, Porterfield Collegiate sport scale model.
For Further Information: Send SASE for full information.

B&D MODELS
P.O. Box 12518
Reno, NV 89510

Offers: Model aircraft plans—old timers and antiques for the reed valve engine: Siamond Zipper, Flying Quaker, Red Zephyr, Miss Philly, Eaglet, Commodore, others.
For Further Information: Illustrated plan book, $2.50.

BALSA USA
P.O. Box 164
Marinette, WI 54143
(800) BALSA US

Offers: Balsa model aircraft video (VHS): *How to Build the Stick 40*, two hours of step-by-step methods for most "trainer type" planes. Also carries balsa model airplane kits.
For Further Information: Send SASE for information.
Accepts: MasterCard, Visa

BLUE RIDGE MODELS
P.O. Box 429
Skyland, NC 28776

Offers: Free flight model aircraft kits (for competition, sport), rubber-powered models (with 13½-inch to 40-inch span) and Dragon Fli helicopter. Carries hand-launched gliders, variety of models. Others.
For Further Information: Catalog, 50¢.
Discounts: "Dealer inquiries invited."

BYRON ORIGINALS, INC.
P.O. Box 279
Ida Grove, IA 51445
(712) 364-3165

Offers: Kits for 28 model R/C aircraft: Biplanes, aerobatics, warbirds, ducted fan jets, amphibians, others. Plus Christen Eagle, P-47 Thunderbolt, F-4U-1 Corsair, Seawind Amphibian, P-51 Mustang, G-17S Staggerwing, F-16 Fighting Falcon, Glasair RG, F-15 Eagle, others.
For Further Information: Catalog, $3.

CARLSON ENGINE IMPORTS
814 E. Marconi Ave.
Phoenix, AZ 85022

Offers: Model aircraft—imported diesel engines: Aurora, Cipolla, D-C, Enya, KMD, Mikro, MK-17, MVVs, RAW, Pfeffer, Silver Swallow and USE.
For Further Information: Catalog, $1.

CHEETAH MODEL
14725 Bessemer St.
Van Nuys, CA 91411
(818) 781-4544

Offers: Model aircraft—slope acrobatic, combat gliders including super model (wingspan 64 inches) and Cheetah (wingspan 48 inches), both with "unbreakable fuselage."
For Further Information: Send SASE for complete information.
Discounts: "Dealer inquiries invited."

CLEVELAND MODEL & SUPPLY CO.
9800 Detroit Ave.
Cleveland, OH 44102
(216) 961-3600

Offers: Model aircraft (C-D) plans (for giant scale models, R/C, electric, rubber, or gas powered) for early bird, warbirds, commercial and racers, private models, homebuilts, jets and others.
For Further Information: Catalog price list, $2; price list, $1.

CS FLIGHT SYSTEMS
31 Perry St.
Middleboro, MA 02346
(508) 947-2805

Offers: Model aircraft—electric flight systems: R/C and other kits, including Astro, Micro-X, Davey, J.M. Glasscraft, Guillow, Goldberg, Topflight, Sig, Airtronics, Easybuilt, and others from over 40 manufacturers. Includes motors, accessories, props, connectors, batteries, carbon fiber sheet, Kevlar mat, tube and solid rods, angle, composite. Also offers model kits, heat guns, irons, films, heat shrink tubing, motors, speed controls, hub kits and Pro control systems.
For Further Information: Catalog, $3.
Discounts: Sells wholesale; quantity discounts.
Accepts: MasterCard, Visa

D & J ELECTRONICS
900 Lucy Rd.
Howell, MI 48843
(517) 546-2644

Offers: Full line of RCD RXs and products for upgrading, plus Focus series R/C systems. Repair service for most R/C systems.
For Further Information: Send SASE for details.
Accepts: MasterCard, Visa, Discover

DGA DESIGNS
135 E. Main St.
Phelps, NY 14532
(315) 548-3779

Offers: Model aircraft—Jet Pilot Kit (pilot bust with modern jet helmet, face mask, oxygen hose, weight 12 ounces), 9 other pilot styles and sizes, 1:8 scale, 1:7 scale, others.
For Further Information: Contact a dealer, or catalog, $1.

DON'S HOBBY SHOP, INC.
1819 S. Broadway
Salina, KS 67401
(913) 827-3222

Offers: R/C engines: Webra, Moki, YS, ASP, MVVs, others, plus Sig kits, JR servos, JR and Futaba radio systems, others.
For Further Information: Send SASE for list.
Store Location: Yes
Discounts: Sells wholesale; quantity discounts.
Accepts: MasterCard, Visa

FLYING SCALE, INC.
1905 Colony Rd.
Metairie, LA 70003

Offers: Plans for 29 scale model rubber aircraft (collectors'): Ryan, Stintson, Boeing, Curtiss, Thompson, plus Japanese, French and German models.

For Further Information: Send SASE for list.

FRANK'S HOBBY HOUSE
19401 N. Cave Creek Rd.
Phoenix, AZ 85024
(602) 992-3495

Offers: Kits and supplies by Ace, Airtronics, Bru-Line, Cox, Du-Bro, Ernst, Futaba, Goldberg, Hobbico, JR, Lanier, Magnum, McDaniel, Midwest, Moki, Panavise, RCD, R/C Sports, Robart, SIG, Webra, YS, others.
For Further Information: Send SASE for list.
Store Location: Yes
Accepts: MasterCard, Visa

GM PLASTICS
7252 Industrial Park Blvd.
Mentor, OH 44060
(216) 953-1188

Offers: Model R/C aircraft kits (machine cut parts, sheeted foam wing design, solid balsa tail feathers, one piece ABS cowl, plans, instructions, hardware, decals).
For Further Information: Contact a dealer or send SASE for details.
Accepts: MasterCard, Visa

GREAT PLANES MODEL MANUFACTURING
P.O. Box 9021
Champaign, IL 61826
(800) 682-8948

Offers: Model R/C aircraft kit—Electro Streak aerobatic model with 4-channel radio (with 3 micro servos). Kit has computer-designed parts, 1:11 scale glider (64.5-inch wingspan), others.
For Further Information: Free brochure.

HERRILLS EXECUFORM
P.O. Box 7853
Laguna Niguel, CA 92607
(714) 495-0705

Offers: Model—aircraft—vacform kits in 1:72 scale (Beech, Boeing, Cessna, Convair, Curtiss, Douglas, Fairchild, Howard, Lockheed, Martin, Northrop, Ryan, Sikorsky, Stinson, Vultee, Waco).
For Further Information: Send SASE for catalog.

HOBBIES & HELIS INTERNATIONAL
201 S. 3rd St. & Rt. 309 N.
Coopersburg, PA 18036
(215) 282-4811

Offers: Model helicopter kits including Hirobo, X-Cell, Kalt, Kyosho, others. Also offers beginner packages/kits. Parts available include rotor blades, fuselages, motors, R/Cs and

others. Tools: Blade balancer, flybar lock, paddle gauges, piston head lock, link pliers, others.
For Further Information: HHI or TSK Catalog, $5 each (specify).

HOBBY HORN
15173 Moran St.
P.O. Box 2212
Westminster, CA 92684
(714) 893-8311

Offers: Model aircraft kits with FF and R/C (1935 to 1941 planes, 46-inch to 108-inch size models), Midway Model Co. full kits (1936 to 1940 planes, 50-inch to 84-inch size models). Model sailplane kits — (electric power or gas) — of Midway Model Co., Electric Model Design. Carries electric systems and parts.
For Further Information: 76-page catalog, $2.
Accepts: MasterCard, Visa

HOBBY SHACK
12480 Bandilier Circle
Fountain Valley, CA 92708

Offers: Model R/C aircraft kits, ARF models and others, by Two Tee, Parma International, others. Models include hydroracing boat, Tamiya Grasshopper II Racer and others. Carries supplies, parts including silk-like material in 2-meter and 5-meter rolls, 11 colors, and Miller deluxe airbrush spray set. Carries Pacer products, R/C model car kits and combos.
For Further Information: Free 96-page Sport Flyer catalog.
Accepts: MasterCard, Visa

HORIZAN MODELS
1296 Franquet St.
Chambly, Quebec J3L 2P6 Canada

Offers: Model airplane kits: Pre-built fiberglass laminated fuselage, balsa covered foam wing panels, complete hardware.
For Further Information: Catalog, $3.

INDOOR MODEL SUPPLY
P.O. Box 5311
Salem, OR 97304

Offers: Model airplanes — endurance rubber models, including copters with an 18-inch span and gliders with a 16-inch span, plus Parlor planes, others. Carries contest/sport scale model aircraft kits, 13-inch scale aircraft kits. Supplies: Balsa, Japanese tissue, others.
For Further Information: Illustrated catalog, $2.

INNOVATIVE MODEL PRODUCTS
P.O. Box 4366
Margate, FL 33063
(305) 978-9033

Offers: Model aircraft kits: Thunderbolt P-47, Mustang P-51D, Hawker Hurricane, other propeller models. Carries dummy radials, PFM adhesive, others.
For Further Information: Catalog, $5.
Accepts: MasterCard, Visa

JET ENGINE TECHNOLOGIES
10241 Ridgewood Dr.
El Paso, TX 79925

Offers: Plans for model jet engine (no machining or welding) — gasoline fueled, produces 3-foot flame and powers planes to 228 mph. You-build "in about 8 hours."
For Further Information: Send SASE for full details.

K & B MANUFACTURING
2100 College Dr.
Lake Havasu City, AZ 86403

Offers: K & B model aircraft and marine engines, fuels, glow plugs, fiberglass cloth, super epoxy resin and primer, microballoon filler, super epoxy thinner and paints.
For Further Information: Send SASE for information.

MIDWEST PRODUCTS CO., INC.
400 S. Indiana St.
P.O. Box 564
Hobart, IN 46342
(219) 942-1134

Offers: Micro-cut woods: Balsa, basswood, hardwoods, carving blocks. Model aircraft kits — electric R/C including trainer (wingspan 50 inches) Aero-Star. Others. Manufacturer.
For Further Information: See your dealer or send for free catalog.

MINIATURE AIRCRAFT USA
2324 N. Orange Blossom Trail
Orlando, FL 32804
(407) 422-1531

Offers: Model aircraft kits — X-Cell Quick-Silver competition helicopter, epoxy-fiberglass, with rear gyro mounting kit, torque rail rotor drive. Others.
For Further Information: Send SASE for information.

MORRIS HOBBIES
1169 Eastern Pkwy.
Louisville, KY 40217
(502) 451-0901

Accepts: MasterCard, Visa

MTA HOBBIES
4172 Pacific Coast Highway, Suite 102
Torrance, CA 90505

Offers: Helicoptor kits by Hirobo, Kyosho, Miniature Aircraft, TSK, others. Parts include engines, combos, bodies, mufflers, others. Also carries hand tools and sets.
For Further Information: Send SASE for list.
Discounts: "10-15%" discount on all Heli parts.
Accepts: MasterCard, Visa

NORTHWEST HOBBY SHOP
P.O. Box 44577
Tacoma, WA 98444
(206) 531-8111

Offers: Model aircraft kits including super sport, aeromaster, others, plus starter packages, electric packages, and fiberglass foam kits with wood and hardware. Accessories include firewall mounts, spinners, nylon racing wheels, axles, racing accessories, props, blues, others.
For Further Information: Send SASE for information.
Accepts: MasterCard, Visa

OLD TIME PLAN SERVICE
P.O. Box 90310
San Jose, CA 95109
(408) 292-3382

Offers: Model aircraft plans: (1) Old Timer F/F Gas Plans, (2) Old Timer Rubber/Towline Plans, (3) Old Timer Flying Scale Plans A through K, (4) Old Timer Flying Scale Plans L through Z.
For Further Information: Each list of plans, $1.50.

PECK-POLYMERS
P.O. Box 710399
Santee, CA 92072

Offers: Model aircraft kits, a variety of rubber power, CO_2, and electric models, plus model aircraft building plans. Carries parts including electric motors, such as "super lightweight" R/C and FSystems, CO_2 engines, others.
For Further Information: Catalog, $2.

QUADROTECH
3148 Kingston Rd., Suite 202
Scarborough, Ontario V1M 2P4 Canada
(416) 931-5564

Offers: Aircraft kits, including Extra 260 (70-inch wingspan R/C), Laser 200, Pitts Special, Salotel, Citabria, others.
For Further Information: Information, $1.

R/C MODELER
P.O. Box 487
Sierra Madre, CA 91025
(818) 355-1476

Offers: Over 875 model plans: Scale aircraft, fun-fly ships, sailplanes, boats, others.
For Further Information: Catalog, $5.

ROBERTS MODEL
18 E. Clay St.
W. Hazleton, PA 18201

Offers: Model aircraft parts (1:72, 1:48 and 1:32 scales) and a complete line of injection molded accessories: Engines, props, control columns, throttles, radio fronts, instrument panels, seats, rubber pedals, guns, spinners, helicopter rotors, wheels, U/C struts, others.
For Further Information: Send business-size SASE for details.

ROSEMONT HOBBY SHOP
P.O. Box 139
Trexlertown, PA 18087
(215) 398-0210

Offers: 1:72 scale aircraft and other kits, Meikraft injected kits. Other aircraft kits from 1919 to modern, all scales, plus armor, WWI to present, all scales.
For Further Information: Catalog, $2 (refundable).
Discounts: "Dealer inquiries invited."
Accepts: MasterCard, Visa, Discover

SABO DESIGNS IN PAPER
P.O. Box 161742
Altamonte Springs, FL 32716

Offers: Model NASA space shuttle—Orbiter kit (8-inch wingspan) printed on gloss paper (for display or hand launch).
For Further Information: Send SASE for complete details.

SHELTON'S HOBBIES
2135 Old Oakland Rd.
San Jose, CA 95131
(800) 228-3237 (except CA), (800) 822-1688 (CA)

Offers: Model products, name brand, 4 to 8 channel systems and servos, plus aircraft parts, components, supplies. Carries R/C model car kits and combos, parts and radios.
For Further Information: Free 136-page catalog.
Accepts: MasterCard, Visa

SIG MANUFACTURING CO., INC.
401-7 Front St.
Montezuma, IA 50171
(515) 623-5154

Offers: Model aircraft kits (balsa, plywood)—classic, biplanes, stunts, sports, multiwing, military, racers, trainers, gliders, others. Includes models for flying confined area, and for one- to four-channel radio equipment. Carries beginners' models, and a variety of scale sizes. Also carries aircraft parts, kit plans, balsa wood, engines and metal sheets (aluminum, brass). Materials: Heavy silk, "Plyspan" tissue, nylon, polyester, flight foam. Stocks paints for foam ARF models, casting materials (resin, fiberglass), control line, radios.
For Further Information: Contact a dealer, or catalog, $3.
Accepts: MasterCard, Visa

DON SMITH
2260 N. Dixie Highway
Boca Raton, FL 33431
(407) 395-9523

Offers: Scale R/C aircraft plans: Messerschmitt, Henschel, Lavochkin, Heinkel, Hawker Sea Furn, Curtis R3C2, others. Cowls, canopies.
For Further Information: Information, $1.

SUPERIOR AIRCRAFT MATERIALS
12020 Centralia
Hawaiian Gardens, CA 90716
(310) 865-3220

Offers: Balsa wood: Sticks, wide sheets, "superlite," planks, others. Carries bargain balsa and birch plywood.
For Further Information: Send SASE for catalog.

TWELVE SQUARED
P.O. Box 21567
Eagan, MN 55121

Offers: Model aircraft kits—1/700 B-2, Bell X-1, Northrop X-4, Heinkel HE-278. Injected kits and conversions: 1:44 scale and 1:72 scale. Carries model stands, others.
For Further Information: Send SASE for illustrated catalog.

VICTORIA PRODUCTS
930 Foul Bay Rd.
Victoria, British Columbia V8S 4H8 Canada
(213) 274-1283

Offers: Model aircraft kits—vacfoam and cast resin types, in 1:72 scale. Vacfoam kits include: Canadair Tutor, Sukhoi, MIG, Bachem, Aero, Blohm, Voss, others. Resin kits are also available.
For Further Information: Send for newsletter.

VINTAGE R/C PLANS
5105 Pine Hill Circle
Howell, MI 48843

Offers: Line of vintage R/C aircraft plans.
For Further Information: Catalog, $2 ($3 foreign).

WESCRAFT
43176 Business Park Dr., #104
Temecula, CA 92590
(909) 695-0735

Offers: Model R/C aircraft kit—B17 with all fiberglass body, sized for .45 to .60 engines. Others.
For Further Information: Send SASE for information.

Model Making—General

Also see Miniature Making, Model Making—Aircraft, Model Making—Railroad and other related categories.

A.J. FISHER, INC.
1002 Etowah Ave.
Royal Oak, MI 48067

Offers: Model ship and yacht fittings to scratch build a competitive R/C model yacht in the 36/600, 1 meter, 50/800 or 20 rater class. Kits of Great Lakes and ocean-going vessels available, plus model building plans and books.
For Further Information: Illustrated catalog, $2.

ACE R/C
116 W. 19th St.
P.O. Box 472
Higginsville, MO 64037
(816) 584-7121, (800) 322-7121

Offers: Model products utilizing Amazing Hinges of latex rubber. Surfaces can be butt-fitted; hinge tension pulls the surfaces together. Others.
For Further Information: Catalog, $3.

AEROSPACE COMPOSITE PRODUCTS
14210 Doolittle Dr.
San Leandro, CA 94577
(510) 352-2022

Offers: Composite materials: Vacuum bagging supplies, carbon fiber laminates, Rohacell (light, rigid foam in 3 thicknesses), carbon or Kevlar mat, glass cloth, carbon fiber (tape, ribbon) fabric tapes. E-Z lam epoxy laminating resin. Others.
For Further Information: Send SASE for complete listing.
Accepts: MasterCard, Visa

AMERICA'S HOBBY CENTER, INC.
146 W. 22nd St.
New York, NY 10011

Offers: Model R/C aircraft, boat and car kits, parts and supplies in known brands for systems (Airtronics, Futaba, Challanger, Cannon), motors (Enya, O.S. Technopower, G-Mark, K & B, Cox, OS, Royal). Also offers kits, starter kits, kits combos with engines or systems for airplanes, boats, ships, cars. Carries Tamiya cars/accessories, glider accessories, retracts, batteries, plugs and engine starters, R/C model car kits/combos: Futaba, Tamiya, Marui, others. Also carries radios, parts, power tools (Dremel, Miller—sprayer set), Taig micro lathe and accessories. Aero Publishers books available.
For Further Information: R/C models catalog, $2.50; airplane catalog, $2.50.

APPLIED DESIGN CORP.
P.O. Box 3384
Torrance, CA 90510

Offers: Tools for model building, etc.: Mini hand belt sander (adjustable tension), mini sandpaper strips, tee-bar aluminum sanding block (2 sizes), Ruff Stuff adhesive sheet sandpapers (3 grains), mini compact hacksaw (10-inch handles wood, plastic, metal and hardened music wire). Others.
For Further Information: Catalog, 50¢.

ARCHER'S HOBBY WORLD
15432 Alsace Circle
Irvine, CA 92714
(714) 552-3142

Offers: Plastic model kits for aircraft, ships, military vehicles by: Ace, Airfix, Arc, Bandai, Crown, Detail Master, DML, ESCI, Fujini, Glencoe, Masegama, Keller, Hobbycraft, IMAI, Italeri, Johan, Lindberg, LS, Matchbox, Mikro, Inicraft, Mitsowa, Model Tech, Monogram, MPC, Pegasus, Pioneer, Red Star, Revell, Skywave, Supermodel, Yaksts, Tamaya, Testors, Trimaster, Union, Verlinden, Williams Bros., WK Models. Vacuform kits by: Airframe, Air Vac, Combat, Contrail, Elliott, Execuform, Falcon, Formaplane, Joystick, Rareplanes, Wings. Also carries decals, finishes, tools, modeling supplies, books.
For Further Information: Catalog, $3.50 (U.S.); $5 overseas.

ARMOR RESEARCH CO.
P.O. Box 8583
Cedar Rapids, IA 52408

Offers: Photo-etched and cast detailing items and accessories for armor models, including tank and artillery ammunition and others. Also offers building information, TM excerpts, photos and scale drawings for a variety of models and items.
For Further Information: Catalog, $5.
Discounts: "Dealer inquiries welcome."

BENSON HOBBY PRODUCTS
7119 N. Chimney Rock Place
Tucson, AZ 85718

Offers: Model electronic accessories for electric R/C, wide range of products.
For Further Information: Send SASE for brochure.

CENTRAL MODEL MARKETING
P.O. Box 772
Aurora, CO 80040
(800) 962-2010

Offers: R/C model car kits, kits with computer-matched pak and charger, or kits with charter and 2-channel, 2-stick radio: Grasshopper, The Hornet, The Falcon, Wizard, Lunch Box, Blackfoot Monster Truck, Midnight Pumpkin, Monster Beetle, Clodbuster, Royal Crusher, Rockbuster, hopped-up Rockbuster, Royal Ripper, Futaba FX-10, Grasshopper II, others.
For Further Information: Catalog, $1.
Accepts: MasterCard, Visa

CLEVELAND MODEL & SUPPLY CO.
9800 Detroit Ave.
Cleveland, OH 44102
(216) 961-3600

Offers: Model aircraft (C-D) plans (for giant scale models, R/C, electric, rubber or gas powered) for early birds, warbirds, commercial and racers, private models, homebuilts, jets, others: Supermarine, Boeing, Beech, Piper Cubs, Fokker, Lindbergs, Waco Taper-Wings, Bristol, Lock Air Express, Curtiss, others.
For Further Information: Pictorial catalog and price list, $2 ($3 outside the U.S.).

CLOVER HOUSE
P.O. Box 62
Sebastopol, CA 95473

Offers: Model N, HO, S and O scale dry transfer alphabets in a variety of type styles, plus stripes, signs and RR lettering. Carries scratch building supplies.
For Further Information: Catalog, $3.

ERIC CLUTTON
913 Cedar Lane
Tullahoma, TN 37388

Offers: P.A.W. diesels for model aircraft, .049 to .35, RC and STD, plus Davies-Charlton diesels (English made) including Dart .03, Merlin .045, Spitfire .06, Sabre .09.
For Further Information: Lists and information, $1.

COASTAL
60 Bretonian Dr.
Brick, NJ 08723

Offers: Lead soldier molds, casting and mold-making supplies for models.

For Further Information: Illustrated catalog, $5; free brochure.

CONCEPT RESEARCH AND DEVELOPMENT, INC.
1003 S. Christensen Rd.
Medical Lake, WA 99022

Offers: Miniature functional catapults (Ballista), plus plans, kits, parts, accessories.
For Further Information: Brochure, $2 (refundable).

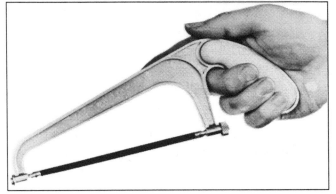
Mini hacksaw. Courtesy of Applied Design Corp.

D & J HOBBY & CRAFTS
96 San Tomas Aquino Rd.
Campbell, CA 95008
(408) 379-1696

Offers: Complete lines of model materials: Imported aircraft, ships and armor kits, fantasy miniatures and games, minitanks and GHQ micro armor, scratch building supplies, and materials by Humbrol, Polly S, Floquil, plus Paasche airbrushes and parts. Decals, books and magazines are available.
For Further Information: Send SASE with specific inquiries.

DANE ART MINIATURES
3138 SW 9th St.
Des Moines, IA 50315

Offers: Detailed parts and accessories for 1/35 scale military models (armor, vehicles, figures), and 1/48 scale military aircraft. Others.
For Further Information: Send SASE for current products list.
Discounts: "Dealer inquiries welcome."

DIAMOND ENTERPRISES
P.O. Box 537
Alexandria Bay, NY 13607
(613) 475-1771

Offers: Live steam model train kits—complete Wilesco & Mamod line. Also offers kits for tractors, marine craft, cars and trucks, plus stationary engines and accessories, including a wide array of parts. Service department.

ing a wide array of parts. Service department.
For Further Information: Catalog, $5.95 (refundable).
Discounts: "Large discounts."

THE DROMEDARY
6324 Belton Rd.
El Paso, TX 79912
(915) 584-2445

Offers: Model ship builder supplies—full lines of tools, rigging and fittings, ship kits (U.S. and plank-on-frame imported), plus a variety of woods, and others.
For Further Information: Catalog, $6 ($7 outside the U.S.).
Accepts: MasterCard, Visa

EVERGREEN SCALE MODELS
12808 NE 125th Way
Kirkland, WA 98034

Offers: Styrene products for model building: Board and batten, ³⁄₁₆-inch and ¼-inch square strips, larger telescoping tubing, wide-spaced clapboard, others. Handbook: Tips/techniques.
For Further Information: Contact dealer, or $1 for handbook.

FLYING SCALE, INC.
1905 Colony Rd.
Metairie, LA 70003

Offers: 29 Scale model rubber aircraft plans (collectors'): Ryans, Stinstons, Boeings, Curtiss, Thompson, plus Japanese, French and German models.
For Further Information: Send SASE for list.

FORMULA 1
5 Keane Ave.
Islington, Ontario M9B 2B6 Canada
(416) 626-5781

Offers: Scale model classic racing and other cars by Tamiya, Fujimi, Heller, Protar, ESCI, Union, Gunze, Monogram, others.
For Further Information: Free price list.
Accepts: American Express, MasterCard, Visa

GALASTIC TRADE COMMISSION
10185 Switzer
Overland Park, KS 66202

Offers: Science fiction models from: Robotech, Star Trek, Thunderbirds, Star Wars, Galactica, Starblazers, Macross, others.
For Further Information: Catalog, $3.
Discounts: "Dealer inquiries are invited."

GOLD MEDAL MODELS
12332 Chapman Ave., #81
Garden Grove, CA 92640

Offers: Photo-etched fittings for a variety of model ships, including WWII Japanese IJN battleships, two types of aircraft recovery cranes, radar, searchlight tower support girders, seaplane transfer carts, catapults, aircraft propellers, ladders, mailing material, others. Separate fittings set for Yamato class. Others.
For Further Information: Send SASE for full information.

HEATH CO.
P.O. Box 8589
Benton Harbor, MI 49023

Offers: R/C Model kits for MRC—Tamaya and other racing cars: Fox Hotshot II competition, All-Terrain Clod Buster. Aircraft—Electric Kyosho Express (61-inch wingspan), Cessna Cardinal, Kyosho R/C sailboat. Carries soldering irons and magnifiers. (Also has electronic kits for variety of products.)
For Further Information: Write for catalog.

HOBBIES NEW
P.O. Box 687
Minot, ND 58702

Offers: Modeler's Helper support vise set (for model aircraft, cars, boats, sailboats). Holds assemblies for installing parts, for engine run up and check out, or when installing radio equipment, changing gear ratios, repairing, adjusting, others.
For Further Information: Send SASE for full details.

HOBBY HOUSE, INC.
8208 Merriman Rd.
Westland, MI 48185
(313) 425-9720

Offers: R/C model car kits/products: Kits by Bolink (1/10 eliminator and basic fiberglass, graphite, Euduro, Enduro conversion and others). Carries Model Racing Products, Associated, Composite Craft, McAllistor, plus NMB bearings, 1/10 bodies (Bolink). MRP bodies: Spider, T-Bird. Also carries TRC tires, Protec chargers, Parma batteries (variety of types).
For Further Information: Send SASE for list.
Accepts: MasterCard, Visa

HOBBY LOBBY INTERNATIONAL, INC.
5614 Franklin Pike Circle
Brentwood, TN 37027
(615) 373-1444

Offers: Model boat/ship items, including unusuals: Electric flight props, fast scale offshore racing cat, 400-watt electric

flight motor, l-meter racing sailboat, 3-meter electric soarer, 4-foot steam launch, wood colored oldtimer props, electric flight propulsion systems and others.
For Further Information: Free catalog ($2 outside the U.S.).

I/R MINIATURES, INC.
P.O. Box 89
Burnt Hills, NY 12027
(518) 885-6054

Offers: Miniature model kits (54mm and 76mm scale), including Christmas and literary figures, and soldiers of most conflicts worldwide. Line of paints.
For Further Information: SASE for details; illustrated catalog, $6.
Discounts: Sells wholesale to legitimate businesses.

When using pewter for models, after assembling, the model may be painted black and polished with 0000 steel wool for an antique look.

K & S ENGINEERING
6917 W. 59th St.
Chicago, IL 60638
(312) 586-8503

Offers: Metal products for model building, etc.: Aluminum tube (8 sizes), round brass tube (20 sizes), copper tube (4 sizes), soft brass fuel tubing, rectangular brass tube (4 sizes), brass strips (20 sizes), square brass tube (7 sizes), brass angles, channel and solid brass rods (many sizes), sheet metal (4-inch × 10-inch), brass (4 thicknesses), tin, aluminum (3 thicknesses), .025 copper, soldering tools (4 models with 30, 60 or 100 watt capacity).
For Further Information: Catalog and price list, 25¢.

THE KIT BUNKER
2905 Spring Park Rd.
Jacksonville, FL 32207

Offers: Line model of aircraft, armor, ships and figures kits (old and new). Also purchases kits, small or large quantity.
For Further Information: Send $1 and SASE with 44¢ postage for list.

MICRO-MARK
340-671 Snyder Ave.
Berkeley Heights, NJ 07922

Offers: Hard-to-find modeler's tools (hand and power types): Saws, including miter cutoff type, Dremel motoshop attachments, Moto-Tool and holders, flexible shaft, drill press attachments, table shaper, disc/belt sander and rotor attachments for Moto-Tools, plus jeweler's drill press, Mini-Vac micro cleaner, Miter-Rite tools, nippers, tweezers,

brushes, file sets, mini bolt cutters, knife blades and sets. Carries Badger airbrush sets and compressors. Others.
For Further Information: 48-page catalog, $1 ($2 outside the U.S.).
Accepts: American Express, MasterCard, Visa

MIRACLE MODELS
P.O. Box 98042
Lubbock, TX 79499

Offers: Brand name model kits, supplies, accessories (and games) by Has Hasagawa, Tamalya, Monogram, MPC, AMT, DML, Dragon, Dremel, Verlinden, Fujimi, Testors, Pactra, Gunze, Floqull, MSC, Avalon Hill, TSR, FASA, Victory, West End, Task Force, GDW, others.
For Further Information: Catalog, $1 (refundable).

MODEL EXPO, INC.
P.O. Box 1000
Mt. Pocono, PA 18344

Offers: Historic ship model kits (from Europe): Replicas (many over 4 feet long) with walnut and mahogany planking, fittings and details in bronze, brass and rare hardwoods— large-scale plans, step-by-step instructions and all materials included. Models include clipper and other sailing ships like the Bluenose II (replica of the last of the tall schooners). Instructional video, *You Take the Helm*, shows how to build the Bluenose, step by step.
For Further Information: Catalog, $1.
Store Location: Yes
Accepts: MasterCard, Visa

NK PRODUCTS
P.O. Box 94
Landing, NJ 07850

Offers: Model diorama accesories at 1/35 scale (a variety of buildings, walls, fences, vehicles, others).
For Further Information: Catalog, $1.75.

OMNI MODELS
P.O. Box 708
Mahomet, IL 61853
(800) 342-6464

Offers: R/C Model car kits and combo deals, plus parts, accessories and electronics by: Advanced, Airtronics, Aristocraft, Associated, Astro Flight, B & B, Bolink, Cox, Dean's, Dynaflite, Futaba, Higley's, KO Propo, Leisure, Losi, McAllistor, MRC, MRP, Novak, Paragon, Parma, Proline, Protec, Ram, Robart, Royal, Sanyo, Schumacher, Tekin, Traxxas, Trinity, Twister, Varicom, World Engines, Yokomo, others.
For Further Information: Send SASE for list.
Accepts: MasterCard, Visa

PRODUCT DESIGN, INC.
16922 NE 124th St.
Redmond, WA 98052
(206) 883-4007

Offers: Model boats (electric) items including the hydro zeta speed controller (for single or twin motors), 180 amps, 600 amp surge, takes up to 20 cells/24 volts. Others.
For Further Information: Write or call for catalog or more details.

CHRIS ROSSBACH
RD 1, Queensboro Manor
Gloversville, NY 12078

Offers: Antique model ignition engines and parts: Precision cast timers, original cylinder heads, point sets, drive washers, spark plugs, tanks. Wide range of engines.
For Further Information: Catalog, $5 ($8 outside the U.S.).

ROYAL PRODUCTS CORP.
790 W. Tennessee Ave.
Denver, CO 80223

Offers: Model R/C products — Head Start systems including heavy-duty starter (standard or jumbo, for engines up to 1:4 scale), power panels, 12V fuel pump (fills or drains model or diesel fuel), locking socket (lock-on battery clip, even fits 4-cycle plugs). Other model aircraft and accessories.
For Further Information: Contact your hobby dealer, or catalog, $4.

SATELLITE CITY
P.O. Box 836
Simi Valley, CA 93062
(805) 522-0062

Offers: Glues for fiberglass or Kevlar — instant and penetrating odorless types.
For Further Information: Send SASE for free tip booklet and fiberglassing instructions.

SQUARE CUT TOOLS
905 N. Harbor City Blvd.
Melbourne, FL 32935

Offers: Model kit or scratch building tools: Balsa cutters (square cut tools of machined zinc plated steel in 3- or 5-piece sets, cutting ⅛-inch to ⁵⁄₁₆-inch squares.
For Further Information: At your dealers, or send for catalog.
Discounts: "Dealer/distributor inquiries invited."
Accepts: MasterCard, Visa

TECH-TOYS
370 Rt. 46 W.
Parsippany, NJ 07054
(201) 227-7012

Model ship.

Offers: R/C model car customizing parts in a variety of scales for on and off road cars, trucks and boats — specializes in ¼ and ⅙. Carries finishing materials and equipment, electronics by: A & L, Advance, Airtronics, Astroflight, Badger, Blue Ribbon, Bolink, Buds, Goldberg, Champion, Cobra International, Composite, Cox, CRP, Custom, Dahms, Deans, Delta, Dremel, Dubro, Duratrax, Floquil, Fox, Futaba, Higley, Houge, JG, K & B, KO Propo, Lavco, M&M, Marui, MCS, MIP, Monogram, Panaconic, Paragon, PDI, Cut, Pro-Shop, Raceco, Race, Sanyo, Tekin, Thorp, Universal, Ungar.
For Further Information: Call or send SASE with inquiry.
Accepts: MasterCard, Visa

TELEFLITE CORP.
11620 Kitching St.
Moreno Valley, CA 92557

Offers: Model rocket motors — you-build (using a rock tumbler and simple handtools), finished product gives 40 pounds of thrust. Electric ignitor from household materials.
For Further Information: Brochure and sample igniter, $2.

32ND PARALLEL
P.O. Box 804
Pismo Beach, CA 93448
(805) 481-3170

Offers: Scale model submarines, 3 models in 1/32 scale with a variety of ballast control systems and options, including working torpedos. Models available from hull kit only, to complete kits with all required parts (less radio) to operate submerged.

For Further Information: Color catalog, $3.

TOWER HOBBIES

P.O. Box 9078
Champaign, IL 61826

Offers: Model R/C equipment, kits and supplies/parts for model cars, boats, planes, tanks, engines, radios, accessories by over 300 manufacturers, including ACE R/C, Astroflight, Dave Brown, Cox, Cressline, Davey Systems, Dremelools, Du-Bro, Future Flight airplane, Flitecraft Models, Futaba (servos, sticks), Carl Goldberg model kits, Great Planes airplane kits, Guillows, Hobbico, Hot Stuff, K & B, Kyosho (aircraft kits, chargers), Master Airscrew, K J Miller, Milt Video, Royal (starter, fuel pump), Sanyo, Supertiger, Top Flite aircraft. Tower Hobbies: Charger, hydrometer, voltmeter, fuel pump, battery, fuels, tools, balsa assortment, heatgun, sealing iron. Others.

For Further Information: Catalog, $3.

THE TOY SOLDIER CO.

100 Riverside Dr.
New York, NY 10024
(212) 799-6348

Offers: Model toy soldiers of plastic and lead. Includes 600 figures from U.S. and foreign manufacturers, dating 1900 to the present (15mm to 70mm scales). Lead soldiers by Authenticast, Bastion, Benbros, Britains, Charbens, Cherilea, Citadel, Crescent, Dorset, Games Workshop, Grenadier, Heritage USA, Herrings, Imperial, Marlborough, Mignot, Minifigs, Ral Partha, S.A.E. Steadfast, Taylor & Barrett Timpo, Trophy, Tunstill, Wend-Al. Plastic soldiers by: Airfix, Atlantic, Auburn, Blue Box, Charbens, Cherilea, Crescent, Deetail, Elastolin, ESCI, Eyes Right, Giant, Hillco, Ideal, Marx, Merton, MPC, Rel, Remsea, Starlux, Superior, Swoppet, Timpo, others.

For Further Information: Send SASE for sample of monthly list; lead or plastics catalog, $7.50 each (specify lead or plastic).

TWELVE SQUARED

P.O. Box 21547
Eagan, MN 55121

Offers: Model aircraft kits—B-1, Bell, Northrop, Heinkel with injected kits and conversions: 1/444 scale and 1/72 scale models kits. Carries model stands for aircraft. Others.

For Further Information: Send SASE for illustrated catalog.

VANGUARD MODEL MARINE

P.O. Box 708, Station B
Ottawa, Ontario K1P 5P8 Canada

Offers: Ship drawings for Canadian warships and government vessels of many types.

For Further Information: Catalog, $2.

VANTEC

460 Casa Real Placa
Nipomo, CA 93444
805-929-5055

Offers: Radio control (18-channel) for boats, subs, robots, quarter scale, plus 6 servo channels for control surfaces, electric drive motors, proportional functions, and eight momentary on-off functions for guns, torpedos, horns, cranes, sub diving pumps; has 4-key on/key off channels for lights, etc.

For Further Information: Specifications, $2.

Accepts: MasterCard, Visa

VINYLWRITE CUSTOM LETTERING

16043 Tulsa St.
Granada Hills, CA 91344
(818) 363-7131

Offers: Model service, including custom lettering—pre-spaced, pre-aligned, custom computer cut in 3M premium cast vinyl, 2 mil thin. Choose from vertical or horizontal text in custom lengths, avaialable in 15 colors and 6 typestyles, including military block, slanted or upright text, ½-inch to 12 inches high.

For Further Information: Write or call for information and sample.

Model Making—Railroad

Also see Miniature Making, Model Making—General and other related categories.

AMERICA'S HOBBY CENTER, INC.
146 W. 22nd St.
New York, NY 10011

Offers: Model railroads, HO and N gauge: Locomotives, cars, coaches (ready-to-run) by Riverossi, Bachmann, MDC, Athearn, International Hobbies, Atlas, Con-Cor, others. Automatic switches, track, crossings, switch machines, couplers, switches, MRC power packs, dual packs also available.
For Further Information: Model Railroad brochures, 75¢.
See Also: Model Making—General

NOEL ARNOLD
84 Twin Arch Rd.
Washingtonville, NY 10992

Offers: Model railroads—the products of 200 manufacturers (locomotives, deisels, cabooses, and a variety of car types)—are available in kits and as parts and accessories, plus layout structures and materials.
For Further Information: Send 75¢ and business-size SASE for newsletter.
Discounts: "Offers discounts."

ASHLAND BARNS
990 Butler Creek
Ashland, OR 97520

Offers: Model railroads blueprints for 77 classic structure designs (barns, depots, minibarns, garages, others)—"simplified, economical."
For Further Information: Comprehensive catalog, $4.

BOOKBINDER'S "TRAINS UNLIMITED"
8420 Midland Pkwy.
Jamaica, NY 11432
(718) 657-2224

Offers: Model railroad, Lionel Standard and O gauge trains, including pre-war and post-war locomotives, diesels, 6464 box cars, accessories, operating cars, Hudsons, tinplate freights and passenger cars, track, switches, transformers and signals (from 1915 to 1985): American Flyer, Bascule Bridge, Lionel cars, N & W Vista Dome passenger cars, Southern RR, Union Pacific RR set, others, all in new, mint, like new, excellent or restored condition.

For Further Information: Illustrated catalog, $5.
Accepts: American Express

CABOOSE HOBBIES
500 S. Broadway
Denver, CO 80209
(303) 777-6766

Offers: Model railroad building kits in HO scale (by Builders in Scale), 150 building kits by Colorado Scale Models.
For Further Information: Send SASE for information.

CENTRAL VALLEY
1203 Pike Lane
Oceano, CA 93445

Offers: Model railroad kits in HO scale black, styrene plastic: Pratt truss bridges, bridge tie sections, girders, fences, railings, steps, ladders, end beams and brake shoes (detailed).
For Further Information: Contact dealer or send SASE for details.

CON-COR
P.O. Box 328
Bensenville, IL 60106

Offers: Model railroad car kits (metal) including 40-foot sliding door boxcars (of the 1940s to the 1960s), including Santa Fe, Southern Pacific, Baltimore & Ohio, Conrail, Southern Railway, SOO Line. N gauge locomotives (Great Northern, Heavy Pacific, Berkshire, Streamlined Hudson (with tender). Other cars and coaches available.
For Further Information: Contact a dealer or send SASE for list.

CUSTOM FINISHING
379 Tully Rd.
Orange, MA 01364

Offers: Model railroad parts in HO scale brass detail: Steam generator stack, high hood bells, side mount bells, modern cab signal box (Conrail, etc.), exhaust stack, RS handbrake, underframe chain guide sets, cooling coils, others.
For Further Information: Send business-size SASE for illustrated listing.

HOBBY SURPLUS SALES

P.O. Box 2170CS
New Britain, CT 06050
(203) 223-0600

Offers: Model railroad items: Lionel, American Flyer, HO, N gauge, LGB. Carries full lines of train repair parts. (Also has other models—R/C, plastic and wood—and model accessories.) "Free shipping in U.S.A. with order."
For Further Information: 128-page catalog, $1.

INTERNATIONAL HOBBY CORP.

350 E. Tioga St.
Philadelphia, PA 19134
(215) 426-ATSF

Offers: Model railroad structures/buildings: IHC carnival series (HO scale carousel and ferris wheel, plus motorizing kits), HO Scale 5 pack gingerbread houses in HO, N or O scale kits. O Scale Pola HO and N scale building kits (block of buildings, antique shop/home, old-time bank, brewery, 3 buildings, pickle factory). HO and O scale model trains, kits by Rivarossi. Model trees—over 15 types—by IHC. Others.
For Further Information: Contact dealer, or order catalogs; IHC catalog ($3.98), Preiser catalog ($7.98), Rivarossi Catalog, all scales ($9.98), parts catalog/Scratch Builders Bible, ($9.98), parts price list ($1.98), ROCO 1:87, HO Military Miniatures Catalog ($3.98). Send SASE for Rivarossi list or HO and N Scale Structures list.

JEFF'S DECAL CO.

1747 Selby Ave.
St. Paul, MN 55104
(612) 646-5069

Offers: Custom decals for all models in sets of 25 plus, matches type styles from any sample, special quality mixed inks available; "free estimates, lowest prices."
For Further Information: Send SASE or call for details, estimates.

KAR-LINE MODEL RAILROAD PRODUCTS

Rt. 1, P.O. Box 7
Stanardsville, VA 22973

Offers: Model railroads in 160 lines; never-lube trucks, couplers; kits or RTR in HO scale.
For Further Information: List, 35¢ or free with business-size SASE.

KEN'S TRAINS

P.O. Box 360
Babson Park, MA 02157

Offers: N scale model trains with New England road names (custom-painted). Line of products from all major manufacturers, including Kato, Green Max, Tomix, others.

For Further Information: Send $1 for list (refundable).
Discounts: "Good prices."
Accepts: MasterCard, Visa

KRATVILLE PUBLICATIONS

2566 Farnam St.
Omaha, NE 68131

Offers: Railroad books including *Steam, Steel & Limiteds* (golden age, 1907-1947); *THE CHALLENGERS*—the story of UP's 4-6-6-4 locomotive; *Motive Power of The Union Pacific* (6th edition), a motive power book covering steam, diesel and electric locomotives; *Union Pacific Streamliners*, a history (1934-1972) of steam powered Forty-Niner and Treasure Island Specials; *Big Boy* the composite, complete story of the world's largest steam locomotive, the UP's 4-8-8-4's. Most books offered have hundreds of photos. Others.
For Further Information: Send SASE for list.

LOCOMOTIVE WORKSHOP

RFD 3, P.O. Box 211-B-1
Englishtown, NJ 07726

Offers: Model railroad economy 0-6-0 kits in O scale brass, plus scale and highrail. Also carries a wide range of O scale kits of Athearn, Lobaugh and Loco Works parts for steam operation.
For Further Information: Send business-size SASE for current newsletter.

MADISON HARDWARE CO.

105 E. 23rd St.
New York, NY 10010
(212) 777-1111

Offers: Old, original Lionel repair parts for model railroads, including engines and cars, plus railroad accessories, figures, parts and others. Carries a full line of HO, N and LGB gauge items.
For Further Information: Send SASE with inquiry or description, including unit number on which part is to be used.

MANTUA METAL PRODUCTS CO., INC.

P.O. Box 10
Woodbury Heights, NJ 08097
(609) 853-0300

Offers: HO gauge model railroad engines, rolling stock and sets, including a series of steam locomotive kits and 25 ready-to-runs—5 diesel locomotives, streamliner and railroad cars (baggage, room, diner, vista-dome observation, combines, coach). Vintage cars include combines, passenger, box, horse, water, log and cabooses. Freight car kits include gondola, flat, hopper, tank, steel refrigerator, steel box, wood stock, boom tender, operating floodlight, Vanderbilt and other tenders, operating crane and covered gondolas. Also carries train sets, track, signals and people. (Also has sporting goods and games.)

For Further Information: Contact dealer, or catalog, $2.

MASTER CREATIONS
P.O. Box 1378
Chino Valley, AZ 86323
(602) 636-5313

Offers: HO scale model railroad structures kits including Grand Hotel with handmade components, metal castings, wood trims, dry transfers, posters, instructions and others. Manufacturer.

For Further Information: Contact dealer, or send SASE for information

WARREN MATT
E. 1489, Highway 54
Waupaca, WI 54981

Offers: Model railroad cabooses, gondolas, hoppers and some steam locomotives, plus kits by Athearn and parts, including cowcatchers, smoke box fronts and others.

For Further Information: List, $2.

O-CAR CO.
P.O. Box 4345
Bangor, PA 18013

Offers: O scale model railroad — full line of traction equipment, trucks, car body details, cars, hardware, finishing kits, others.

For Further Information: Contact dealer, or 65¢ SASE for details.

P & D HOBBY SHOP
31902 Groesbeck
Fraser, MI 48026
(313) 296-6116

Offers: Model railroad components, including conversion for Weaver RS-3, early Weaver RS units and RS-4/5 conversion kits. Parts and parts kits with components and instructions and RS and FA parts are available. Parts include windshield wipers, headlights, flag pole holders, market lights, stacks, steam vents, grills, horns, marker lights, fans, others. Carries O scale model railroad locomotives and cars (40-foot box cars, others).

For Further Information: O Scale list, send business-size SASE with 85¢ stamps.

Accepts: MasterCard, Visa

RAIL ROAD PROGRESS
P.O. Box 233
Gibbsboro, NJ 08026

Offers: HO hopper model railroad car kits (29 styles with lengths, heights, number of panels and types of peaks for most common hopper car users). Manufacturer.

For Further Information: Send SASE for brochure.

RAILROAD BOOK NEWSLETTER
P.O. Box 684
Anoka, MN 55303

Offers: Railroad books, including *Milwaukee Road* — narrow gauge lines, Milwaukee rails and road east, road west, the decline and fall, electrics and Hiawatha story; *Great Northern* — history; *Northern Pacific* — NP diesels, NP steam, Northern Pacific views, Class A, Duluth Union Depot; *Chicago Burlington & Quincy* — high plains route, Highline scrapbook, Burlington route across Iowa; *Chicago Great Western* — complete story, corn belt route, Iowa in merger decade, pencil drawings of CGW depots; *Chicago & North Western* — rails, C & NW power, NW motive power, others.

For Further Information: Send SASE for list.

RAILS 'N SHAFTS
P.O. Box 300
Laurys Station, PA 18059
(215) 799-2530

Offers: Books on America's railroads, including B & O Steam, Canadian national railways, Chessie, C & NW power, Chicago's trains, Colorado rail, North Shore, diesel locomotive rosters, electric locomotive plans, Grand Trunk Western Guide to Tourist Railroads, Pennsylvania, Kansas City Southern, Katy railroad, Lehigh and New England, MR Cyclopedia, Milwaukee electrics and rails, N & W, New York Central, Grand Central, Norfolk & Western, Old Dominion, passenger trains, cabooses, Mexican railroads, Red Arrow, St. Clair, Santa Fe Trails, Seaboard, Southern Pacific, trolleys, traction classics, Union Pacific and others.

For Further Information: Send SASE for catalog.

Accepts: MasterCard, Visa

THE RED CABOOSE
16 W. 45th St., 4th Floor
New York, NY 10036
(212) 575-0155

Offers: Model railroad trains and accessories, including American and foreign prototypes, in N, HO and other scales by Kadee, Atlas, Tivakato, Rivarossi, Mantua, Stewart, Bachmann, Magnuson, Peco, Shinohara, Tichy, Walthers, Kibri, VollmerFaller, Patal (buildings), Fleischman and Con-Cor. Also offers European trains in all scales. Carries LGB and O scale, HO and N scale brass, plus Foredom equipment, Paasche and Badger airbrush sets, Contact resistance soldering units and books. Buys toy trains.

For Further Information: Send SASE or call with specific inquiry.

Accepts: MasterCard, Visa

RESTORATION TRAIN
RD 1, Queensboro Manor, P.O. Box 390
Gloversville, NY 12078

Offers: Line of model railroad restoration parts.
For Further Information: Parts catalog, $15.

RON'S BOOKS
P.O. Box 714
Harrison, NY 10528

Offers: Railroad books on Baja California railways, railroad bridges, Bedford Guilford, B & O steam, Dawn of the Diesel age, Detroit Toledo & Ironton, Erie railroad, E-Units, Interurbans, locos of the Duluth Missable & Iron Range, cyclopedias (steam, diesel), Milwaukee electrics, NP, N&W, NYC, Penn Central, Pennsylvania railroad, PRR, Tri-state steam railroads, Short Line, SP, Sante Fe, Seaboard, trolleys, Union Station, others.
For Further Information: Send business-size SASE for complete list.
Discounts: "Discount prices."

SIGNS OF OLDEN TIMES
P.O. Box 62
Sebastopol, CA 95473

Offers: Over 575 dry transfer lettering sets for model railroads. Carries a full line of scratch building supplies in N, HO, S and O scales.
For Further Information: 58-page catalog, $3.

SUMPTER VALLEY DEPOT
135 NW Greeley Ave.
Bend, OR 97701
(503) 382-3413

Offers: Model railroad cars including O scale engines, cabooses and cars (tank, box, stock, water tank, reefers, others).
For Further Information: Free brass list.

TOY TRAIN HEAVEN
P.O. Box 24
Hughesville, PA 17737

Offers: Model railroad trains, kits and sets: Atlas HO engines, cars, bridges kits, piers, girders, degree crossings, terminals and joiners, track assortment, remote snap switches, others. Carries Model Rectifier HO engines, Mantua RTR HO team locomotives, Athearn HO diesels, Kadee Trucks, couplers and accessories, including Kadee N Gauge Magne-Matic coupler conversions kits, N scale steam locomotives, Atlas N gauge diesels, Kato N Scale trains, Atlas N Scale track, joiners, pier sets and girders, bridges, degree crossings, switches, others. Also carries MRC HO power packs.

For Further Information: Send SASE with requests for information.
Accepts: MasterCard, Visa

TRACKSIDE SPECIALTIES
P.O. Box 460
Manheim, PA 17545

Offers: HO and O scale scratch model railroad builder's items: Drivers, rods, valve gear, cabs, pilots, boiler fronts, lost wax parts, Puffing Billy parts and cars.
For Further Information: List, $1 (refundable).

THE TRAIN MASTER LTD.
P.O. Box 5208
Albany, NY 12205
(518) 489-4777

Offers: N Scale model railroad items, including kits and cars (freight, passenger and box), turntables, locomotives, track, switches and many other parts, model structures and scenery, of major manufacturers: Acme, AMM, Aim, AMI, Arbour, B-R, Bachmann, Bowser, Brawa, Caboose Ind., DMK, EKO, Gloor, Green Max, Faller, Cork, Heljan, Herpa, Kadee, Kato, Kibri, Labelle, Lifelike, Magnuson, Midwest, ML, MLR, Model Dynamics, Model Rectifier, MZZ, MJ Int., Roco, Walthers, others.
For Further Information: N scale price list/catalog, $2 ($1 refundable).

TRAIN WORLD
751 McDonald Ave.
Brooklyn, NY 11218
(718) 436-7072

Offers: Model railroad trains, including LGB collectors' cars, power packs and electronics, box cars and gondolas. Carries over 90 buildings, replacement parts, starter sets with track and transformer, locomotives, street cars, passenger and freight cars, accessories, and electrical items. Also carries Aristo Craft G scale model buildings, Mantua locomotives and cars, plus Lionel releases, engines and cabooses, rolling stock, operating cars including classics, standard gauge classics, collector sets, cars and others. Bowser and Rivarossi trains are available including locomotives, cars, kits and sets. Athearn cars, MRC power packs, plus various operating accessories are also available.
For Further Information: Send SASE for list.
Discounts: "May have closeouts."
Accepts: MasterCard, Visa

VALLEY MODEL TRAINS
3 Fulton St.
Wappingers Falls, NY 12590
(914) 297-7511

Offers: Model railroad building kits in all scales (Z to LBG) and by most manufacturers, including Design Preservation Models series 2 kits for buildings, stores, garages, packing houses and others. Also offers Faller buildings and others. Carries HO scale model automobiles including Cadillac, Buick, Bentley models, Rolls Royce Silver Cloud, Volvo, Mercedes and others.

For Further Information: Send SASE with 45¢ postage for newsletter and list.

WOODLAND SCENICS
P.O. Box 98
Linn Creek, MO 65052

Offers: Model scenics, including all formulated to coordinate colors, turf, and a variety of foilage and lichen in realistic colors. Carries decals — model graphics for letters, lines, numbers (any scale), dry transfers with authentic advertising, posters, signs and railroad heralds (full color).

For Further Information: Contact a dealer or send 4 stamps for catalog.

WORLD OF TRAINS
10518 Metropolitan Ave.
Forest Hills, NY 11375
(718) 520-9700

Offers: Model railroad trains, kits, accessories and parts by Gargraves (track), Lionel (trains, track), LGB locomotives, caboose and cars (passenger, platform gondola, box, flat, hopper, tank, others), plus Bachmann steam locomotives and diesels (HO), Atlas (HO trackage), Bachmann N scale locomotives and N Gauge locomotives, HO and N Gauge powerpacks, and Bachmann N Scale buildings. Also offers transformers and tracks, pre-war and post-war trains and accessories. Buys train collections (old Lionel, American Flyer, M.P.C. and store inventories). Repairs all 027.0 and standard gauges.

For Further Information: Catalog, $2.
Discounts: "May run specials."
Accepts: Discover, MasterCard and Visa

YE OLDE HUFF 'N PUFF
P.O. Box 53
Pennsylvania Furnace, PA 16865

Offers: Wood Craftsman model railroad kits in a range of scales, including HO (freight cars, structures, detail parts), HOn3 (mine train kits and freight cars), S (freight cars, detail parts, figures), On3 freight cars, O freight cars and detail parts. Models available include AG, LW, Sugar Pine, Main Line and Silver Streak. Manufacturer.

For Further Information: Contact dealer. HO = HOn3 scale catalog, $1; S scale list, SASE; O Scale Catalog, $1; On3 scale list, SASE.

Mold Crafts

Includes Cake, Candles, Concrete, Paper, Plaster, Plastics. Also see Ceramics, Metalworking, Sculpture and Modeling and related categories.

AMERICAN ART CLAY CO., INC.
4717 W. 16th St.
Indianapolis, IN 46222
(317) 244-6871

Offers: Molding and modeling supplies: Sculptamold (clay/plaster/papier-mâché), instant papier-mâché, casting compound, carving wax and Superdough modeling compound. Carries modeling tools, Mix-A-Mold (mix powder with water to make reproduction molds in minutes; fill with casting medium), CreaStone (stone-like material, for casting), and Rub 'N Buff wood finishes.
For Further Information: Free information packet.
See Also: General Craft Supplies, Ceramics and Metalworking

BARKER ENTERPRISES, INC.
15106 10th Ave. SW
Seattle, WA 98166
(206) 244-1870

Offers: Candle-making supplies: Dyes, waxes, additives, releases, glaze. Candle molds (plastic, metal) in over 650 shapes: Tapered, novelties, holiday, 2-part and others in a variety of sizes.
For Further Information: Catalog, $2.

BOYD'S
P.O. Box 6232-C
Augusta, GA 30916

Offers: Formulas for mold and modeling materials (from home ingredients) with directions for over 16 air dry and other "clays," mold-making and casting materials, candle molds (also glues, paints), plus hints.
For Further Information: Booklet, $6.

CANDLECHEM CO.
P.O. Box 705
Randolph, MA 02368
(617) 986-7541

Offers: Line of candle-making chemicals, scents, dyes, pigments, perfume and essential oils and others.
For Further Information: Free catalog.

Discounts: Sells wholesale to legitimate businesses.

CASTINGS
P.O. Box 915001
Longwood, FL 32791
(407) 869-6565

Offers: Casting equipment and supplies for creating toy soldiers, Civil War figures/horses, cannons and weapons, cowboys, Indians, and cavalry men, plus action soldiers of WWI and WWII, aircraft, medieval horses/riders, Napoleonic foot soldiers, artillery and riders/horses. Also offers a German marching band mold, carousel molds, chess set molds (fantasy, Waterloo and King Richard's Court) and winter village molds (carolers, Santa, snowman, skaters, boy and girl on sleds, street lamp). Carries paint kits for mold sets, complete introductory starter kits, casting metals and instruction booklets.
For Further Information: Product information, $1.
Discounts: Quantity discounts.

CASTOLITE
4915 Dean
Woodstock, IL 60098

Offers: Liquid plastics for casting, coating, fiberglassing, reproducing and embedding, plus additives and fillers.
For Further Information: Catalog, $2.

CEMENTEX LATEX CORP.
480 Canal St.
New York, NY 10013
(212) 226-5832

Offers: Natural latex molding compounds: High solids type with medium viscosity (brushable or sprayable) to cast plaster, Portland cement and some waxes; also carries a pre-vulcanized type. Stocks latex for casting hollow articles (pour into plaster mold—when used with filler, very hard articles may be obtained), plus 2-part RTV polysulfide rubber for flexible molds (pourable for casting plaster, cement and others). Manufactures and compounds natural and synthetic latex materials.
For Further Information: Send SASE for complete information.

COASTAL ENTERPRISES
60 Bretonian Dr.
Brick, NJ 08723
(908) 477-7948

Offers: Lead soldier molds and mold making and casting supplies—full line. Also offers castings, collectibles and hard to find items.
For Further Information: Catalog, $5.

CRAFT TIME
211 S. State College Blvd., #341
Anaheim, CA 92806

Offers: Plastercraft figures—a full line, ready-to-paint, many with instructions and color guide—including adults, children, houses, scenery, animals, others.
For Further Information: Catalog, $2 (refundable).

CREATIVE PAPERCLAY CO.
1800 S. Robertson Blvd., Suite 907
Los Angeles, CA 90035
(310) 839-0466

Offers: Paperclay modeling material, molds for masks, doll heads, others, plus kits and books.
For Further Information: Send SASE for details.
Discounts: Allows discounts to teachers and institutions; sells wholesale to legitimate businesses.

KEMPER MANUFACTURING CO.
13595 12th St.
Chino, CA 91710

Offers: Cake and candy-making decorator sets. Tools: Flower and leaf cutting, rollers, mini ribbon sculpting, detail carving, bud-setter, others.

For Further Information: Contact dealer or write for literature.
See Also: General Craft Supplies

VAN DYKE'S
P.O. Box 278
Woonsocket, SD 57385

Offers: Molding: Plaster, Hydro-cal, Hydrostone, rock putty, resin putty, Sculpall. Also offers polymer finish kit, scenery resin, fiberglass cloth, chopped strand mat, strands, polyester resin, talc, whiting, color paste and gel wax. Fillers: Granulated cork, paper pulp. Mold-making materials: Silicone rubber, polymold, latex, epoxy putty sticks, plastic resin dyes. Flocking gun, adhesive, airbrush sets, compressors, spray guns, booth, finishes, glues, Dremel MotoToolsets, woodworking and upholstery tools and materials also available.
For Further Information: Catalog, $1.
Discounts: Quantity discounts.
Accepts: MasterCard, Visa
See Also: Furniture Making and Upholstery and Woodworking

WILTON ENTERPRISES
Woodridge, IL 60517

Offers: Cake and candy decorating materials, supplies, tools and equipment including cake pans, sheets, specialty shapes, accessories, special occasion supplies, bags for decorating, cookie cutters and other cutters, cake novelties, decorating sets and icing colors. Also offers candy-making molds and supplies.
For Further Information: Contact dealer or send SASE for information.

Nature Crafts

Also see General Craft Supplies, Basketry and Seat Weaving, Miniature Making, Model Making, Fabrics and Trims and other related categories.

ART BY GOD
3705 Biscayne Blvd.
Miami, FL 33137

Offers: Ostrich eggs, by six and up lots.
For Further Information: Send SASE for price list.

ASHCOMBE FARM & GREENHOUSE
906 Grantham Rd.
Mechanicsburg, PA 17055
(717) 766-7611

Offers: Dried flowers: Silver King artemisia, crested celosia, globe amaranth and others.
For Further Information: Send SASE for full information.
Discounts: Sells wholesale.

BENJANE ARTS
P.O. Box 298
W. Hempstead, NY 11552

Offers: Assorted shells, single and in sets, plus shell craft ideas booklet, supplies and accessories.
For Further Information: Catalog, $5.

CADILLAC MOUNTAIN FARM
4481 Porter Gulch Rd.
Aptos, CA 95003
(408) 476-9595

Offers: Dried flowers, herbs, exotics, supplies.
For Further Information: Send SASE for list.
Discounts: Sells wholesale.

COUNTREE
4573 Blender
Middleville, MI 49333
(616) 795-7132

Offers: Dried flowers: Silver King artemisia, baby's breath, others.
For Further Information: Free price list.

COUNTRY GRAPEVINE
2915 Martinsville Rd.
Martinsville, OH 45146
(513) 685-2706

Offers: Grapevine forms; wreaths in round, heart and oval shapes; plus swags, arches, baskets, wall pockets and trees.
For Further Information: Free price list.

DODY LYNESS CO.
7336 Berry Hill Dr.
Palos Verdes Peninsula, CA 90274
(310) 377-7040

Offers: Potpourri supplies: 36 fragrance oils, fixatives, dried blossoms, herbs, spices (including allspice, chamomile, coriander, frankincense, myrrh, rose hips, sassafras, tilia and others). Carries dried flowers (for wreaths, candle rings, others): Pansies, roses, others. Pressed flowers, quail eggs and books also available.
For Further Information: Send SASE for list.
Discounts: Quantity discounts; sells wholesale.

DOROTHY BIDDLE SERVICE
P.O. Box 900
Greeley, PA 18425
(717) 226-3239

Offers: Flower drying/arranging supplies/equipment: Preservatives, floral clays, foam, picks, pins, wires, tapes, snips, flower presses, holders, beach pebbles, marble chips, moss, adhesives, silica gel. Also carries preserved flat butterflies, ferns, feathers, garden tools, accessories and books.
For Further Information: Catalog, 50¢.
Discounts: Quantity discounts; allows discounts to teachers and institutions; sells wholesale to legitimate businesses.

DRIED NATURALS OF OKLAHOMA
Rt. 1, P.O. Box 847
Ramona, OK 74061

Offers: Assortment of 10 dried weeds, grasses and cultivated material (some bleached and dyed).
For Further Information: Send SASE for price information.

EARTH HEALING ARTS
P.O. Box 162635
Sacramento, CA 95816
(916) 878-2441

Offers: Potpourri blends and supplies, plus herbs and herb blends. (Also has skin care and gift items.)
For Further Information: Catalog, $1 (refundable).

EVERLASTINGS
20220 U.S. 6
Milford, IN 46542
(219) 831-5763

Offers: Line of dried flowers, preserved greens and ferns in bunches. Also carries heather ti trees, hydrangea and peonies.
For Further Information: Send SASE for price list.

When making potpourri, saturate the fixative (e.g., orris root, oakmoss, vetiver, etc.) with the fragrance oil, then mix this in with the assorted petals and herbs. Note: Cut fixatives look nicer in potpourri than powdered fixatives—no dust.
— Tom Thumb Workshops

FLORAL DECOR
P.O. Box 111261
Tacoma, WA 98411
(206) 857-3041

Offers: Naturals: Line of wreaths, arches, swags, others.
For Further Information: Free catalog.

GAILANN'S FLORAL CATALOG
821 W. Atlantic St.
Branson, MO 65616

Offers: Full line of floral supplies. Dried flowers: Roses, larkspur, German statice, heather. Also carries holly wreath bases, ribbons, corsage boxes.
For Further Information: Catalog, $1.
Discounts: "Also sells wholesale—inquire, with resale number."

HERB SHOPPE
215 W. Main St.
Greenwood, IN 46142
(317) 889-4395

Offers: Bulk herbs, potpourri supplies, essential oils, herb bunches and wreaths, others.
For Further Information: Catalog and newsletter, $3 (refundable).

HOFFMAN HATCHERY
Gratz, PA 17030

Offers: Eggs (blown): Goose, guinea, duck, turkey, quail, pheasant—variety of sizes.
For Further Information: Send SASE for price list.

HUNDLEY RIDGE FARM
P.O. Box 253
Perry Park, KY 40363
(502) 484-5922

Offers: Dried flowers and a line of dried herbs including Silver King artemisia, yarrow, blue salvia, sinuata statice, feverfew, globe amaranth.
For Further Information: Send SASE for price list.

J & T IMPORTS
143 S. Cedros, # F
Solana Beach, CA 92075
(619) 481-9781

Offers: Dried/preserved flowers/naturals: Pepper grass, capsia, baby's breath, eucalyptus, pennyroyal, moss, raffia, lycarpodium, larkspur, straws, branches, wreaths, natural twig products, herbs. Also carries floral supplies, decoratives, ribbons and others.
For Further Information: Send SASE for list.
Store Location: Yes
Discounts: Quantity discounts; allows discounts to teachers and institutions; sells wholesale to legitimate businesses.

JURGEN CRAFT PRODUCTS
1202 Chestnut, #2
Everett, WA 98201
(800) 735-7248

Offers: "Flower Preserve" preservative.
For Further Information: Call or write for information.

LILY OF THE VALLEY
3969 Fox Ave.
Minerva, OH 44657
(216) 862-3920

Offers: Over 740 species of herbal plants, dried herbs—perennials, scented species, everlastings, rare and unusuals (including passion vine, carob), others.
For Further Information: Plant and product list, $1 (refundable).
Store Location: Yes
Discounts: Quantity discounts; sells wholesale to legitimate businesses.

LIRA CO.
209 Renwood Circle
Lafayette, LA 70503

Offers: Potpourri blends, ingredients, including essential oils, extracts, spices, herbs (also teas, others).
For Further Information: Catalog, $1 (refundable).
Discounts: Quantity discounts.

LONG CREEK PRODUCTS
P.O. Box 900
Dallas, NC 28034
(800) 542-8734

Offers: Natural wreaths: Straw, birdseed, pine, moss, potpourri, others. Also carries excelsior, pine needles, straw bales. Adhesives, pick machines and glue guns also available.
For Further Information: Call for product list.
Accepts: MasterCard, Visa

MEADOW EVERLASTINGS
16464 Shabbona Rd.
Malta, IL 60150
(815) 825-2539

Offers: 30 plus dried flower/plants and pods: Unusuals and teasels, thistle, yarrow, sea holly, nigella, poppy pods, natural wreaths, plus arches, bunches, swags, bouquets. Carries 18 herbal potpourri ingredients, blends, oils, others.
For Further Information: Catalog, $2 (refundable).
Store Location: Yes
Discounts: Quantity discounts.

Misting dried flowers and herbs with water from a spray bottle before use makes them less brittle and easier to work with.

—Meadow Everlastings

NATURE'S EVERLASTINGS
1005 E. Green St.
Pasadena, CA 91106
(818) 795-9260

Offers: Line of dried flowers, wreaths, supplies.
For Further Information: Send SASE for list.
Discounts: Sells wholesale.

NATURE'S FINEST
P.O. Box 10311, Dept. CSS
Burke, VA 22009

Offers: Over 70 dry herbs and potpourri ingredients. Other dry ingredients: Heliptopin crystals, sea salt, caucarina cones, wood chips, talc, others. Carries over 115 essential oils/fragrances, plus reviving solution, simmer dry mixes and oils, plus fixatives, pomander kits, rolling mixes, scent rings, pressed flowers, sea salt, talc, wood chips, styrax, bath mixes and fizzles. Also offers a variety of containers: Bags, acrylic boxes, bottles, baskets. Ornaments, stencils and rubber stamps are also available.
For Further Information: Catalog, $2.50 (refundable).
Discounts: Quantity discounts; sells wholesale to legitimate businesses.

NATURE'S HERB CO.
P.O. Box 40604
San Francisco, CA 94140
(415) 474-2756

Offers: Over 350 bulk spices and herbs, plus potpourri ingredients in bulk quantities ("1- to 2,000-pound prices"); all products milled and blended in-house. Also has bulk teas and powdered botanicals, and bulk gelatin capsules, and packaged teas and spices.
For Further Information: Send SASE for list.
Discounts: Sells wholesale.

NATURE'S HOLLER
RR 1, P.O. Box 29-AA
Omaha, AR 72662
(501) 426-5489

Offers: Naturals: Wild grapevine curls, bulk, wreaths (variety) buttonbush balls, teasel, cone flowers, corn tassels, sycamore bark/balls, sweetgum, cockleburrs, locust, magnolia. Pods available include okra, milkweed, ninebark. Also offers moss, lichens, wheat, acorns, hickory nuts, bamboo, locust thorns/branches, and a variety of cones, driftwood and slabs. Carries woodware, puzzles, shelves, cutouts and knobs.
For Further Information: Catalog, $2.
Discounts: Quantity discounts.

OUR NEST EGG
205 S. 5th
Mapleton, IA 51034
(712) 882-1940

Offers: Natural eggs: Ostrich, rhea, emu, goose, duck. Egg decorating materials: Line of pearl and metal ornaments/findings. Tools: Markers, cutters, drills, marker-units. Supplies: Braids, ribbons, rhinestones, mirrors, adhesives, finishes, miniatures, hinges, hinge rings, brass tubes and rods. Carries 65 plus egg stands and books.
For Further Information: Send SASE for information; catalog, $4.
Discounts: Quantity discounts.

PEACEFUL ACRES
Rt. 1, P.O. Box 580
Checotah, OK 74426

Offers: Line of botanicals, herbs, spices for crafts, plus silica gel, preservatives, essential and fragrance oils.
For Further Information: Catalog, $1.

PRIDE'S FARM
Rt. 2, P.O. Box 389
East Lebanon, ME 04027

Offers: Line of pressed flowers (apply to most surfaces).
For Further Information: Send SASE for list.

SAN FRANCISCO HERB CO.
250 14th St.
San Francisco, CA 94103

Offers: Full line of herbs, potpourri. 65 potpourri ingredients: Allspice, apple pieces, cedarwood chips, chamomile, cinnamon, coriander, feverfew, ginger root, hibiscus, lavender, lemon verbena, oak moss, orange peel, pine cones, rosebuds, rosemary, rose hips, sage, sassafras, statice flowers, yarrow, others. Also offers 4 potpourri mixes, 29 mix recipes, 6 simmering potpourri recipes, 7 sachet recipes. Carries 24 fragrance oils: Frankincense, exotic spices, floral bouquet, and others. 60 plus botanicals also available.
For Further Information: Free catalog.
Discounts: Sells wholesale.

SHAW MUDGE AND CO.
P.O. Box 1375
Stamford, CT 06904
(203) 327-3132

Offers: Complete line of fragances for gift manufacturing and processing. Custom design and stock compounds available. Manufacturer.
For Further Information: Contact dealer, or send SASE for information.

SIMPLY DE-VINE
654 Kendall Rd.
Cave Junction, OR 97523

Offers: 15 grapevine wreaths: Teardrops, heart, oval, matted back, others. Carries baskets, bundles and cane wreaths. Manufacturer. Special orders service.
For Further Information: Catalog, $1 (refundable).
Discounts: Quantity discounts.

T & D FEATHERS
P.O. Box 428
Olathe, CO 81425

Offers: Assortment of feathers and furs for craft use.
For Further Information: Send SASE for information.

When crushing whole spices for potpourri, try using two bricks. Place the spices on the long edge of one brick and grind with the other brick.

—Nature's Finest

TEXTILE ENTERPRISES, INC.
216 Main St.
P.O. Box 154
Whitesburg, GA 30185
(404) 834-2094

Offers: Dried and painted floral products, Spanish moss, excelsior, wreaths, others. Floral supplies: Foams, wires, tapes, pins. Natural materials: Variety of cones, pods, lotus, grapevine. Wreaths: Statice, twig, wheat, wood based, gypsophia, others. Bells, beads, novelties, baskets.
For Further Information: Catalogs, $5.
Store Location: Yes
Discounts: Quantity discounts; sells wholesale to legitimate businesses.
See Also: Macrame

TOM THUMB WORKSHOPS
P.O. Box 357
Mappsville, VA 23407
(804) 824-3507

Offers: Natural supplies. Dried flowers: Statice, star, tansy, wheat, wild iris, sugarbush, eucalyptus, coxcomb. Cones and pods: Lotus, nigella, teasel, others. Potpourri mixes: Woods, forest, rose, seaside, Tahitian, others. Patterns: Ornaments, dolls. Containers: Boxes, jars, bags. Supplies: Cholla wood, twist paper and other ribbons, floral items, moss, silica, foam. Carries wire, straw and moss wreaths, a full line of spices, herbs and essential oils and books.
For Further Information: Catalog, $1.
Store Location: Yes
Discounts: Quantity discounts.
Accepts: MasterCard, Visa

THE ULTIMATE HERB & SPICE SHOPPE
111 Azalea
P.O. Box 395
Duenweg, MO 64841
(417) 782-0457

Offers: Over 500 bulk herbs/spices, 70 potpourri blends, plus supplies.
For Further Information: Catalog, $2.
Store Location: Yes

VAL'S NATURALS
P.O. Box 832
Kathleen, FL 33849
(813) 858-8991

Offers: Dried miniature roses, pepper berries and other naturals.
For Further Information: Free catalog and price list.
Discounts: Sells wholesale.

Oddities

BOTTLE CAPS UNLIMITED
22533 S. Vermont Ave.
Torrance, CA 90502
(310) 320-6034

Offers: Bottle caps: All popular soda brands (for jewelry, fashions, novelties, others.)
For Further Information: Send SASE for details.

COMMONS
P.O. Box 5012
Central Point, OR 97502

Offers: Modern arrowhead-making techniques.
For Further Information: Send SASE for full details.

HEATH CO.
P.O. Box 8589
Benton Harbor, MI 49023

Offers: Heathkit electronics kits (3 skill levels), including electronic equipment, security and lighting products, weather stations, marine products (sonar, loran, others), clocks, amateur radios, computers, oscilloscopes, DMMs, PC Logic analyzer, plus radio control model cars, planes, boats. Also offers systems trainers, home-study courses in basics, digital tech, electro-optics and others.

For Further Information: Write for catalog.

KELLER ACOUSTICS
P.O. Box 1921
Amherst, NY 14226

Offers: Plans for custom-built speaker systems.
For Further Information: Send SASE for details.

TATE ENTERPRISES UNLIMITED, INC.
P.O. Box 44003
Aurora, CO 80044
(303) 755-5591

Offers: Kits/plans for you-make Atlati spear throwers (ice age spear-weapons) and accessories. Carries Primitive skills books and spears, including target and hunting types.
For Further Information: Free brochure.
Discounts: Quantity discounts; allows discounts to teachers and institutions; sells wholesale to legitimate businesses.

WAWCO INC.
P.O. Box 1026
Ballwin, MO 63022

Offers: Plans/manual for constructing a Halloween Haunted House (to be assembled/disassembled/stored).
For Further Information: Send SASE for full details.

Paints, Finishes and Adhesives

Also see Artist's Supplies, Tole and Decorative Crafts, and categories throughout the book.

ART ESSENTIALS OF NEW YORK LTD.
3 Cross St.
Suffern, NY 10901
(800) 283-5323

Offers: Gold leaf, genuine and composition, sheets and rolls (22 kt patent, 23 kt patent, 22 and 23 kt glass type, white gold, French pale gold, lemon gold, gold metal or composition types). Also offers silver leaf. Supplies: Gilding size and gilding knife, burnishing clay, and other tools and brushes. Carries technical books.
For Further Information: Free catalog.
Discounts: Quantity discounts; allows discounts to teachers, institutions and professionals.

BENBOW CHEMICAL PACKAGING, INC.
935 E. Hiawatha Blvd.
Syracuse, NY 13208
(315) 474-8236

Offers: Fezandie & Sperrle dry pigments for artist's colors.
For Further Information: Free price list.

CREATEX COLORS
14 Airport Park Rd.
East Granby, CT 06026
(203) 653-5505, (800) 243-2712

Offers: Createx colors—non-toxic, water-based liquid dyes, textile paints, airbrush colors, marble colors and others. Manufacturer.
For Further Information: Free catalog.

CRESCENT BRONZE POWDER CO.
3400 N. Avondale Ave.
Chicago, IL 60618
(312) 529-2441

Offers: Metallic pigment colors (86) including over 28 gold shades. Phosphorescents, metallic paints and lacquers, plus glitters, diamond dust, glass tinsel, beads, bronze liquids (heat resistant) and finishes. Manufacturer.
For Further Information: Contact a dealer, or request free color card.

DELTA TECHNICAL COATINGS, INC.
2550 Pellissier Place
Whittier, CA 90601

Offers: Ceramcoat acrylics, fabric colors and fabric paints; Stencil Magic stencils and paints; and Home Decor stains and finishes. Also offers tempera poster markers, Shiva acrylics and Paintstik oil (solid form).
For Further Information: Contact a dealer, or send a SASE for details.
See Also: Batik and Dyeing and Fabric Decorating

THE DURHAM CO.
54 Woodland St.
Newburyport, MA 01950
(508) 465-3493

Offers: Gold leaf (hand beaten) including XX deep patent, glass and surface types.
For Further Information: Send SASE for full information.

GOLD LEAF & METALLIC POWDERS, INC.
74 Trinity Place, Suite 1807
New York, NY 10006
(212) 267-4900

Offers: Gold leaf—22 kt and 23 kt patent gold, glass gold, roll gold. Metallic powders.
For Further Information: Send SASE for full information.

ILLINOIS BRONZE
Lake Zurich, IL 60047
(312) 438-8201

Offers: Judy Martin's Country Colors water-base acrylics, water-base varnish/sealer, and soft pastel Country Colors. Gimme fabric colors: Glitters, Iridescents, Puffs, Dyes and others. Other colors also available. Manufacturer.
For Further Information: See your dealer, or send SASE for information.

SEPP LEAF PRODUCTS, INC.
381 Park Ave. S.
New York, NY 10016
(212) 683-2840

Offers: August Ruhl gold leaf (karat leaf) in variety of shades, plus LeFranc oil size and Gilder's tips. Also offers the instructional video; *Gold Leaf Basics*, with Kent H. Smith.

For Further Information: Contact your dealer or request free catalog. Write for technical data.

U.S. BRONZE POWDERS, INC.
Rt. 202, P.O. Box 31

Flemington, NJ 08822
(201) 782-5454

Offers: Metallic pigments and paints, silver lining paste, others.
For Further Information: Send SASE.

Paper Crafts and Paper Making

Also see General Craft Supplies, Artist's Supplies, and categories throughout the book.

BEE PAPER CO.
P.O. Box 2366
Wayne, NJ 07474

Offers: Aquabee plotter paper—for check plots, charts, graphs, etc., available in grades from economy bond to 100% rag vellum. Sold by sheets or rolls or cut to specifications.
For Further Information: Send SASE for complete information.

GERLACHS OF LECHA
P.O. Box 213
Emmaus, PA 18049

Offers: Paper-cutting supplies: Variety of papers, scissors, pattern packets and other designs.
For Further Information: Catalog, $2.25.

GOLD'S ARTWORKS, INC.
2100 N. Pine St.
Lumberton, NC 28358
(919) 739-9605, (800) 356-2306

Offers: Complete paper-making supplies/equipment: Cotton linter pulp in 5 grades. Also offers raffia, seagrass and abacai (hemp) by the pound. Carries Perma color dry pigments, Texicolor pearlized, plus paper-making kits, molds and deckles. Also carries synthetic cloths, felt, methylcellulose paste powder, jewelry findings, Sculptamold, Marbelex, hydrated pulp. Equipment: Garrett hydropulper/mixer, pulpsprayer, pulp buckets, vats, handwringer units. Books available.
For Further Information: Free catalog.
Store Location: Yes
Discounts: Quantity discounts.

GOOD STAMPS—STAMP GOODS
30901 Timberline Rd.
Willits, CA 95490
(707) 459-9124

Offers: Blank paper goods (14 colors) in business cards, postcards, giant tall and regular greeting cards (scored), book marks, envelopes, stationery. Also offers mixed scrap bag, "Stamper's Sampler," cut-out greeting cards (hearts, stars, trees) with envelopes and tags.

For Further Information: Send SASE for Paper Swatch Book.
Discounts: Quantity discounts.
See Also: Rubber Stamping and Stamp Making

LAKE CITY CRAFT CO.
Rt. 2, P.O. Box 637
Highlandville, MO 65669
(417) 587-3092

Offers: Quilling kits (papers, patterns for standard-size frames), including Honeycomb Posies, Magnetic Charmers, Hearts, Christmas motifs, quotes, announcements, alphabet sampler, floral bouquets and mini-designs. Papers: Over 25 colors and assortments, including parchment paper. Carries mini-shadowbox frames, quilling tools and accessories, plus miniature (1-inch scale) furniture and accessories kits.
For Further Information: Color catalog, $2.
Discounts: Sells wholesale to legitimate businesses.

QUILL-IT
P.O. Box 130
Elmhurst, IL 60126
(708) 834-5371

Offers: Quilling papers (full line of colors, widths), kits, tools, fringers, frames, paper snipping supplies, books.
For Further Information: Catalog, $1 (refundable).

SAX ARTS & CRAFTS
P.O. Box 51710
New Berlin, WI 53151

Offers: Arts/crafts supplies. Paper-making: Kits, vat, molds, felts, cotton linters, unbleached abaca pulp, methylcellulose, retention aid (for colors). Papers (in known brands): Drawing, construction (regular and large), sulphite, Color Kraft, backgrounds, plus plates, bags, Origami packs and papers; features include fadeless colors, corrugation, borders, doilies, precut puzzle sheets, fluorescents, gummed, neons, flint, cellophanes (and colors), crepe and streamers, metallics, tissue (and pomps squares kits), Mod Podge art paper tape, velour, printing types, etching. Offers 11 rice papers—3 pads, 2 assortments—plus boards, scratchboards and books.
For Further Information: Catalog, $3 (refundable).
Discounts: Quantity discounts; allows discounts to teachers and institutions; sells wholesale to businesses.
Accepts: American Express, MasterCard, Visa
See Also: Artist's Supplies and General Craft Supplies

Photography

Also see Artist's Supplies and other related categories.

A & I CAMERA CLASSICS LTD.
2 World Financial Center
New York, NY 10281
(212) 786-4695

Offers: Cameras/equipment: Canon, Nikon, Olympus, Pentax, Konica, Minolta, Nikon, Yashica, Leica, Polaroid, others. Books available.
For Further Information: Send SASE for list.
Store Location: Yes
Accepts: American Express, Discover, MasterCard, Visa

AAA CAMERA EXCHANGE, INC.
43 7th Ave.
New York, NY 10011
(212) 242-5800

Offers: Camera outfits: Beginner—with camera, lens, film, tripod, gadget bag, strap, flash; Dream Kit and Deluxe SLR outfits—with choice/selection of cameras (Canon, Minolta, Fujica, Pentax, Olympus, Ricoh, Yashica). Cameras—these brands, and also Chinon, Mamiya, Konica, others. I.D. cameras: Polaroids, Shackman, Beatti. Lenses: Leitz, Minox, Nikon, Minolta, Canon, Sigma, Soligor, Tamron, others.
For Further Information: Send SASE or call for list.
Discounts: "Reduced/special prices."
Accepts: MasterCard, Visa

ABE'S CAMERAS & ELECTRONICS
1957-61 Coney Island Ave.
Brooklyn, NY 11223
(718) 645-0900

Offers: Cameras: Canon, Nikon, Minolta, Pentax, Olympus. Auto focus cameras: Nikon, Olympus, Pentax, Canon, Minolta, Fuji, Ricoh. Lenses and flashes: Vivitar, Tokina, Sigma, Canon, Tamrac, Minolta, Telesor, others. Video camcorders by Panasonic, Sony and JVC, plus Slik tripods and others.
For Further Information: Send SASE or call for list.
Store Location: Yes
Discounts: "Some reduced prices."
Accepts: MasterCard, Visa

ALBUMS INC.
P.O. Box 81757
Cleveland, OH 44181

Offers: Albums—for weddings, studio, portrait photographers, plus plaques and a line of frames in a variety of styles and sizes (products of Holson, Topflight, Camille, Sureguard, Pro-Craft, Yankee Plak, Lacquer-Mat, Marshall's).
For Further Information: Free wholesale catalog.
Store Location: Yes
Accepts: MasterCard, Visa

B & H PHOTO
119 W. 17th St.
New York, NY 10011
(212) 807-7474, (800) 221-5662

Offers: Still cameras/equipment/accessories: Hasselblad, Bronca, Rollei, Pentax, Mamiya, others. Also offers studio lighting, strobe and tungsten lights, lenses, filters, papers, aids, copy systems and underwater photo equipment. Known brands in used equipment also available.
For Further Information: Free catalog.
Store Location: Yes
Discounts: Quantity discounts.
Accepts: MasterCard, Visa

BACKDROP OUTLET
1524 Peoria Ave.
Chicago, IL 60608
(800) 466-1755

Offers: Line of backgrounds and glamour backdrops and accessories (hand-painted muslin and canvas types), plus stools and other accessories.
For Further Information: Free catalog.

BROMWELL MARKETING
3 Allegheny Center, #111
Pittsburgh, PA 15212
(412) 321-4118

Offers: Cameras, equipment and supplies for large format: View cameras, lenses, tripods, and a full line of accessories and specialty items.
For Further Information: Free catalog.

CAMBRIDGE CAMERA EXCHANGE, INC.
7th Ave. & 13th St.
New York, NY 10011
(212) 675-8600

Offers: Cameras and equipment in known brands: Agfa-Gevaert, Bronica, Cambron, Canon, Casio, Chinon, Exakia,

Fuji, Hasselblad, Kodak, Konica, Leica, Lindenblatt, Mamiya, Praktic, Ricoh, Rollei, Topcon, Vivitar, Contax/Yashica, Polaroid, Passport, others, plus 4 × 5 cameras. Stocks lenses, flashes, exposure meters, tripods, darkroom equipment and used cameras.
For Further Information: Free catalog.
Store Location: Yes
Discounts: Sells wholesale.
Accepts: Discover, MasterCard, Visa

CAMERA WEST
423 Alvarado St.
Monterey, CA 93940
(408) 649-0232

Offers: Cameras and equipment by: Nikon, Ricoh, Olympus, Tokina, Sigawith, Minolta, Chinon, Yashica, Samurai, others. Over 8 tripods.
For Further Information: Send SASE for list.
Discounts: "May run sales."
Accepts: MasterCard, Visa

CAMERA WORLD OF OREGON
500 SW 5th & Washington
Portland, OR 97204
(503) 227-6008

Offers: Cameras and accessories by: Canon, Fuji, Chinon, Nikon, Ricoh, Minolta, Konica, Pentax, Olympus, Yashica, Tamron, others. Video camcorders by: Sony, Panasonic, Chinon, Canon, Hitachi, Olympus, Minolta, Nikon, Quazar, JVC, RCA, Magnavox, Pentax. Camera lenses by Sigma, Tokina, Vivitar and others. Carries flashes, light meters, others.
For Further Information: Send SASE or call for list.
Accepts: MasterCard, Visa

CENTRAL CAMERA CO.
230 S. Wabash Ave.
Chicago, IL 60604
(312) 427-5580

Offers: Cameras/equipment: Nikon, Pentax, others including shutter and SLR's. Carries Ilford papers and film, Metz flash/accessories, Bogen tripods, others.
For Further Information: Send SASE for list.
Store Location: Yes

CHAUCER INDUSTRIES
P.O. Box 366
Bethpage, NY 11714

Offers: PC computer program (for IBM or compatible): Slide Labeling categorizes slides, prints part or all of slide listing, while screen search mode helps locate slides faster; records photo data, recreates or corrects shots.
For Further Information: Send SASE for full details.

COKIN CREATIVE FILTERS
P.O. Box 243
Whippany, NJ 07981

Offers: Conkin system filters, enlargers, most lenses (200 types).
For Further Information: Brochure, $3.50.

DAY LAB
400 E. Main St.
Ontario, CA 91761
(714) 988-3233

Offers: Daylight enlarger-processor to make color or black-and-white prints from negatives or slides in normal room light; works with any chemistry, including Cibachrome.
For Further Information: Send SASE or call for further details.

DELTA 1 CUSTOM PHOTO MANUFACTURING
10830 Sanden Dr.
Dallas, TX 75238
(214) 349-9779

Offers: Darkroom products: Water filters, stainless steel sinks and trays, fans, louvers, mixing tanks, ABS sinks, demand heaters, others.
For Further Information: Send SASE for full details.

DIAL-A-PHOTO, INC.
P.O. Box 5063
Jacksonville, FL 32247
(904) 398-8175

Offers: Dial-A-Photo computer system for all cameras, films. Pocket-sized system helps predict shots in a variety of conditions.
For Further Information: Send SASE for further information.
Accepts: MasterCard, Visa

DORAN ENTERPRISES
2779 S. 34th St.
Milwaukee, WI 53215

Offers: Pictrol soft focus lens converter unit (with most lenses to 2-inch diameter), with dial diffusion.
For Further Information: Free catalog.

EXECUTIVE PHOTO & SUPPLY CORP.
120 W. 31st St.
New York, NY 10001
(212) 947-5290

Offers: Cameras/accessories: Nikon, Minolta, Canon, Pentax, Yashica, Leica, Fuji, Konica, Polaroid passport models, EW Marine underwater equipment, Mamiya, Hasselblad,

others. Lenses: Sligor, Kiron, Tokina, Sigma, Pentax, Canon, Ed-IF, others. Also flashes, tripods, projectors/viewers, studio kits, stands, reflectors, darkroom equipment/supplies, enlarger outfits, film, papers and chemicals.
For Further Information: Write for catalog.

FOCUS CAMERA, INC.
4419-21 13th Ave.
Brooklyn, NY 11219
(718) 436-6262

Offers: Cameras and equipment: Nikon, Hanimex, Contax, Yashica, Konica, Canon, Olympus, Pentax, Vivitar, others. Lenses: Vivitar, Kiron, Sunpak, Sigma, Tokina, Polaroid, Tamron, Canon, Nikon, Metz, others. Also offers carousels, flashes, digital flashes, meters, camera cases and gadget bags, Bogen and Slik tripods, others.
For Further Information: Send SASE or call for list.
Discounts: "May have some below-list prices."
Accepts: MasterCard, Visa

FRANKLIN DISTRIBUTORS CORP.
P.O. Box 320
Denville, NJ 07834
(201) 267-2710

Offers: Line of cameras and other photographic equipment.
For Further Information: Free catalog.

FREE TRADE PHOTO
4718 18th Ave., Suite 127
Brooklyn, NY 11204
(718) 633-6890

Offers: Cameras/accessories/equipment: Canon, Nikon, Pentax, Maxxum, Leica, Olympus, Minox, Minolta. Carries Rokunar SP studio systems, studio lighting, darkroom accessories and others.
For Further Information: Send SASE for list.

FREESTYLE
5120 W. Sunset Blvd.
Los Angeles, CA 90027
(213) 660-3460

Offers: Darkroom supplies/accessories: Stainless tanks/reels, thermometers, film loaders, filters, polarizers, mount boards. Film: Black-and-white by Ilford, Arista, Kodak, Ortho Litho. Carries color and black-and-white papers, film.
For Further Information: Send SASE or call for list.
Accepts: MasterCard, Visa

FUJI PHOTO FILM, U.S.A., INC.
555 Taxter Rd.
Elmsford, NY 10523

Offers: Fuji film in a variety of sizes/types.

For Further Information: Contact dealer, or write for information.

GARDEN STATE CAMERA
101 Kuller Rd.
Clifton, NJ 07011
(201) 742-5777

Offers: Cameras/equipment/accessories: Nikon, Canon, Sigma, Yashica, Pentax, Tokina, Wamron, Samyang, Sunpak, Vivitar, Olympus, Minolta, Konica, others. Carries special camera outfits for beginners and professionals. Buys cameras.
For Further Information: Free catalog.
Store Location: Yes
Accepts: American Express, Discover, MasterCard, Visa

LIGHT IMPRESSIONS
439 Monroe Ave.
P.O. Box 439
Rochester, NY 14603

Offers: Photography supplies: Archival storage and display products, studio and darkroom equipment, photography gear. Wide range of fine art photography books, from classics to most recent, and hard-to-find titles.
For Further Information: Free catalog.
Store Location: Yes
Discounts: Quantity discounts.

MAMIYA AMERICA CORP.
8 Westchester Plaza
Elmsford, NY 10523
(914) 347-3300

Offers: Mamiya photographic equipment — a variety of cameras, interchangeable lenses, others.
For Further Information: Contact dealer, or send SASE for information.

MELROSE PHOTOGRAPHICS
50 E. Butler Ave.
Ambler, PA 19002
(215) 646-4022

Offers: Custom printing, including Cibachrome enlargements. Prints from 35mm to 6×7 transparencies only; photos in a variety of sizes, in pearl or glossy surface. Flush mountings.
For Further Information: Send SASE for full details.
Discounts: Sells wholesale.

MERIT ALBUMS, INC.
19338 Business Center Dr.
Northridge, CA 91324
(818) 886-5100

Offers: Wedding albums and others in a variety of styles and sizes. Also carries proof books, photo mounts and folios by Topflight, Leathermark, Tap, Holson, Camille and Dimension.
For Further Information: Free wholesale catalog.
Accepts: MasterCard, Visa

MIBRO CO., INC.
64 W. 36th St.
New York, NY 10018
(212) 695-7133

Offers: Cameras—SLR outfits: All-in-one, 3-Lens Beginner, All purpose action, Sports minded 3-lens, For-starters, Mini-max pickup/go, Nature lover, Professional, others. Cameras by: Minolta, Pentax, Ricoh, Canon, Fuji, others. Also offers a line of lenses, flashes, tripods, gadget bags, others.
For Further Information: Send SASE or call for list.
Accepts: MasterCard, Visa

MINOLTA CORP.
101 Williams Dr.
Ramsey, NJ 07446

Offers: Minolta cameras and accessories in a variety of types, including a sports action card set camera for continuous autofocus and others.
For Further Information: Contact dealer, or write for information.

MINOX U.S.A.
1315 Jericho Turnpike
New Hyde Park, NY 11040

Offers: Minox photographic equipment, including small full-frame 35mm camera and other models/types.
For Further Information: Contact dealer, or write for information.

THE MORRIS CO.
1205 W. Jackson Blvd.
Chicago, IL 60607
(812) 421-5739

Offers: Camera products, including the Morris Mini slave flash—gives twice the light for group shots or use as a fill light; palm-size, it's triggered by the camera's built-in flash. Manufacturer.
For Further Information: Contact dealer, or send SASE for information.

NEW YORK INSTITUTE OF PHOTOGRAPHY
211 E. 43rd St.
New York, NY 10017

Offers: Photography home study course—30 lesson program covering both the basics and advanced, professional aspects of photography. Includes a mini-course in video techniques, with training materials, cassette tape communication, and individual attention and constructive criticism to enhance learning.
For Further Information: Free *Career Guide* and catalog.

NIKON CONSUMER RELATIONS
19601 Hamilton Ave.
Torrance, CA 90502

Offers: Photographic equipment, including full line of cameras, some with 5-segment Matrix Metering, plus synchronized, cybernetic, rear-curtain fill-flash and other advanced systems. Stocks speedlight and other flashes.
For Further Information: Contact dealer, or write for information.

NRI SCHOOL OF PHOTOGRAPHY
4401 Connecticut Ave. NW
Washington, DC 20008

Offers: Photography and video production home-study course for professional training in still and video photography. Includes instruction in studio, darkroom equipment and techniques for equipment use. Critiques and communication from professional instructors (of the McGraw-Hill Continuing Education Center).
For Further Information: Free catalog.

OMEGA
6210 Holiday Way
Post Falls, ID 83854

Offers: Construction plans for a photographic enlarger stand/light table for enlargements 20-inch × 24-inch and larger without moving the enlarger (light table is removable).
For Further Information: Send SASE for details.

PHOTO MART
P.O. Box 19027
Washington, DC 20036
(919) 945-9867

Offers: Instructional photography videos, including *Basic 35mm, Lighting and Exposure, Design and Composition, Studio, Business, Basic Videography, Basic Darkroom, Ansel Adams, Advanced Subjects, Images, Glamour Photography, Flash, Films, Photographing People.* Subjects include photojournalism, prize photos, action work, sports action, weddings, others. Also offers 13 sample photographer's contracts (blank forms).
For Further Information: Send SASE, or call for list.
Accepts: Discover, MasterCard, Visa

PHOTO SCOPE
5745 Plauche Ct.
New Orleans, LA 70123
(504) 733-0915

Offers: Black-and-white photo finishing; complete services for all sizes.
For Further Information: Write or call for free start-up kit.

PHOTO-THERM
110 Sewell Ave.
Trenton, NJ 08610
(609) 396-1456

Offers: Darkroom equipment, including temperature baths and modular controls in a variety of models of high precision type; "reasonable cost."
For Further Information: Write or call for catalog.

PHOTOGRAPHERS' FORMULARY CO.
P.O. Box 950
Condon, MT 59826
(406) 754-2891

Offers: Full and complete line of photographic chemicals for processing and printing.
For Further Information: Send SASE for list.

PHOTOGRAPHER'S WARE HOUSE
P.O. Box 3365
Boardman, OH 44513

Offers: Photographic lighting equipment: Home studio lighting kits, professional starter kits (strobes, umbrellas/adapters, stands), others. Also offers strobe lights and umbrella outfits, light boxes, soft boxes, slaves, reflectors, others.
For Further Information: Send SASE for list.

PHOTOGRAPHY BOOK CLUB
P.O. Box 2003
Lakewood, NJ 08701

Offers: Photography books at savings for members. When choosing an introductory title at token cost, members agree to purchase more books in the first year of membership. Club bulletins are sent 15 times yearly; card to be returned if selection is declined.
For Further Information: Send SASE for full details.

THE PIERCE CO.
9801 Nicollet
Minneapolis, MN 55420
(612) 884-1991

Offers: Photography studio products: Painted backgrounds (25 including scenics), photography supplies, photo albums and mounts, drapes, printed forms, poly bags, toys, others.
For Further Information: Catalog, $1 (refundable).

PNTA
333 Westlake Ave. N.
Seattle, WA 98109
(206) 622-7850

Offers: Photography studio supplies for lighting effects (diffusion, colored gels, portable lighting kits, Bogo patterns, studio lights, fog and smoke machines, reflector sheets), plus scenic materials (seamless paper, backdrops and 3D materials, including brick, stone, tile and others). Carries studio draperies and tracks, paint, dyes, muslin.
For Further Information: Free catalog and samples.

RONALD L. RUEDIGER & ASSOCIATES
P.O. Box 204
Natrona Heights, PA 15065
(412) 226-9123

Offers: Slide mount imprinter—stamps 6 lines of information (name, copyright, address, telephone, etc.) directly onto plastic and cardboard slide mounts in proper alignment.
For Further Information: Send SASE for full information.
Accepts: MasterCard, Visa

SHOOTERS OF USA LAB
P.O. Box 8640
Rolling Meadows, IL 60008
(708) 956-1010

Offers: Professional developing/printing service for prints, photo business cards, greeting cards, "blow-up" color enlargements (16 inches × 20 inches and up) and other enlargements.
For Further Information: Send SASE for list.
Discounts: Quantity discounts.

SMILE PHOTO
29 W. 35th St.
New York, NY 10001
(212) 967-5900

Offers: Cameras/accessories by Canon, Nikon, Minolta, Ricoh, Nikonos (underwater equipment), Fujica, Yashica, Konica, Olympus, Nikon, Pentax, others. Also offers lenses, cases and studio accessories, including lights, booms, stands, copy systems, lighting assemblies, reflectors, copy stand, umbrellas and slide projectors.
For Further Information: Send SASE, or call for information.
Accepts: Discover, MasterCard, Visa

SOUTHERN CAREER INSTITUTE
Drawer 2158
Boca Raton, FL 33427
(407) 368-2522

Offers: Professional photography home-study course for basic to advanced photography (techniques for a wide range of practices); business and career are all focal points of this study program.
For Further Information: Free catalog.

SPEEDOTRON CORP.
310 S. Racine Ave.
Chicago, IL 60607
(312) 421-4050

Offers: The Speedotron Accelerator portable rechargeable battery pack for hand-held flash systems (quickens the pace of the hand-held flash), a 320V battery pack to use with 1 or 2 hand-held flash units. The accelerator gives up to 400 full-power flashes and fast recycle rate, with interchangeable lead-acid gel cell battery and AC cord.
For Further Information: Contact dealer, or send SASE for information.

STATICMASTER
P.O. Box 5178
El Monte, CA 91734
(818) 444-3852

Offers: Staticmaster brush—cleans negatives, slides and lenses of dust and static. Manufacturer.
For Further Information: Free literature.

TAMRAC
6709 Independence Ave.
Canoga Park, CA 91303

Offers: Camera and video carrying systems (cases) for over 40 models, including Super Pro (compartmentalized, for most photographic equipment, with zip out, fold out, easy accessibility). Other styles include Zoom Traveler, a smaller version with shoulder strap, and the Photographer's Vest style for carrying camera and lenses, etc.

For Further Information: Write for catalog.

THOMAS INSTRUMENT CO., INC.
1313 Belleview Ave.
Charlottesville, VA 22901
(804) 977-8150

Offers: Duplex Super Safelight, a darkroom light with monochromatic light source and special filters to give soft light. Others.
For Further Information: Contact dealer, or call/write for details.

WALL STREET CAMERA
82 Wall St.
New York, NY 10005
(212) 344-0011

Offers: Camera equipment by Bronica, Hasselblad, Rollei, Pentax, Mamiya, Canon, Leica. Press/view cameras: Omega, Sinar, Fiji, Nagaoka. Also offers lenses and light meters (known brands), plus zoom outfits by Olympus and Minolta. Carries Tiltall tripod and Kodak carousels, plus RCA, Olympus, Sony, and other video camcorders and darkroom outfits (enlarger plus accessories). Allows trade-ins of cameras for new models.
For Further Information: Catalog, $1 (refundable).
Discounts: "Some below list prices."
Accepts: MasterCard, Visa

ZONE VI STUDIOS, INC.
Newfane, VT 05345
(802) 257-5161

Offers: Photographic specialties: Zone VI camera—handcrafted field camera with extensions/removable bellows, lenses to 360mm, a mahogany body with brass fittings, plus a case. Also offers archival print washers, tripods and cases, compensating enlarging metronomes, view camera lenses by Schneider, and 4×5 camera outfits, modified meters and cold light enlarger timer. Carries print flatlevers, cold light heads, stabilizers, developing timers, drying screens, paper, chemicals, easels, film washers, darkroom tanks, reels, oversized proofers, magnifiers and books.
For Further Information: Free catalog.

Rubber Stamping and Stamp Making

Also see General Craft Supplies, Artist's Supplies, Paints, Paper Crafts and Paper Making and Fabric Decorating.

A STAMP IN THE HAND CO.
20630 S. Leapwood Ave., Suite B
Carson, CA 90746
(310) 329-8555

Offers: Rubber stamps from favorite companies, many in hand-carved eraser designs: Hearts, paper dolls, tree with hearts, animals. Carries custom stamps, paper, cards.
For Further Information: "Kat-A-Log" and supplements, $3.50.

ACEY DEUCY
P.O. Box 194
Ancram, NY 12502

Offers: Rubber stamp designs including Ugly Ties or Dumb Hats postal stamps, plus assorted people, others. Has unmounted stamps at half price.
For Further Information: Catalog, $1.50.

ACME/STAR
1720 N. Marshfield Ave.
Chicago, IL 60622

Offers: Supplies/equipment: Rubber stamp markers, letterpress and printing items.
For Further Information: Catalog, $2.

ALL NIGHT MEDIA, INC.
P.O. Box 10607
San Rafael, CA 94912
(415) 459-3013

Offers: Rubber stamp designs, including cartoons Stamp-A-Face, sets. Other designs include Winnie the Pooh, teddies, animal designs (and sets), Stamps-On-Wheels, Global Cow, cats, fish, shells, waves, teacher's stamps, messages, birthday, nature, fantasy, musical, country, borders, flowers, classic and love motifs. Also carries bookplates.
For Further Information: Send SASE for list.

ANNE-MADE DESIGNS
P.O. Box 697
Erwin, TN 37650

Offers: Decorative rubber stamps: Whimsical and folk art images, others. Has unmounted stamps at very low cost.
For Further Information: Catalog and card of unmounted stamps, $5.

ARBEN STAMP CO.
413 Main St.
P.O. Box 353
Evansville, IN 47703

Offers: Rubber stamps: Hearts, dolls, holiday motifs, others. Also offers Pollagraphs, embossing powders, glitter, glue, others.
For Further Information: Catalog, $2.50.
Discounts: Sells wholesale.

ART IMPRESSIONS
P.O. Box 20085
Salem, OR 97307
(503) 393-2014

Offers: Original rubber stamps designs including over 1,300 name stamps in 12 designs, plus special occasions and others, both mounted and unmounted.
For Further Information: Catalog, $3.
Discounts: "Wholesale welcome, send copy of business license."
Accepts: MasterCard, Visa

THE ARTERY
1411 N. 25th St.
Boise, ID 83702
(208) 336-2038

Offers: Kite designs—full line from areas worldwide. (And kite jewelry.)
For Further Information: Write for information.
Discounts: "Dealer inquiries invited."

BIZARRO
P.O. Box 16160
Rumford, RI 02916
(401) 728-9560

Offers: Design rubber stamps: Sports figures, map of U.S., alphabet stamp sets, others. Supplies include embossing powders and rainbow stamp pads. Also offers *How to Use Rubber Stamps* books.
For Further Information: Catalog, $2.
Store Location: Yes
Discounts: Sells wholesale.

CALIFORNIA STAMPIN'

5532 Paseo Navarro
Pleasanton, CA 94566

Offers: Over 160 pages of rubber stamps: Printworks, Rubber Stampede, SonLight Impressions, Stampendous and others. Also offers stamp supplies.
For Further Information: Catalog, $4.
Discounts: Has discounts.

Use baby wipes to clean water-based inks from rubber dies.
—Stamp of Excellence

CIRCUSTAMPS

P.O. Box 250
Bolinas, CA 94924
(415) 868-1474

Offers: Scaled images in rubber stamps (to be used with one another) of an array of circus performers in action: Clowns, trapeze artists, lion tamers, Oriental acrobats, jugglers, stilt walkers, band/action animals. Also offers animal bases and animal wagon and cage (in parts). Unmounted stamps sold at half price.
For Further Information: Catalog, $1.

CO-MOTION RUBBER STAMPS

4455 S. Park Ave., #105
Tucson, AZ 85714

Offers: Artistic rubber stamps including Southwestern (saguaro cactus, Indian pottery and designs), teddy bear, penguins, others. Techniques video.
For Further Information: Catalog, $2.
Discounts: Sells wholesale.

DELAFIELD STAMP CO.

P.O. Box 56
Delafield, WI 53018
(414) 646-8599

Offers: Over 400 rubber stamp designs: Holiday (Halloween, Christmas, others), seasonal, others. Also offers stamping accessories, ColorBox items, DSC Art greeting cards.
For Further Information: Catalog and supplement, $4.
Discounts: Sells wholesale.
Accepts: MasterCard, Visa

DIVA RUBBER

P.O. Box 849
Montara, CA 94037

Offers: Rubber stamps by Vivian Jean, Roger Jones, Anne Norcia—unmounted only.
For Further Information: Catalog, $2 (refundable).

DOUBLE D RUBBER STAMPS, INC.

P.O. Box 1
Olivia, MN 56277
(612) 826-2288

Offers: Sign language alphabet rubber stamps and over 900 other designs.
For Further Information: Catalog, $2 (refundable).
Discounts: "Wholesale, send copy of resale permit or license."
Accepts: Discover, MasterCard, Visa

EMERALD CITY STAMPS

7925 Annesdale Dr.
Cincinnati, OH 45243

Offers: Over 1,000 creative rubber stamps: Cosmos, comic faces, fantasy, wild, flowers, shells, trees, bugs, birds, fish, pyramids, vehicles, balloons, special occasion, holiday, slogans and signs, hands, hearts, others. Unmounted stamps sold at half price.
For Further Information: Catalog, $2 (refundable with $20 order).
Discounts: Sells wholesale.

ESTONIA AND FRIENDS

P.O. Box 469
Surfside, CA 90743

Offers: Alphabets and other rubber stamps. Paperphernalia, including calendars, notepapers, silk neckties, others. Unmounted stamps available.
For Further Information: Catalog, $1.

EXQUISITE IMAGES

4188 Piedmont Ave.
Piedmont, CA 94611
(510) 601-6847

Offers: Rubber stamps including body part images: Lungs, brains, kidneys, eyes, hearts, stomach parts, others. Also offers storage and display cases.
For Further Information: Send SASE for list.
Accepts: MasterCard, Visa

FRUIT BASKET UPSET

P.O. Box 23129
Seattle, WA 98102

Offers: Rubber stamp images, including over 100 new designs and 4 new alphabets.
For Further Information: Catalog, $3 (refundable).

GOOD IMPRESSIONS

P.O. Box 33 RB
Shirley, WV 26434

Offers: Rubber stamp images: People, plants, borders, animals, fantasy, cupids, birds, silhouettes, quilting motifs, food, buildings, holiday, alphabets, sign language. Also offers Letter Lock personal stamps—banner and 250-piece alphabet set. Banner slogans, quotations also available.
For Further Information: Catalog, $1.

GOOD STAMPS—STAMPS GOOD

30901 Timberline Rd.
Willits, CA 95490
(707) 459-9124

Offers: Rubber stamps in a variety of designs, including holiday, rainbows, Pot o' Gold, clover, leprechaun, sunrise, clouds, rabbits, ducks, broken egg (pair), 13 heart motifs and others. Blank paper goods are also available.
For Further Information: Catalog, $3. Send SASE for paper swatches.
See Also: Paper Crafts and Paper Making

GRAPHIC RUBBER STAMP CO.

11250 Magnolia Blvd.
North Hollywood, CA 91601
(818) 762-9443

Offers: Rubber stamp designs: Circus, sheep, photographic, castles, borders, people, telephones, bicycles, flowers, Hollywood, dancers, sports, trees, animals, fantasy, quotations, alphabets, transportation, Native American, spiritual, cartoons, others. Also offers embossing powders (kit available), stamp pads, glitter, paper items, printing kits, and techniques video.
For Further Information: Catalog #1 (displaying 3,000 stamps), $4; Catalog #2 (displaying 900 stamps), $3.50.
Store Location: Yes
Discounts: Quantity discounts; sells wholesale to legitimate businesses.

GREGORY MANUFACTURING CO., INC.

P.O. Box 1303
Jackson, MS 39215
(601) 355-1429

Offers: Crystalite acrylic stamp mounts with maple base and handles, available in over 100 sizes packed in units of 10 by size. Shapes available include circles. Also offers indexing tape, double-sided foam tapes, mount strips, molding in over 12 sizes, plus matrix, cushion, stamp gum, handles and engraving blocks/bases.
For Further Information: Free catalog.
Discounts: Quantity discounts.

GUMBO GRAPHICS

P.O. Box 11801
Eugene, OR 97440

Offers: Over 2,000 rubber stamp images and sets, including reproductions, bizarre items, animals, fish, plants, Indians,

abstracts, children, women, men, bugs, birds, beasts, dragons, others.
For Further Information: Catalog, $2.

Stamp small background stamps of stars, hearts, tulips, etc., in pale colors first. Then stamp your message stamps over them in darker colors.

—Stampourri

HAMILTON ARTS

5340 Hamilton Ave.
Cleveland, OH 44114
(216) 431-9001

Offers: Original hand-drawn art rubber stamps—decorative imagery, Mother Goose designs, fantasy, animals, landscapes, bears and toys, others.
For Further Information: Catalog, $2 (refundable).
Discounts: Sells wholesale.

HEARTFELT IMPRESSIONS

P.O. Box 248
Pacific Palisades, CA 90272
(213) 459-6050

Offers: Rubber stamp designs including whimsical, action animals, plus hearts, teacher's slogans, calligraphy slogans, holidays, others.
For Further Information: Catalog, $1.
Discounts: Sells wholesale.

HIPPO HEART

P.O. Box 4460
Foster City, CA 94404
(415) 347-4477

Offers: Rubber stamp designs including mini motifs, animals, birds, borders/corners, fantasy, foods, flora, holidays, sports, leisure, quotes, people, seashore, transportation, teachers, skies, others.
For Further Information: Catalog, $2 (refundable with $20 order).

INKADINKADO

76 South St.
Boston, MA 02111
(617) 338-2600

Offers: Rubber stamps, including a stamp set of solar system, astronauts, rockets, others.
For Further Information: Write for catalog.

JACKSON MARKING PRODUCTS

Brownsville Rd.
Mt. Vernon, IL 62864
(618) 242-1334, (800) 851-4945

Offers: Rubber stamp-making equipment: Precision rubber stamp presses redesigned for industrial use (Mazak and Standard Foundry), hand press and stamp die-cutting machines, and hot stamping and laminating equipment. Also offers mount strip (6 styles), matrix board, stamp gum, cushions, pads and inks, solutions, self-inkers, racks, 64 type styles and handles. Services: Photo engraving of artwork, matrix board molding, rubber die molding.
For Further Information: Free brochure.
Discounts: Quantity discounts.

ED JACOBS
7316 San Bartolo St.
Carlsbad, CA 92009
(619) 438-5046

Offers: Your name custom designed on a Chinese seal. Others.
For Further Information: Write or call for free information.
Discounts: Quantity discounts.

JUDI KINS RUBBER STAMPS
17832 S. Hobart Blvd.
Gardena, CA 90248

Offers: Rubber stamp images (original designs): Seal and heart, ducks, monkey hanging from balloon, elephant, water drops, rabbits, others. Custom stamp service, from customer's designs.
For Further Information: Catalog, $2.
Discounts: Sells wholesale.

KLEAR COPY DESIGN RUBBER STAMPS
55 7th Ave. S.
New York, NY 10014
(212) 243-0357

Offers: Design rubber stamps: Beetle, elephant, lion head, other animals, drinks on tray pocket watch, period images, historical locales and costumes, antiquities, unusuals (Spam, luggage, coins, bottles), Palmer Cox's Brownie. Also offers Christmas designs, ornate alphabets, cupids.
For Further Information: Catalog, $2 (refundable).

L.A. STAMPWORKS
P.O. Box 2329
North Hollywood, CA 91610
(818) 761-8757

Offers: Art rubber stamps: Popeye characters in action, balloon quotes, air mail, animals, circle motifs, Art Nouveau, florals, scenes, people (dancers, mermaids, kids, flappers, 30s ladies, old-timers, silhouettes), holiday themes, teacher's, zodiac, cartoon, borders, others.
For Further Information: Catalog, $5.
Discounts: Sells wholesale.

LADY AND THE STAMP
3358 E. Yorba Linda Blvd.
Fullerton, CA 92631
(714) 996-9592

Offers: Rubber stamp images in an array of designs. Supplies: Stamp pads, papers, pens and markers, embossing powder, ribbon, tissue, glitter supplies. Paper: Stationery, tags, stickers, gift boxes, others.
For Further Information: Send SASE for list.

LASTING IMPRESSIONS
198 Greenwood Ave.
Bethel, CT 06801
(203) 792-3740

Offers: Rubber stamps in dog and cat images—lifelike, variety of species. Others.
For Further Information: Catalog, $2 (refundable).
Discounts: Sells wholesale.

LOVE YOU TO BITS
P.O. Box 2864
Redwood City, CA 94064
(415) 367-1177

Offers: Over 250 original rubber stamp designs: Whimsical holiday motifs, quotes and signs, Christian stamps, stamps in Spanish, animals, flowers, cartoon creatures, others. Has unmounted stamps at half price.
For Further Information: Catalog, $2.
Discounts: Sells wholesale.

Chinese seals on rubber stamps. Courtesy of Ed Jacobs.

LOVING LITTLE RUBBER STAMPS
1 Federal St.
Newburyport, MA 01950
(508) 465-9954

Offers: Over 400 rubber stamp designs—originals and ol-

dies: Special occasion, holiday, quotes, people, money, food, seashore, ecology, buildings, sports, animals, vintage motifs, hands, borders, signs, others.
For Further Information: Catalog, $2.

MEDIAESCAPE INC.

P.O. Box 24107
Denver, CO 80224
(303) 758-8232

Offers: Rubber stamps of the Jewish tradition—full range, "from reverence to pure silliness," including animals, ark, people, quotes, others. Catalog has design tips.
For Further Information: Catalog, $2 (refundable).
Discounts: "Wholesale inquiries welcome."

MOE WABBA

P.O. Box 9121
San Rafael, CA 94912

Offers: Stamp designs including "classical," fantasy, quotes, cartoon, others.
For Further Information: Stamp album, $2 (refundable).
Discounts: Sells wholesale.

MOSTLY ANIMALS

P.O. Box 32266
San Jose, CA 95152
(800) 832-8886

Offers: Line of rubber stamps in animal designs.
For Further Information: Call or write for information.

MUSEUM OF MODERN RUBBER

187 Orangethorpe Ave.
Placentia, CA 92670
(714) 993-1198

Offers: Rubber stamp images (specialty is topical stamps, and "stamps-of-art"): Western images, holiday, cupids, cartoon, V.I.P. people (Stooges, Elvis, others), slogans of the 70s. Unmounted stamps at half price.
For Further Information: Catalog, $3.
Discounts: Sells wholesale.

NAME BRAND

P.O. Box 34245
Bethesda, MD 20827

Offers: Calligraphic rubber stamps—We've Moved, Handmade By, Thank You, Junk Mail, others. Custom stamps (addresses, monograms, names) and logos available.
For Further Information: Catalog, $2 (refundable).
Discounts: "Wholesale inquiries welcome."

NATURE IMPRESSIONS

2007 Leneve Place
El Cerrito, CA 94530
(415) 527-9622

Offers: Over 400 rubber stamp images including New Active interacting images, which feature characters and changes of accessories and clothes. Also offers nature and animal motifs, stamp pads and brush marker pens.
For Further Information: Catalog, $1.35.

NEATO STUFF'S RUBBER-STAMP COOKBOOK

P.O. Box 4066
Carson City, NV 89702

Offers: Rubber stamps in cooking images—5 designs for recipe cards, 80 plus words/phrases used in recipes, plus popcorn and other food motifs. Has unmounted stamps at half price.
For Further Information: Catalog, $3 (refundable).

ONCE UPON A STAMP

356 W. Eagle Lake Dr.
Maple Grove, MN 55369
(612) 425-6053

Offers: Artistic rubber stamps: Duck, cat, mouse with book and candle, frog and flower, ant, rabbit, butterfly, other. Also includes wagon and other motifs, some with left and right versions. Unmounted stamps for half price.
For Further Information: Catalog, $1 (refundable).
Discounts: Sells wholesale.

100 PROOF PRESS

Rt. 1, P.O. Box 136
Eaton, NY 13334
(315) 684-3547

Offers: Over 2,900 rubber stamp images: Holiday, people, make-a-face parts, crowds, hands, bicycles, ethnic, vintage, elves, Native American, dancing, soldiers, photographic, sports, cosmic, dolls, toys, angels, fantasy, animals, birds, others.
For Further Information: Catalog, $3 (refundable).

ORANGE RUBBER STAMP CO.

59 Bacon St.
Orange, MA 01364
(508) 544-2202

Offers: Graphic rubber stamps, including dressed "Uncle Wiggly" rabbits, crow, dog, goat, crocodile, insects, others.
For Further Information: 32-page catalog, $2 (refundable).

PALO ALTO RUBBER STAMPS

3892 El Camino Real
Palo Alto, CA 94306

Offers: Design rubber stamps, including man and camera with tripod, man with newspaper, postmark designs, others.
For Further Information: Catalog, $1.

Instead of spending a lot of money on cards, stationery, giftwrap and especially holiday cards—why not stamp them yourself? Create your own stamp art.

—Moe Wabba

PEACE RESOURCE PROJECT
P.O. Box 1122
Arcata, CA 95521
(707) 822-4229

Offers: Artistic rubber stamps with peace motifs and slogans: "Peace" in several languages, "Create Peace"/Picasso Dove Face, "Wage Peace," "Let Peace Begin With Me" and others. Also offers peace buttons, stickers, T-shirts, and a list of peace organizations.
For Further Information: Write for catalog.
Discounts: Quantity discounts.

POSH IMPRESSIONS
875 E. Birch St.
Brea, CA 92621
(714) 529-9933

Offers: Exclusive rubber stamps of over 40,000 images, plus stickers rolls and "unlimited" accessories. Also offers classes, videos, others.
For Further Information: Catalog, $3.
Store Location: Yes
Discounts: Wholesale discounts.

PRINT GOCCO
434 DeAnza St.
San Carlos, CA 94070
(800) 392-7476

Offers: Hand-stamping system that prints multi-color of any design, includes master-making unit, screens, bulbs, inks, clip art. Line of blank greeting cards and envelopes.
For Further Information: Call or write for information.

PRINT PLAY
P.O. Box 4252
Portland, OR 97208
(503) 274-8720

Offers: Individual words rubber stamp collection—to mix for slogans, etc., or to complement pictorial designs.
For Further Information: Free brochure.

QUAKER CITY TYPE
RD 3, P.O. Box 134
Honey Brook, PA 19344

Offers: Type in a variety of styles, for printing and stamps.
For Further Information: Catalog, $2 (refundable).

QUARTER MOON
P.O. Box 61185
San Jose, CA 95161

Offers: Artistic rubber stamps: Teddy bears, cats, other animals, circus performers, borders, flowers, holiday items, people, alphabets, hearts, train, boat, Asian art, coins, others. Also offers Rollagraph rollerstamps (animals, slogans, Asian dragon, others). Has unmounted stamps at half price.
For Further Information: Catalog, $3.
Discounts: Sells wholesale.

RED BEANS & RUBBER STAMPS
P.O. Box 6481
Altadena, CA 91003

Offers: Line of African-American rubber stamp images "for the ages" in a variety of designs.
For Further Information: Catalog, $1 (refundable).

REMARKABLE RUBBER STAMPS
P.O. Box 2004
Snoqualmie, WA 98065

Offers: Rubber stamps in a wide variety of designs.
For Further Information: Catalog, $2.50.
Discounts: Sells wholesale.

RUBBER BABY BUGGY BUMPERS
1704 N. Evergreen St.
Burbank, CA 91505
(818) 847-7039

Offers: Original rubber stamps by 13 artists, including holiday, characters, fantasy/sci-fi, humorous motifs, others. Unmounted available.
For Further Information: Catalog, $4.
Accepts: MasterCard, Visa

RUBBER DUCK STAMP CO.
P.O. Box 416
Medford, OR 97501

Offers: Rubber stamps, including ducks, rabbits, teddy bears, Easter baskets, flowers, others. Assorted die cuts. Supplies: Pads, inks, wood blocks.
For Further Information: *Ducklog*, $3 (½ refundable).
Discounts: Sells wholesale.

RUBBER LOVER'S BOXARIA
2607-A Nelson Ave.
Redondo Beach, CA 90278

Offers: Boxes for rubber stamps—"e-flute" corrugated

cardboard with instructions, categorizing tips and label space.
For Further Information: Write for catalog.

RUBBER POET
P.O. Box 1011
Rockville, UT 84763

Offers: Repeatable rubber stamp fabric designs, including contemporary, geometric, others.
For Further Information: Catalog, $2 (refundable).

THE RUBBER ROOM
P.O. Box 7149
Redwood City, CA 94063

Offers: Novelty rubber stamps in a variety of designs.
For Further Information: Catalog, $2 (refundable).

Store your stamp pads upside down when you're not using them. This keeps the ink moving from top to bottom of the pad.
—Hippo Heart Rubber Stamps

RUBBER STAMP EXPRESS
1409 Kuehner Dr., Suite 205
Simi Valley, CA 93063

Offers: Rubber stamp designs, including postmark designs, animals (domestic and wild), past cars, aircraft and other vehicles, borders, action people, sports, dancing, babies, face parts, kitchen objects, food, trees, globe, flowers, holidays, surfing, greetings, Southwest and Native American. Supplies: Stationery, blank postage stickers, embossing powder (clear gloss), postcards, gift tags, label paper. Sells unmounted stamps at half price.
For Further Information: Catalog, $4.
Discounts: Sells wholesale.

RUBBERSTAMPEDE
P.O. Box 246
Berkeley, CA 94701
(415) 843-8910

Offers: Rubber stamp designs (mostly original): Plants/trees, flowers, cartoon characters, dinosaurs, fantasy, Noah's ark, people, holiday, slogans, quotations and greetings. Includes animals, both domestic and wild (15 cats, 58 teddies, others). Also offers 17 roller stamps: Borders, footprints, teddies, cat tracks, others. Carries Face Case (parts to mix), love kit motifs, Posh Impression stamps (variety of companies), art maker sets, wrapping papers, ink pads, inks.
For Further Information: 30-page catalog, $2.

SONLIGHT IMPRESSIONS
1520 Commerce St., Suite I
Corona, CA 91720
(714) 278-5656

Offers: Christian design rubber stamp series (in English and Spanish): Peace dove, dove with word "Peace," cross, sun and clouds, lighthouse "Let Your Light Shine," "Born Again" with butterfly, "Love One Another as I Have Loved You" with heart, and other series of designs. Has unmounted stamps at half price.
For Further Information: Catalog, $3.
Discounts: Sells wholesale.

SOUTH WESTAMPS
3445 N. 19th Ave.
Phoenix, AZ 85015
(602) 274-2282

Offers: Rubber stamps: "Close Encounters," holiday motifs, Premium and Economounts, custom stamps, rubber plates. Has unmounted, grab bag specials.
For Further Information: Pieces catalog, $1.
Store Location: Yes

STAMP ADDICTION
3230 E. Flamingo Rd.
Las Vegas, NV 89121
(702) 434-3405

Offers: Precia Prints rubber stamps: Holiday, fantasy, quotes, animals, others.
For Further Information: Catalog, $3 (refundable).
Accepts: MasterCard, Visa

STAMP ANTONIO
1931 NW Military Highway
San Antonio, TX 78213
(210) 342-6217

Offers: Rubber stamps with contemporary Texas/Western motifs, quotes and others produced by over 50 companies.
For Further Information: Flyer, $1 and business-size SASE with 52¢ postage.
Store Location: Yes
Discounts: Sells wholesale.
Accepts: MasterCard, Visa

THE STAMP ATTIC
602 W. Huntington St.
North Webster, IN 46555

Offers: Stamps of fun and fanciful creatures, cartoons, quotations, others. Unmounted stamps at half price.
For Further Information: Catalog, $2 (refundable).

When using different colors in ink pads and markers, always start with the lightest color first. You probably won't need to clean the stamp before changing colors if you follow this rule.
—Graphic Rubber Stamp Co.

STAMP BERRY FARMS
1952 Everett St.
North Valley Stream, NY 11580

Offers: Artistic rubber stamps: Cartoon, signs/banners, vintage figures, dance, sports, music, food, vehicles, textures, quotes, hands, holidays. Over 60 animals, religious, mail, greetings, alphabets, and copyright-free designs. Cartoon sets (hands/feet), special effects sets, custom face stamps from customer's design (photo, passport, etc.). Supplies: Marker sets, paints, paper cards/envelopes and stamp pads. Unmounted stamps at half price.
For Further Information: Catalog, $2 (refundable).

THE STAMP LADIES
P.O. Box 2512
Fallbrook, CA 92088
(619) 723-4438

Offers: Over 2,000 rubber stamps of leading stamp companies; motifs include 500 holiday stamps, full range of others.
For Further Information: Catalog, $3; children's catalog, $2 (refundable).

STAMP OF EXCELLENCE, INC.
1105 Main St.
Canon City, CO 81212
(719) 275-8422

Offers: Line of rubber stamps including special occasion (designs, quotes): Holiday, birthday, baby, bridal, party, Valentine's, springtime flowers. Other subjects include kitchen, mail, "frames," classroom, notecard, Oriental, Native American, cosmic, fantasy, scenic, animals, others. Has unmounted quotations.
For Further Information: Catalog, $3.
Store Location: Yes
Discounts: Quantity discounts; sells wholesale to legitimate businesses.
Accepts: MasterCard, Visa

THE STAMP PAD CO., INC.
P.O. Box 43
Big Lake, MN 55309
(612) 263-6646, (800) 634-3717

Offers: Rubber stamps in over 2,000 pictoral designs or in script or block types. Also offers custom first name stamps in three styles.
For Further Information: Catalog, $1.
Accepts: MasterCard, Visa

STAMPENDOUS!
1357 S. Lewis St.
Anaheim, CA 92805
(800) 869-0474

Offers: Original design rubber stamps, including "Handcrafted by" and other phrases, plus bears, rabbits and other "creative" figures in action. Mini-stamp sets supplies.
For Further Information: Catalog, $3.
Accepts: MasterCard, Visa

STAMPINKS UNLIMITED
P.O. Box 97
Shortsville, NY 14548

Offers: Artistic rubber stamps, including peace motifs/slogans—"Wage Peace" and globe, peace dogs, peace (in several languages, including Chinese character), others. Also offers E. Pobin Allen's carousel/stylized designs and Cindy Pacileo's motifs, including zoo and other animals. Carries mail art, stars, hearts, other animals, birds, old structures, slogans, cathedrals, trees. Also carries greetings and postcard designs, stamp pads, pads, inks, paper products. Unmounted stamps at half price. Custom stamp service available.
For Further Information: Catalog and supplement, $2.50.
Discounts: Sells wholesale.

STAMPOURRI
P.O. Box 3434
La Habra, CA 90632
(310) 69-STAMP

Offers: Artistic rubber stamps: Teacher stamps in English and Spanish, holidays, angels, quotes, mermaids, dogs, inspirational, thanks, party, spring, outdoors, mail, borders. Sets: Bible, Noah's ark, animals, others. Also offers templates and paper products (cards, bookmarks, others).
For Further Information: 35-page catalog, $3.

STARRY NIGHT STAMPS
303 North St.
Catawissa, PA 17820

Offers: Line of "heavenly" rubber stamps including moon faces, others. Has unmounted stamps.
For Further Information: Catalog, $1.50 (refundable).
Discounts: Sells wholesale.

STEWART-SUPERIOR CORP.
1800 W. Larchmont Ave.
Chicago, IL 60613
(312) 935-6025, (800) 621-1205

Offers: Rubber stamp manufacturing equipment/supplies: Vulcanizers, stamp gum, matrix, imprinted stamp pads, cements, daters, seals, photopolymers, acrylic mounts, inks

(over 35 colors), cushions, molding, brushes, bottles, sign makers, others.
For Further Information: Send SASE with inquiry.

TOOMUCHFUN RUBBERSTAMPS
515 E. Grand River Ave.
East Lansing, MI 48823
(517) 351-2030

Offers: Rubber stamp motifs, including special occasions and other stamps "for celebrating"—candles, sun face designs, etc. Unmounted stamps half price.
For Further Information: Write for catalog.
Discounts: "Wholesale inquiries welcome."
Accepts: MasterCard, Visa

UNCLE REBUS STAMP CO.
P.O. Box 334
Rutherford, CA 94573

Offers: Line of rubber stamp designs.
For Further Information: Send stamp for catalog.

VISUAL IMAGE PRINTERY
1215 N. Grove St.
Anaheim, CA 92806
(714) 632-2441

Offers: Rubber stamp designs including "Forest Folk," and other fantasy characters (wizards, dragons, castle, fairies, trees, others).

For Further Information: Catalogs, $3.
Discounts: Sells wholesale.
Accepts: MasterCard, Visa

W.C. WARD STAMPS ETC.
3165 Rainbow Glen Rd.
Fallbrook, CA 92028
(619) 295-5044

Offers: Artistic rubber stamp designs.
For Further Information: Catalog, $2.
Discounts: Sells wholesale.

WOOD CELLAR GRAPHICS
P.O. Box 409
Randolph, NE 68771
(402) 337-1627

Offers: Over 80 new designs. Unmounted available.
For Further Information: Catalog, $3 (refundable); send SASE for flyer.
Discounts: Sells wholesale.

WORKS OF HEART
P.O. Box 15007
Portland, OR 97215

Offers: Artistic rubber stamps, including over 700 original designs, custom stamps and dual-use stamps for fabric and paper. Also offers fabric paints and supplies.
For Further Information: Catalog, $2.
Discounts: Sells wholesale.

Scientific Supplies and Equipment

AMERICAN SCIENCE & SURPLUS
3605 Howard St.
Skokie, IL 60076
(708) 982-0870

Offers: Surplus/unusual items: Laboratory equipment/ supplies/kits, fiber optics and electrical items, lighting, wires, cords, bottles, jars, boxes, tool sets, solders, hemostats, airbrushes, jewelry, military items, and scientific kits and items. Electronics: Magnetics, oscillators, lighting, clocks, motor building, rocketry, telegraphy items, hydroponics, solar energy, transducers, solenoids, AC/DC motors. Science novelties: Kaleidoscopes, mirrors, magnifiers, "wonder" and gravity items. Also offers magnets and bunsen burners.
For Further Information: Catalog available.
Store Location: Yes
Discounts: Quantity discounts.

ANALYTICAL SCIENTIFIC
11049 Bandera Rd.
San Antonio, TX 78250
(512) 684-7373

Offers: Scientific-related products: Chemicals, a variety of equipment, glassware, experiments/projects and books.
For Further Information: Catalog, $3 (refundable).

EDMUND SCIENTIFIC
101 E. Gloucester Pike
Barrington, NJ 08007
(609) 573-6260

Offers: Technical/scientific products: Kits for mini hot-air balloons and steam engines, microscope accessories, optics, ES lens, diffraction grating, kaleidoscopes, science subjects, 16 microscopes and pocket models, eyepieces, prisms, alcohol lamps, tubing, goggles, pH paper, clocks, timers, scales/ balances, 35 plus magnifiers, loupes and electroplating kits. Also offers pencils and drawing sets, plastic bottles, dispensers, fiber optics fibers, light guides, helium-neon laser and others. Solar-related items include panels, cells, photovoltaics, trackers, others. Carries magnets, mirror film, modeling items, motors, fans, components, Dremel tools, measuring items, projectors, light boxes, steam-driven models, jeweler's items, papers.
For Further Information: Write for catalog.

HEGENOW LABORATORIES
1302 Washington
Manitowoc, WI 54220

Offers: Laboratory chemicals and glassware.
For Further Information: Catalog, $2.

PYROTEK
P.O. Box 1
Catasauqua, PA 18032
(717) 256-3087

Offers: Plans/supplies for making rockets—in a variety of sizes and types. Line of fuels, chemicals.
For Further Information: Catalog, $3.

Scrimshaw

Also see Jewelry Making and Lapidary, Tools and Equipment and other related categories.

AN OLD ALASKA IVORY DEALER
1825 Loose Moose Loop
North Pole, AK 99705

Offers: Fossil walrus ivory material (also has finished scrimshaw, carvings).
For Further Information: Send SASE with inquiry.

BOONE TRADING CO.
562 Coyota Rd.
Brinnon, WA 98320
(206) 796-4330

Offers: Raw materials, including fossil walrus ivory (teeth in 3 sizes), tusks, tips, polished pieces, scrap chip tusks. Elephant materials include scrap, tusk tips, slabs, sections, whole and hollow tusks. Also offers mammoth ivory, jewelry blanks, polished slabs, belt buckle blanks, scrimshaw kits, simulated stag, amber and ivory (with some original material/resin), stag antler burrs, crowns, rosettes and sheep horns. Carries books, animal skins, trade beads, ancient coins, others.
For Further Information: Send SASE for list.
Discounts: Quantity discounts; sells wholesale to businesses.
Accepts: MasterCard, Visa

HUNTER'S FOSSIL IVORY CO.
1022 N. 1st Place
Springfield, OR 97477
(503) 747-1973

Offers: Tagua nuts (vegetable ivory) with polished scrimshaw area, plus fossil walrus ivory (small to whole tusks), beads, teeth and scrimshaw kits.
For Further Information: Free catalog, or catalog plus generous sample, $5.

SCRIMSHAW UNLIMITED
1511 Oxford Rd.
Grosse Pointe, MI 48236

Offers: Scrimshaw tracing patterns, findings, tools, ivory. Also offers scrimshaw kits (each with ink, scribe, practice piece, ivory blank, etc.) and finished scrimshaw.
For Further Information: Free catalog.

ALAN ZANOTTI
20 Braunecker Rd.
Plymouth, MA 02360
(508) 746-8552

Offers: Ivory (legal from estates), bone material, fossil ivory, horns, skulls.
For Further Information: Send SASE for list.

Sculpture and Modeling

Also see Ceramics, Metalworking, Mold Crafts and Woodworking.

AMERICAN ART CLAY CO., INC.
4717 W. 16th St.
Indianapolis, IN 46222
(317) 244-6871

Offers: Fimo modeling material for home oven firing of small items, miniatures, jewelry and other sculpting. Available in 36 bright colors. Sculptamold modeling compound, clays, others.
For Further Information: Contact a dealer, or send SASE for details.
See Also: Ceramics

ART STUDIO CASTING
234 Huron St.
Brooklyn, NY 11222
(718) 389-7200

Offers: Custom foundry services in the lost wax process. Moldmaking, fine finishing, patination and fabrication.
For Further Information: Send SASE, or call for full information.

BRI METAL FABRICATORS
72 Knowlton St.
Bridgeport, CT 06608
(203) 368-1649

Offers: Metal sculpture service: Flame cutting, press forming, shearing, machining, plasma cutting, roll forming, welding and finishing.
For Further Information: Send SASE, or call for information.

BRYANT LABORATORY, INC.
1101 5th St.
Berkeley, CA 94710
(415) 526-3141

Offers: Patina chemicals (solvents, acids and dry chemicals for art needs) including silver nitrate, chloride and sulfide, borax, calcium carbonate, eucalyptus oil, gold chloride, mercury, talc, preservatives, others. Lab items: Alcohol lamps, beakers, bottles, filters, bunsen burners, cylinders, clamps, flasks, hydrometers, droppers, funnels, petri dishes, slides, stirrers, test tubes, tubing, others. Books are also available.

For Further Information: Write for price list and formulas.
Discounts: Quantity discounts; allows discounts to teachers and institutions.

DESIGN CONSULTING SERVICE
41355 Covelo Rd.
Willits, CA 95490
(707) 984-8394

Offers: Line of waxes (for plaster mold casting, other).
For Further Information: Send SASE for details.

DICK BLICK
P.O. Box 1267
Galesburg, IL 61402
(309) 343-6181

Offers: Full line of art/sculpture and other materials and equipment: Soapstone, alabaster, stone sculpture tool sets. Modeling: Instant papier-mâchés, Sculptamold, plastercraft gauze, plaster of Paris (and molds), Sculptey, modeling clays, plasticolor. Clays: Mexican pottery, Marbelex, Westwood ovencraft, others. Also offers Egyptian paste, earthenware and other kitchen-fired clays, plus glazes, ceramic and modeling tools/sets and aids.
For Further Information: Catalog, $4.
Store Location: Yes
See Also: Artist's Supplies

DODD & MARBLE
P.O. Box 298
Woodland Hills, CA 91365
(818) 718-2824

Offers: Sculpting marble (large sizes) in black types, pinks, whites, rust-peach, blue-white-purple, beige-white-brown, gray, green and beige. Travertine is available in red, silver and beige. Also offers alabaster and onyx in a variety of colors, plus other stones, a line of bases, soapstone, and tools for stone sculpting.
For Further Information: Free list.
Store Location: Yes
Discounts: Quantity discounts; allows discounts to teachers and institutions; sells wholesale to legitimate businesses and professionals.

DURHAM
P.O. Box 804
Des Moines, IA 50304

Offers: Durham's Rock Hard Water Putty: Molds, carves, sculpts, models or casts (no firing).
For Further Information: Send business-size SASE for handcraft booklet.

HOHEB STUDIOS
689 Washington St.
Ashland, OR 97520
(503) 488-0835

Offers: Custom sculptural enlargement services—works from models or drawings, and enlarges sculpture to any size for final execution in bronze, stone, fiberglass or plaster.
For Further Information: Send SASE with inquiry.

HUCKELBERRY FINN
P.O. Box 305
Gold Hill, OR 97525

Offers: Dental tools and other products for sculpting with polyform clays including Cernit, others.
For Further Information: Free catalog.

LARAN BRONZE, INC.
310 E. 6th St.
Chester, PA 19015
(215) 874-4414

Offers: Lost wax ceramic shell foundry. Custom services: Bronze and aluminum casting, rubber mold making, polyester and fiberglass castings in large sizes and enlarging.
For Further Information: Send SASE with inquiry.

Alabaster and soapstone are recommended for beginning carvers. Keep in mind that when you are carving you are "removing," therefore you should start with as large a stone as possible. This will enable you to be adventurous and will give you an opportunity to experiment without the fear of ending up with nothing but a small pile of chips.

—Montoya/Mas International, Inc.

MONTOYA/MAS INTERNATIONAL, INC.
435 Southern Blvd.
West Palm Beach, FL 33405
(407) 832-4401

Offers: Carving stones (imported), line of marble bases (many sizes/colors), over 1,600 sculpture tools (including hard-to-find), clays and waxes. Services available include art foundry, casting, mounting, repairs and restoration.
For Further Information: Catalog, $3.
Store Location: Yes
Discounts: Quantity discounts; allows discounts to teachers and institutions; sells wholesale to legitimate businesses.

PAUL KING FOUNDRY
92 Allendale Ave.
Johnston, RI 02919
(401) 231-3120

Offers: Custom services, including sculptural and architectural castings, lost wax and French sand processes, bronze, plus aluminum and other non-ferrous metals.
For Further Information: Write or call with inquiry.

POLYFORM PRODUCTS CO.
9420 W. Byron St.
Schiller Park, IL 60176
(312) 678-4836

Offers: Super Sculpey ceramic-like sculpting compound for small work; bake in the kitchen oven to harden. Also offers Sculpey III; both come in sets, multi-packs. Also offers glazes, booklets.
For Further Information: Contact your dealer or write for details.

JERRY PORTER
P.O. Box 3241, University Station
Charlottesville, VA 22903
(804) 293-6858

Offers: Virginia Alberene black soapstone (a soft cross between African wonderstone and Belgian black soapstone) in small to huge pieces direct from the quarry.
For Further Information: Send SASE or call with inquiry.

PREMIER WAX CO., INC.
3327 Hidden Valley Dr.
Little Rock, AR 72212
(501) 225-2925

Offers: Microcrystalline waxes (for sculpting and casting): Victory, available in 3 colors, and Be Square types. Sold in 10 pound lots and up.
For Further Information: Send SASE or call for full information.

THE ROBERT FIDA STUDIO
1100 Storey Blvd.
Cheyenne, WY 82009
(307) 635-5056

Offers: *The Sculptor's Studio* video series with Robert Fida covers moldmaking and casting, including casting with concrete, plaster, hydrostone, hydrocal, pewter, bronze, pecan shell, marble. Also covers gold leafing, finishing techniques for concrete and plaster, shrinking castings, marketing for the visual artist and other topics.
For Further Information: Send SASE for list.

SCULPTURE STUDIO & FOUNDRY
1150 Clare Ave.
West Palm Beach, FL 33401
(407) 833-6950

Offers: Art casting services: Enlargements to any size, mold making, bronze casting with ceramic shell, resin and stone casting, patina.
For Further Information: Send SASE or call with inquiry.

STEATITE OF SOUTHERN OREGON, INC.
2891 Elk Lane
Grants Pass, OR 97527
(503) 479-3646

Offers: Oregon soapstone, an inspected sculpturing/carving stone.
For Further Information: Send SASE for prices.
Discounts: Sells wholesale.

TALLIX
175 Fishkill Ave.
Beacon, NY 12508
(914) 838-1111

Offers: An enlarging studio with a scraping technique that enables enlargements with detail. Enlarges sculpture to any size and any degree of finish.
For Further Information: Send SASE or call for price quotes.

TROW AND HOLDEN CO.
P.O. Box 475
Barre, VT 05641

Offers: Line of stone sculpting and cutting tools: 5 pneumatic carving tools, carbide tip chisels, rippers, chisels (machine, splitter, clean-up, double blade, marble lettering, 4-point, 9-point, marble tooth and cutting types), and carver's and other drills. Also offers slab splitters, striking and mash hammers, paving cutters, busters, wedges and shims, straightedges, air stopcocks, and Stone Lewis lifting dogs.
For Further Information: Free catalog.
Discounts: Allows discounts to teachers and institutions; sells wholesale to businesses.

Sign Making

Also see Artist's Supplies, Paints, Finishes and Adhesives, and Tole and Decorative Crafts.

AMERICRAFT CORP.
904 4th St. W.
Palmetto, FL 34221
(813) 722-6631

Offers: Florida Plastics letters—formed, dimensional, molded and cut-out—plus Side Lites 2-color letters, Sign Language and Bronze-Lite products. Also offers Gravix panels, E-Z Change changeable copy Plexiglas letters, others.
For Further Information: Free catalogs.

ART ESSENTIALS OF NEW YORK LTD.
3 Cross St.
Suffern, NY 10901
or 508 Douglas Ave.
Toronto, Ontario M5M 1H5 Canada

Offers: Gold leaf (genuine and composition) in sheets and rolls (variety of shades/karats), plus glass-type gold leaf. Also offers silver leaf and supplies, such as gilding size, knives, burnishing clay, and other tools and brushes. Books are also available.
For Further Information: Send SASE for product lists.

BARCLAY LEAF IMPORTS, INC.
21 Wilson Terrace
Elizabeth, NJ 07208
(908) 353-5522

Offers: Line of gold leaf and supplies—professional and beginner (including introductory packages).
For Further Information: See dealer, or send SASE for information.

DICK BLICK
P.O. Box 1267
Galesburg, IL 61402
(309) 343-6181

Offers: Arts/crafts/graphics and sign-making supplies: Airbrushes, paints, banners, sign blanks, sign cloth. Also offers sandblaster units, supplies and equipment (for gold leafing, pinstriping, screen printing), plus books on lettering and other topics.
For Further Information: Catalog, $4.

Store Location: Yes
Accepts: American Express, Discover, MasterCard, Visa
See Also: Artist's Supplies and General Craft Supplies

COMMERCIAL SCHOOL OF LETTERING
513 E. Hawthorne St.
Fort Wayne, IN 46806

Offers: A two-volume sign painting video course for beginners. Volume I covers brushes, basic strokes, materials, pricing and more (comes with book, price guide and pinstriping booklet). Volume II covers layout, banners, showcards, trucks and more.
For Further Information: Send SASE for full information.

THE CUTAWL CO.
Rt. 6
Bethel, CT 06801
(203) 792-8622

Offers: Cutawl machine (with knife, chisel and saw blades that cut curves, logos or patterns—blades swivel 360 degrees)—cuts most sign and display materials including Lexan, Plexiglas, Lucite, Fome-Cor, Gatorfoam, plywood, particle board, stencil board, vinyl, cloth, others.
For Further Information: Free catalog.

THE DURHAM CO.
54 Woodland St.
Newburyport, MA 01950
(508) 465-3493

Offers: Gold leaf (hand beaten), including XX deep patent, glass and surface types.
For Further Information: Send SASE for full information.

E-Z SIGN
23 S. Fairview Ave.
Goleta, CA 93117

Offers: Lessons in sign painting.
For Further Information: Sample lesson, $1.

EARL MICH CO.
806 N. Peoria St.
Chicago, IL 60622
(312) 829-1552

Offers: Sign letters, both vinyl and reflective types (computer prespaced or individual die cut), for producing com-

puter digitized logos, punched materials, universal symbols, alphabet sheets, screen printing, police and fire decals, plastic dimensional letters, static lettering. Also offers magnetic sheeting, letters and signs, prespacing tapes, vinyl and reflective material (in sheets, striping, rolls) and other die-cut sign graphics—over 100 colors/type styles.
For Further Information: Write or call for information.
Accepts: MasterCard, Visa

GEMINI INC.
103 Mensing Way
Cannon Falls, MN 55009
(507) 263-3957

Offers: Letters of vacuum formed plastic, injection molded plastic, cast aluminum, cast bronze, flat cut-out plastic and metal types, and edge trim gemlite letters. Also offers aluminum and bronze plaques, custom metal cut-outs, custom formed plastic, and videos and manuals.
For Further Information: Free catalog.

GOLD LEAF & METALLIC POWDERS, INC.
74 Trinity Place, Suite 1807
New York, NY 10006
(212) 267-4900

Offers: Genuine metallic leaf: Gold (variety of shades/karats), palladium, silver leaf and composition leaf products, including gold, bronze, copper, variegated and others. Also offers patinating and gilding supplies and accessories, restoration aids and others.
For Further Information: Send SASE for information.

HARTCO
1280 Glendale-Milford Rd.
Cincinnati, OH 45215

Offers: Sandmask stencils: Vinyl (for sandblasting raw or treated wood, plastic or glass), pin-feed stencil materials, etching tapes and others.
For Further Information: Send SASE for full information.

HAYNES SIGN CO.
Highway 27 S.
Murrells Inlet, SC 29576

Offers: Instructional video on sign painting from veteran painter; includes step-by-step directions, techniques.
For Further Information: Send SASE for details.

KAUFMAN SIGNS
Centertown, MO 65023

Offers: Sign-making materials and equipment, pinstriping items and books.
For Further Information: Free catalog.

LEO UHLFELDER CO.
420 S. Fulton Ave.
Mt. Vernon, NY 10553
(914) 664-8701

Offers: Golf leaf—quality Florentine gold, XX deep patent, glass, surface gold, roll gold. Also offers gold size (quick and slow forms). Importers.
For Further Information: Send SASE for full information.

MULLER STUDIOS SIGN CO.
Ridge Rd.
Stafford Springs, CT 06076
(203) 974-2161

Offers: Sign blanks—constructed of Simpson Signal M.D.O., with mahogany frames and waterproof glue. A variety of stock sizes and shapes (including old-tavern, oval, round, rectangular, other old-world looks). Custom wood signs built to specifications.
For Further Information: Write or call for details.

NEON
P.O. Box 4410
Arlington, VA 22204

Offers: Course in neon lighting, includes free video.
For Further Information: Send SASE for full details.

NUDO PRODUCTS, INC.
2508 S. Grand Ave. E.
Springfield, IL 62703
(800) 826-4132

Offers: White-wood sign panel (smooth vinyl surface, factory laminated to exterior plywood) for hand/screen lettering or vinyl letters (flame resistant), available in a variety of sizes and other substrates. Also offers fiberglass surfaced sign panels.
For Further Information: Write or call for sample.

PETER HORSLEY PUBLICATIONS
115 Riverbirch Cresent SE
Calgary, Alberta T2C 3M1 Canada
(403) 279-0227

Offers: Self-study course in neoncrafting. The course is clearly written with photos and diagrams, complete technical information, basic electricity, design and selling, manufacturing and service/repair. Also supplies source data.
For Further Information: Send for free sample lesson.

RAYCO PAINT CO.
6100 N. Pulaski Rd.
Chicago, IL 60646
(800) 421-2327

Offers: Banner blanks—drill cloth with nylon rope top/bottom, can be lettered on two sides if latex coated—available in 14 sizes, to 4 foot × 40 foot. Full line of screen process, sign and painter's supplies and equipment.
For Further Information: Write or call for catalog.

SCOTT PLASTICS CO.
P.O. Box 1047
Tallevast, FL 34270
(813) 351-1787

Offers: Sign-making materials—raw products and a full line of letters and signs, plus unfinished high density, letter quality foam in 3 thicknesses and by the cut sheet or entire skid. Others.
For Further Information: Free catalog.

SEPP LEAF PRODUCTS, INC.
381 Park Ave. S.
New York, NY 10016
(212) 683-2840

Offers: August Ruhl gold leaf, glass gold, patent gold, palladium leaf, karat gold in a variety of shades and roll gold. Also offers gilder's tips, LeFranc oil size and an instructional video—*Gold Leaf Basics*, with Kent H. Smith. Technical data service available—write.
For Further Information: Free catalog.
Discounts: Sells wholesale to legitimate businesses.

SIGN-MART
1657 N. Glassell
Orange, CA 92667
(714) 998-9470, (800) 533-9099

Offers: Blank vinyl banner material: 3 foot times any length, hemmed and grommeted, for lettering or silkscreen, in 12 colors.
For Further Information: Send SASE for full information.

T.J. RONAN PAINT CORP.
749 E. 135th St.
New York, NY 10037
(212) 292-1100

Offers: Ronan paints in lettering enamels ("one-stroke," solid hiding, colors) for metal, wood, others. Also offers bulletin colors, background enamels, brushing and spraying acrylics, Japan colors, fluorescents, non-tarnish liquid gold, specialty sign finishes.
For Further Information: Contact dealer, or send SASE for information.

TARA MATERIALS INC.
P.O. Box 646
Lawrenceville, GA 30246
(404) 963-5256

Offers: Vinyl banner cloth in three types, including Taravyn 9 oz., reinforced for use with vinyl paints or inks and pressure sensitive graphics; Taravynall 10 oz. reinforced cloth, coated on one side to accept paint, ink, enamel and pressure sensitive graphics; and Taracloth III, smooth moisture-resistant polyflax fabric, triple-coated for paints and pressure sensitive graphics. Also offers Tyvek, Tygerag and Taracloth banner cloth. Manufacturer.
For Further Information: Write for information.

TIP SANDBLAST EQUIPMENT
7075 Rt. 446
P.O. Box 649
Canfield, OH 44406
(216) 533-3384, (800) 321-9260

Offers: Combination sandblaster and paint units, accessories, and 3M Buttercut resist material, available by the yard or roll.
For Further Information: Free catalog.

TRADEMARK SIGN SYSTEMS
4 Hall Rd.
Ithaca, NY 14850
(800) 423-6895

Offers: Carving and sandblasting blanks: Old growth redwood with vertical grain, splined glue joints, matched boards ready to finish.
For Further Information: Color brochures.
Discounts: Sells wholesale to dealers.

WENSCO SIGN SUPPLY
2910 Schoeneck Rd.
Macungie, PA 18062
(215) 966-3555

Offers: Complete line of sandblasting sign supplies (to sandblast wood, glass, stone, brick, others): Sandblast machines, air compressors, tape masking materials. Also offers Sign-Life products, automatic letter-cutting machines, hoods, nozzles, and other parts and supplies. Has custom sandblasting service.
For Further Information: Send SASE for complete information.

YARDER MANUFACTURING CO.
708 Phillips Ave.
Toledo, OH 43612
(419) 476-3933

Offers: Sign blanks—steel and aluminum in stock sizes with "factory-to-you pricing."
For Further Information: Send SASE for full details.

Tattooing

DYVIRG, INC.
4138 E. Grant Rd.
Tucson, AZ 85712

Offers: Line of custom-made, hand-crafted, precision tattoo machines (signed and numbered). Also offers custom repair/tuning service for tattoo machines.
For Further Information: Free catalog.

SPAULDING & ROGERS INC.
Rt. 85, New Scotland Rd.
Voorheesville, NY 12186
(518) 768-2070

Offers: Full line of tattooing equipment/supplies, including tattooing machines with shaders, outliners and needles. Also offers power packs, parts, needle jigs, ultrasonic cleaners, autoclaves, sterilizers, medical supplies, eye loupes, lamps, ink mixers, skin markers, hectograph pencils, stencil cutters. Colors available as inks, cosmetic colors, Sta-Glo sets. Carries over 2,600 designs sets: Animals, figures, cartoons , seaside, emblems, religious, fantasy, Indian, Egyptian, others. Videos and books also available. Manufacturer.
For Further Information: Catalogs (3), $12.
Store Location: Yes

Taxidermy

DAN CHASE TAXIDERMY SUPPLY CO.
13599 Blackwater Rd.
Baker, LA 70714

Offers: Full and complete line of taxidermy supplies and over 500 instructional videotapes on subjects related to taxidermy.
For Further Information: Free catalog.

MCKENZIE TAXIDERMY SUPPLY
P.O. Box 480
Granite Quarry, NC 28072

Offers: Full line of taxidermy supplies, including deer and animal forms.
For Further Information: Free catalog.

REEL MOUNTS
P.O. Box 1541
Amherst, NY 14226

Offers: Fish taxidermy guide, including step-by-step instructions for trophy fish.
For Further Information: Send SASE for full information.

VAN DYKE'S
P.O. Box 278
Woonsocket, SD 57385

Offers: Taxidermy kits for beginners, instructional videos and handbooks. Also offers advanced/professional supplies, a full line for taxidermists and tanners.
For Further Information: Free booklet.

Tole and Decorative Crafts

Also see General Craft Supplies, Artist's Supplies, Miniature Making, Paints, Finishes and Adhesives, Fabric Decorating and other related categories.

ADVENTURES IN CRAFTS
Yorkville Station
P.O. Box 6058
New York, NY 10128
(212) 410-9793

Offers: Decoupage products, including kits, prints, miniature paintings (animals, flowers, Oriental, Goodey's Ladies, Anton Pieck, others) and black-and-white prints (botanicals, borders, birds, animals). Also offers wood products, including a line of boxes, lap desks and screens (3 and 4 panels). Gilding supplies available include Dutch metal gold/silver leaf and marbleizer. Carries repousse moldable epoxy and other adhesives, sizing, box hardware, papers, graining tools, trayer, burnisher, mini-tool sets, plus finishes and books.
For Further Information: Catalog, $3.50.

ANIMAL ART
4122 Irving Ave. N.
Minneapolis, MN 55412

Offers: Natural 3D wooden animal boxes with removable lids. Rabbits, ducks, pigs/piglets, roosters, ducks, cats, dinosaurs, others.
For Further Information: Catalog, $1.

ANNIE'S CALICO CAT ORIGINALS
P.O. Box 1004
Oakdale, CA 95361

Offers: Woodcrafting patterns (full-sized) including cats. Also in wood cutouts.
For Further Information: Catalog, $1.

ART CRAFT WOOD SHOP
P.O. Box 75
Crestline, KS 66728
(316) 389-2574

Offers: Ready-to-paint wood items including table benches, spool cabinets, glove and trinket boxes, others.
For Further Information: Catalog, $3.

B & B PUBLISHING, INC.
P.O. Box 420268
Kissimmee, FL 34742
(407) 870-2121

Offers: Instructional videos by Maureen McNaughton and Linda Wise, plus books on how-to basics and projects.
For Further Information: Free brochure.
Discounts: Sells wholesale to legitimate businesses.

BARCLAY LEAF IMPORTS, INC.
21 Wilson Terrace
Elizabeth, NJ 07208
(908) 353-5522

Offers: Gold leaf: Introductory packages, line of professional supplies.
For Further Information: Send SASE for information.

Practice cutting out of old magazines first. Hold the curved scissors with your thumb and third finger; the index finger under the blade will support and guide it. The points of the scissors face away from the paper. The cutting hand moves only to open and close the scissors; the other hand turns and feeds the paper to the scissors. Relax—you'll cut much better!

—Adventures in Crafts Studio

BEAR WOODS SUPPLY CO.
P.O. Box 40
Bear River, Nova Scotia B0S 1B0 Canada
(902) 467-3703

Offers: Unfinished wood ware, including candle cups, holders, sticks, Shaker pegs, other pegs, wheels, toys (cargo and people, yo-yos, bells, animals, bowling pins), kitchen items, miniatures, line of boxes and shapes, spindles, bars, knobs, beads, game pieces, spools, finials, dowels, others.
For Further Information: Free catalog.
Store Location: Yes
Discounts: Quantity discounts; sells wholesale to legitimate businesses.
Accepts: MasterCard, Visa

BRIDGEWATER SCROLLWORKS
Rt. 1, P.O. Box 585
Osage, MN 56570

Offers: Wood cutouts—over 1,000 shapes, including hearts,

animals, flowers, figures, others. Custom cutting service.
For Further Information: Catalog, $5 (refundable).
Discounts: Quantity discounts.

CAPE COD COOPERAGE
1150 Queen Anne Rd.
Chatham, MA 02633
(508) 432-0788

Offers: Barrel staves—sanded, ready-to-decorate/paint—and hinged-top chests and boxes.
For Further Information: Send SASE for list.

CHARLOTTE FORD TRUNKS
P.O. Box 536
Spearman, TX 79081
(806) 659-3027

Offers: Trunk repair/restoration supplies: Hinges, locks sets, other hardware, finishes, linings. Also offers how-to books to help restore, refinish, line and decorate all kinds of trunks.
For Further Information: Illustrated catalog, $3.

CRANBERRY PAINTER
P.O. Box 1489
Buzzards Bay, MA 02532
(508) 759-4623

Offers: Decorative painting pattern packets, 12 plus motifs (including some to personalize with names/dates/events), and pen and ink supplies.
For Further Information: Brochures, $1 (refundable).

CUPBOARD DISTRIBUTING
114 S. Main St.
P.O. Box 148
Urbana, OH 43078

Offers: Woodenwares, including miniatures, carousel horses and other animals, jointed animals, pull toys, spools, candles, sticks, cups, holders, eggs, fruit, boxes, gameboards, shapes, signs, wheels, pegs, dowels, knobs, school items. Also offers jewelry, including necklace kits, patterns, beads, findings, bells and cord, plus resin figures, hardware, paints, brushes and others.
For Further Information: Catalog, $1.
Accepts: Discover, MasterCard, Visa

CUSTOM WOOD CUT-OUTS UNLIMITED
P.O. Box 518
Massillon, OH 44648

Offers: Wood cut-outs in a wide array of shapes and sizes, plus custom wood cutting services.
For Further Information: Catalog, $1.50 (refundable).

When using a liquid form of paint, use very little paint on your brush. You should be working with a "dry brush."
— Stencil House of NH, Inc.

DARCIE HUNTER PUBLICATIONS
P.O. Box 253
Littlerock, CA 93543
(805) 944-4559

Offers: Books on tole, country folk painting and others.
For Further Information: Catalog for SASE with 52¢ postage.
Accepts: MasterCard, Visa

DESIGNS BY RHONDA
P.O. Box 289
Poplarville, MS 39470
(601) 795-8809

Offers: Designs by Rhonda books, including *Carousel Collection* of patterns/instructions for wood, fabric and others, plus 20 projects with carousels, using brush sculpting techniques.
For Further Information: Contact dealer, or send SASE for details.
Discounts: Sells wholesale.

DUX' DEKES DECOY CO.
RD 2, P.O. Box 66
Greenwich, NY 12834
(518) 692-7703, (800) 553-4725

Offers: Over 50 patterns of carved decoy blanks: Swan, goose, duck, loon, shorebirds, wading blanks (miniature to full-size white pine or basswood).
For Further Information: Write for information.
Discounts: Sells wholesale.
Accepts: MasterCard, Visa

EASY LEAF
947 N. Cole Ave.
Los Angeles, CA 90038
(213) 469-0856

Offers: Line of genuine gold leaf and composition metal leaf in a variety of shades, karats and types. Also offers gold leaf accessories and supplies. Manufacturer.
For Further Information: Free catalog.

FACTORY 2 U, INC.
P.O. Box 250
Glenmont, NY 12077

Offers: Pine woodenware, including pegboards, shelves, shadowboxes, plus over 90 maple/poplar cut-outs. Also offers plaques and sign boards, wreaths, lap desks, 13 baskets, book and other racks, stools, boxes, towel bars, sconces, quilt racks and candleholders. Parts: Pegs, wheels, axles, candle cups, dowels and bases. Also carries plywood sheets and custom cutouts to order.

For Further Information: Catalog, $2 (refundable).
Discounts: Quantity discounts.

FORTÉ INDUSTRIES INC.
P.O. Box 276
Stephenson, MI 49887

Offers: Wood cut-outs and unassembled kits including miniatures, wall units, collector boxes, shadowboxes, basket covers, Christmas shapes. Also offers basswood lumber in 3 widths.
For Further Information: Catalog, $1.

GOLD LEAF & METALLIC POWDERS, INC.
74 Trinity Place, Suite 1807
New York, NY 10006
(212) 267-4900

Offers: Genuine and composition gold leaf in a variety of karats and shades, plus silver, palladium, copper and aluminum leaf, supplies for patinating and gilding and restoration aids.
For Further Information: Send SASE for information.

HERITAGE CRAFT STUDIO, INC.
325 Dreyer Dr. W., Unit 23
Ajax, Ontario L1S 6W6 Canada

Offers: Folk art painting supplies, including woodenware, paints, brushes, books.
For Further Information: Catalog, $1.
Discounts: Sells wholesale.

HERITAGE SAW CO.
11225 6th St. E.
St. Petersburg, FL 33706
(813) 367-7557

Offers: Line of woodenware, paints, brushes, books, plus folk art painting tools and supplies.
For Further Information: Catalog, $2.
Discounts: Sells wholesale.

HOFCRAFT
P.O. Box 72
Grand Haven, MI 49417
(800) 828-0359

Offers: Tole art supplies, including a full line of paints (Priscilla, Permanent Pigment, Shiva), dyes, brushes and handcrafted wood items, plus books.
For Further Information: Catalog, $4.
Discounts: Has discounts.
Accepts: MasterCard, Visa

HOMESTEAD HANDCRAFTS
1301 N. Pines Rd.
Spokane, WA 99206
(509) 928-1986

Offers: Tole decorative painting supplies, including paints (acrylics, fabric, sponging, inks), brushes and cleaners, canvas, mediums, stencils, resin, stains, finishes, unfinished wood. Also offers artist's supplies and tole books.
For Further Information: Catalog, $3.

Tired of those bare walls? Consider the wide range of stencils available and create your own wall murals. Not only could you save money, but you'll also have a unique, decorative feature for market resale of your home.

—Manor House Designs

HOUSE WORKS PLUS
P.O. Box 432
Randolph, VT 05060
or 102 Taylor Ave.
Madison, CT 06443

Offers: Wooden cut-outs, including hearts on strings, peg racks, clam and teddy bear baskets, cat silhouettes, others.
For Further Information: Catalog, $2 (refundable).

JACKIE SHAW STUDIO
13306 Edgemont Rd.
Smithsburg, MD 21783
(301) 824-7592

Offers: 100 videos/books, including *View It 'N Do It* decorative painting lessons by Jackie Shaw, Ardi Hansen, Nancy Michael, Sherry Gunter, others. Subjects include angels, wildflowers, birds/butterflies, animals, simple strokes and faux finishes. Pattern books include subjects such as folk art, wood, fabric painting, tin punch, stenciling, others. Also carries brushes, kits.
For Further Information: Contact dealer, or catalog, $1.
Discounts: Sells wholesale to legitimate businesses.

JENNINGS DECOY CO.
601 Franklin Ave. NE
St. Cloud, MN 56304
(800) 331-5613

Offers: Decoy painting kits including blanks, eyes, paints, patterns.
For Further Information: Free catalog.
Accepts: MasterCard, Visa

KNOTTINGHAM'S CRAFTS
2312 Jonathan Ave.
Rockford, IL 61103

Offers: Unfinished wood cut-outs and patterns of bears, bunnies, hearts, cats, shelves, children's motifs, dinosaurs, minis, others.
For Further Information: Catalog, $2 (refundable).

LADYBUG ART CENTER
1901 E. Bennett St.
Springfield, MO 65804
(417) 883-4708

Offers: Decorative painting instruction/pattern books: Traditional and country designs, including country kids, florals, whimsical animals (rabbits, bears, donkeys, cats, dogs, others), wildlife, Patticakes, characters and animals, Light in the Window angels, Victorian designs, American Reflections scenics, others.
For Further Information: Contact dealer, or send SASE for list.
Accepts: MasterCard, Visa

LAILA'S
22 Strathearn Ave, Units 1 & 2
Bramalea, Ontario L6T 4L8 Canada

Offers: Full line of decoupage prints by a variety of artists in traditional, classics, florals, animals, birds and others. Books also available.
For Further Information: Color catalog, $20, or SASE with inquiry.

LARSON WOOD MANUFACTURING
P.O. Box 672
Park Rapids, MN 56470

Offers: Full, wide range of woodenware, including boxes, plaques, frames, toys, novelties and game parts. Also carries stains, paints, hardware. Manufacturer.
For Further Information: Stencil pattern color catalog, $4.50. Precut stencil color catalog, $4, or both $7 (refundable).

THE MAGIC BRUSH, INC.
P.O. Box 530
Portal, AZ 85632

Offers: Pattern/instruction books for decorative painting, by Sherry C. Nelson, including how to paint realistic birds, butterflies and animals on wood, reverse glass or canvas; carries design/pattern packets.
For Further Information: Send 4 29¢ stamps for catalog.

MANOR HOUSE DESIGNS
1795 Seven Chapel Rd.
Millersville, MD 21108
(410) 721-8945

Offers: Stencil patterns (mylar, acetate) of wreaths, potted flowers, topiaries, tabletop, trompe l'oeil, bird cages and others—detailed cut. Air Nouveau stencil burners. Precut stencils for wall murals.
For Further Information: Stencil pattern catalog, $4.50. Precut stencil catalog, $4.
Discounts: Sells wholesale to legitimate businesses.

NEW ENGLAND COUNTRY DESIGNS
20 Hatheway Rd.
Ellington, CT 06029
(203) 871-0033

Offers: Pattern packets for New England homes in wood and acrylic (miniature collectibles), with instructions, drawings, photos, wood.
For Further Information: Catalog, $2.
Discounts: "Dealer inquiries welcome."

P.C. ENGLISH
Thornburg, VA 22565
(800) 221-9474

Offers: Carved waterfowl blanks (with eyes and color painting patterns) of mallards, wood and goldeneye ducks.
For Further Information: Write for catalog.

PLAID ENTERPRISES
P.O. Box 7600
Norcross, GA 30091

Offers: An instructional video on marbleizing and faux techniques for home decor using waterbase FolkArt acrylic paints.
For Further Information: Send SASE.

RAINBOW WOODS
20 Andrews St.
Newnan, GA 30263
(404) 251-4195

Offers: Unfinished hardwood turnings, including dowels, wheels, axles, candle cups, hearts, napkin rings, eggs, Shaker pegs, boxes, checkers, fruit, balls, knobs, spindles, thimbles and others in wide array of sizes. Jewelry findings.
For Further Information: Free catalog.
Discounts: Quantity discounts; sells wholesale to legitimate businesses.

BARNEY ROBERTI, DAUGHTERS AND SONS
Youngsville, PA 16371

Offers: Wood parts and wood stenciled shapes in country and modern styles, including animals, others.
For Further Information: Catalog, $2.50 (refundable).

Courtesy of Dover Publications.

FAITH ROLLINS

13010 W. 66th St.
Shawnee, KS 66216

Offers: Really Country painting series (pattern/instructional books) by Faith Rollins, including people, traditional motifs, Christmas, plantation folk art, animals, toys, patriotic motifs, scenics, florals, others.
For Further Information: Catalog, $2.
Discounts: "Dealer inquiries welcome."

SANDEEN'S

1315 White Bear Ave.
St. Paul, MN 55106
(612) 776-7012

Offers: Tole-making and folk art supplies: Wood items, paints, books.
For Further Information: Catalog, $2 (refundable).
Accepts: MasterCard, Visa
See Also: Embroidery and Cross-Stitch

SAWDUST AND PAINTINGS

376 E. Rialto Ave.
San Bernardino, CA 92408
(909) 381-3885

Offers: Unfinished wood products—shapes, wheels, others.
For Further Information: Catalog, $2 (refundable).
Store Location: Yes
Discounts: Sells wholesale to legitimate businesses.

SIVERS WOOD IDEAS

7710 Cherry Park, #140
Houston, TX 77095

Offers: Original art patterns for tole, plus wood items.
For Further Information: Portfolio of patterns, $2 (refundable).

STENCIL HOUSE OF N.H.

P.O. Box 16109
Hooksett, NH 03106
(603) 625-1716

Offers: Over 175 stencils (from mylar) designs: Reproductions, children's, florals, traditional, others—for hard surfaces and fabrics. Also offers Paintstiks, acrylics, stencil adhesives, brushes, cleaners and floor cloths. Services include custom designing and stenciling.
For Further Information: Catalog, $2.50 (refundable).
Discounts: Sells wholesale to legitimate businesses.

THE STRAWBERRY TREE, INC.

1 Merrimac St.
Newburyport, MA 01950
(617) 465-5053

Offers: Unfinished pine woodenware, including spice chests in 3 sizes, with 3 to 5 drawers, plus boxes, cut-out shapes, toy items, decoratives, others.
For Further Information: Catalog, $1.

Pet food bowls make the best water containers for decorative painting because they will not tip over or spill.

—Cranberry Painter Decorative Arts

TOFT'S TOLE HOUSE

P.O. Box 249X21
Waynesville, MO 65583

Offers: Precious Littles collection of cut-out patterns/kits in folk designs for bookends and others with photos and instructions.
For Further Information: Catalog, $2.

TREASURES

P.O. Box 9
Huntsville, OH 43324

Offers: Plans/cutting patterns for furniture pieces and home accessories (as shown in books by Jo Sonja, Helan Barrick, Pat Clarke, Folk Art Finish and others) in all shapes full size, plus kits. (Also has assembled items.)
For Further Information: Catalog, $3.
Store Location: Yes
Discounts: Quantity discounts; allows discounts to teachers and institutions; sells wholesale to legitimate businesses.

URSA MAJOR CORP.

695 Mistletoe, #2
P.O. Box 3368
Ashland, OR 97520
(800) 999-3433

Offers: Night Sky Star Stencil kit, including stars stencil for ceiling and luminous paint (invisible in daytime, but shines in the dark 30 plus minutes); stencil can be reused if carefully taken down. Also offers U.S.A. Map Stencil, World Map Stencil.
For Further Information: Free brochures.

VIKING FOLK ART PUBLICATIONS

1317 8th St. SE
Waseca, MN 56093
(507) 835-8043

Offers: Pattern/instructional books for decorative painting, including transparent flowers (acrylics and bronzing powder), traditional and country designs, for all levels of ability. Also offers decorated dimensional frames and sweatshirt designs for fabric dyes.
For Further Information: Contact dealer or send SASE for list.

WEST MOUNTAIN GOURD FARM

Rt. 1, P.O. Box 853
Gilmer, TX 75644
(903) 734-5204

Offers: Gourds in a range of shapes/sizes, cleaned and ready to paint or craft.
For Further Information: Information packet, $2 (refundable).

WHITE PINE DESIGNS, INC.

Rt. 1, P.O. Box 99
Roland, IA 50236
(515) 388-4601

Offers: Raw wood boxes: Pantry, recipe, jewelry, trunks, tissue. Also offers doll toys and furniture.
For Further Information: Catalog, $3.
Discounts: Sells wholesale.

WOLFORD ENTERPRISES

P.O. Box 3321
Fontana, CA 92334

Offers: Little doll pictures (ready to paint) on ivory bristol.
For Further Information: Send SASE for details.

Always read through the entire instructions before beginning to paint an item, so you will have all supplies on hand, be prepared for each step, and find answers to questions before you are halfway through the project.

—B&B Publishing, Inc.

THE WOODEN HEART

Rt. 11, P.O. Box 2260
Elizabethton, TN 37643
(615) 543-5602

Offers: Wood design packets for birdhouses, plates.
For Further Information: Send SASE with 2 stamps for catalog.
Discounts: Sells wholesale to legitimate businesses.
See Also: Fabric Decorating

WORDEN'S WORLD OF CRAFTS, INC.

3359 N. Federal Highway
Pompano Beach, FL 33064

Offers: Paper tole kits (75 designs)—traditional and classic motifs, florals, others.
For Further Information: Free catalog.

Tools and Equipment—Multipurpose

Also see specific arts, crafts and needlecrafts categories.

ARTOGRAPH, INC.
13205 16th Ave. N.
Minneapolis, MN 55441
(612) 553-1112

Offers: Artograph opaque projectors (transfers, enlarges or reduces photos, designs or patterns for tracing), including compact models and others plus floor stands. Manufacturer.
For Further Information: Contact dealer, or write for free booklet.

ATLAS COMPRESSION ENGINEERING
955 Massachusetts Ave.
Cambridge, MA 02139

Offers: Little Atlas embossing press (embosses and patterns metals, leather, plastic, Fimo, others)—all steel unit.
For Further Information: Free information.

BLUE RIDGE MACHINERY & TOOLS, INC.
P.O. Box 536
Hurricane, WV 25526
(304) 562-3538

Offers: Machinery/tools, including lathes, milling machines, and hand and power tools by Unimat, Compact, Maximat, Myford, Sherline, Atlas, Jet and many other manufacturers. Also offers machine shop supplies and accessories.
For Further Information: Catalog, $1.
Discounts: Sells wholesale to legitimate businesses.

BRANDMARK
462 Carthage Dr.
Xenia, OH 45385
(513) 426-6843

Offers: Branding irons in solid brass, with convenient torch heating. The first line of each brand reads "Handcrafted by" and is followed by a custom-made second line of up to 20 letters and spaces maximum. The brands feature ¼-inch letters with line borders. Also offers an electric model.
For Further Information: Send SASE for details.
Accepts: MasterCard, Visa

CARDINAL ENGINEERING
Rt. 1, P.O. Box 163
Cameron, IL 61423
(309) 342-7474

Offers: You-Build Wood-Met Plans: Clamp and spin tools, lathes, turning chisels, saws, routers, air compressors, sanders, drill presses, boring heads and bars, pantographs, gas-fired furnaces and many accessories. Also offers hand tools, drills, measuring items, magnifiers, aluminum and stainless steel, tool steel, brass, music wire and copper tubes. Books are also available.
For Further Information: Catalog, $2.

THE DAN-SIG CO.
P.O. Box 2141
Memphis, TN 38101
(901) 525-8464

Offers: Dazor line of magnifier lamps in a variety of styles and types, including floating arm pedestal and a floating arm model on rollers. Also offers replacement lamps and bulbs.
For Further Information: Contact dealer, or send SASE for details.

DREMEL, INC.
4915 21st St.
Racine, WI 53406
(414) 554-1390

Offers: Power tools, attachments and accessories, including redesigned Moto-Tool high-speed rotary tools, shaft attachments and drill presses, plus 2-speed scroll saws, disc/belt sanders, table saws, engravers, attachments and over 165 bits for over 10 applications. Manufacturer.
For Further Information: Contact dealer, or write for catalog.

The well-known product WD-40 makes an excellent hand cleaner also—just spray it on and rub it in like soap, wipe your hands dry and then wash with your regular soap.
—Cardinal Engineering

THE FOREDOM ELECTRIC CO.
16 Stony Hill Rd.
Bethel, CT 06801

Offers: Flexible shaft rotary power tools, 21 handpieces and accessories tools to cut, grind, buff, polish, sand and deburr.

Also offers bench lathes (variable speeds), hand-piece holders, and power tools and accessories for crafts, jewelry making. Manufacturer.
For Further Information: Contact dealer, or write for free catalog.

FOSTER-TRENT, INC.
2345 Boston Post Rd.
Larchmont, NY 10538

Offers: Craft projector that enlarges pictures, patterns and drawings for prints, plans, photos and gems. Projects images onto wall, wood, paper, fabric or screen.
For Further Information: Send SASE for full details.

GOLD CO.
P.O. Box 24986
Tampa, FL 33623

Offers: Gold foil printer (personalizes business cards, pencils, matches, others).
For Further Information: Write for details.

HARBOR FREIGHT TOOLS
3491 Mission Oaks Blvd.
Camarillo, CA 93012

Offers: Full line of power and hand tools, equipment and accessories by Porter-Cable, Goodyear, Powerwinch, Black & Decker, Stanley, Makita, SK, Skil, Hanson, Industrial, Eastern, Ryobi, Chicago Pneumatic, Campbell Hausfeld, Homelite, Milwaukee, Empire, Vise-Grip, Quincy, others. Usuals, and automobile tools, trailers, dollys, shop cranes, carts, pumps, generators and welding equipment.
For Further Information: Write for catalog.
Store Location: Yes
Accepts: American Express, Discover, MasterCard, Visa

KEMPER TOOLS
13595 12th St.
Chino, CA 91710

Offers: Tools for arts/crafts—tole painting, clay modeling, sculpting, stenciling, ceramics, doll making, bead making, cake decorating, pottery and many others. Includes line tools, palette knives, wire forms, dog sets, brushes, flower makers, cutter sets, clay gun, knives, brushes, plus tools for quilling, carving, piercing, making lace and plaster cleanup. Stocks modeling compound and others. Manufacturer.
For Further Information: Free catalog.

MICROSTAMP CORP.
2770 E. Walnut St.
Pasadena, CA 91107
(818) 793-9489

Offers: Trace Mark micro-marking system (for permanent identification of cameras, most metals, plastics, other smooth firm surfaces). The imprint is virtually invisible, but legible under a magnifying glass.
For Further Information: Send SASE for full details.

NORTHERN
P.O. Box 1219
Burnsville, MN 55337

Offers: Full and complete lines of hand and power tools, parts and equipment including sandblasters, drills, a variety of saw models, gas engines, generators, hydraulic parts, welders and welding sets, winches and jacks, air compressors and air tools, saws, sanders and drill bits. Also offers Pro-Max chainsaws, log splitters, Sawzall kits, portable Migwelder and torches (including pen/pocket), welders, pressure washers, hole shooters (industrial drill use) and drill presses. Carries workbench kits, tool boxes and others.
For Further Information: Free catalog.
Discounts: Has discounts.

NORTON PRODUCTS DEPARTMENT
P.O. Box 2012
New Rochelle, NY 10802

Offers: Craft projector enlarges patterns, pictures, plans, projects, slides, coins, gems, etc., onto wood and other surfaces.
For Further Information: Send SASE for details.
Accepts: MasterCard, Visa

NOVA TOOL CO.
12500 Finigan Rd.
P.O. Box 29341
Lincoln, NE 68529
(402) 464-0511

Offers: Branding irons for hard and soft woods with solid brass heads and deep cut letters. The first line says "Handcrafted by," and the second line consists of up to 20 characters and spaces of choice. Also offers a 3-line model iron.
For Further Information: Free brochure.
Accepts: MasterCard, Visa

PARAGRAVE CORP.
1455 W. Center St.
Orem, UT 84057
(801) 225-8300, (800) 624-7415

Offers: Paragrave hi-tech engraving system (with thin, ultra-high speed drill in Parapak). It engraves glass, metal, wood and other hard surfaces. Demonstration video available.
For Further Information: Send SASE for full information.
Accepts: Discover, MasterCard, Visa

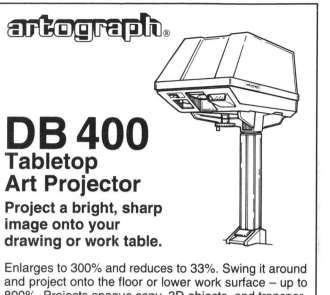

DB 400
Tabletop
Art Projector
Project a bright, sharp image onto your drawing or work table.

Enlarges to 300% and reduces to 33%. Swing it around and project onto the floor or lower work surface – up to 800%. Projects opaque copy, 3D objects, and transparencies (accessory backlight required).

The ideal art projector for graphic artist/illustrators or fine artists.

AVAILABLE FROM:

Art projector. Courtesy of Artograph.

REX GRAPHIC SUPPLY
P.O. Box 6226
Edison, NJ 08818
(201) 613-8777

Offers: The Creator table for draftsman, artist and graphic artist. The table has a white melamine top, heavy gauge tubular steel base (enamel finish), dual position foot rest, rear stabilizing bar and built-in floor levelers. It's adjustable for height and angle and comes in 2 size models.
For Further Information: Send SASE or call for full information.

SMITHY
3023 E. 2nd St.
The Dalles, OR 97058
(619) 449-1112

Offers: Lathe/mill/drill 3-in-1 machine shop (multi-use for any shape or size work in metal, wood or plastic).
For Further Information: Write or call for information.

TESTRITE INSTRUMENT CO., INC.
135 Monroe St.
Newark, NJ 07105

Offers: Stanrite easels—aluminum lights, eight units and High Style studio types, plus portable indoor/outdoor and table models. Also offers Seerite opaque projectors—4 models plus accessories—and Stanrite lighting—north light with reflector. Exhibition lights available.
For Further Information: Free art catalog.

THE TOOL CRIB OF THE NORTH
P.O. Box 1716
Grand Forks, ND 58206
(800) 582-6704

Offers: Power tools by Smart, Freud, Skil, Davis, Performax, Biesemeyer, DeWalt, Powermatic, Black & Decker, Elu, Delta, AEG, Makita, JET, Milwaukee, Accu-Miter, Jorgensen, Panasonic, Ryobi, Bosch, Porter-Cable and others.
For Further Information: Catalog, $3.
Accepts: Discover, MasterCard, Visa

ULTRAVISION
5589 Cote des Neiges
Montreal, Quebec H3T 1Y8 Canada
(514) 344-3988

Offers: Magnifiers in a variety of models, including 3 clipons, Optivisor and other headband types, stand (flexi), hand, Magnistitch with mount or clamp, loupes and linen testers. Also offers Big Eye and other illuminated/lamp magnifiers.
For Further Information: Free catalog.
Discounts: Quantity discounts.

Wine and Beer Making

BEER & WINE HOBBY
180 New Boston St.
Woburn, MA 01801

Offers: Line of wine- and beer-making supplies and equipment.
For Further Information: Free catalog.

THE CELLAR
14411 Greenwood Ave. N.
Seattle, WA 98133
(206) 365-7660, (800) 342-1871

Offers: Full line of equipment/supplies. For beer making, products include mini-brewery kits (4), yeasts, 17 plus malt extracts, hops, brewing equipment (fermenters, brew kegs, controllers, additives), bottling equipment and bottles. Wine-making products include ingredients, kits, supplies, fermentation items, hydrometers, barrels, crushers, presses, pumps, filters, bottling equipment and bottles. Also offers soda pop extracts, dispensers, glassware, videos, books.
For Further Information: Free catalog.
Store Location: Yes
Discounts: Quantity discounts.
Accepts: MasterCard, Visa

GREAT FERMENTATIONS
87 Larkspur St.
San Rafael, CA 94901

Offers: Line of home brew supplies, "pub quality."
For Further Information: Free catalog.

KRAUS
P.O. Box 7850
Independence, MO 64054

Offers: Wine- and beer-making supplies, including fruit presses, crushers, siphons, tubing, hops, malted barley grains, malt extracts, yeasts, heading powders, brewing salts, gypsum, concentrates. Extracts include liqueur, wine, soda pop. Also offers food grade containers, fermenters, fruit presses, grape crushers, hydrometers, wine filter kits, filters, brushes, pitters, sieves, funnels, cappers, labels, bottle capping and corking machines and corks.
For Further Information: Free illustrated catalog.
Accepts: MasterCard, Visa

O'BRIENS CELLAR SUPPLIES
P.O. Box 284
Wayne, IL 60184
(312) 289-7169

Offers: Beer- and wine-making supplies. Wine-making products include additives, concentrates, neutralizers, tannin, nutrients, oak chips, equipment sets, pressure and other barrels, bags, cloths, transferring items, vinometer, balance scales, presses, kits, corkers and cappers. Beer-making products include malt extracts, 16 kits, malt syrups, additives, brewing enzymes, malt grains, grain mills, hops, screw caps, corks, crowns and stoppers. Books are also available.
For Further Information: Free catalog.
Discounts: Quantity discounts.
Accepts: MasterCard, Visa

SEMPLEX
P.O. Box 11476
Minneapolis, MN 55411

Offers: Wine- and beer-making supplies/equipment: Nutrients, clarifiers, filters, yeasts, filter kits, stoppers, bungs, spigots, hand-corking machines, fermentation locks, hydrometers, vinometers, bags, funnels, winebases, 15 concentrates, bottle cappers, bottles, chemicals, beer yeasts and hops, barley, malt extracts and T. Noirot extracts.
For Further Information: Free illustrated catalog.
Accepts: MasterCard, Visa

SPECIALTY PRODUCTS INTERNATIONAL
P.O. Box 784
Chapel Hill, NC 27514

Offers: Beer- and wine-making supplies: Kits, ingredient packs, bottle capper sets, fermenters, siphon units, hydrometers, enzymes, tannin, descalers/sterilizers, malts. Books are also available.
For Further Information: Free catalog.

WILLIAM'S
P.O. Box 2195
San Leandro, CA 94577

Offers: Line of beer-making supplies: Yeast, hops, malts, bottles, equipment, caps, others.
For Further Information: Free catalog and newsletter.

Wood Carving

Also see General Craft Supplies, Construction—Full-Size Structures, Doll and Toy Making—Rigid, Furniture Making and Upholstery, Frames and Picture Framing, Woodworking and other related categories.

BUCK RUN CARVING SUPPLIES
781 Gully Rd.
Aurora, NY 13026
(315) 364-8414

Offers: Detail Master woodburners, Foredom power tools, Miller wildfowl study bills, pewter-cast feet, Kuzalls and Ruby carvers, High-Tech grinders, paints, brushes, others. Books and videos are also available.
For Further Information: Catalog, $2 (refundable).

CHESAPEAKE BAY WOODCRAFTERS
4307 Hanover Ave.
Richmond, VA 23221
(800) 388-9838

Offers: Quality basswood and tupelo blanks, carving cutouts, patterns. Tools: Foredom brand woodburners, grinders, carvers, cutters.
For Further Information: Free catalog.
Accepts: MasterCard, Visa

COXE BLOCKS
555 Redfern Lane
Hartsville, SC 29550
(800) 354-4262

Offers: Carving blocks in over 10 standard sizes (tupelo, juniper). Does custom sawing from patterns or for special sizes.
For Further Information: Send for price sheet.
Discounts: "Welcomes dealer inquiries."
Accepts: MasterCard, Visa

FLEX EYES
5000 Krystal Dr.
Milton, FL 32571
(904) 994-6122

Offers: Eyes for carvers and taxidermists—nonbreakable, painted, adjustable, flexible, with finished front eyeball. Also offers waterfowl and fish eyes.
For Further Information: Write for information.
Accepts: MasterCard, Visa

FOREST PRODUCTS
P.O. Box 12
Avon, OH 44011

Offers: Over 90 basswood carving kits, including ducks, songbirds, shorebirds and birds of prey. Carving supplies: Eyes, cast feet and bandsawed decoy blanks. Tools: Ruby carvers, texturing discs, cutters, Flexi-Craft machines. Books are also available.
For Further Information: Write for catalog.

G. SCHOEPFER, INC.
460 Cook Hill Rd.
Cheshire, CT 06410
(800) 875-6939

Offers: Eyes for decoys, birds, fish: Basic glass, lead crystal, machine glass lenses, others.
For Further Information: Send SASE for price list.
Discounts: Quantity discounts.
Accepts: American Express, MasterCard, Visa

GREGORY D. DORRANCE CO.
1063 Oak Hill Ave.
Attleboro, MA 02703
(508) 222-6255

Offers: Decoy carving blanks and wood. Supplies include cast feet and eyes, diamonds, texturing stones, brushes, and Paasche and Badger airbrushes. Art supplies include Grumbacher, Liquitex, Jo-Sonja, Winsor & Newton, Robert Simmons. Also offers over 300 books.
For Further Information: Write for information.
Store Location: Yes

HIGHWOOD BOOKSHOP
P.O. Box 1246
Traverse City, MI 49685
(616) 271-3898

Offers: Decoy and fish carving books on painting, design, carving techniques, reference, patterns, others. (Also collector's books, outdoor magazines.)
For Further Information: Send 58¢ postage for #18 catalog.
Accepts: MasterCard, Visa

J.H. KLINE CARVING SHOP
Forge Hill Rd., P.O. Box 445
Manchester, PA 17345
(717) 266-3501

Offers: Over 800 patterns of precut wood blanks, Foredom tools, glass eyes, woodburning units, bits, carvers, sanders, abrasives, cast bills and feet.
For Further Information: Catalog, $1 (refundable).

JANTZ SUPPLY
P.O. Box 584
Davis, OK 73030
(800) 351-8900

Offers: Knife supplies: Over 85 blades and blade kits (with handle material, fittings, instructions). Also offers tools (by Dremel, Baldor, Starrett and others). Abrasives and polishing equipment.
For Further Information: Catalog, $3.
Accepts: Discover, MasterCard, Visa

JENNINGS DECOY CO.
601 Franklin Ave. NE
St. Cloud, MN 56304
(612) 253-2253

Offers: Over 1,400 products for carvers: Basswood, tupelo, butternut cut-outs and cut-out kits—wildfowl, Santas, others. Also offers eyes, other accessories. patterns, cork decoy kits and books.
For Further Information: Free catalog.

MDI WOODCARVERS SUPPLY
228 Main St.
Bar Harbor, ME 04609
(800) 866-5728

Offers: Dremel flex shaft kits, points (diamond, ruby, tungsten carbide) and carving books.
For Further Information: Write for information.
Accepts: Discover, MasterCard, Visa

MOUNTAIN WOODCARVERS
P.O. Box 3485
Estes Park, CO 80517
(800) 292-6788

Offers: Stubai (Austrian) woodcarving tools—mid-length, steel (for hand and mallet carving) of professional quality.
For Further Information: Free catalog.

RAZERTIP INDUSTRIES
P.O. Box 1258
Martensville, Saskatchewan S0K 2T0 Canada
(306) 226-2188

Offers: Detail burner unit with 26 tip shapes; small, light pan. Available in Canada only.
For Further Information: Write for dealer or information.
Accepts: MasterCard

RITTER CARVERS, INC.
1559 Dillon Rd.
Maple Glen, PA 19002
(215) 997-3395, (800) 242-0682

Offers: Carving supplies for basswood, white cedar, tupelo and hardwoods. Also offers carving cut-outs, cast pewter feet, glass eyes and other accessories, diamonds, carbides, Jo-Sonja colors. Tools: Foredom; chisels, detailers.
For Further Information: Free catalog.
Store Location: Yes

WOOD CARVERS SUPPLY, INC.
P.O. Box 7500
Englewood, FL 34295

Offers: Carving supplies, including woods, kits, hand and power carving tools, carving knives and books.
For Further Information: Catalog, $2.

WOOD N' THINGS, INC.
601 E. 44th St., #3
Boise, ID 83714
(208) 375-WOOD

Offers: Carving supplies by Foredom and Auto Mach, including gouges, burners, knives, glass eyes, woods and over 200 books.
For Further Information: Free catalog.
Accepts: MasterCard, Visa

Woodworking

Also see General Craft Supplies, Construction — Full-Size Structures, Doll and Toy Making — Rigid, Furniture Making and Upholstery, Frames and Picture Framing, Tools and Equipment, Wood Carving and related categories.

ACCENTS
P.O. Box 7387
Gonic, NH 03839

Offers: 1,000 woodcraft (blueprint) patterns: 200 packet for jigsaws, scroll and bandsaws; 100 Country Critters wind-action whirligigs; 100 yard ornaments (animals, birds, others); country projects patterns and show-stoppers.
For Further Information: Catalog and sample pattern, $2.

ACME ELECTRIC
P.O. Box 1716
Grand Forks, ND 58206

Offers: Power tools, including Delta woodworking machines (Unisaw, sanders, router/shapers, saws, tilting arbors, others), and Powermatic saw units and others. Also offers nailers, drills, jointing systems, jigsaws, cross cutter and miter saws, sanders, shapers, lathes, jointers, routers and saw bosses.
For Further Information: Catalog, $2.
Accepts: MasterCard, Visa

ADAMS WOOD PRODUCTS
974 Forest Dr.
Morristown, TN 37814
(615) 587-2942

Offers: Stock wood legs in maple, cherry, oak, mahogany, walnut in a variety of styles and sizes.
For Further Information: Free brochure.

ADJUSTABLE CLAMP CO.
443 N. Ashland Ave.
Chicago, IL 60622

Offers: Clamps: Jorgensen and Pony clamps in a variety of types for woodworking, furniture repair, maintenance.
For Further Information: Free details. "How-to-clamp-it" catalog, $1.
Discounts: Sells wholesale to dealers.

ADVANCED MACHINERY IMPORTS LTD.
P.O. Box 312
New Castle, DE 19720

Offers: Full line of scroll saw blades, accessories and improvements for almost any scroll saw, plus Hegner precision scroll saws. Also offers lathes, lathe duplicators, jet clamps, workbenches, Felderr systems and others.
For Further Information: Write for information.

ALBERT CONSTANTINE & SON, INC.
2050 Eastchester Rd.
Bronx, NY 10461
(212) 792-1600

Offers: Woodworking/veneering supplies: Kits, 80 plus veneers, veneering tools, marquetry kits, Optivisor, pantograph, chisels, mallets, drawknives, carving tools, woodburners, planes, spokeshaves, scrapers, sharpeners, saws, cutters, measurers, rasps. Also offers joiners, routers, doweling units, planers, sanders, sprayers, engravers, gilding supplies, stains, finishes, furniture plans (full-sized), carving and decoy kits. Tools: Knives, vises, router bits, nailers, woodturning tools. Materials: Lumber, turning blocks. Carries clock parts, dollhouse/furniture kits, model kits, toy parts, upholstery tools/supplies, cane, webbing, guitar/dulcimer parts and woods, lamp parts, workbenches and books.
For Further Information: 116-page catalog, $1.
Accepts: Discover, MasterCard, Visa
See Also: Furniture Making and Upholstery

AMT
4th Ave. & Spring St.
Royersford, PA 19468
(215) 948-0400

Offers: Hand and power tools/equipment: Shaper/routers, mortising machines, saws, lathes, carving tools, planers, jointer-planers, vises, clamps, cutters, trimmers, miter gauges/boxes, flexible shafts, drill presses, sanders, grinders, routers and cutters, radial drills, accessories, parts, knives, chisels and others.
For Further Information: Free catalog.
Accepts: Discover, MasterCard, Visa

ARMOR
P.O. Box 445
East Northport, NY 11731
(516) 462-6228

Offers: Wood products: Balls, pegs, cradles, cups, toy wheels, axle pegs, door harp parts, cut-outs, pins, others. Woodworking plans: Swinging cradle, Adirondack chair, rocking horse, traditional furniture (desks, ice boxes, shelves, cabinets, chairs, spinning wheel, dry sinks, stools, children's items, lamps, clocks, pool and soccer tables, others). Also offers clocks and lamp parts, tools, hardware, furniture trim, dollhouse kits and components, stencils, other craft supplies.
For Further Information: Free catalog.
Accepts: MasterCard, Visa

AVIATION INDUSTRIAL SUPPLY CO.
3900 Ulster St.
Denver, CO 80207

Offers: Tools/equipment: Bosch (saws, drills, sanders, routers, trimmers), Hitachi saws, others.
For Further Information: Write or call for prices.
Accepts: MasterCard, Visa

BADGER HARDWOODS
N. 1517 Highway 14
Walworth, WI 53184
(800) 252-2373, (414) 275-9855

Offers: Hardwood lumber: Red oak, white oak, ash, walnut, cherry, maple, butternut. Also offers oak flooring on ramp, widths and lengths, plus paneling in oak, cherry, butternut, ash and maple.
For Further Information: Free catalog.
Accepts: MasterCard, Visa

BARAP SPECIALTIES
835 Bellows
Frankfort, MI 49635

Offers: Hard-to-find woodworking supplies: Whirligigs, door harps, clocks and parts, chair cane, wood toy parts, lamp parts, lazy Susan bearings, tools/patterns, dowels, spindles, finishing materials. Also offers box and cabinet hardware and others.
For Further Information: Catalog, $1.

BOGERT & HOPPER, INC.
P.O. Box 119
Northport, NY 11768
(516) 261-6173

Offers: Wood parts: Wheels, axles, Shaker pegs, candle cups, dowels, others.
For Further Information: Free catalog.

BURL TREE
3527 Broadway St.
Eureka, CA 95503
(707) 442-1319

Offers: Burlwoods: Redwood, maple, buckeye, manzanita, madrone, oak, myrtle, walnut and related figured woods in a variety of thicknesses.
For Further Information: Send SASE for list.
Discounts: Sells wholesale.

CARTER PRODUCTS CO., INC.
437 Spring Ave. NE
Grand Rapids, MI 49503
(616) 451-2928

Offers: Delta (Rockwell) 14-inch and 20-inch bandsaw guide conversion kits plus other kits for popular brand saws 14 inches and larger (including Grizzly, Grob, Davis, Wells and others).
For Further Information: Free brochure.

CASADE TOOLS, INC.
P.O. Box 3110
Bellingham, WA 98227
(800) 235-0272 ext. 31

Offers: Tools: Carbide-tipped router bits and shaper cutters, cabinet sets and ½-inch shank cabinet door sets. Routers: Dovetail, flush trim, cove bits, roundover, core bull nose, Roman ogee, slot cutter, beading. For the shaper: Straights, flutes, beads, corner rounds. Also offers right arm clamps with pivoting arm and wood shaper units.
For Further Information: Write for catalog.
Accepts: MasterCard, Visa

CASEY'S WOOD PRODUCTS
P.O. Box 365
Woolwich, ME 04579
(800) 45-CASEY

Offers: Factory seconds woodenware: Shaker pegs, beanpot candle cups (by 100 plus lots), turnings, dowels, novelties in first and second quality.
For Further Information: Catalog, $1.

CHERRY TREE TOYS
P.O. Box 369-319
Belmont, OH 43718
(614) 484-4363

Offers: Woodcrafting parts/supplies/kits/plans. Wood parts include pegs, wheels, spindles, knobs, plugs, dowels, others. Also offers door harp parts/accessories, toy wagon kits, whirligigs and musical banks, trains and other vehicles, clock and desk parts, miniature hobby tools and sets, miniature items (including authentic old-time gas pumps, washboards, others), plus hardware, stencils, paints, brushes.
For Further Information: Catalog, $1.
Discounts: Quantity discounts.
Accepts: Discover, MasterCard, Visa

COLONIAL HARDWOODS, INC.
7953 Cameron Brown Ct.
Springfield, VA 22153
(800) 466-5451

Offers: Hardwoods (cut to order) in 120 species, veneers, mouldings, wood to 4-inch thickness, burls and blocks for turners, hardware, finishes and books.
For Further Information: Send SASE for list.

COLONIAL WOODWORKS
P.O. Box 19965
Raleigh, NC 27619

Offers: Architectural interior mantels, mouldings, paneling, windows, custom items, others.
For Further Information: Product and design catalog, $10.

CRAFT SUPPLIES USA
P.O. Box 50300
Provo, UT 84605
(801) 373-0919

Offers: Woodturning equipment/tools/accessories by Henry Taylor, Richard Raffan, Dale Nish and Woodfast, including lathes, workshop units, others. Also offers a line of pens, pencils, fountain and rollerball kits.
For Further Information: Catalog, $2.

CRAFTERS MART
P.O. Box 2342
Greeley, CO 80632

Offers: Wood parts/shapes, including turnings (Shaker pegs, candle cups, balls), wheels, door harp tuning pens, clapper balls, plus harp wire, hangers, others.
For Further Information: Catalog, $2 (refundable).

CRAFTERS OF FINE ARTS
P.O. Box 368
Carson City, MI 48811

Offers: Line of woodworking patterns: Windmills, wells, weather vanes, birdhouses, feeders, planters, whirligigs, jig-sawing items, Christmas designs, animals, butterflies, others.
For Further Information: Catalog, $1.

CRAFTS BY CASH
4215 Hill St.
Mims, FL 32754

Offers: Plans for custom rustic mailboxes—3 full-sized plans with instructions.
For Further Information: Information list, $1.

CRAFTS BY JG'S
Rt. 1, P.O. Box 168
Galena, MO 65656

Offers: Full-sized woodcraft patterns (with painting instructions) for towel bars, memo pads, cows and owls, ducks and pigs, bunnies and chickens.
For Further Information: Send SASE for list, prices.

CRAFTSMAN WOOD SERVICE CO.
1735 W. Cortland Ct.
Addison, IL 60101

Offers: Hardwoods: Veneers, marquetry and inlay, turning blocks, boards, lumber, plywood, dowels, pegs, relief carving and moulding. Tools: Dremel, Foredom and others, plus carving sets, upholstery equipment, flexible shaft, power and jigs, others. Also offers hardware, lamp parts, wooden ship models, 11 dollhouse kits, gauges, plans, adhesives, finishes, books and upholstery supplies.
For Further Information: Write for catalog.

CRAFTY CUT-OUTS
1705 Taylor Ave.
Evansville, IN 47714
(812) 479-0454

Offers: Scroll saw patterns—over 150 designs, all occasion. Word cutouts, alphabets.
For Further Information: Send SASE for list.

CROFFWOOD MILLS
RD 1, P.O. Box 14
Driftwood, PA 15832
(814) 546-2532

Offers: Pennsylvania hardwoods—15 species, over 2,000 sizes, 12 species, to 2 inches thick, kiln-dried. Also offers random board and specialty packs, dimension cuts, thin woods. Unique: Sapwood cherry or walnut, others.
For Further Information: Free catalog.
Discounts: "Small orders welcome."

CROWN CITY HARDWARE CO.
1047 N. Allen Ave.
Pasadena, CA 91104

Offers: Over 1,000 reproductions of European hardware (restorations, others) for cabinetry, furniture, doors, windows of iron, brass, wood, porcelain—"olde worlde pieces" authentically produced.
For Further Information: Catalog/history, $25.

CUSTOM WOOD CUT-OUT'S UNLIMITED
P.O. Box 518
Massillon, OH 44648
(216) 832-2919

Offers: Wood cut-outs: Animals, fowl, birds, holiday/novelty shapes, figures, fish and quotes. Also offers necklace parts, ornaments, racks, toys, child's furniture and stools.
For Further Information: Catalog, $2 (refundable).
Discounts: Quantity discounts; sells wholesale to legitimate businesses.

DAKOTA WIND
P.O. Box 866
Jamestown, ND 58402

Offers: Wood cut-out patterns including Windowsill Cats series.
For Further Information: Catalog, $1.

DEER CREEK PRODUCTS
3038 NW 25th Ave.
Pompano Beach, FL 33069

Offers: Over 500 wood patterns for toys: Circus, mermaids, bears, clowns, rockers, playthings, trains, dinosaurs, others. Also offers shelves, signs, ornaments, door stops, weather vanes, kitchen items, decorations, plaques, organizers, tables, chairs, TV trays, lamps, others.
For Further Information: Send SASE for list.

DESIGNCRAFT
729 Grapevine Highway, Suite 358
Hurst, TX 76054

Offers: 300 scroll saw patterns for bookends, puzzles, frames, novelties, others (uses Easy Trace transfer system).
For Further Information: Send SASE for full details.

Beech, birch and maple are comparable, somewhat the same color and subdued figure. They finish the same and machine alike. Hard maple tends to tear out when machining. All are light in color—from light brown to creamy beige.

—Croffwood Mills

DOYEL ENTERPRISES
P.O. Box 315
Yorba Linda, CA 92686
(714) 666-1770

Offers: Radial arm saw fence system (cuts angles with one saw groove, adjustable to 47 degrees), aluminum. Others.
For Further Information: Send SASE for details.
Accepts: MasterCard, Visa

DREMEL
P.O. Box 1468
Racine, WI 53401

Offers: Line of woodworking machinery, power tools and accessories, kits and sets. Manufacturer.
For Further Information: Write for free brochure.

E.C. MITCHELL CO.
88-90 Boston St.
P.O. Box 607
Middleton, MA 01949
(508) 774-1191

Offers: Flexible sanding/abrasive cords and tapes (for grooves, slots and holes) in 18 sizes.
For Further Information: Send SASE for list.

EAGLE AMERICA CORP.
P.O. Box 1099
Chardon, OH 44024
(216) 276-9334

Offers: Full line of router bits, laminate trims, groove and edge formers, moulding and other cutters. Router accessories and sets.
For Further Information: Free catalog.
Discounts: Allows discounts for schools, technical institutes, volume users, woodworking clubs, guilds, associations.
Accepts: MasterCard, Visa

ECON ABRASIVES
P.O. Box 865021
Plano, TX 75086
(214) 377-9779

Offers: Sandpaper and sander accessories: Belts, discs, sheets, wide belts, rolls, flap wheels, pump sleeves, cabinet paper, finish paper, jumbo cleaning sticks, plus abrasive belts, bar clamps.
For Further Information: Free catalog.
Discounts: Has discounts.

EDLCO
P.O. Box 5373
Asheville, NC 28813
(704) 255-8765

Offers: Over 20 species of hardwoods and softwoods, including Appalachian woods and hard-to-find imported woods—select and project grades.
For Further Information: Write or call for catalog.
Discounts: Quantity discounts.

FARRIS MACHINERY
1206 Pavilion Dr.
Grain Valley, MO 64029
(800) 872-5489

Offers: "K5" home workshop wood machining center, saws,

planes, molds, mortises; takes up less than 12 square feet of space, runs on 110V AC power.

For Further Information: Free information kit; VHS video, $14.95.

FORMBY'S WORKSHOP
Olive Branch, MS 38654

Offers: Formby's products for wood: Furniture refinisher dissolves old varnish, lacquer or shellac and conditions the wood.

For Further Information: Free booklet, "Successful Refinishing."

FOURTH DIMENSION
85 Helmar Dr.
Spencerport, NY 14559

Offers: Patterns/instructions for wood cut-outs: Bunnies, sheep, frogs, skunks, raccoons, pigs, flamingos, others.

For Further Information: Catalog, $1.

FROG TOOL CO. LTD.
700 W. Jackson Blvd.
Chicago, IL 60661
(312) 648-1270

Offers: Hand woodworking tools: German carving, Swedish carving, hammers, screwdrivers, Japanese sharpening items, doweling jigs, bevelers, cutters, drills, measuring items, planes, drawknives, spokeshaves, musical instrument tools, saws, veneering/turning tools, panovise, woodburning tools, lathes, dowels, table hardware, sanding items, log cabin tools, finishes, workbenches. Power tools: Grinders, Foredom tools and handpieces, burrs. Plans and books also available.

For Further Information: Catalog, $5.

Discounts: Quantity discounts; sells wholesale to legitimate businesses.

Accepts: MasterCard, Visa

See Also: Furniture Making and Upholstery

GARRETT WADE CO., INC.
161 Avenue of the Americas
New York, NY 10013
(212) 807-1757, (800) 221-2942

Offers: Full line of hand tools, including the new advanced precision honing guide (sets micro bevels), "blind nailer" tool (like a positioning jig), scrapers with prepared edges for longer use, multi-angle aluminum gauges, bandsaw blades (including 1/16-inch narrow, in raker style, and "cabinetmaker's special" skip-tooth and unset raker), and other scroll and cabinet styles. Also offers saw setting gauges, gap filling glue, and other common and unique hand tools.

For Further Information: Free catalog.

GENEVA SPECIALTIES
P.O. Box 636
Lake Geneva, WI 53147
(800) 556-2548

Offers: Woodworking plans/kits: Novelty clocks, log and birdhouses, holiday/novelty cutouts, child's furniture, toys, novelty lamps, rocking horses, furniture (shelves, cupboards, cabinets, desks, trunks). Also offers clocks (and parts), musical movements and kits, lamp and electrical parts, classic toy plans and parts, dowels and other turnings, hardware, woodburners, paints, brushes, stencils, decoy kits (fish, fowl) and plans for flower and other carts with metal liners.

For Further Information: Free catalog.

Discounts: Quantity discounts.

Accepts: Discover, MasterCard, Visa

GILLIOM MANUFACTURING, INC.
P.O. Box 1018
St. Charles, MO 63302
(314) 724-1812

Offers: Power tool kits (to-construct), including 12-inch bandsaws, 18-inch bandsaws, 10-inch tilt/arbor saws, lathe/drill press combinations, 9-inch tilt table saws, 6-inch belt sanders, spindle shapers and circular saw tables. Kits include step-by-step plans and all necessary metal parts and components (except wood and motor). Also offers some accessory kits, including a speed reduction kit for cutting steel that fits the 18-inch bandsaw. Power tool plans available (individually, or a set at a savings).

For Further Information: Brochure, $2.

GRIZZLEY IMPORTS, INC.
2406 Reach Rd.
Williamsport, PA 17701
Order line (800) 523-4777, (717) 326-3806

Offers: Shop equipment: Sanders (drum, combo, others), saws (heavy duty, band, others), planers, jointers, shapers, dust collectors, others.

For Further Information: Write or call for information.

Accepts: MasterCard, Visa

HARRIS TOOLS
76 Quentin Rd.
Brooklyn, NY 11223
(800) 449-7747

Offers: Line of old-style hand tools including wooden spokeshave (with adjustable mechanism) and others.

For Further Information: Catalog, $1 (refundable).

HOGUE
P.O. Box 2038
Atascadero, CA 93423
(805) 466-4100

Offers: Exotic woods (cut-off sizes, others): Rosewood, gonedlo alves, pau ferro, coco bolo, others. Use for jewelry, inlays, knife handles, parquet tables.
For Further Information: Send SASE for information.

HOME LUMBER CO.
499 Whitewater St.
Whitewater, WI 53190
(800) 262-5482

Offers: Woodworking tools/equipment by DeWalt, Makita, Bostitch, Ryobi, others.
For Further Information: Send SASE for list.
Accepts: Discover, MasterCard, Visa

HORTON BRASSES
Nooks Hill Rd.
P.O. Box 120
Cromwell, CT 06416
(203) 635-4400

Offers: Full line of cabinet and furniture hardware for homes and antiques, including handles, knobs, latches, hinges and slides in many styles (brass, antiqued, others).
For Further Information: Catalog, $4.

HOUSE OF STARR
P.O. Box 783
Angels Camp, CA 95222

Offers: Patterns for woodcrafting (and fabric painting, etc.), each in 3 sizes.
For Further Information: Patterns list, $1.

HOW-TO BOOK CLUB
Blue Ridge Summit, PA 17214

Offers: Member's prices "up to 50% off" and a bonus book plan. Club news bulletins are sent 14 times yearly; can order, or return form and decline. Members receive introductory books at near-nothing cost and agree to purchase at least 3 books during 2 years. How-to/project books include toy making, home accessories, furniture making, grandfather clocks, outdoor building, pine projects, frames/framing, clock making, remodeling, wood turning, power tool references.
For Further Information: Send for details and current book list.

HOWEE'S INC.
Rt. 7, P.O. Box 633
Joplin, MO 64801
(417) 623-0656

Offers: Wood turnings, including wheels, pegs, spindles, candle cups, knobs, rings, spools, fruits, hearts, finials, boxes, smokestacks, miniatures, beads, bells, buckets, dolls, bowling pins, dowels. Also offers hardware, hinges.
For Further Information: Free catalog.
Discounts: Quantity discounts; sells wholesale to legitimate businesses.

HTC
120 E. Hudson
P.O. Box 839
Royal Oak, MI 48068
(800) 624-2027

Offers: Mobile machine bases (shop on wheels) in a variety of models of welded steel construction.
For Further Information: Free catalog.

INTERNATIONAL TOOL CORP.
1939 Tyler St.
Hollywood, FL 33020
(800) 338-3384

Offers: Full line of woodworking equipment/tools in known brands: Porter-Cable, Delta, Aeg, Senco, Stanley, Skil, Hitachi, Ryobi, Mirka, Milwaukee, Bosch, Freud, DeWalt, Felker, others.
For Further Information: Send SASE for list.
Accepts: Discover, MasterCard, Visa

INTERNATIONAL VIOLIN CO.
4026 W. Belvedere Ave.
Baltimore, MD 21215

Offers: Violin and guitar kits, tools, parts, accessories, tone wood, strings, cases, bows, others.
For Further Information: Catalog, $1.

KAYNE & SONS FORGED HARDWARE
100 Daniel Ridge Rd.
Candler, NC 28715
(704) 667-8868

Offers: Hardware, including household, reproduction, handforged and furniture. Also offers locks, tools and accessories, fireplace items, custom handforging, repairs and restorations.
For Further Information: Catalog, $4.

KLINGSPOR'S SANDING CATALOGUE
P.O. Box 3737
Hickory, NC 28603

Offers: Woodworking equipment: Random, Porter-Cable, Bosch, Ryobi, Delta, others. Includes belt and orbit sanders, sanding center units, drums, sheet and detail sanders. Also offers Dremel Moto-tool, mini grinders, vacuums, others.
For Further Information: Write for catalog.

KNOTWHOLE PUBLISHING
5629 Main St.
Stratford, CT 06497

Offers: Woodworking index/PC information base, guide to published woodworking plans/techniques (12,700 plus projects, plans and tips from 27 woodworking magazines, updated annually).
For Further Information: Send SASE for full details.

LARSON WOOD MANUFACTURING
P.O. Box 672
Park Rapids, MN 56470

Offers: Woodenware (in a variety of sizes/shapes): Plaques, frames, boxes, toys, novelties, game parts. Also offers hardware, paints, stains, finishes, others. Manufacturer.
For Further Information: Catalog, $3 (refundable).

LEICHTUNG WORKSHOPS
4944 Commerce Pkwy.
Cleveland, OH 44128

Offers: Over 400 hand and power woodworking tools, with unusual/exclusive tools for workbench, cabinetry to sharpen, clamp, dowel, instrument-make, mat, frame. Includes tools for miniature crafting, mini-welding, others. Also offers wood and clock parts, woodburners, paints, brushes, abrasive cords/tapes, blade sharpeners for chain saws and mowers and others.
For Further Information: Free catalog.
Accepts: Discover, MasterCard, Visa

LINDEN PUBLISHING
179 Davidson Ave.
Somerset, NJ 08873

Offers: Woodworking books—over 300 titles on finishing, turning, joinery, carving, tools, furniture, wood/timber, toys, carpentry, blacksmithing, cabinetmaking, coach building, others.
For Further Information: Catalog subscription, $1.

LOBO POWER TOOLS
9031 E. Slauson Ave.
Pico Rivera, CA 90660
(310) 949-3747

Offers: Woodworking equipment including saws, planers, shapers, lathes, jointers, sanders, routers, milling units, tool grinders, others.
For Further Information: Send SASE for list.

MACBETH HARDWOODS
930 Ashby Ave.
Berkeley, CA 94710
(510) 843-4390

Offers: Basswood—kiln dried, 1 inch through 5½ inch thicknesses—and Jelutong in clear, KD, rough. Also offers lumber and carving blocks and a variety of other hardwoods.
For Further Information: Send SASE for stock list.

MAFELL NORTH AMERICA, INC.
80 Earhart Dr.
Williamsville, NY 14221
716-626-9303

Offers: Erika pull-push combination radial arm saw unit as table/radial arm saw (and accessories for customizing). Also offers other stationary or timber-framing tools.
For Further Information: Catalog, $1.

MANNY'S WOODWORKERS PLACE
555 Broadway St.
Lexington, KY 40508
(606) 255-5444

Offers: Woodworking books and videos on a variety of instructional subjects.
For Further Information: Catalog, $2.

MANZANITA DECORATIVE WOOD
P.O. Box 111
Protrero, CA 92306
(619) 478-5849

Offers: Manzanita burls—full range of sizes, full inventory.
For Further Information: Call, or send SASE with inquiry.
Discounts: Sells wholesale.

MARLIN INDUSTRIES, INC.
Rt. 70, P.O. Box 191
Cashiers, NC 28717
(704) 743-5551

Offers: Carving machines for professionals and hobbyists, including Sign Carver (machine follows templates) and Sulpi-Carver series.
For Further Information: Brochure and price list, $1.

MARLING LUMBER CO.
P.O. Box 7668
Madison, WI 53707
(800) 247-7178

Offers: Makita power tools, cordless driver-drill (2-speed, variable speed), 25-piece ratchet set, ⅜-inch cordless drill (variable speed), finishing sander, ⅜-inch drill and others.
For Further Information: Send SASE or call for information.
Accepts: MasterCard, Visa

MASTERCRAFT PLANS WEST

P.O. Box 625

Redmond, WA 98073

Offers: Patterns (full-sized) in packets: Jigsaw items, birdhouses, shelves, windmills, tool houses, donkeys with carts, garden furniture, gifts and novelties, country crafts, variety designs, others.

For Further Information: Send SASE for catalog.

MCLS, LTD.

P.O. Box 4053

Rydal, PA 19046

Offers: Woodworking tools—33 plus router bits, including reversible combination rail/stile set, raised panel types, tongue/groove, drawer pull, multiform molding maker, others. Router speed controls.

For Further Information: Send SASE for catalog.

MEISEL HARDWARE SPECIALTIES

P.O. Box 70

Mound, MN 55364

Offers: Door harp plans/kits in 5 designs. Also offers hardware parts kits, tuning pins, clapper balls, music wire and plastic eyes.

For Further Information: Catalog, $1.

Accepts: MasterCard, Visa

MIDWEST DOWEL WORKS, INC.

4631 Hutchinson Rd.

Cincinnati, OH 45248

(513) 574-8488

Offers: Dowels, plugs and pegs in a variety of sizes and woods: Oak, walnut, hickory, maple, cherry, mahogany, teak. Treated dowels are available.

For Further Information: Write for catalog.

Discounts: Quantity discounts.

MONTERY WOODWORKS

214 Ophir, P.O. Box 158

Johannesburg, CA 93528

Offers: Wood products, including plugs, pegs, blocks, dowels, wheels, others.

For Further Information: Catalog and coupon, $1.

OLDE WOODEN BUCKET

P.O. Box 312

Port Richey, FL 34673

Offers: Wooden bucket plans.

For Further Information: Send SASE for details.

OLSON CATALOG SALES

16 Stony Hill Rd.

Bethel, CT 06801

(203) 792-8622

Offers: Bandsaw blades, including flex-back, new furniture band, thin gauge for bench top and 3 wheel saws. Saws are welded to length or are available in 100-foot coils. Scroll saw blades are available in plain or pin end, and fret, spiral and jeweler's type.

For Further Information: Free catalog.

Discounts: Has discounts.

ORIGINAL WOOD DESIGNS

P.O. Box 1141

Los Banos, CA 93635

(209) 826-5541

Offers: Manzanita burlwood—raw burls, finished pieces and slabs in a range of sizes.

For Further Information: Contact for prices.

PACIFIC STANDARD LUMBER CO., INC.

P.O. Box 610

Garberville, CA 95542

(800) 256-8479

Offers: Tropical hardwoods from Fiji (selected with a perpetual yield in mind—milled, dried): Damanu, yako, buabua, salu salu, dakua, kauvula, mahogany, vesi.

For Further Information: Free brochure/samples.

Accepts: MasterCard, Visa

Ash is hard to tell from red oak when finished, but it has a more pronounced oak-like figure than the "real McCoy." Ash is not porous and does not require filler as does red oak.

—Croffwood Mills

PENN STATE INDUSTRIES

2850 Comly Rd.

Philadelphia, PA 19154

(215) 676-7609

Offers: Woodworking machines/accessories—line of air guns, dust collectors, planers, sanders, scroll saws, lathes and suplicators, carving and drill tools, grinders, router bits, shaper cutters, speed control units, corner clamps, others.

For Further Information: Free catalog.

Accepts: Discover, MasterCard, Visa

PERFORMAX PRODUCTS, INC.

12211 Woodlake Dr.

Burnsville, MN 55337

Offers: Power tools: Component drum sander, with radial

saw attachment or stand alone, plus manual or power feed option conveyor unit and a 22-inch drum sander with open end.

For Further Information: Write or call for free brochure.

PLANFAN
P.O. Box 473
Bridgeport, NE 69336

Offers: Complete plans to build gun cabinets in 4 styles.
For Further Information: Send SASE.

POPULAR SCIENCE BOOK CLUB
P.O. Box 1763
Danbury, CT 06813

Offers: Book club for do-it-yourselfers. Members receive bulletins 15 times yearly and can choose or return form within 10 days; "up to 75% discounts" on books. Members choose introductory books at near-nothing cost and agree to purchase a specified number of others within a year; may cancel afterward. Subjects include woodworking skills, home workshops, house building, wiring, plumbing, home improvement, remodeling, repair, carpentry, masonry, furniture making, toys, tools, others.
For Further Information: Write for current book list.

PORTA-NAILS, INC.
P.O. Box 1257
Wilmington, NC 28402
(919) 762-6334, (800) 634-9281

Offers: Woodworking machines: Dowel mate, ring master, panel template, router arc attachment, router mate, universal router system (3 tools from 1), others.
For Further Information: Contact dealer, or write for brochure.

RB INDUSTRIES, INC.
1801 Vine St.
P.O. Box 369
Harrisonville, MO 64701
(800) 487-2623

Offers: RBI Hawk line of scroll saws—beginner/pro models. Others.
For Further Information: Free information kit.

SEVEN CORNERS ACE HARDWARE, INC.
216 7th St. W.
St. Paul, MN 55102
(800) 328-0457

Offers: Woodworking equipment/tools/accessories by Milwaukee, Makita, Freud, Biesmeyer, Bosch, Porter Cable, Ryobi, Delta, Jorgensen, DeWalt, Dremel, Hitachi, David White, Senco, others—bench top, power and hand tools.

Also offers ladders (fiberglass, aluminum types), air tools, variety of kits, sets.
For Further Information: Send SASE for list.
Accepts: Discover, MasterCard, Visa

SHOPSMITH, INC.
3931 Image Dr.
Dayton, OH 45414
(513) 898-6070

Offers: Workshop power tools: All-in-one units, scroll saw—20-inch variable speed model, with sawdust blower.
For Further Information: Send SASE for further details.

SKIL CORP.
4300 W. Peterson Ave.
Chicago, IL 60646

Offers: Power tools: Drills, cordless drill (with 5-position variable torque clutch, 2-speed, with 7.2 volt rechargeable battery pack), variety of saws, others. Manufacturer.
For Further Information: Send SASE for information.

STEVE WALL LUMBER CO.
Rt. 1, P.O. Box 287
Mayodan, NC 27027
(919) 427-0637, (800) 633-4062

Offers: Woodworking machinery including Mini-Max and Delta units, Hawk and planer-molder, others. Also offers lumber (kiln dried rough, sold by board): Aromatic red cedar, cherry, red or white oak, hard maple, mahogany, walnut, butternut and others. Craft wood mixtures.
For Further Information: Catalog, $1.
Accepts: MasterCard, Visa

SUN DESIGNS
173 E. Wisconsin Ave.
Oconomowoc, WI 53066
(414) 567-4255

Offers: Design plan books for 55 gazebos (mix and match designs for railings, fascia, etc.), bird houses/feeders, toys, backyard structures, cupolas and bridges, privies. Construction plans, all designs.
For Further Information: Send SASE for full details.
Discounts: Sells wholesale to legitimate businesses.
Accepts: MasterCard, Visa

THE TAUNTON PRESS
63 S. Main St., P.O. Box 5506
Newtown, CT 06470
(203) 426-8171

Offers: Instructional videos for professionals on Shaker tables, mortise-and-tenon joints, joinery, router jigs, shop tips, wood finishing, tiling, carving (ball-and-claw), chip tips/ techniques. Books also available.

For Further Information: Free catalog.

Discounts: Sells wholesale to businesses.

TAYLOR DESIGN GROUP

P.O. Box 810262
Dallas, TX 75381
(214) 484-5570

Offers: Incra jigs and joints and templates for double-double. Through Dovetail and Cornerpost Eagletail.

For Further Information: Free catalog; video brochure, $6.

THE TOOL CRIB OF THE NORTH

P.O. Box 1716
Grand Forks, ND 58206

Offers: Name brand woodworking machinery/power tools/ accessories: Wedge, Bosch, Panasonic, Makita, Skil, Freud, Milwaukee, Selta, Englo, Porter Cable, Black & Decker, others.

For Further Information: Catalog, $3.

Store Location: Yes

Discounts: Quantity discounts.

TOOLMARK CO.

6840 Shingle Creek Pkwy.
Minneapolis, MN 55430
(612) 561-4210

Offers: Wood lathe accessories for wood turning including spindle duplicators, duplicator systems, bowl turners, Unicenter systems, woodshavers, steady rests, safety shields.

For Further Information: Free literature and price list.

TOOLS, INC.

1567 N. Harbor Blvd.
Fullerton, CA 92632
(714) 525-3581

Offers: Power tools: Hitachi plunge router, Bosch top handle jigsaw kit, Porter-Cable finish sander, omni-jig dovetail machine with template and template guide kit, biscuit joiner, Elu variable speed plunger router, carbide blades, and a variety of sets.

For Further Information: Send SASE for list.

Accepts: Discover, MasterCard, Visa

TOTAL SHOP

P.O. Box 25429
Greenville, SC 29616
Order line (800) 845-9356

Offers: Total shop multi-purpose machine (converts to 5 basic power tools). Other units: Bed jointers, shapers, sanders, planers, saws, dust collectors, others.

For Further Information: Catalog, $1.

TREMONT NAIL CO.

8 Elm St.
P.O. Box 111
Wareham, MA 02571
(800) 842-0560

Offers: Old-fashioned steel cut nails, 20 types from old patterns: Rosehead, wrought-head, others.

For Further Information: Free catalog.

Discounts: Quantity discounts; allows discounts to teachers and institutions; sells wholesale to legitimate businesses and professionals.

TREND-LINES, INC.

375 Beacham St.
Chelsea, MA 02150
(617) 884-8882, order line (800) 767-9999

Offers: Over 3,000 woodworking tools: Saws, routers, planers, bands, jointers, grinders, drills, planer jointers, sanders, mortisers, drill presses, laminate sitters, trimmers, Dremel tools, others. Accessories: Sawhorses, supports, airbrushes, nail/spray guns, sand blasters, vises, measuring and carving/turning tools and router bits. Also offers wood sign layout kit, dollhouse kits, project plans, turning items, folding table legs, metal wheels, cedar liners/blocks, finishes.

For Further Information: Free catalog.

Discounts: "May run sales."

Accepts: Discover, MasterCard, Visa

UNICORN UNIVERSAL WOODS

4190 Steeles Ave.
West Woodbridge, Ontario L4L 3S8 Canada
(416) 851-2308

Offers: 70 species of lumber, millwork, plywoods, veneers, others.

For Further Information: Free catalog.

Discounts: Sells wholesale.

VAUGHN & BUSHNELL MANUFACTURING. CO.

11414 Maple Ave.
Hebron, IL 60034

Offers: Vaughn hand tools, including hammers, picks and axes.

For Further Information: Contact dealer, or send SASE for information.

VEGA

Rt. 3, P.O. Box 193
Decatur, IL 62526
(800) 222-8342

Offers: Woodworking tools/equipment: Saw fences—profes-

sional, utility, radial, mitre, others. Lathe duplicators — 3 models; lathes — bench, heavy, bowl. Also offers sanders, MSC jointmakers, bandsaws, tenon jigs, mitre gauges, stock feed systems and video tapes.
For Further Information: Contact for information.

WHOLE EARTH ACCESS
2990 7th St.
Berkeley, CA 94710
(415) 845-3000

Offers: Power tools: Porter-Cable saws, drills, laminate trimmers, routers, removers, sanders. Also offers Skil drill kits, saws, Freud router bits, carving and Forstner bits. Carries Milwaukee drills, sanders, chainsaws, jigsaws, others. Hitachi router, plane, saws, sanders. Makita drills, saws, sanders and Delta shop machinery are also available.
For Further Information: Send SASE for list.

WILKE MACHINERY CO.
3230 Susquehanna Trail
York, PA 17402
(717) 764-5000

Offers: Bridgewood woodworking machinery, including shaper units, planers, jointers, others.
For Further Information: Catalog, $1.

WILLIAMS & HUSSEY
Riverview Mill, P.O. Box 1149
Wilton, NH 03086
(800) 258-1380

Offers: Molder-planer unit (cuts moldings and planes hardwood) with "two-minute" cutter changes — for professionals and hobbyists. Manufacturer.
For Further Information: Free information kit.

THE WINFIELD COLLECTION
1450 Torrey Rd.
Fenton, MI 48430
(313) 629-8158

Offers: Full-size country woodcraft patterns: Frames, cutouts, self-sitters, swivel leg figures and animals, country scenes, animals, holiday items, candleholder motifs, action toys, racks, stools, boxes, baskets, weather vanes, vehicles, dinosaurs, carousels, others.
For Further Information: Catalog, $1.
Discounts: Sells wholesale.

THE WOODWORKERS' STORE
21801 Industrial Blvd.
Rogers, MN 55374
(612) 428-2199

Offers: Wood veneers and kits (35 species), tools, inlay/

bandings, wood strips, wood trims, moldings, parts, hardware (for furniture), upholstering rush and caning, flexible shaft and carving tools, clock parts, musical movements, finishes. Also offers a variety of hardwood lumber and plans (furniture, dollhouses, toys, others).
For Further Information: Catalog, $2.
Accepts: Discover, MasterCard, Visa

WOOD MOULDING & MILLWORK PRODUCERS ASSOCIATION
P.O. Box 25278
Portland, OR 97225

Offers: Booklet: *500 Wood Moulding Do-It-Yourself Projects* (for birdhouses, bookshelves, door trims, drawer dividers, planters, others), plus illustrated traditional projects and scores of new ways to use moulding.
For Further Information: Copy of booklet, $4.05.

WOOD-PLY LUMBER CORP.
100 Bennington Ave.
Freeport, NY 11520
(516) 378-2612

Offers: Over 60 species of exotic/domestic hardwoods: Lumber, plywood, veneers, turning blocks and burls.
For Further Information: Send SASE for list.

WOODARTIST
P.O. Box 31564
Charleston, SC 29417

Offers: Antique birdhouse plans for bluebirds, martins, other birds.
For Further Information: Send SASE for price list.

WOODCRAFT SUPPLY CORP.
210 Wood County Industrial Park
P.O. Box 1686
Parkersburg, WV 26102
(800) 542-9115

Offers: Woodworking tools: Sculptor's/carving, punches, adzes, hooks, rasps, files, rafflers, and measuring and layout tools/equipment. Also offers planes, vises, framing tools/equipment (also for musical instruments), plus tools to dowel, turn, log build, do marquetry and veneering. Carries branding irons and power tools by Dremel, Rockwell, Foredom. Specialty: Planes, vises, saws, miters, clamps. Also carries glass domes and inserts, lamp and clock parts, musical movements, hardware, woodware, plans and books.
For Further Information: Free catalog.
Discounts: Quantity discounts; allows discounts to teachers and institutions.
Accepts: MasterCard, Visa

WOODCRAFTERS

11840 N. U.S. 27

Dewitt, MI 48820

Offers: Woodcraft patterns: Windmills, wishing wells, weather vanes, birdhouses, whirligigs, jigsawing. Wood parts also available.

For Further Information: Catalog, $1.

Accepts: MasterCard, Visa

WOODMASTER TOOLS

2908 Oak St.

Kansas City, MO 64108

Offers: Woodmaster power-feed machine (planes/molds/sands) to frame, mold, do casings, tongue and groove. Also offers picture frame patterns and drum sanders.

For Further Information: Free information kit.

Believe it or not, poplar wood makes an attractive substitute for cherry when appropriately stained. The subdued irregular figure of cherry is picked up in the poplar flat-sawn boards.

— Croffwood Mills

WOODWORKER'S BOOK CLUB

P.O. Box 12171

Cincinnati, OH 45212-0171

(513) 531-8250

Offers: Each month brings a free issue of the club newsletter, describing the main selection and dozens of other selections. You have at least ten days to make up your mind. Drop a note to find out what the latest membership opening offer is. Currently, it's a free book plus a half-price book, with no obligation ever to buy another book, which is a great deal for any book club to offer. The club name describes the type of selections you'll find.

For Further Information: Call for information.

WOODWORKERS SOURCE

5402 S. 40th St.

Phoenix, AZ 85040

(602) 437-4415

Offers: Hardwoods—exotic and domestic—from over 75 species: Lumber, plywood, veneers, turning squares and blanks. Collector's hardwoods sample kit (30 woods from worldwide).

For Further Information: Send SASE for list.

WOODWORKER'S SUPPLY

5604 Alameda Place NE

Albuquerque, NM 87113

Offers: Woodworking machinery: Routers, borers, saws, shapers, scrolls, planers, sanders, pantographs, plus wood turning items, cedar lining and veneers. Bosch power tools: Laminates, trimmers, drills, router. Porter-Cable routers and others. Also offers hardware, lights, cutters, drawer slides, lock sets, folding table legs, latches, hinges, doweling tools/aids, picture framing guns and Framemate items (miter box, clamps, others). Carries a full line of routers and other bits, plus edge banding systems, joining machines and drill presses.

For Further Information: Free catalog.

Discounts: Quantity discounts.

Accepts: MasterCard, Visa

WOODWORKS

213 Cutting Horse

Fort Worth, TX 76117

(817) 218-4447

Offers: Wood turnings: Candle cups, Shaker and other pegs, bean pots, hearts, toy wheels, axle pegs, spindles, door harp parts, eggs, apples, others—most by 100-piece lots. Also offers jewelry findings, hardware and pattern packets.

For Further Information: Free catalog.

Store Location: Yes

Discounts: Quantity discounts; sells wholesale to legitimate businesses.

Accepts: MasterCard, Visa

Needlecrafts, Sewing and Fiber Arts

Batik and Dyeing

Also see Artist's Supplies, Fabric Decorating, Fabrics and Trims, General Needlecraft Supplies, Rug Making, Spinning and Weaving and other related categories.

AKITO'S ART MATERIALS IMPORT
3347 N. Clark St.
Chicago, IL 60657

Offers: Fabric dyes and equipment, and Oriental art supplies, including a variety of brushes, inks, papers.
For Further Information: Catalog, $1.50.
See Also: Artist's Supplies

ALJO MANUFACTURING CO.
81-83 Franklin St.
New York, NY 10013
(212) 226-2878

Offers: Dyes: Direct dyes (for cotton and rayon), acid dyes (for silk, wool, batik, tie-dye, printing), Zymo-Fast vat dyes (for cotton, batik, tie-dye), alcohol/water-base dyes (for hand painting on silk), cold process fiber reactive dyes (for painting on silk, cotton, rayon, wool, batik), acid dyes for nylon (7 fluorescent colors), acetate nylon disperse-type dyes (for nylon, synthetics). Also offers tjanting tools, beeswax, paraffin, plus chemicals/agents.
For Further Information: Free catalog.
Discounts: Quantity discounts; allows discounts to teachers, institutions and professionals.

BROOKS & FLYNN, INC.
P.O. Box 2639
Rohnert Park, CA 94927
(707) 584-7715

Offers: Equipment and supplies for marbling, tie-dye, batik, silk painting: Procion MX dyes (90 colors), Chromasilk liquid dyes, Tulip fabric paints, Deka fabric paints. Also offers silk fabrics and silk scarves from China, brushes, T-shirts and others.
For Further Information: Free catalog.
Accepts: American Express

CALIFORNIA COLORS
1075 W. 20th St.
Upland, CA 91786

Offers: Microwave dye kits with dye for 10 to 60 pounds of wool and instructions.

For Further Information: Send SASE for details.

DELTA TECHNICAL COATINGS
P.O. Box 3584
South El Monte, CA 91733
(213) 686-0678

Offers: Fabric dyes, Deka Iron-on (for transfers), Ceramcoat acrylics and Marble-Thix powder, which creates marbleized patterns when combined on fabric with acrylics or fabric dye. Offers other colors and mediums.
For Further Information: See your dealer. Business-size SASE with inquiry.

DHARMA TRADING CO.
P.O. Box 150916
San Rafael, CA 94915
(800) 542-5227

Offers: Fabric dyes: Procion reactive, Jacquard silk type, Tinfix, Deka series L. Also offers fabric paints, waxes (paraffin, sticky, beeswax, inkodye resist), plus Gutta and Deka silk resists, chemicals, containers, tjantings (3) work frame, fabric pens, syringes, steamers. Fabrics: T-shirt, other cottons, velveteen, silks, plus silk/cotton scarves, garments for dyeing (T-shirts, pants, T-dress, others).
For Further Information: Free catalog.
Store Location: Yes
Discounts: Quantity discounts; sells wholesale to businesses.
Accepts: MasterCard, Visa
See Also: Fabric Decorating

HOUSTON ART & FRAME, INC.
P.O. Box 56146
Houston, TX 77256

Offers: Dylon Micro-Dye (from England) for cotton, cotton/polyester, linen, silk. Available in 6 colors for tie-dye in microwave oven.
For Further Information: Contact dealer, or send SASE for details.

IVY IMPORTS, INC.
12213 Distribution Way
Beltsville, MD 20705
(301) 595-0550

Offers: Visionart instant set silk dyes and kits including "Dyeing to Quilt" kit, others. Features Batik Tintout dyes, Pientex ink dyes (all fabric). Also offers fabric paints, additives, resists, steamers, brushes, silk scarves (8 sizes) and instructional videos with Diane Tuckman or Naomi Barsky (on Tinfix and Pientex). Color and book sets available.

For Further Information: Catalog, *Grapevine* booklet, $4.50.

Discounts: Sells wholesale to businesses.

See Also: Fabric Decorating

RUPERT, GIBBON & SPIDER

P.O. Box 425
Healdsburg, CA 95448
(707) 433-9577, (800) 442-0455

Offers: Line of silk fabrics (over 15), jacquards, imported cottons, silk and cotton scarves. Also offers jacquard silk dyes, gutta resist, vertical fabric steamers, Deka paints, dyes, brushes, patterns and books.

For Further Information: Free catalog, referrals to nearest store.

Discounts: Quantity discounts; sells wholesale to legitimate businesses.

TEXTILE RESOURCES

20592 Bloomfield St.
Los Alamitos, CA 90720
(213) 431-9611

Offers: Textile decorating—dyes, chemicals, waxes, variety of fabrics and materials for hand application.

For Further Information: Write or call for brochure.

Clothing and Accessories

Also see Costumes—Ethnic, Historic, Special Occasion, Doll, Toy and Clothes Making—Soft, Fabrics, Outdoors and Outerwear, Sewing and related categories.

ALPEL PUBLISHING
P.O. Box 203-CSS
Chambly, Quebec J3L 4B3 Canada
(514) 658-6205

Offers: Patterns/instruction books, including: *Easy Sewing for Infants* (with 70 patterns), *Easy Sewing for Children* (75 patterns for 3 to 10 years old), *Easy Sewing for Adults* (78 patterns), and *Easy Halloween Costumes for Children* (60 costumes for 3 to 12 years old). Books also have ideas and patterns for accessories, plus mini-patterns. Duplicut vinyl grid sheets for enlarging patterns are also available.
For Further Information: Free brochure; with sample infant pattern, $1.
Discounts: Quantity discounts.
See Also: General Craft Supplies and Costumes

ARTFUL ILLUSIONS
P.O. Box 278
Ector, TX 75439
(903) 961-2816

Offers: 27 Artwear clothing patterns: Designer jackets in a variety of styles, shredded cloth design jackets, Sante Fe blouses and skirts, vests, coats, others.
For Further Information: Catalog, $1.50.
Discounts: Sells wholesale to legitimate businesses.

AUDITORE PATTERN DESIGN
12629 N. Tatum Blvd.
Phoenix, AZ 85032

Offers: Pocket shopping bag patterns (for foldable bags); training packets (teaches sewing or pattern making), plus *Learn to Make Patterns.*.
For Further Information: Catalog, $2.

BBD, INC.
P.O. Box 75
Mt. Angel, OR 97362

Offers: Baby diaper patterns (with adjustable Velcro fasteners, extra center padding, elastic legs) for tiny to toddler sizes.
For Further Information: Send SASE for list.

Discounts: "Distributor inquiries welcome."

BONFIT AMERICA, INC.
5959 Truimph St.
Commerce, CA 90040
(800) 342-9555

Offers: "Patterner" units: No paper, adjustable for custom fit of clothing and for pleats, darts, yokes, basques, panels, flares. Create skirts, pants, bodices and other men's/women's clothes (elegant, casual, sports, maternity, sleep and bridal wear designs—with storage bag). Designer kits.
For Further Information: Send SASE for details.
Accepts: American Express, Discover, MasterCard, Visa

BURDA PATTERNS
P.O. Box 67028
Marietta, GA 30066
(800) 241-6887

Offers: Line of fashion patterns, variety of sizes/styles/items.
For Further Information: Send business-size SASE (double-stamped) for mini-catalog.

CABINET OF VINTAGE PATTERNS
3522 Deerbrook
Windsor, Ontario N8R 2E9 Canada

Offers: Clothing patterns—reproductions of women's and children's patterns of 1905-1930, including long and short skirts and dresses, jackets, tops, others.
For Further Information: Catalog, $4.

Recycle your newspapers into countless Christmas ornaments. Spray paint white angels, green wreaths, red bows. Use wire coat hangers for support and staples or hot glue to fasten pieces. Decorate with spray glitter, gold paint, etc. Glue on trims, fabrics.

—Seams Sew Easy

CAMPBELL'S
P.O. Box 400
Gratz, PA 17030

Offers: Vintage and ethnic garment patterns: Over 100 of 1950s and before, including patchwork garment patterns, country craft patterns, buttons, semi-precious beads, acces-

sories. Also offers patterns from the 19th Century, plus books on period clothing.
For Further Information: Catalog, $4.50.

CARDIN ORIGINALS
15802 Springdale St., #1
Huntington Beach, CA 92649
(714) 897-2437

Offers: Garment patterns, including a rag "fur" coat (all cotton, in one pattern piece). Others.
For Further Information: Catalog, $2.
Discounts: Sells wholesale.

CHARTRU ENTERPRISE
P.O. Box 177
Platteville, CO 80651

Offers: All occasion wallet pattern (with checkbook holder, license pocket, credit card section, coin purse). Also offers accessories and patterns.
For Further Information: Send SASE for details.

CITY SAFE TRAVELWEAR
1075 NW Murray Rd., #13
Portland, OR 97229
(503) 643-1968

Offers: Pattern for travel vest with 10 hidden pockets, lined, multi-sized.
For Further Information: Send SASE for details.

CREATE-A-TIE
P.O. Box 3015-CS
Renton, WA 98056
(206) 226-2419

Offers: Clip-on tie and bow-tie patterns in children's through adult sizes (includes 3 tie clips, full-sized pattern). Tie clips.
For Further Information: Send SASE for information.
Discounts: Quantity discounts; sells wholesale to legitimate businesses.

DONNA SAYERS FABULOUS-FURS
700 Madison Ave.
Covington, KY 41011
(606) 291-3300

Offers: Manmade furs/leathers kits (or buy by yard) for coats, jackets, accessories (10 colors each of furs/leather). Patterns and books also available.
For Further Information: Free catalog—with coupons.

DOS DE TEJAS
P.O. Box 1636
Sherman, TX 75091

Offers: Sewing patterns: Tote and garment bags, "chameleon" vest, broomstick skirt, "Hobo walkabout" bags, no-sew hats, and companion hardware to patterns.
For Further Information: Send SASE for brochure.
Accepts: MasterCard, Visa

DOUBLE D PRODUCTIONS
4110 Willow Ridge Rd.
Douglasville, GA 30135

Offers: Square dance apparel patterns—over 60 items, including full skirts, petticoats, tops, others.
For Further Information: Catalog, $1.

To thread a needle easily, wet the eye of the needle instead of the thread.

—Lois Ericson

EDA'S PATTERNS
P.O. Box 1125
Helotes, TX 78023

Offers: Belt bag design patterns (secure inside pockets, belt or shoulder option, "no bulge" look).
For Further Information: Send SASE for details.

ELIZABETH LEE DESIGNS
P.O. Box 696
Bluebell, UT 84007

Offers: Classic nursing wardrobe patterns for breastfeeding mothers.
For Further Information: Free newsletter/catalog.

EMILY'S SISTER
4636 SW Loop 820, #118
Fort Worth, TX 76109

Offers: Patterns for boot skirts, multi-sized in 3 Western styles.
For Further Information: Send SASE for list.

LOIS ERICSON
P.O. Box 5222
Salem, OR 97304
(503) 364-6285

Offers: Creative sewing books: *Design and Sew It Yourself* (techniques, drawings), *Print It Yourself*, and *The Great Put On* (progressive techniques).
For Further Information: Free book list.

Discounts: Quantity discounts; sells wholesale to legitimate businesses.

FAIR WINDS PATTERN CO.
819 N. June St.
Hollywood, CA 90038

Offers: Patterns for classic clothing of a bygone era (1900 to 1945).
For Further Information: Brochure, $1.

FASHION BLUEPRINTS
2191 Blossom Valley Dr.
San Jose, CA 95124
(408) 356-5291

Offers: Classic ethnic clothing patterns—over 20 designs in blueprint format, multi-sized, for women, men, children—some fashionable today. Patterns include wrap dresses, tunics, pants, jackets, vests, tops, robes, shirts, coats, others—with Oriental, Far Eastern, African, Mexican, European origins. Early American patterns that adapt to today: Prairie skirt, gown, apron, shirts.
For Further Information: Catalog, $2.
Discounts: Sells wholesale to businesses.
See Also: Costumes—Ethnic, Historic, Special Occasion

FASHION DESIGN METHODS
264 H St.
P.O. Box F110-10
Blaine, WA 98230

Offers: *Hundred Hats*, a book of full-sized patterns for pillbox hats, fezes, fedoras, safari hats, sailor's hats, Bretons caps, turbans, berets, fur hats and others. Includes directions for making blocks and equipment, design- and pattern-making instructions, tips on sewing by machine or hand, plus glove and bag patterns.
For Further Information: Send SASE for details.

FASHION TOUCHES
170 Elm St.
P.O. Box 804
Bridgeport, CT 06601
(203) 333-7738

Offers: Service: Custom-covered belts and buttons from customer's fabrics.
For Further Information: Catalog, $1.
Store Location: Yes
Discounts: Allows discounts to teachers and institutions.

FAY'S FASHION FABRICS
155 Webster Dr., #508
Pensacola, FL 32505
(904) 455-2410

Offers: Half-slip instructions—7 styles with fabric.
For Further Information: Send SASE for details.

JACKIE FEARS
2931 St. Johns Ave.
Billings, MT 59102

Offers: Discontinued patterns—most brands and sizes, 1989 to present.
For Further Information: Send $5 for complete list or $2 per brand.

FRENCH CAMEL PATTERN CO.
12235 Rocker Rd.
Nevada City, CA 95959

Offers: Line of fashion sewing patterns.
For Further Information: Send business-size SASE for brochure.

FRIENDS PATTERNS
P.O. Box 1753
Homestead, FL 33030

Offers: Amish clothing patterns for men, women and children: Mennonite dresses, other dresses, aprons, bonnets, children's caps, broadfall pants (men's, boys), sack coats, shirts, vests. Also offers Amish dolls and swimsuits—classic designs.
For Further Information: Illustrated catalog, $1 (refundable).

GENNY'S PATTERNMAKING
P.O. Box 66
Truckee, CA 96160

Offers: Patterns produced from a garment, picture or sketch.
For Further Information: Send business-size SASE for brochure.

GHEE'S
2620 Centenary Blvd., #3
Shreveport, LA 71104
(318) 868-1154

Offers: Handbag-making supplies: Metal frames in a variety of sizes and shapes, magnetic closures, chains, handbag accessories and notions.
For Further Information: Catalog, $1.

GREAT COPY PATTERNS
P.O. Box 085329
Racine, WI 53408
(414) 632-2660

Offers: Great Copy patterns: Sewer's cardigan, embellishment kit for appliqué designs.

The Santa Fe Collection Pattern. Courtesy of Artful Illusions.

For Further Information: Send SASE for information.

GREAT FIT PATTERNS
2229 NE Burnside, Suite 305
Gresham, OR 97030
(503) 665-3125

Offers: Modular patterns for sizes 38-60 (18W-40W): Basic pattern shapes (little fitting required) with interchangeable pieces for knits and weaves: Tops (includes coats, jackets, vests, sweaters, dresses), skirts/pants and accessories.
For Further Information: Catalog, $1.
Discounts: Sells wholesale to fabric stores/retail outlets.

HARRIET'S
P.O. Box 1363
Winchester, VA 22604
(703) 667-2541

Offers: Patterns and costumes (from eras between 1690 and 1910—especially Victorian).
For Further Information: Adult catalog, $7; Children's catalog, $3.

HESSON COLLECTABLES
1261 S. Lloyd
Lombard, IL 60148
(312) 627-3298

Offers: Old, original fashion prints and plate reprints of fashion plates, plus old mail-order catalogs.
For Further Information: Send SASE with specific inquiry.

JEAN HARDY PATTERNS
2151 La Cuesta Dr.
Santa Ana, CA 92705

Offers: Men's and women's riding clothes patterns for English, Western and saddle seat riding. Action patterns include tennis dress, skirts, blouses, sport sets, pep-squad skirts, dresses, body suits, square dance dresses and skirts and sport sets. Others.
For Further Information: Catalog, $1.

JOY
1377 Osceola St.
Denver, CO 80204

Offers: Jumpsuit patterns (drop-seat style) in misses, boys, girls sizes.
For Further Information: Send SASE for list.

THE KWIK-SEW PATTERN CO.
3000 Washington Ave. N.
Minneapolis, MN 55411

Offers: Patterns for dance dresses, petticoats, ruffled panties, and Western-style patterns for men.
For Further Information: See your dealer, or send SASE for information.

LEOPARDS SPOTS
2951 Marina Bay Dr., Suite #150
League City, TX 77573

Offers: Split wrap pants/skirt pattern (front wraps to cover pants).
For Further Information: Send SASE for details.

Make accessories with rubber bands as base for "scrunchies" for pony tails.

—Fashion Touches

LOGAN KITS
Rt. 3, P.O. Box 380
Double Springs, AL 35553
(205) 486-7732

Offers: Garment kits (and refills) including patterns/fabric (some elastic) for lingerie items, nightgowns, men's under-

wear, girl's lingerie. Also offers a master pattern for a baby wardrobe. A variety of fabrics is included with kits.
For Further Information: Brochure, $1.50.
Discounts: Sells wholesale; quantity discounts.

MARY WALES LOOMIS
1487 Parrott Dr.
San Mateo, CA 94402
(415) 345-8012

Offers: Books, including *Make Your Own Shoes* (sandals, slippers, handbags). Illustrates the use of sewing machine and shoemaker's cement. Also publishes a book on belt making.
For Further Information: Send SASE for full information.
Discounts: Sells wholesale to legitimate businesses.

THE MOTHER NURTURE PROJECT
916 Royal Blackheath Ct.
Naperville, IL 60563

Offers: Breastfeeding pattern aids (clothes have hidden nursing openings): Jumper, tops, Modest Mariner coverups, pop-over top, dresses (tee, cowl neck, other), knit turtleneck blouse. Also offers cooperative clothes patterns (for breast feeding and body transition): 5 dresses, 2-piece dress, pleated, ruffled and other tops, jumpsuits, sun dresses, swimsuits, jumpers, actionwear (pants, skirts, tops), slips, loungers. Also has ready-made clothes.
For Further Information: Catalog, $3.

PREEMIE-YUMS
2527 Wilark Dr. NW
Salem, OR 97304

Offers: Preemie patterns/kits for infants 4 to 6 pounds, and readywears.
For Further Information: Send $1 and business-size SASE for brochure.

QUEEN SIZE PATTERNS
RD 4, P.O. Box 135
Meyersdale, PA 15552

Offers: Queen-size bra patterns (35 and up, cup size 4 inches up) and bra kits.
For Further Information: Send SASE for measuring instructions and details.
Discounts: "Dealers and seamstresses welcome."

R INDYGO JUNCTION
P.O. Box 30238
Kansas City, MO 64112

Offers: Over 25 clothing and craft patterns (adult, children's), including jackets, shirts, appliqués, others.
For Further Information: Catalog, $3 (refundable).

Discounts: Sells wholesale.

SEAMS SO EASY
P.O. Box 2189
Manassas, VA 22110
(703) 369-5897

Offers: Swimwear patterns: Sweetheart bikini, tanga, thong, bandeau, boomerang, kitty kat and 12-in-1 types, plus men's briefs, fringe patterns, beach coverups, others.
For Further Information: Send SASE for list.
Accepts: American Express

SEW LITTLE PATTERN CO.
P.O. Box 3613
Salem, OR 97302

Offers: Master sewing patterns (full-size) each with 4 sizes and 16 or more garments—in full, European styling for all bodies, both regular/serger styles. Offers quick/easy playwear—preemies to 12 months, layette or "Cabbage Patch" clothes, toddlers garments with "grow features." Doll patterns are also available.
For Further Information: Brochure, $1.
Discounts: Quantity discounts; sells wholesale.

SEW SASSY LINGERIE
815 Cornelia Dr. SE, Dept. CSS
Huntsville, AL 35802

Offers: Lingerie kits/fabrics. Kits include teddies, short and long pj's, gowns, robes, underwear, poncho/capes. Larger girls sizes available in a wide array of styles. Also offers Kwik-Sew and Stretch & Sew patterns. Fabrics include stretch, woven and Cuddleskin. Notions: Closures, garters, strap holders, Do-Sew tracing material and books.
For Further Information: Catalog, $2 (refundable).

Use 2 to 4 mil plastic for tracing multi-sized patterns. A permanent marker pen will write on the plastic.

—Logan Kits

SOSEW PRESS
210 Estates Dr., Suite 401
Roseville, CA 95678
(916) 783-0524

Offers: "Me" vest pattern: Patchwork—each square is a fabric picture about a person.
For Further Information: Send SASE for details.

SUITABILITY
12485 Cedar Rd., #3
Cleveland, OH 44106

Offers: Equestrian clothing patterns including Western duster, others.
For Further Information: Free catalog.

SUITABLES
P.O. Box 700685
San Antonio, TX 78270

Offers: Instructions for no-sew fabric covered shoes and fabric covered belts.
For Further Information: Send SASE for details.

THE THREAD BARE PATTERN CO.
P.O. Box 1484
Havelock, NC 28532

(800) 4-PATTERN

Offers: Large collar patterns (with appliqués), plus other clothing/accessory patterns.
For Further Information: Catalog, $2 (refundable).

THE THRIFTY NEEDLE
3233 Amber St.
Philadelphia, PA 19134
(800) 324-9927

Offers: Sew-A-Sweater kit (no knit—cut and sew like a T-shirt): Cotton, wool, acrylic materials.
For Further Information: Send $2 for swatches.

Costumes — Ethnic, Historic, Special Occasion

Also see Clothing and Accessories, Doll, Toy and Clothes Making — Soft, Fabrics and Trims and other related categories.

ALPEL PUBLISHING
P.O. Box 203-CSS
Chambly, Quebec J3L 483 Canada

Offers: Easy-Sew pattern book: Children's traditional costumes (3 to 12 year olds) and pirates, Peter Pan, robots, others; includes accessories and patterns to be enlarged. Makeup and wigs are also covered. Carries Duplicut wipe-clean, vinyl grid sheets for pattern enlargement.
For Further Information: Free brochure with sample infant's pattern, $1.
See Also: Clothing and Accessories

AMAZON DRYGOODS
2218 E. 11th St.
Davenport, IA 52803
(319) 322-6800

Offers: Nineteenth Century-inspired products: Over 700 historic/ethnic clothes patterns from 1390 to 1950, with emphasis on the 1800s — coats, cloaks, hats, bonnets, gowns, suits, corsets, lingerie, underwear, formal clothes, everyday, work outfits and military uniforms (sizes for most patterns: Ladies, 6 to 44 plus, men's 32 to 48 plus). Supplies: Hoop wire, boning, stays, ostrich feathers, specialty fabrics (including fancies), uniform wools, tradecloth, veilings. Indian/frontier patterns available.
For Further Information: 3 catalogs, $12 (bulk), $15 (first class).
Accepts: MasterCard, Visa

ATIRA'S FASHIONS
3935 S. 113th St.
Seattle, WA 98168

Offers: Middle Eastern patterns (men's, women's), plus imported accessories, custom bras for Renaissance look, beaded fringe and dance accessories.
For Further Information: Catalog, $4.
Store Location: Yes

BAER FABRICS
515 E. Market St.
Louisville, KY 40202
(502) 583-5521, (800) 769-7776

Offers: Special bridal collection of fabrics: Taffetas, satins, chiffons, organzas, nettings and laces in a range of colors, plus trims, notions, supplies.
For Further Information: Notions catalog, $3.
Store Location: Yes
Discounts: Quantity discounts; allows discounts to teachers, institutions and businesses.
See Also: Fabrics and Trims

BALTAZOR'S
3262 Severn Ave.
Metairie, LA 70002

Offers: Bridal/fine hand-sewing supplies: Fabrics, laces, bridal accessories, plus lace-making and smocking items.
For Further Information: Catalog, $2.

BIRCH STREET CLOTHING
P.O. Box 6901
San Mateo, CA 94403

Offers: Sewing pattern for 6 halloween costumes from sweatshirts for children 6 months to 10 years of age: Jester, devil, skeleton, others.
For Further Information: Send SASE for list.

There is no error that cannot be corrected when making a bridal gown. Hem too short? Add lace ruffle to make up the difference. Bodice too small? Add a strip of fabric in the vertical bust seam. Cover with appliqués.

— Brides 'N Babes

BRIDALS INTERNATIONAL
45 Albany St.
Cazenovia, NY 13035
(800) 752-1171

Offers: Imported bridal fabrics and laces for designer look gowns; patterns from major companies.
For Further Information: Catalog, $8.50.
Store Location: Yes

BRIDES 'N BABES
P.O. Box 2189
Manassas, VA 22110

Offers: Wedding supplies, including you-make bridal gowns and accessories, brides' maids gowns, party favors. Also of-

fers instructions for bridal headpieces (hats, veils, combs, garlands, halos, coronets, cascades, nosegays, corsages, rice roses, others).
For Further Information: Send business-size SASE for brochure.

CAMPBELL'S
P.O. Box 400
Gratz, PA 17030

Offers: Historic patterns for over 100 multi-sized vintage designs covering 1805 through 1950 by Past Patterns: Day and evening gowns, ball gown bodices, skirts, undergarments, cloaks, jackets, others. Accessories include pewter buttons. Books are also available.
For Further Information: Catalog, $4.50.

CELEBRATIONS BY POST
11120 Gravelly Lake Dr. SW
Tacoma, WA 98499

Offers: Bridal hardware for home sewing: Austrian crystals, sequins, luster pearls, rhinestones, crystals, bridal buttons/loops, veilings, English net, milliner's wire, boning, horsehair, petticoats, hoop skirts, others.
For Further Information: Free brochure.

THE CROWNING TOUCH
4838 Balthazar Terrace
Fremont, CA 94555
(510) 794-LOVE

Offers: Bridal veiling (precut, edged, gathered) in a variety of lengths and styles.
For Further Information: Send SASE for samples.

THE CUTTING CORNER
4112 Sunset Dr.
San Angelo, TX 76904
(915) 942-9780

Offers: Pageant and bridal fabrics, including laces, sequins, silk, iridescents, metallics, velvets, taffetas, satin, lamé, glitter dot, others. Also offers fringes, rhinestones, other trims and appliqués.
For Further Information: Catalog with samples, $10 (refundable with $75 purchase).

DOERING DESIGNS
68935 233rd St.
Dassel, MN 55325

Offers: Selection of Scandinavian costume patterns—women's, men's, children's multi-sized. Braid and pewter also available.
For Further Information: Brochure, $1.

Russian cossack uniform from Folkwear Pattern. Courtesy of the Taunton Press.

HARRIET A. ENGLER
P.O. Box 1363
Winchester, VA 22604

Offers: Garment patterns (men's, women's) of Civil War era, a variety of day and evening gowns, undergarments, blouses, skirts, coats, trousers, jackets, shirts, hats and crinolines for hoop skirts.
For Further Information: Catalog, $7; children's, $3.

FASHION BLUEPRINTS
2191 Blossom Valley Dr.
San Jose, CA 95124

Offers: Classic ethnic clothing patterns—over 20 designs in blueprint format, multi-sized for women, men, children: Korean and Chinese jackets, dresses (Thai, Judean, nomad, Mexican, Volga, African). Also offers clothes from the East Indies, Kashmir, Japan, plus Early American fashion patterns.
For Further Information: Catalog, $1.
Discounts: Sells wholesale.

FOLKWEAR

The Taunton Press
63 S. Main St.
P.O. Box 5506
Newtown, CT 06470
(203) 426-8171

Offers: 66 folkwear sewing patterns (for men, women, children—multi-sized): Ethnic (of Gaza, France, Syria, Turkey, Afghan, Japan, China, Russia, Croatia, Tibet, Hong Kong, Austria, Bolivia, Australia, Morocco, India, Native American, others) and vintage (Edwardian, Victorian, Early American from the 1920s to 1950s).
For Further Information: Catalog, $3.
Discounts: Sells wholesale.
Accepts: MasterCard, Visa

HEIDI MARSH PATTERNS

810 El Caminito
Livermore, CA 94550

Offers: Civil War-era garment patterns—copies of originals—for men, women and children, including a variety of long dresses, bodices, skirts, jackets, coats, others.
For Further Information: Catalog, $1.

KIMBERLY FABRICS

P.O. Box 8006
Central Valley, CA 96019
(800) 638-7491

Offers: Fabrics for skaters, Western wear, costumes, bridal and other special occasions. Materials include sequins, brocades, lamé, laces, taffetas, cottons, sparkle sheers, lycra, others. Kimmy kits offer little girl patterns/fabrics for bride, angel or princess and others. Trims include sequin appliqués, fringe, Venice and other lace and Western appliqués.
For Further Information: Catalog, $3.

MEDIEVAL MISCELLANEA

6530 Spring Valley Dr.
Alexandria, VA 22312

Offers: Patterns for garments of the medieval era—a variety of gown styles, headgear, others. Also offers fabrics, supplies, equipment and jewelry reproductions.
For Further Information: Catalog, $2.
Discounts: "Dealer inquiries welcome."
See Also: Sewing

NEWARK DRESSMAKER SUPPLY

6473 Ruch Rd.
P.O. Box 2448
Lehigh Valley, PA 18002
(215) 837-7500

Offers: Sewing and needlecraft supplies, aids and fabrics.

Bridal supplies include pearl buttons, looping, hair boning, 15 appliqués, bands, garters, flowers (garlands, sprays), accessories, veils, fabrics (laces, satins, moire, organza, esprit, nylon net, tulle, illusion). Also offers pressing items, fabric paints, sequins, rhinestones, beads, others.
For Further Information: Catalog, $1.
Discounts: Quantity discounts.
See Also: General Needlecraft Supplies

O.F.A. INC.

P.O. Box 44211
Philadelphia, PA 19144
(215) 849-2530, (800) 217-2530

Offers: 18 Traditional African patterns (for men, women, children, dolls) of Ghana, Nigeria, Senegal, Gambia. Includes a sew-by-numbers pattern/fabric set. Service: Traditional African clothing, custom made.
For Further Information: Brochure, $1.
Discounts: Quantity discounts to teachers and institutions; wholesale to legitimate business.

OLD WORLD ENTERPRISES

29038 Kepler Ct.
Cold Spring, MN 56320

Offers: Patterns styled after garments of the 19th Century (screened on brown paper) for sizes 8 through 12, including gowns for day and evening, bustled styles, men's informal suits, frocks, coats.
For Further Information: Catalog, $2.

PAST PATTERNS

P.O. Box 758
Grand Rapids, MI 49510

Offers: Historic garment patterns of the late 1800s to the present (on brown paper), including authentically styled gowns, blouses, suits, petticoats, nightwear, men's dusters and suits. Also offers a full line of garments from 1911 to the 1950s for women, children. (All patterns in today's sizes.)
For Further Information: Catalog, $4; information flyer free.
Accepts: MasterCard, Visa

PATTERNS OF HISTORY

816 State St.
Madison, WI 53703
(608) 264-6428

Offers: Patterns for garments of the 19th Century, including gowns in a variety of styles.
For Further Information: Send business-size SASE for list.

PEGEE OF WILLIAMSBURG
P.O. Box 127
Williamsburg, VA 23187
(804) 220-2722

Offers: Historical fashion patterns. 1776 era garments: Cloaks, women's and girls' dresses, and men's and boys' shirts, breeches, waistcoats and military coats. 1800s garments: Scarlett's Barbecue Party Dress and Green Velveteen Dress (from her mother's portiers), hoop skirt, Empire dresses.
For Further Information: Brochure, $2.
Discounts: Sells wholesale to businesses.

RAINMENTS
P.O. Box 6176
Fullerton, CA 92634

Offers: Historical fashion patterns (1100 to the 1950s) by 24 companies. Also offers corset kits and supplies, millinery patterns and supplies and costume books.
For Further Information: Catalog, $5.

Fabrics better suited to sew-in interfacing include metallics, beaded or sequinned, rayon, fake furs, leather vinyl and open-work fabrics.

— Baer Fabrics

RENEGADE
P.O. Box 7089
Phoenix, AZ 85011

Offers: Medieval chain mail-making kit, including instructions, patterns, metal links.
For Further Information: Send SASE for details.

ROSEBAR
93 Entin Rd.
Clifton, NJ 07014
(201) 777-0078, (800) 631-8573

Offers: Bridal and evening wear fabrics/laces: Silk, taffeta, satin, Barcelona lace, others. Suitable for the bride, bridal party, mother of the bride and casual/honeymoon.
For Further Information: Send SASE for details.

THE TAUNTON PRESS
63 S. Main St.
Newtown, CT 06470
(203) 426-8171

Offers: 80 folkwear vintage and ethnic patterns: Algerian suit, Russian Cossack uniform, dresses of Gaza, Afghani Nomad, Syrian, Hong Kong Cheongsam, Austrian Dirndl, Russian settlers and children's prairie. Also offers outerwear of Turkey, Japan, China, Tibet, Bolivia, Seminole, Morocco, Belgium, South Asia, Australia, Hungary, Scotland.
For Further Information: Free catalog.
Discounts: Sells wholesale to legitimate businesses.

TEXUBA
517 Boccaccio Ave.
Venice, CA 90291
(310) 827-8535, (800) 858-5550

Offers: Vintage kimonos and obis in 200-pound bales at reduced cost per unit.
For Further Information: Call, or send SASE for details.

TRIPLE D BRAND
1153 S. Lee St., #265
Des Plaines, IL 60016

Offers: Country and Western shawl patterns, jacket country and Western classic and fringed styles.
For Further Information: Free catalog.

VICTORIAN BRIDAL & GIFTS
2 Goverment Rd., #203
Toronto, Ontario M8X 1V6 Canada
(416) 236-7255

Offers: Bridal pattern designs for handbags, potpourri pillows/hangers, fabric frames/books, headpieces, hairbows, ribbon/fabric flowers, others. Ready-mades available.
For Further Information: Brochure, $2 (refundable).

Doll, Toy and Clothes Making—Soft

Also see Doll and Toy Making—Rigid, Miniature Making, Fabrics and Trims, Knitting and Crochet and other related categories.

ABBOTT
8600 N. Charlotte St.
Kansas City, MO 64155

Offers: Reversible rag doll patterns: Red Riding Hood (and Grandma and the Wolf), Cinderella, Goldilocks and the 3 bears, plus a black-white, awake-asleep, topsy-turvy princess. Also offers doll and clothes patterns: Mary Poppins, black, kewpee, Lulu, others.
For Further Information: Send SASE for list.

LYN ALEXANDER DESIGNS
P.O. Box 8341
Denver, CO 80201

Offers: Authentic period design patterns for antique or reproduction dolls. Dresses: Party, Indian, 1800s, Gibson Girl (bride, lingerie). Also offers 1880 plus French and German girl's Bru (1886) outfits, 1900 to 1930 dresses, plus infants' and large sizes. Hats: 1908 to 1924 styles. Carries patterns for underwear, leggings and cape coats, plus bodice patterns and shoe patterns (and for leather shoes). Books are also available.
For Further Information: Catalog, $2.
Discounts: Sells wholesale.

ALL ABOUT DOLLS
49 Lakeside Blvd.
Hopatcong, NJ 07843
(201) 770-3228

Offers: Line of soft doll kits, doll blanks and supplies (including plastic armatures for soft bodies, others).
For Further Information: Catalog, $2.
Accepts: American Express, Discover, MasterCard, Visa

ANTOINETTE DESIGNS
906 Lincoln St.
Rockville, MD 20850

Offers: Soft sculpture doll patterns (dollhouse scale, to 22 inches) with historic, storybook and international costumes, including a 10-inch soft sculpture ballerina doll pattern.
For Further Information: Send business-size SASE for list.

ATLANTA PUFFECTIONS
P.O. Box 13524
Atlanta, GA 30324
(404) 262-7437

Offers: Over 75 soft doll patterns including Puff Ima Mouse doorstop, Nanny and the Twins, others. Supplies (to support patterns).
For Further Information: Color catalog, $1.50; send SASE for brochure.
Discounts: Sells wholesale to legitimate businesses.

BY DIANE
1126 Ivon Rd.
Endicott, NY 13760
(607) 754-0391

Offers: Fuzzy Friends toy kits/patterns including teddy bears, sea creatures, other wild and domestic animals and hand puppet kits/patterns. Also offers animal eyes, noses and joint sets, music boxes and furs (synthetic, mohair).
For Further Information: Catalog, $2.
Discounts: Quantity discounts; sells discount to teachers and institutions; sells wholesale to legitimate businesses.

CABIN FEVER CALICOES
P.O. Box 550106
Atlanta, GA 30355
(404) 873-5094

Offers: Soft doll patterns: 3-inch country folks, and on up to 24 inches. Includes antique-look, country, doorstop doll, Topsy-Turvy and animals. Also offers a full line of quilting patterns and kits, fabrics, aids (scissors, markers, batting), fabric packs (shade groups), stenciling/cutting tools and books.
For Further Information: Catalog, $1.
See Also: Quilting

MARY CANTRELL
505 Pratt Ave.
Huntsville, AL 35801
(205) 533-4972

Offers: Soft sculpture doll patterns (with clothes) by Miss Martha, plus 17 assorted books.
For Further Information: Send SASE for information.

CAROLEE CREATIONS
787 Industrial Dr.
Elmhurst, IL 60126

Offers: Full line of easy-sew cloth doll patterns (full-sized): Clowns, kitties, cowboys, little girls (8 inches and up), little boys and babies and layettes. Also offers Amish, ethnic and other dolls. Animal and other long-legged creatures and critters are available. Supplies include furs, hair wigs, loom tools and fabrics. Books are also available.
For Further Information: Color catalog, $1.
Accepts: MasterCard, Visa

CARVERS' EYE CO.
P.O. Box 16692
Portland, OR 97216
(503) 666-5680

Offers: Glass or plastic eyes, noses, joints, growlers and eye glasses for teddy bears and dolls.
For Further Information: Send $1 for information.

JEAN CAVINESS
150 Old Marietta Rd.
Canton, GA 30114

Offers: Old Black Mammy soft doll patterns (full-size, with instructions): 20-inch Jemima (big mammy type), 22-inch Honey Chile (fat baby with pigtails all over head), 17-inch Liza Jane (pickaninny girl with pigtails all over head).
For Further Information: Send SASE for list.

When using felt for bodies, interface it with fusible interfacing. Use the grain of the interfacing opposite the grain of the felt.

— Let's Talk About Dollmaking Magazine

CHARLES PUBLISHING
P.O. Box 577
Weatherford, TX 76086

Offers: Crochet patterns: Roger Rabbit, country goose, California Raisins, Santa, Sylvester, Tweetie, Dumbo, tyrannosaurus, stegosaurus, others.
For Further Information: Send SASE for list.

CLONZ
P.O. Box 60333
Santa Barbara, CA 93160

Offers: "Transfer magic," allowing you to iron a photograph onto a 28-inch portrait doll (or other fabric).
For Further Information: Send SASE for details.

THE CLOTH DOLL — PATTERNS
P.O. Box 1089
Mt. Shasta, CA 96067

Offers: Pattern Fair soft doll patterns by Judi Ward (22-inch

Oriental, 22-inch boy, 30-inch bed doll, 22-inch girl and boy dolls). Also offers Gracie and baby dolls, sailors and schoolgirl dolls. Henry & Hannah 16-inch dolls by Lyn Alexander — toddler twins, with 2-piece wardrobes of period costumes — are also available.
For Further Information: Send SASE for list.

CR'S CRAFTS
P.O. Box 8-41 CB
Leland, IA 50453

Offers: Doll and animal patterns, kits, supplies: Teddies (and posable Bears filled with plastic beads), monkeys, wrap-around puppets, dolls (plastic heads). Also offers craft fur, fabrics, fiberfill, animal parts, animal voices (cow, lamb, bear, puppy, bird, cat), cow and other bells, music boxes and doll parts. Others.
For Further Information: 112-page catalog, $2, ($4 Canada).
Discounts: Quantity discounts.

CURIOUS CHARACTERS LTD.
2609 S. Blauvelt Ave.
Sioux Falls, SD 57105

Offers: Soft sculptured doll patterns including 20-inch Amanda baby, Emily newborn hand puppet, Sunday's Child 16-inch preemie doll/puppet, Toby and Lucy chimps (and outfits) and others. Also offers "sculpture skin" fabric, hair, doll needles and Nyloop fabric for chimps face/hands/feet.
For Further Information: Send SASE for brochure.

D PALM'S TENDER FACES
2222 Foothill Blvd.
La Canada, CA 91011

Offers: Doll patterns (using your photo and reproduction medium), 22 inches and up for sizes: male, female, child. Transfer medium also available.
For Further Information: Brochure, $1.

DARLINDA'S PATTERNS PLUS
1060½ N. Main St.
Logan, UT 84321

Offers: Over 200 soft doll patterns, including cows, babies, others.
For Further Information: Free catalog.

DAR'S QUIET CORNER
1308 Grant
Grand Haven, MI 49417
(616) 846-0247

Offers: Doll body patterns for Donna RuBert, Terri DeHetre and Connie Walser Derek dolls, others. Also offers Loc-Line armatures.
For Further Information: List, $2 (refundable).

DOLL EMPORIUM PATTERN CO.
1546 S. Wallis Ave.
Santa Maria, CA 93454
(805) 925-2245

Offers: Doll clothing patterns (full-sized) for specific dolls (as released by the artist); multiple designs per pattern.
For Further Information: Contact nearest distributor; catalog, $3.50 (with coupon).

THE DOLLHOUSE FACTORY
157 Main St.
P.O. Box 456
Lebanon, NJ 08833
(908) 236-6404

Offers: Full line of name brand dollhouses and supplies—needlework, wood, lighting, components, accessories, wallpapers, furniture, moldings, hardware, masonry. Kits and tools also available.
For Further Information: Catalog, $5.50.

DOLLS DELIGHT, INC.
P.O. Box 3226
Alexandria, VA 22302
(800) 257-6301

Offers: Doll clothing patterns (for 18-inch dolls), plus ready-to-wear items.
For Further Information: Send SASE for list.
Accepts: MasterCard, Visa

EMMALINES
1588 W. 950 N.
Provo, UT 84604

Offers: Patterns for 11½-inch fashion dolls: Fairy Tale designs.
For Further Information: Send business-size SASE for details.

To stiffen a fabric craft project, but not too much, use Krylon clear acrylic spray paint. It will not discolor the project.
—Atlanta Puffections

ENDANGERED SPECIES
231 Islamorada Lane
Naples, FL 33961

Offers: Soft animal kits on preprinted designer fabric (stuff/stitch): Fat Cat, rhino, Pokey Bear and others. Pre-embroidered doll kits also available.
For Further Information: Send SASE for details.

EVERYTHING NICE
56330 Ledien Dr.
Macomb, MI 48042

Offers: Crochet patterns in the Victorian style, including intricate designs in a variety of sizes.
For Further Information: Catalog, $1.

FABRIC CHALET
491 E. Woodmen Rd.
Colorado Springs, CO 80919
(719) 552-1214

Offers: Imported fabrics for reproduction doll clothes: Silk, velveteen, cottons, taffeta, others. Also offers small laces.
For Further Information: Samples, $5.
Store Location: Yes
Accepts: MasterCard, Visa

FABRIC PATTERNS
3270 Whitbeck Blvd.
Eugene, OR 97405

Offers: Soft sculpture doll patterns including ample-plump woman figure (17-inch) and Emota male figure (jointed, posable) 24-inch.
For Further Information: Send SASE for list.

FANCYWORK AND FASHION
4728 Dodge St.
Duluth, MN 55804
(218) 525-2442

Offers: Doll costumes pattern book for 17 complete fairy tale outfits: Rapunzel, Snow White, Cinderella, Sleeping Beauty, Gretel, Dorothy, Heidi, Goldilocks, Princess, others—for 18- to 19-inch modern dolls. Accessories patterns are also available.
For Further Information: Send SASE for list.
Accepts: MasterCard, Visa

GABRIELE'S DOLL STUDIOS
P.O. Box 880-91Y
Blaine, WA 98230

Offers: Soft doll kits with a Dollmaking System of fabric bodies with faces hand-screened on muslin: Baby clowns, Victorian French fashion (18 inches) with French fashion patterns. French faces: Bru, Juneau, Steiner (allows more than one doll per kit).
For Further Information: Catalog, $2.

GINGER SNAP JUNCTION
7301 W. 64th Place
Arvada, CO 80003

Offers: Soft dolls and toys: Snowmen buddies, kittens, 16-

inch doll on a 9-inch mop, cat and mouse, others.
For Further Information: Brochure, $1.50.
Discounts: Sells wholesale.

GOLDEN FUN KITS
P.O. Box 10697
Golden, CO 80401
(303) 279-6466

Offers: Soft toy patterns for animals and dolls. Also offers eyes, noses, squeakers, joints, animal voices (growlers, others), musical movements, doll/animal joints, doll pellets.
For Further Information: Catalog, $1.
Discounts: Quantity discounts.

SALLY GOODSPEED
2318 N. Charles St.
Baltimore, MD 21218
(410) 235-6736

Offers: Line of 1920s boudoir doll patterns.
For Further Information: Free brochure.

GUILIANI CREATIONS
1737 River City Way
Sacramento, CA 95833

Offers: Cloth doll kits/patterns (a silkscreened face is included in kits; patterns are full-sized) including very tall girl dolls: 18 inches to 4 foot sizes.
For Further Information: Catalog, $1.
Accepts: MasterCard, Visa

HAND OF THE CREATOR
P.O. Box 7941
Beverly Hills, CA 90212

Offers: Barbie fashion patterns — Hollywood glamour designs in over 5 styles.
For Further Information: Send SASE for list.

HAPPY HEARTS
653 SW 2nd St., #164
Lee's Summit, MO 64063
(816) 525-2746

Offers: Doll costuming items: Feathers (small ostrich plumes, pompoms and boas; marabou and boas; pheasant fluff; peacock). Also offers elegant laces and trims, and an assortment of fabrics and accessories.
For Further Information: Catalog, $2 (refundable).

JUDY HOLLAWAY
13650 E. Zayante Rd.
Felton, CA 95018
(408) 335-4684

Offers: Contemporary/heirloom reproduction supplies: Patterns, imported fabrics, laces, smocking supplies, trims, others. Also offers custom-made dresses.
For Further Information: Catalog, $5.

JOSEPH'S COAT
26 Main St.
Peterborough, NH 03458
(603) 924-6683

Offers: 19th-Century heirloom cloth doll kits (by Gail Wilson): Snowman, angel, Santa, Pinnochio, Humpty Dumpty, and other dolls and character dolls.
For Further Information: Send SASE for catalog.

Try using a sliver of soap when marking a pattern on the back side of fur. This will give a nice line to cut by.
— Golden Fun Kits

KAREN'S DOLL KLOSET
P.O. Box 71
Clementon, NJ 08021

Offers: Doll clothes hangers, plus doll stands and accessories for dollhouse dolls. Also offers magnifying glass work station and organizer — containers.
For Further Information: Catalog, $1 (refundable).

KARRES
P.O. Box 4534
Marietta, GA 30061

Offers: Cloth doll patterns, including French clowns (with full-size cutout templates for doll and costumes), Earth Angel and smaller Earth Angel (and clothing and instruction book). Also offers Universal Toddler boy or girl for 8 sizes — 12 inches to 36 inches, with porcelain or vinyl head, arms and legs, and 8 ethnic variations.
For Further Information: Send SASE for full information.

THE KEZI WORKS
P.O. Box 17631
Portland, OR 97217

Offers: Cloth doll patterns and instructions, including Marianne, an 18-inch porcelain-look, fully jointed girl with old-fashioned costume. Also offers Country Dreamer and California Dreamer series of dolls.
For Further Information: Flyers, $1.

LEDGEWOOD STUDIO
6000 Ledgewood Dr.
Forest Park, GA 30050

Offers: Heirloom sewing supplies for antique doll costumes:

Braids, French laces, silk ribbons and taffeta, China silk fabric, Swiss batiste, Swiss embroidery, small beads, buttons, metal buckles, jacquard ribbons, and other fabrics and trims. Doll costume patterns are also available.
For Further Information: Illustrated catalog, $2 and business-size SASE.

SYLVIA MACNEIL
2325 Main St.
West Barnstable, MA 02668
(508) 362-3875

Offers: Antique fabrics (1860 to 1900): Silk taffeta, faille, cottons, woolens, others.
For Further Information: Send business-size SASE for list.

MAGIC CABIN DOLLS
Rt. 2, P.O. Box 39
Westby, WI 54667
(608) 634-2848

Offers: Doll-making (natural fibers) kits/patterns. Also offers skintone cotton knits, accessories and yarns: Mohair, alpaca, boucle.
For Further Information: Free catalog.
Discounts: Quantity discounts; allows discounts to teachers and institutions; sells wholesale to legitimate businesses.

MAGIC THREADS
Studio 719 P St., #3
Lincoln, NE 68508
(402) 477-6650

Offers: Cloth storybook doll patterns: 15-inch dolls—elves, Rapunzel, knight, sprite, Raggedy, mermaid, dragon, others. 22-inch Santas (with quilt/block robes designs). Also offers supplies: Fringes, eyes, lamé, others.
For Further Information: Send business-size SASE for brochure
Discounts: Sells wholesale.

MATERIAL MEMORIES
P.O. Box 39
Springville, NY 14141

Offers: Folk art doll/toy patterns (full-sized): From a 5-inch Raggedy up to a 15-inch Guardian Angel, plus animals, round bottom-standable dolls, black kids/watermelons, Amish, cherubs, babies, topsy-turvy, others. Birth certificated. Also offers curly chenille.
For Further Information: Catalog, $1.
Discounts: Sells wholesale.

MIMI'S BOOKS & SUPPLIES
P.O. Box 662
Point Pleasant, NJ 08742
(908) 899-0804

Offers: Patterns for Universal Toddler 16-inch cloth doll, with ethnic variations. Cloth body accepts porcelain head (patterns full-size). Also offers tub-time toddlers' clothing patterns and other patterns for 12-inch to 36-inch dolls.
For Further Information: Send SASE for list.

EDWINA L. MUELLER
228 Dogwood Lane
Washington, NJ 07882

Offers: Doll fashion patterns: Adaptation of old Patsy doll wardrobe (fits 8- to 9-inch toddler dolls), patterns from Dorita Alice Doll Fashions (Barbie and Batman outfits), others for 11½-inch fashion dolls.
For Further Information: Send business-size SASE for list.

MUFFY'S BOUTIQUE
1516 Oakhurst Ave.
Winter Park, FL 32789
(407) 644-8883

Offers: Patterns by Yesterday's Children (professional, for doll costumes). Also offers Swiss batiste, French laces, silks, trims, silk ribbons, others.
For Further Information: List, $1 and SASE; catalog, $3.50; pattern catalog, $2.50.

MY SISTER & I PATTERNS
3385 Sam Rayburn Run
Carrollton, TX 75007

Offers: Ragg-Bagg doll patterns, including 24-inch Inga, Teddy and the Bear, others.
For Further Information: Catalog, $2.50.

PATCH PRESS
4019 Oakman St. S.
Salem, OR 97302

Offers: Cloth doll patterns, including Ballerina/Good Fairy (21-inch jointed doll with ballerina and fairy costumes) and others.
For Further Information: Send SASE for information.

The biggest mistake beginning doll makers make is using cheap stuffing. Poor quality stuffing causes lumps no matter how well you make the doll. Always buy good quality stuffing at fabric or craft stores.

—Magic Threads

PATTERNCRAFTS, INC.
P.O. Box 25639
Colorado Springs, CO 80936

Offers: Cloth doll/toy patterns, including Udder Bliss whim-

sical cow in 5-inch, 9-inch and 13-inch sizes. Others.
For Further Information: Catalog, $1.

PLATYPUS
P.O. Box 396, Planetarium Station
New York, NY 10024
(212) 874-0753

Offers: Soft doll and animal patterns (full-sizes) in booklets. Doll patterns include 8-inch pocket dolls to 24-inch mannequin proportional figured; includes boy, girl, jester, mermaid, others. Other patterns available include pocket dolls, platypus, holiday items and soft toys such as trains, animal silhouettes, others. Supplies: Muslin, fur, notions. Booklets available.
For Further Information: Catalog with free pattern, $1.50.
Discounts: Sells wholesale.

THE QUILTING B
315 3rd Ave. SE
Cedar Rapids, IA 52401
(319) 363-1643

Offers: Line of textured yarns for Santa beards and doll hair.
For Further Information: Send SASE for list.

RAGPATS
P.O. Box 175
Caroga Lake, NY 12032

Offers: Doll and toy animal patterns: over 200 commercial designs, plus 1930s to 1970s designs and artists' designs — copied from originals.
For Further Information: Catalog, $3.

ROBBIE'S DOLL CREATIONS
7102 Longmeadow, #109
Madison, WI 53717
(608) 831-1744

Offers: Molded-face doll supplies (Swiss imported), 100% cotton Euro-tricot, 30 plus doll masks.
For Further Information: Free catalog.

ROSE OF SHARON
1109 Lead Ave. SW
Albuquerque, NM 87102

Offers: Soft, exotic animal patterns: Carousel animals, dragons, tropical birds, others.
For Further Information: Catalog, $1.

SEW LITTLE PATTERN CO.
P.O. Box 3613
Salem, OR 97302

Offers: Full-size patterns for folk art styles (with X eyes and round bottom — use for doorstops, decoratives, etc.). Styles include Farm Folks, Rabbits family, Sweet Innocence girls, layette pattern for Cabbage Patch and others.
For Further Information: Brochure, $1.
Discounts: Quantity discounts.
See Also: Clothing and Accessories

SEW SPECIAL
9823 Old Winery Place, Suite 20
Sacramento, CA 95827
(916) 361-2086

Offers: Original soft sculpture kits/patterns for country decor: Sewing basket, pincushion, machine covers, broom covers/dolls, cats, cows, others. Also offers puppet pals dolls, crayon apron, tote, soft doll and animal patterns, doll pairs patterns.
For Further Information: Catalog, $2.
Discounts: Sells wholesale.

For small dolls, try using cotton swabs or a small paint brush to apply blush to your doll faces. Spraying "lightly" with hair spray will help set the blush.

— Sew Special

THE SEWING CENTIPEDE
P.O. Box 218
Midway City, CA 92655

Offers: Soft doll/toy patterns (full-sized) including 19-inch rag dolls (with real rag hair), Pig and Mouse, doorstop Clara Belle Cow and Clover Cow broom cover. Other kitchen broom covers include Beehive Bears and geese in braided fabric wreath. Also offers Greta Goose centerpiece, 24-inch clown doll, baby doll with movable arms and legs. Body fabrics are available in muslin and other shades. Carries eyes for animals.
For Further Information: Color catalog, $2.

SOMETHING SPECIAL
502 N. Canal
Carlsbad, NM 88220
(800) 272-6992

Offers: Doll pellets by pound, bisque (flesh shades) and doll-making kits.
For Further Information: Send SASE for list.

STANDARD DOLL CO.
2383 31st St.
Long Island City, NY 11105
(718) 721-7787

Offers: Doll-making supplies, including doll parts, body patterns (8 inches to 36 inches), voices/sounds/growlers, line of music boxes, shoes and other accessories, pellets, chenille, fabrics (flesh, others), plus lace and other trims and aids. Mini-zippers and buttons, tags, bags, boxes, magnifiers and books are also available. Carries porcelain and other dolls.

For Further Information: Catalog, $3.
Discounts: Quantity discounts.
Accepts: American Express, MasterCard, Visa
See Also: Doll and Toy Making—Rigid

CYNTHIA THIELE
Alexander Creek Lane, #4
Anchorage, AK 99695

Offers: Demuremaids soft sculpture doll patterns.
For Further Information: Send SASE with inquiry.

TREASURES FROM HEAVEN
68 N. Broadway Dr., #2
Blackfoot, ID 83221
(208) 785-1166

Offers: Doll clothing for a variety of sizes.
For Further Information: Brochure, $2.

UNICORN STUDIOS
P.O. Box 370
Seymour, TN 37865

Offers: Musical movements and voices (full line of tunes, electronic types, windup types): Music, animal and doll voices (12), accessories, mini-light sets, kits, wooden boxes (28), animal and doll parts. Also offers Wyndo cards, instructions and books.
For Further Information: Catalog, $1 (refundable).

VIV'S RIBBONS & LACES
212 Virginia Hills Dr.
Martinez, CA 94553
(510) 933-7758

Offers: Doll sewing/French hand-sewing supplies: Silk and other ribbons, ribbon rose maker, old/new French and English cotton laces, plus other laces and trims. Also offers buckles, jewelry findings and books on silk ribbon embroidery, millinery, others.
For Further Information: Catalog, $3.50 (refundable).
Discounts: Quantity discounts; allows discounts to teachers and institutions; sells wholesale to legitimate businesses.
Accepts: MasterCard, Visa

Embroidery and Cross-Stitch

Also see Bead Crafts, General Needlecraft Supplies, Miniature Making, Needlepoint, Quilting, Sewing and other related categories.

A & L DESIGNS
P.O. Box 122
Summit Station, PA 17979

Offers: Counted cross-stitch for church/clergy: Fabrics, kits, patterns.
For Further Information: Brochure and swatches, $3.50.

ART POINT, INC.
116 S. School St.
Ukiah, CA 95482
(707) 462-4541

Offers: Services, including cross-stitch or needlepoint canvas, custom-printed from the customer's color photograph — a person, pet, house, scene, artwork, etc. (with instructions).
For Further Information: Send SASE for further details.

AUNT MARY'S HOBBY
20 SW 27th Ave.
Pompano Beach, FL 33069

Offers: Embroidery supplies including threads, evenweaves and other fabrics, notions and sewing aids, plus designs and books.
For Further Information: Stitchery catalog, $1.50; cross-stitch catalog, $1.50.
See Also: Needlepoint

BAYBERRY STITCHERY
P.O. Box 441
Acton, MA 01720

Offers: Cross-stitch/embroidery supplies: Threads (by DMC and Balger, including metallics), home accessories for cross-stitch, paperweights, wire frames and bellpulls. Also offers fabrics: Aida, Jobelan, Alma, Rustico, Floba, Fiddlers in tube-style and others. Carries waste canvas, totes, bags, folding stands and charted design books.
For Further Information: Catalog, $3; sale flyers, $3 for a year.

BEA ENGELBRECHT
P.O. Box 46
Glide, OR 97443

Offers: Plastic canvas tissue-box patterns: Lighthouse, tugboat, outhouse, log cabin, motor home, 18-wheeler, others.
For Further Information: Send SASE for full details.

BETTEKARIL'S NEEDLECRAFTS
P.O. Box 5008
Brandon, MS 39047
(601) 992-3266

Offers: Supplies for cross-stitch (and crochet, knitting, others). Threads: DMC, metallics, filaments, Ginnie Thompson Flower, yarns. Fabrics: Aida, and 35 plus unusuals (including Colorado, Dublin, Gretchen, Kappie, others). Also offers kits, waste canvas, sewing notions, cross-stitch projects with inserts, perforated paper, stands, totes and design/chart books. Custom framing and finishing service is also available.
For Further Information: Catalog/Needle Arts Guide, $5 (refundable).
Discounts: Discounts available.

CANTERBURY DESIGNS, INC.
P.O. Box 204060
Martinez, GA 30917
(706) 860-1674

Offers: Over 80 cross-stitch books, leaflets, kits: Original and reproduced samplers, scenes, miniatures, holiday motifs, baby, florals, Amish quilts, borders, others. Pine wood accessories: Racks, bread boards, picture frames, cutouts and towel holders, others. Also offers Kali cross-stitch fabric pieces/assortments.
For Further Information: Catalog, $2.
Discounts: Allows discounts to teachers and institutions; sells wholesale to legitimate businesses.

COMPUCRAFTS
P.O. Box 326
Lincoln Center, MA 01773

Offers: Cross-stitch software for Apple II computers. Also has software for weaving.
For Further Information: Send SASE for complete information.

CRAFT HAPPY
293 Clarlyn Dr.
Rt. 1, P.O. Box 28
Keswick, Ontario L4P 3C8 Canada
(416) 476-2480

Offers: Needle Magic punch embroidery supplies: Yarns (acrylics, metallics), transfers, accessories, glues, others.
For Further Information: Free price list.

CRAFTS BY DONNA
P.O. Box 1456
Costa Mesa, CA 92628
(714) 545-8567

Offers: Supplies/kits for Brazilian embroidery, battenberg lace, trapunto, ribbon embroidery, others.
For Further Information: Mini-kit and catalog, $2 (specify interest).

CROSS CREEK
5131 Industrial Blvd.
Maple Plain, MN 55359

Offers: Embroidery floss (324 colors), organizer system, scroll-rods needlework frame, Aida fabric in 15 colors, fray check and other cross-stitch items.
For Further Information: Send SASE for list.
Discounts: Sells wholesale; quantity discounts.
Accepts: MasterCard, Visa.

CROSS STITCHED MIRACLES
P.O. Box 32282
Euclid, OH 44132

Offers: Full line of cross-stitch supplies and 3,500 books.
For Further Information: Catalog, $4.75 (U.S.); $6 (Canada).

DAISY CHAIN
P.O. Box 1258
Parkersburg, WV 26102

Offers: Embroidery fabrics including silk gauze, a ver a soie silk, others. Also offers Balger metallic ribbons, gold and platinum plated needles, accessories, charted design cross-stitch books, resource books, needleworker's hand cream.
For Further Information: Catalog, $2.
Discounts: Quantity discounts.

DIGI-STITCH
11101 E. 41st St., Suite 349
Tulsa, OK 74146

Offers: Service: Color or black-and-white photos transformed to charted cross-stitch patterns on paper with symbols for DMC floss colors; "highly detailed" portraits, children, babies, animals, homes, automobiles.
For Further Information: Send SASE for complete details.
Accepts: MasterCard, Visa.

DMC CORP.
P.O. Box 5161
Clinton, IA 52732

Offers: Full line of DMC yarns (tapestry, Persian, Medicis), pearl and matte cotton threads, and 360 colors of long-staple cotton embroidery floss.
For Further Information: See your dealer, or send SASE for details.

EMBROIDERY MACHINE
P.O. Box 599
Pawtucket, RI 02862

Offers: Automatic punch embroidery tool ("up to 500 stitches a minute"). Use with all punch patterns/materials, it's push button. Spool on the end feeds thread. Available in 3 needle sizes, battery-powered. Also offered as kit. Pattern books are available.
Accepts: MasterCard, Visa.

THE ETC SHOP
P.O. Box 142
Freeport, NY 11520

Offers: Perforated paper in 5 colors, window cards (2 sizes, round, heart-shaped), others.
For Further Information: Send SASE for catalog.

FANCYWORK
2708 Slaterville Rd.
P.O. Box 130
Slaterville Springs, NY 14881
(607) 539-6610

Offers: 5,000 cross-stitch books—most all design categories: Country, classic, contemporary, holiday motif, men, women, children, babies, whimsical, Oriental, Western, nautical, early American, flowers, wild and domestic animals, scenes, geometrics and many others in mini to large sizes. Accessories for cross-stitch are also available.
For Further Information: Catalog, $2.
Store Location: Yes
For Further Information: Catalog, $2.75 prepaid.

GRAPHS FOR CRAFTS
50 Kerrick Rd.
Reading, PA 19607

Offers: Service: Any photograph or art work converted into graphs for cross-stitch or needlepoint. Graph is up to 30 colors; useful for gifts, preserving memories. Popular subjects

include pets, homes, logos, special designs, others (photo image size 1 inch and up).
For Further Information: Send business-size SASE for more information.

HEARTDROPS
P.O. Box 181
Oneonta, NY 13820

Offers: Cross-stitch fabrics (Aida, Hardanger, linens, Lugana, Jobelan, Davos, patterned, others). Also offers cross-stitch frames and accessories, over 1,000 graph designs and others.
For Further Information: Catalog, $5 (refundable).

HH DESIGNS
P.O. Box 183
Eastchester, NY 10709

Offers: Line of candlewick (colonial needlecraft) pillow kits—simple embroidery stitches in a variety of designs.
For Further Information: Catalog, $1.

THE HOMESTEADER
P.O. Box 18324
Spartanburg, SC 29318

Offers: Cross-stitch fabrics, including Aida, plus cross-stitch designs and coordinating "shaped" mats and frames.
For Further Information: Catalog, $2.

IN STITCHES
10611 Abercorn Extension
Savannah, GA 31419

Offers: Custom cross-stitch service: Hand charting of photos of home, car, logos, others.
For Further Information: Catalog, $1 (refundable).

INTERNATIONAL HOUSE OF BUNKA
19 Tulane Crescent
Don Mills, Ontario M3A 2B9 Canada
(416) 445-1875

Offers: Bunka needle craft (punch) tool and supplies—kits, threads, patterns, accessories. Teach-yourself manual and custom framing service also available.
For Further Information: Write or call for price lists.
Discounts: Sells wholesale.

JUST COUNTIN'
P.O. Box 559
La Center, WA 98629

Offers: Cross-stitch supplies/accessories. Fabrics: Linens, cottons, Evenweaves, rayons, blends and poly by Aida, Congress, Jobelan, Fiddlers, Tabby, others. Also offers DMC floss, waste canvas, notions, accessories with inserts, mounting boards, perforated paper cards, pine items, framing mats, porcelain bases, and 800 plus design/chart books.
For Further Information: Catalog, $2.

JUST NEEDLIN'
14503 S. Hills Ct.
P.O. Box 433
Centreville, VA 22020

Offers: Cross-stitch fabrics: Aida (colors), Alice, Alma, Anne, coverner block, Damask, Davos, Fiddlers, Floba, Gloria, Hampton, Hearthside, Hopscotch, Jobelan, Klostern, Linda, linens, Loomspun, Melinda, Monza, Patrice, Rustico, Shenandoah, others. Also offers DMC, Balger, Ginny Thompson and filament threads. Carries perforated papers, projects (with inserts), hoops, scroll frames, magnifiers and other aids, and over 1,200 design chart booklets.
For Further Information: Catalog, $3 (refundable).
Discounts: Has discounts.
See Also: Paper Crafts and Paper Making

KEMP'S KRAFTS
5940 Taylor St.
Coloma, MI 49038

Offers: Plastic canvas/needlework projects for doll furniture.
For Further Information: Send SASE for list.

KREINIK MANUFACTURING CO., INC.
9199 Reistertown Rd., Suite 2098
Owings Mills, MD 21117
(800) 624-1928

Offers: French silk yarns and threads for needlepoint, cross-stitch, embroidered smocking and other; includes Soie d'Alger and other silks, Balger metallics.
For Further Information: Send SASE for sample (specify interest).
Discounts: Sells wholesale.

LJ ORIGINALS, INC.
516 Sumac Place
De Soto, TX 75115
(214) 223-6644

Offers: Transgraph-X needleart kit (clear plastic grid kits)—converts drawings into charts for any counted needle art (5 to 25 count-per-inch); calculates size, reduces and enlarges patterns.
For Further Information: Catalog, $1 (refundable).
Discounts: Quantity discounts; sells wholesale to legitimate businesses.

MARILYN'S NEEDLEWORK & FRAMES
4336 Plainfield Ave. NE
Grand Rapids, MI 49505

Offers: Stoney Creek Collection cross-stitch designs/kits, plus a wide selection of fabrics. Also offers Balger blending filaments, Wheatland craft frames, cross- stitch books by top designers and DMC floss. Carries needlepoint, crewel and longstitch designs.
For Further Information: Catalog, $5.

MARY JANE'S CROSS 'N STITCH, INC.
5120 Belmont Rd.
Downers Grove, IL 60515

Offers: Over 1,200 stitchery books and leaflets, embroidery fabrics (Aida, Evenweave, others) and DMC floss.
For Further Information: Catalog and guide, $5 (refundable).

MEISTERGRAM
3517 W. Wendover Ave.
Greensboro, NC 27407

Offers: Monogramming and embroidery equipment and supplies (also training, service and marketing know-how).
For Further Information: Write for information.

MORNING GLORY NEEDLEWORKS
77 E. 8th St., Suite 165
Holland, MI 49423

Offers: Blackwork and whitework charts, including samplers, bookmark band samplers, mini-samplers, and other original and reproduction samplers.
For Further Information: Send business-size SASE for chart and catalog.

NEEDLECRAFT ORIGINALS
P.O. Box 1679
Grand Centre, Alta T0A 1T0 Canada

Offers: Service: Custom-designed cross-stitch and needlepoint charts from any photo (house, person, baby, scene, car, logo, sketch or artwork, others).
For Further Information: Send SASE for complete details.
See Also: Needlepoint

OZARK PUNCH SUPPLIES
P.O. Box 114
Duenweg, MO 64841

Offers: Wide array of punch embroidery supplies.
For Further Information: Free catalog.
Discounts: Sells wholesale; quantity discounts.

PANTOGRAMS MANUFACTURING CO., INC.
6807 S. MacDill
Tampa, FL 33611
(813) 839-5697

Offers: Monogramming system equipment. Manufacturer.
For Further Information: Write or call for information.

To protect individual charts or patterns, store them in a photo album. This allows you to categorize your patterns using several albums and attaching index tabs. You can categorize by pattern type (floral, baby) or by needle art (cross-stitch, knitting).

—BetteKaril's Needlecrafts

ANNE POWELL LTD.
P.O. Box 3060
Stuart, FL 34995
(407) 287-3007

Offers: Counted cross-stitch charts, kits, Glenshee linen, Solingen embroidery scissors, plus antique sewing tools, informative books and gift items for needlecrafters.
For Further Information: Catalog, $5.
Discounts: Sells wholesale to legitimate businesses.

PRETTY PUNCH CRAFTS LTD.
10 Pinelands Ave.
Stoney Creek, Ontario L8E 3A5 Canada
(416) 662-8116

Offers: Needle punch embroidery accessories: Kits (acrylics and lusters, metallics, other), needle packs, and 600 color-coded iron-on transfers.
For Further Information: Free brochure, price list and nearest dealer.
Discounts: Sells wholesale to businesses.

PURE CHINA SILK CO.
Rt. 2, P.O. Box 70
Holdrege, NE 68949
(308) 995-4755

Offers: Silk embroidery threads in 14-yard skeins and multi-strand twist threads in 64 colors for embroidery, cross-stitch, needlepunch, petit point, etc.
For Further Information: Color card, $1.25.
Discounts: Quantity discounts.

ROBIN DESIGNS
12909 Turkey Branch Pkwy.
Rockville, MD 20853

Offers: Service: Custom cross-stitch kits from photographs.
For Further Information: Send SASE for brochure.

ROBISON-ANTON TEXTILE CO.
P.O. Box 159
Fairview, NJ 07022
(201) 941-0500

Offers: Super Luster embroidery floss on 1-pound cones of

6-strand mercerized cotton; available in 228 colors. Specializes in cones for kit manufacturers.
For Further Information: Contact dealer, or send SASE for information.

EVA ROSENSTAND
P.O. Box 185
Clovis, CA 93613

Offers: Cross-stitch kits and designs from Denmark in a wide array of traditional and classic designs—people, scenes, flowers, animals, other motifs.
For Further Information: Catalog, $4.50.

SANDEEN'S
1315 White Bear Ave.
St. Paul, MN 55106
(612) 776-7012

Offers: Norwegian and Danish Embroidery/handcraft supplies: Swedish kits, Hardanger supplies, brackets, others.
For Further Information: Needlecraft catalog, $3 (refundable).
See Also: Tole and Decorative Crafts

SEW ORIGINAL NEEDLEART
6423 Ming Ave.
Bakersfield, CA 93309

Offers: Evenweave fabrics selection, threads (metallics, DMC, others), fibers, stitching aids, kits, books.
For Further Information: Catalog, $3.

THE SQUARE STITCHERS
119 Fant Lane
Union, SC 29379
(803) 427-2625

Offers: Cross-stitch maps designed as single charts of 200 × 160 squares, including the U.S., Europe and others.
For Further Information: Brochure and cross-stitch book, $2.

STITCH IN TIME
P.O. Box 317
Spring Lake, MI 49456

Offers: Service: Custom color cross-stitch charting from photographs—any subject.
For Further Information: Send SASE for brochure.

STITCH 'N STUFF
24401 Carla Lane, NS
North Olmsted, OH 44070

Offers: Counted cross-stitch supplies, DMC floss, fabrics, accessories, plastic canvas, yarn, books, others.

For Further Information: Catalog, $1 (refundable).
Discounts: Quantity discounts.

STITCHERS' DELIGHT
2480 Iris St.
Lakewood, CO 80215
(303) 233-6001

Offers: Colorado cross-stitch graphs and kits, books, fabric and accessories.
For Further Information: Catalog, $1 (refundable).

THE STRAWBERRY SAMPLER
#7 Olde Ridge Village
Chadds Ford, PA 19317
(215) 358-9145

Offers: Cross-stitch kits (some with framing kits): Samplers, florals, Oriental, Danish, traditional, quotations, holiday motifs, samplers, state; many designs are printed on home accessories. Kits: Afghans, pillows. 85 Fabrics: Klostern, Aida, Fiddler, Loomspun, Rustico, Congress, Hardanger, linens, Jobelan, afghan types. Magnifiers, waste canvas. Also offers accessories, framing supplies/kits and design books.
For Further Information: Color catalog, $3.50.
Accepts: MasterCard, Visa

STRINGS 'N THINGS
1228 Blossom Terrace
Boiling Springs, PA 17007
(712) 258-6022

Offers: Threads: Schurer, Marlitt, Nordiska cotton, silk, metallic, wool, tatting, embroidery/tapestry cottons, cutwork, Pearl cotton, DMC and Baroque (and other) crochet cottons, metallics, Persian wool, Balger filaments and braid.
For Further Information: Send business-size SASE for brochure.
Discounts: Quantity discounts.

THERON TRADITIONS
222 Williams St., #125
Glastonbury, CT 06033

Offers: Counted thread kits: Overdyed floss, variety of stitches, linen fabric, color photo, stitch charts and graph, including samplers, quotations, others.
For Further Information: Contact your dealer, or catalog, $1.50. "Shop inquiries welcome."

THREAD ARTISTS
Rt. 1
St. Catherines, Ontario L2R 6P7 Canada

Offers: Bunka embroidery Teach Yourself kit: Bunka needle, floral kit, instructions, catalog of supplies. (Florals include tulips, rose, hibiscus, violets, others.)

For Further Information: Send SASE for full information.

THUMBELINA NEEDLEWORK SHOP
P.O. Box 1065
Solvang, CA 93464
(805) 688-4136

Offers: Full line of counted thread designs (charts and kits with Aida floss, chart): In classics, traditional, other motifs.
For Further Information: Supply catalog, $1; other counted thread embroidery catalogs: (1) Danish Handcraft Guild, $2.75; (2) Permin Christmas Designs/kits, $2.25; (3) Permin Designs in kits, $2.25; (4) Eva Rosenstand/Clara Weaver, $4.50; (5) Charts or kits, no Christmas, $2.75.

THE YARN SHOP
360 N. Westfield St.
Feeding Hills, MA 01030
(800) 525-2685

Offers: Home accessories to embroider: Linens and jewelry blanks, frame sets/knobs. Fabrics: Linens, Aida, others. Also offers adjustable hoop stand/holder, mat/mounting boards, dazor magnifier, waste canvas and stitch kits, aids, graph paper and pattern books.
For Further Information: Free catalog.
Accepts: MasterCard, Visa

Fabric Decorating

Also see Bead Crafts, General Needlecraft Supplies, Batik and Dyeing, Embroidery and Cross-Stitch, Fabrics and Trims and Sewing.

THE ART STORE
935 Erie Blvd. E.
Syracuse, NY 13210
(315) 474-1000

Offers: Fiber arts/crafts supplies and equipment: Jacquard textile and silk paints, batik, screen printing, marbling, beads, others.
For Further Information: Complete list, $3.
See Also: General Craft Supplies

BEJEWELED WHOLESALERS
P.O. Box 8096
Pembroke Pines, FL 33084-0096
(305) 433-5700

Offers: Line of studs, BeDazzler rhinestones and setters, rims, settings, pearls, fringes, conchos, sew-on jewels, others.
For Further Information: Catalog, $1.

BLUEPRINTS-PRINTABLE
1504 #7 Industrial Way
Belmont, CA 94002

Offers: Printable clothing/accessories: Silks, rayons and cottons (blueprint sensitized fabrics). Also offers hair clips, buckles, earrings, handbags.
For Further Information: Catalog and fabric samples, $3.

BY JUPITER!
6801 N. 21st Ave.
Phoenix, AZ 85015

Offers: Fabric fading kit: Compound and instructions for 6 yards of fabric.
For Further Information: Send SASE for details.

COLLINS CREATIONS
Rt. 1, P.O. Box 1562
Streetman, TX 75859

Offers: Ultrasuede appliqué patterns (and instructions) in a variety of designs for surface decorating.
For Further Information: Catalog, $2 (refundable).

COLORCRAFT, LTD.
14 Airport Park Rd.
East Granby, CT 06026

Offers: Createx colors (acrylics), kits, plus glitter powders, adhesives, mediums, "perma seal," marble colors, foils, others. Instructional videos on fabric painting are also available.
For Further Information: Contact dealer, or write for catalog.
Accepts: MasterCard, Visa

CRAFT INDUSTRIES LIMITED
P.O. Box 38
Somerset, MA 02726
(508) 676-3883

Offers: Surface decorating colors: Country Classics dyes for wool and other fabrics, fabric paints (neon, puff, pearl), tie-dye kits, marbling paints.
For Further Information: Send SASE for list.

When decorating clothing and jewelry, there are many more options besides the usual rhinestones and nailheads. Try something unusual, like little squares of Friendly Plastic glued to a shirt and edged in puff paint.

—Fashion Craft

CREATIVE CRYSTAL CO.
P.O. Box 1232
Burlington, CT 06013
(800) 578-0716

Offers: The Bejeweler electric rhinestone setter (plus instructions, patterns, supplies, stand); German-made.
For Further Information: Send SASE for details.
Accepts: MasterCard, Visa

DECART, INC.
Lamoille Industrial Park, P.O. Box 309
Morrisville, VT 05661
(802) 888-4217

Offers: Deka line of fabric paints in a full array of colors. Manufacturer.
For Further Information: See your dealer, or send SASE for information.

DELTA TECHNICAL COATINGS, INC.
2550 Pellissier Place
Whittier, CA 90601
(213) 686-0678

Offers: Delta fabric dyes, colors, glitter, Shiny and Swell Stuff and Stichless glue, plus Ceramcoat acrylics, Shiva Signa-Tex acrylic paints and Marble-Thix powder (water base) for marbling.
For Further Information: Send business-size SASE for free color guide.

DESIGNS BY DEBBIE MITCHELL
304 W. Cheryl Ave.
Hurst, TX 76053
(817) 282-6890

Offers: Iron-on transfer designs, including whimsical animals (bears, reindeer, chickens, others), holiday motifs, others; by packets. Books also available.
For Further Information: Catalog, $4.

DHARMA TRADING CO.
P.O. Box 150916
San Rafael, CA 94915
(800) 542-5227

Offers: Fabric paints, Pientex silk inks, Deka-silk and metallics, Texticolor iridescent, Versatex textile paint, dyes. Also offers fabric pens, brushes, jars, gloves, squeeze bottles. Carries T-shirt and other cotton fabrics, T-shirts, T-dresses and pants, silk fabrics, silk and cotton scarves, and a line of dyes and batik products.
For Further Information: Free catalog.
Discounts: Quantity discounts.
Accepts: MasterCard, Visa
See Also: Batik and Dyeing

DORSET DESIGNS
1442A Walnut St., #356
Berkeley, CA 94709

Offers: Imported laces: Lyon, Valenciennes, Maline (French), plus edging from England, cotton embroideries from Switzerland, others.
For Further Information: Catalog, $5.50 (refundable).
Discounts: "Wholesale inquiries welcome."

EXTRA SPECIAL PRODUCTS CORP.
P.O. Box 777
Greenville, OH 45331
(800) 648-5945

Offers: Surface decoratives: Flex-O-Mirro, "Razzles" sequin pieces and "grass," Fuzzy Wuzzy iron-on velour sheets, foils, copper sheets, templates, black transfers, jewelry findings, others.

For Further Information: Free catalog.
Discounts: Allows discounts to teachers, institutions and professionals; sells wholesale to legitimate businesses.

FABDEC
3553 Old Post Rd.
San Angelo, TX 76904
(915) 653-6170

Offers: Procion fiber dye kit, dyes for silkscreen, stencil, airbrush, batik; will dye yarn, fabrics, paper, wood, baskets. Also offers additives, tjantings (3), wax, paper and natural fabrics: Cottons (mercerized, muslin, duck), viscose rayon, challis.
For Further Information: Send SASE for lists.
Discounts: Quantity discounts; large order discounts on pound orders.
Accepts: MasterCard, Visa

Use only fabrics that are well-washed and well-rinsed.

—Fabdec

FC&A'S TRANSFER PATTERNS
103 Clover Green
Peachtree City, GA 30269

Offers: Iron-on transfer patterns (for clothing) in country designs, whimsical and other animals, Southwest motifs, 20s, circus clowns, dinosaurs, bows, holiday motifs, others; by packets.
For Further Information: Send SASE for list.

FLORA MULTIMEDIA & CO.
4801 Marble Ave. NE
Albuquerque, NM 87110
(505) 255-9988

Offers: Silkscreen printing video (with workbook) for home workshop—presents progressive techniques to print on fabrics (and other flat surfaces); includes supply sources data.
For Further Information: Send SASE for details.
Accepts: American Express

G.H.T.A. CO.
5303 Holly Springs Dr.
Houston, TX 77056

Offers: Cotton and 50/50 blend plain clothing: T-shirts and sweatshirts, leggings, long T-shirts, golf shirts, shorts, others.
For Further Information: Catalog, $2.
Discounts: Sells wholesale.

GRAMMA'S GRAPHICS
20 Birling Gap, Dept. TCSS-P4
Fairport, NY 14450
(716) 223-4309

Offers: Sun print kits. Images are derived through printing photo negatives, objects, stencils or cutouts, on fabric treated with solution. Sun exposure makes prints in blue. Designs are washable. Also offers untreated cotton fabric by the yard, blank note cards, gift tags/envelopes. Classroom sun kits and print papers are also available.
For Further Information: Brochure, $1 and business-size SASE.
Discounts: Sells wholesale; quantity discounts.

HILTON
P.O. Box 1016
San Juan, TX 78589

Offers: Iron-on appliqué motifs: Southwest, autumn, floral, Christmas, plus trial assortments. Carries other boutique items for surface decorations.
For Further Information: Catalog, $2 (refundable).

ILLINOIS BRONZE
Lake Zurich, IL 60047
(312) 438-8201

Offers: "Gimme" fabric decorating products: Glitters, Iridescents, Slicks, Puffs, Dazzling Dyes, Beachstreet Dyes, See-Through Sparkle Tints, Precious Metal, Fabri-coat, Fabric mediums, Glitter Glue, all in a wide range of colors. Also offers acrylic paints (country brights, pastels) and others. Manufacturer.
For Further Information: See your dealer, or send SASE for information.

IMAGINATION STATION
P.O. Box 2157
White City, OR 97503
(800) 338-3857

Offers: Service: Photographs transferred to fabric: Black-and-white, color, sepia. Enlarges, reduces, customized to order (photos returned).
For Further Information: Free brochure.
Accepts: MasterCard, Visa

IVY IMPORTS, INC.
12213 Distribution Way
Beltsville, MD 20705

Offers: Visionart instant set silk dyes and the Silk Experience kits. Fabrics: Silk, cottons. Also offers Tinfix and Silktint colors, fabric pens, paints, additives, resists, brushes and steamers. Instructional videos with Diane Tuckman and Naomi Barsk, plus silk painting books are also available.

For Further Information: Contact your dealer, or send SASE for information.
Discounts: Quantity prices, discounts to teachers, institutions and businesses.

CAROLYN KYLE ENTERPRISES, INC.
2840 E. Black Lake Blvd. SW
Olympia, WA 98502
(206) 352-4427

Offers: Line of imported glass "jewels" for surface decorating.
For Further Information: Send SASE for information.

Try sponge brushes to apply dye in stripes or designs.

—Fabdec

LAURATEX FABRICS
153 W. 27th St.
New York, NY 10001
(212) 645-7800

Offers: Cotton fabrics prepared for painting and screen painting: Sateen, ottoman, batiste, linens.
For Further Information: Send SASE for information.

M & M TRIMS
91 S. Main Plaza
Wilkes-Barre, PA 18701
(717) 825-7305

Offers: Swarovski rhinestones and other trims for surface decorating.
For Further Information: Brochure, $1 and SASE.

PENTEL OF AMERICA, LTD.
2805 Columbia St.
Torrance, CA 90503

Offers: Line of Fabrifun pastel dye sticks (for natural fabrics). Also offers artist's pastels, watercolors, crayons, pens and adhesives.
For Further Information: See your dealer, or send SASE for information.
Discounts: Quantity discounts.

PHOTOTEXTILES
P.O. Box 3063
Bloomington, IN 47402

Offers: Service: Customer photographs and artwork transferred to fabric. Also offers Crazy Quilter Cuties antique graphics on fabrics.
For Further Information: Free brochure.
Store Location: Yes
Discounts: Quantity discounts; allows discounts to teachers

and institutions; sells wholesale to legitimate businesses.

PRINTABLES

P.O. Box 1201
Burlingame, CA 94011

Offers: Clothes for surface designers—casual and dressy styles in sizes XS to XL in preshrunk, PFD, cotton sheeting, and rayon challis, plus silk selections in several colors (but not preshrunk). Also offers basic clothing ready for artistic embellishment, silk scarves, quilted cotton and silk hand-bags, belts, jackets and earrings in cotton, silk and leather.
For Further Information: Catalog and fabric samples, $2.

PRO CHEMICAL & DYE, INC.

P.O. Box 14
Somerset, MA 02726
(508) 676-3838

Offers: Full line of dyes for silkscreen, handpainting, batik, other, including permanent cold-water types that are wash-fast. Also offers pigments, marbling items, fluorescents and auxiliaries.
For Further Information: Free catalog.
Discounts: Sells wholesale; quantity discounts.

QUALIN INTERNATIONAL

P.O. Box 31145
San Francisco, CA 94131

Offers: Silk scarf blanks imported from China, with hand-rolled hems. Also offers scarf assortments and silk fabrics.
For Further Information: Send SASE for list.
Discounts: Quantity discounts.

RIBBONS & LACE

P.O. Box 30070
Mesa, AZ 85275

Offers: Line of decorative trims: Laces, ribbons, beads, craft supplies.
For Further Information: Catalog, $2.99 (refundable).
Discounts: Sells wholesale.

SAVOIR FAIRE

3020 Bridgeway, Suite 305
Sausalito, CA 94965

Offers: French dyes (Tinfix and others) for brushes, plus steam ovens and stretcher frames.
For Further Information: Send SASE for full information.

SILKPAINT CORP.

P.O. Box 18
Waldron, MO 64092
(816) 891-7774

Offers: Silkpaint! brand resist, Fiber-Etch cellulose dissolving medium for cotton, linen and rayons, plus silkpaint kits and air-powered resist pens.
For Further Information: Free catalog.
Discounts: Allows discounts to teachers and institutions; sells wholesale to legitimate businesses.
Accepts: MasterCard, Visa

When sewing (on machine) long bias strips, stabilize the cuts before sewing with strips of masking tape on either side. Remove tape after sewing.

—Phototextiles

SOHO SOUTH

P.O. Box 1324
Cullman, AL 35056
(800) 280-6520

Offers: Fabric dyes and paints, marbling materials, beads, decorative findings, silk scarves and fabric.
For Further Information: Free catalog.

SUREWAY TRADING ENTERPRISES

826 Pine Ave., #5
Niagara Falls, NY 14301

Offers: Line of silk fabrics and scarves, French dyes for painting and airbrush.
For Further Information: Free catalog.
Discounts: Sells wholesale; quantity discounts.

TAYLOR VON OTTERBACH

56 San Marco Ave.
St. Augustine, FL 32084
(904) 825-4999

Offers: Silk clothing blanks in crepe de chine, designed for dye or paint—60 styles in 3 sizes; 33 styles in 1X to 3X.
For Further Information: Free catalog.

TEXTILE COLORS

P.O. Box 887
Riverdale, MD 20738
(800) 783-9265

Offers: FabricArts all-fabric paints and mediums, dyes, sample and other painting kits. Also offers silk and wool fabrics and silk scarves. Carries tools, brushes, accessories, chemicals, cleaners, videos and books.
For Further Information: Catalog and color charts, $2.
Discounts: Quantity discounts; allows discounts to teachers, institutions and professionals.

TRADITIONS
P.O. Box 176
Madisonville, TN 37354

Offers: Specialty laces, ribbons, pearls and others for surface decorating.
For Further Information: Catalog, $2.

J. TREAR DESIGNS
2121 Slater St.
Santa Rosa, CA 95404
(707) 523-2840

Offers: All cotton clothing (for painting or dyeing): Fleece, crinkle cotton, sheeting and cotton lycra.
For Further Information: Catalog and swatches, $1.
Discounts: Quantity discounts.

WEB OF THREAD
3240 Lone Oak Rd., Suite 124
Paducah, KY 42003
(502) 554-8185

Offers: Machine embroidery threads, couching braids, cords, ribbons (silk, rayon, metallics, others).

For Further Information: Catalog, $2.

THE WOODEN HEART
Rt. 11, P.O. Box 2260
Elizabethton, TN 37643
(615) 543-5602

Offers: Line of fabric pattern packets: Decorative designs (tole-like whimsical and country) including holiday motifs, scenes, rabbits, flowers for dolls.
For Further Information: Send 2 stamps for brochure.
Discounts: Sells wholesale.
See Also: Tole and Decorative Crafts

YESTERDAYS
P.O. Box 4308
Scottsdale, AZ 85261
(602) 201-5732

Offers: Service: Iron-on transfers made from photos, drawings or sketches—full-color up to 11-inch × 17-inch; for fabric surfaces.
For Further Information: Send SASE for full details.
Accepts: MasterCard, Visa

Fabrics and Trims

Also see most other categories in Section II.

ARISE
6925 Willow St. SW
Washington, DC 20012

Offers: Line of Artse silk (Japanese and Indonesian, other), including scrap and piece bags, others. Also offers cotton/Ikat bags and kimono bundles (5 and up).
For Further Information: Send SASE for information.

ASF
4115 Brownsville Rd.
Pittsburgh, PA 15227

Offers: Fabric club featuring silks, wools, cottons, others.
For Further Information: Bimonthly swatches, $10 yearly.
Discounts: Has discounts.

BAER FABRICS
515 E. Market St.
Louisville, KY 40202
(502) 583-5521

Offers: Fabrics: Sample 1—Ultrasuede facile, Caress and Lamous in over 125 solid colors, printed and embossed suedes, $7.50 a set; Sample 5—Liberty of London lush cotton prints (some discount), $5 a set; Sample 6—fashion collection of cotton prints, jacquards, madras plaids, linen tweeds, fancies, knits, polyester crepe de chine prints (discounted), $5 a set; Sample 10—action collection of lycra, lycra/cotton stretch fabrics (solids, prints, metallics), ripstop nylon and nylon taffeta (discounted), $5 a set.
For Further Information: Notion catalog, $2; sample sets as above.
See Also: Costumes—Ethnic, Historic, Special Occasion

BARBEAU FINE FABRICS
1308-A Birch St.
Fort Collins, CO 80521

Offers: Members get 4 mailings yearly of fashion fabric swatches: Silks, wools, cottons, others.
For Further Information: Swatch service, $12 yearly (with binder).

SONYA LEE BARRINGTON
837 47th Ave.
San Francisco, CA 94121
(415) 221-6510

Offers: Hand-dyed/marbled cotton fabrics: Over 200 solids, variety of patterns.
For Further Information: Swatches, $5.

BEAD DIFFERENT
1627 S. Tejon St.
Colorado Springs, CO 80903
(303) 473-2188

Offers: Stretchable fabrics: Glitterskin, spandex, lycra, stretch satin, others.
For Further Information: Send SASE for special prices for 10 or 25 yards.

THE BINDING STITCH
8 Taunton Ave.
Dennis, MA 02638

Offers: Dressmaker cotton velveteens (25 colors).
For Further Information: Swatch cards, $10.

SUZANNE BOEHM
P.O. Box 695
Asheville, NC 28802

Offers: Handwoven fabrics from natural fibers; variety of colors, patterns, solids.
For Further Information: Samples, $5 (refundable).

BRITEX-BY-MAIL
146 Geary St.
San Francisco, CA 94108
(415) 392-2910

Offers: Fashion fabrics in a variety of domestic/imported cottons, blends, silks, linens, rayons, woolens, knits, spandex, others.
For Further Information: Swatch service available. Specify needs, describing garment/yardage and fiber wanted, price restrictions; for personal consultation include $5.
Store Location: Yes
Discounts: Sells wholesale to legitimate businesses.
Accepts: MasterCard, Visa

BUTTERFLY NYLON OUTLET
P.O. Box 416
Lacey's Spring, AL 35754
(205) 881-5458

Offers: Lingerie fabrics, laces.
For Further Information: Catalog with samples, $3 (with $5 rebate).

CAMILLE ENTERPRISES
P.O. Box 615
Rockaway, NJ 07866

Offers: Designer fabrics in a full array of colors and textures.
For Further Information: Fabric swatches, $3 (refundable).

CAROLINA MILLS
P.O. Box V, Highway 76 W.
Branson, MO 65616
(417) 334-2291

Offers: Fabrics: London Fog line, polyester doubleknits, polyester gabardines, windbreaker fabric, wools and wool blends.
For Further Information: Color cards for three fabrics, $2.

CENTURY LEATHER
P.O. Box 256
Wakefield, MA 01880

Offers: Garment leathers: French butts, English sides, shoulders, both suedes and smooth-sided types, plus dyes and finishes.
For Further Information: Catalog and swatches, $1.

CINEMA LEATHERS
1663 Blake Ave.
Los Angeles, CA 90031
(213) 222-0073

Offers: Line of garment leathers, including suedes and others—lamb, pig, cow, novelties, foils, others.
For Further Information: Send SASE for information.
Store Location: Yes
Discounts: Quantity discounts; sells wholesale to legitimate businesses.

CODE FELT LTD.
P.O. Box 130
Perth, Ontario K7H 3E3 Canada
(613) 267-2464

Offers: Felt, burlap, vinyl, other fabrics and craft items.
For Further Information: Shade cards, coupon, $3.
Store Location: Yes
Discounts: Quantity discounts; allows discounts to teachers and institutions; sells wholesale to legitimate businesses.

Accepts: MasterCard, Visa

COMMONWEALTH FELT CO.
P.O. Box 150
Easthampton, MA 01027

Offers: Perfection brand felt by the piece in assortments or by yard; also offers felt appliqué shapes and letters.
For Further Information: See your dealer, or send SASE for prices.

COTTON EXPRESS
4400 Country Club Dr.
Wilson, NC 27893
(919) 399-7639

Offers: Cotton knit fabrics: Jersey, interlock, mesh, others.
For Further Information: Brochure, swatches, $4.

THE COTTON SHOPPE
P.O. Box 3168
Key Largo, FL 33037
(307) 852-9618

Offers: Lines of known-brand fabrics including Hoffman, RJR, others.
For Further Information: Over 250 swatches, $6 ($8 international).

D'ANTON
3079 Oasis Rd. NE
West Branch, IA 52358
(319) 643-2568

Offers: Full line of luxury garment leathers: Suedes, smooth and fun types in a variety of colors, textures and finishes.
For Further Information: Information list, $1 and SASE.
Discounts: Quantity discounts; sells wholesale to legitimate businesses and professionals.

Looking for a way to mark suede without leaving lines? Chalk works great. Brush it off after the pattern is cut out.
—Leather Unlimited Corp.

DAZIAN, INC.
2014 Commerce St.
Dallas, TX 75201
(214) 748-3450

Offers: Boutique and theatrical fabrics/trims: Satin, nylon silks, laces, flameproof types, patent, buckram, felt, chronoline, muslin, velvet, fluorescents and novelties including metallics, coated and pearlized. Also offers spangles, sequins, rhinestone motifs, appliqués, crowns, tiaras, fringes, mir-

rors, jewels, feathers, hats, millinery and hoop wires, boning, plastic fringes, leis and metallic trims.
For Further Information: Free catalog and samples.
Discounts: Sells wholesale; quantity discounts.

DIMPLES
101 Sunset
Collinsville, IL 62234

Offers: Line of children's fabrics; seasonal selections.
For Further Information: Swatch mailings (1 year), coupon, $5 (Canada, $8).

ELSIE'S EXQUISIQUES
513 Broadway
Niles, MI 49120
(616) 684-7034

Offers: Trims: Silk and satin ribbons, imported trims, ribbons, silk ribbon roses, others.
For Further Information: Send SASE with specific inquiry.
Discounts: Sells wholesale to businesses.

FABRIC GALLERY
146 W. Grand River
Williamston, MI 48895
(517) 655-4573

Offers: Fashion fabrics: Imported/domestic silks, wools, cottons. Line of buttons, others.
For Further Information: Swatches service, $8.
Store Location: Yes

FABRICATIONS FABRIC CLUB
P.O. Box 2162
South Vineland, NJ 08360

Offers: Members of this fabric club, on payment of a yearly fee, receive coordinated swatch collections of designer and other quality fabrics 4 times yearly.
For Further Information: Send SASE for full details.
Discounts: "Prices are reasonable."

FABRICS UNLIMITED
5015 Columbia Pike
Arlington, VA 22204
(703) 671-0325

Offers: Ultrasuede and many other designer fabrics (including Adele Simpson, Calvin Klein, others and exclusives).
For Further Information: Send SASE for information; ultrasuede color card (over 30 colors), $4.
Discounts: Quantity discounts; allows discounts to teachers, professionals and institutions.

FAY'S FASHION FABRICS
1155 Webster Dr.
Pensacola, FL 32505
(904) 455-2410

Offers: Line of lingerie fabrics.
For Further Information: Catalog, samples, coupon, $3.
Discounts: Sells wholesale.

FIELD'S FABRICS
1695 44th SE
Grand Rapids, MI 49512
(616) 455-4570

Offers: Fabrics: Cuddleskin brushed back satin sleepwear, Polo cotton interlock, silks, velvets, Canton fleece, cotton twills, washable bridal satins, metallic fabrics, Pendleton wools.
For Further Information: Specify swatch sets, $2 each. Swatches, $10 (refundable) for: Ultrasuede, Facile, Caress and Ultraleather in 50 colors.
Accepts: Discover, MasterCard, Visa

G STREET FABRICS
11854 Rockville Pike
Rockville, MD 20852
(301) 231-8998

Offers: Fabric sample charts, $10.00 each as below: (1) Liberty of London cotton prints; (2) pinwale cotton corduroy; (3) cotton batiks; (4) cotton crepe georgette; (5) iridescent moire taffeta; (6) polyester/cotton poplin; (7) Ultrasuede; (8) Facile; (9) silk gabardine; (10) silk shantung; (11) doupioni silk twill suiting; (12) silk charmeuse and crepe de chine; (13) rayon velvet; (14) wool crepe; (15) wool gabardine; (16) wool jersey; (17) wool chiffon flannel; (18) acetate taffeta and satin; (19) anti-static polyester lining; (20) linen in four weights. Other fabrics available. Has sample subscription service with monthly sample mailings, and a custom sample service. Refundable.
For Further Information: Inquire with SASE.
Accepts: MasterCard, Visa

GREAT AMERICAN SEWING FACTORY
Ossining, NY 10562

Offers: Sewing trims, including laces (eyelet, cluny, flat, ruffled, others), ribbon assortments, Christmas trims, elastics, velcro, appliqués and other trims, plus threads.
For Further Information: Catalog, $1 (refundable).

GS INDUSTRIES
149 W. Chicago Ave.
Chicago, IL 60610

Offers: Line of activewear/swimwear fabrics: Lycra, cottons, nylons in a variety of prints, colors, textures.

For Further Information: Swatch booklet, $10 U.S. ($8, Canada).

H.E. GOLDBERG & CO., INC.
9050 Martin Luther King Jr. Way S.
Seattle, WA 98118

Offers: Tanned furs and skins: Large/small quantities—fox, beaver, mink, calfskin, lambskin, muskrat, raccoon, rabbit skin, opossum, reindeer, ermine, others.
For Further Information: Catalog, $1.
Accepts: Discover, MasterCard, Visa

HERMES LEATHER
45 West 34th St., Room 1108
New York, NY 10001
(212) 947-1153

Offers: Line of garment leathers/suedes; hides, pig suede, cabretta, others.
For Further Information: Send SASE for swatch card.
Store Location: Yes
Discounts: Sells wholesale to legitimate businesses.

J. FLORA
1831 Hyde St.
San Francisco, CA 94109

Offers: Soft suede scraps (for trims, appliqués, crafts) by pound of mixed colors.
For Further Information: Send SASE for list.
Discounts: Quantity discounts.

JEHLOR FANTASY FABRICS
730 Andover Park West
Seattle, WA 98188
(206) 575-8250

Offers: Specialty fabrics: Sequined and beaded fabrics, "cracked ice," metallics, brocades, lamés, satins, chiffons, lycra, stretch satin and nude sheers, stretch suiting. Trims: Rhinestones, glass beads and jewels, beads, sequins, spandex, appliqués/trims, fringe, feathers, others.
For Further Information: Catalog, $5 (refundable).
Store Location: Yes
Discounts: Quantity discounts.

JOYCE'S
P.O. Box 381
Morrisville, NY 13408

Offers: Line of children's fabrics including Ultrex nylon, Polarfleece. Prints include Minnie, Mickie, Barbie, Snoopy, Dalmations, Batman, Flintstones, trolls, others.
For Further Information: Samples, $1 and business-size SASE (2 stamps).

Nap on suede goes downward—like stroking a cat's fur.
—D'Aton

KAGEDO
55 Spring St.
Seattle, WA 98104
(206) 467-9077

Offers: Kagedo vintage and antique Japanese silks. Fine kimono and obi fabrics for textile artists; small custom-sorted orders.
For Further Information: Samples, $3; send SASE with inquiry.

KIEFFER'S LINGERIE FABRICS
P.O. Box 7500
Jersey City, NJ 07307

Offers: Full line of lingerie fabrics: Nylons, faux cuddleskin, sheers, stretches, laces. Also offers elastics, filler, straps, girdle fabrics, novelties, nylon/lycra swimwear fabrics and linings, plus polyester knits, polycottons, sweatshirt fleece and knits, velours, stretch fabrics; thermal and 2-way action fabrics. Carries threads, ribbing, facings, notions, scissors, Sew Lovely patterns, sequin novelties, laces.
For Further Information: Free catalog.
Discounts: Quantity discounts; allows discounts to institutions; sells wholesale to legitimate businesses.

CHERYL KOLANDER'S
5806 N. Vancouver Ave.
Portland, OR 97217
(503) 286-4149

Offers: Line of silk fabrics: Aurora silk and other types, naturally dyed.
For Further Information: Free brochure; color chart/samples, $15.

L.P. THUR FABRICS
126 W. 23rd St.
New York, NY 10011
(212) 243-4913

Offers: Line of unique/hard-to-find fabrics: Lycra, rayons, cottons, craft, theatrical, costume and designer fabrics, trims, glass beads, buttons, others.
For Further Information: Send SASE for samples.
Store Location: Yes
Discounts: Sells wholesale.

LACE HEAVEN
2524 Dauphin Island Pkwy.
Mobile, AL 36605
(205) 478-5644

Offers: Fabrics: Lace, lycra, velour, tricots, stretch lace, T-shirt knits, nylon parachute and interfacings, silks, flannels, others. Also offers lace inserts, trims and notions.
For Further Information: Catalogs, $4 (refundable).
Store Location: Yes
Discounts: Quantity discounts.

LAS MANOS
P.O. Box 515
Lower Lake, CA 95457
(707) 994-0461

Offers: Guatemalan handwoven cotton fabrics—traditional and contemporary designs, variety of bright colors.
For Further Information: Samples, $3.
Discounts: Sells wholesale

THE LEATHER FACTORY, INC.
3847 E. Loop 820
P.O. Box 50429
Fort Worth, TX 76105
(817) 496-4414

Offers: Leather skins for garment making: Cowhide, deerskin, elk, rabbit, thin velvet suedes, others. Lining leathers: Kip, pigskin, others. Exotic leathers: Python, cobra, whipsnake skins, embossed splits in alligator or ostrich grains.
For Further Information: Catalog, $3.
See Also: Leather Crafts

LEATHER UNLIMITED CORP.
7155 Country Highway B
Belgium, WI 53004
(414) 999-9464

Offers: Garment leathers: Sides, deerskin, sheepskin, chamois, elk, exotic animal prints (by special order—zebra, leopard) others. Also offers dyes, kits, others.
For Further Information: Catalog, $2 (refundable).
Store Location: Yes
Discounts: Quantity discounts; sells wholesale to legitimate businesses.
See Also: Leather Crafts

LOGAN KITS
Rt. 3, P.O. Box 380
Double Springs, AL 35553

Offers: Fabrics by the pound: Lingerie and activewear selections.
For Further Information: Send business-size SASE and $1 for fabrics brochure.
See Also: Clothing and Accessories

M.R. ANDREWS
1130 Fremont Ave., #178
Seaside, CA 93955

Offers: African fabrics—variety of prints.
For Further Information: Swatches and price list, $5.

THE MATERIAL WORLD
5700 Monroe St.
Sylvania, OH 43560
(419) 885-5416, (607) 535-4105

Offers: Line of quality fashion fabrics—imported and domestic silks, wools, cottons, blends, others; coordinated selections from areas worldwide.
For Further Information: Send $7.50 to receive collection of swatches 4 times a year.

MESSER'S FIBER DESIGNS
2 W. 6th St.
Maysville, KY 41056

Offers: Traditional and custom handwoven cotton warp with rag filler for rugs, placemats, hangings.
For Further Information: Send SASE for price list.
Discounts: Sells wholesale.

MICHIKO'S CREATIONS
P.O. Box 4313
Napa, CA 94558

Offers: Ultrasuede in 50 colors, by yard or remnants by yard. Also offers Ultrasuede samplers (40 colors in each package), Ultrasuede scraps by the pound.
For Further Information: Free samples, ideas and information; swatches, $5 (refundable).

MILL END STORE
121st & Broadway
Beaverton, OR 97005
(503) 646-3000

Offers: Fabrics: May include imported cottons, wools, silks, drapery and upholstery fabrics, nylons, polyesters, velvets, velveteen, others. Also offers patterns, notions, yarns, needlework items.
For Further Information: Send SASE for brochure or with inquiry.

MONTEREY MILLS
1725 E. Delavan Dr.
Janesville, WI 53546
(608) 754-8309

Offers: Synthetic furs: Shags, shearling, plush, toy animal types, closeouts, remnants. Also offers stuffings.
For Further Information: Sample package, $4.
Store Location: Yes
Discounts: Quantity discounts.
Accepts: MasterCard, Visa

NATURAL FIBER FABRIC CLUB
521 5th Ave.
New York, NY 10175

Offers: On payment of fee, members in this natural fabrics club receive 4 scheduled mailings of swatches of fashion fabrics from areas worldwide, plus a handbook and illustrated sewing aids catalog. Portfolio of swatches of 24 basic fabrics in stock: Cottons, wools, silks. Unscheduled mailings. Members get savings from retail cost.
For Further Information: Send SASE for full details.
Accepts: MasterCard, Visa

OLD MILLWORKS
P.O. Box 9013
Dickson City, PA 18519

Offers: Fabrics: Cuddlecloth flannel-backed satin, "jewel tones" and pastels, plus lightweight flannel, others.
For Further Information: Swatches, $1 and business-size SASE.

ON MY GOODKNITS INC.
P.O. Box 8658
Allentown, PA 18105
(610) 439-8862

Offers: Line of cotton fabrics: Interlocks, jerseys, ribs, French terry and fleece in custom colors. Also offers fabric development services, consulting. (Single roll minimums.)
For Further Information: Send SASE for list.

OPPENHEIM'S
120 E. Main St.
North Manchester, IN 46962
(219) 982-6848

Offers: Fabrics, (including irregulars): Linen-look and many other cottons, knits, satins, polyester and polycottons, calicos, rug weavers' scraps, faux fur, needlecraft and bridal fabrics, taffetas, muslin netting, cheesecloth. Specialty fabrics: Wool remnants, Ultrasuede scraps, Christmas. Also offers trims, stamped goods and quilt blocks, pillow forms, upholstery squares, "thermal suede" lining, rubber sheeting, poly doll cloth, wool mattress pads, polyfill and trims. Carries cut/sew and other sewing projects, plus remnants and package bargains.
For Further Information: Catalog, $1.
Accepts: MasterCard, Visa

ORNAMENTAL RESOURCES, INC.
P.O. Box 3010
Idaho Springs, CO 80452
(303) 567-4987

Offers: Embellishments (some rare/unique): Beads, chains, rhinestones, jewels, shells, appliqué motifs and antique bullion, tassels, brass stampings, feathers, findings, supplies. Also offers display forms, tools, others.
For Further Information: Catalog in 3-ring binder, $15 (with a year's supplements).

PELLON DIVISION
119 W. 40th St.
New York, NY 10018

Offers: Pellon Wonder Under transfer fusing material (heat press to fuse to fabrics; has peel-off backing), Pellon Craft-Bond backing material (fusible), and Pellon Tru-Grid enlarging material.
For Further Information: Contact dealer, or send SASE for information.

PENNYWISE FABRICS
1650 Highway 124
Harrisburg, MO 65256

Offers: Natural fabrics: Cottons, silk, wool, linen, others.
For Further Information: Samples, $2 and business-size SASE.

PHILIPS BOYNE
1646 New Highway
Faringdale, NY 11735
(800) 292-2830

Offers: Fine shirtings: Woven fabrics, imported/domestic in cottons, silks, blends, novelties. Also offers yarn dyed in stripes, checks, plaids.
For Further Information: Sample package, $3 (refundable).
Accepts: MasterCard, Visa

QUALIN INTERNATIONAL
P.O. Box 31145
San Francisco, CA 94131
(415) 647-1329

Offers: Silk fabrics (also blanks, scarves, others) of natural white, plus silk painting supplies.
For Further Information: Send business-size SASE for catalog.

REDSTONE FIBERS
16909 N. County Road 25E
Loveland, CO 80538

Offers: Cotton fabric handwoven to specifications. Choice of color, pattern, weight; preshrunk, 50-inch width.
For Further Information: Samples, $6.

SAWYER BROOK DISTINCTIVE FABRICS
P.O. Box 2864
Key Largo, FL 33037

Offers: Collection of imported and domestic fabrics—natural cottons and blends, silks, linens, denims, outing flannels, batik fabrics, others.
For Further Information: Send SASE for samples.
Accepts: MasterCard, Visa

Use a hot knife to cut out organza or tissue lamé or any other synthetic fabrics that frays. The hot knife seals the edge—no more fraying.

—Jehlor Fantasy Fabrics

SELECT FABRICS-B
P.O. Box 177
Charlie Lake, British Columbia V0C 1H0 Canada

Offers: Handwoven fabrics, including unique/originals, others.
For Further Information: Samples, $8.

SEW FAR, SEW GOOD
848 Dodge Ave., Suite 105
Evanston, IL 60202

Offers: Fabrics for girls, boys, infants: Knits, wovens, Disney, OshKosh, holiday and other motifs.
For Further Information: Brochure, swatches, $3.

SEW NATURAL
State Route 612, P.O. Box 97
Dothan, WV 25833
(304) 465-0910

Offers: Fabrics: Cottons (twill, ticking, wovens, chambrays, interfacing, bird's eye, flannel, knits), silk, others. Also offers tapes, batting (wool, cotton), elastics, cutters/mats, other aids. Patterns: Children's, Albala's, others.
For Further Information: Send SASE for catalog.

SPECIAL EFFECTS
P.O. Box 781061
Wichita, KS 67278

Offers: "Ice Crystal" fabrics: Intricate patterns, hand-dyed cottons.
For Further Information: Complete samples, $4.

SPECIALTIES
4425 Cotton Hanlon Rd.
Montour Falls, NY 14865
(607) 594-2021

Offers: Lingerie fabrics: Nylon, tricot, silky and cotton wovens, laces, cotton knits, foundation materials, others. Also offers notions, patterns, threads, accessories and lingerie kits.

For Further Information: Catalog, $2.
Accepts: MasterCard, Visa

STRETCH & SEW FABRICS
3697 La Mesa Blvd.
La Mesa, CA 91941
(619) 589-8880

Offers: Fabrics, including dyed to match rib, interlocks, fleeces, others. Line of patterns.
For Further Information: Catalog of patterns, $3.
Store Location: Yes
Discounts: Allows discounts to teachers and institutions; quantity discounts.

SUNCOLORS
P.O. Box 838
Carmel, NY 10512

Offers: Handwoven Guatemalan cottons—variety of patterns and colors.
For Further Information: Swatchbook, $3 and SASE (refundable).

SUNFLOWER STUDIO
2851 Road B ½
Grand Junction, CO 81503
(303) 242-3883

Offers: Traditional natural fiber fabrics (handwoven, hand-dyed)—18th- and 19th-Century adaptations.

SUPPLIES 4 LESS
13001 Las Vegas Blvd. S.
Las Vegas, NV 89124

Offers: Variety of laces (eyelet, ruffled, flat, others), appliqués, ribbons in colors, belt cordings, flowers, fabrics, others.
For Further Information: Catalog, samples, $2.50
Discounts: "Some discounts."

TANDY LEATHER CO.
P.O. Box 2934
Fort Worth, TX 76113

Offers: Variety of garment leathers.
See Also: Leather Crafts

TESTFABRICS
P.O. Drawer O
Middlesex, NJ 08846

Offers: Fabrics, including specialty types for museums, universities, others.
For Further Information: Free catalog.
Discounts: Sells wholesale.

Accepts: MasterCard, Visa

THREADS AT GINGERBREAD HILL
356 E. Garfield
Aurora, OH 44202
(216) 562-7100

Offers: Fashion fabrics: Imported/domestic/designer silks, wools, cottons, synthetics, others.
For Further Information: Swatches 4 times yearly, $8.

ULTRAMOUSE LTD.
3433 Bennington Ct.
Birmingham, MI 48009
(313) 646-8712

Offers: Ultrasuede scraps in assorted colors, by 8 ounce lots. Other scrap materials.
For Further Information: Send $2 for catalog.

ULTRASCRAPS
P.O. Box 339
Farmington, UT 84025
(801) 229-9468

Offers: Ultrasuede scraps by the pound—assorted colors/sizes. Also offers specially cut package pieces or yardage.
For Further Information: Send SASE for list.

UTEX TRADING
710 9th St., Suite 5
Niagara Falls, NY 14301
(416) 596-7565

Offers: Couture silk fabrics: Prints, crepe de chine, China colors, Thai and Fuji silks, raw silk noil, doupioni organzas, knits, charmeuse, jacquards, crepe satin, twill, boucles, tussah, others—dress/suit weights. Also has a branch office in Toronto, Canada.
For Further Information: Send SASE for brochure. Sample deposits: White silks, $8; colored silks, $12 per set.

General Needlecraft Supplies

Also see General Craft Supplies and specific categories in Section II.

AARDVARK ADVENTURES
P.O. Box 2449
Livermore, CA 94551
(800) 388-2687

Offers: Line of cross-stitch/embroidery fabrics: Aida, Congress cloth, Hardanger, Lugana, others. Threads: Natesh rayons, metallics, iridescents and Mettler brand, plus a variety of yarns. Trims: Ribbons, braids, buttons, tassels, shisha, diffraction foil, lamé, others. Surface decorating: Paints, glitters, silk scarves, needlepoint canvases. Aids: Tweezers, scissors, stabilizers, Sculpey, beads, shells, trims, others. Also offers rubber stamps and books.
For Further Information: Catalog, $2 (refundable).
Store Location: Yes
Discounts: Sells wholesale to legitimate businesses.
Accepts: MasterCard, Visa

AFRICAN FABRIC
407 Corte Majorca
Vacaville, CA 95688

Offers: African fabrics: Cotton yardage, swatches. Also offers patterns for African wildlife vest (appliqué), Yo-Yo vest, Christmas quilt, wall hangings and placemats. Spool insert for tube-type threads also available.
For Further Information: Send business-size SASE for information.

AMERICAN HANDICRAFTS/MERRIBEE
P.O. Box 2934
Fort Worth, TX 76113
(817) 921-6191

Offers: Needlecraft kits/tools/equipment/supplies: Knitting, crochet, cross-stitch, plastic canvas, quilting, others.
For Further Information: Free catalog.

THE AN*SER
P.O. Box 548
Penngrove, CA 94951

Offers: Fabrics: Zweigart, Mono, Interlock, Hardanger, Aida lines, others. Threads: Floss, metallics, silk, wool. Also offers tools, magnifiers, lamps, and over 3,000 cross-stitch charts.

For Further Information: Catalog, $5 (refundable).

BALTAZOR'S
3262 Severn Ave.
Metairie, LA 70002
(504) 889-0333

Offers: Sewing supplies: Fabrics, lace-making supplies, smocking and laces, bridal accessories, others.
For Further Information: Catalog, $2.

BECK'S WRAP 'N WEAVE
2815 34th St.
Lubbock, TX 79410
(806) 799-0151, (800) 658-6698

Offers: Knitting kits, yarns, tools, weaving and lace-making yarns and items. Also offers books; runs specials.
For Further Information: Catalog, $2.
Discounts: Quantity discounts.
Accepts: MasterCard, Visa

BUFFALO BATT & FELT CORP.
3307 Walden Ave.
Depew, NY 14043
(716) 688-4111

Offers: Polyester stuffing in pound bags, Super Fluff bags or bulk rolls. Also offers super resilient stuffing in bulk rolls, quilt batts of Super Fluff in queen/king size or rolls, traditional weight quilt batt (crib to queen/king sizes), comforter-style, high loft quilt batts, 2 inches thick.
For Further Information: Brochure and swatches, $1 (refundable).
Discounts: Quantity discounts.

CRAFT GALLERY
P.O. Box 145
Swampscott, MA 01907
(508) 744-2334

Offers: Needlecraft kits: Crewel, silk, mini-rugs, cross-stitch, counted thread, needlepoint, lace-making, embroidery, antique doll. Also offers DMC needlepoint canvases, frames, magnifier lamps, markers, thimbles, scissors and needles. Threads, machine and hand: DMS, machine embroidery, tatting, quilting, plus knitting/crochet yarns and accessories. Carries ribands, lace net, iron-on transfers, shisha, scissors, and a variety of canvases. Fabrics: Aida, Linda, Hardanger,

Wool Davos, Herta, Rustico, others. Patterns/books also available.
For Further Information: Catalog, $2.
Discounts: Allows discounts to teachers, institutions and professionals.

CREATIVE CRAFT HOUSE
P.O. Box 1386
Santa Barbara, CA 93102

Offers: Line of trims: Braids in a variety of styles and widths, plastic and other beads, rhinestones, naturals.
For Further Information: Send SASE for list.

F & W PUBLICATIONS
1507 Dana Ave.
Cincinnati, OH 45207

Offers: *The Fiberworks Directory of Self-Published Books on the Fiber Arts* and other needlecraft books.
For Further Information: Send SASE for information.

BETTE S. FEINSTEIN
96 Roundwood Rd.
Newton, MA 02164

Offers: Hard-to-find needlework books: Needlepoint, embroidery, fibers, sewing, others. Search service available.
For Further Information: Catalog, $1.

GRANNY'S QUILTS SEWING CENTER
4509 W. Elm
McHenry, IL 60050
(815) 385-5107

Offers: Quilting and sewing supplies: Cotton fabrics, patterns, notions, kits, stencils, and Viking, Pfaff sewing machines.
For Further Information: Catalog, $2.
Store Location: Yes

Cotton stuffing used in heirloom dolls and bears creates the feel of antique equals.

— Morning Glory Products

HALLIE'S HANDWORKS
6307 NE 2nd Ave.
Miami, FL 33138

Offers: Judaic needlework: Patterns, stitchery supplies (threads, aids, others). Also offers gifts.
For Further Information: Send SASE for catalog.

HANDWORKS
Rt. 1, P.O. Box 138
Afton, VA 22920
(800) 346-2004

Offers: Line of children's sewing projects, knitting baskets, others.
For Further Information: Send SASE for list.

HEARTLAND CRAFT DISCOUNTERS
Rt. 6 E., P.O. Box 65
Geneseo, IL 61254
(309) 944-6411

Offers: Needlecraft (and other) supplies/tools: Kits, wedding supplies/accessories, including headpieces, figures, flowers, others. Threads/yarns for embroidery, knitting, crochet, plastic canvas, sewing, others. Also offers tools/equipment/accessories, plus animal parts: Eyes, paws, others.
For Further Information: Catalog, $2 (includes monthly flyers).
See Also: General Craft Supplies

HERRSCHERS
Hoover Rd.
Stevens Point, WI 54481
(800) 441-0838

Offers: Tools/equipment: Frames (quilt, scroll, adjustable, tapestry), magnifiers, adjustable dressmaker forms, Fiskars scissors. Kits: Cross-stitch, crewel, cloth dolls, crochet, candlewicking, latch hook, needlepoint, quilts, holiday items and thread-its. Also offers stamped table linens and pillowcases, yarns, (DMC and Star floss), fiberfill, fabrics (flour sacking, toweling, flannel, linen, Hardanger, Aida, toweling), towels, canvases, laces, trims.
For Further Information: Catalog, $2.

IDENT-IFY LABEL CORP.
P.O. Box 204
Brooklyn, NY 11214
(718) 436-3126

Offers: Personalized labels on white cotton, with stock phrases. Name tapes (1 line).
For Further Information: Free brochure.
Discounts: Quantity discounts; allows discounts to institutions.

INTERWEAVE PRESS
201 E. 4th St.
Loveland, CO 80537
(800) 645-3675

Offers: Needlecraft books: Weaving titles and patterns, dyeing, spinning, textiles, yarn guide, knitting, sweaters, care of spinning wheels.

For Further Information: Contact dealer, or free catalog.
Discounts: Sells wholesale to legitimate businesses.

JANALEESE DESIGNS
P.O. Box 125
St. Thomas N5P 3T5 Canada

Offers: Kits/supplies: Counted cross-stitch, embroidery, needlepoint pictures and tablecloths.
For Further Information: Catalog, $2.

KATHLEEN B. SMITH
P.O. Box 48
West Chesterfield, MA 01084

Offers: 18th-Century needlework items: Natural dye worsted yarns, silk floss, silk/cotton tapes, fabrics, kits for canvas work and samplers—all-natural fibers.
For Further Information: Catalog, $3.

LACIS
2982 Adeline St.
Berkeley, CA 94703

Offers: Books: Needlework, costume and embroidery titles.
For Further Information: Catalog, $4.

MADEIRA MARKETING LTD.
600 E. 9th St.
Michigan City, IN 46360

Offers: GlissenGloss metallic threads: Subdued, antique, shimmer or multi-ply sparkly metallics in a variety of colors for needlepoint, plastic canvas and cross-stitch.
For Further Information: Needlework guide, $1; metallics color card, $6.

MAGIC NEEDLE
Rt. 2, P.O. Box 172
Limerick, ME 04048

Offers: Quilting kits, patterns, silk ribbons, embroidery materials, buttons, others.
For Further Information: Catalog, $1 (refundable).

MARY MAXIM
2001 Holland Ave.
P.O. Box 5019
Port Huron, MI 48061
(313) 987-2000

Offers: Kits: Quilting, cross-stitch, crewel, embroidery, others. Also offers cloth doll supplies, notions, sewing aids, threads, quilting frames and stands, holiday items, stencils, batting and fiberfill, pillow forms and other supplies.
For Further Information: Free catalog.

Metallic and rayon threads are slippery. To control them and keep them from falling off the spool on the machine, and off the machine, use surgitube on each spool. This can be purchased at any pharmacy and is available in a variety of sizes to fit most kinds of spools. The thread stays clean and neat.

—Aardvark Adventures

MORNING GLORY PRODUCTS
302 Highland Dr.
Taylor, TX 76574
(800) 234-9105

Offers: Polyester and cotton quilt batting, pillow forms and stuffing.
For Further Information: Contact your dealer, or send SASE for information.

MOUNT CASTOR INDUSTRIES
P.O. Box 488
East Orleans, MA 02643

Offers: Patterns based on people's names—charted, computer-generated designs for needlepoint, counted cross-stitch, quilts.
For Further Information: Send $1 and business-size SASE for information.

NANCY'S NOTIONS
P.O. Box 683, Dept 32
Beaver Dam, WI 53916
(414) 887-0391

Offers: Sewing, quilting and serging products: Glass locked beads, charted needlework designs and kits, hoops, appliqués, Gosling drapery tapes, shade tapes, reflective tapes and material, machine embroidery and other threads. Also offers rag rug items, quilted clothing patterns and many others, plus instructional videos—many on machine sewing, knitting, cross-stitching, quilting, decorating, rug braiding, weaving.
For Further Information: Free catalog.
Store Location: Yes
Discounts: Quantity discounts; allows discounts to teachers, institutions and professionals; sells wholesale to legitimate businesses.
See Also: Sewing

NEWARK DRESSMAKER SUPPLY
P.O. Box 2448
Lehigh Valley, PA 18002
(215) 837-7500

Offers: Needlecraft/sewing items. Threads: Swiss Metrosene, machine rayon, silk, Coats & Clark, elastic, cotton, upholstery, metallics, ribbon floss, overlocks, stretch nylon,

Candlelight. Also offers zippers (including doll sized), buckles, bow-tie clips, silk and dry flowers, ribbons, over 50 laces, metallics, bindings, tapes, elastics, buttons. Carries fabrics, appliqués, scissors, cutters, bridal items, veiling, flowers, others. Doll items: Heads, eyes, stands, others. Also carries stencils, adhesives, paints, sequins/rhinestones, beads.
For Further Information: Free catalog.
Discounts: Quantity discounts; sells wholesale to legitimate businesses.
Accepts: MasterCard, Visa
See Also: Costumes—Ethnic, Historic, Special Occasion

PEDDLER'S WAGON
P.O. Box 109
Lamar, MO 64759
(417) 682-3734

Offers: Pre-owned needlework books and magazines.
For Further Information: List, $2.

POSTON'S WORLD OF IDEAS
300 S. Prosperity Farms
North Palm Beach, FL 33408

Offers: Crewel and other kits and supplies, doll parts and dolls, fabrics, a variety of plastic and other beads, needlecraft equipment and aids and quilting frames.
For Further Information: Write for catalog.

R.L. SHEP
P.O. Box 668
Mendocino, CA 95460
(707) 937-1437

Offers: Out-of-print books on textiles and costumes; reprints of Edwardian and Victorian titles.
For Further Information: Free brochure.
Discounts: Sells wholesale to legitimate businesses.

S & S ARTS & CRAFTS
P.O. Box 513
Colchester, CT 06415
(800) 243-9232

Offers: Group/bulk packs/supplies: Latchhook, plastic canvas, looper weave and cross-stitch, plus kits, frames and items. Also offers felt, fur, burlap, lace, cords, netting and low-cost projects.
For Further Information: Free catalog.
Discounts: Quantity discounts.
See Also: General Craft Supplies

SIMMONS BOOKS
501 Main St.
Los Lunas, NM 87031
(505) 865-8765

Offers: Out-of-print needlework books—a wide array of categories including embroidery, needlepoint, machine/hand sewing, others.
For Further Information: Catalog, $1.

SNOWFLAKE DESIGNS NEEDLEWORK SHOP
114 N. San Francisco St.
Flagstaff, AZ 86001
(602) 779-2676

Offers: Handpainted needlepoint, fibers, canvas, even weaves, linens, plus counted cross-stitch supplies, charts, yarns and knitting kits.
For Further Information: Catalog subscription, $3.50.
Store Location: Yes
Accepts: MasterCard, Visa

STUDIO BOOKS
P.O. Box 7804
Huntington Beach, CA 92615

Offers: Used and out-of-print fiber arts books in a variety of categories.
For Further Information: Catalog, $2

SUSAN BATES, INC.
P.O. Box 24998
Greenville, SC 92616

Offers: Full line of sewing notions and aids, knitting and crochet hooks, crochet tools and accessories.
For Further Information: Contact dealer, or send SASE for information.

Price your homemade items for sale by figuring cost of materials and multiplying by 4.

—WSC

THE TAUNTON PRESS
63 S. Main St.
P.O. Box 5506
Newtown, CT 06470
(203) 426-8171

Offers: 80 folkwear patterns in ethnic and vintage styles. Also offers knitting patterns, books, including fabric/fiber sourcebooks and knitting titles, and instructional videos.
For Further Information: Free catalog.
Discounts: Sells wholesale to legitimate businesses.
See Also: Costumes—Ethnic, Historic, Special Occasion

TAYLOR BEDDING MANUFACTURING CO.
P.O. Box 979
Taylor, TX 76574

Offers: Line of fiberfill, batting, pillow forms, others.
For Further Information: Contact dealer, or send SASE for information.

TAYLOR'S CUTAWAYS & STUFF
2802 E. Washington St.
Urbana, IL 61801

Offers: Fabrics by the pound: Polyester, satin, felt, cottons, blends, silks. Remnants: Velour fleece, tricot. Fabric packs: Craft velvet, calico, cotton prints, solids. Also offers precut fabric squares, lace, trims, ribbons, buttons, doll and animal parts, growlers, eyes, shrink-art items, potpourri fragrances, silica gel, satin ornaments, iron-on transfers and patterns.
For Further Information: Brochure, $1.
Discounts: Quantity discounts.

TEXTILE REPRODUCTIONS
P.O. Box 48
West Chesterfield, MA 01084
(413) 296-4437

Offers: Products naturally dyed with vegetable dyes, including embroidery threads, fabrics, trimmings, wool blend felt, silk ribbons, needlecraft tools and books.
For Further Information: Catalog, $4; catalog with samples, $12.

UCCB PRESS
P.O. Box 5300
Sydney, Nova Scotia B1P 6I2 Canada
(902) 539-5300 ext. 604

Offers: Grid craft pattern software—pattern designs for knitting, needlepoint, rug hooking, others on computer program.
For Further Information: Send SASE for details.

VICTORIAN VIDEO PRODUCTIONS
P.O. Box 1540
Colfax, CA 95713

Offers: Instructional videos on lace making, weaving, appliquéing, basketry, stenciling, needlepoint, spinning; 1 to 2 hours each.
For Further Information: Free catalog.
See Also: Basketry and Seat Weaving, Lace Making and Spinning and Weaving

WOODEN PORCH BOOKS
Rt. 1, P.O. Box 262
Middlebourne, WV 26149
(304) 386-4434

Offers: Used and out-of-print books (fiber art and related categories): Sewing and dressmaking—garments, pattern design, historical/ethnic costumes, fabric design, Godey's Lady's books, French, bridal, children's, smocking, Civil War uniforms, leather and fur, tailoring. Needlework: Beaded bags, wig making, silk making on color, masks, embroidery, lace making, crochet, knitting, quilting, dyeing, needlepoint, others.
For Further Information: Send $3 for next three catalogs.

WSC
P.O. Box 212
Alamogordo, NM 88311
(505) 437-2934

Offers: Over 150 Indian patterns/kits in crochet, needlepoint, latchhook.
For Further Information: Catalog, $3.
Discounts: Quantity prices; wholesale to legitimate businesses.

YARNWORKS
519 Main St.
Grand Junction, CO 81501
(303) 243-5365

Offers: Supplies/equipment: Hand and machine knitting, weaving, spinning, basketry, cross-stitch, needlepoint, dyeing and crochet. Knitting: Needles-Inox (W. Germany), Takumi (Japanese), accessories, holders, bags. Weaving: Glimakra, Schacht looms. Reeds, heddles, loom accessories, dyes, warping mills and other accessories, tapestry looms, umbrella swifts, winders. Also offers yarns of many manufacturers, porcelain buttons, crochet hooks, Knitking and White knitting machines, Ashford and Louet spinning wheels and books.
For Further Information: Send SASE for information.
Discounts: Quantity discounts.

YLI CORP.
P.O. Box 109
Provo, UT 84603

Offers: Threads: Woolly, nylon serging threads in 78 solids and 5 variegated combinations. Also offers Candlelight metallic yarns—for serger, sewing machine bobbin, hand/machine knitting, needlepoint, weaving and others in 18 colors on 75- to 5,000-yard cones. Ribbons: Silk, Spark organdy, synthetic silk, fancies. Carries silk threads in 215 colors, silk batting, Olfa rotary cutters and mats.
For Further Information: Catalog and Candlelight color chart, $2.50.

Home Decorating

Also see most other categories where home accessories are listed.

AMERICAN BLIND & WALLPAPER FACTORY
28237 Orchard Lake Rd.
Farmington Hills, MI 48334
(313) 553-6200

Offers: Wall coverings—all national brands (traditional, classic, contemporary, florals, textured, embossed, etc.), plus shades and blinds.
For Further Information: Write or call for quote on specific brand; give pattern book name and pattern number.
Discounts: Has discounts.
Accepts: Discover, MasterCard, Visa

ANDREAE DESIGNS
35673 Ashford Dr.
Sterling Heights, MI 48312
(313) 826-3404

Offers: Line of laser-cut stencils: Victorian decorative designs (swags, wreaths, hatboxes, hats, vines, children's murals, others).
For Further Information: Catalog, $3.50.

BENNINGTON'S
1271 Manheim Pike
Lancaster, PA 17601

Offers: Top brands of wallpaper (any book or pattern), plus coordinating fabric or borders.
For Further Information: Write for price quote (give book name, pattern number).
Discounts: Has discounts.
Accepts: MasterCard, Visa

DESIGNER SECRETS
P.O. Box 529
Fremont, NE 68025

Offers: Designer fabrics, wallcoverings, window treatments, bedspreads, furniture accessories.
For Further Information: Catalog, $2.
Discounts: Has discounts.

DOBRY ENTERPRESS
P.O. Box 112
Severna Park, MD 21146
(410) 437-0297

Offers: Instruction books on custom draperies, cloud shades, no-sew drapery swags and jabots.
For Further Information: Free literature.
Discounts: Quantity discounts; allows discounts to teachers and institutions; sells wholesale to legitimate businesses.

FABRIC CENTER
484 Electric Ave., P.O. Box 8212
Fitchburg, MA 01420

Offers: Full line of home decorating fabrics.
For Further Information: Free brochure; catalog, $2.

THE FABRIC OUTLET
P.O. Box 2417
South Hamilton, MA 01982

Offers: Waverly and Robert Allen decorator fabrics, Waverly wall coverings.
For Further Information: Send fabric name, number, yardage.
Discounts: Has discounts.
Accepts: MasterCard, Visa

HOME FABRIC MILLS
882 S. Main St.
Cheshire, CT 06410
(203) 272-3529

Offers: Decorator fabrics: Chintz, wovens, textures, prints, tapestries, jacquards, lace, others. Also offers fire-retardant contact fabrics, trims, accessories.
For Further Information: Free brochure.
Discounts: Has discounts.

HOMESPUN
P.O. Box 3223
Ventura, CA 93006
(805) 642-8111

Offers: Seamless cotton drapery fabrics—10 feet wide, heavily textured selections (for drapes, wall coverings, upholstery, bedspreads, tablecloths, clothing).
For Further Information: Catalog and swatches, $2.
Discounts: "At factory direct prices."

Accepts: MasterCard, Visa

INSTANT INTERIORS
P.O. Box 1793
Eugene, OR 97440
(503) 689-4608

Offers: Instant decoration how-to booklets: *Bed Covers*, *Easiest Furniture Covers*, *Fabric Space Makers*, *Table Toppings*, *Lampshades*, *Quickest Curtains* and *Pillows and Cushions*.
For Further Information: Contact dealer, or send SASE for catalog sheets.

LOWERY/HORN ASSOCIATES
431 Rodi Rd.
Pittsburgh, PA 15235

Offers: Over 80 banner-making patterns; fabrics and other supplies.
For Further Information: Catalog, $1.

A "cloud shade" is defined as a drapery that is gathered at the top, and moves up and down. These shades are particularly easy for beginners.

— Dobry Enterprises

MARLENE'S DECORATIVE FABRICS
301 Beech St.
Hackensack, NJ 07601
(800) 992-7325

Offers: Major manufacturer's decorator fabrics for draperies, slipcovers, upholstery, including 118-inch Tergal, voiles and batiste fabrics.
For Further Information: Send SASE with specific inquiry.
Discounts: Quantity discounts.

MCKIBBEN & CO.
P.O. Box 470
Hampton, FL 32044
(904) 468-1440

Offers: Original precut stencil motifs: Ferns, palms, florals, trellis, chintz, rose, decorative containers, others.
For Further Information: Catalog, $3.50.

ROLLERWALL, INC.
P.O. Box 757
Silver Spring, MD 20918

Offers: Embossed paint rollers for wall patterns (florals, traditional, colonial, contemporary designs).
For Further Information: Send SASE for list.

SHEFFIELD SCHOOL OF INTERIOR DESIGN
211 E. 43rd St.
New York, NY 10017

Offers: Interior Decorator home-study course—taped/printed lessons on color, fabrics, furniture, accessories; individualized taped analyses of student's room designs.
For Further Information: Free illustrated catalog.

T & M CREATIONS
P.O. Box 3264
Traverse City, MI 49685
(616) 947-5695, (800) 767-9229

Offers: Instructional videos on slipcover making, cushions, drapery making.
For Further Information: Send SASE for details
Discounts: Quantity discounts.
Accepts: MasterCard, Visa

VIDEO INSTRUCTIONAL PROGRAMS
781 Golden Prados Dr.
Diamond Bar, CA 91765
(714) 861-5021

Offers: Instructional videos: *Home Decorating* (shade and curtain treatments, including Roman, balloon, cloud) and *Instant Decorating* (for bed, bath, living rooms—dust ruffles, pillow shams, furniture, others). Booklets: *Quickest Curtains* and *Bed Covers*. Also offers over 35 sewing videos, including embroidery, monogramming, decorative serger items, others. Can also rent videos—rental applies to purchase.
For Further Information: Send SASE for list.

WARM PRODUCTS, INC.
16120 Woodinville-Redmont Rd., # 4
Woodinville, WA 98072
(206) 488-4464

Offers: Insulated windowshade lining system in natural needled cotton batting.
For Further Information: Free instructions/brochures.
Discounts: Quantity discounts; allows discounts to teachers and institutions; sells wholesale to legitimate businesses and professionals.

YOWLER & SHEPPS
3529 Main St.
Conestoga, PA 17516

Offers: Wall stenciling designs in a variety of styles/motifs.
For Further Information: Catalog, $2 (refundable).
Disounts: "Wholesale inquiries welcome."

Knitting and Crochet

Also see General Needlecraft Supplies, Rug Making, Spinning and Weaving, Yarns and other related categories.

EMMA ADAMS
125 Dantzler Lane
Summerville, SC 29483

Offers: Religious filet crochet patterns: Praying hands, beatitudes, child's prayer, serenity prayer, Madonna and Child, Head of Christ, Nativity scene, others.
For Further Information: Send SASE for full list.

ALDEA'S
P.O. Box 667
Beaumont, CA 92223
(714) 845-5825

Offers: Machine knitting instructional videos by Alvina Murdaugh covering basics, converting hand to machine knitting, techniques, maintenance, tips, ribber techniques, gifts. Also offers a variety of clothing titles (coats, sweaters, dresses, skirts, pants, others).
For Further Information: Send SASE for list.
Discounts: Sells wholesale.
Accepts: MasterCard, Visa

ALL BRANDS
9789 Florida Blvd.
Baton Rouge, LA 70815
(504) 923-1285, (800) 866-1261 (for quotes).

Offers: Knitting machines: Brother, Knitking, Singer (Studio), Toyota-Elna Knitcraft, Bond/Baby Knit/Simplicity Bulkys. Also offers machine accessories. Service contracts available. Buys some products.
For Further Information: Send SASE for brochure (specify product interest).
Accepts: MasterCard, Visa
See Also: Sewing

ANNIE'S ATTIC
1 Annie Lane, P.O. Box 212B
Big Sandy, TX 75755
(800) LV-ANNIE

Offers: Crochet kits/patterns: Afghans, scarves/hats, slippers, Pocket Pals, buttons, bows, jewelry, rugs, doilies, bath and flower sets, potholders, layette items, baby outfits, sweaters, collars, fashion and other doll clothes, toys, bas-

kets, others. Also offers plastic canvas kits, yarns, knitting and canvas accessories and instructional videos.
For Further Information: Free catalog.
Store Location: Yes
Discounts: Sells wholesale; quantity discounts.
Accepts: American Express, Discover, MasterCard, Visa

APOLLO KNITTING STUDIO
2305 Judah St.
San Francisco, CA 94122
(415) 664-2442

Offers: Instructional videos (VHS or Beta) for machine knitting, beginner or advanced, with Nobu Mary Fukuda.
For Further Information: Send SASE for full details.
Discounts: "Dealer inquiries welcome."

ASCEND
P.O. Box 135
Kew Gardens, NY 11415

Offers: Instructions for crocheting your favorite knitting patterns.
For Further Information: Instructions, $1.

AUNTIE KNITS, INC.
212 Rock Rd.
Glen Rock, NJ 07452
(201) 447-1331

Offers: Over 40 sweater kits (yarns by major companies) in a variety of styles, including cardigans, pullovers, vests, others.
For Further Information: Free catalog.

BARE HILL STUDIOS/FIBER LOFT
Rt. 111
P.O. Box 327
Harvard, MA 01451

Offers: Natural fiber yarns for machine/hand crochet and knitting: Rowan, Tahki, Elite, Crystal Palace. Also offers mill ends. Exotic fibers: Silks, angoras, ribbons.
For Further Information: Fiber samples, $2.75; complete sample card (over 500 colors), $5.
Discounts: Quantity discounts.

BARKIM, LTD.
47 W. Polk St., Suite 100
Chicago, IL 60605
(312) 548-2211

Offers: Yarns from New England, Canada, Norway, Iceland. Also offers Guernsey wool (England), Rowan kits and yarns, and Shetland and Aran yarns. Carries mini-kits and other patterns.
For Further Information: Catalog and yarn samples, $4 (refundable); send SASE for newsletter.
Accepts: American Express, Discover, MasterCard, Visa

BAY COUNTRY BOUTIQUE
Rosecroft Rd.
St. Mary's City, MD 20686
(301) 862-4220

Offers: Knitting yarns and kits, patterns, implements. Also offers a quarterly knitting newsletter, TKGA correspondence course and over 100 books.
For Further Information: Send SASE for list.

BENDIGO WOOLLEN MILLS
P.O. Box 27164
Columbus, OH 43227
(614) 236-8111

Offers: Line of Australian cabled wool yarns for knitting—hand washable.
For Further Information: Send for free shade cards.
Accepts: MasterCard, Visa

BLACK SHEEP WOOLS
P.O. Box 9205
Lowell, MA 01853
(508) 937-0320

Offers: Brand name yarns—mill ends and discontinued styles.
For Further Information: Samples, $3.
Store Location: Yes
Discounts: Has discounts.

BETTE BORNSIDE CO.
2733 Dauphine St.
New Orleans, LA 70117

Offers: Hand knitting yarns in over 200 shades/styles, plus knitting patterns, accessories and books.
For Further Information: Catalog, $4.

BRAMWELL YARNS, U.S.A.
P.O. Box 8244
Midland, TX 79708
(915) 699-4037

Offers: Bramwell imported yarns, knitting publications, knitting machine accessories.
For Further Information: Write or call for nearest dealer.
Discounts: Sells wholesale.

BUSHFIELD
Romney, IN 47981

Offers: Books: Crochet, knitting and other needlecrafts.
For Further Information: List, $2 (refundable).

BY SHIRLEY MCKIBBEN
3720 Hood Ct.
Turlock, CA 95380
(209) 668-0550

Offers: Machine knitting instructional videos by Shirley McKibben (5) and others, including repair for Toyota machines.
For Further Information: Send SASE for list.

CAM BOOKS
2534 Main
Torrington, WY 82240

Offers: Over 170 knitting and crochet books.
For Further Information: List, $1 (refundable).
Discounts: Has discounts.

CHARLES PUBLISHING
P.O. Box 577
Weatherford, TX 76086

Offers: Line of crochet patterns: Known characters and creatures (Roadrunner, Coyote, Hulk, Cheerleader, dinosaurs, others).
For Further Information: Send SASE for complete list.

CHARMOR'S
108 S. Division St., Suite 4
Auburn, WA 98001

Offers: Knitting machines: Melrose, Brother, White, Heirloom. Yarns: Brown Sheel Wool, Yarn Country. Monthly knitting club.
For Further Information: Send SASE for details.

CLOSE-KNIT YARNS
45 Green Valley Ct.
Howard, OH 43028

Offers: Yarns: Tahki, Lane Borgosesia, Brown Sheep, Ironstone kits.
For Further Information: Send SASE for brochure; samples, $5.

CONCEPTS
P.O. Box 1219
Troy, NY 12181

Offers: Crochet patterns: Tissue holders, pillows, totes, animals, holiday items, afghans, others.
For Further Information: Brochure, $1 (refundable).

P. COX EXPRESSIONS
1256 Pocket Rd. NW
Sugar Valley, GA 30746

Offers: Machine knitting yarns: Rayons, cottons, linens, silks, acrylics.
For Further Information: Color card collection, $3.

CREATE SOMETHING BEAUTIFUL
P.O. Box 1794
Wallingford, CT 06492
(203) 269-9270

Offers: Original sweater kits. Brand name knitting/crochet yarns: Alpaca, cottons, wools, others.
For Further Information: Brochure and over 100 yarn samples, $3.
Accepts: MasterCard, Visa

CROCHET COTTAGE
P.O. Box 80072
Midland, TX 79708

Offers: Crochet patterns: Old-fashioned dolls, tissue cover dolls in whimsical motifs, others.
For Further Information: Send SASE for list.

CUNIBERTI ENTERPRISES
P.O. Box 308
Englewood, NJ 07631
(201) 569-8772

Offers: Imported and designer yarns: Wools, cottons, linens, novelty, blends, acrylics—from England, Switzerland, Italy and U.S.
For Further Information: Complete set of color cards, $3.
Discounts: Offers value packs; sells wholesale.
Accepts: MasterCard, Visa

CUSTOM KNITS & MANUFACTURING
Rt. 1, P.O. Box 16
Lake Park, MN 56554
(218) 238-5882

Offers: Wood yarn trees: Rotating floor model (for 72 cones of yarn) or ceiling model. Also offers yarn plyer, pom-pom maker, cone holder.
For Further Information: Free catalog.
Store Location: Yes

Discounts: Quantity discounts; allows discounts to teachers and institutions; sells wholesale to legitimate businesses.
Accepts: MasterCard, Visa

D'ARGENZIO'S
5613 Berkshire Valley Rd.
Oak Ridge, NJ 07438
(201) 697-1138

Offers: Knitting kits: S.C. Huber, Los Manos, North Island, Prism, Rowan, others. Also offers yarns, knitting machines, instructional videos and books.
For Further Information: Information and prices, $5.

DESIGNS BY ANNE LTD.
671 Rosa Ave., #205
Metairie, LA 70005
(504) 482-7863

Offers: Yarns, current and discontinued types, plus out-of-print and other books.
For Further Information: Send SASE for list (books or yarn).

DESIGNS BY ROBERTA
Rt. 1, P.O. Box 28
Charlotte Hall, MD 20622

Offers: Crochet booklets: Monthly verses, all occasion verses and patterns for holiday trims, frigies, lapel pins, others.
For Further Information: Send SASE for information.

DISCOVERY BOOKS
P.O. Box 8556
Honolulu, HI 96830

Offers: Crochet afghan patterns in a variety of original Hawaii designs.
For Further Information: Catalog, $1.

EWE & EYE
P.O. Box 646
Mahopac, NY 10541
(800) 220-YARN

Offers: Supplies and yarns for hand/machine knitting. Also offers knitting machines, sweater kits (including features from Vogue), accessories, instructional videos and books.
For Further Information: Catalog, $4 (refundable).

EXQUISICAT
P.O. Box 6321
Richmond, VA 23230
(804) 784-4024

Offers: Washable wool yarns—mohair, alpaca, and Little Dorrit sock yarns (cones).

For Further Information: Color card, $2 (refundable).
Discounts: Sells wholesale.

THE FIBER STUDIO
9 Foster Hill Rd., P.O. Box 637
Henniker, NH 03242

Offers: Natural yarns and equipment for knitting, crocheting (also for weaving and spinning) with cottons, wools, mohairs. Also offers close-out yarns.
For Further Information: 60 yarn samples, $4; equipment catalog, $1.

FIBERS & MORE
P.O. Box 65085
Vancouver, WA 98665
(206) 576-0642, (509) 922-1483

Offers: "Projects-to-Go" kits—designs for knitting, hand-weaving (placemats, scarves, blankets, sweaters, dye projects, others).
For Further Information: Catalog of kits, $2.
Accepts: MasterCard, Visa

FIBRES
P.O. Box 135
Osterville, MA 02655
(508) 428-3882

Offers: Current yarns: Silk City, Aarlen, Brentwood, Classic Elite, Melrose, Plymouth, Reynolds, Valentino, Flatura de Crosa, Scotts Woolen Mill, Knitting Fever and Schaffhauser.
For Further Information: Price list, order data, $2.50 (refundable).
Accepts: MasterCard, Visa

FINGERLAKES WOOLEN MILL
1193 Stewarts Corners Rd.
Genoa, NY 13071
(800) 441-WOOL

Offers: Fingerlake yarns: Wools, angora/wool blends and Unspun in 23 colors. Spinning kits also available.
For Further Information: Send SASE for list.
Discounts: Sells wholesale.

ALICE FOWLER ORIGINALS
P.O. Box 787
Colorado Springs, CO 80901

Offers: Patterns/instructions for knit and crochet baby sets, sweaters, caps, booties, others.
For Further Information: Catalog, 50¢.

GOSSAMER THREADS & MORE
575 4th Ave.
Durango, CO 81301
(303) 247-2822

Offers: Knitting yarns: Wools, linens, cottons, silks, plus lace knitting items.
For Further Information: Send SASE for details.
Accepts: MasterCard, Visa

TERESA DANE GOTO
6740 Samuel Ct.
Anchorage, AK 99516
(907) 345-2031

Offers: Fashionable Beginnings machine-knitted garment patterns for mothers-to-be, nursing mothers and children: Sweaters, skirts, jogging pants. Patterns include hidden-zippered outfits and baby and older boy and girl patterns.
For Further Information: Send SASE for list.
Discounts: Sells wholesale.

GRAND VIEW COUNTRY STORE
U.S. Rt. 2
Berlin, NH 03570
(603) 466-5715

Offers: Yarns, original knitting kits, patterns and basket kits.
For Further Information: List, $3.
Store Location: Yes

GRANNY HOOKS
35230 Law Rd.
Grafton, OH 44044

Offers: Crochet hooks (all types/sizes, including jumbo).
For Further Information: Send business-size SASE for brochure.

HANDIWORKS
P.O. Box 13482
Arlington, TX 76094

Offers: "Rag Elegance" (fabric strip) knitting and crochet patterns, including sweatshirt with knit/crochet yoke, unattached collars, crochet vest, others.
For Further Information: Color cards (15) and price list, $3.
Discounts: Sells wholesale.

HAZELCRAFTS
P.O. Box 175
Woburn, MA 01801

Offers: Over 70 knitting books, patterns for a variety of sweaters, coats, hats and other accessories, purses, skirts, tops, dresses. Also offers baby and children's patterns, men's items, others.

For Further Information: Send business-size SASE for list.

HOWES HOUSE
114 Pascack Rd.
Hillsdale, NJ 07642

Offers: Knitting/crochet patterns: Bibs, sweaters, sweatshirts, afghans, baskets, animals and puppets, tissue covers, golf club covers, spiral animals and people, shade pulls, leg warmers, others. Also offers patterns for holidays: Ornaments, pumpkins, others. Patterns for plastic canvas items are also available.
For Further Information: Send SASE for list.

JANKNITS
1500 Cohagen Rd.
Ingomar, MT 59039
(406) 354-6621

Offers: Line of knitting books by Janet Mysse, including *Affordable Furs*, featuring fur/leather combined with knitting, plus items for children and dolls.
For Further Information: Send SASE for full information.
Discounts: Sells wholesale.

KATHE'S KITS
1505 Mayfair
Champaign, IL 61821
(217) 355-5400

Offers: Knitting machine kits: Chenille rayon, angora, cotton, wool—includes designer coats and jackets, children's designs, others. Also offers Knitpicky knitting machines—computer interface models.
For Further Information: Catalog, $3 (refundable).

If a cotton yarn is giving you trouble it may need some moisture. Spray it with a plant mister or refrigerate it overnight.
— Bonnie Triola

KNIT KNACK SHOP, INC.
Rt. 3, P.O. Box 104
Peru, IN 46970
(317) 985-3164

Offers: Extensive line of machine knitting books, Hauge D100 Linker for knitting machine, others.
For Further Information: Send SASE for price list.
Discounts: Sells wholesale.

THE KNIT WORKS
2417 Lebanon Ave., Suite A
Belleville, IL 62221
(618) 277-4111

Offers: Cone yarns—Tamm line, metallic threads (over 300 colors), Amber yarns (15 lines including natural fibers—over 200 colors).
For Further Information: Contact your dealer, or send SASE for list.
Discounts: Sells wholesale.

KNIT-O-GRAF PATTERN CO.
958 Redwood Dr.
Apple Valley, MN 55124
(612) 432-5630

Offers: Pictoral knitting patterns for 4-ply yarns: Cardigan and pullover sweaters, puppet mittens, afghans, socks, others.
For Further Information: Color catalog, $1.25.

KNITKING
1128 Crenshaw Blvd.
Los Angeles, CA 90019

Offers: Knitting machines, including Compuknit III and others, plus accessories, a line of yarns and pattern books.
For Further Information: Free brochures.
Store Location: Yes

KNITTING CIRCLES
Cedar Beach
Charlotte, VT 05445

Offers: Circular knitting kits (pattern and yarn). Support/service.
For Further Information: Catalog, $4.

KNITTING MACHINES & YARNS BY BET
829 Lynnhaven Pkwy.
Virginia Beach, VA 23452
(804) 463-0009

Offers: Brother knitting machines (punchcard and electronic models).
For Further Information: Send for information.
Discounts: May run sales.
Accepts: MasterCard, Visa

KNITTING MACHINES OF FLORIDA
380 Semoran Commerce Place, Suite 107
Apopka, FL 32703

Offers: Cone yarns: Amber, Bouquet, Spindlecraft types. Also offers Craft Cascade acrylics, others.
For Further Information: Send SASE for yarn sample sheets.
Discounts: Sells wholesale.
Accepts: MasterCard, Visa

KRUH KNITS

P.O. Box 1587
Avon, CT 06001
(203) 674-1043

Offers: Knitting machines and machine accessories, computer programs, audio tapes, electronic patterns. Also offers finishing tools, furniture, lamps, aids, videos, yarn winders, motors, gauge helps, punchcards, ravel cords, sewing aids, washing solutions. Carries a full line of yarns.
For Further Information: Catalog, $2.

KRYSTAL DESIGNS

107 W. 7th St.
Junction City, KS 66441

Offers: Hand and machine knitting yarns and Singer knitting machines.
For Further Information: Yarn samples, $3.50 (refundable).

LAUREL YARNS

P.O. Box 216
Jericho, NY 11753

Offers: Line of cone yarns in a variety of types, colors, shades, plys.
For Further Information: Send $1 for samples.

LOST ART YARN SHOPPE

821 W. Front St.
Traverse City, MI 49684

Offers: Yarns/kits: Skacel, Rowan, Brown Sheep, Elite, Manos, Pingouin, Reynolds, Renaissance, others. Also offers knitting needles, accessories, patterns, books and rug braiding items.
For Further Information: Send for catalog; price lists and samples, $4 (refundable).
Store Location: Yes

MACHINE KNITTERS VIDEO MAGAZINE

637 Nicollet Ave.
North Mankato, MN 56003

Offers: Instructional videos by subscription: Knitting techniques and patterns, new products, personalities—studios, styles, reviews, events, maintenance ideas, others.
For Further Information: Send SASE for full information.

MARTHA JEAN'S

P.O. Box 347
Chewelah, WA 99109

Offers: Early 1900s crochet Camisole patterns, chart for Lily, Iris, Rose or other yokes, plus camisoles, baby items and household accessories.
For Further Information: List, $2.

MILL HOUSE YARN OUTLET

P.O. Box 9016
North Dartmouth, MA 02747

Offers: Cone yarns (for knitting machines, etc.) by 20-pound lots or larger. Offers a variety of acrylics, cotton mixed yarn types, others.
For Further Information: Send SASE for more information.

ALYCE MISNER

P.O. Box 2351
Big River, CA 92242

Offers: Line of hand knitting charts, kits and patterns.
For Further Information: Send SASE for information.

N.S.D. PRODUCTS

P.O. Box 880
Brandon, MS 39043
(601) 825-6831

Offers: Camel crochet (uses crochet hooks but looks like knitting)—basic instruction books and patterns.
For Further Information: Free flyers.
Discounts: Sells wholesale.
Accepts: MasterCard, Visa

THE NEEDLEWORK ATTIC

4706 Bethesda Ave.
Bethesda, MD 20814
(301) 652-8688

Offers: Sweater kits in a variety of color choices for selected styles, plus Rowan yarns and kits, and books.
For Further Information: Send SASE for information.

NEWTON'S KNITS

2100 E. Howell, Sp. 209
Anaheim, CA 92806
(714) 634-0817

Offers: Toyota knitting machines and Yarn Country cone yarns in a range of colors.
For Further Information: Contact your dealer, or send SASE for nearest location.
Discounts: Sells wholesale.

NORTHEAST KNITWORKS

P.O. Box 109
Freeport, ME 04032
(207) 865-1939

Offers: Cone yarns: Alpaca, mohair, blends, others.
For Further Information: Color cards, $5 (refundable).
Discounts: Quantity discounts.

NORTHSTAR KNITS
1293 NW Wall St., #1501
Bend, OR 97701

Offers: Collection of knitting kits, sweatshirts and sweatshirt yoke kits. Kits: Sweaters, accessories sets, T-shirt yokes, legwarmers. Also offers knitting/crochet accessories, yokes (striped, with "legwarmers" on pants), flower patterns with pearl centers, other. Accessories: Knitting needles, crochet hooks, others.
For Further Information: Catalog sheets, $4.50 (refundable).
Discounts: Allows discounts to teachers, institutions and professionals; sells wholesale to businesses.

PASSAP—U.S.A.
271 W. 2950 S.
Salt Lake City, UT 84115
(800) PASS-301

Offers: Passap knitting machines, including the Electronic and other models. Also offers steam presses and irons. Manufacturer.
For Further Information: Write for nearest dealer; free brochures.

PATTERNS
P.O. Box 2021
Superior, WI 54880

Offers: Crochet afghan patterns: Mile-A-Minute, Indian Paintbrush, Tequila Sunrise, Indian Tears, Rickrack, Navajo Crazy Quilt, Amish, Grandma's Love, Fan, Indian Arrow, others.
For Further Information: Send SASE for list.

PATTERNWORKS
P.O. Box 1690
Poughkeepsie, NY 12601

Offers: Knitting accessories/aids: Line of needles including bamboo, interchangeables, flex, others. Aids: Needle cases, ball winders, guides, calculators, rulers, graphs, gauges, finishing items, counters, knitting frame. Also offers knitting patterns, lines of yarns, books and videos.
For Further Information: Free catalog.
Discounts: Allows discounts to teachers and institutions.

PEACE WEAVERS
Rt. 3, P.O. Box 572
Berryville, VA 22611

Offers: "Peace fleece" yarn pack—Soviet and American wools spun into 20 colors of yarn, available by the skein, or in knitting kits for a global (map) sweater pattern.
For Further Information: Send business-size SASE for brochure; samples, $2.

PENELOPE CRAFT PROGRAMS, INC.
P.O. Box 1204
Maywood, NJ 07607
(201) 368-8379

Offers: Software (for IBM or compatible PC/XT/AT or PS/2 with at least 19K and PC/MS-DOS 2.11 or higher): Knit One adjusts knitting patterns to specified gauge and size.
For Further Information: Send SASE, or call for more information.
Discounts: Sells wholesale.
Accepts: American Express

PIGEON HILL FARM
Milbridge, ME 04658
(800) 321-TESS

Offers: Tess' designer yarns—handspun and/or hand-dyed wools, alpaca, angora, mohair, silks and blends.
For Further Information: Send SASE for brochure.

RAFTER-FOUR-DESIGNS
P.O. Box 3056
Sandpoint, ID 83864

Offers: Rag rug knitting instructions—beginning or advanced.
For Further Information: Send business-size SASE for brochure.

RITTERMERE-HURST-FIELD
15 Keele St. S.
P.O. Box 59
King City, Ontario L0G 1K0 Canada
(416) 833-0635

Offers: "Sweaters in a Sac" country sweaters knitting kits—variety of styles and designs.
For Further Information: Brochure, $1.

P.G. ROBERTS CO.
514 Loves Park Dr.
P.O. Box 2468
Loves Park, IL 61132

Offers: Interchangeable Delrin knitting needles—over 300 combinations, with sizes 5 to 15, 2 extenders, 2 stitch stops; in case.
For Further Information: Send SASE for list.
Discounts: Sells wholesale.

SAMI'S KNIT WIT
6477 Oakwood Dr.
Piedmont, CA 94611

Offers: Knitking, Singer and Toyota machines and accessories. Yarns: Erdal, Waterloo Co., Aarlan, Phentex, Noro,

Robin, Vendome, Leisure Arts, Brentwood, Bonnie Triola, Silk City, Scott's Woolen, Bouquet, Heirloom, others. Also offers discontinued dye lots, mill ends, close-outs.
For Further Information: Catalog/newsletter subscription, $5.
Accepts: American Express, MasterCard, Visa

SCHOOLHOUSE PRESS
6899 Cary Bluff
Pittsville, WI 54466
(715) 884-2799

Offers: Handknitting tools, wool yarns, over 100 books and videos.
For Further Information: Samples, $3.
Accepts: MasterCard, Visa

THE SEWING CENTER
2581 Piedmont Rd. NE
Atlanta, GA 30324
(404) 261-5605

Offers: Singer knitting machines—5 models for a variety of skill levels.
For Further Information: Send SASE for information.

SEW-KNIT DISTRIBUTORS
9789 Florida St.
Baton Rouge, LA 70815
(504) 923-1260

Offers: Knitting machines and accessories by Brother (fits Knitking), Toyota, Singer (fits Studio), Intarsias, Swiss-Made Passap. Also offers videotapes, ribbers, links, winders, hobbys, laces, hand punches, transfers, strippers, tools, bed extensions, Dazor lamp, tilt stand metal, Susaman irons, Jiffy steamers, Baby Lock sergers and Knit Bond, Read Pleaters, Stanley Pleaters, Baby Lock models. Carries dress forms, blocking cloth, sweater eggs and dryer, others.
For Further Information: Send business-size SASE for accessory price lists.
Accepts: American Express, Discover, MasterCard, Visa

SKACEL COLLECTION, INC.
224 SW 12th St.
Renton, WA 98055
(206) 255-3411

Offers: Knitting yarns, patterns and books: Schaffhauser Wolle, Scholler Wolle, Astermann Wolle, Mondail cashmere, and effect and jewelry yarns. Also offers turbo needles.
For Further Information: Send for information.

THE SPINNING WHEEL
307 Main St.
Ames, IA 50010
(515) 232-3288

Offers: Rauma (Norwegian) sportweight wools, yarn kits, pewter buttons, clasps.
For Further Information: Catalog and color card, $3.

SPRING HOUSE YARNS CO.
649 Wexford Bayne Rd.
Wexford, PA 15090

Offers: Handspun yarns: Wools, silks, mohair, and a selection of exotic fibers spun for softness and texture—in natural shades and dyed colors.
For Further Information: Brochure, $1.50.
Discounts: Sells wholesale.

STEPHANIE'S STUDIO & YARN
Rt. 1, P.O. Box 14
Bybee, TN 37713

Offers: Cone yarns for knitting machines: Jade, spiral twist cottons, ravel cord, acetate, acrylics, blends, wools, mohair, metallics—by the pound or cones.
For Further Information: Send SASE for list.
Discounts: Quantity discounts.
Accepts: MasterCard, Visa

D.J. STEVENS
109 S. Hubbards Lane
Louisville, KY 40207
(502) 895-0143

Offers: Knitting machine design patterns (for all machines—punchcard, mylar and electronic): Zoo animals, country designs, action figures and sports, florals, birds, logos, emblems, others.
For Further Information: Send business-size SASE for catalog.

STONEBRIER YARN & DESIGN CO.
P.O. Box 953
Carefree, AZ 85377
(602) 488-1040

Offers: Designer yarns and accessories by Lane Borgosesia, Di Crosa, Melrose, Vendome, Anny Blatt, Shewe and other name brands.
For Further Information: Price list, $3.

THE STRING SLINGER
P.O. Box 23272
Chattanooga, TN 37422
(815) 843-0272
or P.O. Box 5232, Station B
Victoria, British Columbia V8R 6N4 Canada

Offers: Instructional knitting machine videos (and workbooks): *Machine Knitting* series—for Japanese machines—and the *Passap Tutorial Series*.
For Further Information: Send SASE for full information.

STUDIO LIMESTONE
253 College St.
P.O. Box 316
Toronto, Ontario M5T 1R5 Canada
(416) 864-0984

Offers: Yarns/kits: Rowan, Annabel Fox, Fox Fibre, Vaturuguai. Also offers patterns, bond knitting frames, buttons (pewter, earth), Britany and Addi Turbo needles and needlepoint kits.
For Further Information: Shade cards set, $25 (refundable); price list, $2.

STUDIO PRODUCTS, INC.
10002 14th Ave. SW
Seattle, WA 98146

Offers: Line of designer electronic knitting machines.
For Further Information: See your dealer, or send SASE for details.

SUZY'S
P.O. Box 904115
Tulsa, OK 74105
(918) 742-8369

Offers: *Knit Repair* instructional video: Repair yarns, finishing, tools and hints.
For Further Information: Send for details.
Accepts: MasterCard, Visa

TD CREATIONS
421 Horn Ave. S.
Moorhead, MN 56560

Offers: Crochet patterns for 15-inch doll bodies and 15-inch fashion dolls: Old-fashioned dresses and matching hats in ruffled, striped, hoop or straight styles with a lacy look.
For Further Information: Send SASE for list.
Accepts: MasterCard, Visa

BONNIE TRIOLA
343 East Rd.
Erie, PA 16509
(814) 825-7821

Offers: Cone yarns for machine knitters, weavers: Wool/rayon, cotton/rayon, ribbon, cable cotton, Italian Florentine, angora. Also offers yarns by Tamm, Millor, and odd-lot and/or designer yarns.
For Further Information: Catalog and mailings, $10.

Discounts: Allows discounts to teachers and institutions; sells wholesale to legitimate businesses.

VIDEO INSTRUCTIONAL PROGRAMS
781 Golden Prados Dr.
Diamond Bar, CA 91765
(714) 861-5021

Offers: Instructional videos, including machine knitting with Alvina Murdaugh and over 30 sewing videos. Videos can be rented—rent can apply to purchase.
For Further Information: Send SASE for video list.

THE WEAVER'S LOFT
308 S. Pennsylvania Ave.
Centre Hall, PA 16828
(814) 364-1433

Offers: Full line of knitting yarns and supplies.
For Further Information: Free catalog; sample set, $8 (refundable).
Discounts: Has discounts.
See Also: Spinning and Weaving

WESTRADE SALES, INC.
2711 #3 Rd.
Richmond, British Columbia V7E 4P3 Canada
(604) 270-8737

Offers: Cone knitting yarns from Forsell and Bramwell in 30 styles and a full line of colors, plus blends and Shetland-type mixtures.
For Further Information: Send SASE for list.

When knitting with our Un-Spun yarn, do not knit too tight; it is quite strong after being knitted, but somewhat fragile beforehand. If it breaks, just overlap the two ends and keep on knitting; you'll be amazed at how soft and light the finished garment is!

—The Woolery

JOYCE WILLIAMS
P.O. Box 7091
Springfield, MO 65801

Offers: Crochet afghan patterns for large hooks: Weekend Wonder, Deep Forest, Blue Skies, Autumnfest, Grassy Knoll, Rainbows, others.
For Further Information: Brochure, $1 (refundable).

WKMG
P.O. Box 1527
Vashon, WA 98070
(206) 463-2088

Offers: Machine/hand knitting pattern books: Iris Bishop, Bramwell, Kathleen Kinder, Mr. Le Warre (on French electronic machines), Val Love, Tami Nobuyuki (beginner workbooks), *Nicely Knit*, Patons, Wendy Phillips, Golden Unicorn, Jill Stern, Pat Varvel, Mary Weaver, Sandra Williams, others. Also offers McCall's machine knitting patterns and fabric paints (Tulip, Delta) with instructions.

For Further Information: Catalog, $1.50.

Discounts: Some quantity pricing.

See Also: Publications

THE WOOL ROOM

Laurelton Rd.
Mt. Kisco, NY 10549
(914) 241-1910

Offers: Bond and studio knitting machines and knitting needles. Yarns: Rowan, Crystal Palace. Also offers spinning/weaving equipment, fleece, fibers, basketry supplies.

For Further Information: Send $1 and SASE for catalog.

Discounts: Quantity discounts; allows discounts to institutions and teachers.

YARN FOR EWE

2720 Crown Point Ct.
Sidney, OH 45365
(513) 492-3315

Offers: Knitting yarns, supplies, books.

For Further Information: Send business-size SASE for list.

Discounts: Has discounts.

YARN N CRAFT PARADISE

P.O. Box 8056
Nutter Fort, WV 26301

Offers: Yarns: Bucilla, Patons, Caron, others in cotton, wool, acrylic, blends. Also offers pattern books for knitting, crochet and other needlecrafts, plus knitting needle sets, tools, accessories.

For Further Information: Catalog, $3 (refundable).

YARN-IT-ALL

2223 Rebecca Dr.
Hatfield, PA 19440
(215) 822-2989

Offers: Brother knitting machines—Electronic fine needle, bulky punch card and other models, plus ribbers. Also offers Brother stands/tables, accessories. Yarns: Melrose, Phentex, Millor, others. Videos, patterns and books are also available.

For Further Information: Free catalog.

Store Location: Yes

Discounts: Quantity discounts.

YARNARTS

P.O. Box 950
Saratoga Springs, NY 12866

Offers: Crochet patterns, computer designed, including picture cover sheets, diagrams and graphs (allows lifelike details) for doll fingers, toes, ears, noses, hands, arms, legs, bums, dimples, etc. Patterns available include a 16-inch Elvis, 24-inch and 16-inch girls, babies, plus animals, aliens, others.

For Further Information: Send SASE for list.

Lace Making

Also see General Needlecraft Supplies, Knitting and Crochet, Yarns and other related categories.

CARPENTERS' CRAFTS
P.O. Box 1283
Alton, IL 62002

Offers: Video: *Learn the Art of Tatting Lace*, with a progression of instructional techniques. Shuttle and thread kits are also available.
For Further Information: Send SASE for prices.
Accepts: MasterCard, Visa

CINDY'S STITCHES
588 Roger Williams
Highland Park, IL 60035
(708) 433-5183

Offers: Threads, tools and supplies for lace making—bobbin, tatted, needle and knitted types. Also offers silk ribbon, smocking and Brazilian cross-stitch items and books.
For Further Information: Call for catalog.
Store Location: Yes

CRAFT GALLERY
P.O. Box 8319
Salem, MA 01971
(617) 744-6980

Offers: Tatting cotton threads and patterns, Battenberg ornament kits, Tatsy patterns and threads, plus imported and other threads in cotton, linen, others. Also offers lace bobbins (including antique English style), lace pins, shuttles (imported, rosewood, board and flat types, others), blank napkins, handkerchiefs and lace sets. Aids include wrist ball holders and other needlecraft helps. Books include a full line of lace-making techniques and titles.
For Further Information: Catalog, $2.
See Also: General Needlecraft Supplies

GLIMAKRA LOOMS 'N YARNS, INC.
1304 Scott St.
Petaluma, CA 94954
(707) 762-3362

Offers: Linen threads in a variety of colors and plies. Equipment and supplies: Lace plates, rolls, pillows, kits, bobbin winders, bobbins and fancy bobbins, pricking tools, pins, glass beads, tatting shuttles. Also offers a variety of pattern sets, plus instructional videos (on bobbin and needle lace), and books, including titles on Batsford, Battenberg, lace braid, bobbin and needlepoint types, Cluny, Russian and others.
For Further Information: Lace book catalog, $1; sample color card, $2.
See Also: General Needlecraft Supplies and Spinning and Weaving

VICTORIAN VIDEO PRODUCTIONS
1304 Scott St.
Petaluma, CA 94954
(707) 762-3362

Offers: Instructional videos: (1) *Needlelace Medallions*—basics; (2) *Bobbin Lace*—covering graduated levels of instruction in basic twist, cross, Torchon ground and others, including finishing. Offers many other craft and needlecraft videos.
For Further Information: Free catalog.
Discounts: Allows discounts to schools and libraries; sells wholesale to businesses.

Macrame

Also see General Needlecraft Supplies, Knitting and Crochet, Yarns and related categories.

ACORN CRAFTS
3954 W. Twelve Mile Rd.
Berkley, MI 48072

Offers: Line of macrame supplies, aids and books.
For Further Information: Catalog, $3.

AL CON ENTERPRISES
P.O. Box 1060
Quincy, FL 32351
(800) 523-4371

Offers: Al Con brand macrame braid/cord—full line of colors (6mm to 8mm). Macrame kits for hangers and baskets. Accessories: Metal rings (rounds, rectangles, square), purse spring closure frames, macrame boards, T-pins, wool beads, dowel rods. Also offers books and chair weaving kits/supplies and video.
For Further Information: Free catalog and sample.
Store Location: Yes
Discounts: Sells wholesale; quantity discounts.
See Also: Nature Crafts

BRIAN'S CRAFTS UNLIMITED
1421 S. Dixie Freeway
New Smyrna Beach, FL 32168

Offers: Macrame supplies: Synthetic cords (indoor/outdoor), Maxi twist in solids and blends, metallics, braid/tube (2mm to 6mm). Accessories: Rings (brass, bamboo, Dee, split key, metal rectangles, plastic), purse snaps, owl eyes, box wreath frames, pre-drilled Marbella beads and wood blocks. Also offers chair frames, ceramic and wood beads, fusing tools, books and other craft supplies.
For Further Information: Catalog, $1 (refundable).
Accepts: MasterCard, Visa
See Also: General Craft Supplies

SUNCOAST
9015 U.S. 19 N.
Pinellas Park, FL 34666

Offers: Maxi-Cord macrame cord (6mm polypropylene) in over 28 solid colors and over 18 mixed color rolls. Also offers cord color chart and other craft supplies.
For Further Information: Full crafts catalog, $2.
Discounts: Has discounts.

TEXTILE ENTERPRISES, INC.
216 Main St.
P.O. Box 154
Whitesburg, GA 30185
(404) 834-2094

Offers: Macrame supplies: Cords (twists, braids in colors, heathers, mixed), wire braid, fancy cords, waxed linens, jute, braided metallics, cotton cables. Accessories: Purse closures, full line of rings (wood, bamboo, rattan, others), purse handles, metal rings/frames (holiday and other shapes), lampshades (Tiffany style and others), plus table frame kits, wall brackets, ceiling hook sets, others.
For Further Information: Catalog, $5.
Discounts: Sells wholesale; quantity discounts.

Needlepoint

Also see General Needlecraft Supplies, Embroidery and Cross-Stitch, Yarns and related categories.

ARTS ARRAY
P.O. Box 5415
Santa Maria, CA 93456
(805) 937-7798

Offers: Line of European "tapestries" (hand-silkscreened color on Penelope double-weave) and kits: Over 500 motifs by Royal Paris, Tapex, Margot Seg, Rico, others in traditional and classic designs—religious, Renaissance, florals, wildlife, seasonal, masterpieces, whimsical subjects, others. Also offers petit point kits (over 26) in classic designs.
For Further Information: Catalog, $2.
Discounts: May run sales.

AUNT MARY'S HOBBY
20 SW 27th Ave.
Pompano Beach, FL 33069

Offers: Hand-painted needlepoint canvases, kits and pre-work in traditional pet designs: Ducks, birds, cats, dogs, horses. Also offers flowers, animals, fish, hearts, motifs for toilet seat cover monograms. Needlepoint canvases include mini-sizes. Carries Royal Paris brand canvases: Hunting/wildlife scenes and others.
For Further Information: Needlepoint catalog, $1.50 (refundable).
See Also: Embroidery and Cross-Stitch

CUSTOM NEEDLEWORK DESIGNS
P.O. Box 9
Oreland, PA 19075
(215) 572-6313, (800) 767-6313

Offers: Custom service. Needlepoint canvas or kit—color design created from your photograph, drawing, others.
For Further Information: Free brochure.

Petit point is worked on single strand canvas, for Cordovaor Silk Screen Gauze with cotton thread, silk or split wool. Petit point may also be worked on Penelope canvas by separating the canvas with a needle and working over the single strands. This is done when a combination of the two stitches is to be worked on one canvas using half the amount of thread or wool.

—Jean McIntosh

GITTA'S CHARTED PETIT POINT
289 Lakeshore Rd. E.
Port Credit, Ontario L5G 1H3 Canada
(416) 274-7189

Offers: Needlepoint/petit point (and cross-stitch) charts/kits in over 45 traditional motifs: Victorian, Renaissance, Eskimo, florals, fowl, others. Fabrics: Linens and others. Brand name threads: Wools, cottons. Also offers canvases, silk-screen mesh and custom needlework framing.
For Further Information: Catalog, $4.
Discounts: Allows discounts to teachers and institutions; sells wholesale to businesses.

JEAN McINTOSH LTD.
P.O. Box 232
Pembina, ND 58271
or 1115 Empress St.
Winnipeg, Manitoba R3E 3H1 Canada

Offers: Needlepoint and petit point kits and charts: Traditional and classic designs in a wide range of motifs, including florals, scenic tapestries, others. Also offers cross-stitch materials.
For Further Information: Catalog, $4.
Store Location: Yes
Discounts: Sells wholesale to legitimate businesses.

PICTUREPOINT-THD
P.O. Box 1505
McKinney, TX 75070
(214) 548-2251

Offers: Needlepoint (or cross-stitch) design service: 16-point color chart and DMC color guide created from a favorite photo, paper or fabric sample (person, pet, home, boat, others).
For Further Information: Send SASE for details.

STUDIO LIMESTONE
253 College St.
P.O. Box 316
Toronto, Ontario M5T 1R5 Canada
(416) 864-0984

Offers: Rowan and Ehrman needlepoint kits. Yarns: Rowan, Annabel Fox, Fox Fibre, Valuruguai and others. Also offers books and knitting supplies.
For Further Information: Sample shade cards, $25 (refundable); price list, $2.

Outdoors and Outerwear

Also see Clothing and Accessories, Fabrics and Trims, Knitting and Crochet, Quilting, Sewing and other specific categories.

ALTRA
100 E. Washington
New Richmond, IN 47967

Offers: Precut outerwear sewing kits: Jackets, pullovers, coats, wind pants, sweats, parkas, sweaters, gaiters, knickers, vests, insulated coveralls (for adults and children), bunting items, hoods, robes, booties. Fabrics: Nylon, blends, pile blends. Notions: Guides gauge, reflective tape (washable), snip clips, side-release buckle, hook/loops, zippers, threads, appliqués, letters, webbings. Insulations: Down, Thinsulate, needlepunch. Also offers hardware, luggage kits (nylon types), ribbing. Carries ready-made outerwear.
For Further Information: Catalog, $1.
Discounts: Allows discounts to teachers and institutions.

FROSTLINE KITS
2525 River Rd.
Grand Junction, CO 81505

Offers: Precut outerwear kits (coats, jackets, baby wear, others) for adults, children: Robes, comforters, others—ready-to-sew.
For Further Information: Write for catalog.
Discounts: Has discounts.

THE GREEN PEPPER
3918 W. 1st Ave.
Eugene, OR 97402
(503) 345-6665

Offers: Sewing patterns: Polar Plus whitewater jackets for adults and children, plus other patterns for stretch outerwear fabric. Fabrics: Raschel, nylon spandex tricot, others. Also offers Teflon press cloths and threads.
For Further Information: Catalog, $2.

Tie your next color of thread to the thread you no longer need, then pull thread through machine when changing colors (saves tedious rethreading).

— Timberline Sewing Kits

HANG-EM HIGH FABRICS
1420 Yale Ave.
Richmond, VA 23224
(804) 233-6155

Offers: Fabrics: Ripstop nylons, dacron (and adhesive). Supplies: Webbing, repair tapes, swivels, tubing and tubes (fiberglass, carbon, vinyl).
For Further Information: Write for price list.
See Also: Kite Making

MARINE SEWING
6801 Gulfport Blvd.
St. Petersburg, FL 33707
(813) 345-6994

Offers: Line of outdoor fabrics: Canvas, vinyls, others (for boating/camping and outdoor items). Also offers notions for outdoor-fabric sewing.
For Further Information: Catalog, $3 and business-size SASE.

OUTDOOR WILDERNESS FABRICS
16195 Latah Dr.
Nampa, ID 83651

Offers: Outdoor fabrics: Gore-Tex, Ultrex, Taslan, Supplex, Ballistics, Cordura, others. Also offers insulations, no-see-um netting mesh, hardware, supplies.
For Further Information: Free price list; full samples, $4.
Accepts: MasterCard, Visa

PINE RIVER TEXTILES, INC.
10443 A 12th St.
Edmonton, Alberta T5N 1R7 Canada
(403) 488-9523

Offers: Line of outdoor/activewear fabrics: Ripstop, nylons, canvas, denim, others. Also offers known-brand patterns, threads, batting.
For Further Information: Catalog, $2.

QUEST OUTFITTERS
2590 17th St.
Sarasota, FL 34234
(813) 378-4620

Offers: Line of outdoor fabrics, wear and gear kits and sewing supplies.
For Further Information: Free catalog.

THE RAIN SHED
707 NW 11th St.
Corvallis, OR 97330
(503) 753-8900

Offers: Outerwear patterns/kits/supplies. Brand patterns by Sew Easy, Daisfiber by Kingdom, Coat Craze, Four Seasons, Green Pepper, Stretch'N Sew, Suitability, Travel Pals. Pat-

GreenPepper Patterns. Courtesy of The Rainshed.

terns: Parkas, pants, vests, jackets, coveralls, suits, gaiters, caps, nightshirts, rompers, robes, swimsuits, riding outfits, totes, caddies, comforters, windsocks. Luggage: Daypacks, cases, bags (ski, duffle, flight, diaper, thermal bottle). Fabrics: Coated/uncoated nylons and Taslan, Supplex, Techtile, cordura, vinyls, packcloth, waterproof/breatheables, wicking knits, mesh, fleece, lycra, blends/cottons, camouflage, insulations. Also offers reflective tapes, webbings, cords, repair

tapes, velcro, notions, tools (snaps/setters, eyelets, hot tips, cutters, scissors) and hardware.

For Further Information: Catalog, $1.

SEATTLE FABRICS

3876 Bridge Way N.
Seattle, WA 98103
(206) 632-6022

Offers: Outdoor/recreational fabrics: Ultrex, Gore-Tex, Supplax, Polarplus, lycra, taffeta, ripstop, oxford, packcloth, cordura, Sunbrella, Textilene, closed cell foam, mosquito netting, heat-seal packcloth, others. Also offers hardware, sewing notions, webbing, flags. Custom orders.

For Further Information: Price list, $3.

Store Location: Yes

TIMBERLINE SEWING KITS

P.O. Box 126-CS
Pittsfield, NH 03263
(603) 435-8888

Offers: Outerwear kits: Jackets, vests, parkas, foot mittens, gaiters. Luggage kits: Cargo bags, travel bags, totes, bike bags, logs. Comforter patterns also available. Fabrics: Nylons, Cordura, taffeta, ripstop, water-repellent types. Also offers goose and duck down.

For Further Information: Brochure, $1; fabrics list on request.

Store Location: Yes

Discounts: Sells wholesale to teachers and institutions.

Accepts: MasterCard, Visa

Quilting

Also see General Needlecraft Supplies, Fabrics and Trims, Sewing and other related categories.

ANGIE'S
P.O. Box 968
Frisco, TX 75034

Offers: Cotton print fabrics from known manufacturers, including fat quarter and yardage assortments for quilting and other uses.
For Further Information: Send SASE for current product list.

GLORIA ASKEW
P.O. Box 893
Opelika, AL 36803

Offers: Fabric squares assortments—solids or prints.
For Further Information: Send SASE for list.

BEST COTTONS
10 Mansfield
Gloucester, MA 01930

Offers: Cotton calico prints in a variety of designs/colors (low prices).
For Further Information: Send SASE for information.

BREWER FABRIC SHOP
570 Stillwater Ave.
Bangor, ME 04401

Offers: Quilting fabrics—calicos, solid shades: Jinny Beyer, Palette, Hoffman, RJR, P & B, Marcus Brothers, others.
For Further Information: Over 1,400 swatches, $8 (with $3 rebate).

BUSY BEE
P.O. Box 1031
Decatur, GA 30031

Offers: Full line of quilting supplies: Threads, templates, notions, fabrics, and a variety of patterns and precut quilting kits.
For Further Information: Catalog, $2.

CABIN FEVER CALICOES
P.O. Box 550106
Atlanta, GA 30355
(404) 873-5094

Offers: Quilting patterns/kits/supplies. Patterns include original Sioux designs (and fabric peaks): Peace Pipe, Eight-Pointed Star, mini-quilt motifs. Also offers pillow kits, fabric packs (¼- to 1-yard assortments), yardage (sheeting, homespun, others), batting, pillow forms, notions and aids, threads (Swiss Metrosene and others), templates (Plasti-graph, Lam-I-Graph, others). Carries rotary cutters, projectors, quilting frames, patterns for quilt clothing and soft toys, videos.
For Further Information: Catalog and cotton swatches, $3.
See Also: Doll, Toy and Clothes Making—Soft

JAMES CARROLL ANTIQUES
P.O. Box 239
Franconia, NH 03580

Offers: Vintage fabric collection—30s through 50s cotton prints (plaids, paisleys, florals, juveniles); fat quarters assortments.
For Further Information: Send SASE for list.

JEAN CAVINESS
150 Old Marietta Rd.
Canton, GA 30114

Offers: Old quilt patterns—traditional advertisements (Campbell's Soup Girl and others), animals, florals, others.
For Further Information: Send SASE and $1.50 for sample and list.
See Also: Doll, Toy and Clothes Making—Soft.

CLOTH OF GOLD
1220 Spartanburg Highway
Hendersonville, NC 28792
(800) 316-0947

Offers: Over 100 prints and solids in 100% cotton fabrics, including perm-press muslin. Long quarters assortments, others.
For Further Information: Call for information; sample card, $2.
Accepts: MasterCard, Visa

If you want a prize-winning quilt, study old quilts for color tips, borders, batting and binding. They teach a lot.

—Jane C. Smith, Quiltmaker

COLONIAL PATTERNS
340 W. 5th St.
Kansas City, MO 64105

Offers: Aunt Martha's line of quilting designs—a variety of classic motifs.
For Further Information: See your dealer, or write for information.

CONTEMPORY QUILTS
5305 Denwood Ave.
Memphis, TN 38120

Offers: Construct-your-own quilting frame kit: Instructions and ratchet accessories, for all size quilts.
For Further Information: Send SASE for full details.

DOVER ST. BOOKSELLERS
8673 Commerce Dr.
P.O. Box 1563
Easton, MD 21601
(401) 822-9329, (800) 235-5358

Offers: Over 600 quilting/patchwork books: Techniques, patterns, garments, accessories, others.
For Further Information: Catalog, $2.
Store Location: Yes
Discounts: Quantity discounts.

EXTRA SPECIAL PRODUCTS CORP.
P.O. Box 777
Greenville, OH 45331
(513) 548-3793

Offers: Quilting aids—rulers, seamers, templates, grids, magnifiers, stenciling and other tools. Also offers plans for build-your-own quilt frames, Dream Seamer, learn-to-appliqué set.
For Further Information: See your dealer, or write for catalog.
See Also: Metalworking

FAIRFIELD PROCESSING CORP.
P.O. Box 1157
Danbury, CT 06813

Offers: Poly-fil polyester fiberfill, Extra-Loft traditional, low-loft, cotton classical and ultra-loft battings. Also offers pillow inserts. Manufacturer.
For Further Information: Contact dealer.

FRUGAL FOX
P.O. Box 369
Fontana, WI 53125

Offers: Line of quilt batting and fiberfill, pillow forms, others.
For Further Information: Send business-size SASE for price list.

THE GIBBS MANUFACTURING CO.
606 6th St. NE
Canton, OH 44702
(216) 455-5344

Offers: Gibbs quilting hoops and framing, and basketry supplies.
For Further Information: Free catalog/brochures.
Discounts: Quantity discounts; allows discounts to teachers, institutions and professionals; sells wholesale to legitimate businesses.

GINGER'S NEEDLEWORKS
P.O. Box 92047
Lafayette, LA 70509
(318) 232-7847

Offers: Cotton fabric collections/squares in designer prints, solid shades (30 plus piece assortments).
For Further Information: Catalog, $2; over 400 samples, $6.

GUTCHEON PATCHWORKS, INC.
917 Pacific Ave., #305
Tacoma, WA 98402

Offers: 100% cotton fabrics in over 200 prints and coordinating solids. Manufacturer.
For Further Information: Fabric samples, $3.

HAPCO PRODUCTS
46 Mapleview Dr.
Columbia, MO 65202

Offers: Quilting accessories, including Hapco snap frames, others.
For Further Information: See your dealer, or write for information.

HINTERBERG DESIGN, INC.
2100 Northwestern Ave.
West Bend, WI 53095
(414) 338-0337

Offers: Quilting hoops, adjustable height and tilt, 2 sizes.
For Further Information: Send SASE for details.
Accepts: MasterCard, Visa

HOMECRAFT SERVICES
340 W. 5th St.
Kansas City, MO 64105

Offers: Aunt Martha's precut quilt kits in a variety of patterns, plus hot-iron transfer sets in traditional motifs, others.
For Further Information: Picture catalog, $1.

Courtesy of Dover Publications.

KEEPSAKE QUILTING
P.O. Box 1459
Meredith, NH 03253

Offers: Quilting supplies: Patterns, stencils, a variety of aids, fabric medleys, quilting kits, over 600 cotton fabrics (solids, plaids, patterns, textured, others), specialty fabric assortments, batting and muslin. Also offers "hundreds" of quilting books and gifts for quilters.
For Further Information: Free catalog (or $1 by 1st class mail).

KEN QUILT MANUFACTURING CO.
113 Pattie St.
Wichita, KS 67211
(316) 262-3438

Offers: Professional model quilting machines, variable speed to full 3500 RPM; four-way quilting operations.
For Further Information: Send stamp for literature and prices.

LA MAISON PIQUEE
P.O. Box 1891
Milwaukee, WI 53201
(414) 332-4590

Offers: Quilting patterns: Set of 19th-Century designs, Bicentennial sampler of colonial America. French quilting explained in *Quiltbroidery*.
For Further Information: Send SASE for pattern list.
Discounts: Quantity discounts; allows discounts to teachers and institutions; sells wholesale to legitimate businesses.

DIANNE LARSON QUILTWORKS
3583 Richie Rd.
Verona, WI 53593
(608) 829-3583

Offers: "Art-in-A-Pinch" quilt hangers (wood, press-method).
For Further Information: Free brochure.

MADISON QUILT CO.
121 S. Main St.
Madison, GA 30650
(800) 442-8639, (706) 342-8639

Offers: Members of this fabric club receive over 400 4-inch square samples: RJR, MEH, Hoffman, A. Henry, F & B, plus quarterly updates.
For Further Information: Send SASE for full details.
Discounts: Has discounts.
Accepts: MasterCard, Visa

MAGIC NEEDLE
Rt. 2, P.O. Box 172
Limerick, ME 04048

Offers: Crazy-quilting items, silk ribbons, line of threads, other supplies and aids.
For Further Information: Catalog, $1.

MOUNTAIN MIST
100 Williams St.
Cincinnati, OH 45215
(513) 948-5276

Offers: Cotton and polyester quilt batting, cotton-covered pillow forms, polyester stuffing. Line of quilt patterns with templates in florals, inspirational and other designs. Manufacturer.
For Further Information: Contact dealer, or send SASE for information.

NEEDLEARTS INTERNATIONAL
19411 Village Dr.
Sonora, CA 95370

Offers: Quilting stencils—over 300, in international designs (Celtic, Oriental, Arabic, others), including Sashiko Japanese embroidery/quilting patterns, supplies and books. Also offers patterns for unusual quilting projects and garments, imported cottons (from Japan, Malaysia, Indonesia, others) and design books.
For Further Information: Catalog, $2.

NOLTING'S LONGARM MANUFACTURING
Rt. 3, Highway 52 E, P.O. Box 147
Stover, MO 65078
(314) 377-2713

Offers: Nolting's longarm quilting machines in 4 sizes (16 inches to 36 inches). Manufacturer.
For Further Information: Send SASE for full details.

THE PATCHWORKS
126 E. Main St.
Bozeman, MT 59715
(406) 587-2112

Offers: Line of reproduction fabric collections including Victorian, Heritage, 30s Novelties, others.
For Further Information: Catalog, $2; samples, $4 each.

PIONEER QUILTS
801 Columbus St.
Rapid City, SD 57701
(605) 342-6227

Offers: Quilt-A-Kits—114 custom-marked designs for quilt blocks, pillows, others. Includes blocks for all bed sizes with florals, animals, old-fashioned, special occasion, Christmas motifs. Also offers granny ball kits and the book *Adventures in Quilting*, by Rose and Eatinger.
For Further Information: Send SASE for information.
Discounts: Sells wholesale to businesses.

Have a hard time choosing colors? Use this formula:
1. Choose a large print (your favorite).
2. A solid (chintz is better).
3. A visual fabric (striped, plaid—not calico).
4. Fill in with small calicoes.

—Jane C. Smith, Quiltmaker

QUILT IN A DAY
1955 Diamond St., Unit A
San Marcos, CA 92069
(619) 436-8936

Offers: Instructional videos and books by Eleanor Burns. Supplies: Threads, patterns, others.
For Further Information: Free catalog.
Store Location: Yes
Discounts: Allows discounts to teachers and institutions; sells wholesale to legitimate businesses.

THE QUILT PATCH
208 Brigham St.
Marlborough, MA 01752
(508) 480-0194

Offers: Quilting supplies, including a full line of threads, stencils, aids, others. Fabrics: Cotton prints and solids, designer fabrics. Also offers books, instructional videos and handcrafted quilts.
For Further Information: Catalog, $1; with swatches, $4.

QUILTING BOOKS UNLIMITED
1911 W. Wilson
Batavia, IL 60510
(708) 406-0237

Offers: Over 1,000 quilting book titles—classic, contemporary and other motifs for quilts, clothing and home accessories; covers a variety of techniques/methods. Also offers sewing notions, over 1,000 bolts of 100% cotton fabrics.
For Further Information: Catalog, $1.
Store Location: Yes
Discounts: Allows discounts to teachers and institutions; quantity discounts.

QUILTS & OTHER COMFORTS
6700 W. 44th Ave.
P.O. Box 394
Wheat Ridge, CO 80034
(303) 420-4272

Offers: Quilting patterns/precut kits: Designer, classics, heirloom, contemporary, old favorites, children's and others—all bed sizes. Also offers pillow kits, easy-patchwork kits. Fabrics: Solid cottons by the yard, muslins, color packets. Aids: Templates, patterns, frames (hoops, stands), notions, cutters, threads, bindings, linings. Carries quilt clothing patterns and books.
For Further Information: Catalog, $2.50.
Discounts: Allows discounts to teachers and institutions; sells wholesale to legitimate businesses.

QUILTWORK PATCHES
209 SW 2nd St.
Corvallis, OR 97333

Offers: Precut quilt kits/patterns: Traditional, others. Also offers cotton fabrics, including precut assortments, squares, coordinated pieces, plus battings, patterns, stencils, templates, Q-Snap PVC quilt frames and others (hoops, stands, floor models). Carries cutters, scissors, markers, threads and books.
For Further Information: Catalog, $1; fabric samples, $2.

QUILTWORKS
2920 N. 2nd St.
Minneapolis, MN 55411

Offers: Quilting fabrics: Concord, Marcus, Meritex, Wamsutta, Peter Pan, Bernartex, Hoffman, Dan River, others. Full line of supplies.
For Further Information: Send SASE for list.
Discounts: Sells wholesale.

ST. PETER WOOLEN MILL
101 W. Broadway
St. Peter, MN 56082
(507) 931-3734

Offers: Natural wool batting, recarding service.
For Further Information: Free brochure.
Discounts: Sells wholesale.

THE SEWING ROOM

35353-CS Law Rd.
Grafton, OH 44044

Offers: Quilting stencils (precut, clear plastic) in over 600 designs: Geometrics, florals, borders, classics, animals, storybook, vehicles, old-fashioned motifs, alphabets, others. Marking tools are also available.
For Further Information: Catalog, $1 (refundable).
Discounts: Sells wholesale.

JANE C. SMITH, QUILTMAKER

RFD 1, P.O. Box 518A
South Berwick, ME 03908
(207) 676-2209

Offers: Line of quilting booklets including *Trip Around the World*, and others by Jane C. Smith. Also offers the book *Quilt in a Day*, plus teacher's work kit and quilting kit.
For Further Information: Free brochure.
Discounts: Quantity discounts; allows discounts to teachers, institutions and professionals; sells wholesale to legitimate businesses.

THE STEARNS TECHNICAL TEXTILES CO.

100 Williams St.
Cincinnati, OH 45215
(513) 948-5277

Offers: Mountain Mist cotton batting (no prewashing), with Glazene finish, plus Gray poly-batting.
For Further Information: See your dealer, or write for information.

THE TEXTILE DETECTIVE

P.O. Box 422
Andover, MA 01810

Offers: Quilting teacher directories—lists lectures and workshops.
For Further Information: Send SASE for full details.

J. WENGLER

311 Preston Ave.
San Antonio, TX 78210
(512) 532-3356

Offers: Quilting frames—two models available in double, queen or king sizes; collapsible and adjustable, in storage cases.
For Further Information: Send SASE for brochure.

Rug Making

Also see General Needlecraft Supplies, Knitting and Crochet, Spinning and Weaving, Yarns and other related categories.

ANDERSON HANDCRAFTED PRODUCTS
Star Route, P.O. Box 87
Leonardtown, MD 20650

Offers: Rug-hooking frames: Hardwood, adjustable (height/angle), portable; with guards; 9-inch × 22-inch working area; floor model. Optional lap stand.
For Further Information: Send SASE for details.

BAR-B WOOLIES
5308 Roeding Rd.
Hughson, CA 95326
(209) 883-0833

Offers: Lines of custom hand-spun and commercial hand-dyed yarns for rug hooking.
For Further Information: Samples, $4 and SASE.

PATSY BECKER
18 Schanck Rd.
Holmdel, NJ 07733
(909) 946-3485

Offers: Line of Patsy rug-hooking designs in whimsical/folk art style motifs.
For Further Information: Catalog, $3.

BRAID-AID
466 Washington St.
Pembroke, MA 02359
(617) 826-2560

Offers: Rug-making/weaving supplies: Hooking/braiding wools by yard, primitive and Scotch burlaps, monk's cloth, cottons, homespuns, rug warp. Wool remnants available by pound. Kits: Rug-braiding, accessory kits. Tools/equipment: Cutter units, hooks, shears, magnifiers. Also offers patterns, shirret items, Braid-Klamp and Braid-Aids, dyes, yarns.
For Further Information: Color catalog, $4; free price lists.
Discounts: Allows discounts to teachers.

CANADA'S CENTER
P.O. Box 487
Aurora, Ontario L4G 3L6 Canada
(416) 773-2633

Offers: Rittemere-Hurst-Field line of rug-hooking designs and supplies.
For Further Information: Catalog, $6 (Canadians add GST).

COUNTRY BRAID HOUSE
RFD 2, Clark Rd., P.O. Box 29
Tilton, NH 03276
(603) 286-4511

Offers: Braided rug kits (with wool, tools). Hooking and braiding video.
For Further Information: Send for brochure.

DIFRANZA DESIGNS
25 Bow St.
North Reading, MA 01864
(508) 664-2034

Offers: Hooked rug patterns/kits (burlap, precut wool fabrics): Traditional and contemporary designs (for brick covers, tapestries, chair seats, pillows) including unusuals, florals, special occasion/personalized, New England motifs, others.
For Further Information: Catalog, $5.
Discounts: Allows discounts to teachers; sells wholesale to legitimate businesses.

THE DORR MILL STORE
P.O. Box 88
Guild, NH 03754
(603) 863-1197

Offers: Wool fabric (exclusive decorator colors for hooking, braiding, quilting) and tweeds. Also offers hooking kits in a variety of traditional designs.
For Further Information: Free supply list; swatches, $3 (collection of 166 shades).

EARTH GUILD
33 Haywood St.
Asheville, NC 28801

Offers: Rug punches: Old style, heavy-duty, punch needle. Hooks: Latch, traditional types. Rug braiding: Braid-Klamp, Braidkin, Vari-Folder Braid Aid braiders. Yarns: Cottons, linens, wool, rug wools, heavyweight, Berbers, Navajo wool, others. Also offers primitive and Scotch burlap, cutters, dyes, equipment, others.
For Further Information: Free catalog.
Store Location: Yes

Discounts: Quantity discounts; allows discounts to teachers and institutions; sells wholesale to legitimate businesses.
Accepts: American Express, MasterCard, Visa
See Also: General Craft Supplies and Spinning and Weaving

EHB DESIGNS
132 Rosedale Valley Rd.
Toronto, Ontario M4W 1P7 Canada
(416) 964-0634

Offers: Line of acid dyes for rug making.
For Further Information: Color chart, instructions, $3; free price list.

The tighter you can keep your pattern stretched, the easier it is to keep everything flat and smooth.

—Sea Holly Hooked Rugs

EMMA LOU'S HOOKED RUGS
8643 Hiawatha Rd.
Kansas City, MO 64114
(816) 444-1777

Offers: Original Heartland hooked rug designs on monk's cloth or burlap. Rug-hooking kits.
For Further Information: Catalog, $4.50.

JANE MCGOWN FLYNN, INC.
P.O. Box 1301
Sterling, MA 01564
(508) 365-7278

Offers: Over 300 rug-hooking designs—traditional, classic, others (on burlap or cotton). Hooks: Pearl K. McGown, pencil. Frames: Puritan, hoops. Cutters: Frazaer, Rigby. Supplies/aids: Binding, shears. Also offers Dorr wool backgrounds/swatches, colors by Maryanne, burlap (Scottish, primitive) and cotton, books, custom stamping on backing or odd/large sizes.
For Further Information: Catalog, "Designs to Dream On," $7.50.
Discounts: Allows discounts to teachers and institutions.

FORESTHEART STUDIO
21 South Carroll St.
Frederick, MD 21701
(301) 695-4815

Offers: Belgian linen backing fabric—by yard, 15-yard lot or bolt. Also offers rug wools, dyes, rug-hooking frames and cutters.
For Further Information: Send SASE for list.
Discounts: Quantity discounts.

FOX HOLLOW FIBERS
560 Milford Rd. S.
Earlysville, VA 22936

Offers: *Australian Locker Hooking—A New Approach to a Traditional Craft*, by Joan Z. Rough: Hooking unspun wool into machine-washable rugs, clothing and wall hangings; illustrated instructions, locker hook.
For Further Information: Send SASE for prices.

GINNY'S GEMS
5167 Robinhood Dr.
Willoughby, OH 44094
(216) 951-1311

Offers: Full line of patterns (burlap, monk's cloth) for hooked rugs: Navajo, other Indian and Southwestern designs (Kachinas, pottery, symbolic, others), Oriental and Eastern patterns. Dry dyes and dye formula books available.
For Further Information: Catalog, $4.
Discounts: Allows discounts to teachers and institutions; sells wholesale to legitimate businesses.

GLIMAKRA LOOMS 'N YARNS, INC.
1302 Scott St.
Petaluma, CA 94954
(707) 762-3362

Offers: Yarns, including rug warps in wools (Klippans Matt and Asbo Rya types), cotton rug warp (Bockens 12/6) and other weaving yarns. Also offers books on rug weaving, rag rug weaving, dyeing, color, others.
For Further Information: Send SASE for price list; CUM Rya catalog, $2.50.
Accepts: MasterCard, Visa
See Also: Lace Making and Spinning and Weaving

GREAT NORTHERN WEAVING
P.O. Box 361
Augusta, MI 49012
(616) 731-4487

Offers: Braid-Aid braiding tools, reel aid, Fraser cutters, palm looms. Yarns/threads: Linens, cottons, cotton rags (on coils), rug roping and filler cotton, fuzzy loopers, warps.
For Further Information: Catalog, $1.
Discounts: Quantity discounts.
Accepts: MasterCard, Visa

JACQUELINE DESIGNS
237 Pine Point Rd.
Scarborough, ME 04074
(207) 883-5403

Offers: Rug-hooking patterns in traditional and primitive designs (on cotton, homespun, linen, wool, burlap with pre-cut wool strips): Florals, fruits, pictorals, scenics, Christmas

motifs, others. Also offers bliss cutters, wool yardage, custom-dyed swatches, precut stripettes, frames (Puritan, hoops), others.
For Further Information: Catalog, $6.
Store Location: Yes
Discounts: Allows discounts to teachers and institutions; sells wholesale to legitimate businesses.

Sew the rug binding on first, then you can hook the outside border row really close to it. You shouldn't see any burlap when you turn the binding under.

—Sea Holly Hooked Rugs

MAJIC CARPET
205 Locke St. S.
Hamilton, Ontario L8P 4B5 Canada
(416) 522-8669

Offers: Rug hoops (hardwood), plus hooking supplies and patterns.
For Further Information: Pattern catalog, $5.

MANDY'S WOOL SHED
Rt. 1, P.O. Box 2644
Litchfield, ME 04350
(207) 582-5059

Offers: Wool fabric (for hooking, braiding, weaving): Tweeds, plaids, solids in pastels, white wool.
For Further Information: Samples set (100), $3.
Store Location: Yes
Discounts: Quantity discounts.

MAYFLOWER TEXTILE CO.
P.O. Box 329
Franklin, MA 02038

Offers: Puritan lap frame (to stretch rug, smooth onto frame sides, tighten; removable) and frame stand.
For Further Information: Order from dealer or teacher.

MILLER RUG HOOKING
2251 Ralston Rd.
Sacramento, CA 95821
(916) 925-8017

Offers: Traditional rug-hooking kits (with hand-dyed wool fabrics).
For Further Information: Color flyer, $4.

MISTY MOUNTAIN FIBER WORKSHOP
Rt. 1, P.O. Box 129
New Castle, VA 24127
(703) 544-7134, (800) 257-2907

Offers: Wool: Tahki, Plymouth, Dyed in the Wool, others. Also offers rug-hooking equipment, fibers, accessories and books, plus looms and spinning wheels.
For Further Information: Free catalog.

MORTON HOUSE PRIMITIVES
9860 Crestwood Terrace
Eden Prairie, MN 55347

Offers: Primitive rug-hooking designs, including those of Tish Murphy, others.
For Further Information: Catalog, $4.

PAT MOYER
308 W. Main St.
Terre Hill, PA 17581
(215) 445-6263

Offers: Rug-hooking (wool strips) kits/patterns on burlap: Traditionals—scenes and florals, abstracts, children's, geometrics, Indian/Southwest, others. Also offers kits/patterns for chair pads, rounds, hearthsidings. Dial-a-Harmony color wheels available.
For Further Information: Free brochure.

NEW EARTH DESIGNS
Beaver Rd.
Lagrangeville, NY 12540
(914) 223-2781

Offers: Rug-hooking designs (silkscreen printed) in Oriental, primitive and traditional motifs, with color photos.
For Further Information: Catalog, $6 (refundable).

JANE OLSON RUG STUDIO
5400 W. 119th St.
Inglewood, CA 90304
(310) 643-5902

Offers: Rug-hooking patterns (burlap or monk's cloth), McLain and Potpourri swatches, Cushing dyes, frames (Bliss, Puritan Lap, Pittsburgh Craftying) and hoops. Also offers Braid Klamp aid set and other aids, plus scissors, hooks, needles, cutters (Fraser, Bliss), linen, and other cords and books. Service: Custom dyeing.
For Further Information: Catalog, $3.
Discounts: Allows discounts to teachers and institutions; sells wholesale to legitimate businesses.

ORIENTAL RUG CO.
214 S. Central Ave.
Lima, OH 48501
(419) 225-6731

Offers: Rug-weaving supplies: Carpet warps, rug filters, rags, looper clips (by bales), others. Also offers Beam counters, loom parts, cutters, floor looms.

For Further Information: Free brochure and price list.
Discounts: Factory direct prices.

VIVILY POWERS
36 Fairview St.
Manchester, CT 06051

Offers: Wool swatches—5-value transitional and gradation types, plus swatchettes.
For Further Information: Descriptive list of 300 swatches, 50¢.
Discounts: Allows discounts to teachers.

Hold the hook in the direction you want the loops to go—keep loops even!

—Jacqueline Designs

R & R MACHINE CO., INC.
433 Duggins Rd.
Stoneville, NC 27048

Offers: Supplies for hooking and braiding, and shirred-wool fabric by the yard or pound, plus others. Also offers rug hooks, braiding sets, needles, rug cutter units, others.
For Further Information: Patterns and supplies catalog, $6.

RAFTER-FOUR DESIGNS
P.O. Box 40
Cocolalla, ID 83813

Offers: Folk art rag rugs (using traditional methods): Braided, Amish knot, Bohemian, patched, fabric tapestry, others (also knitted, crocheted, shirred).
For Further Information: Catalog, $2.

RED CLOVER RUGS
2 Mill St., Frog Hollow
Middlebury, VT 05753
(802) 388-0872, (800) 858-YARN

Offers: Red Clover rug patterns—over 100, for punch needle, hooking. Also offers hooking kits and over 360 colors of wool rug yarns.
For Further Information: Catalog, $3.

RIGBY
P.O. Box 158
Bridgton, ME 04009
(207) 647-5679

Offers: Cloth-stripping machines (4 models), cuts from ³⁄₃₂-inch wide—for braiding, weaving, hooking. Cutter regrinding service.
For Further Information: Free catalog.

Discounts: Allows discounts to teachers; sells wholesale to legitimate businesses.

RITTERMERE-HURST-FIELD
P.O. Box 59
King City, Ontario L0G 1K0 Canada

Offers: Rug-hooking designs: Wide array of traditional, classic and other designs, plus scenics, florals, animals, geometric motifs, many others. Also offers rug kits, rug hooks, wools, other supplies and aids and knitting kits.
For Further Information: 110-page catalog, $6.

ROCKY MOUNTAIN RUG CRAFTS
P.O. Box 2932
Durango, CO 81302
(303) 884-4192, (800) 331-5213

Offers: Line of rug-hooking and braiding supplies, Dorr and Woolrich wool, for primitive, folk art, Southwest and traditional designs.
For Further Information: Catalog, $4.
Accepts: MasterCard, Visa

THE RUGGING ROOM
10 Sawmill Dr.
Westford, MA 01886
(508) 692-8600

Offers: 200 plus rug hooking patterns, including pictorals, primitives, animals, geometrics, others. Service: Custom designing and repairs.
For Further Information: Catalog, $3.50.
Discounts: Quantity discounts; allows discounts to teachers, institutions and professionals; sells wholesale to legitimate businesses.

RUMPLESTILTSKIN'S
20360 NW Phillips Rd.
Hillsboro, OR 97124

Offers: Tuft-hooking needles (eggbeater type)—electric and hand models.
For Further Information: Send business-size SASE for information.

RUTH ANN'S WOOL
RD 4, P.O. Box 340
Muncy, PA 17756

Offers: Woolrich rug-hooking wool: Natural, white and 28 colors.
For Further Information: Information and color card, $2.
Discounts: Allows discounts to teachers.

Hooked loops should be as high as the strip is wide.

— DiFranza Designs

NANCY SAWYER'S RUG SHOP

32 Main St.
P.O. Box 611
Yarmouth, ME 04096

Offers: Remnant wool — seconds and discontinued patterns, plus hooking and braiding supplies.
For Further Information: Send SASE for price list.

SCOTT GROUP

5701 S. Division Ave.
Grand Rapids, MI 49548

Offers: Discounted rug yarns — wools (cones, skeins and by the pound). Full range of colors.
For Further Information: Send SASE with inquiry (send sample or requirements).

SEA HOLLY HOOKED RUGS

1906 M. Bayview Dr.
Kill Devil Hills, NC 27948
(919) 441-8961

Offers: Traditional rug-hooking kits/patterns. Wools: Hand-dyed by the yard or pound. Also offers hooks, rug shears, cutters, frames, burlap, rug binding, and other aids and supplies. Books are also available.
For Further Information: Send SASE for brochure.
Discounts: Allows discounts to teachers and institutions; sells wholesale to legitimate businesses.

SHILLCRAFT

8899 Kelso Dr.
Baltimore, MD 21221
(410) 682-3060

Offers: Latchhook kits (for rugs, pillows) — designs stenciled on canvas with precut wool or acrylic yarn (interchangeable colors available), traditional and contemporary motifs: Kamariah and Persian, florals, animals, Southwestern, children's, patriotic, inspirational, Christmas, others. Tools and aids, and Victorian lampshade kits, cross-stitch, and other needlecraft kits and yarns.
For Further Information: Catalog, $1.
Discounts: Sells wholesale to legitimate businesses.

SPINDLE HILL

3251 Main St.
Coventry, CT 06238
(203) 742-8934

Offers: Mill end hooking wools — random colors, by pound (5-pound minimum). Also offers hooked rug repair service (for clean rugs).
For Further Information: Send SASE for information.

SWEET BRIAR STUDIO

866 Main St.
Hope Valley, RI 02832
(401) 539-1009

Offers: Traditional and primitive supplies, custom designs and designer patterns.
For Further Information: Send for catalog.
Store Location: Yes

TRIPLE OVER DYE

187 Jane Dr.
Syracuse, NY 13219
(315) 468-2616

Offers: TOD dye formulas books (over 100 formulas per book) — *TOD Book I* and *TOD Book II* by Lydia Hicke, *TOD Book III* by Janet Matthews. Includes TOD snips (8 shade samples to put with each formula in TOD books).
For Further Information: Free brochure.
Discounts: Quantity discounts; allows discounts to teachers and institutions.

VERMONT RUGS

P.O. Box 485
Johnson, VT 05656
(802) 635-2434

Offers: Cotton denim strips with chenille edge, rug strips (blends) — by 25 pounds and up lots.
For Further Information: Send SASE and $1 for sample.
Discounts: Quantity discounts.

W. CUSHING & CO.

P.O. Box 351
Kennebunkport, ME 04046
(800) 626-7847

Offers: Rug-hooking swatches: Perfection, Jacobean, spot dyed, studio, plus Dorr background wools, plaids and tweeds. Lines of rug designs: Joan Moshimer, Frost, Edward Sands, Ruth Hall, Pearl K. McGown, others. Also offers known-brand frames, Cushing Perfection dyes, rug hooks and books.
For Further Information: Sampler, $3.

WHISPERING HILL FARM

Rt. 169, P.O. Box 186
South Woodstock, CT 06267

Offers: Rug-hooking supplies, including backing fabrics (primitive and fine burlap, linen), others.
For Further Information: Catalog, $2.75.

THE WOOL WINDER
Rt. 1
Manilla, Ontario K0M 2J0 Canada
(705) 786-1358

Offers: Line of rug-hooking and braiding supplies, including Canadian Woolrich and primitive wools.
For Further Information: Price lists, $1.

WOOL WORKS, PLUS
1246 Oak Ridge Dr.
South Bend, IN 46617
(219) 234-2587

Offers: Line of rug-hooking and braiding supplies and accessories.
For Further Information: Send for information.

YANKEE PEDDLER HOOKED RUGS
57 Saxonwood Rd.
Fairfield, CT 06430
(203) 255-5399

Offers: Rug-hooking wool by yard or pound, line of other supplies including hooks, frames, new designs for spot-dyed wools, others.
For Further Information: Catalog, $4; business-size SASE for flyer.

YESTERYEARS RUG HOOKING STUDIO
Rt. 1
Meaford, Ontario N0H 1Y0 Canada
(519) 538-2425

Offers: Ash hoops in three sizes, plus rug hooks and other supplies.
For Further Information: Send for information.
Store Location: Yes

Sewing

Also see other categories of Section II.

ABRAHAM'S SEWING NOTIONS
13104 Mason
Grant, MI 49327

Offers: Sewing notions, laces, ribbons, buttons, threads, others.
For Further Information: Catalog, 50¢.

ALL BRANDS
9789 Florida Blvd.
Baton Rouge, LA 70815
(504) 923-1285

Offers: Sewing machines, sergers and knitting machines: Elna, Viking, White, Necchi, Riccar, Brother, Simplicity, Singer; commercial brands—Johnson, Thompson, Singer, Juki, others. Monogrammers—Toyota, Brother, Melco, others. Also offers smocking pleaters, machine accessories, cabinets, tables, pressing equipment, warehouse locations.
For Further Information: Send SASE for list (specify interest).
Discounts: Has discounts.
Accepts: American Express, Discover, MasterCard, Visa

AMAZON DRYGOODS
2218 E. 11th St.
Davenport, IA 52803
(319) 322-6800

Offers: 19th Century-inspired products: Over 700 historic/ethnic clothes patterns, up to the 1950s, with emphasis on the 1800s: Men's and women's clothing including corsets, military uniforms. Supplies/aids: Hoop wire, boning, stays, feathers. Fabrics: Nainsook, batiste and other cottons, flannels, taffeta, satins, gold "boullion" frize, tradecloth. Also offers hat veilings, trims, military buttons and yard goods (blue, butternut, gray wool, etc.). Books available on costuming, fashions, accessories and lace making, Victorian and Indian clothing. Carries ready-made historic clothes, shoes, hats, accessories, plus washboards, buckets, washtubs, others.
For Further Information: Catalog, $2; pattern catalog, $4.
Accepts: American Express, MasterCard, Visa

AMERICAN & EFIRD, INC.
P.O. Box 507
Mount Holly, NC 28120
(704) 827-7556

Offers: Maxi-Lock polyester cone threads (for sergers and other sewing machines) in a full line of colors.
For Further Information: Contact your dealer, or send SASE for details.

AMICI CREATIVE ARTS
P.O. Box 163
Rio Vista, CA 94571
(707) 374-6548

Offers: Lingerie fabrics: Tricots, cotton knits, stretch lace, angel skin, lycra, others. Patterns: Swik Sew, Primary Patterns, others. Also offers laces, elastics, bra parts, iron-on transfers, Gingher scissors, books.
For Further Information: Catalog, $2.

ATLANTA THREAD & SUPPLY CO.
695 Red Oak Rd.
Stockbridge, GA 30281
(404) 389-9115

Offers: Sewing supplies/aids (some known brands): Cone threads, closures, markers, linings/pockets, interfacings, shoulder pads. Also offers pliers, measurers, dress forms, hampers, caddys, gauges, notions, pleaters, cords, weights, pressing aids (irons, machines, steamers). High-speed sewing machines: Tacsew, Singer, Pfaff, Consew. Racks: Counter, spiral, adjustable, garment, others. Also offers cutting machines.
For Further Information: Free catalogs.
Discounts: Quantity discounts.

BABY LOCK, SPA, INC.
P.O. Box 31715
Seattle, WA 98103
(206) 783-8087, (800) 422-2952

Offers: Line of Baby Lock sergers and overlockers.
For Further Information: Brochure.

BARBECK ENGLISH SMOCKING
1113 Caroline St.
Fredericksburg, VA 22401

Offers: Smocking/pleating machine, design patterns and books.
For Further Information: See your dealer, or send SASE for details.

THE BEE LEE CO.
P.O. Box 36108
Dallas, TX 75235

Offers: Sewing supplies: Threads, buttons, zippers, laces, trims, Western trims, snap fasteners (pearl, others).
For Further Information: Free catalog.

BERNINA
3500 Thayer Ct.
Aurora, IL 60504
(708) 978-2500

Offers: Bernina brand sewing machines and serger machines.
For Further Information: Send SASE for information.

To stabilize the grain and prevent sagging on circular skirts, use matching thread and straight stitch two rows in each quarter of circle.

— Fit For You

BERNINA SEWING CENTER
660 Denison St.
Markham, Ontario L3R 1C1 Canada

Offers: Bernina sewing machines and serger machines.
For Further Information: Send SASE for information.

BIRCH STREET CLOTHING
P.O. Box 6901
San Mateo, CA 94403

Offers: Pattern for children's travel pillow that converts to rest mat, plus patterns for children's clothing.
For Further Information: Catalog, $1.

A BUNCH OF BUTTONS
420 N. Main St.
Grapevine, TX 76051
(817) 488-0585

Offers: Ceramic buttons (handcrafted) in almost 300 original shapes, sizes, colors: Animals, vehicles, bows, hearts, cosmic, critters, teddies, babies, Western, fruit, holiday motifs, alphabets, classics, others. Service: Custom buttons (bisque, Lad molds).
For Further Information: Catalog, $2 and SASE.
Discounts: Quantity discounts.

THE BUTTON SHOP
7023 Roosevelt Rd.
Berwyn, IL 60402
(312) 795-1234

Offers: Sewing supplies: Line of zippers, bindings, interfacings. Threads: Mercerized, specialty, invisible, machine, carpet, metallics, including Swisse and others. Buttons: Usuals, military, decoratives. Also offers trims, elastics, tapes, cords, bra parts, pockets, ribbons, knit cuffs, measurers, closures, buckles, markers, notions. Carries old treadle and other sewing machine parts, plus new parts.
For Further Information: Free catalog.
Discounts: Sells wholesale; quantity discounts.

BUTTONS UNLIMITED
12819 SE 36th, #431
Bellevue, WA 98006

Offers: Line of buttons—classic and unusual designs, shapes, styles.
For Further Information: Catalog, $2 (refundable).

CALICO CUPBOARD
P.O. Box 245
Rumney, NH 03266
(800) 348-9567

Offers: Sewing kits (precut, ready-to-sew): Baby quilts, table runners, placemats, others.
For Further Information: Free catalog.

CATHERINE'S OF LEXINGTON
Rt. 6, P.O. Box 1227
Lexington, NC 27292
(704) 798-1595

Offers: Serger threads: Industrial polyester, polywrap, wooly nylon stretch, machine embroidery, lingerie nylon. Also offers cone thread racks, aids, stands, books. Service: Scissor sharpening.
For Further Information: Free catalog; with color cards, $2; SASE for information.
Discounts: Allows discounts to teachers and institutions.

CLOTILDE, INC.
1909 SW 1st Ave.
Fort Lauderdale, FL 33315
(305) 761-8655

Offers: Complete line of sewing supplies/tools/aids, including latest, unusuals, innovative: Gauges and templates, needles, threaders, markers, cutters, scissors, weights, tapes, glues, closures. Trims: Sequin appliqués, glass beads, ribbons. Threads: Cottons, metrosene, serger, stretch, cone, metallics. Aids: Craft drill, magnifiers, mini-vacuum kit, machine attachments, pressing aids. Handbag parts: Snaps,

chains, frames, plus patterns. Also offers interfacings, boning, bra cups and instructional videos by Clotiles.
For Further Information: Free catalog.
Discounts: Has discounts; sells wholesale to businesses.
Accepts: MasterCard, Visa

COATS & CLARK, INC.
30 Patewood Dr., #351
Greenville, SC 29615
(803) 234-0331

Offers: Sewing supplies/aids: Closures, threads, tapes, trims by J & P Coats, Anchor, Susan Bates (hooks/needles). Also offers embroidery hoops/frames, needlework accessories lines and Red Heart, Patons and Jaeger yarns.
For Further Information: Contact dealer, or free order form.
Discounts: Allows discounts to teachers and institutions; sells wholesale to legitimate businesses.

Serging machines do not like a 3-ply thread. Use only 2-ply, and preferably industrial thread used by large manufacturers.

—Catherine's of Lexington

CREANATIVITY
P.O. Box 335
Thiensville, WI 53092
(414) 242-5477

Offers: Nativity patterns/kit of soft figures: Holy Family, angel, kings, sheep, camel, donkey; starter set includes stable.
For Further Information: Send SASE for details.
Accepts: American Express, Discover, MasterCard, Visa

CSZ ENTERPRISES, INC.
1288 W. 11th Street, Suite 200
Tracy, CA 95376
(209) 832-4324

Offers: Dress forms and pants forms kits: Exactly duplicates body (make own or custom made). Also offers instructional videos and form stands.
For Further Information: Send SASE for information.

CUMMINGS
P.O. Box 133
Fair Oaks, CA 95628

Offers: Publications on writing and marketing pattern designs, selling original designs to magazines, others.
For Further Information: Send SASE for full details.

THE CUTTING EDGE
P.O. Box 430
Perryville, MO 63775
(314) 547-7562

Offers: Serger cone threads: Metallics, colors, wooly nylon, Sulky rayon, ribbon floss, synthetic ribbons, packs. Aids: Threader, totes, irons, neck lamps, others. Also offers cone stands, trees and serger books.
For Further Information: Send business-size SASE for brochure.
Discounts: Quantity discounts; allows discounts to teachers and institutions; sells wholesale to legitimate businesses.

DELECTABLE MOUNTAIN CLOTH
125 Main St.
Brattleboro, VT 05301

Offers: Buttons in a variety of sizes, styles, colors.
For Further Information: Send $1 and SASE for list.

DOGWOOD LANE
P.O. Box 145
Dugger, IN 47848
(800) 648-2213

Offers: Handmade porcelain buttons (folk shapes), classic clothing patterns, others.
For Further Information: Catalog, $2.50.

DRITZ CORP.
P.O. Box 5028
Spartanburg, SC 29304
(800) 845-4948

Offers: Dritz sewing aids: Cutting mats and rotary cutters, measuring devices, grommets/kits, rivets, snaps, tools. Other aids available include grippers, holders, seam hams, press items, weights, notions, metallic threads and thread sets, machine accessories, belt/buckle kits, line of scissors, shears and snips, line of elastics, trims, cords.
For Further Information: Contact dealer, or send SASE for information.

DURANGO BUTTON CO.
1021 C.R. 126
Hesperus, CO 81326

Offers: Line of Southwestern buttons—traditional to exotic: Silver, ceramic, rock art, gemstone, rare coins, cowboy, red brass types.
For Further Information: Catalog, $2 and SASE.

EASTMAN MACHINE CO.
779 Washington St.
Buffalo, NY 14203
(716) 856-2200

Offers: Chickadee professional electric rotary shears—cuts material to ½-inch thick. Manufacturer.
For Further Information: Send SASE for full details.

ELNA, INC.
7642 Washington Ave. S.
Eden Prairie, MN 55344
(612) 941-5519, (800) 848-ELNA (in the U.S.), (416) 856-1010 (in Canada)

Offers: Sewing machines, including budget-priced, others, plus machine accessories and attachments.
For Further Information: Contact dealer, or send SASE for full details.

VICTORIA FAYE
P.O. Box 640
Folsom, CA 95763
(916) 983-2321

Offers: Imported sewing supplies: French and English laces, Swiss embroideries, silk fabrics and ribbons, other ribbons. Also offers sewing kits and other trims, lace motifs, jabots and collars (Swiss, English, French), plus original design patterns for dolls, teddies.
For Further Information: Catalog, $5 (refundable); silk ribbon color guide, $2.50.
Accepts: MasterCard, Visa

Tweezers are a must for serger sewing. Keep yours handy at all times by hanging them on the thread carriage on your serger. No lost tweezers ever again!

—The Cutting Edge

FIT FOR YOU
781 Golden Prados
Diamond Bar, CA 91765
(909) 861-5021

Offers: Known-brand apparel patterns. Accessories/aids: Appliqués, tapes, bindings and other trims, cutters/mats, fusings, gauges, closures, Velcro. Also offers weights, notions, tables, markers, repair tools, threads (wooly nylon, cone types), knitted bands for appliqués, instructional videos (also for rent), square dance apparel patterns of 7 manufacturers, books and no-wind music boxes.
For Further Information: Catalogs, $1 (specify: Square Dance, Western), business-size SASE with specific inquiry.
See Also: Knitting and Crochet

SHERMANE FOUCHE
P.O. Box 410273
San Francisco, CA 94141

Offers: Designer pattern collection of women's jackets, trousers, others.

For Further Information: Send SASE for details.

GINSCO TRIMS
242 W. 38th St.
New York, NY 10018

Offers: Lines of sewing trims: Braids, tassels, fringe, cords, edgings, pearls, metallics, frogs, buttons, ruffles, crests, emblems, others.
For Further Information: Catalog, $5 (refundable).

GREENBERG & HAMMER, INC.
24 W. 57th St.
New York, NY 10019
(212) 246-2836

Offers: Fabrics, sewing notions, accessories and supplies for dressmakers, costumers, milliners, others. Also offers professional steamers.
For Further Information: Free catalog and swatchbook.
Store Location: Yes
Discounts: Sells wholesale.

HANCOCK FABRICS
3841 Hinkleville Rd.
Paducah, KY 42001
(800) 845-8723

Offers: Fabrics: Drapery, upholstery, quilting, dress/fashion, others. Line of quilting supplies.
For Further Information: Free catalog.
Store Location: Yes
Discounts: Sells wholesale; quantity discounts.

THE HANDS WORK
1585 Tennyson St.
Denver, CO 80204
(303) 534-4251

Offers: Handcrafted porcelain buttons: Animals, fruits, vehicles, geometrics, flowers, hearts, others.
For Further Information: Catalog, $2.
Discounts: Quantity discounts; sells wholesale to legitimate businesses.

HOME-SEW
P.O. Box 4099
Bethlehem, PA 18018
(215) 867-3833

Offers: Sewing supplies: Aids, ribbons, laces, threads, buttons, elastics, barrettes, web belting, poly boning, fringes, bindings, tapes, scissors, cutters, bridal appliqués, others.
For Further Information: Catalog, 50¢.
Discounts: Sells wholesale; quantity discounts.

ISLANDER—VIDEO DIVISION

P.O. Box 66
Grants Pass, OR 97526
(503) 479-3906, (800) 944-0213

Offers: Sewing instructional videos, by Margaret Islander: Industry shortcuts, shirt making, skirts, others—industrial techniques adapted to home sewing.
For Further Information: Send SASE for brochure.
Accepts: MasterCard, Visa

JUKI AMERICA

5 Haul Rd.
Wayne, NJ 07470
(201) 633-7200
or 3555 Lomita Blvd.
Torrance, CA 90505
(213) 325-5811

Offers: Juki Lock server, models for 1-, 2-, or 3- to 4-thread convertible overlock machines.
For Further Information: Contact a dealer, or send SASE for details.

J KULIL IMPORTS/EXPORTS

3423 Huntley Terrace
Crete, IL 60417

Offers: Mini-sewing machines, hand operated, cordless (rechargeable, battery operated).
For Further Information: Send SASE for details.

A quick way to dress up or to make unique a ready-to-wear blouse or denim shirt is to replace the plain buttons with unique buttons. You instantly have a fashion statement!

—The Hands Work

LIFE INDUSTRIES

205 Sweet Hollow Rd.
Old Bethpage, NY 11804
(516) 454-0055

Offers: Remay pattern cloth: Heavy-duty stabilizer sold by 6-yard lot.
For Further Information: Send SASE for details.
Accepts: MasterCard, Visa

LIFETIME CAREER SCHOOLS

101 Harrison
Archbald, PA 18403

Offers: Dressmaking home-study course—speed-up methods and factory shortcuts included—for home sewers and professionals.
For Further Information: Free booklet.

LIVE GUIDES

10306 64th Place W.
Mukilteo, WA 98275
(206) 353-0240

Offers: Generic serger instructional video—all aspects of serger sewing on nine models of sergers (purchase or rent).
For Further Information: Send SASE for full information.
Accepts: MasterCard, Visa

MAGIC MOUSE CREATIONS

126 Windmere Trail
Moneta, VA 24121

Offers: Sewing accessory patterns: Baskets, boxes, "ultimate pocket," others.
For Further Information: Catalog, $1.

MARY'S PRODUCTIONS

217 N. Main
P.O. Box 87
Aurora, MN 55705
(218) 229-2804

Offers: Sewing books: Appliqué, accents, sweatshirts, travel gear/gifts, others. Videos: *Designer Sweatshirts*. Also offers appliqué designs, thin squeakers.
For Further Information: Free brochure.
Discounts: Sells wholesale.

MELCO INDUSTRIES, INC.

1575 W. 124th Ave.
Denver, CO 80234
(800) 36-MELCO

Offers: Stellar 1 computerized embroidery system unit, to automatically embroider designs, lettering, monograms, others.
For Further Information: Send SASE for information.

NANCY'S NOTIONS

P.O. Box 683, Dept. 32
Beaver Dam, WI 53916
(414) 887-0391, (800) 833-0690

Offers: Sewing Aids/Notions: Scissors, cutters, measurers, third hand, weights, markers, papers, machine accessories, hoops, charted designs/kits, laces, appliqué press sheets and fusibles, interfacings, reflective tape/material, serger aids, rag rug items. Threads: Mettock, wooly nylon, rayon, metallics, Sulky rayon. Patterns: Quilted clothes, larger-women fashions (sizes 38 to 60). Video series, with Nancy Zieman—sewing, altering, tailoring, home decor, art, monogram, quilting techniques.
For Further Information: Free catalog.
Discounts: Allows discounts to teachers, institutions and professionals.

NATIONAL THREAD & SUPPLY CO.
695 Red Oak Rd.
Stockbridge, GA 30281
(800) 331-7600 ext. A202

Offers: Sewing threads—over 40 types, including Coats & Clark serging thread (in 250 colors). Also offers Wiss and Gingher scissors, Sussman irons, Dritz notions, others.
For Further Information: Free catalog.
Accepts: American Express, MasterCard, Visa

NATURAL FIBER FABRIC DIRECT
10490 Baur Blvd. SN 1093
St. Louis, MO 63132

Offers: Natural fashion fabrics (cotton, sateen, silks, wools, others), sewing and tailoring aids; members' savings.
For Further Information: Send SASE for brochure.

When pleating fabric, be sure to trim selvage edges. It's much easier on the pleater needles.

—The Smocking Bonnet

NEW HOME SEWING MACHINE CO.
171 Commerce Rd.
Carlstadt, NJ 07072
(201) 933-9026

Offers: My Lock sergers—electronically controlled: 1-needle/3-thread model with rolled hem capability; 2-needle/3- or 4-thread convertible, electronic speed controller.
For Further Information: Send SASE for information and nearest dealer.

PATCHOGUE SEWING MACHINE CENTER, INC.
75 E. Main St.
Patchogue, NY 11772
(516) 475-8282

Offers: Sewing machine parts, attachments, accessories for home/commercial models, hard-to-find items.
For Further Information: Catalog, $3 (refundable).
Store Location: Yes
Discounts: Allows discounts to teachers and institutions.

THE PERFECT NOTION
566 Hoyt St.
Darien, CT 06820

Offers: Sewing notions: Hard-to-find Sergers and accessories, electric and manual rotary cutters, irons and pressing aids, scissors, rulers, gauges, curves, skirt markers, bow-tie hardware, how-to books, others.
For Further Information: Catalog, $1.
Accepts: MasterCard, Visa

PFAFF AMERICAN SALES CORP.
610 Winter Ave.
Paramus, NJ 07652
(201) 262-7211

Offers: Pfaff brand sewing machines including electronic models. European manufactured.
For Further Information: See your dealer or write for information.

PROFESSIONAL SEWING SUPPLIES
P.O. Box 1427
Seattle, WA 98111

Offers: Sewing supplies: Chakoner markers, magnetic holder. Threads: Cotton basting, silk. Also offers Japanese shears, thimbles, interfacings, tapes, waist banding, third hands, cutter sets, notions.
For Further Information: Send 25¢ and SASE for catalog.
Discounts: Sells wholesale; quantity discounts.

PURCHASE FOR LESS
231 Floresta Way
Portola Valley, CA 94028

Offers: Books on quilting—appliqué, patchwork, foundation method, samplers, imagery, modular, traditional and contemporary, basics, advanced, shortcuts, others. Sewing subjects include clothing/quilting, serging, cutting, colors, couture, embroidery, other fiber arts.
For Further Information: Catalog, $2.
Discounts: Discounted throughout.

ROSEMARY'S SEWING SUPPLY
2299 Duncan Rd.
Midland, MI 48640
(517) 835-5388

Offers: 100% cotton flannel (by yard): Solids, prints, children's, double-napped, diaper. Also offers quilt bundles, patches, receiving blanket flannel, muslin, pellon. Threads: Cone and others. Carries aids, accessories, quilt batts, scissors, measuring tools.
For Further Information: Send SASE with 2 stamps for information.
Discounts: Quantity discounts.

SARAH'S SEWING SUPPLIES
7267-A Mobile Highway
Pensacola, FL 32526
(904) 944-2960

Offers: Sewing notions: Zippers, adjustable patterns, pins, needles, threads, aids, others.
For Further Information: Free catalog.

SEW/FIT CO.
5768 W. 77th St.
Burbank, IL 60459
(708) 458-5600

Offers: Sewing aids: Rotary cutting mats in two sizes.
For Further Information: Free catalog.
Discounts: Quantity discounts; allows discounts to teachers and institutions; sells wholesale to legitimate businesses.

SEWIN' IN VERMONT
84 Concord Ave.
St. Johnsbury, VT 05819
(802) 748-3803, (800) 451-5124

Offers: Singer brand sewing machines and sergers, irons, presses and accessories.
For Further Information: Free brochures.
Store Location: Yes

To determine the correct size of thread to use for garment construction, pull a thread from the fabric (the thread that goes across the fabric). Match the size of the fabric thread with the sewing machine thread.

—Things Japanese

SEWING MACHINE DISCOUNT SALES
5960 E. Florence
P.O. Box 2277
Bell Gardens, CA 90201
(213) 562-3438

Offers: Singer sewing machines, including school model (heavy-duty—for all fabrics/leather). Threads: Wooly nylon, Dual Duty, machine embroidery, polyester, cone types.
For Further Information: Send business-size SASE for catalog.
Discounts: Has discounts.
Accepts: MasterCard, Visa

SIERRA OAKS
2475 Fawn Hill
Auburn, CA 95603

Offers: Igloo pet bed patterns—3 sizes.
For Further Information: Send SASE for details.

SILKPAINT CORP.
18220 Waldron Dr.
P.O. Box 18
Waldron, MO 64092
(816) 891-7774

Offers: Fiber-Etch cellulose dissolving medium (removes plant fibers from between embroidery for "instant cutwork"). Also offers silk-painting items.

For Further Information: Free catalog.
Discounts: Allows discounts to teachers and institutions; sells wholesale to legitimate businesses.
See Also: Fabric Decorating

SINGER SEWING CENTER
1669 Texas Ave. S.
College Station, TX 77840

Offers: Singer, Necchi, Pfaff, Elna and other sewing machines, plus serger attachments. Sewing equipment: Flower stitch attachment, embroiderer's delight, spiral stitch attachment, automatic buttonholer (with 5 templates). Also offers Stitch'N'Trim overlock attachments.
For Further Information: Send SASE for list.
Accepts: American Express, Discover, MasterCard, Visa

THE SMOCKING BONNET
16012 Frederick Rd.
Lisbon, MD 21765
(800) 524-1678

Offers: English smocking/French hand sewing: Patterns, smock gathering machines. Fabrics: Broadcloth, batiste, others. Threads: DMC, Swiss-Metrosene. Also offers a variety of laces, other aids.
For Further Information: Catalog, $3.
Store Location: Yes
Discounts: Allows discounts to teachers and institutions; sells wholesale to legitimate businesses.

SOUTH SAVVY
P.O. Box 136
Apple Valley, CA 92307

Offers: Southwestern soft accessories patterns: Cactus varieties, cactus-shaped potholder/mitts, pillows, wreaths, others. Woodcraft plans for fabric appliqués also available.
For Further Information: Send SASE for list.

SPEED STITCH
3113-D Broadpoint Dr.
Punta Gorda, FL 33983
(813) 629-3199

Offers: Sewing threads: Sulky rayon, machine cottons, basting, metallics, wooly nylon, Metrocor, rayon ribbon floss. Patterns/kits: Pillows, vests, others. Patterns: Quilts, clothing, patchwork, others. Handbag items: Frames, clasps, snaps. Kits and books: Charted needlework, cutwork, quilting, others; fabric paints/dyes. Also offers battings, cutters, boards, hoops, stabilizers, machine attachments, magnifiers, and *Sewing With Nancy* videos.
For Further Information: Catalog, $3 (refundable).
Discounts: Quantity discounts; allows discounts to teachers, institutions and professionals.

SUBURBAN SEW 'N SWEEP, INC.
8814 Ogden Ave.
Brookfield, IL 60513
(708) 387-0500

Offers: Singer Sewing machines, pressers, others.
For Further Information: Call or write for models available.
Accepts: MasterCard, Visa

SURE-FIT DESIGNS
P.O. Box 5567
Eugene, OR 97405
(503) 344-0422

Offers: Personal fitting system, including starter package: Dress kit with master pattern, templates, book, designing stylus, tracing vellum, instructional video.
For Further Information: Send SASE for full details.

THINGS JAPANESE
9805 NE 116th St., Suite 7160
Kirkland, WA 98034
(206) 821-2287

Offers: Silk filament threads—full color shades and metallics.
For Further Information: Brochure and samples, $2.
Discounts: Allows discounts to teachers and institutions; sells wholesale to legitimate businesses.

THE THREAD BARE PATTERN CO.
P.O. Box 1484
Havelock, NC 28532
(800) 4-PATTERN

Offers: Line of sewing supplies.
For Further Information: Catalog, $2.

THREAD DISCOUNT SALES
10222 Paramount Blvd.
Downey, CA 90241
(310) 928-4029

Offers: Sewing machines: Sergers, standard—Singer, White models. Threads: Rayon, machine, serger, embroidery, overlock, wooly nylon, metallics. Also offers ironing presses, others.
For Further Information: Catalog, $2.
Store Location: Yes
Discounts: May run sales. Quantity discounts; allows discounts to teachers and institutions; sells wholesale to legitimate businesses.

TIMBERLINE SEWING KITS
Clark St., P.O. Box 126
Pittsfield, NH 03263

Offers: Sewing kits: Totes, garment and cargo bags, packs, bike bags, drawstring sacks, billfolds, wallets, accessory pouches, belts. Also offers comforter kits (4 bed sizes) and outerwear clothing kits (jackets, vests, others). Manufacturer.
For Further Information: Catalog, $1.
Discounts: May run sales. Allows discounts to teachers and institutions.

To keep a "designer" sweatshirt looking good, turn it inside out before laundering. This will protect the decorations and the outer fabric. Write a "care label" to give with each sweatshirt you decorate so the person who receives the shirt knows the best way to launder it.

—Mary's Productions

TREADLEART
25834 Narbonne Ave.
Lomita, CA 90717
(800) 327-4222

Offers: Sewing threads: Sulky rayon (35 variegated colors), DMC machine embroidery threads. Also offers sewing machine accessories: Walking foot (quilting). Carries fusible interfacings, stabilizers, needles, hoops, scissors, cutters, patterns, books.
For Further Information: Catalog, $1.50.
See Also: Publications

UNIQUELY YOU
112 Edwardia Dr.
Greensboro, NC 27409
or 2186 St. Catherine St. W.
Montreal, Quebec H3H 1M7 Canada

Offers: Uniquely You adjustable body form with zippered cover for easy-pin or basting onto unit; five basic sizes.
For Further Information: Inquire at dealers, or send SASE for information.
Accepts: MasterCard, Visa

VAN EPS
312 Willow Dr.
Little Silver, NJ 07739
(800) 382-5130

Offers: Swatch service (3 mailings per year) for couture fabrics (yearly fee), imported/domestic: Cottons, silks, linens, woolens. Also offers patterns, trims, others.
For Further Information: Send SASE for full details.
Store Location: Yes

VIKING SEWING MACHINE CO.
22760 Berea Rd.
Cleveland, OH 44111
(800) 358-0001

Offers: Viking Husqvarna sewing machines and other models.
For Further Information: Send SASE for information and nearest dealer.

WHITE SEWING MACHINE CO.
11750 Berea Rd.
Cleveland, OH 44111

Offers: Elna sewing machines.
For Further Information: See your dealer, or write for information.

WONDERFUL WORLD OF HATS
897 Wade Rd.
Siletz, OR 97380
(503) 444-2203

Offers: Millinery/hatmaking instructional videos and home-study courses: 15 study units covering all hat types (pillbox, helmet, gaucho, sailor, square, others), including designing, refurbishing, pattern drafting, construction, color, blocking and linings.
For Further Information: Catalog, $3.

A WORK OF HEART
P.O. Box 1355
Grass Valley, CA 95945

Offers: Chatelaine kits (ribbons, rings, sewing items, instructions) in a variety of color combinations. Sewing items: Seam rippers, Gingher embroidery scissors, needle case, stiletto, beeswax, others.
For Further Information: Send SASE for list.

YLI CORP.
45 W. 300 N.
Provo, UT 84601
(801) 377-3900

Offers: Threads: Wooly nylon serging, Candlelight metallic yarns (for serger, sewing machine bobbin, hand/machine knit, needlepoint, weaving, other).
For Further Information: Catalog and Candlelight color chart, $2.50.

Spinning and Weaving

Also see General Needlecraft Supplies, Knitting and Crochet, Lace Making, Rug Making, Yarns and other related categories.

AVL LOOMS
601 Orange St.
Chico, CA 95928
(916) 893-4915

Offers: Weaving looms: Baby Wolf portable, Baby Dobby to dobby loom. Also offers computer software for IBM, MAC and Apple II, plus weaving equipment/aids.
For Further Information: Catalog, $2.
Discounts: Quantity discounts; allows discounts to teachers and institutions; sells wholesale to legitimate businesses.

AYOTTES' DESIGNERY
Maple St., P.O. Box 287
Center Sandwich, NH 03227
(603) 284-6915

Offers: Home-study course in handweaving: Series of lessons—beginner to professional levels. Also offers yarn club membership and yarn sales: Cottons, wools, mohairs, linens, silks, novelties, close-outs reduced. Weaving looms and equipment also available.
For Further Information: Catalog, $1.
Store Location: Yes
Discounts: Quantity discounts.

BECK'S WARP 'N WEAVE
2815 34th St.
Lubbock, TX 79410
(806) 799-0151

Offers: Supplies/equipment/tools and looms for weaving, plus Ashford spinning wheels. Yarns: Cottons, wools, mill ends, others. Also offers supplies for lace making, basketry, silk/metallic embroidery, cross-stitch.
For Further Information: Catalog and yarn samples, $1.
Discounts: Quantity discounts on yarns.

CAROL LEIGH'S SPECIALTIES
7001 Hill Creek Rd.
Columbia, MO 65203
(314) 874-2233

Offers: Triangular frame looms: Adjustable, weaves six sizes per loom, includes loom stand and tools; U.S. made.

For Further Information: Send for information.

CASTLEGATE FARM
424 Kingwood-Locktown Rd.
Flemington, NJ 08822
(908) 996-6152

Offers: Romney fleece—greased and washed; plus handspun and millspun yarns.
For Further Information: Brochure, fleece samples, $2.50.
Store Location: Yes

COBUN CREEK FARM
Rt. 10, P.O. Box 15
Morgantown, WV 26505
(304) 292-1907

Offers: Coopworth wool fleece—colored, white.
For Further Information: Send 25¢ and SASE for wool sample.
Discounts: Quantity discounts.

COTTON CLOUDS
5176 S. 14th Ave. CS
Safford, AZ 85546
(602) 428-7000, (800) 322-7888

Offers: Cotton yarns, cotton spinning fibers, spinning wheels, looms, patterns, knitting machines, books.
For Further Information: Catalog and over 450 samples, $6.50 ($5 refundable).
Store Location: Yes
Discounts: Quantity discounts; sells wholesale to legitimate businesses.

COTTON CREEK CO.
218 Main St., #194
Kirkland, WA 98033

Offers: Yarns: Chenilles, textures, rayons, plus space-dyed yarns and cotton rug filler.
For Further Information: Samples and price list, $2.50.

COYOTE PINES RARE BREED
P.O. Box 487
Balgonie, Saskatchewan S0G 0E0 Canada
(306) 771-2797

Offers: Karakul roving, handspun, natural-colored yarns.
For Further Information: Sample kit, $3.

CREEK WATER WOOL WORKS
P.O. Box 716
Salem, OR 97308
(503) 585-3302

Offers: Weaving looms: Ashford, Cascade, Glimakra, Louet, Schacht. Spinning wheels: Ashford, Cascade, Clems & Clems, Country, Craftsman, Haldane, Lendrum, Louet, Redgates, Restoration Arts, Reeves, Peacock, Schacht. Custom handcrafted spinning wheels: Cascade, Fox, Joslin and Van Eaton. Accessories: Bench and hand carders, others. Also offers equipment/aids, dyes, additives and books.
For Further Information: Catalog, $3.
Discounts: Quantity discounts.
Accepts: MasterCard, Visa

CRYSTAL PALACE YARNS
3006 San Pablo Ave.
Berkeley, CA 94702
(510) 548-9988

Offers: Ashford spinning wheels and looms. Coned and balled yarns: Cottons, linens, rayons, wools, silk and silk blends, others. Japanese aids: Winders, swift, twister. Fibers: Wools (Romney, Merino, mohair, blends, camel, goat, silks), others. Also offers books.
For Further Information: Contact dealer, or send business-size SASE with inquiry.
Store Location: Yes
Discounts: Quantity discounts; sells wholesale to legitimate businesses and professionals.

When first learning how to spin, try using a drop spindle and some carded wool. This is a good, inexpensive introduction to the craft of yarn making. Then, when you have mastered the drop spindle, you will be ready for a spinning wheel. Spinning on a wheel is much faster and more relaxing.
— The Woolery

CURTIS FIBERS
Rt. 1, P.O. Box 15
Ritzville, WA 99169

Offers: Fibers for spinning, including hard-to-find types, popular domestic and imported yarns.
For Further Information: Free catalog; fiber samples, $3; yarn samples, $3.

CUSTOM COLORS
4743 Balsam St.
Las Vegas, NV 89108
(702) 645-4227

Offers: Yarns: Custom color cottons, blends (spinning), Pima cotton and silk, cotton/ramie and other cotton blends. Also offers cotton roving, silk batts (multicolor). Spinning

equipment: Schacht, Ashford, Roberta, Elec, plus spindles.
For Further Information: Samples, $5.
Discounts: Sells wholesale.
Accepts: MasterCard, Visa

CUSTOM HANDWEAVING
P.O. Box 477
Redondo Beach, CA 90277

Offers: Yarns and spinning fibers: Mohair, alpaca, cashmere, others.
For Further Information: Send $5 for samples.

CYREFCO
P.O. Box 2559
Menlo Park, CA 94026

Offers: Cyrefco weaving looms — counter balance, counter march looms; Pegasus dobby system — for Cyrefco, Glimakra and other looms.
For Further Information: Catalog, $2.

DAFT DAMES HANDCRAFTS
P.O. Box 148-B
Akron, NY 14001

Offers: Yarns, including pearl and mercerized cottons, cotton flake, silks, Shetland wool/polyesters and rayon chenille. Natural cotton warps.
For Further Information: Send 75¢ for each sample.

DORSET LOOMS
P.O. Box 520
Stillwater, NY 12170
(518) 664-3668

Offers: Dorset looms — crossbuck design, folding floor models.
For Further Information: Write or call for brochure.
Discounts: Sells wholesale.

DUNDAS LOOM CO.
P.O. Box 7522
Missoula, MT 59807
(406) 728-3050

Offers: Looms, including table models (4- 8- 12-harness types), tapestry looms. Also offers treadle stands, weaving accessories.
For Further Information: Brochure, $1.
Discounts: Sells wholesale.

EARTH GUILD
33 Haywood St.
Asheville, NC 28801

Offers: Spinning wheels: Country Craftsman, Reeves,

Louet, Schacht. Weaving looms: Rigid-Heddle, Tapestry, table, folding, floor (Schacht, Louet, Beka) and children's. Yarns: Warps, wefts—cotton, linen, Euroflax, Marysville, Ironstone, metallics, Maysville, Harrisville, Christopher, others. Dyes: Natural Procion, Lanaset acid wool. Also offers spinning wheel construction plans, wheel accessories, loom accessories/tools, fibers, netting/knotting, rug making and other crafts supplies. Books are also available.
For Further Information: Free catalog.
Store Location: Yes
Accepts: American Express, MasterCard, Visa
See Also: General Craft Supplies and Rug Making

EATON YARNS

P.O. Box 665
Tarrytown, NY 10591
(914) 631-1550

Offers: Finnish weaving yarns: Wools, cotton chenille, textured and others, plus seine twines. Also offers linens and linen warp.
For Further Information: Color cards, $1 each.
Discounts: Sells wholesale.

EDGEMONT YARN SERVICE, INC.

P.O. Box 205
Washington, KY 41096
(606) 759-7614

Offers: For weaving: Maysville carpet warp, fillers, yarns, including cottons, wools, plus rags, loopers, jazz strings. Weaving looms and loom parts: Schacht table, Lil Bea 2-harness and Orco models floor looms. Also offers loom parts.
For Further Information: Samples and prices, $3.
Store Location: Yes
Discounts: Quantity discounts; sells wholesale to legitimate businesses.

A Cotton Glossary:
1. *Carded Yarn*. Not combed. Carding machines straighten, clean and untangle the fibers before they are spun into yarn.
2. *Combed Yarn*. Yarns have been carded and combed, an advanced form of carding. Combing separates the long, choice, desirable fibers of the same length from short, immature, undesirable stock. Only the best grades of fiber may be combed. Combed yarns are always superior to carded.

—Cotton Clouds

THE EWE TREE

61 Geoppert Rd.
Peninsula, OH 44264
(216) 650-6777

Offers: Dyed-cotton loopers for weaving—15 colors and natural; minimum order 30 plus pounds.
For Further Information: Send SASE for samples.
Discounts: Production weaver program with volume discounts.

FAIRMOUNT FARM FLEECES

Fairmount Farm, Thomas Rd.
Rindge, NH 03461
(603) 899-5445

Offers: Fleece for spinning and weaving: Natural colors—white, cream, light/dark grays, browns, blacks. Also offers Finnsheep and Finnsheep Xs.
For Further Information: Send business-size SASE for information, samples.
Store Location: Yes

FIBER LOFT

Rt. 111, P.O. Box 327
Harvard, MA 01451

Offers: Weaving/spinning equipment by Leclerc, Schacht, Harrisville, Ashford, Louet. Natural fibers/blends: Alpaca wools, cottons, mohairs, rayons by Harrisville, Elite, Tahki, Plymouth, Crystal Palace, others. Exotics, fibers: Silks, angora, ribbon, cashmere, others.
For Further Information: Yarn samples, $3.50; fiber samples, $2.75.
Discounts: Quantity discounts; sells wholesale to businesses.

THE FIBER SHOP

Rt. 2, P.O. Box 290
Farmland, IN 47340
(317) 468-6134

Offers: Spinning/weaving equipment, including Charkha wheels, Gaywood dyes, knitting and crochet accessories. Fibers: Wools, blends, cottons, exotics, flax, others.
For Further Information: Free catalog.
Accepts: MasterCard, Visa

THE FIBER STUDIO

Foster Hill Rd., P.O. Box 637
Henniker, NH 03242
(603) 428-7830

Offers: Yarns: Novelties, Shetlands, rug wools, chenilles, cottons, silks, brushed mohair, perle cottons (3/2 to 5/2), Berbers wool, 10/6 rug linen, Tahki wools. Spinning fibers: New Zealand fleeces, yak, mohair, camel hair, alpaca, silk rovings, flax. Also offers weaving looms and spinning wheels, studio knitting machines, exotic wood buttons, mill ends and close-outs.
For Further Information: Catalog, $1; yarn samples, $4; fibers samples, $4.

FILOSE
P.O. Box 10598
Portland, OR 97210

Offers: Line of hand-dyed yarns.
For Further Information: Samples $10 (refundable); send SASE for information.

FIRESIDE FIBERARTS
625 Tyler St.
Port Townsend, WA 98368
(503) 385-7505

Offers: Weaving looms: Floor, tapestry and other types. Also offers weaving accessories, yarns, spinning supplies and equipment, basketry items and books.
For Further Information: Catalog, $2.

FLEECE & FROMAGE FARMS
Siam Rd.
Windham, NY 12496

Offers: Chemical-free yarns, Rambouillet raw fleece, and ready-to-spin roving and batting.
For Further Information: Samples, $1 (specify interest).

FLOCK OF MANY COLORS
2100 Swan Highway
Bigfork, MT 59911
(406) 837-4294

Offers: Montana wools: Raw, natural-colored fleece (black, grays, white), mohair—specializes in long fleeces.
For Further Information: Samples, $3.

FLUME FARM
18101 N. U.S. Highway 666
Cortez, CO 81321

Offers: Hand-picked Karakul and mohair fleeces (white and colors).
For Further Information: Send $2 for samples and prices.

FORT CRAILO YARNS CO.
Broadway & Wisner Ave., P.O. Box G
Newburgh, NY 12551
(914) 562-3623

Offers: Crailo handweaving yarns: Full line of wools (worsted, rya, spun and lite spun), cottons (8/1 to 8/6).
For Further Information: Samples and list, $2.
Store Location: Yes
Discounts: Quantity discounts.

FRICKE ENTERPRISES
8702 State Rd. 92
Granite Falls, WA 98252
(206) 691-5779

Offers: Wool carders—chain-drive drum carders, metal and wood frames, motorized and manual models, bench carders. Also offers third-hand attachment for manual carders, cotton and wool hand cards, batt picker, spinning wheels.
For Further Information: Send SASE for catalog.
Discounts: Sells wholesale to legitimate businesses.

GAYWOOD DYES
P.O. Box 88952
Seattle, WA 98138
(206) 395-0327

Offers: Australian spinning/weaving supplies. Offers dyes for wool, mohair, silk, fur, nylon and cashmere. Also offers Gaywood sliver in a variety of shades, covered Correidale wool fiber, nooramunga spinning wool (Merino cross).
For Further Information: Contact supplier, or send SASE for information.

GILMORE LOOMS
1032 N. Broadway Ave.
Stockton, CA 95205
(209) 463-1545

Offers: Handweaving looms: 4/8 harness types to 54-inch sizes, flat heddles. Also offers Little Gem 18-inch (4-harness) and 23-inch 8-harness looms for weaver chair use; folds, with back wheels. Inkle loom also available.
For Further Information: Free brochure.

Use your spinning wheel to ply leftover commercial yarns into unusual novelties.

—Straw into Gold

THE GLEANERS YARN BARN
P.O. Box 1191
Canton, GA 30114

Offers: Mill end yarns and threads in natural, synthetic and blends, in a variety of sizes and types.
For Further Information: Sample catalog and mailing list (1 year), $3.

GLIMAKRA LOOMS 'N YARNS, INC.
1304 Scott St.
Petaluma, CA, 94954
(707) 762-3362

Offers: Swedish weaving looms: Floor jack 4-harness, Swift Little Loom, tapestry/Gobelin model, AKTIV collapsible floor 8-harness model, space saver and therapeutic models. Also offers weaving frames, belt looms, loom accessories/aids, including umbrella swift, warping frames and mill, others. Yarns: Line of wools, cottons, linens, cottolins, Irish linen rug warp, others.

For Further Information: Catalog, $2.50; yarn samples (1,000), $15 (Canada, $20).

GOOD WOOD
Rt. 2, P.O. Box 447A-3
Bethel, VT 05032
(802) 234-5534

Offers: Heddle rigid-frame, 2-harness looms, 2 sizes.
For Further Information: Send for information.
Accepts: MasterCard, Visa

GREAT NORTHERN WEAVING
P.O. Box 361
Augusta, MI 49012

Offers: Rug-weaving supplies: Cotton rags on coils, 8/4 cotton warp, rug filler, loopers. Also offers weaving equipment, books and rug braiding supplies.
For Further Information: Catalog, $1.
Discounts: Quantity discounts.

HANDWEAVERS GUILD OF AMERICA
2402 University Ave. W., Suite 702
St. Paul, MN 55114
(612) 646-0802

Offers: Publications: Spinning wheel plans for Tyrolese model, spindle plans, directories, others. Beginner weaving video also available.
For Further Information: Send SASE for list.

GARY HARTMAN
175 Lawn Ave.
Hamilton, OH 45013

Offers: Loopers (natural, six colors dyed), by the pound; minimum 20 pounds.
For Further Information: Samples, $2.

HEIRLOOMS
Rt. 2, P.O. Box 239
Milton-Freewater, OR 97862

Offers: Pre-wound warp kits for wool scarves.
For Further Information: Send business-size SASE for brochure.

HERITAGE LOOMS
Rt. 6, P.O. Box 731
Alvin, TX 77511
(409) 925-4161

Offers: Looms: Table and inkle types. Also offers shuttles, weaving supplies and loom repair service.
For Further Information: Catalog, $1.

HUNT VALLEY CASHMERE
6747 White Stone Rd.
Baltimore, MD 21207

Offers: Cashmere fibers and yarns in a variety of shades.
For Further Information: Send business-size SASE for catalog.

16-harness computer-aided loom. Courtesy of J-Made Looms.

ICELANDIC WOOL
P.O. Box 53
Camden Wyoming, DE 19934
(800) 777-9665

Offers: Icelandic wool for spinning and weaving (also knitting and felt work).
For Further Information: Send for information.

IHANA BRUSHING SERVICE
6400 W. 99th St.
Overland Park, KS 66202

Offers: Professional brushing service for blankets, scarves, yardage, other woven woolens.
For Further Information: Send $1 for information.

IN SHEEP'S CLOTHING
24 Audubon Ave.
Providence, RI 02908

Offers: Home-grown angora, fiber and yarn — specify preference.
For Further Information: Free catalog; samples, $2.

J-MADE LOOMS
P.O. Box 452
Oregon City, OR 97045
(503) 631-3973

Offers: Standard and computer-aided weaving looms: Floor and table models (4, 8, 12 and 16 harnesses). Accessories and aids: Warp beam kits, shuttles, raddles, warping frame, heddles, reeds, loom parts, weaving tools, others.
For Further Information: Catalog, $3.
Store Location: Yes
Discounts: Quantity discounts; allows discounts to teachers and institutions; sells wholesale to legitimate businesses.

JAGGER SPUN
Water St.
P.O. Box 188
Springvale, ME 04083
(207) 324-4455

Offers: Coned wool yarns (worsted, Merino, ragg, heathers) and wool/silk blends for weaving and machine knitting.
For Further Information: Catalog, $6.
Discounts: Allows discounts to teachers and institutions; sells wholesale to legitimate businesses.

KESSENICH LOOMS
P.O. Box 156
Allegan, MI 49010
(616) 673-5204

Offers: Looms: four table models (10-inch to 25-inch) and four floor models (30-inch to 46-inch).
For Further Information: Brochure, $1.

KINGS VALLEY ANIMAL FAMILY
39968 Ward Rd.
Monmouth, OR 97361
(503) 929-2100

Offers: Fleece: Romney, all-natural colors and white.
For Further Information: Send SASE for fleece list; samples, $2 (refundable).

KNOTS & TREADLES
103 E. Pittsburgh St.
Delmont, PA 15626
(412) 468-4265

Offers: Video rental library—via UPS. Also offers weaving/spinning supplies and equipment, dyes, sheep motifs (on fabrics, ribbons, stickers, others), plus books.
For Further Information: Write for information.

LA LANA WOOLS
136 Paseo Norte
Taos, NM 87571
(505) 758-9631

Offers: Handspun yarns (plant-dyed and textured), carded blends, fleeces. Also offers Schacht equipment.
For Further Information: Sample card set, $15.

LAMBSPUN BULKY SAMPLE CLUB
140 W. Oak St.
Fort Collins, CO 80524
(303) 484-1998

Offers: Yarns and fibers by the pound: Cashmere, silk, alpaca, kid mohair, Merino, others.
For Further Information: Send $5 for six list mailings.
Discounts: Sells wholesale.

LIZARD HISS STUDIO
P.O. Box 20542
Sun Valley, NV 89433

Offers: Line of rug yarns—variety of plies, shades.
For Further Information: Send SASE for details.
Discounts: Has discounts.

Recipe for washing wool: 1 large box Ivory Snow (2 pounds), 1 quart denatured alcohol, 2 ounces eucalyptus oil. Mix together (do not use wood to mix it). Keep in a jar. When needed, drop a handful of the mix in hot water.

—The Wool Room

LOOM EXCHANGE
P.O. Box 9937
Seattle, WA 98109
(206) 782-6083

Offers: Used looms listings.
For Further Information: Publication, $1 and SASE ($4.50 in Canada).

LOUET SALES
P.O. Box 267
Ogdensburg, NY 13669
(613) 925-4502

Offers: Handweaving looms: Floor models, 4, 8 harness. Also offers extension sets, benches and spinning wheels.
For Further Information: Catalog and list of dealers, $1.

THE LUNATIC FRINGE
161 Ave. C
Apalachicola, FL 32320
(904) 653-8747

Offers: The tubular spectrum color gamp kit—brilliant colors by the ounce, pound or ton. (Also has handmade jewelry, including shuttle pendant.)
For Further Information: Send for information.

MACOMBER LOOMS
Beech Ridge Rd.
P.O. Box 186
York, ME 03909
(207) 363-2808

Offers: Macomber handweaving looms: Traditional Ad-A-Harness Looms and Ad-A-Cad/Cam Systems; also offers floor models and accessories.
For Further Information: Write or call for catalog.

THE MANNINGS
P.O. Box 687
East Berlin, PA 17316
(717) 624-2223

Offers: Weaving looms by Dorset, Leclerc, Galliger. Also offers spinning wheels, rug yarns in variety of plies, skeined wool for dyeing, dyes and books. Specialty yarns: Fawcett, CUM, Maypole, Lily, others.
For Further Information: Catalog, $1.

MAURICE BRASSARD ET FILS, INC.
1972 Simoneau, CP 4
Plessisville, Quebec G6L 2Y6 Canada

Offers: Weaving yarns: Cottons, polyester, orlon, linen, boucle, silk—all in several colors. Also offers Lamieux yarn (wool) and Nilus Leclerc looms.
For Further Information: Free price list; list with samples, $7.95.

MOUNTAIN LOOM CO.
P.O. Box 1107
Castle Rock, WA 98611
(800) 238-0296

Offers: Looms: 12-inch to 28-inch table models; 4-, 8- and 12-harness models. Also offers portable floor, tapestry and countermarch floor-style looms. Carries Maru Dai for Kumihimo, Roberta Electric spinner, Cottage Industry Machines by Ertoel, plus accessories and books.
For Further Information: Free catalog.
Accepts: MasterCard, Visa

THE MUSK OX CO.
512 Little Sleeping Child Rd.
Hamilton, MT 59840

Offers: Musk Ox Qiviut—golden fleece of the Arctic; raw clean fiber (minimal guardhair) in 4-ounce and up lots.
For Further Information: Samples, $3 (refundable) and SASE.

NORSK FJORD FIBER
Rt. 2, P.O. Box 152
Lexington, GA 30648
(706) 743-5120

Offers: Norwegian, Swedish supplies/yarns for spinning, knitting. Also offers felting supplies, plus fleece and rovings in a variety of animal shades.
For Further Information: Catalog, $1; sample cards: (1) Fleece and rovings, $3, (2) Spelsau yarns, $3.

NORTHWEST LOOMS
P.O. Box 1854
Ridgecrest, CA 93556
(619) 375-3179

Offers: Handweaving looms—table models including with open reed and open-top heddles, jack-type table looms, up to 16 harnesses.
For Further Information: Write for information.

NORWOOD LOOMS
P.O. Box 167
Fremont, MI 49412
(616) 924-3901

Offers: Weaving looms: Workshop, folding, floor models—4-, 8- and multiple-harness. Also offers loom benches, shuttles, warping boards, other equipment, plus quilting frames and hoops. Manufacturer.
For Further Information: Send SASE for brochure.
Discounts: Sells wholesale to legitimate businesses.

OCTAVIA'S JEWELS
P.O. Box 308
Gladwyne, PA 19035

Offers: Line of cotton yarns—10/2, 16/2, 20/2 and finger styles; variety of colors.
For Further Information: Send SASE for samples, information.

ORIENTAL RUG CO.
214 S. Central Ave.
Lima, OH 45801
(419) 225-6731

Offers: Rug-weaving loom—floor model, weaves 36 inches wide. Loom accessories: Beam counter, loom parts, rag cutter. Also offers carpet warps, rug fillers, rags, looper clips, prints.
For Further Information: Free brochure and price list.

For spinners, wash wool in very hot water with dish soap and washing soda, soak only a few minutes. Leave out soap if you want it "in-the-grease".

—Flock of Many Colors

PINE CREST ANGORA RANCH
P.O. Box 3867
Prescott, AZ 86302
(602) 776-0505

Offers: Mohair (long staple, no second cuts): Raw and hand scoured/carded, by the pound.
For Further Information: Send SASE for prices.

PINTLER SHEEPCAMP
530 Faucher
Moxee, WA 98936
(509) 453-0183

Offers: Roving: Romney, mohair, Lincoln and blends in white and natural shades, plus Lincoln silver fleeces.
For Further Information: Send business-size SASE for list.

THE RIVER FARM
Rt. 1, P.O. Box 471
Fulks Run, VA 22830
(800) USA-WOOL

Offers: Fleece—black, brown, gray, white Corriedale (skirted, sorted). Weaving looms and spinning wheels: Schacht, Ashford, Country Craftsman, Louet.
For Further Information: Catalog, $1.
Accepts: MasterCard, Visa

RIO GRANDE WEAVER'S SUPPLY
216 Pueblo Norte Rd.
Taos, NM 87571
(505) 758-0433, (800) 765-1272

Offers: Rio Grande weaving loom and spinning wheel. Rio Grande yarns: Hand-dyed wool rug/tapestry/apparel types. Also offers Glimakra and Schacht equipment, wool warp yarns, natural and synthetic dyes, fleeces (scoured, dyed, carded), plus videos and books.
For Further Information: Catalog, $1.
Store Location: Yes
Discounts: Quantity discounts.

SUZANNE RODDY—HANDWEAVER
1519 Memorial Dr.
Conroe, TX 77304
(409) 756-1719

Offers: Weaving and spinning equipment. Looms: Glimakra, Harrisville, Kyra, Louet, Tools of the Trade. Spinning wheels: Ashford, Clemes & Clemes, Haldane, Lendrum, Louet, Peacock, Tennessee Great Wheel. Looms and wheels accessories also available.
For Further Information: Catalog, $3; free price list.
Discounts: Has discounts.

ST. PETER WOOLEN MILL
101 W. Broadway
St. Peter, MN 56082
(507) 931-3734

Offers: Wool batting, wool roving, alpaca roving, curly mo-
hair. Service: Custom scouring and carding of new and used wool.
For Further Information: Free brochure.
Store Location: Yes
Discounts: Quantity discounts; allows discounts to teachers and institutions; sells wholesale to legitimate businesses.

SCANDINAVIAN DESIGNS
607 E. Cooper St.
Aspen, CO 81611

Offers: Prism mohair yarn dyed in five values; mohair cones (15 colors).
For Further Information: Dye color cards, $5.

SCARBROUGH
125 Moraine
P.O. Box 1727
Estes Park, CO 80517
(303) 586-9332

Offers: Equipment: Schacht, Ashford, Louet, Lendrum, Jensen, Norwood, Cranbrook, Harrisville, AVL, LeClerc, Clemes. Also offers natural dyestuffs, Meck wool combs, accessories, spinner's sample pack, plus instructional videos and books.
For Further Information: Fiber samples, $3.50; catalog, $2.50.
Accepts: MasterCard, Visa

LOIS SCARBROUGH
125-B Moraine
P.O. Box 1727
Estes Park, CO 80517
(303) 586-9332

Offers: Looms and wheels: Schacht, Harrisville, Louet, Norwood, Cranbrook, AVL, LeClerc, Ashford, Glimakra, Dundas, Jensen, Friendly, Inkle, rigid heddle, cardweaving, tapestry, Navajo and 4-harness styles. Harrisville yarns, kits, supplies and folkwear patterns also available.
For Further Information: Catalog, $5.
Accepts: American Express, Discover, MasterCard, Visa

SCHACHT SPINDLE CO., INC.
6101 Ben Place
Boulder, CO 80301

Offers: Spinning wheels: For fine/medium weight yarns. Weaving looms: Floor models, table, tapestry and rigid-heddle type table models, plus inkle looms. Accessories and tools: Winders, shuttles, beaters, heddles, spindles, umbrella swift, others.
For Further Information: See your spinning supply shop; catalog, $2.

SCHOOLHOUSE YARNS
25495 SE Hoffmeister Rd.
Boring, OR 97009
(503) 658-3470

Offers: Finnish weaving yarns: Wool blanket type and other wools, worsted, plus linens and linen warp, cotton chenille, seine twines and cotton Pilvi. Also offers cotton bias strips, and Toika looms and loom equipment.
For Further Information: Toika catalog, $2; sample cards, 1¢ each.

Use your washing machine to spin out water in your wool.
—Cobun Creek Farm

SHANNOCK TAPESTRY LOOMS
10402 NW 11th Ave.
Vancouver, WA 98685
(206) 573-7264

Offers: Shannock tapestry looms—high-tension, heavy-duty, professional type, with roller beams and weaving accessories.
For Further Information: Write for information.

SILK CITY FIBERS
155 Oxford St.
Paterson, NJ 07522
(201) 942-1100

Offers: Cone yarns (color coordinated, over 1,000 shades) including Contessa, Avanti, Majesty, Chenille, Katrinka, Slinky, Soie Rustique. Also offers cottons: Stonewash, lace, perle, stripe, fancy, others. Carries Metallique, Prima Donna, English wool, Montego, others.
For Further Information: Send business-size SASE for introductory material.

THE SILK TREE
1551 Johnston Street, #15
Vancouver, British Columbia V6H 3R9 Canada
(604) 687-7455

Offers: Line of silk yarns and fibers.
For Further Information: Samples, $5.

SILVER CLOUD FARM
1690 Butler Creek Rd.
Ashland, OR 97520
(503) 482-5901

Offers: Romney sheep and Angora goat fleeces for hand-spinning.
For Further Information: Send SASE for prices.

SPIN 'N WEAVE
2927 E. Grant Rd.
Tucson, AZ 85716
(602) 321-0588

Offers: Supplies, fibers and yarns for weaving, spinning, dyeing (also crochet and basketry).
For Further Information: Send 98¢ stamps for new yarn samples.

STEEL HEDDLE
P.O. Box 546
Greenville, GA 30222
(404) 672-4238

Offers: Reeds: Steel Heddle brand, in standard and pattern reeds. Also offers custom-made reeds.
For Further Information: Send for order information/prices.
Discounts: Sells wholesale.

STRAW INTO GOLD
3006 San Pablo Ave.
Berkeley, CA 94702
(510) 548-5241

Offers: Ashford spinning wheels, plus yarns by Crystal Palace, Chanteline and Villawool. Also offers coned yarns, wheel accessories, knitting needles and books.
For Further Information: Send SASE (52¢ postage) for lists.
Store Location: Yes
Discounts: Quantity discounts.
See Also: Batik and Dyeing

TREENWAY CRAFTS LTD.
725 Caledonia Ave.
Victoria, British Columbia V8T 1E4 Canada
(604) 383-1661

Offers: Spinning wheels by Ashford and others. Also offers weaving and spinning accessories, yarns, including Silk Merchant silks.
For Further Information: Samples and price list, $3; catalog, $3.

VICTORIAN VIDEO PRODUCTIONS
P.O. Box 1540
Colfax, CA 95713
(916) 346-6184

Offers: Instructional weaving videos: Factual, techniques—tapestry, beginner harness, cut Pilr rug, card, weave drafting, rigid heddle, others. Also offers tapes on hand spinning fundamentals, dyeing, other needlecrafts and basketry.
For Further Information: Free catalog.
Discounts: Sells wholesale to legitimate businesses.
Accepts: MasterCard, Visa

When winding, always form yarn on straight sided tubes. Place the yarn on holders so that the yarn will unwind from the tubes in a clockwise direction. This avoids additional twisting and kinking of the yarn.

— Ayottes' Designery

THE VILLAGE WEAVER
5609 Chaucer
Houston, TX 77005
(713) 521-0577

Offers: Weaving and spinning equipment: Norwood, Schacht, LeClerc, Cranbrook, Glimakra, Harrisville, Ashford, Louet, Brother. Also offers weaving and spinning accessories and machine knitting equipment.
For Further Information: Catalog, $2 (with classes information).

VRESEIS LTD.
P.O. Box 3892
Santa Susana, CA 93093

Offers: Cotton yarns, sliver and fabrics — naturally colored.
For Further Information: Samples, $8.

THE WEAVER-ARTISANS OUTLET
Clarion St., P.O. Box 80
Smicksburg, PA 16256
(814) 257-8891

Offers: Sock loopers for rug weaving — natural, 50 dyed colors.
For Further Information: Color card, $5.
Discounts: Sells wholesale.

WEAVER'S CABIN
20578 317th St.
Avon, MN 56310
(612) 845-7115

Offers: Weaving products by Schacht, Harrisville, Norwood, Louet, Glimakra. Yarns: Pearl cottons, linen/cotton rug warp, mohair, silk, alpaca, others. Dyes: Gaywool, Procion.
For Further Information: Catalog, $2; catalog and yarn samples, $5.

THE WEAVER'S LOFT
308 S. Pennsylvania Ave.
Centre Hall, PA 16828
(814) 364-1433

Offers: Weaving and spinning supplies and yarns.
For Further Information: Free catalog; sample set, $8 (refundable).
Discounts: Has discounts.
See Also: Knitting and Crochet

WEAVER'S SHED
1616 Mabry St.
Tallahassee, FL 32310

Offers: Bulky handspun (for weaving, basketry), variegated Norwegian Spelsau yarns, others.
For Further Information: Price list and samples, $1.

THE WEAVER'S SHOP & YARN CO.
39 Courtland
P.O. Box 457
Rockford, MI 49341
(616) 866-9529

Offers: Weaving looms: Glimakra, Schacht, LeClerc, Norwood, Cranbrook, Harrisville.
For Further Information: Catalog, $3.

THE WEAVING & KNITTING SHOP
3173 Walnut St.
Boulder, CO 80301
(300) 443-5545

Offers: Weaving looms: Schacht, Glimakra, Harrisville, Norwood, Cranbrook, Louet. Also offers spinning equipment, yarns, and knitting and basketry supplies. Service: Custom weaving.
For Further Information: Free catalog; yarn sample packet, $9.50.
Store Location: Yes
Discounts: Quantity discounts; allows discounts to institutions.

THE WEAVING EDGE
3350 British Woods Dr.
Roanoke, VA 24019
(703) 992-3536

Offers: Fibers for spinning and felt making — acid-dyed Romney fleece (wide range of colors grouped by season).
For Further Information: Send SASE and $2 for each sample.

THE WEAVING STUDIO
1409 E. Davenport St.
Iowa City, IA 52245

Offers: Weaving looms, spinning supplies, yarns, fibers, books.
For Further Information: Send SASE.
Discounts: Allows discounts to teachers and institutions.

WEAVING WORKS
4717 Brooklyn Ave. NE
Seattle, WA 98105
(206) 524-1221

Offers: Weaving looms, spinning wheels and accessories, plus traditional and fashion yarns in a variety of fiber types. Also offers dyes, books, basketry supplies, and hand and machine knitting supplies.
For Further Information: Catalog, $1 (refundable).

WEBS

Service Center Rd.
P.O. Box 147
Northampton, MA 01061
(413) 584-2225

Offers: Yarns. Cottons: Berroco, Berkshirt, Hampshire. Also offers knitting types, wools and wool blends (worsteds) in webs and standard brands, mill ends and close-outs. Books also available.
For Further Information: Samples, $2.
Store Location: Yes
Discounts: Quantity discounts; allows discounts to institutions.

THE WOOL ROOM

Joe's Hill Rd.
Brewster, NY 10509
(914) 279-7627

Offers: Weaving/spinning looms: Schacht, Harrisville, Norwood/Cranbook, Wolf. Spinning wheels: Sickinger (Australia), Maja (New Zealand), Schacht, Indian Charka, Jensen, Reeves, Louet, Country Craftsman, Curry Great Wheel. Yarns: Manos, Euroflex, Crystal Palace, Harrisville. Mohair fibers: Corriedale, Shetland, Jacob. Also offers dyed Gaywool sliver, tops (mohair, cottons, ramie, wools, linens, others), loom accessories, dyes.

For Further Information: Catalog, $1; send SASE for information (specify interest).

THE WOOLERY

Rt. 1
Genoa, NY 13071
(315) 497-1542

Offers: Weaving looms: Glimakra, Harrisville, LeClerc, Schacht, Norwood/Cranbrook. Also offers accessories, spinning wheels, hand-spinning equipment and supplies, dyes, Fingerlakes yarns (wools/blends), kits. Services: Scouring, picking and blending of scoured wool, carding, spinning.
For Further Information: Catalog, $2.
Store Location: Yes
Discounts: Sells wholesale to legitimate businesses.

WOVEN DREAMS

P.O. Box 6934
Los Osos, CA 93412
(805) 528-8806

Offers: Weaving looms and wheels, plus yarns by Crystal Palace, Harrisville Designs, Ashford, Wilde Yarn, Schacht, Classic Elite.
For Further Information: Send SASE for details.

YOLO WOOL PRODUCTS

41501 County Rd. 27
Woodland, CA 95776
(916) 666-1473

Offers: Sliver for spinning, weaving yarns, plus wool batting and knitting yarns.
For Further Information: Flyers, samples, $2.
Discounts: Quantity discounts; sells wholesale to legitimate businesses.

Yarns—Multipurpose

Also see General Needlecraft Supplies, Knitting and Crochet, Spinning and Weaving and other related categories.

ALLEGRO YARNS
3535 Pierce St. NE
Minneapolis, MN 55418

Offers: Swiss and Swedish wool yarns. Brand name yarns: Berocco, Bryspun, Cascade, Jaeger, Patons, Wendy, Renaissance Hayfield, Jaeger.
For Further Information: Samples, $1.

BLACK SHEEP WOOLS
P.O. Box 9205
Lowell, MA 01853
(508) 937-0320

Offers: Line of natural-fiber yarns.
For Further Information: Samples, $3.
Store Location: Yes
Discounts: Has discounts.

BROADWAY YARN CO.
P.O. Box 1467
Sanford, NC 27331

Offers: Yarns for weaving, crochet, knitting, macrame: Poly/cottons, nylon, wools and blends, polyester. Also offers loom selvage, others.
For Further Information: Swatch cards, $3 (refundable).
Discounts: Sells wholesale.

CREATIVE YARNS
9 Swann St.
Asheville, NC 28803
(704) 274-7769

Offers: Knitting yarns: Towan, Plymouth, Tahki, Brown Sheep. Also offers handpainted needlepoint canvas, silks, Paternaya, metallics.
For Further Information: Catalog, $3.50.
Accepts: MasterCard, Visa

CUSTOM KNITS & MANUFACTURING
Rt. 1
Lake Park, MN 56554
(218) 238-5882

Offers: Line of Nomis yarns–full range of colors, cones.

For Further Information: Color cards, $2.

DAVIDSON'S OLD MILL YARNS
P.O. Box 8
Eaton Rapids, MI 48827
(505) 388-5408

Offers: Mill end yarns: Variety of types and colors.
For Further Information: Send 4 SASE for quarterly samples.

FIESTA YARNS
P.O. Box 2548
Corrales, NM 87048
(505) 897-4485

Offers: Hand-dyed yarns—mohair, rayon, cotton, silk, wools—in a variety of plies, colors, textures.
For Further Information: Color cards, $6.

FINGERLAKES YARNS
Stewarts' Corners
Genoa, NY 13071
(800) 441-9665

Offers: Yarns: Soft wools and angoras in 29 colors. Un-Spun yarns also available.
For Further Information: Samples, $3.
Discounts: Sells wholesale.

THE GLEANERS YARN BARN
P.O. Box 1191
Canton, GA 30114
(404) 479-5083

Offers: First-quality mill end yarns: Cottons, rayons and blends, cotton/nylon, acrylics, wools, polyesters, orlon, lyrux, angora blends, wool rug, boucle and novelty types. Available by the pound.
For Further Information: Current samples (year's mailing), $3.
Store Location: Yes
Discounts: Quantity discounts.

MARTHA HALL
462 Main St.
Yarmouth, ME 04096
(207) 846-9746

Offers: Hand-dyed yarns: Mohair, silks, linens, cottons, cashmere, alpaca, natural Maine wools. Also ribbons, totes, baskets and books.

For Further Information: Catalog, $2; yarn sample set (230), $12.

JAMIE HARMON
RD 2, P.O. Box 170-150 R
Richmond, VT 05477

Offers: Handspun and naturally dyed wool yarn, worsted weights, others. Also offers Rainbow Ridge children's sweater kits.
For Further Information: Samples and brochure, $4.

MARR HAVEN
772 39th St.
Allegan, MI 49010

Offers: Soft American yarn (Rambouilet) by skeins or cones—natural shades.
For Further Information: Free brochure.

If you have a textile that is hard and you would like to soften it, rinse it in creme rinse.

—The Gleaners Yarn Barn

DEBBIE HAZY
607 Seabrook Dr.
Indiana, PA 15701
(412) 349-4899

Offers: Knit roping yarn for placemats, rug weft or braiding.
For Further Information: Sample pack, $2.
Discounts: Has discounts.

HUMMINGBIRD FIBERS
1227 Valerian Ct.
Sunnyvale, CA 94086

Offers: Yarns for knitting and weaving—cottons, rayons, synthetics—allergy-free types.
For Further Information: Samples, $6 (refundable).

THE KNITTIN' KITTEN
P.O. Box 1330
Cedar Ridge, CA 95924

Offers: Soft yarns for cabled hoods and scarves.
For Further Information: Pictures and samples, $2.

OGIER TRADING CO.
410 Nevada Ave.
P.O. Box 686
Moss Beach, CA 94038
(415) 728-9216

Offers: Line of imported fashion and novelty yarns—variety of weights, colors, styles.
For Further Information: Color card subscription, $8 (refundable).

ON THE INCA TRAIL
P.O. Box 1861
Taos, NM 87571

Offers: Bolivian alpaca yarns in fine, sport, worsted and bulky (spun to specification), colors and naturals.
For Further Information: Send SASE for order information.

JOHN PERKINS INDUSTRIES, INC.
P.O. Box 8372
Greenville, SC 29604
(803) 277-4240

Offers: Hand and machine yarns: Single, plied, novelty, fancy, natural, colors, bleached, variegated, on cones, cakes, dyetubes. Also offers specialty yarns, ultra fancy, special assortments by pound-up.
For Further Information: Send SASE for list.

QUALITY YARNS
570 Westbank Rd.
Glenwood Springs, CO 81601
(800) 845-YARN

Offers: Variety of yarns including wools, cottons, linens, metallics, silks.
For Further Information: 64 sample cards, $20; selected samples, $5.

F. RYAN
2215 Louise Lane
Norman, OK 73071
(405) 360-0140

Offers: New England wool and mohair sport and worsted yarns.
For Further Information: Color samples, $5 (refundable).
Discounts: Has discounts.

STONE FOX FIBRE WORKS
1544 East River Rd.
Grafton, WI 53024

Offers: Natural fiber handspun yarns: Llama, alpaca, wool, silk, angora, mohair.
For Further Information: Samples and price list, $3 (refundable).

SWEATERS, ETC.
943 Kensington Ave. SW
Grand Rapids, MI 49503

Offers: Handspun yarns and natural fibers—natural and dyed colors.
For Further Information: Send SASE for price list; sample cards, $3.

TE AWA WOOLS

P.O. Box 5236
Fullerton, CA 92635

Offers: New Zealand wool yarns, soft, natural and heather colors (for knitting, crochet, weaving).
For Further Information: Send SASE for brochure.

THE UNIQUE

11 E. Bijou St.
Colorado Springs, CO 80903

Offers: Line of Rauma yarns; close-out yarns.
For Further Information: Color cards, $3.50 each.

WEAVER'S WAY

P.O. Box 70
Columbus, NC 28722

Offers: Brand name yarns—Mercerized/Perle, natural and novelty cotton yarns, wools. Also offers weaving equipment.
For Further Information: Catalog, sample cards set, $3 (cash).

WILDE YARNS

3737 Main St.
P.O. Box 4662
Philadelphia, PA 19127
(215) 482-8800

Offers: Yarns, including wools in naturals, white, Berber, dyed Berber, 3-ply, 2-ply warp/weft, bulky, clothing—undyed naturals, novelties, carded.
For Further Information: Sample pack, $6.
Store Location: Yes
Discounts: Allows discounts to teachers and institutions; sells wholesale to legitimate businesses.

YARN BARN

918 Massachusetts St.
Lawrence, KS 66044
(913) 842-4333

Offers: Weaving and knitting yarns, and weaving and spinning equipment, dyes and books.
For Further Information: Catalog, $1.
Store Location: Yes
Discounts: Quantity discounts.

THE YARN BASKET

5114 Top Seed Ct.
Charlotte, NC 28226

Offers: Full line of types, color shades and plies of natural yarns for weaving and knitting.
For Further Information: Sample card and prices, $5 (refundable).

YARN COUNTRY

P.O. Box 6500
Concord, CA 94524

Offers: Yarns: Brunswick, Reynolds, Pingouin, DMC, Patons, others in wools, blends, cottons, rayon, acrylic. Also offers accessories, cross-stitch and canvas items.
For Further Information: Catalog, $3; 400 samples, $8.
Accepts: MasterCard, Visa

Resources

Associations

Also see General Craft Supplies and Publications. Include a business-size, stamped, self-addressed envelope with inquiries to associations.

ACADEMY OF MODEL AERONAUTICS
1810 Samuel Morse Dr.
Reston, VA 22090

Offers: This Model Aviation association provides members with a *Competition Newsletter*, *AMA News* and *Model Aviation Magazine*, and the opportunity to get liability insurance coverage for accidents arising from the operation of model aircraft, cars and boats. The association endorses and encourages a safety code among members regarding the flying of model aircraft. Members have access to the AMA Museum. Membership begins every January 1st.
For Further Information: Send SASE for full information.

AMERICAN CRAFT COUNCIL
40 W. 53rd St.
New York, NY 10019

Offers: This association promotes excellence and education in all arts and crafts—textiles, needlecrafts, sculpture, pottery and many others. Their magazine, *American Craft*, reflects this emphasis.
For Further Information: Send SASE for full information.

AMERICAN QUILTER'S SOCIETY
P.O. Box 3290
Paducah, KY 42002

Members of this society of professional and amateur quilters join to carry on this American tradition. They receive *American Quilter* magazine 4 times yearly, the *Update* bimonthly newsletter, admission to the Annual National Quilt Show (that awards over $40,000 in cash prizes), receive member discounts of up to 20% on books and other resources, and participate in the Quilts for Sale program service (for members who wish to show their quilts for sale in a quarterly publication). They also share experiences, ideas and advice with other members nationwide.

AMERICAN SOCIETY OF ARTISTS, INC.
P.O. Box 1326
Palatine, IL 60078

This is a professional service organization for artists and artisans; membership is juried—inquiries should include 4 slides of work. Members receive group insurance and product discounts, and *A.S.A. Artisan* and art/craft fair bulletins.

AMERICAN SOCIETY OF GEMCUTTERS
P.O. Box 9852
Washington, DC 20016

Members of this association receive *American Gemcutter* magazine monthly, plus gem cutting evaluations and instructions with regional and national awards for excellence. Also offers marketing assistance through participation in a national marketing plan to sell cut stones. Offers other educational and supplemental services, design library supplements, access to the Gemcutters National Library, others.

ASSOCIATION OF TRADITIONAL HOOKING ARTISTS
50 Cape Florida Dr.
Key Biscayne, FL 33149

This rug-hooking association of guilds (ATHA) has a publication issued bimonthly—with news, views, tips and techniques on the craft.

COTTAGE INDUSTRY MINIATURES TRADE ASSOCIATION
1376 Mary Lee Way
San Jose, CA 95118

This is an association for those in the handcrafting miniatures business.

DOLL MAKERS ASSOCIATION
6408 Glendale St.
Metairie, LA 70003

This is a nonprofit doll-maker's organization devoted to fostering the art and sharing knowledge to aid beginners; holds yearly conventions. Instructors teach all aspects of the craft: Mold making, French handsewing, wig making, others.

GREETING CARD ASSOCIATION
1350 New York Ave. NW, Suite 615
Washington, DC 20005

This organization caters to artists, photographers and writers in the greeting card industry. Members receive a monthly newsletter of marketing and business trends and ideas. Membership is composed of large to small publishers and others. Publications available include a market list and information on copyright basics, publicity, owning/operating a store, starting a business, sales representatives, PR, how to succeed, others. Publishes a membership directory and monthly *CardNews*. The association was formed to network within and promote the industry.

HANDWEAVERS GUILD OF AMERICA
120 Mountain Ave., B101
Bloomfield, CT 06002

This association celebrated its 20th anniversary in 1988. It promotes excellence in the fiber arts by uniting a diverse group of craftspeople worldwide, through educational services and a biennial convention. Members receive *Shuttle, Spindle & Dyepot* quarterly journal, slide and textile kits, videos, information on exhibits, informational publications, library book rental, suppliers and educational directories.
Accepts: MasterCard, Visa

INTERNATIONAL GUILD OF MINIATURE ARTISANS
P.O. Box 71
Bridgeport, NY 13030
(315) 699-3903

The IGMA was founded to establish a standard of quality and promote excellence in the field of artistic miniatures; individuals may join as general members and after six months may apply for Guild Artisan Membership (by submitting samples of their work). Pays an initiation fee if accepted. Among the primary goals of the association: Encouragement, education. Events: Exhibits, shows—with awards for excellence.

INTERNATIONAL SCULPTURE CENTER
1050 Potomac St. NW, #250
Washington, DC 20007

A subscription to *Sculpture Magazine* automatically entitles one to a membership in this nonprofit organization devoted to professional development of sculptors, and an appreciation of sculpture worldwide. Among other member benefits: Free registration in Sculpture Source (a computerized slide registry linking sculptors with purchasers; non-artists get a discount on first-time use), group health and fine arts insurance rates, discounts, priority registration to events, use of a resources library. (Professional level memberships receive additional benefits.)

THE KNITTING GUILD OF AMERICA
P.O. Box 1606
Knoxville, TN 37901

This is an association of knitting teachers, designers, manufacturers and shop owners, etc., that offers members a master knitter program, correspondence courses, a national design competition and national convention; also offers the bimonthly magazine, *Cast On*, with designs and how-to information, and product and other news. Local guilds meet and share educational programs.

THE KNITTING GUILD OF CANADA
P.O. Box 159
St. Clements, Ontario N0B 2M0 Canada

This guild of machine and hand knitters connects knitters from coast to coast in Canada. It offers a quarterly magazine, teacher registry, and information on all aspects of knitting.

MARITIME SHIP MODELERS GUILD
1675 Lower Water St.
Halifax, Nova Scotia B3J 1S3 Canada

This guild is dedicated to sharing expertise in ship model construction. Bimonthly meetings are held, along with monthly workshops. Club members are interested in a wide range of styles and types of model construction.

NATIONAL ASSOCIATION OF MINIATURE ENTHUSIASTS
P.O. Box 69
Carmel, IN 46032

Members of this miniatures crafting organization network with others and receive the *Miniature Gazette* quarterly.

NATIONAL CLOTH DOLLMAKERS ASSOCIATION
1601 Provincetown Dr.
San Jose, CA 95129

This association whose members love and make cloth dolls is open to any who shares that experience.

NATIONAL INSTITUTE OF AMERICAN DOLL ARTISTS
Kripplebush Rd.
Stone Ridge, NY 12484
(914) 687-7949

This is an organization of professional doll artists and its devoted patrons. For patrons membership information, contact: Elsie Orr, 2600 Leix Way S., San Francisco, CA 94080.

NATIONAL SOCIETY OF TOLE AND DECORATIVE PAINTERS
P.O. Box 808
Newton, KS 67114

Since its inception in 1970, this nonprofit organization has grown to over 30,000 members, including students, teachers, designers and the business community. It has chapters in the U.S and Canada (each chapter sponsors workshops and holds meetings). Members receive a monthly publication and are entitled to attend the convention and events.

THE PROFESSIONAL ASSOCIATION OF CUSTOM CLOTHIERS
1375 Broadway
New York, NY 10018

This is a sewing industry association (ACCI), that includes primary and secondary resources uniting all facets of industry under various membership divisions. The association holds the largest trade show in the country in the spring and fall. Their "Statement and Object" to members: To create a greater appreciation among the public for craft, needlework and other related products; to educate and foster cooperation among both the public and industry. A bimonthly newsletter disseminates news and events data to members.

SOCIETY OF ANTIQUE MODELERS
209 Summerside Lane
Encinitas, CA 92024

Members of this flying old-timers society receive 6 issues of *Sam Speaks* and join in model free flight and R/C flying.

SOCIETY OF CRAFT DESIGNERS
6175 Barfield Rd. NE, Suite 220
Atlanta, GA 30328

Members of this Society are composed of designers, editors, manufacturers and others who are involved in the crafts industry and who hold an annual convention and other noteworthy events for the promotion of excellence of design. It also fosters professionalism in the marketplace, education for its members, and conducts seminars and a referral service listing. A bimonthly newsletter and other reference material is offered.

SOCIETY OF GILDERS
42 Maple Place
Nutley, NJ 07110

This society sponsored its first gilding exhibition in the fall of 1988, with lectures and exhibitors from the picture frame, furniture, gilding supply and signmaking industries; members may attend events, and receive a newsletter.

SURFACE DESIGN ASSOCIATION
4111 Lincoln Blvd., Suite 426
Marina Del Rey, CA 90292

This is a nonprofit, educational association. Members receive a quarterly journal with surface design data, news, and technical and business information.

UNITED FEDERATION OF DOLL CLUBS, INC,
6B East St.
Parkville, MO 64152

Clubs are helpful for doll makers, as a way of sharing ideas, techniques and more. Write the above federation for the address of the nearest doll club.

Books and Booksellers

Also see specific categories throughout the book.

AMERICAN J. SMITH
140 Waite Rd.
Boxboro, MA 01719

Offers: Worldwide book search for out-of-print and hard-to-find books.
For Further Information: Send SASE for details.

BETTER HOMES & GARDENS CRAFTS CLUB
Meredith Corp.
150 E. 52 St.
New York, NY 10016

Offers: New members choose 3 books for $1 plus shipping and handling and agree to buy 2 more books within 12 months at member price; they offer a wide selection of craft titles.
For Further Information: Request materials from above address.

BETTERWAY BOOKS
F&W Publications
1507 Dana Ave.
Cincinnati, OH 45207

Offers: Publisher of a variety of woodworking and craft titles, including *The Woodworker's Source Book*, by Charles Self, *Make Your Woodworking Pay for Itself*, by Jack Neff, and *The Good Wood Handbook*, by Jackson/Day.
For Further Information: Free catalog.

CRAFTER'S CHOICE
Book of the Month Club
Camp Hill, PA 17012

Offers: Members of this book club choose 3 introductory books at nominal cost, agree to purchase 2 more books within the year at member prices; crafts and needlecraft titles are chosen from brochures printed 15 times yearly.
For Further Information: Send SASE with inquiry.

CREATIVE NEEDLECRAFTS CLUB
Rodale Press Inc.
P.O. Box 10220
Des Moines, IA 50381-0220

Offers: New members choose 1 book for $1 plus postage and handling and agree to buy 2 books within the next year; they offer many craft and needlecraft titles.
For Further Information: Request materials from above address.

DOVER PUBLICATIONS, INC.
31 E. 2nd St.
Mineola, NY 11501

Offers: Craft/needlecraft books including a series of copyright-free design books, and cut-and-use stencil books. Craft books include glass crafts, silkscreen, paper, woodworking, needlecrafts (quilt, knit, crochet, lace, cross-stitch, others). Also offers textiles, photography, architecture, art instruction, children's activities, Indian crafts and designs, stencil books, plus non-art/craft titles.
For Further Information: Free catalog.

BETTE S. FEINSTEIN
96 Roundwood Rd.
Newton, MA 02164

Offers: Books, both out of print and new; including needle and fiber crafts (quilting, customers, textiles, dress making, patchwork, cutwork, stamp work, ethnic and historic clothing, others), needlecraft and sewing booklets and old magazine issues. Service: Book searching.
For Further Information: Lists, $1.

LARK BOOKS
50 College St.
Asheville, NC 28801

Offers: Arts, crafts and needlecraft books: Woodworking, kaleidoscopes, paper, gold leaf, eggs, nature, ceramics, basketry, others. Needlecrafts: Embroideries, art, quilts, textiles, silk painting, knitting, rug making, weaving, lace making, doll making, others.
For Further Information: Free catalog.

MEREDITH BOOKS
Locust at 17 St.
Des Moines, IA 50309-3023

Offers: Publishers of a variety of craft titles.
For Further Information: Request catalog from above address.

NORTH LIGHT BOOK CLUB
P.O. Box 12171
Cincinnati, OH 45212-0411
(513) 531-8250

Offers: Each month you'll get a free issue of *North Light Magazine*, offering 100 or more books on all areas of fine art—each book discounted at least 20% off the retail price. North Light also provides book excerpts, step-by-step lessons, tips from reknowned art instructors, and devotes a full page to a club members' work in each issue. Drop them a note or call to find out what the latest new member offer is. Currently, it's a book of your choice free with another one for just half price.
For Further Information: Call number above or write.

NORTH LIGHT BOOKS
1507 Dana Ave.
Cincinnati, OH 45207

Offers: Arts/crafts how-to books. Fine artists titles: Watercolor, pastel, oil, acrylic, airbrush, screen printing, design, graphics, drawing, perspective, pencil, others. Crafts titles: Gift making, silk painting, dough craft, paper sculpture, nature projects, home building, log homes, play houses, masonry, woodworking, furniture making, molding and others.
For Further Information: Free catalog.
Discounts: Quantity discounts; allows discounts to teachers and institutions; sells wholesale to legitimate businesses.

PUBLISHERS CENTRAL BUREAU
1 Champion Ave.
Avenel, NJ 07001

Offers: General book categories, but has some arts/crafts/needlecrafts/hobbies titles: Woodworking, paper and artists' titles, folk art, needlecrafts, plus armor, railroads, anatomy, books useful for designs.
For Further Information: Write for catalog.

RODALE PRESS INC.
33 E. Minor St.
Emmaus, PA 18098

Offers: Publishers of craft titles.
For Further Information: Request catalog from above address.

ROSS BOOK SERVICE
3718 Seminary Rd.
Alexandria, VA 22304

Offers: Books on textile arts, sewing, embroidery, dress making, tapestries, design, dyeing, laces, quilting, arts, embroidery, soft sculpture, fabric decorating, textile history, crafts.
For Further Information: Send SASE for lists—specify interests.

STERLING PUBLISHING CO. INC.
387 Park Ave. S
5th Floor
New York, NY 10016-8810

Offers: Publishers of various craft titles.
For Further Information: Request catalog from above address.

STOREY PUBLISHING
Schoolhouse Rd.
Pownal, VT 05261

Offers: 90 country skills booklets, including: Rug making, furniture, stencils, curtains and quilts, insulated window shutters, homemade wine, clay flowerpots, canoes, solar heated pit greenhouse, chair caning, hearth and root cellar construction, pole woodshed, cold frame construction and other country booklets.
For Further Information: Free catalog.
Discounts: Quantity discounts; sells wholesale to legitimate businesses.
Accepts: MasterCard, Visa

WOODWORKER'S BOOK CLUB
P.O. Box 12171
Cincinnati, OH 45212-0171
(513) 531-8250

Offers: A free monthly issue of the club newsletter, describing the main selection and dozens of other selections. You have at least 10 days to make up your mind. Drop a note to find out what the latest membership opening offer is. Currently, it's a free book plus a half-price book, with no obligation ever to buy another book. The club name describes the type of selections you'll find.
For Further Information: Call for free information.

General Craft Business

Also see Supportive Materials and Aids. This category aids those who have gone from hobby status to professional with crafts work—those who are suppliers, service providers or otherwise in business, and those who desire to be in business.

AD-LIB PUBLICATIONS
51 N. 5th St.
Fairfield, IA 52556

Offers: Books/databases: *Directory of Book, Catalog and Magazine Printers*, by John Kramer (1,000 printers of these and other bound publications). Lists are specialty detailed for choices. Other marketing books: Made easier, direct response forms, marketing, specialty publishers. Databases: *PR Flash: The National Publicity Database*—for book marketing (and other use). *Book Marketing Opportunities*: Also lists reviewers, columnists, TV and radio stations, bookstore chains, mail-order, others.
For Further Information: Send SASE for information.

AMERICA ONLINE
(800) 827-6364

Offers: Computer bulletin board service: On-line data communications, marketing or information resource, technical assistance. Charged by month; has trial membership.
For Further Information: Call for details.

AMERICRAFT
Stillwaters
Wendell, MA 01379
(800) 866-2723

Offers: Marketing to mail-order gift catalogs buyers; all craft categories except jewelry.
For Further Information: Call or send SASE for information.

ART STUDIO WORKSHOP
P.O. Box 424
Devault, PA 19432

Offers: Marketing data on craft shows, artists/galleries, others.
For Further Information: Issue, $3.70.

ARTIST CREATED
(303) 442-2148

Offers: Listings of over 1,400 craft galleries and gift shops; cost depends upon specified area (all or state/region).
For Further Information: Call for detailed information.

BOARDWATCH
8500 W. Bowles Ave., Suite 210
Littleton, CO 80123
(800) 933-6038

Offers: Monthly publication listing computer bulletin board services.
For Further Information: Send SASE for full details.

If you are thinking of making the leap from craft hobbyist to professional, the most valuable advice I can share with you is *prepare*, *research* and learn all you can about the business of crafts—not just the techniques. Diligence pays off in a profitable career.

—Sylvia Landman

BOLLINGER
499 Bloomfield Ave.
Montclair, NJ 07042
(800) 526-1379

Offers: Craft business insurance to home-based operations: 3 liability limits, property, craft show and theft coverages, plus additional options.
For Further Information: Call for quick quote or brochure.

BARBARA BRABEC PRODUCTIONS
P.O. Box 2137
Naperville, IL 60567

Offers: Books by Barbara Brabec (a home-based business authority): *Homemade Money* (5th Edition), *How to Select, Start, Manage, Market and Multiply the Profits of a Business at Home* (published March 1994), *Creative Cash, Making Money with Your Crafts, Needlework, Designs & Know-How*. Carries other business resource publications.
For Further Information: Free *Guides to Success* catalog.

BUSINESS COMPUTING CONSULTANTS
P.O. Box 1049
Meredith, NH 03253
(603) 279-6032

Offers: Craft shop system of computer software for craft

retailers. Comes with on-site training workshop for management/sales staff, plus an off-the-shelf retail/accounting package.
For Further Information: Call or write for information.

CARRIS POTTERY
105 Monticello Rd.
Oak Ridge, TN 37830
(615) 483-7167

Offers: Computer program for display-items method of marketing crafts.
For Further Information: Free brochure.

COMPUSERVE
(800) 848-8990

Offers: Computer service including bulletin board that serves as a communication, data and marketing resource. Provides crafts (and other) forums, technical assistance. Has trial membership.
For Further Information: Call for full details.

CULTURAL CENTERS OF COLOR/NEA
1100 Pennsylvania Ave.
Washington, DC 20335
(202) 682-5400

Offers: Report on national survey (1990); lists culturally oriented arts organizations.
For Further Information: Send SASE for information.

Sales reps were asked what would be the most important advice to give a craftsperson using a rep for the first time. Over and over, reps repeated the same problem areas:
1. Poor promotional literature.
2. Not paying reps their commissions on time.
3. Not willing to communicate with the reps.
4. Not being able to fill orders promptly.

—Northwoods Trading

CUSTOM DATA SOLUTIONS
P.O. Box 1002
Fort Lee, NJ 07024
(201) 224-3336

Offers: Computer software: Craft mall operations, vendor lease/business, reports totals, rental income, check printing, customer database, mailing labels.
For Further Information: Call or send SASE for information.

DIRECT MARKETING ASSOCIATION
1730 K St. NW
Washington, DC 20006

Offers: Resource for data regarding mail-order operations.
For Further Information: Send for information.

FEDERAL TRADE COMMISSION
Enforcement Div., B.C.P.
Washington, DC 20580

Offers: Data on the legalities of mail-order operations.
For Further Information: Contact with inquiry.

FIRST NATIONS ART, INC.
69 Kelley Rd.
Falmouth, VA 22405
(703) 371-3505

Offers: Aids Native American artists in finding wholesale outlets for their work. Buyers' guide lists authentic Native arts and crafts.
For Further Information: Send SASE for details.

THE FRANCISCO ENTERPRISE
572 143rd St.
Caledonia, MI 49316
(616) 877-4185

Offers: *The Craftmarket Listing*: Market of crafts to best prospects—over 2,000 active craft gallery, gift shop and boutique buyers who appreciate direct mail marketing. Includes: Mailing labels, sourcebook, card decks, disks, tapes sequenced in alphabetical order and/or zip code order.
For Further Information: Send SASE for information.

THE FRONT ROOM PUBLISHERS
P.O. Box 1541
Clifton, NJ 07015

Offers: Publications on marketing/home business: *Directory of Craft Shops*, *Directory of Wholesale Reps for Artisans*, *Pattern Designer Directory . . .*, *Market Your Handcrafts to Shops/Galleries*, and *How to Purchase Supplies Wholesale*. Also offers special reports on selling, debts, credit, crafter's directory, others.
For Further Information: Free *Learning Extension* Catalog.

LIFESTYLE CRAFTS
2164 Riverside Dr.
Columbus, OH 43221
(614) 486-7119

Offers: *Buyers' Resource Directory* with a buyers' service card referral program meant for anyone who wholesales a product line; allows readers to contact any of 15,000 shop buyers.
For Further Information: Write or call for sample copy.

MINORITY BUSINESS DEVELOPMENT
Hoover Blvd., 14th/Constitution NW
Washington, DC 20230
(202) 482-1936

Offers: Provides Commerce Department with advice and funding for minority businesses.
For Further Information: Send or call for information.

The number one problem a craftsperson has getting his foot in the door is that he/she, when first contacting a rep, does not use business stationery and does not have good sheets or 8½ × 11 professional color photos.

—Northwoods Trading

NORTH LIGHT BOOKS
1507 Dana Ave.
Cincinnati, OH 45207

Offers: Business-oriented books: *Artist's Market*, *Photographer's Market*, *The Crafts Supply Sourcebook*, and titles on marketing and self-promotion, selling specific crafts, graphics and cartoons and others.
For Further Information: Free catalog.
Discounts: Quantity discounts; allows discounts to teachers and institutions; sells wholesale to legitimate businesses.

NORTHWOODS TRADING CO.
13451 Essex Ct.
Eden Prairie, MN 55347

Offers: *Directory of Wholesale Reps for Craft Professionals* lists those interested in crafts with descriptions of each company, and tips and data on presenting crafts work. An aid to making the right connections.
For Further Information: Catalog, $15.95.

OLIVER PRESS
P.O. Box 1628
Wheat Ridge, CO 80034

Offers: Business resource books for quilting/others, most by Jeannie M. Spears: *Pricing Your Work*, *Bookkeeping*, *Shops: Start-Up Steps*, *Selling Your Work Through Galleries*, *Copyrights, Patents and Ethics for Quilters*.
For Further Information: Send SASE for catalog.

THE REP REGISTRY
P.O. Box 2306
Capistrano Beach, CA 92624
(714) 240-3333

Offers: Registry service. Over 4,000 sales representatives for the work of professional craftspeople.
For Further Information: Send SASE for details.

REVENUE SERVICE CO., INC.
P.O. Box 200205
Denver, CO 80220

Offers: Nationwide collection service for crafts accounts collecting.
For Further Information: Send SASE for details.

RT MARKETING INSTITUTE
P.O. Box 4564
North Hollywood, CA 91607

Offers: Video: *How to Market Your Arts and Crafts*, by Howard L. Cossman. Steps to market original work.
For Further Information: Send SASE for information.

SILVER LINING
(800) 828-4143

Offers: Business computer software for consignment shops, craft malls, other professional use. Covers sales, accounts receivable, inventory tracking, wholesale/retail pricing, consignment inventory—for IBM compatibles.
For Further Information: Call for details.

SYLVIA'S STUDIO
1090 Cambridge St.
Novato, CA 94947
(415) 883-6206

Offers: Reprints on crafts business topics by Sylvia Landman. Lists of college manuals for home self-study courses. Booklets: (1) *How to Start Your Own Teaching Studio*, (2) *How to Sell Your Designs to the Craft Magazine Market*, (3) *The Business of Marketing Your Arts & Crafts*. Also offers home business audio tapes: Starting a business, mail-order, marketplace data, time management/organization. Others.
For Further Information: Send SASE with 3 first-class stamps for catalog.

Publications

Publications in your areas of interest can be treasures of source information, technical inspiration and networking cooperation. Check a newsstand or library for a single issue of a publication that interests you. If you inquire regarding subscriptions to publications, include a business-size, stamped, self-addressed envelope, or, try requesting a current single issue of the publication and include a check or money order of at least $6.00 to cover cost and postage.

AMERICAN CRAFT
P.O. Box 585
Ridgefield, NJ 07657

This is the magazine of the American Craft Council—a showcase of excellence in crafts—and that is one of the member benefits. Profiles of crafts and craftspeople are given as points of education and inspiration.

AMERICAN INDIAN ART MAGAZINE
7314 E. Osborn Dr.
Scottsdale, AZ 85251

This is a quarterly magazine fostering Native American art, with features on all aspects, historic and contemporary.

AMERICAN QUILTER
P.O. Box 3290
Paducah, KY 42002

This official magazine of the American Quilter's Society displays quilts and techniques that promote the art form and preserve the craft. Among the features: Who's who, historical notes, show listings and events, more. (See Associations.)

AMERICAN WOODWORKER
P.O. Box 139
Emmaus, PA 18049

This home woodworking project magazine presents techniques and how-to's from the masters, with detailed instructions and in-depth buyer's guides.

ARTS & CRAFTS CATALYST
P.O. Box 433
South Whitley, IN 46787

This is a bimonthly magazine listing arts and crafts festivals, shows, and other events throughout the U.S. (listings include professional show directors and mall shows). Includes details on place, time, deadlines and fees involved. Has classified advertising.

THE ARTISTS' MAGAZINE
1507 Dana Ave.
Cincinnati, OH 45207

This monthly magazine abounds with features for artists (and craftspeople): Profiles of known pros, and an array of projects, shows, business, problem-solving, markets, showplaces and more. Has advertising.

ARTNEWS
5 W. 37th St.
New York, NY 10018

This award-winning magazine features news reporting on the art world to art lovers—with analysis, criticism and exemplary graphics.

BEARHUGS
300 E. 40th St.
New York, NY 10016

Distributed internationally, this monthly bear-lovers publication shows, features and informs about—bears.

BERRY HILL PRESS
7336 Berry Hill (MB)
Palos Verdes, CA 90274

Naturals/florals, potpourri and related topics are features of this quarterly publication meant for designers and other interested parties. Issues include potpourri recipes, product information and news features. Has classifieds.

BETTER HOMES AND GARDENS CRAFT & WEAR
1716 Locust St.
Des Moines, IA 50309

Send SASE for information.

BIAS LINE
115 S. Manhattan Ave.
Tampa, FL 33609

This newsletter is geared to costumers and technicians with technical data and business/marketing topics. Patterns for period apparel may be shown with details as to fabrics and techniques. Book reviews and product information are regular features.

BLACK SHEEP NEWSLETTER
1690 Butler Creek Rd.
Ashland, OR 97520

This quarterly newsletter is meant for growers, spinners and textile artists interested in black sheep wool and other animal fibers. Upcoming events and book reviews are included. Has advertising.

THE BUSINESS OF HERBS
Rt. 2, P.O. Box 246
Shevlin, MN 55676

This bimonthly newsletter reports trade news, market tips, grower resources, sources and more. Herbal facts, interviews, ideas, forums, book reviews, events and business ideas round out issues. Advertising.

CAROL'S BITS & PIECES
P.O. Box 33305
Kansas City, MO 64168

This illustrated monthly newsletter for sewers presents creative projects and shares hints, tips and know-how while analyzing today's fashion patterns and techniques.

THE CARRIAGE TRADE
Rt. 2, Lot 8 Dalrymple, P.O. Box 18
Camlachie, Ontario N0N 1E0 Canada

This quarterly knitting magazine presents projects and patterns, product and book reviews and more.

CARTOON WORLD NEWSLETTER
P.O. Box 30367
Lincoln, NE 68503

This monthly newsletter presents a comprehensive list of new art and cartoon markets.

CARTOONIST PROFILES
P.O. Box 325
Fairfield, CT 06430

Edited by a cartoonist syndicated for 27 years, this quarterly magazine explores how cartoonists became successful through profile features.

CAST ON
P.O. Box 1606
Knoxville, TN 37901

This is the official publication of the Knitting Guild of America sent to members in order to foster education and communication. Features knitting projects of known designers, plus letters, tips and hints, book reviews and Guild activities. Has advertising. (See Associations.)

CERAMIC ARTS & CRAFTS
30595 W. Eight Mile Rd.
Livonia, MI 48152

This monthly magazine focuses on how-to's in hobby ceramics, with color projects, materials list and instructions. A variety of techniques are given in each issue, as are "News & Views" and "Show Listings." Has advertising and classifieds.

CERAMIC SCOPE
3632 Ashworth N. Ave.
Seattle, WA 98103

This magazine is published bimonthly. Circulation is limited to dealers, distributors, manufacturers, importers and teachers in the hobby ceramics field. Industry news/views are given, events profiled and shop/studio business covered. Regular features: Seminar listings, "Showcase" (by state, with dates/details) and new products. Has advertising.

CERAMICS MAGAZINE
30595 W. Eight Mile Rd.
Livonia, MI 48152

This ceramics publication presents mold designs and products from known manufacturers, decorating techniques, contributions by world famous ceramic artists, articles by professionals, tips and shortcuts. Includes paper patterns on clay carbon graph paper. National show listings are given through reviews. Has advertising.

THE CHART CONNECTION
2240 W. 3800 S., #J201
West Valley City, UT 84119

Network communication to locate, sell or buy charts for cross-stitch.

CLASSIC CROSS-STITCH
P.O. Box 50281
Boulder, CO 80301

This is a bimonthly magazine of traditional cross-stitch designs, with charts, instructions, product information and more.

CLASSIC TOY TRAINS
P.O. Box 1612
Milwaukee, WI 53201

This quarterly magazine for collectors and operators also serves to inspire model railroad crafters. Among the classics presented are Lionel, American Flyer, LGB and others.

THE CLOTH DOLL
P.O. Box 1089
Mt. Shasta, CA 96067

This quarterly magazine is oriented to soft doll-making, with at least 3 patterns per issue, plus a variety of topics, including needle sculpturing, sewing, ideas and inspiration, detailed techniques and marketing data. Doll- and toy-making know-how are presented by pros. Includes: reviews, search-sources and insert patterns. Has advertising.

COLOR TRENDS
8037 9th Ave. NW
Seattle, WA 98117

This magazine is devoted to color and dyes, with actual dyed fabric, yarn and paper samples included, plus dye instructions, yarn painting, designer fabrics data, color innovations, more; published twice yearly.

COTTAGE CONNECTION
P.O. Box 14460
Chicago, IL 60614

This is a newsletter of the National Association for the Cottage Industry. It provides news and information on general business and laws, advertising, copyrights and more; includes book/video reviews and calendar—for professionals, suppliers and distributors.

COUNTED CROSS-STITCH
306 E. Parr Rd.
Berne, IN 46711

This counted cross-stitch magazine published bimonthly brings a variety of charted design projects for household accessories and other items. A "Stitching Hotline," product and book reviews and designer data round out the content. Has advertising.

COUNTRY HANDCRAFTS
P.O. Box 572
Milwaukee, WI 53201

This magazine presents country-oriented crafts/needlecrafts projects—vintage techniques upgraded to today's crafting, and more. Among the projects are how-to's with diagrams and illustrations.

COUNTRY NEEDLECRAFT
P.O. Box 11309
Des Moines, IA 50340

A selection of country patterns and designs appear in this monthly magazine, as do projects for a variety of needle-crafts. Regular features: Techniques, tips, book reviews, reader's networking, and business aspects of needlecrafts. Has advertising.

CRAFT INTERNATIONAL
247 Centre St.
New York, NY 10013

This publication focuses on the contemporary international arts and crafts movement, covering all areas of the globe, with news, fellowships and other noteworthy information.

THE CRAFT MARKETING NEWS
P.O. Box 1541
Clifton, NJ 07015

This bimonthly is published for all wanting to market their talent—with listings of shops wanting handcrafts and reports on business, plus wholesale suppliers, profiles. Has advertising.

CRAFTERS' LINK NEWSLETTER
59999 Myrtle Rd.
South Bend, IN 46614

This newsletter is geared to increasing profits in crafts work with down-to-earth business data and profiles of successful craftspeople.

CRAFTER'S SOURCELETTER
P.O. Box 575749
Murray, UT 84157
(801) 977-9048

This newsletter reviews suppliers of art and craft materials, sources for patterns, kits and fabrics. (Also has Sewer's SourceLetter and Stitcher's SourceLetter.)

CRAFTS
News Plaza
P.O. Box 1790
Peoria, IL 61656

How-to techniques and some full-sized, fold-out patterns are included in colorful monthly issues of this magazine that presents an array of crafts/needlecrafts techniques. Has advertising.

THE CRAFTS FAIR GUIDE
P.O. Box 5508
Mill Valley, CA 94942

This quarterly publication covers in detail, and through reviews, over 1,000 fairs throughout the West. Fairs are rated for sales/enjoyment; invaluable for show marketing. Shows listed by dates/town/state. Advertising.

CRAFTS 'N THINGS
701 Lee St., Dept. C552
Des Plaines, IL 60016

This crafts/needlecrafts magazine provides a wealth of projects per issue (with pattern sheets, illustrations, directions) in a range of techniques with instructions. Include source data. Ideas, letters, product news and "Showcase" are given in each issue. Has advertising.

CRAFTS PLUS
130 Spy Ct.
Markam, Ontario L3R 5H6 Canada

Published 8 times yearly, this crafts magazine provides a wide variety of crafts and needlecrafts projects. Columns include "Coming Events in Canada" listings, plus product and Canadian dealers information. Has advertising.

CREATIVE CRAFTS & MINIATURES
P.O. Box 700
Newton, NJ 07860

Crafts, needlecrafts and miniatures are covered in this magazine in how-to features with patterns, diagrams and illustrations. Readers' letters, product and book reviews and store listings are regular features. Has advertising.

CROCHET TODAY FASHIONS
306 E. Parr Rd.
Berne, IN 46711

This quarterly crochet magazine features fashions and accessories for the entire family; includes over 15 patterns per issue (illustrated and graphed). Has advertising.

CROCHET WORLD
306 E. Parr Rd.
Berne, IN 46711

This bimonthly crochet magazine presents illustrated project patterns for adult and children's apparel, dolls and doll clothes, toys and home decor items. Projects are marked for level of ability, easy to advanced. "Potpourri," reader-trades/wants, and "Show-It-Off" are among regular features. Has advertising.

CROSS QUICK
P.O. Box 58322
Boulder, CO 80302

Cross-stitching design/charts are a main attraction of this bimonthly magazine that presents holiday, country, classics, keepsake and other motifs, using large charts in three colors. Other features: Contests, stitchers, "Cross Quick" projects.

CROSS-STITCH & COUNTRY CRAFTS
3000 Walnut St.
P.O. Box 52416
Boulder, CO 80302

Every bimonthly issue of this magazine has at least 23 original cross-stitch patterns and designs with color photos (close-up, hands-on) as aids, plus chart ratings and skein data; includes heirloom and country motifs. "Finish It Tonight" projects and designer originals are included.

CROSS-STITCH! MAGAZINE
207 E. Broadway
Big Sandy, TX 75755
(903) 636-4011

Send SASE for information.

THE CROSS STITCHER
701 Lee St., Dept. CSS2
Des Plaines, IL 60016

This bimonthly magazine is devoted to cross-stitching, providing a variety of pattern illustrations, features and other information.

DARKROOM & CREATIVE CAMERA
7880 Merrimac
P.O. Box 48312
Niles, IL 60648

This bimonthly magazine is geared to darkroom and photochemistry, processing, printing, etc., and this is reflected in articles—technical, how-to's and reviews.

DARKROOM PHOTOGRAPHY MAGAZINE
9021 Melrose Ave.
West Hollywood, CA 90069

This magazine (published 8 times yearly) presents darkroom topics for professional and amateur photographers, including manipulation, processing, printing, how to build equipment, tools and products guides, special effects and others.

DECORATIVE ARTIST'S WORKBOOK
1507 Dana Ave.
Cincinnati, OH 45207

This magazine is dedicated to decorative and tole painting, with color worksheets and patterns for demonstrations led step-by-step by professionals such as Jo Sonja Jansen, Priscilla Hauser and others. Includes marketing ideas, seminar updates, product news and book reviews. Has advertising.

DECORATIVE ARTS DIGEST
14 Main St.
Park Ridge, IL 60068

This monthly magazine of tole and decorative painting presents how-to's from prominent artists (and a featured artist per issue), with updated techniques for all media, color illustrations for projects, and over 85 original patterns a year. Includes product/book reviews, calendars, questions/answers. Has advertising.

THE DOLL ARTISAN
9 River St.
Oneonta, NY 13820

This is a bimonthly magazine for production doll makers (and those interested in doll making); a publication of the Doll Artisan Guild.

DOLL CASTLE NEWS
P.O. Box 247
Washington, NJ 07882

This is a bimonthly magazine about dolls and doll making. Includes articles on museums, plus miniatures listings, a paper doll section, clothes patterns and needlework. Regular departments include questions/answers, show calendar and news. Has advertising.

DOLL DESIGNS
306 E. Parr Rd.
Berne, IN 46711

This bimonthly magazine is meant for doll and toy craftspeople. Includes features on composition, cloth, soft-sculpture, ceramic and other dolls, technical how-to's, styles and trends of today and vintage toys. Houses, furniture and clothing are covered, and profiles of doll artists included. Columns: Letters, shows, tips, questions/answers. Has advertising.

THE DOLL READER
900 Frederick St.
Cumberland, MD 21502

This publication appears 8 times yearly, with a sister publication (*The Teddy Bear and Friends*).

DOLL WORLD
306 E. Parr Rd.
Berne, IN 46711

This is a bimonthly magazine for doll lovers, doll crafters and collectors. It presents features on a variety of patterns, informative articles of all eras and areas worldwide. Includes doll shows, paper dolls, pattern reviews. Has advertising.

DOLLCRAFTER
30595 W. Eight Mile Rd.
Livonia, MI 48152

This bimonthly magazine aids the reader to make or collect dolls.

DOLLMAKING PROJECTS & PLANS
169 5th Ave.
New York, NY 10010

Magazine of crafting techniques and plans, data and sources for dolls—cloth, ceramic, vinyl and others. Includes directions for projects with diagrams, patterns, illustrations. Features include trends, news, calendar of events and collector's data. Has advertising.

EARLY AMERICAN LIFE
P.O. Box 8200
Harrisburg, PA 17105

This magazine on early America offers crafts, examples of quality craftsmanship, building, decorating and renovation ideas; gives source data and a calendar of events (arts/crafts and folk festivals, historic exhibits).

FIBERARTS, MAGAZINE OF TEXTILES
50 College St.
Asheville, NC 28801

This magazine presents articles on quilting, weaving, stitchery, knitting, soft sculpture and others, plus historical design and techniques and fiber data. Regular features include show and opportunities data.

FINE PRINT
1610 Bush St.
San Francisco, CA 94109

The artistry of book printing and binding are presented in this quality magazine.

FINE TOOL JOURNAL
P.O. Box 4001
Pittsford, VT 05763

This magazine on tools for craftspeople and collectors features absentee auctions, tools for sale, technical and historical information, coming events calendar and other topics. It is issued quarterly.

FINESCALE MODELER
P.O. Box 1612
Waukesha, WI 53187

This bimonthly magazine covers scale modeling: Aircraft, boats, cars, figures, fantasy/sci-fi, dioramas, others. Professional technical data, articles on scratch building and others are given. Includes events, new products, reviews, tips. Has advertising.

FOR THE LOVE OF CROSS STITCH
P.O. Box 56099
Little Rock, AR 72215

Twenty exclusive cross-stitch projects are a focal point of every issue of this magazine, with colorful charts, country designs, adaptions of paintings and lithographs and more. Book reviews, product information, letters and hints are also presented.

HANDWOVEN
306 N. Washington Ave.
Loveland, CO 80537

This weaving magazine is issued 5 times yearly, with photographed weaving projects (and instructions), plus articles of lore, history, techniques and profiles. Includes woven fashions, accessories, fabrics. Two researched theme issues are included each year.

THE HERB COMPANION
306 N. Washington Ave.
Loveland, CO 80537

This bimonthly magazine for herb growers and enthusiasts presents herbs and their uses—culinary, in crafts, potpourris—plus growing, cultivating, drying and other herbal topics. Regular features include "In Basket" (letters), a calendar of events and book reviews.

THE HERBAL CONNECTION
P.O. Box 245
Silver Spring, PA 17575

Send SASE for catalog.

HERBAL CRAFTS QUARTERLY NEWSLETTER
Rt. 13, P.O. Box 357
Mappsville, VA 23407

Herbal crafting is the focal point for this publication—past features included spice and sachet wreath making, flowers. Regular columns: Hints, product and book reviews, letters.

HERBALGRAM
P.O. Box 201660
Austin, TX 78720
(512) 331-8868

This quarterly journal is published by the American Botanical Council and the Herb Research Foundation. Includes reviews, media coverage, herb data, updates, legalities, conference data, book reviews and an events calendar—all edited by an advisory board.

HERBAN LIFESTYLES
84 Carpenter Rd.
New Hartford, CT 06057

This bimonthly newsletter is devoted to herbs.

HOME SHOP MACHINIST
2779 Aero Park Dr.
P.O. Box 2820
Traverse City, MI 49685

Metalworking and machining how-to articles are presented in this magazine.

THE HOMEOWNER
3 Park Ave.
New York, NY 10016

Home remodeling and improvement are major themes for this monthly magazine, with how-to's, technical data, professional experiences, profiles and more.

HOMESEWING TRADE NEWS
300 Sunrise Highway
P.O. Box 286
Rockville Centre, NY 11571

Meant for the sewing, craft and yarn industries, this publication offers a resource directory with subscription.

HOOK & NEEDLE TIMES
P.O. Box 798
Marysville, WA 98270

This monthly knitting and crochet newsletter has patterns, tips, feature profiles, inspiration and humor.

HOOKED ON CROCHET
207 E. Broadway
Big Sandy, TX 75755

An assortment of crochet patterns (illustrated, diagrammed, with directions) make up this bimonthly magazine—projects for personal and home decor.

HOW MAGAZINE
P.O. Box 12575
Cincinnati, OH 45212

The focal point for this bimonthly magazine is graphics—design, technique, concepts as given by contemporary art directors, production people, computer-graphics professionals and others—with coverage of techniques, tools, problem solving, color separations, papers, computer systems, business, legalities, PR, more.

INTERNATIONAL SCULPTURE
1050 17th St. NW, #250
Washington, DC 20036

Members of this organization receive a magazine of information on business, projects, exhibits and more.

JEREMIAH JUNCTION, INC.
P.O. Box 710
Manchester, CT 06045

This counted cross-stitch magazine is published 6 times yearly, with 20 to 25 design projects per issue, in color, with clear charts. Designs include country motifs, scripture, others.

THE JOY OF HERBS
P.O. Box 7617
Birmingham, AL 35253

This is a quarterly publication on herbs with news, features, product resources and advice, including crafts projects using naturals, herbs and spices, herb growing and cultivation. Herb recipes are included, as are regular features: "Question/Answers," "Coming Events," "Book Reviews," "Suppliers Directory" and more. Has advertising.

KIT CAR
8490 Sunset Blvd.
West Hollywood, CA 90069

Specialty cars constructed from kits is this bimonthly magazine's focus. Each issue illustrates and details a showcase of models. Technical features aid car builders in installation and operation. Regulars: News, assembler's guide and swaps. Has advertising.

KITELINES
P.O. Box 466
Randallstown, MD 21133

This is the comprehensive international journal of kiting—the only magazine of its kind—the source of news, plans, techniques, reviews of new kites and books, profiles of kiting personalities, in-depth features. With event and supplier lists. Has advertising.

KNITTING NEWS
306 E. Parr Rd.
Berne, IN 46711

This knitting newsletter features patterns, news, book reviews and more. It is issued quarterly.

KNITTING WORLD
306 E. Parr Rd.
Berne, IN 46711

Packed with knitting patterns and directions, this bimonthly magazine covers knitwear and accessories for all members of the family. Features: Machine knitting, hints and innovations. Has advertising.

LACE CRAFTS QUARTERLY
3201 E. Lakeshore Dr.
Tallahassee, FL 32312

This lace-making magazine presents how-to articles throughout—on hand and machine techniques, plus in depth information on lace, care/repair, latest products—and reviews of designs, books and events. Full-sized patterns are included with instructions. Has advertising.

LAPIDARY JOURNAL
P.O. Box 80937
San Diego, CA 92138

A monthly publication of jewelry making and the lapidary arts, including outstanding photography of gemstones, technical data and articles on expeditions, equipment, shows, projects and events. Extensive advertising and classifieds.

LEATHER CRAFTERS JOURNAL
4307 Oak Dr.
Rhinelander, WI 54501

This bimonthly publication features leather crafting for all ages and skill levels; provides how-to articles using full-sized patterns with illustrations. Source information given for tools and supplies.

THE LEATHER CRAFTSMAN
P.O. Box 1386
Fort Worth, TX 76101

This leather crafting magazine is published bimonthly, with a wide range of leather projects (with patterns, illustrations, directions) for home and personal items and accessories—like lamp bases, saddles, guitar covers, purses and others. Regular columns include book reviews, guild news, new products data, calendar of events and "Help." Has advertising.

LEISURE ARTS
104 Riverwood Rd.
North Little Rock, AR 72118

A range of creative arts are represented in this bimonthly magazine—counted cross-stitch, knitting and crochet, and a variety of other crafts projects are presented by noted professionals. Includes unique projects charts, diagrams and directions. Departments: Letters, tips, reviews and "Show Your Style." Has advertising.

LET'S TALK ABOUT DOLLMAKING MAGAZINE
300 Nancy Dr.
Point Pleasant, NJ 08742

Current materials, techniques, products and resources for doll-making are included in the four issues that are published irregularly.

LEVEL 3 PHOTOGRAPHIC ARTS
309 N. 3rd St.
Philadelphia, PA 19106

This is a quarterly photography newsletter presenting reviews, interviews and more.

MAKING IT!
300 Sunrise Highway
P.O. Box 286
Rockville Centre, NY 11571

This publication is meant for custom dressmakers and other interested seamstresses.

MCCALL'S NEEDLEWORK & CRAFTS
P.O. Box 5063
Harlan, IA 51537

This bimonthly magazine presents readers with professional projects that are diagrammed or charted and color illustrated for easy crafting. Emphasis: Needlecrafts, basics and innovations for fashions and accessories and some crafts. Features books, buyer's guide, shows. Has advertising.

METALSMITH
12653 Muirfield Blvd.
S. Jacksonville, FL 32225

This quarterly magazine is published by the Society of North American Goldsmiths and offers reviews, aesthetics, criticism, profiles of master metalsmiths, technical papers, surveys of galleries and other business. (See Associations.)

MIND YOUR OWN BUSINESS AT HOME
P.O. Box 14850
Chicago, IL 60614

This newsletter of the National Association for the Cottage Industry presents aspects of home-based business.

MINIATURE COLLECTOR
170 5th Ave.
New York, NY 10010

This magazine gives readers a look into the world of dollhouses and other scale miniatures, with professional articles, "Projects & Plans" and "Showcase" features. Household furnishing, houses, buildings and architectural details are illustrated. Departments: Auctions, news, calendars, new products. Has advertising.

MINIATURES DEALER MAGAZINE
Clifton House
Clifton, VA 22024

Presented for retailers in the dollhouse and miniatures trade, this monthly magazine deals with how-to's, innovative techniques for marketing and personality profiles.

MINIATURES SHOWCASE
P.O. Box 1612
Waukesha, WI 53187

This is a quarterly magazine that shows artisans and miniature collections, utilizing detailed close-up photography of dollhouses, people and accessories, along with descriptions and explanations. Projects—scratch-building, finishing, assembling—are also shown. Each issue includes "Letters," a "Collectors Guide" and more. Has advertising.

MODEL AIRPLANE NEWS
P.O. Box 428
Mount Morris, IL 61054

Model aircraft is this monthly magazine's focus—carried through step-by-step projects (illustrated, diagrammed and described), articles on products/use, and "Field and Bench Review" of aircraft. Regulars: "Clubs," "Plans Mart," others. Has advertising.

When sending checks for catalogs or mail order merchandise, always write the company's address and phone number (if known) on the back of the check. If there's a problem later on you'll have the information you need with the canceled check.

—Crafter's SourceLetter

MODEL RAILROADER
P.O. Box 1612
Waukesha, WI 53187

The authoritative monthly magazine of scale model railroading has ideas for beginners and veterans; projects include directions, railroad showcasing, new products. Has advertising.

MODERN MACHINE KNITTING
264 H St.
P.O. Box 110
Blaine, WA 98230

This monthly machine-knitting magazine features illustrated project patterns and sources of supplies.

NATIONAL STAMPAGRAPHIC
1952 Everett St.
North Valleystream, NY 11580

This quarterly magazine is about rubber stamps of the artistic kind. It presents the creations of stamp artists throughout, with technical features, personal profiles and more. Features: Exchanges, hints. Has advertising and "Classi-Rubber-Fieds."

NEEDLE & CRAFT
P.O. Box 2012
Harlan, IA 51537

This bimonthly magazine presents easy-to-do projects in needlecrafts—cross-stitch, quilting, knitting and crochet and crafts (how-to's and diagrams throughout).

THE NEEDLECRAFT SHOP, INC.
207 E. Broadway
Big Sandy, TX 75755

Send SASE for information.

NEEDLEPOINT NEWS
P.O. Box 5967
Concord, CA 94524

This is a bimonthly magzine of how-to's, designs, profiles and technical data—all related to needlepoint. Business-related information may be included.

NEEDLEPOINT PLUS
P.O. Box 5986
Concord, CA 94524

This bimonthly publication is written by and for needle-pointers. Newest trends and designs are presented with diagrams, charts, photos, book reviews.

NEEDLEWORDS
306 E. Parr Rd.
Berne, IN 46711

Published quarterly, this publication abounds with counted cross-stitch graphed patterns (some in color), trends, techniques. Features: Finishing, primers, "World of Stitches" projects and basics. Has advertising.

NORTHWEST PHOTO NETWORK
1309 N. 77th St.
Seattle, WA 98103

Photography is the focus of this quality, tabloid-sized publication for commercial photographers and others; it offers events, techniques, specialties, marketing and business data, galleries, marketing and photographs. Has advertising.

NORTHWEST WOOLGATHER'S QUARTERLY
P.O. Box 70401
Seattle, WA 98107

This quarterly publication presents articles on weaving, spinning, fiber-raising, dyeing, knitting, basketry, quilting and related topics. Also presents book reviews, shows and exhibits reviews and more.

NUTSHELL NEWS
21027 Crossroads Circle
P.O. Box 1612
Waukesha, WI 53187

This is a monthly magazine of miniatures that offers reports on shows, profiles of craftspeople and displays of their work, plus how-to tips and techniques, visits to museums/collections and more. Miniature projects are diagrammed and directed. Regulars: Shows, letters, reviews, mini-market, others. Has advertising.

OLD-TIME CROCHET
306 E. Parr Rd.
Berne, IN 46711

This quarterly crochet magazine features patterns from cover to cover—classic and traditional apparel, accessories and home decor. Has advertising.

OPEN CHAIN PUBLISHING
P.O. Box 2634
Menlo Park, CA 94026

For subscription call (415) 366-4440.

ORNAMENT
P.O. Box 35029
Los Angeles, CA 90035

Ornaments of the ancient, contemporary and ethnic kind are the focus in this quality magazine that presents jewelry and clothing. Original designs are beautifully photographed. Includes: News, features, galleries and shops data, collecting, resources. Has advertising.

OUTDOOR & TRAVEL PHOTOGRAPHY
1115 Broadway, 8th Floor
New York, NY 10010

This photography magazine focuses on the outdoors, nature and travel. Published quarterly, it presents topics unique to this specialty; adds a "Readers Portfolio" for submission of work and resume.

PAIRS
1090 Cambridge St.
Novato, CA 94947

This quarterly newsletter is meant for couples in business, including craftspeople. Features reflect that with "Pairs and Spares" issues column, "Understand Me" differences, tips/ideas, interviews and more.

PAPERCUTTING WORLD
584 Castro St., #360
San Francisco, CA 94114

Here's a quarterly for cut-paper artists, craftspeople and paper suppliers. Among the features are how-to's, interviews, product and book data and paper-cutter fiction.

THE PATTERN CONNECTION
2240 W. 3800 S., #J201
Salt Lake City, UT 84119

This bimonthly publication networks used/out-of-print patterns for crafts and needlecrafts; free pattern listings.

PHOTO OPPORTUNITY
P.O. Box 838
Montclair, NJ 07042

Profiles of professionals, strategies for studios and business places, promotions are given in this bimonthly magazine. Regularly featured: Success pointers and resources, events calendar and profiles. Has advertising.

PHOTOGRAPHER'S FORUM
614 Santa Barbara St.
Santa Barbara, CA 93101

Send SASE for information.

PHOTOGRAPHIC MAGAZINE
8490 Sunset Blvd.
West Hollywood, CA 90069

This is a monthly how-to magazine that features techniques and special effects (darkroom, lighting, tools, equipment, others). Presents/reviews cameras and video products. Has advertising.

PLASTIC CANVAS! MAGAZINE
23 Old Pecan Blvd.
Big Sandy, TX 75755

With plastic canvas stitchery the focal point, this bimonthly magazine covers basics and projects for many accessories.

POPULAR PHOTOGRAPHY
1515 Broadway
New York, NY 10036

This monthly magazine includes techniques and equipment,

innovations, workshops listings, problem solving and new products. Has advertising.

POPULAR WOODWORKING
P.O. Box 5986
Concord, CA 94524

This bimonthly magazine presents project ideas, techniques and other data; includes step-by-step instructions, color photos and technical diagrams to aid in projects.

POTPOURRI FROM HERBAL ACRES
P.O. Box 428-MB
Washington Crossing, PA 18977

This networking publication is issued quarterly. Features ideas, tips, recipes, crafts and news in herbs.

PRIMER
82 Colfax Rd.
Springfield, NJ 07081

This newsletter for the decorative painting and crafts industry is published bimonthly. It addresses topics of business interest, evaluates advertising, copyrights, business promotion, accounting, marketing and others.

THE PROFESSIONAL QUILTER
P.O. Box 1628
Wheat Ridge, CO 80034

From a pro/business standpoint, this quarterly magazine offers features on management and marketing; organization of studio, home, business; teaching, designing; issues of ethics, economics and more. Includes valuable input from professionals. Regulars: Reviews, resources, competitions/shows, news, computer data. Has advertising.

PROFESSIONAL STAINED GLASS
245 W. 29th St.
New York, NY 10001

This monthly magazine presents fine examples of contemporary and other stained glass, plus glass topics. Includes color photographs, diagrams and description. Regular departments include "Design," "Video and Book" reviews, "Techniques" and "Product Updates." Includes "Notable Works" and artists. Has advertising.

PROFITABLE CRAFT MERCHANDISING
News Plaza
P.O. Box 1790
Peoria, IL 61656

This monthly magazine is published for retailers, manufacturers, publishers, importers, distributors and designers; presents product information from a craft merchandising level, with new trends, projects, news and views in crafts, needlecrafts and creative sewing. Reports trade shows, events, reviews, news. Includes Retailer Assistance Cards and an Annual Craft Market Handbook with subscription. Has advertising.

THE QUALITY CRAFTS MARKET
15 W. 44th St.
New York, NY 10036

This service publication of the National Information Center for Crafts Management and Marketing presents business and marketing for pros—pricing, sales, consignment, shops, networking, buyers, others.

QUICK & EASY NEEDLECRAFT
207 E. Broadway
Big Sandy, TX 75755

Send SASE for information.

QUICK & EASY PLASTIC CANVAS!
23 Old Pecan Blvd.
Big Sandy, TX 75755

What *Plastic Canvas! Magazine* does for projects, this bimonthly magazine does for easy-quick projects (with the same full color illustrations, charts and directions) throughout each issue.

QUILT WORLD
306 E. Parr Rd.
Berne, IN 46711

This bimonthly magazine presents full-sized patterns throughout—motifs, diagrams, photographs for a variety of quilts—from heritage to contemporary style. Includes international news, "Notes & Quotes," "Pieces and Patches" rundown, book reviews, "Quilters Queries & Quotes," "Show Directory" and "Classifieds."

QUILTER'S NEWSLETTER MAGAZINE
P.O. Box 394
Wheatridge, CO 80034

Each issue of this magazine is packed with 50 to 100 quilt photos, plus news, lessons, features, hints, contests. Project how-to's are diagrammed, with full-size patterns for 5 to 15 quilts. Features: Noted quilters, show calendars, club/guilds, more. Has advertising.

QUILTING TODAY
P.O. Box 549
New Milford, PA 18834

This bimonthly magazine is packed with color pictures, original projects with step-by-step instructions and full-size pat-

terns. Includes articles on quilt shows and guild news. Quilters/designers share know-how with readers on mastering techniques.

R/C MODELER MAGAZINE
144 Sierra Madre Blvd.
P.O. Box 487
Sierra Madre, CA 91024

This is a magazine devoted to radio control models.

RADIO CONTROL CAR ACTION
251 Danbury Rd.
Wilton, CT 06897

This R/C car magazine features the newest models and trends, plus photo features on cars, bodies, accessories, driver models. Includes information on engines, parts, pit tips, plus articles, product news and advertising.

RAILROAD MODEL CRAFTSMAN
P.O. Box 700
Newton, NJ 07860

Model railroads—actual lines, and modeling kits and scratch-building protypes—are covered in this monthly magazine. Model landscaping and kit hints are given. Departments: Letters, exchanges and dealer directory.

ROCK & GEM
2660 E. Main St.
Ventura, CA 93003

This jewelry-making/rockhound magazine is published monthly to present and review lapidary equipment; covers field trips, collecting, prospecting, identification through photos and descriptions. Has advertising.

RUBBERSTAMPMADNESS
408 SW Monroe, #210
Corvallis, OR 97333

A world of rubber stamping is represented in this bimonthly publication that is color-covered; includes reviews of catalogs, news, mail art, how-to's, letters and trends. Has advertising.

RUG HOOKING
500 Vaughn St.
Harrisburg, PA 17110

This bimonthly magazine is devoted to all aspects of rug hooking, with illustrated projects (4 to 5 per issue) from rug-hooking experts to instruct and inspire. Features techniques, designing, dyeing and profiles with photos. Departments: Answers, letters, events, resources. Has advertising.

SAC

P.O. Box 159
Bogalusa, LA 70429

Monthly publication gives nationwide news (and in-depth reports) on upcoming arts/crafts shows in the South (given by state). Mall shows advertised. Show listing form/resources.

THE SCALE CABINETMAKER

P.O. Box 2038
Christiansburg, VA 24068

This is a quarterly magazine for those who build miniatures. Includes how-to features with directions and other data useful to scale crafters.

SCALE SHIP MODELER

7950 Deering Ave.
Canoga Park, CA 91304

Covering all aspects of model boating, this magazine gives informative articles, with color photos—techniques, kit reviews, showcases, events. Features: Product/book reviews, letters, museums/clubs, wants and product news. Has advertising.

SCULPTURE

P.O. Box 91110
Washington, DC 20090

This is the magazine of the International Sculpture Center (a nonprofit organization devoted to the advancement of contemporary sculpture). Examples of superb sculpture abound throughout each issue. "News Commissions," "Exhibitions" and "Reviews" are included. Has advertising.

SERGER BOOKLET SERIES

2269 Chestnut, Suite 269
San Francisco, CA 94123

This booklet series on serger technology is published bimonthly by professionals—covers basics to advanced data.

SEW BUSINESS

1500 Knoll Trail Dr., Suite 112
Dallas, TX 75248

This industry magazine is published monthly, offering readers news, new trends and marketing developments, through a range of sewing categories. Reports: Events, business, forecasts, markets, trade association, news, updates, products video/book reviews.

SEW NEWS

P.O. Box 1790
Peoria, IL 61656

This sewing publication appears monthly, reporting on fashions, fabrics, sewing savvy and projects. Features projects and suggestions (illustrated) on color, dyeing, coordinating, others. Sewing patterns reviewed, hints given; includes resources, product data, book reviews, tips, latest products, videos, shoppers. Has advertising.

SEWER'S SOURCELETTER

2240 W. 3800 S., #J201
Salt Lake City, UT 84119

Sources of supplies, news and descriptions of suppliers for variety of craft interests is the main focus of this quarterly publication. Has classifieds.

SEWING BOOKLET SERIES

2269 Chestnut, Suite 269
San Francisco, CA 94123

This booklet series is issued bimonthly, with in-depth reports on the latest sewing methods, written by sewing professionals.

THE SEWING CIRCLE

P.O. Box 200504
Cartersville, GA 30120

Published 8 times yearly, this newsletter is devoted to old sewing patterns—finding, buying and selling them.

THE SEWING UPDATE

2269 Chestnut, Suite 269
San Francisco, CA 94123

This bimonthly newsletter features fashion-sewing information—articles by professionals (Nancy Zieman, Gail Brown, Robbie Fanning and others), innovative ideas—simple to advanced—technical data, reviews, plus product, equipment and pattern news and business topics.

SHUTTLE, SPINDLE & DYEPOT

2402 University Ave. W., Suite 702
St. Paul, MN 55114

This is the official magazine of the Handweaver's Guild of America (see Associations). Issues have technical data, illustrations and descriptions of the finest examples of weaving, spinning and dyeing. Issues also have guild news, product coverage and advertising.

SIDELINE BUSINESS

P.O. Box 351
Emmaus, PA 18049

This monthly publication guides those with at-home businesses to market craftswork and ideas.

SIGN CRAFT MAGAZINE

P.O. Box 60031
Fort Myers, FL 33906
(813) 939-4644

Recognizing sign making as an art, this bimonthly magazine presents photos, ideas, data on design, materials, business. Includes photo displays of signs, and newest products are shown. Regulars: Letters, tips and news. Has advertising.

SIMPLY CROSS STITCH

207 E. Broadway
Big Sandy, TX 75755

Send SASE with inquiry.

SMALLMARK

1850 Laguna St., Suite 1H
Concord, CA 94520

This quarterly miniatures newsletter is meant for the ½-inch to 1-inch scale enthusiast—how-to's, artist profiles, news and show reviews are included, as are updates, resources and more.

SOUTHERN ARTS & CRAFTS

P.O. Box 159
Bogalusa, LA 70429

This monthly publication gives nationwide news (and in-depth reports) on upcoming arts/crafts shows in the South; detailed data given. Includes letters, comments, show listing forms, resources. Has advertising.

SPIN-OFF

306 N. Washington Ave.
Loveland, CO 80537

This is a quarterly magazine on spinning. Presents articles on aspects of spinning and fibers, projects from fleece to finish—illustrated, with directions and historical information. Regulars: Reviews, calendars, news, answers, Spinning Guild news, tips. Has advertising.

STITCH 'N SEW QUILTS

306 E. Parr Rd.
Berne, IN 46711

An array of quilt patterns appears in every issue of this bimonthly magazine, including traditional, contemporary and unique quilts. Color photos show the finished quilt; suggestions and tips appear to improve the quilting craft. Regular features include general instructions and advertising.

STITCHER'S SOURCELETTER

P.O. Box 575749
Salt Lake City, UT 84157

Send SASE for information.

STRATEGIES

P.O. Box 838
Montclair, NJ 07042

Subtitled the *Self-Promotion Newsletter for Photographers*, this business newsletter is geared to it as fine art. Careers, exhibitions, portfolios, grants and other data is given in all bimonthly issues.

STREET ROD ACTION

7950 Deering Ave.
Canoga Park, CA 91304

This hot rod magazine is geared to hot rod kits and building—with features, product information and resources, plus events, NSRA news, book reviews, tips, showcases, color photos. Has advertising.

STROKES 'N STITCHES

P.O. Box 818
Mead, WA 99021

This bimonthly publication for artists and textile painters shares printed patterns and designs for appliqué, embroidery, punch needle, textile painting (and stencil designs).

SUNSHINE ARTISTS U.S.A.

1736 N. Highway 427
Longwood, FL 32750

This monthly magazine is a calendar of art/craft shows and events nationwide. Listings given by state are definitive. Has advertising.

SURFACE DESIGN JOURNAL

311 E. Washington St.
Fayetteville, TN 37334

This is a quarterly publication of the Surface Design Association, with information on dyes, application, business topics, news, reviews, show data.

TEDDY BEAR REVIEW

170 5th Ave.
New York, NY 10010

This quarterly publication on teddy bears presents teddy history; projects are shown, as are profiles, holiday topics, collections and more.

THE TEDDY TRIBUNEE

254 W. Sidney St.
St. Paul, MN 55107

This magazine is published 5 times yearly, and features

"news and views of the bear world," articles, trends, events, reviews. Has advertising.

THREADS MAGAZINE
P.O. Box 5506
Newtown, CT 06470

Much that can be created with threads is presented in this quality magazine. Design, details and techniques for art wear, needlecrafts and related topics are given and illustrated. Regular features: Letters, answers, technical tips, calendars, conferences, workshops, competitions, book reviews, suppliers and more. Has advertising.

TOLE WORLD
P.O. Box 5986
Concord, CA 94524

This bimonthly painting magazine is project-packed with presentations of well-known artists, an array of technical aids and features.

TOY SOLDIER REVIEW
127 74th St.
North Bergen, NJ 07047

This is a quarterly international magazine for toy soldier enthusiasts—craftspeople, collectors, others.

TRAINS
P.O. Box 1612
Waukesha, WI 53187

This monthly magazine is meant for the railroad hobbyist and model railroader. Issues are loaded with detailed articles about railroads and the railroad world of yesterday and today. Color photographs enhance features. Has advertising.

TREADLEART
25834 Narbonne Ave.
Lomita, CA 90717

This bimonthly magazine is geared to sewing embellishment—projects, hints, topics—illustrated, diagrammed and described.

VINTAGE CLOTHING
P.O. Box 1422
Corvallis, OR 97339

This newsletter covers yesterday's clothing—learning about, reconstruction of, caring for and more.

THE WATER COLOUR GAZETTE
619 Hamilton Ave., Unit 1
Winnipeg, Manitoba R2Y 1Z3 Canada

Send SASE for information.

WESTART
P.O. Box 6868
Auburn, CA 95604

This semi-monthly tabloid has a readership of artists, craftpeople and students. It features profiles and current reviews.

WILDFOWL CARVING & COLLECTING
P.O. Box 1831
Harrisburg, PA 17105

This magazine is meant for the bird-carving enthusiast, whether craftsperson or collector. Features give inspiration, instruction and recreation through color photos of masterpiece carvings. Professional carving pointers are given, with habitat reference photos and information on every facet of this American art form.

WILDLIFE PHOTOGRAPHY
P.O. Box 691
Greenville, PA 16125

As the title suggests, this is a publication for those who photograph in the wild.

WKMG
P.O. Box 1527
Vashon, WA 98070

This bimonthly magazine is a guide to machine knitters. Technical artists assist beginners; patterns are given for a variety of machines and rated for levels of ability. Issues list seminars and special events, "Clubs & Guilds," include a "Dealer Directory," and give letters, yarn and product news. Has advertising.

WOMEN ARTIST NEWS
P.O. Box 3304, Grand Central Station
New York, NY 10164

This bimonthly magazine may profile artists/craftspeople who work in crafts and fiber crafts. Published for critics, museums, galleries, teachers, other enthusiasts. Shows articles on history, opinions and related. Reviews exhibitions/events, books. (Supported in part by funds from the New York State Council on the Arts.)

WOMEN'S HOUSEHOLD CROCHET
306 E. Parr Rd.
Berne, IN 46711

This quarterly crochet publication features projects from cover to cover—for home and personal accessories.

WOOD
P.O. Box 55054
Boulder, CO 80302

This is a bimonthly woodworking magazine featuring projects from cover to cover — with specifications, directions, diagrams and illustrations. Has advertising.

WOODWORK
P.O. Box 1529
Ross, CA 94957

This quarterly magazine covers woodworking today, with topics for all skill levels. Presents cabinetmaking design and how-to's, profiles of professionals and their work, details on tools and equipment. Includes quality photography and diagramming throughout for projects and other features — on contemporary and other furnishings. Regular features: Letters and "Events Calendar." Has advertising.

THE WOODWORKER'S JOURNAL
517 Litchfield Rd.
P.O. Box 1629
New Milford, CT 06776

Send SASE for information.

THE WORKBASKET
4251 Pennsylvania Ave.
Kansas City, MO 64111

This home magazine presents features on knitting, crochet, sewing, embroidery, quilting, other needlecrafts and crafts. Projects are diagrammed. Has advertising.

WORKBENCH
700 W. 47th St., Suite 310
Kansas City, MO 64112

This do-it-yourself woodworking magazine covers projects for home improvement, furniture and accessories making/repair and more — with detailed directions and photographs. Regular features include "Product News," "Equipment Guide," "Calendar of Woodworking Shows," "Letters," "Workbench Solver," "Carpenter's Apprentice" and resources. Has advertising.

Supportive Materials and Aids

Also see General Craft Supplies.

A.I.M. DISPLAYS
P.O. Box 718
Franklin, NC 28734
(800) 524-9833

Offers: Aluminum display panels: Diamond shaped with folding hinges and leveler feet in a variety of sizes.
For Further Information: Free brochure.
Store Location: Yes
Discounts: Quantity discounts; allows discounts to teachers/institutions.

ACTION BAG CO.
501 N. Edgewood Ave.
Wood Dale, IL 60191
(312) 766-2881

Offers: Bags: Ziplock and other plastic bags in a variety of sizes, including Floss-A-Way and bolt bags for fabrics, plus cotton drawstring bags, retail shopping bags and shipping supplies. Manufacturer.
For Further Information: Free catalog.
Discounts: Sells wholesale.

ADLER SALES, INC.
P.O. Box 8317
Richmond, VA 23226
(804) 288-4480

Offers: Custom-built display cases (for miniatures and others): Walnut bases, optional mirror-backed, multi-sizes.
For Further Information: Free list.

ALPHA IMPRESSIONS
4161 S. Main St.
Los Angeles, CA 90037
(213) 234-8221

Offers: Labels—woven and custom printed.
For Further Information: Free brochures.
Store Location: Yes
Discounts: Quantity discounts.

ALUMA PANEL, INC.
2410 Oak St. W.
Cumming, GA 30131
(800) 258-3003

Offers: Sign blanks and stands: Aluminum, styrene and D-board types, variety of sizes. Also offers flexible magnetic sheeting, sparcal vinyl, corrugated plastic, blank banners, sandblast stencil, chromatic paints.
For Further Information: Send SASE for list.

AMERICAN CARDSERVICE CORP.
3303 Harbor Blvd.
Costa Mesa, CA 92626
(800) 576-3061, op. 333

Offers: Credit card portable processor system for American Express, Discover, MasterCard and Visa; approvals within a minute without phone line.
For Further Information: Call for information.

BADGE-A-MINIT
348 N. 30th Rd.
P.O. Box 800
La Salle, IL 61301
(815) 224-2090

Offers: Badge-A-Minit Starter kit: You-make, with original design fronts, others. Kit features machine, supplies, directions.
For Further Information: Free color catalog.

CHARM WOVEN LABELS
P.O. Box 30027
Portland, OR 97230
(503) 252-5542

Offers: Personalized woven labels with stock phrases: From the Needles of, Custom Made by, Original, Handmade by, Hand Knit by, Made Especially for You, Fashioned by or blank (you choose). Care instruction labels.
For Further Information: Free brochure.

CHIMERA STUDIOS, INC.
3708 E. Hubbard St.
Mineral Wells, TX 76067

Offers: "Flame Pruf" additive, by quart.
For Further Information: Send SASE for details.

COLLECTORS HOUSE
704 Ginesi Dr., Suite 11
Morganville, NJ 07751
(908) 972-6190, (800) 448-9298

Offers: Displays—jewelry tray, bracelet T-bar, necklace stand/easel, Allstate portable and table top showcases, Riker Mount display boxes (butterfly cardboard with glass top, variety of sizes, with cotton, velvet).
For Further Information: Send for information.
Discounts: Quantity discounts.

CREATIVE ENERGIES, INC.
1609 N. Magnolia Ave.
Ocala, FL 34475
(904) 351-8889

Offers: Display systems—Public Hanging stackable panel unit (indoor/outdoor), Earth Mounds collapsible pedestable for 3D, staking/weight systems for all canopies. Also offers triple truck dolly, Light-Dome canopy and zippered side curtains for all canopies.
For Further Information: Free brochure.

DANA LABELS, INC.
7778 SW Nimbus Ave.
Beaverton, OR 97005
(503) 646-7933

Offers: Custom-printed labels—garment labels, size tabs, tags, care and content labels. Also offers paper shipping, embossing and cosmetic labels, pressure sensitive and others.
For Further Information: Brochure, $1.

DEALERS SUPPLY
P.O. Box 717
Matawan, NJ 07747
(800) 524-0576

Offers: Display supplies—fire-retardant fitted table covers, showcases, display grid modules, KD Kanopies, folding tables, lighting, booth signs, black lights, alarms and security aids and others.
For Further Information: Free catalog.
Accepts: MasterCard, Visa

DESIGNER PAPER PRODUCTS
45 Prospect St.
Yonkers, NY 10701
(800) 831-7791

Offers: Packaging—boxes for apparel, jewelry, gifts, plus paper bags, shopping bags, tissue, wrapping papers, patterned bags, printing.
For Further Information: Free catalog.

DIANNA TZARINA
1099 Atlantic Dr., Bldg. 4
West Chicago, IL 60185
(800) 932-1099

Offers: Display cases, including mirror-back doll (and other) cases in standard and custom sizes.
For Further Information: Free list.
Discounts: Has discounts.
Accepts: MasterCard, Visa

DISPLAYBRIGHT
108 Echo St.
Santa Cruz, CA 95060
(800) 995-1723

Offers: Portable halogen display lighting (use with Abstracta and other systems).
For Further Information: Send SASE for list.

DOVER PUBLICATIONS, INC.
31 E. 2nd St.
Mineola, NY 11501
(516) 294-7000

Offers: Copyright-free design books—black on glossy white, clip/use: Borders, holiday motifs, seasons, art nouveau/deco, contemporary motifs, patriotic, sports, office, children's, silhouettes, old-fashioned, travel, transportation, health, symbols, florals, borders, ethnic, early ads, calligraphy.
For Further Information: Free catalog.
Store Location: Yes

FLOURISH CO.
5763 Wheeler Rd.
Fayetteville, AR 72703
(501) 444-8400

Offers: White tarps—standard and custom sizes—and Protector canopies.
For Further Information: Free brochure.

GRAPHCOMM SERVICES
P.O. Box 220
Freeland, WA 98249
(206) 331-5668

Offers: Custom labels and hangtags, tagging equipment, self-inking stamps, merchandising and advertising specialties. Service: Design.
For Further Information: Free catalog.
Discounts: Quantity discounts.

H & H DEVELOPMENT
P.O. Box 4082
Evergreen, CO 80439
(303) 674-5608

Offers: Instant Shelter display booth: Portable, free-standing with poly top, truss frame, self-contained, in a variety of sizes.
For Further Information: Send SASE for information.

Accepts: MasterCard, Visa

HEIRLOOM WOVEN LABELS
P.O. Box 2188, Grand Central Station
New York, NY 10163

Offers: Woven labels — wide range of colors/styles, personalized.
For Further Information: Send SASE for list.

IDENT-IFY LABEL CORP.
P.O. Box 204
Brooklyn, NY 11229

Offers: Personalized labels on white cotton, with stock phrases: Original by, Handmade by, Made Especially for You by, Hand Knit by, Made With Love by Mother (Grandmother), Made With Tender Loving Care, Hand Woven by, Fashioned by and blank style (you-add). Name tapes (1 line).
For Further Information: Send SASE for list.
Discounts: Quantity discounts.

J & N IMPORTS
P.O. Box 12272
Birmingham, MI 48012
(313) 642-2672

Offers: Jewelry boxes — velvet ring, earring and pendant types by the dozen.
For Further Information: Write or call for free sample.

JENKINS
3950 A Valley Blvd.
Walnut, CA 91789
(909) 594-1349/1471

Offers: Canopies for indoor/outdoor use, canopy connectors, hardware, sawhorses, signs and sign frames, racks, other accessories.
For Further Information: Send SASE for list.

JOHNSON'S INSTANT SHELTERS
7656 SE 123rd Lane
Bellview, FL 32526
(904) 245-2923

Offers: Canopies, including a double truss model with polyester, in 3 sizes, many colors, zippered side panels (with door), bags, stakes.
For Further Information: Call or write for information.
Accepts: MasterCard, Visa

KIA PHOTOGRAPHY
453 Main St.
Nashua, NH 03060
(603) 888-0357

Offers: Promotional items — color postcards, catalog sheets, brochures, greeting cards, others — 1,000 minimum.
For Further Information: Send SASE for list.

L & L STITCHERY
P.O. Box 43821
Atlanta, GA 30336
(404) 691-2239

Offers: Personalized woven labels: Fabric sew-ons, name tapes.
For Further Information: Free brochure.

M.D. ENTERPRISES DISPLAY SYSTEMS
4907 W. Hanover Ave.
Dallas, TX 75209
(214) 352-2802

Offers: KD Kanopy display system: Panels covered in heavy fabric, knock-down panels, tubular construction, easy-adjustable.
For Further Information: Send SASE for list.

MADE IN THE SHADE E-Z UP
P.O. Box 231
Cool, CA 95614
(800) SHADE-2-U

Offers: E-Z Up portable shelters — canopies and accessories in a variety of sizes, basic units and others.
For Further Information: Free brochure and list.
Store Location: Yes
Discounts: Quantity discounts; allows discounts to teachers and institutions; sells wholesale to legitimate businesses and professionals.

ELAINE MARTIN, INC.
P.O. Box 261
Highwood, IL 60040
(708) 945-9445

Offers: Show/display equipment — snap joint canopies in 3 standard colors, with slant, flat or peak roof models. Also offers folding tables, director chairs.
For Further Information: Free catalog.
Discounts: Quantity discounts; sells wholesale to legitimate businesses.
Accepts: MasterCard, Visa

JOHN MEE CANOPIES
P.O. Box 11220
Birmingham, AL 35202
(205) 967-1885

Offers: KD Majestic canopies, 3 sizes. EZ-UP 500 canopies, 4 sizes with double truss frame and polyester top. Also offers package specials, and items from Show-off, Graphic Display

Systems, Armstrong, including replacement tops, chairs, others.
For Further Information: Write or call for free catalog.
Accepts: MasterCard, Visa

KYLE MURRAY TRAILERS
P.O. Box 8250
Greenwood, SC 29649
(803) 229-4666

Offers: Cargo trailers—single and tandem axle models, in 4 sizes each; optional double rear doors.
For Further Information: Send SASE for information.

NAME MAKER, INC.
P.O. Box 43821
Atlanta, GA 30336
(800) 241-2890

Offers: Fabric labels (small quantities, up), plus retail program for craft and fabric shops.
For Further Information: Send SASE for list.

NEW VENTURE PRODUCTS
7441 114th Ave., #605
Largo, FL 34643
(800) 771-SHOW

Offers: The Showoff Line of canopy and display systems—portable, easy-set-up displays in a variety of sizes and types.
For Further Information: Call or write for information.

NEWSTECH
12447 Pinebrook
South Lyon, MI 48178

Offers: Hand tags, business cards and self-stitch labels in a variety of orginal designs to-be-personalized, plus tying yarns and cords.
For Further Information: Catalog, $2.
Discounts: Quantity discounts.
Accepts: MasterCard, Visa

NORTHWEST TAG & LABEL, INC.
111 Foothills Rd., Suite 221
Lake Oswego, OR 97034

Offers: Labels on satin, nylon, polyester: Care content, size tabs, in stock, and custom labels, size stickers. Also offers hang tags in a variety of types, and custom-made labels to specification.
For Further Information: Brochure, $1.

OZARK NOVELTY
P.O. Box 28 MB
Webb City, MO 64870
(417) 673-5171

Offers: Jewelry showcases—aluminum framed, hinged glass lid.
For Further Information: Free catalog.
Accepts: MasterCard, Visa

PACKAGING UN-LIMITED INC.
1121 W. Kentucky St.
Louisville, KY 40210
(502) 584-4331, (800) 234-1833

Offers: Boxes—corrugated, gift, hat, jewelry, custom-sized, others. Also offers bags, bubble and foam wraps, tissue, foam peanuts, tape, mailing tubes, folders (optional printing).
For Further Information: Free brochure.

PANELS BY PAITH
Rt. 6, P.O. Box 656
Roxboro, NC 27573
(800) 67-PAITH

Offers: Plaques in over 5 shapes/sizes of bases and domes for display.
For Further Information: Free catalog.

PGS MARKETING, INC.
4940 Viking Dr., #208
Minneapolis, MN 55435
(800) 488-9039

Offers: Display pegboard gondola spinner system—four-sided, rotates (for limited space).
For Further Information: Send SASE for list.

THE PLASTIC BAG OUTLET
190 W. Passaic St.
Rochelle Park, NJ 07662

Offers: Plastic bags—hi-density T-shirt handle bags (4 sizes), loop handle bags, tote handle bags (3 sizes), and super reinforced tote handle bags.
For Further Information: Send SASE for list.
Accepts: MasterCard, Visa

PLASTIC BAGMART
554 Haddon Ave.
Collingswood, NJ 08108
(609) 858-0800

Offers: Plastic bags—clear, zip-lock, carryout types—plus shipping tapes, bubble pack bags, tissue, others.
For Further Information: Free price list.
Store Location: Yes
Discounts: Quantity discounts; sells wholesale to legitimate businesses and professionals.

POLYBAGS PLUS
P.O. Box 3043
Port Charlotte, FL 33949

Offers: Polybags, zipclose bags, cotton drawstring bags, floss organizers, heavy-duty piece bags selection. Others.
For Further Information: Send SASE for brochure.

SAKET CO.
7249 Atoll Ave.
North Hollywood, CA 91605
(818) 764-0110

Offers: Plastic bags in all sizes, small and large quantities, for crafts/hobbies, commercial and office use, industry. Cellophane bags.
For Further Information: Free catalog.
Store Location: Yes
Discounts: Quantity discounts; allows discounts to teachers and institutions; sells wholesale to legitimate businesses and professionals.

SPRINGHILL GIFTS
13 Spring St.
Stamford, CT 06901

Offers: Labels and business cards (optional craft logos).
For Further Information: Samples, $2 (refundable).

STERLING NAME TAPE CO.
P.O. Box 110
Winsted, CT 06098
(203) 379-5142

Offers: Custom labels printed with name, logo, artwork, etc., in one or more ink colors with care or content information on back.
For Further Information: Sample kit, $1.

THE WOOD FACTORY
21 Musick
Irvine, CA 92718
(714) 472-WOOD

Offers: Wood displays and accessories, including trees, shelving, cabinets, contemporary designs.
For Further Information: Free catalog.

YAZOO MILLS, INC.
305 Commerce St.
New Oxford, PA 17350
(717) 624-8993

Offers: Mailing tubes—in a full line of lengths and any quantity, with end plugs for most standard sizes; sold by carton.
For Further Information: Free catalog.

Index